The AA KEYGuide
Scotland

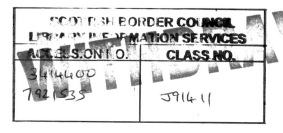

Contents

KEY TO SYMBOLS

✚ Map reference
✉ Address
☎ Telephone number
🕐 Opening times
💷 Admission prices
🚌 Bus number
🚆 Train station
⛴ Ferry/boat
🚗 Driving directions
ℹ Tourist office
🎏 Tours
📖 Guidebook
🍴 Restaurant
☕ Café
🏬 Shop
🍸 Bar
🚻 Toilets
① Number of rooms
🅿 Parking
🚭 No smoking
❄ Air conditioning
🏊 Swimming pool
🏋 Gym
❓ Other useful information
🛍 Shopping
🎭 Entertainment
🎤 Nightlife
🏅 Sports
★ Activities
♥ Health and Beauty
👶 For Children
▷ Cross reference
★ Walk/tour start point

HOW TO USE THIS BOOK

Understanding Scotland is an introduction to the country, its geography, economy and people. **Living Scotland** gives an insight into Scotland today, while **The Story of Scotland** takes you through the country's past.

For detailed advice on getting to Scotland—and getting around once you are there—turn to **On the Move**. For useful practical information, from weather forecasts to emergency services, turn to **Planning**.

Out and About gives you the chance to explore Scotland through walks and tours.

The **Sights**, **What to Do**, **Eating and Staying** sections are divided geographically into six regions, which are shown on the map on the inside front cover. These regions always appear in the same order. Towns and places of interest are listed alphabetically within each region.

Map references for the **Sights** refer to the atlas section at the end of this book or to the individual town plans. For example, Perth has the reference ✚ 317 J10, indicating the page on which the map is found (317) and the grid square in which Perth sits (J10).

UNDERSTANDING SCOTLAND

Scotland is an area of northern Britain, a separate kingdom until 1707. Extending over 78,722sq km (30,414sq miles) it covers around one-third of the landmass of Britain, but with just 5 million inhabitants, has less than one-tenth of the total population. It has Britain's highest mountain, Ben Nevis (1,343m/4,406ft) and deepest lake, Loch Morar (over 305m/1,000ft). You could probably drive overland from one end to the other within 24 hours, if you wanted and weather permitting—reaching the extremities of the islands would take you a little longer. But don't be fooled by the size on a map: There's enough to explore here to take a lifetime of discovery.

Unmistakably Scottish scenes: turreted Castle Fraser, left, and magnificent Glen Affric, right

GETTING PAST THE CLICHÉS

Scotland sells itself to the world as a land of misty mountains and big scenery, romantic and tragic history, tartan McHaggisry with a beating Celtic heart. Anybody who comes to these shores looking for this image is unlikely to go away disappointed—the mountains are undoubtedly majestic, the history rich and well told, and yes, some Scotsmen wear kilts.

But, of course, Scotland has a great deal to offer beyond the clichés, as any visitor who scratches the surface of this intriguing and contradictory land will soon discover. And it is the little personal discoveries—a glimpse of a hidden fairy-tale castle between the trees, the heady scent of a heather moor on a hot day, the unexpected sight of an otter nosing along the shore, a cheery conversation with the only other walkers on a bare mountainside, a fresh-washed beach of pure shell sand in a turquoise bay, a superb meal of fresh seafood in a pub you've chanced upon in a place where you can't begin to pronounce the Gaelic name—which make any visit here memorable.

LAND AND ECONOMY

Most of the population lives around the urban centres of Edinburgh and Glasgow, Dundee and Aberdeen.

Approximately half of Scotland is covered by natural or semi-natural vegetation, which includes heather moorland, peat bog and woodland, both natural and afforested. Around 11 per cent of the land is used for arable agriculture (predominantly cereals and vegetables), and slightly more for improved grazing.

The heavy manufacturing industry of the 19th and early 20th centuries (such as shipbuilding) for which Scotland was once renowned, has given way to light industry, including electronics and technology centred on Silicon Glen, the area between Glasgow and Edinburgh. Industrial production across the country includes woven textiles, brewing and distilling, and fisheries and tourism both make significant contributions. Oil and natural gas are extracted from beneath the waters of the North Sea.

RELIGION

The Protestant, Presbyterian Kirk or Church of Scotland is the established (official) religion in Scotland. Unlike the Church of England, it does not have the monarch at its head, but is governed by its General Assembly, with a leader, the Moderator, elected annually. About one third of Scottish Christians are Catholics.

GOVERNMENT

Queen Elizabeth II is the hereditary monarch of Britain, including Scotland. The British government, based at Westminster, London, holds overall power; it is made up from the political party with the most elected Members of Parliament (MPs). The Westminster parliament, which makes the laws for Britain, includes 59 Scottish MPs.

Since 1999, Scotland has also had its own parliament, based in the capital, Edinburgh, and with 129 elected members (MSPs). The Scottish government (or Scottish Executive) is made up of MSPs from the political party holding the most seats. The role of the First Minister (currently Jack McConnell) within Scotland is approximately equivalent to the role of the Prime Minister within the whole of Britain. Powers devolved

from Westminster include matters of education, health and environmental policies in Scotland; Westminster retains control of defence, fiscal policy, foreign affairs and national security.

At a more local level of government, Scotland is divided into 32 unitary authorities, shown below. Of these, the biggest in area is the Highland Region (2,611,906ha/6,529,765 acres, pop. 208,000), and the smallest is the City of Dundee (5,500ha/13,750 acres, pop. 145,000). The largest population falls within the City of Glasgow (pop. 612,000), the smallest in Orkney (pop. 19,810).

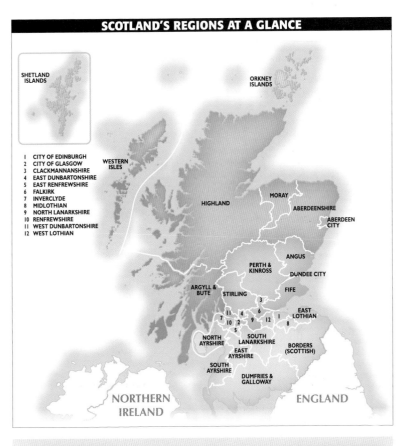

SCOTLAND'S REGIONS AT A GLANCE

SHETLAND ISLANDS

ORKNEY ISLANDS

I CITY OF EDINBURGH
2 CITY OF GLASGOW
3 CLACKMANNANSHIRE
4 EAST DUNBARTONSHIRE
5 EAST RENFREWSHIRE
6 FALKIRK
7 INVERCLYDE
8 MIDLOTHIAN
9 NORTH LANARKSHIRE
10 RENFREWSHIRE
11 WEST DUNBARTONSHIRE
12 WEST LOTHIAN

WESTERN ISLES

HIGHLAND

MORAY

ABERDEENSHIRE

ABERDEEN CITY

ANGUS

PERTH & KINROSS

DUNDEE CITY

ARGYLL & BUTE

STIRLING

FIFE

EAST LOTHIAN

NORTH AYRSHIRE

SOUTH LANARKSHIRE

EAST AYRSHIRE

BORDERS (SCOTTISH)

SOUTH AYRSHIRE

DUMFRIES & GALLOWAY

NORTHERN IRELAND

ENGLAND

UNDERSTANDING THE REGIONS

To help you find your way through the information in this book, we have divided the country into six areas. **Edinburgh** and **Glasgow** have their own sections, matching their very different identities and appeal for the visitor, the former with a genteel, cultured, 18th-century outlook, the latter proud of its image as a gritty Victorian industrial city. **Southern Scotland** covers the Dumfries and Galloway, Borders and Lothians area, which is rich in rolling hills, wide green valleys, appealing small towns and a history centred on conflict with English neighbours. **Central Scotland** takes in the wooded heart of the country and extends eastward across the fertile Perthshire farmland into Fife, encompassing mansions and fishing villages, modern engineering and a history of rebellion and skirmish. The **Highlands and Islands** is a mantle for the wild high country of the mainland and the stunningly beautiful islands of the western coast, with remote fortifications, lonely glens and Britain's last areas of wilderness. The northern isles of **Orkney and Shetland** have an identity that is shared as much with Scandinavia as with the Highlands, which rightly earns them their own division within the book.

BEST PLACES TO STAY

Cosses Country House, Ballantrae (▷ 270) A country house in a woodland garden setting near the coast, in the southwest

Lochgreen House, Troon (▷ 273) Comfort and fine food in this stylish hotel, judged the Automobile Association's Hotel of the Year for 2003–04

Gleneagles, Auchterarder (▷ 277) Two convincing reasons to stay at this top hotel: the golf, and Andrew Fairlie's sublime cooking in the restaurant

Ballachulish House, Ballachulish (▷ 285) A magnificent Highland setting for a lovely guesthouse with top-class facilities and service

Isle of Eriska (▷ 286) Enjoy the luxurious facilities of this superb hotel, set on a private island off the west coast

A grand ruin at Kelso, one of the great Border abbeys

BEST PLACES TO EAT

Restaurant Martin Wishart, Edinburgh (▷ 251) Modern European cooking is the passion at this minuscule, minimalist restaurant in fashionable Leith

The Peat Inn, at Peat Inn (▷ 256) Top French cooking at a former coaching inn, set in the heart of Fife—an established favourite

The Buttery, Glasgow (▷ 258) Tuck into the very best of modern Scottish cuisine in this award-winning city-centre restaurant

The Applecross Inn, Applecross (▷ 261) Splendid food in a cosy coastal pub, well worth the spectacular drive over a high mountain pass to get there

Three Chimneys Restaurant, Colbost (▷ 264) Rustic chic and a culinary delight in the wild beauty of north Skye

Fine dining: Scottish seafood is the tops

BEST LANDSCAPES

Loch Lomond and the Trossachs National Park (▷ 98) Classic landscapes of lochs and wooded hills in Scotland's first national park

Glencoe (▷ 127) A dramatic valley scarred by a historic tragedy, with some of the best mountain climbing and winter sports

Lewis and Harris (▷ 135) Remote beaches of white shell sand and sparkling turquoise seas reminiscent of the Caribbean (but colder!)

The Cairngorms (▷ 122) Britain's highest mountain plateau, with ancient woodlands, unusual wildlife and alpine flora

Grey Mare's Tail (▷ 61) A waterfall is the focus of this miniature beauty in Dumfriesshire

Lochs and glens set the scene: Loch Katrine, above, and Glencoe, left

BEST CASTLES

Edinburgh Castle (▷ 71–73) The biggest and best, an icon of Scottish history and identity and dominating the capital

Crathes (▷ 124) Fairy-tale turrets and an outstanding garden mark out this ancient Highland beauty

Blair Castle (▷ 90) Everything you expect of a romantic castle in the heart of Scotland, with a fascinating history and its own private army

Culzean Castle (▷ 60) A stately 18th-century mansion in a spectacular clifftop setting in the southwest, surrounded by verdant parkland

Eilean Donan (▷ 126) A picture-perfect treasure in a dream setting of loch and mountains, tucked away in the northwest

Edinburgh Castle, symbol of power in the capital city

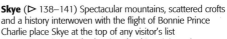

BEST ISLANDS

Skye (▷ 138–141) Spectacular mountains, scattered crofts and a history interwoven with the flight of Bonnie Prince Charlie place Skye at the top of any visitor's list

Arran (▷ 57) Described as 'Scotland in miniature', a charming and accessible island often overlooked in the race to the Highlands

Shetland (▷ 147–148) A remote group of islands quite unlike any other, with its own vibrant traditions and culture

Lewis and Harris (▷ 135) Ancient sites and quiet beauty on the western edge of Europe

Islay (▷ 131) A superb museum, great birdwatching and seven distilleries in one small jewel of an island

Skye's Cuillin Mountains are paradise to climbers

BEST ANCIENT SITES

Skara Brae (▷ 145) A Neolithic village revealed under the shifting sands of Orkney

Kilmartin (▷ 132, 134) A unique concentration of chambered cairns dating back to 3000BC, near the ancient capital of Dalriada

Mousa Broch (▷ 148) Scotland's best preserved broch, or stone tower, on a tiny Shetland island

Calanais (▷ 135) A stone circle and avenue second only to Stonehenge in importance, on Lewis

Sueno's Stone, Forres (▷ 126) A Pictish cross slab in the northeast, vividly carved with battle scenes

Monoliths on Lewis, above, and an ancient Orkney village right; below and right, exotic flora at Inverewe

BEST GARDENS

Inverewe Gardens (▷ 133) A remarkable semi-tropical garden thrives on the wild northwest coast

Logan Botanic Garden (▷ 63) Shelter under the natural umbrella of the giant gunneras at this exotic delight in the far southwest

Royal Botanic Garden, Edinburgh (▷ 86) An accessible green oasis near the heart of the city, with glasshouses and planting for all seasons

Crarae Gardens (▷ 123) For Highland glen read Himalayan gorge in this outstanding woodland garden

Threave (▷ 66) The National Trust for Scotland's teaching garden in the southwest, famous for its riot of spring bulbs

A Viking resident of the Museum of Scotland, below

BEST GALLERIES/MUSEUMS

Museum of Scotland (▷ 78–81) Scotland's chief national treasure house, in the heart of Edinburgh

Burrell Collection (▷ 106–108) Exquisite art treasures from around the world, gathered by one extraordinary Glaswegian man

National Gallery of Scotland (▷ 82) An outstanding collection of fine art from around the world, most notably Scottish painting

New Lanark World Heritage Site (▷ 65) An industrial village brought back to life

The Tenement House (▷ 117) Reveals the domestic scale of life in a very ordinary Glasgow tenement (apartment)

TOP 20 EXPERIENCES

Take a walk—it doesn't have to be the whole of the West Highland Way, but pick something to suit your level of fitness and see some of the real Scotland (▷ 199–236).

Eat a top-class meal of fresh-cooked modern Scottish fare—the seafood and the beef are world-famous (▷ 237–265).

Taste a dram of single malt whisky. You can add a drop of water if you like, and if you've never tried it, Cragganmore is a good one to start with (▷ 242–243).

Listen to some live traditional music in a bar and see if you can stop your toes tapping to accordion and fiddle (▷ 149–198).

Climb up Calton Hill for a great view across Edinburgh (▷ 70). Also excellent views from the castle, and from Salisbury Crags.

Visit an island, and allow yourself time to slow down and enjoy the experience. Skye is so easy with the bridge now, while Harris and Lewis or Shetland are more of a challenge (▷ 138–141, 135, 147–148).

Take your credit card and go shopping—the designer clothes in Glasgow and Edinburgh are beckoning you (▷ 150–51).

See and hear a pipe band, still one of the great spectacles of Scotland. Catch them at a Highland games and other events, or satiate your senses at the World Pipe Band Championships (▷ 157).

Get lost in the Museum of Scotland, Edinburgh. It's easily done, but you're bound to find something interesting around the next corner to illuminate another bit of the country's rich history (▷ 78–81).

Make your way to some remote extremities on the map—the Rhinns of Galloway, the Mull of Kintyre, Cape Wrath, John o'Groats, Hermaness, Fraserburgh—you'll see so much more of the real Scotland off the beaten track (▷ 55–148).

Watch a sunset over the Western Isles. You may have to share your vantage point with the midges, so come prepared (▷ 130–131).

Take a railway trip, sit back and enjoy the scenery—the West Highland route from Fort William to Mallaig is the most famous (▷ 193).

Bag a Munro (▷ 15), but take sensible precautions in the hills.

Party with the local people at a festival—or join in a ceilidh; the Scots know how to have a good time (▷ 156–157).

Find a sheltered spot and watch for wildlife—gannets and puffins around the cliffs, red deer and golden eagles in the hills, otters and seals on the seashore (▷ 55–148).

Look up your ancestors at a clan site, and find out if there's a tartan for you. With so many modern inventions on the books, you don't need a Scottish last name to find something suitable (▷ 168, 306).

Explore Edinburgh's New Town to enjoy the splendours of the open spaces and the 18th-century architecture (▷ 84–85, 208–209).

Look up some Scottish art—Raeburn and Ramsay at the National Gallery, the Scottish Colourists at the Gallery of Modern Art, the new wave at Glasgow's GoMA (▷ 82, 88, 105).

Follow the trail of a great Scot to discover the architecture of Charles Rennie Mackintosh, or the poetry of Robert Burns (▷ 114–115, 58–59).

Enjoy a traditional cup of tea in a Glasgow tea room (▷ 188).

Terrific views from Calton Hill
Left, listen for a roaring stag in the late summer

On the edge in Orkney, remote and beautiful

Enjoy pipe bands galore at the Edinburgh Tattoo

Chase up stories and legends of the life of Robert Burns, and try Tam O'Shanter for a riotous taste of his poetry

Living
Scotland

Intense colours typify John Lowrie Morrison's very Scottish paintings—this is Tobermory, on Mull

The Loch Ness Monster, a national joke

Billy Connolly, an international joker

Clan and Family

The Duke of Wellington crowned with a traffic cone outside Glasgow's Gallery of Modern Art: The Scots have a healthy irreverence of authority

Scots names are easy to spot, like the Scots accent. They reflect family origins and migrations—Ewan MacGregor (Gaelic), Magnus Magnusson (Scandinavian), Robert Bruce (French), Sean Connery (Irish), Alexander Fleming (Flemish).

The Scots are by descent divided roughly fifty-fifty into Highland and Lowland, but often think of their families as more than nuclear, and claim Highland clanship. They wouldn't have done this 150 years ago, when 'teuchters' (a derogatory term for Highlanders) were low-status. Modern clan gatherings and reunions can pump much needed cash into the countryside, and make the worldwide extended family more than a myth, helping to hold modern rambling and changing relationships together.

Many English have gone native in the North, from the radical playwright John McGrath to novelists Anne Fine and Kate Atkinson. And novelist William McIlvanney, playwright John Byrne, actor Sean Connery and comedian Billy Connolly emerged from the Irish communities in Scotland.

The new Scots

More 'new Scots' have come from the over-crowded and overheated mainland of Europe, and they are a positive factor, enriching the blend. Italians came from Barga and Frosinone to sell fish and chips and ice cream (Europe's best!). They turned out commercial and cultural dynamos, from hotel magnate Lord Forte to racing driver Dario Franchitti, sculptor Eduardo Paolozzi, actors Tom Conti and Daniella Nardini, Archbishop Mario Conti and art entrepreneur Ricky Demarco. Jewish migrants brought the centenarian socialist Manny Shinwell and novelist Muriel Spark, not to speak of the legendary foul-mouthed stand-up comedian Jerry Sadowitz. And in 1997 Mohammad Sarwar, from Glasgow, became Britain's first Muslim MP.

Morag, a stuffed sheep (precursor of clone Dolly), looks over the shoulder of a newspaper reader at the Royal Museum

The success of Harry Potter has made an Edinburgh author's fortune

Former milkman Sean Connery, one of Scotland's best-known exports

Alfresco in Glasgow: The modern city is developing a reputation for chic

Home and household

Urban Scots are European-style flat-dwellers, with houses that vary from 'wally closes' (Glasgow's spectacular Victorian palazzos, so-called for their art nouveau tiled corridors) to the modern high-rises. Households are growing in number, even if the population is not: from 1.9 million in 1980 to 2.2 million in 2004. Many of these are single-person households—divorce, social mobility, falling birth rates and even the legalisation of homosexuality in the 1970s may be contributory factors—but it adds up to a lively city life. Post-1918 suburbs have bourgeois bungalows or 'cooncil hooses' (council-owned housing). But many folk still dream of escape to a 'but an' ben' (single-roomed cottage) on the land rather than the usual summer on a Spanish beach.

Religion

In the 1960s the Kirk (Church of Scotland) dominated the Scottish Sabbath: In the 21st century its place has been taken by the supermarket. The Kirk likes to think of its Presbyterian structure as Scotland's true democracy, and elected its first female Moderator (leader) in 2003. Its General Assembly in May still draws headlines, and it copes with a huge amount of social work in a society proudly secular until real trouble hits. The Catholic Church, which numbers about a third of Scottish Christians, grew with Irish immigration after 1800. Its hierarchy is doctrinally conservative though socially radical, and its separate state school system is regularly argued over. Pietism—encompassing the Free and Free Presbyterian Kirks—persists among the Gaels. Alternative faiths also thrive, with Buddhists at Eskdalemuir and Arran and New Agers at Findhorn.

Tolerance

Do the Scots hate the English? Ignore football-tabloid prejudice, it hasn't stopped them marrying each other by the thousand. Prejudices are more about class than nation: 'He's English, but he's not a Yah.' You hear that often. A Yah is a wealthy young English person at a Scottish university with a very loud voice. So just how tolerant are the Scots? Asylum-seekers in Glasgow—the modern migrants—face mixed prospects. The new Parliament was lambasted by the late Cardinal Thomas Winning and the fundamentalist bus billionaire Brian Soutar for trying to repeal anti-gay legislation. Piety tends towards 'the divided self', illustrated by the writers who needed two voices— including Hugh MacDiarmid/Chris Grieve, Lewis Grassic Gibbon/James Leslie Mitchell—to deal with the complexity of the place.

Hard cash

Wealth and poverty have always been here, with little material difference between the dwellings at Skara Brae (2500BC) and a 19th-century croft. In the 20th century progress avalanched in, bringing cars, phones and computers. Scotland today is developing an entrepreneurial middle class, and has 69 out of the top 1,000 of Britain's mega-rich, according to an annual poll in the *Sunday Times* newspaper. The biggest fortune is that of Dutch oil and gas heir Paul van Vlissingen, of Letterewe in Wester Ross, a gentle soul respected for his ecological work. In Scotland, double the UK percentage of millionaires cashed in on sport or the arts—Sean Connery, Jackie Stewart, Annie Lennox—though the mother of them all is Edinburgh-based writer J. K. Rowling: Harry Potter has earned her a cool £500 million.

The thistle, a prickly symbol of Scotland for 500 years

Stag hunting is important to the economy, but venison is not widely eaten: Most is exported to European markets

Scotland's opportunities for hill-walking are boundless

Landscape and
Nature

Look at a geological map of Europe and see it go crazy when it hits the west coast of Scotland. No wonder people come here for the scenery.

The country's complex landscape has always impinged on the lives of its people, who invented geological study in the 1780s. In the far northwest the rocks are over 3 billion years old, but it was events of 300–400 million years ago that gave Scotland many of its distinctive peaks, such as Arthur's Seat (▷ 70). The ice ages created U-shaped glaciated valleys like Glencoe (▷ 127), and Glen Rosa on Arran. The blanket bog of the Flow Country of Caithness and Sutherland was laid down thousands of years ago, and is the largest remaining area of such peatland in Europe.

In economic terms, three quarters of the land is useless—loch, marsh, rock—but there's also the rich red earth of the Borders and Strathmore, which produced a world-changing agriculture in Perthshire, Aberdeenshire, Ayrshire and Fife. Today these areas are known for their cereal crops, and rich harvests of potatoes and raspberries.

Stone-built

Scotland is stone-built, so no town is like the next. Volcanic rocks like granite—grey and pink—in the north, compete with sedimentaries like old red sandstone. Classical Edinburgh is built of indestructible, silver-grey Craigleith sandstone, lethal to the men who quarried and carved it. Glasgow's red Cairnpapple and creamy Dunbarton or Lanark sandstones are softer, and turn dramatically dark with time. Roofs are incredibly varied: thatch and turf for centuries, followed by tiles (originally from the Low Countries, brought as ballast in trading ships) and later slate from Ballachulish and Easdale, and corrugated iron. Harling—coating a building with a layer of small stones embedded in mortar—is a distinctive Scottish feature, from cottages to castles.

Wind turbines are replacing hydroelectricity as the green energy source of the future

Poor recyclers

Modern Scots have one of the world's worst recycling records. By the end of the 1990s the Scots were refilling their mined and quarried land with more landfill waste than anyone else in Europe. Government targets for increasing recycling have resulted in major improvements, but over 7 million tonnes of waste is still being buried in Scotland every year, and less than 20 per cent of waste is being recycled.

The hardy Scottish Blackface-cross is the mainstay of upland farming

Roadsign at the Famous Grouse distillery, Glenturret: Red grouse rely on the management of heather moors for their survival

SLOW
GROUSE CROSSING

Land conflicts

Scarcely a week goes by without an environmental flurry in the Scottish press, provoking wild words. At Lingerbay on Harris, plans by construction giant Lafarge to create a vast 'super quarry' have finally been abandoned after a planning appeal that lasted more than a decade. Remote Glensanda on the shores of Loch Linnhe was not so lucky—this is the largest quarry in Europe with 6,000 tonnes of granite an hour being loaded on to ships, mostly bound for European and US road schemes. Windfarms and open-cast coal mining continue to exercise rural communities and environmentalists throughout Scotland, with the usual boundary lines of jobs and money versus ecological interests often blurred by aggressive lobbying on both sides.

Hedging their hogs

Since 2003, there has been an annual battle in the Western Isles over the fate of their hedgehogs. Their population has soared thanks to the abundance of birds' eggs. So bad did the problem get that Scottish Natural Heritage, the body charged with preserving the nation's wildlife, decreed that the whole hedgehog population on the Western Isles should be culled. Hedgehog preservation societies rushed from the mainland to save the Uist hedgehogs. Early attempts by SNH staff to trap and kill the creatures failed, and the preservation societies smuggled a handful to the mainland for rehabilitation. The bulk of the islands' 4,000-strong population however remained. By 2005 SNH were trying a new approach, but their plan to hunt out the hedgehogs with dogs may fall foul of anti-hunting legislation.

In the blood

The texture of Scotland—the feel of lava stone, sandstone or granite; of heather, bracken, sand and marram grass; of seaweed, sheep-cropped grass, hedges, wool—has always fed the Scottish imagination, reflected in art, design, poetry and architecture. And while peat may be despised by farmers for its acidity, it's a valuable fuel when dried, and perfumes Harris Tweed and whisky alike.

Puffins, known as the penguins of the air, make nest burrows in the sloping cliffs all around the Scottish coastline in summer

The ultimate game fishing is for wild salmon in Scottish rivers

Haggis is a tasty dish of minced offal, onion, spices and oatmeal

Many Scottish pubs are still dens for serious drinking

Throwing the hammer at the Highland Games

Walkers manufacture some 10,000 mouth-watering tonnes of shortbread each year

Scottish golfer Colin Montgomerie has won the European Tour Order of Merit a record eight times

Keeping Body and Soul
Together

Summertime street entertainment, Dundee

Downhill skiing is a popular winter sport

Scotland's weather is constantly varying, with a vocabulary to suit. There is no direct English translation for 'dreich', which means cold, raw, grey, damp. Be prepared: not just for rainy days, but for that sudden prospect of brilliance when you've got to get out of the city or miss the sight of a lifetime.

The need to defy the elements has partly created the landscape. Heating for homes was necessary from the start, and tree-felling by the early settlers left much of the land covered with bog. Coal mining was followed by whaling for blubber-oil, and then by William Murdoch's gas lighting and James Young's shale-derived paraffin, but it was in the 1980s—thanks to offshore oil and nuclear energy—that the Scots finally caught up with the rest of Britain on central heating.

The climate has bred a culture of hard outdoor labour, powered by drink and high-fat food, and countered by hard enjoyment: the military sports of the Highland gatherings, and dancing for men. Highland culture shows the traces of traditional hunting in fishing, deerstalking and shooting, reflecting short winter and long summer days.

Playing the game

The Scots have been 'fitba-daft' (soccer crazy) since the 1860s, when Saturday afternoons became work-free and footballs cheap. The Glasgow Boys' Brigade ran the biggest amateur league in Europe and many players went on to local and national teams. Class and sectarian conflict still pervade the Old Firm of (Protestant) Rangers and (Catholic) Celtic, but what do bought-in European players know of such grievances? While many spectators are content to watch from the sofa at home or down the pub, tickets to the big games still sell out fast. Rugby Union was always more genteel, but a working-class sport in the Borders. The Rugby Sevens are an exciting introduction to the game. In the Highlands, shinty—a form of field hockey—prevails.

Stephen Hendry has won snooker's World Championship seven times

Celtic and Rangers do battle at Hampden Park

Irn Bru: Those in the know swear by the bottled stuff

Sporting heroes

While golf is viewed as an elitist game in much of Britain, in Scotland, where it was invented, golf was and is pretty democratic, with public courses readily available. At the opposite end of the scale it has become big bucks as 'corporate golf', producing heroes such as Sam Torrance and Sandy Lyle. Curling—the sliding of polished granite stones along the ice—is a peculiarly Scottish pastime that developed in the 18th century. Colder winters once saw curlers at their open-air 'bonspiels'; now it's played on indoor rinks, and is gaining a new following thanks to a gold medal performance by a Scottish ladies team at the 2002 Winter Olympics, watched by millions on television. TV has also taken snooker and motor-racing, Scottish specialties, into the very big time, with names such as David Coulthard.

Munros with mobiles

Scotland has been a leisure-landscape since the Victorians came north to shoot and fish. Youth hostels and Munro-bagging—climbing the peaks over 3,000ft (914.4m)—inspired worker-climbers in the 1930s into the perils and triumphs of hard rock. It's an unforgiving and little-tracked country, prone to fog and downpour, which needs warm clothes, waterproofs, good boots, maps and compasses and emergency rations. Twenty-eight volunteer mountain rescue teams around the country do sterling work to rescue the stranded, but it's important to remember that, no, you won't survive a Highland blizzard by taking your mobile phone. Walkers in Scotland have the right to roam in the countryside—although they are obliged to consider the rights of other land users, including farmers and gamekeepers.

Eating and drinking

Scottish fish is legendary, and fish farms are now worth more than shipbuilding. Herring grilled in an oatmeal crust, with gooseberry sauce, is the food of the gods. And try the national dish, haggis, traditionally served with 'bashed neeps and tatties' (mashed turnips and potato). Meaty broths with barley or lentils are still served in the pubs. A few selected menus, like the great Scottish fry-up (bacon, eggs, sausages, tomatoes, mushrooms, with fried bread or potato scones) are fine if eaten once; repeated, they're a heart attack on a plate. And if whisky (▷ 242–243) is not your thing, drink the orange fizz called Irn Bru—claimed to be more popular here than Coca-Cola. It was devised to quench the thirsts of those given to stirring molten iron—and is also noted as a hangover cure.

Shopping

A recent survey put Edinburgh and Glasgow among the Top 10 happening cities of Britain—at No. 2 and No. 7, they both scored more highly for 'buzz' than London (No. 9). Wander through the shopping steets and modern malls of either city and you might wonder how a country with a population of just 5 million can sustain quite so many trendy designer boutiques. Part of the answer lies with visitors, who like to shop—each year, they spend over £250 million on clothes alone. Cheap flights from Norway and Denmark have allowed a new wave of Viking invaders into the country, and Glasgow has become the unofficial shopping capital of Scandinavia.

The lion rampant, a flag dating to the 13th century

Presiding Officer George Reid, MSP, the public face of the Scottish Parliament

The Forth Rail Bridge, a Scottish icon since 1890

Pillars of
Society

Scotland has a proud tradition of education of the individual for the betterment of the community, and laws for the provision of free, compulsory education for all children age 5–16 have been in place since 1872. In a land where settlements may be tiny and remotely scattered, there are some very small schools indeed. The island of Canna, for instance, has a primary school with just two pupils.

The pattern of tertiary education owes more to historic links with continental Europe than with neighbouring England. While the older universities, established back in the 15th century, may major on familiar academic subjects, vocational colleges offer a diversity of practical qualifications for the 21st century. For instance, the recently formed UHI Millennium Institute, which undertakes university-level education at 15 locations across the Highlands and Islands, offers degrees relevant to local interests including Gaelic and Media Studies, and Mariculture Science (marine aquaculture), moving the tradition forward.

Common Riding to re-establish town boundaries is an ancient tradition of the Borders

Monarchs of the Glens

Who owns Scotland? The Duke of Buccleuch, of Bowhill and Drumlanrig (▷ 57) is the last grandee, with 81,000ha (200,000 acres). The State, through the Forestry Commission and the Ministry of Defence, owns huge tracts, as do the banks and building societies who lend to home-buyers. Around 60 per cent of households rented 'cooncil hooses' in 1980, a number now halved, leaving problematic high-rises and run-down housing in the cities. Housing associations are seen as a way out for 'excluded Scots', whose situation is dramatized in the novels of James Kelman and Irvine 'Trainspotting' Welsh.

Glasgow-born Lorraine Kelly presents her own morning TV show, LK Today

The Garden Lobby of the new Scottish Parliament building by Holyroodhouse

Parliament House

The hammerbeam hall behind St. Giles Cathedral in Edinburgh has housed, since 1707, the Scots legal hierarchy. This runs from local Justices of the Peace (JPs) to Sheriff Courts, the High Court and Court of Session. Scottish judges wear robes with huge red crosses and are called Lord. Their principles, even after centuries of British legislation, are closer to European law than to English. If you are involved in a serious accident or a death, you will encounter the Procurator-Fiscal (an examining magistrate), who has no English counterpart. The final courts of appeal are the House of Lords and increasingly the European Court. Scotland's advocates (barristers) and writers (solicitors) have changed a lot since Sir Walter Scott's claret-fuelled day: Solicitors are (unlike in England) efficient house agents and property managers.

Scapegrace Oor Wullie has appeared in thousands of comic strip episodes since 1936

Provost and bailie adieu

Local government is increasingly less local in Scotland. The old burghs—once 175 of them, with their provosts, bailies (JPs) and councillors the great engine of local government—have now vanished under 32 multi-purpose councils. The land areas they cover range from tiny Clackmannan to Highland (bigger than Belgium), though community councils in many small towns still deal with parking, sports facilities and amenities. Despite their novelty and occasional unpopularity, the new councils have been regarded as a success story, especially for the effective way they have dealt with emergencies such as the outbreak of foot and mouth disease in 2001.

Westminster— who cares?

The leaders of two of the three main political parties at Westminster— Labour's Tony Blair and the Liberal Democrats' Sir Menzies Campbell— are Scots-born (Edinburgh and Glasgow). Scotland sends 59 elected representatives (MPs) south to the London parliament (41 Labour, 11 Liberal Democrats, 6 Scottish Nationalists, 1 Conservative). While Scotland's own parliament has certain legislative powers (▷ 5), Westminster has reserved control of defence, foreign affairs, currency, economic policy and media, and the Secretary of State for Scotland continues as a role within the Cabinet. As for relations to Edinburgh's Scottish Executive? First Minister Jack McConnell says he has more dealings with the European Parliament in Brussels…

Europe ahoy!

Scotland's best-kept political secret is its eight Members of the European Parliament (or MEPs), elected by proportional representation on an all-Scotland list, who go to Brussels and Strasbourg. The European Union's Committee of the Regions has been disappointing, but the Scotland Europa office in Brussels (www.scotland europa.com) is a good contact point. Scotland's EU record is mixed— severe setbacks in fisheries policy, envy of 'Celtic Tiger' Ireland's nifty Brussels manoeuvring for extra funds—but Scots regard themselves as more European than the rest of Britain. Since 2002 you can sail direct from Zeebrugge in Belgium to Rosyth: The trip is not cheap, nor at 16 hours as Superfast as the company name, but it is very comfortable, and makes the Forth Bridge literally the gateway to the North.

A modern brooch to a traditional design by Hector Russell, and (far right) an imitation leather kilt for the 21st century, by Geoffrey Tailor Kiltmakers

Ace percussionist Evelyn Glennie, on the gamelan

19th-century Wemyss ware revived in the 21st by Griselda Hill

Glasgow's cutting-edge Scottish Exhibition and Conference Centre, nicknamed 'the Armadillo'

Culture and the Arts

Local heroics

Think global, act local: This really works in cultural activities that enrich communities across the country through drama, music, literature and history groups, writers in residence, craftworkers' circles, small publishers and museums. The last have gone from 150 to over 400 since the 1960s, and range from the fortress-like Museum of Scotland (▷ 78–81) to little treasures such as the Wick Heritage Centre (▷ 142). Schools and village halls are pressed into service for community activities that pull people together, although the competition with an evening in front of the television may be tough. National movements tend to stress youth and nativism, but how much of this activity could survive without the input of the retired and the incomers?

Scotland makes a distinct but misleading cultural impression. Only one culture? Hugh MacDiarmid exploded: 'Scotland small? Our…intricate multifold Scotland small?' An intensely regional popular culture contains far more variety than just Scots and Gaelic. The Lowland country folk have their ballads, Common Ridings, dances with fiddle and accordion bands, and exhausting strathspeys and reels (local dances are held all over the country). Scandinavian themes have influenced Orkney and Shetland from the Sagas onwards, celebrated in the stunning Orkney Festival in the great medieval cathedral at Kirkwall and in Viking Up Helly Aa festivals across Shetland.

Once denounced as 'speaking common', dialect is now being encouraged. Bizarrely, the self-appointed guardian of Scottish dialect, the Boord o' Braid Scots, is in Northern Ireland (where the Protestants demanded funding to match Gaelic resources now awarded to the Catholics). Doric, the full-strength Scottish dialect, is at its strongest in the northeast, and sounds almost like another language.

Who wants Ed Fest?

Not Edinburgh, at first. For long after its start in 1947 residents much preferred the excitement of the Military Tattoo at the castle, where the prancing cavalry was supplied by the Co-op's milk-float horses. Folk came around after seeing the injection of huge amounts of tourist cash and businesses drawn to the city by this annual world-famous festival. Today there are 30 or so big productions in the official Edinburgh Festival, and something close to a thousand on the Fringe, with spin-offs such as the Book Festival (▷ 175). Since being designated Europe's culture capital for 1990, Glasgow has developed its own cultural festivals, led by the fabulous folk fest, Celtic Connections, in January.

Storyteller Mairi Hedderwick's enchanting red-headed creation, Katie Morag (above)

Ewan MacGregor in *Trainspotting* (1995)

Taking part in the Fringe

Painting…

…was almost unknown among the Scots until the 18th century, but then grew up very rapidly via Allan Ramsay, Henry Raeburn, David Wilkie, the Glasgow Boys of the 1880s and the Scottish Colourists of the 1900s, and can be seen in world-class galleries in Glasgow and Edinburgh (Scottish art schools have always looked to Europe, not to London). Modern painting remains representational with many strong individual styles: Peter Howson, John Bellany, Stephen Campbell. Good paintings from the Royal Scottish Academy and other artist-run bodies can be bought at reasonable prices in many private galleries. The sensationalism of Young British Artists? It's at this point you know you are in a different country: Scots don't really care. For the same daft prices you could get a D. Y. Cameron, an Elizabeth Blackadder or a Stephen Conroy. No contest.

Written for kids

Scotland has a rich tradition of storytelling for children, from the yarns of Robert Louis Stevenson to J. M. Barrie's creation, Peter Pan. Modern classics include Mollie Hunter's historical fiction and Joan Lingard's haunting tales of displacement for older children. A firm favourite with youngsters, Mairi Hedderwick's beautifully illustrated Katie Morag adventures on the Isle of Struay made their first appearance in 1984, loosely based on the author's own experiences of living on the Hebridean island of Coll (▷ 131). Look, too, for her several illustrated accounts (for adults) of travelling around Scotland. Also popular is Maisie the kilted cartoon cat, who lives in an Edinburgh where even the street names and bus numbers are familiar.

Gaelic awake! Or Gaelic: a wake?

Although the language issue marks literary politics in Wales, Scots Gaelic, with fewer than 60,000 speakers, seems headed for its deathbed. Or will projects like Gaelic pre-school playgroups and Sabhal Mór Ostaig, the Gaelic college on Skye backed by the nationalist-inclined financier Sir Iain Noble, snatch it back to life? To hear Gaelic spoken as a natural, first language in everyday use, travel to the Western Isles. Gaelic culture is celebrated each year at the Mod, a festival with competitions in writing and song, which moves from town to town. For a glimpse into the pattern and rhythm of this lyrical language, try the poetry of Skye-born Sorley MacLean (1911–96)—in translation, of course.

Ian Rankin, author of the Inspector Rebus novels, paints a gritty portrait of the Scottish crime world

Furious fiddling from the Shetland band Fiddlers' Bid takes the folk tradition forward for the next generation

Birling (spinning) at a ceilidh

Space-age architecture at Glasgow's Science Centre

Music

Robert Burns celebrated a contradictory power in the Calvinist psalm and the secular—often bawdy—ballad. Hamish Henderson rediscovered many of these after 1945, and singers from Jeannie Robertson to Jean Redpath, fiddlers, and folk-bands such as the Battlefield Band, have kept the tradition alive and kicking. Contemporary music runs from the Singing Kettle for children, via an Atlantic jazz scene through to tough brassy ladies—Annie Ross, Lulu, Annie Lennox, Shirley Manson. Political pop is belted out by folk-rockers such as Runrig and the Proclaimers. And the British pop charts are enriched by bands like Texas and Franz Ferdinand. There is a relatively thin heritage of classical and stage music, but Scotland has inspired others over the centuries, including Hector Berlioz *(Waverley)* and Lerner and Loewe *(Brigadoon)*.

For the children: The *Jacobite* steam train shares the West Highland line with a *Hogwarts* special

Public building

Charles Rennie Mackintosh's buildings in Glasgow (▷ 114–115) proved a hard act for architects to follow. The city's titanium-clad millennium Science Centre, by the Building Design Partnership, cost a cool £75 million (▷ 111) and suggests a new confidence in the design of public structures. And Sir Norman Foster's SECC (1997), nicknamed the Armadillo, has helped raise the profile of regeneration in the heart of the city. In Edinburgh, the colossally expensive Parliament building of the late Enrico Miralles at Holyrood was completed in July 2004 and is a stunner (▷ 173). Meanwhile Benson and Forsyth's 1999 striking fortress-like Museum of Scotland (▷ 78–81) is still courting controversy, as the confusion of its interior structure is rationalized.

Viking fun at the Up Helly Aa fire festival, Shetland

The Story of Scotland

Hunter-Gatherers to Macbeth

As history has retreated from the landscape, it has regrouped in museums—Scotland has more than 400 of them, mostly opened since the 1960s. Most notable is the Museum of Scotland in Edinburgh (▷ 78–81): Here it's immediately apparent just how complex the Scottish past has been.

It's not, for a start, that of an ethnically homogeneous nation. Human settlement goes back to the retreat of the ice-cap after 10,000BC, when hunter-gatherer communities foraged here in summer. The absence of trees over much of northern Scotland meant the extensive use of stone, and elaborate buildings—settlements, temples, passage graves—testify to a sophisticated culture, in touch with Europe, contemporary with the pyramids. This was followed, in the Bronze and Iron Ages, by farming communities.

Scotland was only temporarily held by the Romans, and on their departure in the fifth century the land was divided between the Britons in the southwest, the Scots (who straddled the Irish Sea) and the Picts in the Grampian region. The Angles pressed north along the east coast, and in the eighth century came waves of Vikings from Scandinavia. They ravaged and looted, then settled in Orkney and Shetland and along the west coast.

Remarkably, by the 11th century there was something like national unity, first under the MacAlpins and ultimately under the MacMalcolms. After 1066 this unified kingdom faced the power of the Norman kings of England. Yet they managed to coexist for almost 250 years before a formal struggle for independence began.

AD43

The Norman-Scots

There was no Norman conquest of Scotland, but after 1066 Scottish monarchs increased their own power, and their chance of good relations with England (which then had huge French possessions) by encouraging the immigration of Norman, Flemish and Breton knights, merchants and monks. Names like Fraser, Bruce and Stewart stem from this period, and many Norman-Scots had big estates in England for which they paid homage to the English king.

Below, a reconstructed Iron-Age longhouse above the beach at Bosta on Lewis shows how snug such a dwelling could be

Early stone structures remain on Orkney: the village of Skara Brae (above) and Maes Howe (right)

Recording history

The Scots were bad at this in the early days: Documentation really only dates from the 1400s. Up to that time, the records kept in abbeys were the basis for medieval history—monks had to be meticulous in recording dates, as they wanted hard facts about when land was taken over or benefactors died. The Wars of Independence (▷ 24–25) would later impose a national framework on these records, in the accounts of chroniclers Walter Bower (1385–1449) and Andrew of Wyntoun (c1350–1420), and Archdeacon Barbour's *The Bru* (c1375). Many of the records on which they were based were lost at sea in 1652, as Oliver Cromwell tried to move them south.

The case for Macbeth

William Shakespeare, writing in 1606, got the story for his play from Wyntoun, via the translated *Chronicles* of Wyntoun's French contemporary Jean Froissart. The real Macbeth was Mormaer (Great Steward) of Moray at a time when Scottish kings had to be acceptable to these regional magnates. He became king in 1040 by defeating and killing Duncan I (his junior) in battle, and ruled with some success, even feeling secure enough to visit Rome in 1050. In 1057 he was in turn challenged and killed by Malcolm Canmore, Duncan's son, who became Malcolm III. History is always written by the victors.

Left, illumination from the *Book of Kells*, which may have been created on Iona; in an age when records were handwritten, the documentation of history was laborious

Rome's special daughter

In AD663 Oswiu, King of Northumbria, rejected Celtic forms of Christianity for the Roman version. The Scottish kingdoms followed suit. David I (c1080–1153) radically expanded the number of bishoprics from three to nine and invited in the monastic orders, encouraged by the papacy, which was then greatly reviving in its strength. In this he was influenced, like all of Northern Europe, by Pope Urban's preaching of the First Crusade in 1095. Popes and kings soon fought over Church autonomy. In 1175 the bishopric of Glasgow was taken from the authority of the Archbishop of York, to become a 'special daughter' of Rome, with a direct reporting line. The rest of the Church in Scotland soon followed.

Roman mask, AD80

Pictish crosses

You'll find the frozen eloquence of these in the Perth area and around the Moray Firth. The greatest, such as Hilton of Cadboll, have pre-Christian symbols and scenes on one side—discs, broken lances, lively hunting scenes, battles and feasts—and Christian symbols on the other. The Picts, dominant here in the seventh century, left few records other than these. In the eighth century they submitted to a takeover by the Scots, driven eastward by Viking raids.

Pictish stone carving combined Celtic and Christian imagery—see it at Meigle (▷ 99)

1200

Arcaded cloisters at Iona, where the Irish monk Columba arrived in AD563 (▷ 130–131)

Stylized Pictish decoration on two plaques from seventh century AD, discovered at Norrie's Law, Fife

The Price of Freedom

The so-called Wars of Independence were as much a struggle for mastery in Scotland between several great Norman-Scots families, as against the English. The background to this was the stand-off in Europe between an increasingly powerful Plantagenet monarch in England, and the rulers of France who were out to evict him from his French possessions.

Edward I was the most formidable English king: legalistic, reforming, but also the ruthless conqueror of Wales. He attempted to secure overlordship on his terms. Scots noblemen were not in principle hostile, but they resented being taxed to support Edward's French wars. Between 1295 and his death in 1307, Edward invaded Scotland four times. He was opposed by a minor noble, William Wallace (c1274–1305), who raised a force and defeated Edward's army at Stirling Bridge in 1297. Wallace intrigued with possible allies abroad, and was ultimately captured, hanged and dismembered at Smithfield, London in 1305.

This was the signal for an ambitious campaign by Robert Bruce, Earl of Carrick (1274–1329), to take over the Scots throne and provide the focus for an increasingly national resistance. Edward II's Scots allies were steadily swept aside by Bruce. In 1314 Edward suffered a crushing defeat at Bannockburn, and Bruce's recognition within Scotland as Robert I was confirmed. England finally came to terms in 1328.

William Wallace (left) became one of Scotland's first national heroes
Right, the Declaration of Arbroath, 1320

A declaration

In 1320 the nobility, bishops and 'community of the realm' petitioned Pope John XXII to support their right to independence. Their words made up one of the finest pieces of political rhetoric of all time:

We are bound to him (King Robert) for the maintaining of our freedom both by his right and his merits, as to him by whose salvation has been wrought unto our people, and by him... we mean to stand. Yet if he should give up what he has begun, seeking to make us or our kingdom subject to the king of England or the English, we would strive at once to drive him out as our enemy.... For, as long as a hundred of us remain alive, we will never on any conditions be subjected to the lordship of the English. For we fight not for glory, or riches, or honour, but for freedom alone...

1200

Edward III at the gates of Berwick, from Froissart's *Chronicles*

The auld alliance

Scotland's special relationship with France lasted from 1295 to 1560—more lasting was the Scots taste for French wine, architecture, philosophy and culture, which still continues. Most Scottish attempts to invade England, at the request of their French allies, were disastrous, and there was only one significant use of French troops in Scotland, in James III's reign (1460–88): They were not popular. Clerics and chroniclers portrayed the alliance as a national cause, perhaps to stifle popular discontent. Meanwhile the Anglo-Scottish split widened. Scotland was hit less severely than England by the Black Death (1349-50), but from parity with the pound sterling the currency began to sink into the cellar, and trade was menaced by English piracy.

Lords of the Isles

Relations between MacDonald and Campbell are, even today, cool. In the Middle Ages half the Scots people lived in the Highlands, and were dominated by Clan Donald, whose power ran from Donegal in Ireland to Inverness and Lewis. As Lords of the Isles they conducted their own diplomacy for their own ends. Post-reformation kings gave preference to the Protestant Clan Campbell, based at Inveraray. Despite a setback stemming from the Massacre at Glencoe, 1692, the Argathelians (as the followers of the Campbell Duke of Argyll were known) dominated politics until population shifts moved authority into the hands of Edinburgh lawyers.

The Stewarts...

...(later Stuarts) were a Breton family, who became Stewards to the Bruces, until one married Robert I's daughter and became Robert II in 1371. Stewart monarchs, provided they lived to grow up, were intelligent, determined, and, given a chance, greedy. They defeated the great nobles, most dramatically the Douglases of the south-west, and their most successful king, James IV (1488–1513), played the Renaissance monarch, extorting greater autonomy for the Scottish Church, which he and his son then looted. It's from this period that Scotland's oldest intact secular stone buildings date: Most castles and halls built before this time were of timber, plaster and wattle.

Left, Robert the Bruce statue, Bannockburn

Border ballads

The Scots ballads have been compared to the Greek epics. Sung or declaimed in the halls of the Border towers and carried by gypsies and tinkers, they retold the battles, loves and tragedies of the 'debatable land'. Their language could vary in the same ballad from the plodding to the sublime. Some were set down by Allan Ramsay in the 1720s, and later by Sir Walter Scott and James Hogg, although Hogg's mother complained, 'If you write them down, folk winnae sing them nae mair'. This seemed to be the case, yet folklorist Hamish Henderson encountered the remarkable Jeannie Robertson in 1946—a tinker woman, illiterate, who still had more than 100 of the great ballads off by heart.

James III of Scotland (1452–88), whose policies brought about a war with England in 1480

1513

William Wallace was played by Mel Gibson (above) in the 1995 movie *Braveheart*, which captured the spirit of Scottish nationalism

Castles like those at Caerlaverock (above) and Duart (left) were built in this age of conflict

A Covenanted People

The Auld Alliance was wearing thin by 1513, and there was a mounting crisis as Church property declined, leading to weakness and corruption. Reform was delayed until it was too late. France was backing the Counter-Reformation (the radical reform movement within the Roman Catholic Church), while Scots intellectuals embraced the Protestantism associated with John Calvin (1509–64) and Geneva.

Again the fulcrum was an active and insensitive English monarch, Henry VIII. Following his defeat of James IV at Flodden in 1513, Henry drove repeatedly into Scotland, leaving a trail of burned towns and abbeys behind him, but also an increasingly resistant Scots population. The French continued to use their advantage to effect, but eventually their great hope, Mary of Guise (widow of James V and mother of Mary Stewart), a fervent Counter-Reformer, drove the Scots away. John Knox led Protestant riots at Perth in 1559 and, when the French left in 1560, founded the Protestant Church of Scotland (the Kirk). A year later Mary Stewart arrived.

Catholic Mary (1542–87), Queen of Scotland at one week old, had married the Dauphin in France. The accidental death of the French King in 1559 made her Queen of both France and Scotland. Her husband died when she was 18, and in 1561 she returned to a Scotland which had become radically Protestant. The contrast between the splendour of the French court and 'black Genevan' kirk was stark.

Below, the Sealed Knot re-enact a battle of the Civil War

1513

The trouble with Mary

Mary, backed by the might of France, was handsome, intelligent and athletic; she was also impulsive and uncalculating. She wed her cousin Henry Stewart, Lord Darnley, whom she called King Henry I. Unstable and probably syphilitic, a Catholic, then a waverer, he alienated his wife by murdering her secret lover David Riccio. Mary revenged herself through her new love, the Earl of Bothwell, who had Darnley murdered in 1567. She married Bothwell, but he lacked a power base. The two were opposed by the Protestant nobility, and overthrown at a skirmish east of Edinburgh. Mary was forced to abdicate, and her baby son was crowned James VI at Stirling in 1567. She was finally executed for treason by Elizabeth I.

Mary, Queen of Scots (right), made her home at Holyroodhouse in Edinburgh (below)

Hard times for Highlanders: *The Massacre of Glencoe*, by James Hamilton (▷ 127)

The wisest fool...

...was a great survivor. James VI (1566–1625) reigned for nearly 60 years. His early years were marked by intrigue and unstable regencies, until he was formally made Elizabeth of England's heir in 1583. He resumed the Stewart drive to power, subordinating the Kirk and the nobility and even trying to take on the Highlands. He was successful and conceited, with a tendency to lecture. As an enlightened patron he grasped at the wealth he encountered after reaching the English—or 'Great British' as he preferred—throne in 1603 as James I. However, he overestimated both his control over Scotland, and the permanency of his management of English politics, for he failed to confront the Puritans in the English Parliament.

James VI and I

Kirk and covenant

Scots Calvinists had a fairly political attitude to religion, which was framed by covenants: contracts between man and God, and man and his rulers. James VI/I had outmanoeuvred them, but his successor was proud, obstinate and not very bright. In 1638 Charles I's attempts to impose Anglican forms on the Kirk led to the National Covenant and military confrontation. Charles lost these Bishops' Wars (1639–40) and, bankrupt, conceded power to the London Parliament. He reneged and the Civil War broke out in 1642. The Scots initially co-operated with the Parliamentarians, but when leader Oliver Cromwell didn't play along with their attempt to impose Presbyterianism throughout Britain, they again courted the King, and failed.

The Killing Time

The monarchy was restored to the joint Crown in 1660, and with it the Edinburgh parliament. While most ministers made their peace with the new regime, a minority in the southwest did not and were expelled from their parishes. Their supporters, the Covenanters, started an intermittent rebellion of risings and guerrilla attacks, which was met with force—the Killing Time—by Charles II's commissioners. Casualties were low, but martyrdom and repression created a lasting culture of popular resistance. In 1688 Catholic King James VII and II was overthrown and exiled. A Jacobite campaign to restore him failed when its leader, Viscount Dundee, was killed at Killiecrankie (▷ 95). New monarchs William and Mary restored the rights of Kirk and parliament, though with bad grace.

Left, a leather mask worn as a disguise by a Covenanting minister who feared for his life in the Killing Time

Darien, famine and union

In the 1690s there were years of severe famine, with many deaths. About a quarter of the country's wealth vanished when the ill-fated attempt to create a Scottish trading post on the isthmus of Darien, in Panama, failed due to fever, and English and Spanish interference. The Westminster Parliament worried what would happen when Anne, last of the Stuart monarchs, died, while the Scots Parliament threatened an independent foreign policy. This led to an extended political crisis (1701–07), in which the Scots nobility, merchants and Kirk were bribed into a formal union with England.

THE Several Journals of the Court of Directors of the COMPANY of SCOTLAND Trading to Africa and the Indies;

1707

The Darien Scheme (above) promised much but left the coffers empty (left). The battle at Killiecrankie (below) was another blow to the Jacobites

A COVENANTED PEOPLE 27

Enlightenment and Progress

The Union was undertaken for reasons of short-term expediency. Its boasted advantages took over 20 years to materialize, but this was a period of relative calm, and the Jacobites (followers of the exiled Stewarts) got little support on the three occasions they attempted invasion. The cultural foundations of later social revolution were laid, notably among lawyers, in the Kirk and in the universities. England needed Scotland: Its trade routes were free from French raiding, and Glasgow's dominance of the tobacco trade was an economic breakthrough.

Society started to adopt the new opportunities, and classical architecture and art flourished. Intellectually Scotland overtook England, with William Robertson (1721–93) and David Hume (1711–76) emerging as leading historians. Law, science, agricultural improvement: These were rapidly disseminated by clubs and societies, along with road building, land enclosure and efforts to create a Scottish militia. By the 1780s a French visitor said he could stand at Edinburgh's toll booth and 'within half an hour take fifty men of genius by the hand'. The Enlightenment was typified by economist Adam Smith (1723–90) and philosophers Thomas Reid (1710–96) and Adam Ferguson (1723–1816), scientifically radical but socially conservative thinkers who feared the social impact of the new commercialism. By the 1780s, Scotland rivalled England in industrial and urban growth. The downside was the clearance in the Highlands after 1745 of tenant crofters to make way for huge-scale sheep farming.

The last war on British soil

In 1745 Prince Charles Edward Stewart (1720–88), son of the Old Pretender to the throne, James III, raised an army at Glenfinnan. Supposedly backed by the French, this turned into a move that menaced the government in London. The Jacobites took Edinburgh before swinging southward. But few joined the cause in England; the French didn't invade, and the dispirited army retreated to Culloden (▷ 125) where it was crushed by an army of (predominantly Scots) soldiers under George II's son, the Duke of Cumberland. The prince fled.

Left, *Prince Charles Edward Stewart*, by Antonio David, 1732

1707

On 19 August 1745 Bonnie Prince Charlie landed at Glenfinnan (right) to raise an army

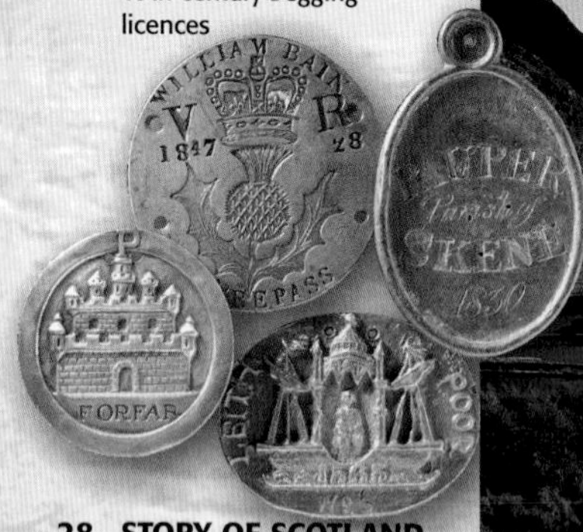

19th-century begging licences

New town, new village

New Pitsligo, Gavinton, Helensburgh: Some 120 such villages were built by 'improving' lairds, as a means of easing their people away from the self-governing townships to the rationally structured 'muckle farm' (great farm), the linen industry or the first factories. The new villages were designed to keep people on the land, as the cultured classes were worried about the social dangers posed by the growth of large towns. They contained the amenities—schools, church, dispensary, library—which 17th-century Scotland had so conspicuously lacked, and were laid out in symmetrical rectangles with well-proportioned houses and gardens. Edinburgh's New Town (▷ 84–85) would follow the same principle on a grander scale.

'Ossian' (1762)

Poet James Macpherson (1736–96) was of Gaelic origins and claimed to have discovered manuscripts of a lost third-century Celtic epic poem about the legendary hero Fingal, as told to his son Ossian. Its impact was like that of *The Lord of the Rings* two centuries later—but could it be a fake? This question divided the literary pundits of Edinburgh and London. English lexicographer Dr. Samuel Johnson's doubts led to his journey north in 1773, with his friend James Boswell in attendance, as recounted in his classic *A Journey to the Western Isles of Scotland*. Johnson was right, as Macpherson failed to produce his 'original' manuscripts. Yet for a generation of European writers, on the eve of the romantic movement, 'Ossian' provided a powerful cultural input.

Brothers in arms

The Union and southern wealth gave access for Scots professionals to wealthy English patrons, and opened up the Grand Tour of Europe to the local nobility. Clever Scots, travelling with aristocrats on the Grand Tour, codified the rules of classical architecture. By the mid-18th century the Scots laird's (landowner's) house was Palladian in style, and his architects—including Sir William Chambers (1726–96) and brothers Robert (1728–92) and James (1730–94) Adam, who also left their mark on London as architects of the king's works—were among the best in the world.

Portrait of an age

The great portrait painter Sir Henry Raeburn (1754–1823) was an Edinburgh orphan, raised in a charity school. He studied under Sir Joshua Reynolds, but forewent the grand style for intimate, psychologically profound studies of the lairds, clergy, lawyers and professors of 'improving' Scotland. He became the visual counterpart to literary giant Sir Walter Scott, although doubt has recently been cast on whether the celebrated portrait of Reverend Robert Walker (below) is one of his works.

The memorable portrait, *The Reverend Robert Walker Skating on Duddingston Loch*

Far left, handwritten manuscript of Robert Burns's poem, *Queen Mary's Lament*

Left, economist and philosopher Adam Smith, whose grave is in Edinburgh's Canongate kirkyard (▷ 70)

1815

Adam Smith's ground-breaking *Wealth of Nations* (1776) examined the effects on different economic groups of the pursuit of self-interest

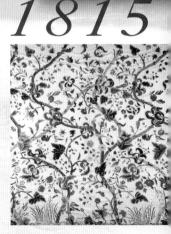

Fine crewelwork from 1719, in the Museum of Scotland

The World's Workshop

In 1859 Samuel Smiles, Haddington-born doctor, radical and railway entrepreneur, published *Self-Help*, a collective biography of innovators and reformers which claimed that success depended on moral integrity and hard work rather than intelligence and scientific training. It's a process that could describe Scotland's industrial progress to that date.

The needs created by the Napoleonic Wars (1800–15) had boosted the cotton, wool, linen and iron industries. Scotland's real breakthrough came in 1828, however, when gasworks engineer J. B. Neilson (1792–1865) devised a means of smelting the high-grade mixture of iron and coal called blackband, found in the Monkland district of Glasgow: It gave a very pure form of iron, which could be cast or turned with great accuracy. This changed the pace of industrialization, attracting engineers and industrialists to Clydeside like a magnet. Steam engines were built, first for textile manufacture, then for ships and sugar-cane crushers. By 1848 Scotland was connected to England by two railway lines, and locomotive-building was starting. By 1900, Glasgow had what was, outside Philadelphia, the world's greatest railway engineering complex.

The new industrial Scotland was not a safe place to live. Houses were tiny and sanitation rudimentary. Cholera killed thousands between 1832 and 1866. In 1871 three-quarters of Glasgow families lived in houses of two rooms or fewer. A primitive poor law couldn't cope with industrial unemployment. The school system—advanced by English standards, with most of the population literate—buckled under the strain and had to be radically reformed in 1872.

Wee Frees

Disruption was the word of the year in 1843. The Kirk split and lost control of the poor law and education. Failure to end the intrusion (imposition) of clergy by landowners resulted in a third of the clergy leaving to form the Free Church of Scotland. Religion was a vital part of the social fabric: Social life revolved round the churches, and the hundreds of thousands of poorly paid, ill-treated Irish immigrants—the *gastarbeiter* of Scotland's economic miracle—depended on their priests. From the initiative of one such priest, Father Walfrid, in Glasgow's poverty-racked East End, came in 1888 a young men's soccer team, the now legendary Glasgow Celtic.

1815

GLASGOW DISTRICT SUBWAY
ROUND THE CITY IN HALF AN HOUR

Holyrood Glass Works, Edinburgh
GLASS CUTTING & ENGRAVING

Above, jute workers in Dundee; right, manufacturing in Edinburgh; top, poster for Glasgow's underground railway, opened in 1896

Sun pictures

Portrait photography was taken to new heights by two young Scottish pioneers. David Octavius Hill (1802–70) was a keen recorder, and painted a portrait of the first steam train to arrive in Glasgow in 1831. In 1843 he was commissioned to paint the heroes of the Disruption of the Kirk (see Wee Frees, left). To make the job easier, along with his friend and chemist Robert Adamson (1821–48), he set out to record the men first by taking photographs, using the calotype method invented by William Henry Fox Talbot only two years before. The pair revealed a remarkable talent for the new art form, and opened a studio on Calton Hill for portraits, as well as recording landscapes and scenes such as the fishermen of Newhaven. Their work is now in the National Portrait Gallery (▷ 87).

Below right, an engine-maker's plate identifies its Glasgow origins

Below, Arroll and Fowler's iconic Forth Rail Bridge

Steam at sea

The first successful steamboat in the world sailed on the Forth and Clyde Canal in 1802. In 1812, Henry Bell of Helensburgh put Europe's first commercial steamer, *Comet*, into service on the Clyde, and by 1840 there were regular transatlantic services. But the engines used sea water, which kept efficiency low and fuel consumption high. In the 1850s and 1860s Glasgow engineers Randolph and Elder, along with the scientist James Thomson (brother of William, Lord Kelvin) devised a combination of compound cylinders and condensers which drastically cut fuel consumption. Within three decades the cargo steamer had taken over from the sailing clipper. The world's first commercial turbine steamer, *King Edward VII* (1901) carried Glasgow holiday-makers as part of a huge fleet.

Iron bridges, northern lights

Scots roads were primitive. In 1720 it took two weeks to get from Edinburgh to London. The great civil engineers like Thomas Telford (1757–1834) made fortunes by building roads and canals throughout Britain and Europe, and training up the generation who would build the railways. Telford's bridges at Dean and Craigellachie were the forerunners of masterpieces like Arroll and Fowler's Forth Bridge (1883–90) and Robert 'Concrete Bob' MacAlpine's West Highland Railway (1894–1901). Robert Stevenson (1772–1850), grandfather of writer Robert Louis Stevenson (▷ 88), understood the importance of rail, but his lasting achievement was the chain of 23 powerful lighthouses, including the Bell Rock, constructed in often hellish weather, to protect the shipping on which Scotland's trade depended.

Doctors as heroes

The Scots universities gave Britain its medical élite, notably the Medical Officers of Health in the 1850s—Edinburgh's Henry Littlejohn and Glasgow's William Russell—who ensured that the cities were adequately drained and supplied with clean water, in great projects such as Glasgow's Loch Katrine pipeline (1859). Medical missionaries like David Livingstone (1813–73) and researchers like Ronald Ross (1857–1932), who conquered the malaria-bearing mosquito, and Robert Philip (1857–1939), who did the same for tuberculosis, became role models. Robert Knox, the surgeon who notoriously employed body-snatchers William Burke and William Hare in the 1820s to supply corpses for his Edinburgh dissection room, and preached 'scientific' racism, did not.

1922

Below, photographic portrait of Sandy Linton and his family by Hill and Adamson, 1845

Above, the bars on board the new Clyde steamers rarely closed: hence the phrase 'steamin' drunk'

A *Scottish* World

Scots had always sought careers and fortunes abroad, from the medieval philosopher Duns Scotus to John Paul Jones (1747–92) and Samuel Greig (1735–88), founders respectively of the US and Russian navies. The enormous expansion of the Scots economy in the 19th century accelerated this involvement, and nearly every family saw up to a third of its members emigrate.

The country is marked by this experience, from tangible signs like Madras College in St. Andrews, founded out of Indian trade profits, to an absorption with overseas commerce and missionary work. Alexander Duff (1806–78) created the English-language educational system in India. David Livingstone's reputation crowned a golden age of missionary effort. He was succeeded by many others. New Zealand was partly settled by Free Church migrants under the Rev. Norman MacLeod. Many politicians were of Scots origins; The first Australian federal prime minister, Andrew Fisher (1862–1928), was a former miner from Ayrshire.

Meanwhile, Thomas Blake Glover (1838–1911), builder of the first Japanese railway, and Richard Henry Brunton (1841–1901), who gave Japan a lighthouse system, helped build up a formidable trade competitor.

Emigration posters from 1920 (far right) and 1914 (below); right, David Livingstone, the missionary pioneer

New Scotland

The largest number of Scots emigrants headed for Canada, where they effectively became the ruling élite. The great agitator for self-government in the 1830s was William Lyon Mackenzie from Dundee, and the first federal prime minister after 1867 was Sir John A. MacDonald from Glasgow. The Maritimes saw considerable Gaelic settlement, preserved in local Mods and music, notably in Cape Breton. The great romancer John Buchan was a popular Governor General (1935–40), and his last novel, *Sick Heart River* (1941), expresses an inclusive Canadian nationalism.

1850

ANCHOR DONALDSON PASSENGERS · AGE SATISFIED PASSENGERS

Urgently Wanted

600 MEN FOR CANADA

300 FOR WINNIPEG FARE £4 10/-

300 FOR TORONTO FARE £3 10/-

available sailing dates are:
"Athenia" 29th July   "Andania" 6th Aug.

tion Forms can be obtained from

B AGENCY

ANCHOR LINE

GLASGOW & NEW YORK via Londonderry WEEKLY

Nabobs

Scots made a lot of money out of India, by sheer rapacity as well as trade. Returning home (if they survived) they bought estates and lived well, creating an early Scots taste for fiery curries which continues to this day. Jute from Calcutta brought wealth to Dundee (▷ 93). British administration was reformed, and a later generation immersed themselves in the culture of the East. In 1885 the Indian Congress was founded by a Scot, Allan Hume; a later supporter was Sir Patrick Geddes (1854–1932), the friend of Gandhi and Nehru, whose legacy of humane town-planning is being rediscovered in Scotland, not least with a proposal to make the whole central belt into a linear park focused on the reopened Forth and Clyde Canal.

Drug barons

On a hillside overlooking the village of Lairg in Sutherland is an Indian temple commemorating Sir John Matheson, a tacksman's son from the shores of Loch Shin. In the 1830s Matheson, with his partner Robert Jardine, broke into the oriental trade previously monopolized by London's East India Company. They sold opium to the Chinese and claimed they were advancing Christianity and Western civilization, despite provoking two wars (1839–42 and 1856–60). There were few voices raised against them in their home country, where they were regarded as better landlords than most. Until very recently their descendants, known as Taipans, dominated the Royal Bank of Scotland.

Tourists

Dr. Johnson was followed in his Highland tour by many English artists of the Romantic era— including poets William Wordsworth and Samuel Taylor Coleridge, painter J. M. W. Turner and philosopher John Ruskin. Another visitor, teenage Mary Shelley, brought Scotland into her horror masterpiece *Frankenstein* (1818). German composer Felix Mendelssohn got to Staffa and Fingal's Cave in 1829 and wrote his *Hebrides* overture; US poet Ralph Waldo Emerson visited essayist Thomas Carlyle at Craigenputtoch in 1833, the start of a life-long correspondence; and English pioneer of tourism Thomas Cook followed hard on the heels of Queen Victoria's residence at Balmoral (1848).

A self-made man

A weaver's son who left Dunfermline in 1848 for the US, Andrew Carnegie (1835–1919) became a telegraph operator on the railroads. From there he moved into steel, founding a company which became the largest iron and steel works in the country. He bought out the opposition and crushed the trade unions, and eventually sold out for £89 million in 1901. He returned to Scotland and built a castle at Dornoch. Carnegie gave subsidies to Scots students, funded some superb libraries and endowed an international peace institution.

Below left, Thomas Lipton (1850–1931) from Glasgow founded a tea and grocery empire

Right, tourist Mary Shelley

1914

Above, Carnegie Hall, Dunfermline was named after the great philanthropist

Far left, Lords Strathcona and Mountstephen built the Canadian Pacific Railway in the 1880s

Left, loading a loco for export at Glasgow docks

A SCOTTISH WORLD 33

A Difficult Country

Scots casualties in World War I were huge, as much as 40 per cent over the overall British level, and by concentrating industry on munitions production (who would buy them in peacetime?) and selling shipping, banking and railways to London bodies, the war damaged Scotland's ability to compete. In 1921 unemployment rose to over 20 per cent, and stayed there for 20 years. For the first time, the Scots began to question both the capitalist system and the Union.

One result was 'Red Clydeside'. Before 1914 the Labour movement was little represented here outside the coalfields, but the huge munitions drive of the war radicalized the engineers, the women and the unskilled workers of Glasgow. It was led by charismatic men including John Wheatley (1869–1930), architect of social housing, and James Maxton (1885–1946). Their shadow lay long over the whole of the 20th century, inspiring communist, Labour and nationalist alike.

Another result was the remarkable intellectual movement—the Scottish Renaissance, headed by fire-eating nationalist Hugh MacDiarmid (1892–1978). The manifesto was his long, witty and lyrical poem 'A Drunk Man looks at the Thistle', written during the General Strike of 1926. The renaissance was probably less about nationalism than about struggling free from the religious inhibitions that remained from the 19th century—and about giving a voice to women—but it fundamentally altered Scots' perceptions of themselves. They were no longer the lieutenants of Empire.

Right, humanitarian James Maxton was a leader of the Independent Labour Party

Women in politics

In the 1900s the Scots were ardent suffragettes, with notable stars including World War I heroine Dr. Elsie Inglis, who was a nurse in the Balkans, birth-control pioneer Marie Stopes (1880–1958) and writers Naomi Mitchison (1897–1999) and Rebecca West (1892–1983). The vote came in 1918, but only a handful of women were actually elected to Parliament, perhaps because of the élitist 'grouse moor' image of the Tories on the right and the legacy of male-dominated trade unionism on the left. This situation changed dramatically with the establishment of the Scottish Parliament in 1999. It now has the second highest female representation in Europe.

1914

Right, *Whisky Galore!* hit cinema screens in 1949
Below, a mobile bank brought finance to the remoter population in the 1950s; top, banknotes from 1969

American factories...

...weren't new in Scotland. But after 1945 US firms, worried about being excluded from Europe—not least by communist-dominated regimes—set up satellite factories to assemble mainly consumer goods in designated development areas. This brought Caterpillar tractors and Hoover cleaners to the Glasgow area, Westclox to Dundee (Scotland produced more clocks than Switzerland for a time) and most notably IBM to Greenock, the first settlement in Silicon Glen. The jobs were welcome, even to trade unionists who were often excluded from the factories, and their 'all workers together' spirit was a far cry from the rigidities of old-style heavy industry.

Axeman Beeching

Railway building occurred in Scotland between 1840 and 1880, when about 50 per cent of the people still lived on the land; by the 1900s trains were coming under pressure from trams and buses in the central belt. By the 1950s about a third of the railway system was hopelessly uneconomic, and when Prime Minister Harold Macmillan appointed Dr. Richard Beeching from ICI to rationalize it, Scotland was going to be hard hit. Huge swathes of the country—the Borders, Buchan, Galloway—lost their lines. A fierce political resistance saved the Highland lines to Wick, Kyle of Lochalsh, Oban and Mallaig, routes that are now kept alive partly by their scenic appeal for visitors.

New Towns

The Labour government of 1945–51 tackled the appalling overcrowding of the old city centres with an agenda of building New Towns. East Kilbride and Glenrothes were started in the late 1940s, followed by Cumbernauld, Livingston and Irvine in the 1960s and 1970s. They were well equipped with schools, shops and sports facilities—unlike so many city housing schemes—and found it easy to attract new industries, notably the technology manufacturing of Silicon Glen, but this overspill hit the older cities badly. Glasgow had over a million people in 1945, and scarcely 600,000 in 2001.

Below and right, architect Charles Rennie Mackintosh made his mark on Glasgow in the early 1900s

New art

In the later 19th century, Scottish painters had rejected the Victorian stag-and-glen sentimentalism for the sharpness of the French Barbizon school and, later, the Post-Impressionists. They were never very interested in urban subjects, despite the fact that 75 per cent of Scots lived in big towns. This tradition lasted; Scots art in the 1970s was as conservative—or as exciting—as it had been a century earlier. One major difference from English painting is that the Scots have always preferred representational art. They feel closer to German expressionism than to French and American abstraction. This applies to a recent, talented generation: Elizabeth Blackadder (1931–), John Bellany (1942–), Stephen Conroy (1964–) and Peter Howson (1958–).

1973

Above left, workers at IBM at Greenock, 1960s

Left, BP's oil and gas complex at Grangemouth

Tulips and Fruit, a painting by Scottish Colourist Samuel John Peploe, c1919

The Road to Home Rule

In 1945 the Scottish National Party (SNP) returned its first MP to Westminster—and its last for over 20 years. Although a Covenant in support of home rule got over 2 million signatures, and some young nationalists 'liberated' the Stone of Scone (▷ 72, 99) from Westminster Abbey, home rule was really a non-topic. The economic downturn of the 1960s stirred things up, and the SNP did so well in later polls that Prime Minister Harold Wilson set up a Royal Commission to investigate the possibility of change for Scotland. When this reported in 1973, things had shifted radically.

In the mid-1960s the government had allocated sections of the North Sea for oil exploration, without much confidence that it would prove economic. In November 1973 the Yom Kippur War and Arab pressure on the US pushed up the price of crude oil by a factor of four. This made North Sea oil exploitable and focused international attention on Scotland, where support for the SNP soared. A moderate measure of devolution was rejected at a referendum in 1979, just when the black stuff, and the profits, were coming ashore, but the issue of home rule did not go away.

1973...

A Scottish Parliament

In 1977 the people of Scotland voted in favour of a new Scottish Parliament, partly elected by proportional representation. It met for the first time in July 1999.

In the same year First Minister Donald Dewar commissioned a new Parliament building to be constructed opposite Holyrood Palace. It was to cost £70 million. By the time it was finally completed in July 2004, the cost had soared to £430 million, and a lot of criticism was directed at MSPs.

But the Executive and Parliament has generally performed well. Problems over school exams were resolved, foot-and-mouth disease was met with a co-ordinated policy, and steps have been made towards bettering Scotland's poor record on pollution and recycling. Whether it can deal with the complex problems of re-engaging industry and coping with an ageing population is another matter.

Left, strike protests in the 1980s; below, the Falkirk Wheel

Above, Queen Elizabeth II was greeted warmly on her Golden Jubilee tour, 2002

On the Move

ARRIVING

ARRIVING BY AIR

There are non-stop flights from leading European cities to Edinburgh, Glasgow (International and Prestwick) and Aberdeen airports. From the US, there are regular flights from New York (Newark) to Glasgow (Continental Airlines) and Chicago to Glasgow (American Airlines); there is a variety of regular flights from Canada to Glasgow, Edinburgh and Aberdeen. Visitors from Australia and New Zealand fly to a London airport and then take a domestic flight to Scotland.

London's Heathrow and Gatwick airports are served by all major cities worldwide, and both destinations are connected to Edinburgh, Glasgow, Inverness and Aberdeen by regular daily flights. London's three other airports—Stansted, Luton and London City—also connect with Scotland, and are mainly associated with low-cost airlines such as ScotAirways, Ryanair and easyJet. Other airports in the UK and Ireland also serve international flights with connections to Scotland, including Birmingham International, Manchester and Leeds Bradford.

Glasgow, Edinburgh and Aberdeen airports have information desks, a small number of high street and souvenir shops (including a

The UK's main international airports, including Edinburgh and Glasgow, are operated by BAA

pharmacy), bureaux de change, restaurants, car-rental firms and left-luggage facilities.

Travellers arriving from destinations outside the UK will have to go through customs and passport controls in the normal way. No passport controls are required for travellers within the UK, but most airlines require proof of identity on check-in, such as a passport.

Contacts:
- British Airways, tel 0870 850 9850
- bmibaby, tel 0870 264 2229
- easyJet, tel 0905 821 0905
- Flybe, tel 0871 700 0535
- Ryanair, tel 0906 270 5656
- ScotAirways, tel 0870 606 0707

TIP
You'll find World Duty Free stores in the main airports. If you are flying within the European Union (EU), you can save money on the liquor and tobacco brands in the blue sector of the store; the green sector offers bigger discounts for passengers flying outside the EU.

Edinburgh Airport
Edinburgh's international airport is located at Ingliston, 6 miles (9.6km) west of the city, off the A8.

All public buses depart from the arrivals area in front of the terminal building. Airlink runs services into the middle of Edinburgh every 10 minutes on weekdays, slightly less often at weekends, and every 30 minutes in the evening; buy tickets at the tourist information point inside the airport, from the ticket booth, or on the bus (bright blue livery). The bus route brings you in past the zoo and Murrayfield sports stadium, and goes all the way along Princes Street to Waverley Bridge and the railway station, right in the city centre. A map showing the location of stops is available from the information desk, and there is a map of the route inside the bus.

The airport has a small selection of high street and souvenir shops, including a pharmacy (Boots). Cash machines are located by the

DESTINATION
Edinburgh to city centre
Glasgow to city centre
Glasgow Prestwick International to city centre
Aberdeen to city centre

bureaux de change in the departure lounge.
● Edinburgh EH12 9DN, tel 0870 040 0007 (general enquiries); www.baa.com

Glasgow International Airport

The main airport is located at Paisley, northwest of Glasgow city centre.

All buses depart from the front of the terminal building. CityLink and Fairline Coaches run services into the middle of Glasgow every 10 minutes on weekdays, slightly less often at weekends, and every 30 minutes in the evening, from bus stop 1. Buy your ticket at the Travel Centre information desk or on the bus. Buses go through to Glasgow's Buchanan Street bus station: A map showing stops is available from the transport information desk. Coach (long-distance bus) services collect and drop off on Bute Road, by International Arrivals.

The airport is linked into the National Cycle Network via a route which runs into Paisley, to join up with National Route 7 (Inverness to Carlisle) and

National Route 75 (Leith to Gourock). For information, contact Sustrans, tel 0117 929 0888.

The airport has a small selection of high street and souvenir shops, including a pharmacy (Boots). Cash machines are located by Travelex on the first floor, and similarly in the International Departures lounge. Bureaux de change are open at all hours. There is a children's play area on the first floor and in the International

Departures lounge. There is also an area providing work spaces with pay phone and modem points.
● Paisley PA3 2ST, tel 0870 040 0008; www.baa.com

> ### TIP
> Departing from Glasgow: Check-in desks 1–38 are in the main terminal building, but 40–64 are in the nearby St. Andrews Building, signposted.

The Edinburgh airport bus link is a great introduction to the city

GETTING FROM THE AIRPORTS			
BUS	**CAR**	**TRAIN**	**TAXI**
Frequent Airlink service to Waverley train station in city centre 25 min, £3 single, £5 return	At Ingliston, west of city centre off A8; 30 min–1 hour	No direct rail link	From arrivals area in front of the main terminal, around £20
Frequent CityLink or Fairline service 905 (bus stop 1) to Buchanan Street bus station, 20 min, £3.30 single, £5 return	In Paisley, 8 miles (12.9km) northwest of the city centre via M8, exit 28; 30 min	Bus to Paisley Gilmour Street station, for frequent connections to Glasgow Central, 11 min, £2.20	From outside door 5, Domestic Arrivals, 20 min, around £17
Regular bus service to Glasgow Central train station, 50 min, £5.10	At Prestwick 45 miles (72km) southwest of Glasgow via A77; 40 min	Regular train service to Glasgow Central train station, 44 min, £5.40	20 min, around £14
Regular service with First Aberdeen into the city centre, £1.30	By Dyce, 7 miles (11.3km) northwest of the city centre via the A96; 15 min	No direct rail link	15 min, around £14

Edinburgh's Waverley train station lies between the Old and New Towns

Glasgow Prestwick International Airport

Glasgow's second airport is a long way from the city centre, but has a direct train link to the city. Prestwick deals mainly with charter holiday flights, plus low-cost flights with Ryanair from London (Stansted), Brussels, Dublin, Frankfurt, Oslo and Paris. Facilities include a small selection of shops, a café, cash machines and a bureau de change.

● Prestwick KA9 2PL, tel 01292 511000; **www**.gpia.co.uk

INTERNATIONAL AIRPORTS AND FERRY PORTS

Aberdeen Airport

Aberdeen airport is known as the world's largest commercial heliport, thanks to its status as the main transport hub for North Sea oil workers, and lies 7 miles (11.3km) northwest of the city. It caters for flights from mainland Europe and Scandinavia, as well as domestic flights.

Internet access is available in the departure lounge. The bureau de change is opposite the information desk. Dyce, the nearest train station, is a short taxi ride away.

● Dyce, Aberdeen AB21 7DU, tel 0870 040 0006; **www**.baa.com

ARRIVING BY TRAIN

In theory, it is possible to travel from one end of Britain to the other by train in a day. Intercity trains on major routes travel at 140mph (225kph), so journeys from London to Edinburgh can take just over four hours. Connecting trains to smaller destinations are likely to be slower and less frequent.

Virgin trains from England follow the east coast route to Edinburgh and the west coast route to Glasgow. GNER trains travel up the eastern side to Edinburgh, and go on to Glasgow, Inverness and

Aberdeen. Tickets for both companies can be bought at any main line station, but note that your ticket will specify which train you can catch, and that tickets are not generally transferable between the different companies.

High-speed Eurostar trains from France (Paris and Lille) and Belgium (Brussels) reach London in less than three hours. Passports are required for travel and, on arrival, you must also pass through customs, before continuing your journey to Scotland.

Both Edinburgh Waverley and Glasgow Central train stations are main hubs for onward travel within Scotland, and both are well served with tourist information desks (including accommodation information), cafés, shops and banking services. Electronic screens indicate from which platform you need to catch your train.

● National Rail Enquiry Service, tel 08457 484950 (daily, 24hrs); www.nationalrail.co.uk

ARRIVING BY COACH

If you travel to Britain by long-distance bus you will probably arrive at London's Victoria Coach Station. The main coach company for connections from England and Wales to Scotland is National Express. Coaches arrive at the main hubs of St. Andrews

The distinctive red-liveried Zeebrugge ferry on the Firth of Forth

Square bus station in Edinburgh, and Buchanan Street bus station in Glasgow.

● National Express, tel 08705 808080; www.nationalexpress.com

ARRIVING BY FERRY

There are two direct routes by vehicle and passenger ferry from Northern Ireland: Belfast to Stranraer, and from Larne to Cairnryan or Troon. For onward travel, Stranraer is served by a rail and coach link. Cairnryan is linked to Stranraer by public bus service. Troon is also on the rail network.

● Stena Line, tel 08705 707070 (reservations); www.stenaline.co.uk
● P&O Irish Ferries, tel 0870 2424 777; www.poirishsea.com Overnight vehicle and passenger ferries from Zeebrugge in Belgium arrive at Rosyth, 13 miles (21km) east of Edinburgh.
● Superfast Ferries, tel 0870

234 0870 (reservations); www.superfast.com

A weekly car and passenger ferry in summer links Shetland with Denmark, Iceland, Norway and the Faroes.

● Smyril Line, Holmsgarth Terminal, Lerwick, Shetland, tel 01595 690845; www.smyril-line.com

ARRIVING BY CAR

Driving into Scotland from England, the two major routes are the A1(M)/M1/A1 on the eastern side of the country, and the M6/A74(M) up the western side. Both routes can become very congested around urban areas at peak times of the day and around holiday weekends (▷ 295).

If you are planning to drive to Britain from the Continent, Eurotunnel operates the train service for cars, caravans and motorcycles through the Channel Tunnel to southern England. On your arrival at Folkestone leave the terminal on the M20 northbound, joining it at junction (intersection) 11a, for major connecting routes north to Scotland.

Bilingual road signs are a common sight in northwest Scotland

GETTING AROUND

ON THE MOVE

For all public transport timetable enquiries within Britain, call Traveline, tel 0870 608 2608 (daily, 8am–8pm); www.traveline.org.uk. If you're planning to explore widely using public transport, then look out for deals such as the Freedom of Scotland Travelpass, which can be bought at any train station, travel agent, Britrail outlet in North America and Europe, or by phone from First Scotrail, tel 08457 550033. The Travelpass covers you for 8 days, or 15 days, and costs £92 or £124 (adult rates). This gives either 4 or 8 days of free travel within that period on the entire network of First Scotrail trains, Strathclyde Passenger Transport Service trains, GNER and Virgin trains within Scotland, and all Caledonian MacBrayne (CalMac) ferries. It also covers some CityLink, Stagecoach and Highland Bus services, and allows for discounted travel on other services such as the Orkney ferry.

GETTING AROUND IN EDINBURGH

Lothian Buses are the main public bus operators in the city, identifiable by their maroon and white livery, or red and white. Bus stops are labelled with the name of the stop (eg Waverley Bridge), then a list of the bus companies that stop there, then night services, then regular services with bus numbers.

There are lots of different tickets, but an exact-fare system operates, so you need to have correct money—no change is given. The standard adult fares are 80p or £1; concessions pay a 40p flat rate before 9.30am Mon–Fri, and travel free at all other times. A child age 5–15 pays 60p to travel any distance. When you get on the bus, put the exact fare into the slot in front of the driver, then tear off your ticket from the machine behind the driver.
- Lothian bus information, tel 0131 555 6363.
- Get timetables and tickets at the Travel Shop, 27 Hanover Street (Mon–Sat 8.15–6), and at Waverley Bridge station (Mon–Sat 8.15–6, Sun 9.30–5).
- An enlarged route map and timetable on the bridge outside Waverley Station has additional information about the night bus service into the suburbs.

Driving here is dogged by narrow streets, one-way systems, 'red' routes, residents'-only parking and dedicated bus routes. On-street parking is generally pay-and-display between 8.30am and 6.30pm Mon–Sat. There are plenty of signed parking areas,

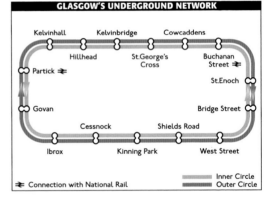

GLASGOW'S UNDERGROUND NETWORK

Kelvinhall Kelvinbridge Cowcaddens
Hillhead St.George's Cross Buchanan Street
Partick
St.Enoch
Govan
Bridge Street
Cessnock Shields Road
Ibrox Kinning Park West Street

Connection with National Rail

Inner Circle
Outer Circle

mostly to the south of Princes Street. The biggest is at Greenside Place, off Leith Street.

GETTING AROUND IN GLASGOW

For information about buses, local trains and the underground network within the city, contact the Strathclyde Passenger Transport (SPT) centre at Buchanan Street bus station on Killermont Street (Mon–Sat 6.30am–10.30pm, Sun 7am–10.30pm; tel 0141 333 3708). The SPT also has information about the ferry to Kilcreggan and Helensburgh.

Glasgow's underground (the 'clockwork orange') forms a 6-mile (9.7km) loop from the west of the city into the centre and Buchanan Street bus station—particularly useful for access to the Museum of Transport, Kelvingrove Art Gallery and Museum (Kelvinhall), the Hunterian Museum (Hillhead), Rangers' stadium (Ibrox) and

St. Enoch shopping centre (St. Enoch). Trains operate from around 6.30am Mon–Sat, 11am Sun, and stop around 11pm Mon–Sat, 5.30pm Sun. Buy tickets from the station booking offices, or from the automatic ticket machines available in many stations. A single ticket (one-way ticket) costs £1, a return £2, with reductions for children. The Discovery ticket allows a day's unlimited travel for just £1.70, if travelling after 9.30am.

Glasgow is bisected by a motorway, and its streets follow a more regular grid pattern than Edinburgh's. But driving is still complicated, and you'd do best to park in one of the public car parks such as Mitchell Street (NCP) or Albion Street (Universal Parking). The underground network also makes 'park and ride' a more attractive option: Park at Kelvinbridge, to the north of the centre (£1.20), or Shields Road, to the south (£1), and catch a train into the city.

Ferries

In addition to the ferry ports of Rosyth, Stranraer, Cairnryan and Lerwick for overseas arrivals and departures, there are also many domestic terminals serving the islands of Scotland. The ferries may carry foot passengers, bicycles, cars, caravans and local freight, and vary in size, facilities and frequency according to the route. Some services may be disrupted by tides and bad weather conditions, so always check sailings in advance.

BUYING TICKETS

Information about timetables and fares is available direct from the ferry companies, or from tourist information centres. Tickets can be reserved in advance from the ferry operator, through travel agents and tourist information offices. When reserving you will be asked for details such as the make or size of the vehicle and number of passengers. Reserving in advance is recommended, especially at holiday times.

On vehicle ferries the price includes the vehicle and a number of passengers (usually up to five). Some fares may be paid on the ferry, by cash or cheque only. Tickets will be either one-way or return, and usually specify the time of the ferry you should catch. Many factors affect the ticket price—such as length of stay, size and type of vehicle—so discuss your needs with the operator before booking.

If you want to explore several islands, an Island Rover ticket (from Caledonian MacBrayne) lasts 8 or 15 days and offers a significant saving. An 8-day pass for two people with a car costs £323; for a foot passenger, or a bicyclist, it is just £48.50. Island Hopscotch tickets are tailored to 26 of the most popular routes through the islands, and offer better value than tickets bought individually. For example, the cost of a car and two people on the route from Mallaig to Skye, the Uists, Harris and Lewis and back to Ullapool is £311.

If travelling with a vehicle, you should usually check in at the ferry terminal 30 minutes before departure. Foot passengers need check in only 10 minutes before.

INDEPENDENT FERRY ROUTES			
DESTINATION	**TIME TAKEN**	**RESTRICTIONS**	**CONTACT**
Gourock–Kilcreggan/Helensburgh	10/40 min	Foot passengers only	Clyde Marine Services Ltd, tel 01475 721281 www.clyde-marine.co.uk
Ardgour–Corran	2 min		Tec Services, Highland Council, tel 01397 709000
Oban–Kerrara	5 min	Foot passengers only	D. McEachan, tel 01631 563665
Islay–Jura	5 min		Serco Denholm, tel 01496 840681
Iona–Staffa	50 min	Foot passengers only; Apr–end Oct	David Kirkpatrick, tel 01681 700358
Mull–Staffa	30 min	Foot passengers only; Apr–end Oct	Gordon Grant, tel 01681 700338
Mull–Staffa/Treshnish	1 hour	Foot passengers only; Apr–end Oct	Turus Mara, tel 01688 400242/08000 858786 www.turusmara.com
Port Appin–Lismore	10 min	Foot passengers only	Argyll & Bute Council, tel 01631 730686
Seil–Easdale	5 min	Foot passengers only	Argyll & Bute Council, tel 01631 562125
Seil–Luing	5 min	Mon–Sat	Argyll & Bute Council, tel 01631 562125
Glenelg–Skye	5 min	Easter–end Oct	R Macleod, tel 01599 511302
Gairloch–Skye	1 hour 30 min	Foot passengers only; April–end Oct	West Highland Seaways Ltd www.overtheseatoskye.com

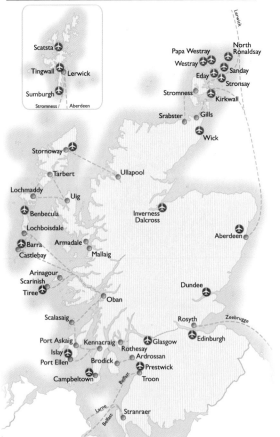

ON BOARD

Larger ferries are generally comfortable, with refreshments, toilets and TVs, and cabins can be booked for longer journeys. Boarding may involve steep ramps, so take care with strollers (pushchairs). On passenger ferries larger luggage may be stored out on the deck to leave the inside clear. Smoking is allowed in designated areas only.

Vehicles can be driven straight into the back of the ferries. You can then go up to the decks, or may be able to stay in your car.

Western Isles

The access ferry ports are Stornoway on Lewis (from Ullapool), Tarbert on Harris (from Uig and Lochmaddy), Lochmaddy on North Uist (from Uig on Skye), Lochboisdale on South Uist (from Oban and Castlebay) and Castlebay on Barra (from Oban).

At the time of writing, the main inter-island ferries for the Western Isles are operated by Caledonian MacBrayne Ltd, known familiarly as CalMac, but this may change in the future as routes are put out to competitive tender. The vessels currently take in islands which include Skye, Arran, Bute, Islay, Mull, Lewis and Harris, and the Uists.

● CalMac, The Ferry Terminal, Gourock PA19 1QP, tel 01475 650100/08705 650000; www.calmac.co.uk

The islands are served by a network of regular but infrequent buses linked in to the ferry services, Mon–Sat. For example, in summer there are four to five buses a day between Stornoway

and Leverburgh, on route W10.
● For timetables and ticket prices, contact the tourist office at 26 Cromwell Street, Stornoway, Isle of Lewis HS1 2DD, tel 01851 703088.

Orkney and Shetland

NorthLink Orkney and Shetland Ferries operates overnight ferries from Aberdeen to Orkney and Shetland, from Scrabster (by Thurso) to Orkney, and between Lerwick in Shetland and Kirkwall in Orkney. Reclining seats or cabins can be booked for the

The CalMac livery of black and white, with red and gold funnels, is a familiar sight in the islands

longer crossings. The cost for a foot passenger to Lerwick starts at £19.80.
● NorthLink Orkney and Shetland Ferries Ltd, Kiln Corner, Ayre Road, Kirkwall, Orkney KW15 1QX, tel 0845 600 0449; www.northlinkferries.co.uk

From May to September, a foot passengers only ferry operates between John o'Groats and Burwick on Orkney. It takes 40 minutes and there is a 45-minute connecting coach service to Kirkwall for every crossing.
● John o'Groats Ferries Ltd, The Ferry Office, John O'Groats, Caithness KW1 4YR; tel 01955 611353/611342; www.jogferry.co.uk

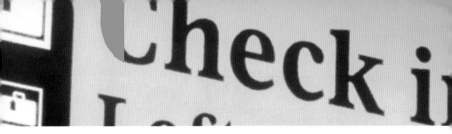

Domestic Flights

Domestic air travel is relatively expensive in Britain but, with an increasing number of low-cost airlines competing for passengers, prices are coming down. If you are flexible about travelling dates and times, some real bargains can be had. However, check carefully what the price includes, such as taxes, credit-card reservation fees and other charges, and be aware that some advertised fares are one-way only. All domestic flights and those to destinations within the European Union (EU) carry a £10 departure tax (usually included in the price). For flights to other destinations the charge is £20.

REGIONAL AIRPORTS
For details of Edinburgh, Glasgow and Aberdeen airports, ▷ 38–40.

The 10 main regional airports are Campbeltown, Islay, Tiree, Barra, Benbecula, Stornoway (Lewis), Sumburgh (Shetland), Kirkwall (Orkney), Wick and Inverness. These are all operated by Highlands and Islands Airports Ltd (HIAL), and their website gives useful information on each one. For a map of airports, ▷ 44.
● HIAL, tel 01667 462445; www.hial.co.uk

Smaller additional airports include the remote Fair Isle.

INVERNESS AIRPORT
Inverness (Dalcross) Airport serves as the main hub for

Loganair flights to the island of Barra (▷ 121) land on the beach, tide permitting

access to the Highlands and Islands (as well as some holiday charter flights to Zurich and Mediterranean destinations). It is located 10 miles (16km) east of Inverness, off the A96 via the B9039.

There is a regular bus service into Inverness every 90 minutes. There is no direct train link, with Inverness and Nairn offering the nearest train stations.
● Dalcross, tel 01667 464000.

BUYING A TICKET
You can reserve tickets direct from the airlines by phone or online, or through travel agents. If reserving online the tickets will be posted to you. If time is short you can collect them at the airport, but some companies may charge for this.

If you have reserved far enough in advance you may be able to amend or cancel tickets, but a fee will be charged.

TIP
Useful websites for flights and information include:
www.cheapflights.co.uk
www.thisistravel.co.uk
www.ba.com
www.worldairportguide.com

ON BOARD
● For security reasons no sharp objects (including scissors and cutlery) are allowed in hand luggage. Lists of prohibited items are displayed throughout the airports. Any items found will be confiscated.
● These are relatively short flights with few frills, but simple refreshments will be available on longer journeys.
● Smoking is not allowed anywhere on the planes, and only in designated areas of airports.

Coaches and Buses

Coaches (long-distance buses) run from Edinburgh's St. Andrews Square bus station and Glasgow's Buchanan Street bus station to all parts of the country and are a slower but less expensive alternative to train travel, reaching many more destinations. Journey times can be long (with some changes necessary) but the vehicles are comfortable, with air-conditioning, toilets and sometimes refreshments for longer trips.

Citylink is the main coach operator for destinations across Scotland, linking Edinburgh, Glasgow, Aberdeen, Dundee, Perth, Inverness, Scrabster (for Orkney), Ullapool, Skye, Fort William, Oban, Campbeltown, Stranraer, Dumfries and many stops in between. They can be identified by the blue and yellow livery.

● Scottish Citylink Coaches, Buchanan Street Bus Station, Killermont Street, Glasgow G2 3NP, tel 08705 505050 (8am–9pm); www.citylink.co.uk

A wide variety of guided coach tours is available—contact travel agents and tourist information offices for more information.

Rural bus services are limited across the country

TIPS

● If seats are available, you can buy a ticket on the day from the coach driver.
● You can reserve by phone, online at sites such as **www.citylink.co.uk** and **www.nationalexpress.com**, at main coach stations and at travel agents.

to you, sent to key locations for personal collection or even sent to you by SMS text message.

BUYING TICKETS

Ticket types include standard singles or returns, plus various saver tickets reservable in advance. Look out for deals such as the Citylink Explorer Pass, which gives unlimited travel over 3, 5 or 8 days (adult £39, £62 or £85), plus discounts on ferry travel. National Express Brit Xplorer cards are available for 7, 14 or 28 days (adult £79, £139 or £219).

Discount cards are also available for passengers over age 60, students and young people.

Baggage allowances are up to two medium-size suitcases and one item of hand luggage per person, with no guarantee that any excess will be carried. Folded and covered bicycles are acceptable.

● It is cheaper to reserve in advance and travel midweek. For example, the single adult Apex fare (reserved at least 5 days before travel) between Edinburgh and Inverness is around £17, and between Glasgow and Skye around £25. Pre-paid tickets can be sent

BUSES

Local buses are reasonably comfortable and often make a pleasant alternative to trains. Major towns and cities usually have frequent buses, but services can be erratic elsewhere, notably in very rural areas, with perhaps only one or two buses a week. Some night services (denoted by an 'N' prefix) are available in major towns and cities.

Tourist information offices can provide information and timetables. Timetables can look daunting, so check them carefully for services that run only on

COMPARATIVE JOURNEYS BY TRAIN AND COACH		
Prices are based on a midweek adult day-return ticket (round-trip ticket)		
JOURNEY	**BY TRAIN**	**BY COACH**
Edinburgh – Inverness	£34 (3 hours 17 min)	£26.70 (4 hours)
Edinburgh – Aberdeen	£19.50 (2 hours 25 min)	£11 (3 hours 30 minutes)
Edinburgh – Glasgow	£10.20 (50 min)	£6 (1 hour 10 minutes)
Edinburgh – Thurso	£49 (next day return; 7 hours 55 min)	£38.40 (8 hours)
Glasgow – Inverness	£19.50 (3 hours 15 min)	£26.70 (4 hours)
Glasgow – Kyle of Lochalsh	£26.50 (next day return; 6 hours 30 min)	£37.40 (5 hours)

school days or are otherwise restricted.

Several bus companies may compete in urban areas. In some cases their services may overlap, but tickets will be company-specific. Stagecoach is the main operator in southwest, east central and northeast Scotland. Rapsons operates local buses in the Highland region, and Orkney and Shetland.

The Royal Mail Postbusservice (tel 08457 740740; www.postbus.royalmail.com) also carries passengers around remoter parts of the country in minibuses. Fares are inexpensive, but note that buses are scheduled to serve the mail first and passengers second, so may set off very early in the morning.

BUS STOPS

Urban bus stops are usually denoted by a sign on a pole giving the number(s) of the buses serving that stop, its location and the destination (direction of travel), sometimes accompanied by sheltered seats. In contrast, rural bus stops may be difficult to spot and are unlikely to have much information.

● Buses will stop at main bus stops if passengers are waiting to get on or off. At a 'request stop' (usually intermediate stops and rural stops), hold out your arm to hail the bus you want.

● Check the number and destination on the front before you get on, or check with the driver, as the stop will probably serve many different routes. At night treat all stops as request stops.

ON BOARD

Keep your ticket until the end of the journey because inspectors regularly board the buses to check tickets and catch fare-dodgers.

● Tickets are usually bought from the driver as you board.

● Children under 5 travel free, and those aged 5–15 travel for half fare. Card concessions for students and seniors are also available.

● Some driver-only buses have two doors: one at the front, where you board, and one midway, where you get off.

● Show your pass or have your change ready to pay the driver when you board. Drivers and conductors prefer the exact fare but they will give change. Tell the driver or conductor where you want to go and he or she will tell you the fare.

● On all buses press the red button once to get off and the bus will call at the next scheduled stop.

Taxis

Taxis are generally an expensive way of getting around in Britain, but very convenient for shorter trips. If you are planning a longer trip by taxi, agree a fee in advance. There are basically two types of taxi: the traditional black London-style cab (found in major cities) and the minicab. The black cabs are world famous and, despite the fact that they now feature advertising and come in shades other than black, the design remains distinctive. All private taxis are licensed and regulated and should have meters. Vehicles can range from ordinary saloon (sedan) and estate cars (station wagons) to seven-seater 'people carriers'. A notice confirming that a vehicle is licensed to carry passengers should be displayed on the back of the vehicle.

FINDING A TAXI

You'll find designated taxi stands outside train stations and large hotels, near shopping malls and at other major points within cities. Taxi cabs can also be hailed in the street: Look for an illuminated orange TAXI light on the top and hold out your arm to attract the driver's attention.

Private taxis and minicabs can be reserved by phone; look in the *Yellow Pages* phone book for local companies, or ask at your hotel.

Taxis can be scarce to find at busy times, especially on Friday

Once-black taxis now come in all colours

and Saturday nights in the city, so reserve a ride home in advance if you're going out on the town.

● Avoid minicab drivers touting at airports and stations as they may overcharge and may be unlicensed or uninsured. Take licensed cabs from taxi stands or reserve with a recommended minicab firm in advance.

● Unlike black cabs, it is acceptable to sit in the front passenger seat of ordinary taxis.

● A tip of around 10 per cent of the total fare is expected and customary, but not compulsory.

Trains

Train services across Britain generally work efficiently and are not too crowded outside peak periods. More than 20 different companies now operate the country's railway. This can lead to differing facilities and some curious price anomalies as each company determines its own fare structure.

Train services are subject to delays, so allow plenty of time for your journey, especially if you have to change trains. Essential engineering work is usually carried out at weekends and public holidays, and can severely disrupt services. Details are displayed at relevant stations, or check in advance with National Rail (www.nationalrail.co.uk).

FIRST SCOTRAIL

First Scotrail operates the majority of train services within Scotland, between 335 stations, as well as the overnight sleeper services that link Edinburgh, Glasgow, Fort William, Aberdeen and Inverness with London. For planning ahead, their website (www.firstscotrail.com) has a useful table, which shows the resources available at every station, including car parking, buffet services and access for travellers with disabilities.

The Railbus scheme offers scheduled onward bus links to non-rail destinations such as Callander, St. Andrews and Ullapool, tel 08457 550033.

● National Rail Enquiry Service, tel 08457 484950 (daily, 24 hours); www.nationalrail.co.uk

Detailed information for the whole network—including operating companies, timetables, fares and engineering works—is available from National Rail Enquiries (see above). Their useful free leaflet *Map and Guide to Using the*

Scotrail trains link across the country with certain bus routes

National Rail Network is available from stations.

Staffed stations usually have free timetables of local services, and almost all stations display timetables. Note that there are different services for weekdays, Saturday and Sunday (generally more limited).

● There are two classes of train travel: first and standard. First is more expensive but guarantees you a seat on crowded trains as well as complimentary drinks and newspapers. Otherwise standard class is perfectly acceptable and you can reserve a seat if you reserve in advance.

● Sleeping compartments can be reserved with First Scotrail on some overnight services to and from Scotland (tel 08457 550033).

Avoid weekday rush hours (7–9.30am and 4–7pm) if possible. Note that the evening rush hour often starts earlier on Friday, especially before public holidays. Allow plenty of time, especially to make connections.

If you are planning to continue your journey via England and the Eurostar train into continental Europe, ask about discounted fares to London International.

● Eurostar, tel 08705 186186; www.eurostar.com

TIPS

● The West Highland Line is a spectacular scenic route between Glasgow and Mallaig; vintage steam trains sometimes travel it in the summer. First Scotrail, tel 08457 550033; www.firstscotrail.com
● The *Royal Scotsman* is a luxury train that takes passengers on tours of 1–4 nights; tel 0131 555 1344; www.royalscotsman.com
---

BUYING TICKETS

You must always have a valid ticket for your journey in advance or you may be liable to a fixed fine. Your ticket or rail pass must be available for inspection on any train, along with any relevant documentation. You can buy a ticket in person for any destination run by any company from any train station, either from the ticket office or from automated machines (usually for shorter journeys). Most travel agents also sell train tickets.

You can also buy tickets online through www.thetrainline.com or www.qjump.co.uk, which give prices and fast reservation for different types of ticket for any journey. If there is no means of purchasing a ticket in advance, you will be sold one on the train.

● Seat reservations are not usually necessary, but are advisable at peak times and are compulsory for certain services, in which case there is no extra charge involved.

Main stations have every modern facility

TYPES OF TICKET

The variety of ticket types, pricing and restrictions offered by different rail companies can be bewildering. For example, GNER, which runs trains between London and Scotland, offers return fares from London to Edinburgh from £39 to £296. Broadly, the earlier you reserve your ticket in advance (up to 10 weeks) and the more flexible you can be about which days and times you travel, the less money you are likely to have to pay. There may also be significant reductions for up to four people travelling together.
● A cheap-day return is best for a day out, but you can buy and use it only after 9.30am.
● Except for certain 'rover' or 'open' tickets your journey(s) must be on the date(s) shown on the ticket and you cannot break the journey (that is, get off en route and join a later train).

Other discounts
● Children under 5 travel free and 5 to 15-year-olds pay half price for most tickets, but check as there are exceptions.
● Britrail Pass: Unlimited rail travel in Britain and Northern Ireland for non-UK residents only, but it can only be purchased abroad.

Britrail passes also come in family and group forms, offering considerable savings to accompanying passengers. As well as regional passes for Scotland, there are passes for London and Wales and combinations with Irish and European passes. For information: www.britrail.com
● Railcard: A young person's railcard (age 16–25 and mature students in full-time education) costs £20 and is valid across the country. You'll need a passport-size photograph and proof of eligibility to buy a railcard.
● Freedom of Scotland Travelpass, ▷ 42.

AT THE STATION
Most train stations have electronic information displays showing departure times, station stops, platform numbers and estimated time of arrival. Departures and arrivals for each platform may be shown at larger stations. Smaller country stations may have few facilities.
● Some urban stations have automatic barriers. Put your ticket into the slot on one side to open the barrier: It will pop out at the top. If you need help, go to the staffed gate at the side of the barrier. The barriers retain used tickets at the end of a journey.
● Major stations have facilities in varying degrees, ranging from basic newsagents and cafés to specialist shops, minimarkets, travel offices, restaurants, dry-cleaners, bureaux de change and pubs. Small or rural stations are usually pretty spartan.
● Smoking is allowed on station platforms and concourses, but not in shops.
● Few stations have left-luggage facilities for security reasons. Larger stations have information desks where you can report lost property.

ON THE TRAIN
Facilities and conditions on board trains vary, depending on the route. Generally, all trains have toilet facilities, ranging from the basic to larger, wheelchair-accessible booths with baby-changing facilities. Many trains have at-seat trolley service for refreshments, and some longer routes also have buffet cars where you can buy drinks and snacks.
● Smoking is banned except in designated smoking carriages (where provided).

MAIN TICKET OPTIONS		
In approximately descending order of price.		
TICKET	**RESTRICTIONS**	**VALIDITY**
Open one-way	None	On the date shown, or on either of the two following days.
Day one-way/day return	None	Date shown; return same day.
Saver return	Peak travel restrictions	Return within one calendar month.
SuperSaver return	Not available for travel before 9.30am, on Fri, summer Sat and peak holidays	Return within one calendar month.
Cheap-day return	Not before 9.30am	Return the same day.

Driving

The most flexible way to get around Scotland is by car. On the whole, motorists drive safely, roads are good and signposting is efficient. Note that the wearing of seatbelts is compulsory. Major routes are well served with rest stop areas and petrol (gas) stations, but on rural routes these may be few and far between. Drink driving laws are strictly enforced—the best advice is not to drive after drinking alcohol.

ON THE MOVE

DRIVING ON THE LEFT
Vehicles drive on the left side of the road. Remember this particularly when: first moving off from the side of the road; turning from one road into another road; driving on a road with few other cars or at night; approaching a roundabout/traffic circle (keep left, go clockwise round, see also tips below); and meeting another vehicle on a single-track road. Do not overtake on the left.

SPEED LIMITS
The speed limit in built-up areas is generally 30mph (48kph). Outside built-up areas it is generally 60mph (97kph) on single carriageways and 70mph (113kph) on two-lane carriageways and motorways.

FUEL
Most garages are self-service. Higher octane unleaded petrol

Enjoying the open road

TIPS: SINGLE-TRACK ROADS

Many of the minor country roads in Scotland are single track for all or some of their length.
- Passing places are marked with a post, usually topped by a square or diamond-shaped white sign. Don't park in a passing place.
- Keep your speed down. Visibility is often limited, and you need time to slow down and pull in to let approaching vehicles past.
- If the nearest passing place is on the right side of the road, wait opposite to allow approaching traffic to pass you.
- If the driver behind you is in a hurry, pull into a passing place and let them past. An impatient driver on your tail is a liability.
- When passing a vehicle that has pulled into a passing place, check ahead first for approaching vehicles or pedestrians.
- If you meet another vehicle and there is no passing place in sight, be prepared to reverse back to a space.
- Look out for livestock on the road. Slow down and be prepared to give way to cattle and particularly sheep, who can wait until the last second before bolting across in front of you. Deer can also be a surprise hazard at night.
- Be courteous—if somebody has pulled in for you to pass, give them a wave of thanks.
- Towing a caravan (trailer) on single-track roads demands extra vigilance; be prepared to pull in to let following traffic pass.

MAKING IT EASY AT ROUNDABOUTS/TRAFFIC CIRCLES

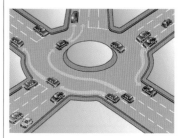

When reaching a roundabout give priority to traffic on your right, unless directed otherwise by signs, road markings or traffic lights. Look forward before moving off to make sure traffic in front has moved. Watch out for vehicles already on the roundabout; be aware they may not be signalling correctly or at all.

Approach mini roundabouts in the same way. Vehicles MUST pass round the central markings.

(gas), unleaded 95 octane petrol and diesel are sold.

CLAMPING AND TOWING AWAY

If your car is parked illegally it may be clamped; the notice posted on your windscreen explains how to get it released. Vehicles are usually released within one hour of payment. If your vehicle is removed it will cost at least £125 to get it back. Vehicles must be collected in person and you must produce identification.

BREAKDOWN AND ACCIDENTS

Several organizations in the UK can assist you in the event of breakdown, including the Automobile Association (AA). Check whether membership in your home country entitles you to reciprocal assistance.

At the scene of an accident

If you are involved in a road-traffic accident, stop and remain at the scene for a reasonable period and give your vehicle registration number, your name and address, and that of the vehicle owner (if different), to anyone with reasonable grounds for asking for those details. If you do not exchange those details at the scene, you must report the accident at a police station or to a police constable within 24 hours.

CAR RENTAL

Arranging a rental car through your travel agent before arriving saves money and allows you to find out about deposits, drop-off charges, cancellation penalties and insurance costs in advance. Established car rental firms have offices throughout Britain; smaller, local firms and online agents may offer better deals; check the *Yellow Pages*. For further information and contact details, ▷ 293.

- You must have a valid driver's licence (an international driver's licence is not required).
- Most rental firms require the driver to be at least 23 years old and with at least 12 months of driving experience.

DISTANCE CHART (MILES IN GREEN, JOURNEY TIME IN BLUE)

225	348	548	319	413	216	131	512	235	357	103	321	301	358	240	538	331	434	501	150	410	150	229	505	357	
Aberdeen	359	449	330	425	233	228	314	252	133	226	338	312	322	042	340	342	236	512	205	241	247	240	516	159	
	Aviemore	405	107	129	138	225	712	144	323	449	215	050	214	439	737	020	515	117	202	307	228	121	121	557	
		Ayr	302	450	409	426	729	415	316	650	456	323	151	455	755	349	507	519	359	208	442	338	523	604	
95			**Campbeltown**	152	112	156	633	117	219	420	159	025	110	359	658	051	411	221	133	203	202	052	225	507	
185	180			**Dumbarton**	203	251	738	153	408	515	136	131	258	505	803	128	559	112	228	351	252	147	147	623	
249	192	161			**Dumfries**	054	546	025	257	318	111	055	222	313	611	124	427	252	032	240	055	035	259	431	
152	147	43	123			**Dunfermline**	541	113	259	233	159	139	235	308	606	209	422	338	028	247	019	106	343	426	
216	209	59	210	92			**Dundee**	605	413	502	651	626	602	237	225	655	356	825	518	521	600	553	829	146	
111	112	76	171	53	108			**Durness**	312	337	052	100	227	333	631	129	447	243	051	256	114	049	303	450	
68	99	121	184	88	151	47			**Edinburgh**	358	352	242	149	140	439	308	152	437	236	107	318	226	442	248	
207	133	313	298	255	341	245	232			**Fort William**	423	403	459	228	526	433	422	602	252	506	252	330	607	346	
125	126	83	179	60	78	17	60	258			**Fraserburgh**	140	306	419	717	202	533	246	138	336	201	129	321	537	
156	61	130	132	88	177	115	119	166	136			**Galashiels**	132	353	651	033	433	203	115	225	142	035	207	510	
41	93	226	289	193	256	152	108	198	166	154			**Glasgow**	328	628	158	340	328	209	055	251	148	332	437	
161	161	92	209	91	61	53	96	294	33	168	201			**Inveraray**	303	422	159	552	245	247	327	320	556	122	
150	144	36	133	15	76	40	85	277	49	102	190	78			**Inverness**	721	433	850	544	546	626	618	855	325	
173	133	86	75	44	133	96	108	238	105	72	213	134	58			**John o'Groats**	459	133	145	251	211	104	137	540	
106	32	212	197	154	240	144	130	104	158	66	100	194	176	138			**Kilmarnock**	629	359	259	441	417	633	210	
223	149	329	314	271	357	261	248	93	275	183	218	311	294	255	120			**Kyle of Lochalsh**	314	420	341	234	036	709	
172	166	15	157	38	58	62	107	299	70	125	212	82	23	81	198	315			**Newton Stewart**	224	045	042	319	405	
183	109	204	206	162	251	187	174	153	201	74	177	237	176	146	80	179	199			**Perth**	303	209	425	355	
235	229	52	214	95	48	134	170	362	107	183	275	109	86	138	261	379	64	256			**Oban**	116	346	445	
86	84	100	161	67	128	29	21	217	43	104	126	79	64	86	116	233	86	159	150			**St Andrews**	239	438	
181	105	120	88	78	167	105	117	210	126	44	201	158	92	38	110	227	115	118	171	96			**Stirling**	714	
80	111	110	192	87	145	40	13	244	55	131	120	91	75	117	143	260	96	187	160	31	125			**Stranraer**	
120	114	65	145	35	92	22	55	247	38	97	160	70	29	70	146	264	51	171	114	34	87	52			**Ullapool**
235	229	52	200	72	125	170	362	133	182	275	133	86	138	261	379	64	256	25	149	172	160	114			
160	86	266	243	200	294	198	184	68	212	111	154	248	230	183	57	132	252	86	315	169	155	197	200	315	

ROAD SIGNS AND DRIVING TIPS

Classes of signs
Plates below signs qualify their message

Junctions and roundabouts

| Give way to traffic on major road | Stop and give way | Crossroads | Roundabout | Mini roundabout (roundabout circulation) | No through road |

Traffic conduct

No stopping (clearway) · National speed limit applies · Speed limit applies · One-way travel · No overtaking · No entry for vehicular traffic

The road ahead

Road narrows on both sides · Double bend, first to left · Two-way traffic straight ahead · Cycle route ahead · Road works · Slippery road

VISITORS WITH A DISABILITY

A wide range of information for visitors with disabilities can be found in VisitScotland's publication *Practical Information for Visitors with Disabilities,* available directly from the tourist board or from tourist offices (▷ 301).

TRIPSCOPE
TRIPSCOPE operates a nationwide travel advice and information service for people with mobility problems. Advice is offered on any aspect of travel, whether it's planning journeys in private or public transport.

This service is available throughout the UK for the price of a local rate telephone call to TRIPSCOPE's Helpline. Requests are also dealt with by letter, textphone, fax and email.

All helpline staff have personal experience of disability and can discuss travel needs to help reduce pre-travel anxiety and stress en route.
● TRIPSCOPE, The Vassall Centre, Gill Avenue, Bristol BS16 2QQ
Helpline tel/textphone 08457 585641,
fax 0117 939 7736;
enquiries@tripscope.org.uk

BY AIR
Airlines make special provision for their passengers with disabilities, and most have departments dedicated to answering inquiries and making the arrangements for people who have special requirements. Some budget airlines may make a charge for providing assistance. As with all specific requirements, the travel agent or airline should be given prior notice of what is needed.

BY BUS AND COACH
Scheduled coach and bus travel in the UK is not widely accessible for wheelchair users, or for any person with a severe walking problem. The vehicles currently used on scheduled coach (long-distance bus) services have high, steep steps which even the ambulant disabled may find difficult to negotiate. People with sufficient mobility can use scheduled coach services, but the staff are not allowed to lift or give any other physical assistance with boarding.

BY TRAIN
While manual and powered wheelchairs—up to a maximum width of 67cm (26in)—can be accommodated on trains, large powered wheelchairs, strollers (pushchairs) and scooters are excluded from virtually all passenger rail services because of their size. Many trains carry lightweight portable ramps for use at unstaffed stations.

Be aware that many smaller stations are either unstaffed or only staffed at peak times. Information about both these and alternative, more accessible stations can be obtained when reserving assistance from the disabled passengers' assistance telephone line provided by each rail company.

For discounted rail fares, the Disabled Persons Railcard is available to people with a range of disabilities, and is also valid for their carers.

● Further information can be found in the booklet *Rail Travel for Disabled Passengers*, available from train stations (see also www.disabledpersons railcard.co.uk).

BY CAR

Everyone travelling in a motor vehicle is required by law to wear a seatbelt when the vehicle is fitted with them. This applies to people with disabilities, with few exceptions. If it is considered that a person should not wear a seatbelt for medical reasons, a doctor's certificate will be required.

Vehicle rental

Some of the major vehicle renters in the UK can make vehicles with hand controls available. Similarly, wheelchairs, scooters and other mobility and medical aids can be rented both in the UK and abroad. TRIPSCOPE (tel 08457 585641) or the Automobile Association (AA) helpline (tel 0800 262050) can supply contact details.

Roadside stops and accommodation

All motorway services are required to provide full access to all their facilities, including toilets, rest rooms, restaurants and shops.

Most of the lodge type of hotels, such as Travelodge, Travelinn and Premier, have at least one, and usually several, accessible rooms on the ground floor.

Holiday Care is a charity that specializes in information about access to serviced accommodation. It can assist with details of hotels, bed-and-breakfast accommodation and guesthouses that can accommodate people with disabilities.

A wheelchair-friendly path at Ben Lawers, in central Scotland

● Holiday Care, 7th floor, Sunley House, 4 Bedford Park, Croydon CR0 2AP, tel 08451 249971, textphone 08451 249976, fax 08451 249972; **www.**holidaycare.org.uk

Motorway breakdown

For people who are deaf or hard of hearing, all emergency motorway phones have an inductive coupler for use with the 'T' switch on hearing aids. For people who are profoundly deaf or without access to such hearing aids, when using a standard motorway phone, repeat twice the name, car registration number, disability and the nature of the emergency to enable the operator to deal with the call.

Parking

For many years, motorists with disabilities in the UK used to have the Orange Badge to assist with parking. It has now been superseded by a European Union (EU) scheme using an identical Blue Badge in all member states; however, UK regulations may differ from those of other countries. The AA has produced a multi-lingual booklet that outlines the details.

● AA Disability Helpline, tel 0800 262 050.

TOURIST ATTRACTIONS

Places of interest such as stately homes, museums and theme parks are required to make their attractions accessible to people with disabilities, but the degree to which this is possible with older buildings may vary. Most major attractions have already taken considerable steps to provide or improve access, and both the National Trust for Scotland and Historic Scotland include access information in their standard guides (▷ 302).

GOING SHOPPING

Shopmobility is a scheme operating in around 20 major shopping centres throughout Scotland to help people with disabilites do their own shopping. There are around 200 Shopmobilities across the UK. They offer a wide selection of mobility aids such as wheelchairs, pavement scooters and walking aids. In Scotland the service is free, but donations are welcome.

● Shopmobility Scotland, c/o Shopmobility Dundee, Overgate Centre, Overgate Lane, Dundee DD1 1UF, tel 01382 228525, fax 01382 224621; email shopmobility–dun@btconnect. com

This chapter is divided into the six regions of Scotland (▷ 5). Places of interest are listed alphabetically in each region. At the front of each regional section, that region's key sites are listed. To locate the sights in each region, turn to the atlas (▷ 307–327).

The Sights

For an explanation of the symbols used in this section, ▷ 2. The abbreviations NTS and HS indicate respectively properties owned by the National Trust for Scotland and Historic Scotland (▷ 302).

SOUTHERN SCOTLAND

Southern Scotland spans the Borders and Lothians area, shaped by hills, wide green valleys, small towns and a history of conflict with the English. It is a landscape associated with the poet Robert Burns, the artists of Kirkcudbright and the novelists Walter Scott and John Buchan.

KEY SIGHTS

Whiting Bay, on the southeast coast of Arran

The south corner tower of triangular Caerlaverock Castle

Drumlanrig Castle, a privately owned mansion

ABBOTSFORD

🗺 314 K12 • Melrose TD6 9BQ
☎ 01896 752043 🕐 Jun–end Sep Mon–Sat 9.30–5, Sun 9.30–5; mid-Mar to end May, Oct Mon–Sat 9.30–5, Sun 2–5 🎫 Adult £5.00, child £2.50 (under 8 free) 🚻 ♿
www.scottsabbotsford.co.uk

This overblown, turreted grey mansion is a must for an insight into the eclectic mind of the writer Sir Walter Scott (1771–1832), best known for epic romantic poems such as *The Lady of the Lake*, and novels including *Ivanhoe*. Abbotsford was the home he built for himself in 1812 on the banks of the River Tweed, 2 miles (3.2km) west of Melrose, and it is filled with historical curiosities, some of which—like the condemned criminals' door from the old Tolbooth in Edinburgh (▷ 70)—are built into the fabric of the house. View the great man's library, the gracious dining room with windows looking down to the river, and a bristling armoury, its walls covered with guns, knives and other paraphernalia. The overall effect is one of mock, almost theatrical antiquity—a distillation of his novels.
Don't miss Scott's collection of nick-nacks of the famous, including Rob Roy's purse, James IV's hunting bottle, a pocket book worked by Flora Macdonald, and many more.

ARRAN, ISLE OF

🗺 312 E12 🛈 The Pier, Brodick KA27 8AU, tel 01770 302140 ⛴ Ferry from Ardrossan to Brodick or Kintyre to Lochranza (summer)

Often described as 'Scotland in miniature', this scenically attractive island caught between the Ayrshire coast and the Kintyre Peninsula has been a popular holiday resort for generations of Clydesiders. The mountain of Goat Fell (874m, 2,867ft) dominates the skyline to the north, and the opportunities for outdoor activities include walking, golf and horseback riding around the island. The red sandstone Brodick Castle (NTS, castle: Apr–end Oct daily 11–4.30; country park: all year daily 9.30–dusk) is the single biggest attraction, with its extensive collection of porcelain and silver, 19th-century sporting pictures and trophies, and wooded country park.

BIGGAR

🗺 313 H12 🛈 115 High Street ML12 6DL, tel 01899 221066, seasonal

Equidistant from Glasgow and Edinburgh, the bustling Borders town of Biggar has retained its character, with a broad main street and wide central square surrounded by shops and tea rooms. The town's heritage is preserved in a range of interesting museums, well signed from the centre. These include Gladstone Court (Easter to mid-Oct Mon–Sat 11–4.30, Sun 2–5) with its re-creation of an indoor 'street' of shops, and the Greenhill Farmhouse Museum (May–end Sep daily 2–5), linked to the 17th-century persecution of the Covenanters (▷ 26–27).

BURNS NATIONAL HERITAGE PARK

See pages 58–59

CAERLAVEROCK CASTLE

🗺 313 H15 • Glencaple, Dumfries DG1 4HD ☎ 01387 770244 🕐 Apr–end Sep daily 9.30–6.30; Oct–end Mar Mon–Sat 9.30–4.30, Sun 2–4.30 🎫 (HS) adult £4, child £1.60 🚻 ♿
www.historic-scotland.gov.uk

The remains of three huge round towers mark out the corners of this ruined, triangular castle of pink sandstone, once the fortress home of the Maxwell family. It is set close to the Solway shore some 8 miles (12.8km) southeast of Dumfries; two sides were protected by an arm of the sea, while the third had a moat, earthworks and a mighty gatehouse to ward off attack. The castle dates from the 13th century, and saw plenty of action before extensive rebuilding in the 15th. In the 1630s it was remodelled for more comfortable living, and an outstanding feature from this time is the ornately carved façade within.

CULZEAN CASTLE AND COUNTRY PARK

See page 60

DRUMLANRIG CASTLE, GARDENS AND COUNTRY PARK

🗺 313 H13 • Thornhill DG3 4AQ
☎ 01848 330248 🕐 Castle: May–end Jun Sat–Thu 12–4; July to mid-Aug daily 12–4. Gardens and country park: end Mar–end Sep daily 12–4 🎫 Adult £7, child £3 (under 5 free), family £20. Park and gardens only, adult £3, child £2, family £10.50 🚻 ♿
www.buccleuch.com

This imposing 17th-century mansion lies amid green hills 18 miles (29km) north of Dumfries, and is one of several homes of the Duke of Buccleuch, one of the wealthiest landowners in Scotland. Four square towers guard the corners, each topped by little turrets that give this castle its unmistakable skyline; the famous view is the one up the straight avenue as you approach. Inside, admire the wooden panelling and carved oak staircase; the art collection is internationally famous.

Outside you can wander through the formal gardens, visit the craft workshops and forge, and even rent a bicycle to explore the grounds.

Burns National Heritage Park, Alloway

Pay homage at the birthplace of Scotland's national bard, and gain an insight into what all the fuss is about.

Burns's birthplace on the high street of Alloway, built in 1757

The original manuscript of 'Auld Lang Syne'

Burns toured the countryside as a tax collector

BASICS

✚ 312 F13 • Murdoch's Lone KA7 4PQ
☎ 01292 443700 🕐 Apr–end Sep daily 9.30–5.30; rest of year daily 10–5
🎟 Adult £5, child £2.50 (under 5 free), family £12.50 🅿 £2 🍴 At museum and Tam o' Shanter Experience
🛍 At museum and Tam o' Shanter Experience 🔧
www.burnsheritagepark.com

SEEING THE BURNS NATIONAL HERITAGE PARK

Robert 'Rabbie' Burns (1759–96) is Scotland's most famous poet and songwriter, his birthday (25 January) celebrated worldwide at haggis suppers. He was born into poverty in a tiny cottage in Alloway. With the nearby museum and other buildings in the park opposite, it is the focus of the Heritage Park.

HIGHLIGHTS

STATUE HOUSE

Tam o'Shanter is a ballad telling the story of drunken Tam, making his way home on his mare, and spying on a party of witches. They chase him, and the mare loses its tail in the flight (hence the naming of many Scottish waterfalls, ▷ 61). Sculptor James Thom created vivid statues that bring the ballad characters to life. Now in the Statue

The Burns Memorial dominates the park (right of picture)

House, they originally toured the country to raise funds for a permanent memorial to Burns.

Burns's parents are buried at Alloway's Auld Kirk (church)

BURNS MONUMENT

The Burns cult sprang up quickly after he died, with public subscription funding the first stones of the Burns Monument in 1820. At the opposite end of the park, it is a venue for events, and there are views over his beloved Alloway from the roof. There's an audio-visual presentation at the Tam o' Shanter Experience, and you can see the stone bridge, the Auld Brig o' Doon, which featured in his poetry.

BACKGROUND

Burns's weaknesses were many: Attempts at farming failed, and his loves and illegitimate children were the stuff of legend—he married Jean Armour in 1788, but only via liaisons with Elizabeth Paton, Mary Campbell and others. Yet his love of life, and celebration of humanity with all its foibles, was extraordinary, and is why his poetry is still enjoyed. Burns's writings ranged from shrewd and witty observations about everyday life and his beliefs in a universal brotherhood, to the deeply romantic and the downright bawdy. Songs like 'Ae Fond Kiss' and 'Auld Lang Syne' are integral to Scottish culture. Burns died in Dumfries, where you can see his house (Apr–end Sep Mon–Sat 10–1, 2–5, Sun 2–5; Oct–end Mar Tue–Sat 10–4) and visit his grave.

The poet's writing set, contained in a leather case

The Grey Mare's Tail waterfall flows into the Tail Burn (stream)

DRUMLANRIG CASTLE, GARDENS AND COUNTRY PARK

See page 57

GLEN TROOL

⊞ 312 F14 ⓘ Glentrool Visitor Centre, Newton Stewart, tel 01671 840302 ⓒ Park: open access all year. Visitor centre: Mar–end Sep daily 10–5; Sep–end Oct Sat, Sun 10-4.30, Mon–Fri 10.30–4 ▢
www.forestry.gov.uk

The Galloway Forest Park covers around 76,000ha (187,720 acres) of wild moorland and loch. While much of it is given over to commercial conifer forestry, Glen Trool remains an area of outstanding natural scenic beauty, with semi-ancient oak woodland that is seen at its best in the autumn.

From the visitor centre east of Glentrool village, walking and bicycling routes lead through the park, and the Southern Upland Way long distance path also passes nearby. Bruce's Stone, at the end of the road by the loch, commemorates a victory by Robert the Bruce against an English force in 1307 (▷ 202–203).

Bruce's Stone, a landmark beside Loch Trool

Terraced gardens on the south side of the castle

CULZEAN CASTLE AND COUNTRY PARK

A fine 18th-century mansion by master architect Robert Adam, in an outstanding coastal setting.

⊞ 312 F13 • Maybole KA19 8LE ☎ 01655 884455 ⓒ Castle: Easter–end Oct daily 10.30–5; country park: all year daily ⓖ (NTS) Castle and country park: adult £12, child £8, family £30. Park only: adult £8, child £5, family £20
📖 Guidebook £3.95 🍴 Home Farm Restaurant ▢ Old Stables Coffee House ⊞ Country Park shop and plant centre 📷
www.culzeancastle.net

RATINGS	
Good for kids	●●●●
Historic interest	●●●●
Outdoors	●●●●
Photo stops	●●●●●

Culzean (pronounced 'Cullane') is the National Trust for Scotland's most popular property. That's partly thanks to the surrounding country park—228 lush green hectares (563 acres) of wild gardens and leafy woodland riddled with trails. You can discover a walled garden, an aviary, a deer park and lots of follies dotted around.

The golden stone castle, romantically set right at the edge of the cliffs, is handsome rather than beautiful, with its baronial towers and castellated roofline. It is reached via a bridge, and rises high above a terraced garden. Inside, it is an 18th-century show home, the masterpiece of Scottish architect Robert Adam, who worked on it from 1777 to 1792 for the powerful Kennedy family, who had dominated this part of Ayrshire since the 12th century.

Highlights include the graceful oval staircase and the Circular Saloon. The top floor was granted to General Eisenhower in 1945, for his lifetime, as a thanks from the people of Scotland for American help during World War II; there are photographs and mementoes of his visits, and for an exclusive thrill, you can even stay in the Eisenhower apartment.
Don't miss Lofty sea views to the craggy island of Ailsa Craig from the Circular Saloon.

60 SOUTHERN SCOTLAND C–J

Haddington's Nungate Bridge was built in the 16th century

Hermitage Castle, remodelled in the 14th century

Jedburgh lies on the old road to Scotland

GRETNA GREEN

🔲 314 J14 🔋 The World Famous Old Blacksmith's Shop Centre DG16 5EA, tel 01461 338441; seasonal 🚌 Gretna Green

Gretna Green's fame rests on its location on the border, and its historical association with runaway lovers from England. Several sites claim to be the original location where, under Scottish law, marriages could simply be declared in front of witnesses—and that was that. You can pay a fee and relive a version of the ceremony at the World Famous Old Blacksmith's Shop Centre (Apr–end Jun, Sep-end Oct daily 9–6; Jul, Aug daily 9–7; Nov–end Mar daily 9–5), a fairly tacky tourist trap. Despite some attractive corners, Gretna itself is unlovely. It became a boom town during World War I, when a huge munitions factory was built here: The Devil's Porridge at nearby Eastriggs (mid-May to end Oct Mon–Sat 10–4, Sun 12–4) tells the story. The town has a designer outlet shopping complex.

GREY MARE'S TAIL

🔲 313 J13 🔋 Unit 1, Ladyknowe, Moffat DG10 9DY, tel 01683 220620 🅾 Visitor centre: Apr–end Oct 🅿 Free, donations requested 🚗 ❓ For information about guided walks, tel 01556 502575 www.nts.org.uk

A spectacular waterfall is the focus of an unexpected Highland scene in the Borders, just off the A708, 8 miles (12.9km) northeast of Moffat. The waterfall tumbles straight down for 200ft (61m), over the lip of a hanging valley, its source Loch Skeen, invisible from below. Steep paths lead to the top of the falls (stout footwear essential), with a view of wild loch and upland scenery that makes the climb worthwhile.

If you'd like to venture farther, there's are guided walks on offer—check with the senior ranger or the tourist information office at Moffat.
Don't miss Peregrine falcons nest nearby; watch them in the visitor centre, via a live television link.

HADDINGTON

🔲 314 K11 🔋 Quality Street, North Berwick EH39 4HJ, tel 01620 892197

This handsome, businesslike market town is set in prime agricultural country on the River Tyne, 18 miles (29km) east of Edinburgh. It was granted the status of a royal burgh in the 12th century (the nearby port of Aberlady, now silted up, was its gateway to trade with continental Europe), and later became the county town for East Lothian. Protestant reformer John Knox was born here in c.1505. The original medieval town was laid out to a triangular street plan which can still be traced along High Street, Market Street and Hardgate. Painted in bright, warm colours, the 18th-century Georgian buildings of the High Street create a pleasing and harmonious façade. The graciously proportioned Town House was built by William Adam in 1748. St. Mary's Church dates from the 15th century.

HERMITAGE CASTLE

🔲 314 K14 • Newcastleton TD9 0LU ☎ 01387 376222 🅾 Apr–end Sep daily 9.30–6.30 🏴 (HS) Adult £2.50, child £1 🏛

The dark sandstone walls of this lonely Border fortress loom high above the marshy ground beside the river known as Hermitage Water, 15 miles (24.1km) south of Hawick. The lack of windows indicates that this was never a homey castle, rather a grim place

for fighting and foul deeds.

The Douglas family took over a simple rectangular building in the 14th century and remodelled it to the massive and forbidding structure seen today. It's easy to imagine the wooden fighting platform which once ran around the outside, near the top of the walls. One owner was boiled alive for his crimes of murder and witchcraft, and another, who starved a rival to death in the dungeon, was murdered in a nearby wood. Mary, Queen of Scots, made a flying visit in 1566 on a gruelling 80-mile (129km) round trip to visit her lover Bothwell. It's a place steeped in atmosphere and history.

JEDBURGH

🔲 314 K13 🔋 Murray's Green TD8 6BE, tel 0870 608 0404

Jedburgh has witnessed many conflicts—in fact, so frequently was the town's castle attacked, rebuilt and attacked again that it was finally demolished in 1409. In its place is the former county jail, now Jedburgh Castle Jail and Museum (Easter–end Oct Mon–Sat 10–4.30, Sun 1–4).

The broken tower and red sandstone walls of the ruined abbey (HS, Apr–end Sep daily 9.30– 6.30; rest of year 9.30–4.30) still dominate the town centre. This was one of the great medieval Border abbeys, and the shepherding skills of the monks were the basis on which the town's weaving industry and wealth grew.

Mary, Queen of Scots, stayed in a fortified, crow-step gabled house (Mar–end Nov Mon–Sat 10–4.30, Sun 11–4.30) in 1566, famously leaving it briefly to visit her lover Bothwell, who lay wounded after a scrap at Hermitage Castle.
Don't miss At her house, Mary, Queen of Scots' death mask.

Kelso Abbey was ruined by the English in 1545

JOHN MUIR COUNTRY PARK

⊞ 318 K11 ⓘ 143A High Street, Dunbar EH42 1ES, tel 01368 863353
🚉 Dunbar
www.edinburgh.org

John Muir (1838–1914) was a native of Dunbar, who emigrated in 1849 and became the founder of the National Parks system in the US. He is recalled by the country park of 733 ha (1,810 acre) that stretches along the coast to the west of Dunbar. The park offers walkers and birdwatchers a good variety of habitats, and all within easy reach of Edinburgh. The overall impression here is one of openness and space—a landscape of horizontals with long beaches and salt marsh, as well as cliffs and rocky shores, backed by woodlands.
Don't miss The view of the Bass Rock from the rocky headland at the far west of the park.

KELSO

⊞ 314 K12 ⓘ Town House, The Square TD5 7HF, tel 0870 608 0404

One of the most elegant of the Borders towns, Kelso has a wide cobbled square at its heart. A poignant fragment is all that remains of Kelso Abbey, once the largest of the Border abbeys, destroyed by the English in 1545. Nearby is the handsome five-arched bridge over the River Tweed built by John Rennie in 1803. From the parapet there is a fine view across to Floors Castle (Apr–end Oct daily 10–4.30). This is the largest inhabited house in Scotland, a monument to the wealth and privilege of the dukes of Roxburghe. It was started in 1718, and remodelled by William Playfair from 1838 to 1849. Fine art, tapestries and French furniture are all on view.

Admiring Hornel's paintings at his home, Broughton House

KIRKCUDBRIGHT

A small artists' town on the Dee estuary.

⊞ 313 G15 ⓘ Harbour Square DG6 4HY, tel 01557 330494

This pretty harbour town (the name is pronounced Kirkoobree) lies southwest of Castle Douglas on the road to nowhere, which is perhaps why it has retained so much

RATINGS				
Historic interest	●	●	●	
Photo stops	●	●	●	●
Specialist shopping	●	●	●	
Walkability	●	●	●	●	●

character. The street plan is medieval, the gap-toothed castle ruin at its heart 16th-century, and its fame as a centre for painters dates from 1901, when artist and 'Glasgow Boy' E. A. Hornel (1864–1933) settled here, among others. Broughton House, on the High Street, where he lived and worked, is now a gallery and museum (NTS, House and garden: Apr–end Jun, Sep–end Oct daily 12–5; July, Aug 10–5; Garden only: Feb–end Apr 11–4). It is said that local residents approached Hornel and his friends for their advice whenever their house frontages needed repainting—and this is the explanation for the harmonious shades seen in the High Street today.

More paintings by Kirkcudbright artists, including Jessie M. King, S. J. Peploe and Charles Oppenheimer, can be seen in the Tolbooth Art Centre (Jun–end Sep Mon–Sat 11–5, also Sun 2–5). Other items, including book illustrations and pottery, are on show at the Stewartry Museum on St. Mary Street (open as Tolbooth). And for 21st-century art that you can buy, don't miss the tiny Harbour Cottage Gallery, down by the old harbour.
Don't miss Hornel's Japanese-style garden at Broughton House.

The old heart of Kirkcudbright is easily explored on foot

Semi-tropical plants at Logan Botanic Garden

LOGAN BOTANIC GARDEN

312 E15 • Port Logan, Stranraer DG9 9ND ☎ 01776 860231
Mar–end Oct daily 10–6; rest of year daily 10–5 Adult £3.50, child £1, family £8 Self-guiding audio tour. Free guided walks Apr–end Sep every second Tue
www.rbge.org.uk

This frost-free corner of the Rhinns of Galloway, in the far southwest, serves as an annexe for tender plants from the Royal Botanic Garden in Edinburgh (▷ 86), and is a plant-lover's delight. Exotic species from the southern hemisphere thrive on the acid soil, including palm-like cordyline, trachycarpus and the ever-popular tree-ferns (*Dicksonia*). Feature plants include Himalayan poppies and South African proteas, and there are bright floral displays throughout summer in the walled garden. The rhododendrons and primulas of the woodland garden are perhaps more familiar to local gardeners.

MELLERSTAIN HOUSE

314 K12 • Gordon TD3 6LG
☎ 01573 410225 Easter and May–end Oct Sun–Mon, Wed–Fri 12.30–5; also Oct 12.30–5 Adult £5.50, under 16 free
www.mellerstain.com

A superb 18th-century mansion northwest of Kelso, this great house is famous for its Adam architecture and elegant interiors, and is still the family home of the Earl of Haddington. Architect William Adam started work on the house in 1725. The large central block was completed in 1778 by his son Robert (1728–92), who went on to design the interior. The delicate plasterwork throughout—but especially in the music room, library and drawing room—is outstanding.

MELROSE

An enticing combination of historic small town and splendid, ruined abbey.

314 K12 Abbey House TD6 9LG, tel 0870 608 0404; seasonal
www.scot-borders.co.uk

RATINGS	
Historic interest	●●●●
Photo stops	●●●●
Shopping	●●●
Walkability	●●●●●

The Romans built a massive fort here, by a bridge over the River Tweed, and called it Trimontium after the three peaks of the nearby Eildon Hills. There's little left to see, but the Three Hills Roman Heritage Centre in the middle of this compact Borders town sets it all in context (Mar–end Oct daily 10.30–4.30).

The more visible history of Melrose dates from 1136, when David I founded the pink sandstone abbey, which lies just below the town centre (HS, Apr–end Sep daily 9.30–6.30; rest of year Mon–Sat 9.30–4.30, Sun 2–4.30). Severely battered by the English in the 14th century, it was later rebuilt, and then robbed of its stones by the Douglases, who used them to build a house. Repairs in the 19th century were at the instigation of novelist Sir Walter Scott; the ruins are majestic, and the stone carving outstanding—take time to look upward to identify saints, dragons, flowers and a pig playing the bagpipes.

Otherwise, it's a genteel town to explore, with delicatessens, an excellent bookshop, and Priorwood Gardens, dedicated to the art of growing flowers which can be dried (NTS, Apr–end Dec Mon–Sat 10–5, Sun 1–5; Jan–end Mar Mon–Sat 12–4).
Don't miss The burial spot of Robert the Bruce's heart in the abbey, marked by an engraved inscription.

Gothic buttresses and pinnacles on the abbey roof

THE SIGHTS

Decommissioned aircraft find a home at East Fortune

Explore down a real mine at Wanlockhead

The parish church at Peebles overlooks the River Tweed

MELROSE

See page 63

MUSEUM OF FLIGHT

⊞ 318 K11 • East Fortune Airfield, East Fortune EH39 5LF ☎ 01620 880308 ◉ Apr–end Oct daily 10–5; Nov–end Mar Sat–Sun 10–4 🅿 Adult £5, conc £4, child under 12 free; additional charges for special exhibitions ▢ ⊞ www.nms.ac.uk/flight

Lying 3 miles (5km) north of Haddington, this is Scotland's national collection of historic aircraft, with more than 50 aircraft offering everything from a Glasgow-built flying machine that inspired the Wright brothers, to the majestic Concorde-G-BOAA. A number of planes from the World War I era are also on display, including a Messerschmitt Komet and a Vickers Supermarine Spitfire. The museum site itself captures a fascinating picture of another age, with original hangars and other buildings forming the most complete record of a World War II airbase in Britain. It was also the site of the launch of the famous airship, *R34*, for the first ever east-to-west Atlantic crossing in 1910.
Don't miss Percy Pilcher's Hawk glider, built in 1896, and said to have inspired American aviation pioneers Orville and Wilbur Wright.

MUSEUM OF LEAD MINING

⊞ 313 H13 • Wanlockhead, by Biggar ML12 6UT ☎ 01659 74387 ◉ Mar–end Oct daily 11–4.30; Jul, Aug daily 10–5 🅿 Adult £5, child £3.50, family £16.85 ▢ ⊞ www.leadminingmuseum.co.uk

Drive up to Wanlockhead, Scotland's highest village (468m/1,535ft) set amid the windswept, heathery domes of the Lowther Hills, and you arrive in a different world. A heritage trail from the visitor centre around the settlement shows you the workings of a community where generations of miners toiled to extract lead. You can wander into Straitsteps Cottages for a taste of family life here in 1740 and 1890, and discover the little lending library, founded in 1756 and thought to be the second-oldest in Europe. Best of all, you can follow a miner into the hillside, down the workings of an old lead mine, to see how the men really worked.

NEW ABBEY

⊞ 313 H15 🛈 64 Whitesands, Dumfries DG1 2RS, tel 01387 253862

Sweetheart Abbey is a most romantic name, and indeed the picturesque ruins which dominate this unassuming little Galloway community, south of Dumfries, tell a sad tale of devotion. The Cistercian abbey (HS, Mar–end Sep daily 9.30–6.30; Oct–end Mar Sat–Wed 9.30–4) was founded in the 13th century by Devorgilla, Lady of Galloway and wife of John Balliol. After he died she carried his heart in a casket with her for the next 20 years, and then was buried with it before the high altar of the abbey church here.
Nearby New Abbey Corn Mill (HS, open as abbey) is an 18th-century water-powered mill for grinding oatmeal, preserved in full working order.
Shambellie House Museum of Costume (Apr–end Oct daily 10–5) is set in a mid-19th-century house, typical of this period. Rooms are brought to life by tableaux of clothed figures, covering different periods. The main location for the National Museum of Scotland's costume collection, the museum is a must for fashion enthusiasts.

NEW LANARK WORLD HERITAGE SITE

See page 65

PEEBLES

⊞ 313 J12 🛈 High Street, Peebles EH45 8AG, tel 0870 608 0404

The broad main street of this bustling Borders town, 35 miles (56km) south of Edinburgh, always seems busy, its small shops and family businesses (few high street multiples here) doing a brisk trade. Visitors come here to shop and enjoy the feel of a pleasant country town. Walks, trails and cycleways lead into the wooded countryside, starting with the gentle walk upstream from the park along the River Tweed to Neidpath Castle (Easter and May–end Sep Wed–Sat 10.30–5, Sun 12.30–5), a 14th-century tower set high above the river. (You can continue the walk past the castle and return on the other bank via a disused railway bridge.)

ROSSLYN CHAPEL

⊞ 317 J11 • Roslin EH25 9PU ☎ 0131 440 2159 ◉ Mon–Sat 9.30–6, Sun noon–4.45 🅿 Adult £6, children free ▢ ⊞ www.rosslynchapel.org.uk

In a mining village 6 miles (10km) south of Edinburgh, this is the most mysterious building in Scotland. A church was founded here in 1446 by William St. Clair, Third Earl of Orkney. It was to be a large cruciform structure, but only the choir was ever built, along with parts of the east transept walls. It is linked with the Knights Templar and other secretive societies, and believed by some to be the hiding place of the Holy Grail, a

The deeply carved Prentice Pillar in Rosslyn Chapel

role publicized in Dan Brown's novel *The Da Vinci Code*. Inside is a riot of medieval stone carving. Every part of roof rib, arch, corbel and pillar is encrusted with decorative work—mouldings, foliage and figures of all kinds, including representations of Green Men, the Seven Deadly Sins and other religious themes.

Don't miss The famous Prentice Pillar with its spiralling strands of foliage and winged serpents, necks intertwined, biting their own tails.

SCOTTISH MARITIME MUSEUM

312 F12 • Harbourside, Irvine KA12 8QE ☎ 01294 278283 Easter–end Oct daily 10–5 Adult £3, child (5–16) £2, family £7
www.scottishmaritimemuseum.org

Though much of Irvine is modern, the town has some interesting old buildings by the waterfront and one of these houses the Scottish Maritime Museum. As well as scale models there are a number of real boats to explore—the *Spartan* is a Clyde puffer (steamboat), which plied its trade up and down the west coast connecting the remote communities; the *Garnock* is a tug, used on the Clyde. There are some fascinating displays about Scotland's seafaring past, many housed in the impressive Linthouse Engine Shop, a restored structure from the Alexander Stephens yard in Govan. Dubbed the 'cathedral to Scottish engineering', this is where some of Scottish shipbuilding's greatest products had their massive engines fitted. Also restored in the complex is a tenement apartment, now depicting life as it would have been experienced by a shipyard worker in the early part of the 20th century.

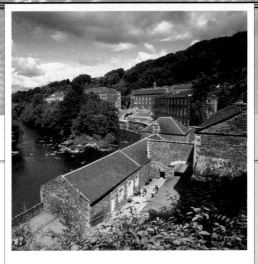

An industrial community that showed how life could be better

NEW LANARK WORLD HERITAGE SITE

An outstanding example of industrial heritage brought very much to life in this village and cotton mill site, restored as a living, working community.

313 H12 • New Lanark Mills, Lanark ML11 9DB ☎ 01555 661345 Visitor centre: daily 11–5; Jun–end Aug 10.30–5 Adult £5.95, child £3.95 (under 3 free), family £16.95–£19.95 Lanark (1 mile/1.6km) £1.75 Owen's Warehouse, open all day for snacks and lunches Gift shop in Owen's Warehouse, also branch of the Edinburgh Woollen Mill
Facilities for visitors with disabilities include adapted chair for the 'dark ride'; induction loop in audio-visual show and 'dark ride' www.newlanark.org

RATINGS				
Good for kids	●	●	●	
Historic interest	●	●	●	●	●
Outdoors	●	●	●	
Photo stops	●	●	●	●

TIP
● The free leaflet 'Discover New Lanark World Heritage Site', available to download from the internet and from tourist information offices, includes a simple site map—invaluable for planning your exploration.

Glasgow philanthropist David Dale (1739–1806) first developed a cotton manufacturing plant and settlement in this steep-sided valley in 1786. However, it is his son-in-law, the Welshman Robert Owen (1771–1858), who is most clearly identified with the village, which he purchased in 1799. A benevolent idealist, over the next two decades he established a Utopian society here—a model community with improved conditions for the workers and their families, complete with school (it is claimed, with the first day nursery and playground in the world), institute for adult education and co-operative village store. The site later declined; in 1973 the New Lanark Conservation Trust started to restore the site, with the stunning results seen today.

The workers' houses are lived in once more, though the mill no longer manufactures cotton. Understand it through the curious Millennium Experience 'dark ride', complete with tableaux and sound effects. You can also explore a millworker's cottage, Robert Owen's house and the school. You can even stay here, in the 3-star New Lanark Mill hotel or self-catering cottages.

Don't miss The walk to the three waterfalls that lie upstream, particularly after rainfall when they are at their best.

Gannets are the big attraction at the Scottish Seabird Centre

Turreted Thirlestane Castle dates back to 1590

The rugged coastline at St. Abb's, home to thousands of seabirds

THE SIGHTS

SCOTTISH SEABIRD CENTRE

➕ 318 K11 • The Harbour, North Berwick EH39 4SS ☎ 01620 890202
🕐 Apr–end Oct daily 10–6; rest of year Mon–Fri 10–4, Sat–Sun 10–5.30
🎟 Adult £6.95, conc £4.50, family £13.95–£21.95. Joint admission and train tickets available from Edinburgh
🚉 North Berwick ☐ 🚻
www.seabird.org

Perched on the edge of the sea, the Seabird Centre is the key to the birdlife of the Firth of Forth, and in particular the famous gannet colony that inhabits the Bass Rock (Jan–end Oct). Interactive displays and wildlife films inform. Panoramic views to the islands are excellent—enjoy them from the café with its outdoor terrace, or follow the spring nesting activity of puffins and other seabirds in close-up on a television link. In winter, fluffy white seal pups can be observed on the Isle of May, home to Britain's largest grey seal colony.

ST. ABB'S HEAD NATIONAL NATURE RESERVE

➕ 314 L11 • St. Abbs, Eyemouth TD14 5QF ☎ 01890 771443 🕐 Open access all year. Visitor centre: Apr–end Oct daily 10–5 🎟 Donations; parking £2–£4 ☐
www.nts.org.uk

Seabirds nest in their thousands here. It's a wild and beautiful landscape at any time of year, with the spectacular cliffs of soft red sandstone, sculpted by wind and waves, reaching 100m (300ft) above sea-level. Fulmars, kittiwakes, guillemots, puffins and razorbills are the most prominent breeding species, and when they are in residence in late spring, the cliffs become an astonishing vertical city.

A circular walk to the lighthouse brings you past

Mire Loch, where little grebes and tufted duck may be seen.

TANTALLON CASTLE

➕ 318 K11 • near North Berwick ☎ 01620 892727 🕐 Apr–end Sep daily 9.30–6.30; rest of year Sat–Wed 9.30–4.30 🎟 (HS) adult £3.30, child £1.30 🚻
www.historic-scotland.gov.uk

Twenty days of blasting from King James V's cannons in 1528 could not destroy this mighty fortress, 3 miles (4.8km) east of North Berwick. Set high on a clifftop promontory, and protected by the sea on three sides, it was almost impregnable, rendered so by the huge curtain wall, 15m (50ft) high and 3.7m (12ft) thick, which still stands. From the 14th century Tantallon was the stronghold of the Red Douglases, Earls of Angus; it was wiped out in 1651, in the Civil War.

THIRLESTANE CASTLE

➕ 314 K12 • Lauder TDU 6RU ☎ 01578 722430 🕐 Easter, Jul, Aug Sat–Thu; mid-Apr to end Jun, Sep Mon, Wed, Thu, Sun 10–3 (last admission) 🎟 Adult £5.50, child £3 (under 5 free). Grounds only: adult £2, child £1 ☐
www.thirlestanecastle.co.uk

Thirlestane is one of the most sumptuously decorated great houses in Scotland. A simple pink sandstone tower house just east of Lauder was transformed from 1670 to 1676 for the Duke of Lauderdale, Secretary of State, by architect William Bruce and master craftsman Robert Mylne—who were also working on Holyrood Palace (▷ 83). Curious semi-circular stair-towers punctuate the outer walls, but it is the plasterwork of the ceilings that is the remarkable feature, created by Dutch masters. Deep garlands of flowers are adorned with gilded highlights.

Don't miss The ceiling of the long drawing room, which took five years to create.

THREAVE GARDEN AND ESTATE

➕ 313 G15 • Castle Douglas DG7 1RX ☎ 01556 502575 🕐 Garden and estate: all year daily. Visitor centre and countryside centre: Apr–end Oct daily 9.30–5.30; Mar and Nov, Dec 10–4. House: Mar–end Oct Wed–Fri and Sun, 11–3.30 (guided tours only, admission by timed ticket) 🎟 Garden: adult £10, child £8, family £20 ☐ 🚻
❓ Electric wheelchairs available
www.nts.org.uk

Threave is the National Trust for Scotland's investment in the future—a teaching garden, where horticulturalists come to learn and try out new ideas. Glorious in its own right, it offers a mixture of established splendours such as a vast walled garden, alongside less formal, more experimental areas. Threave House dates from 1872, and was the heart of an estate that today covers 480ha (1,200 acres) of prime countryside. **Don't miss** Quintessential herbaceous borders in summer, and the early spring daffodils—around 200 different varieties.

VIKINGAR!

➕ 312 F12 • Greenock Road, Largs KA30 8QL ☎ 01475 689777
🕐 Vikingar! Experience: Apr–end Sep daily 10.30–5.30; Oct, Mar 10.30–3.30; Nov, Feb Sat, Sun 10.30–3.30; Dec, Jan closed 🎟 Adult £4, child £3 (under 5 free), family £12.20 🚉 Largs ☐ 🚻
www.vikingar.co.uk

Vikingar! is a lively reminder that the Norse had a major impact in the shaping of Scotland. The centre tells of the Vikings in Scotland from the early invasions to final defeat at the Battle of Largs in 1263, using models, impressive audio-visual effects

The 12th-century priory church at Whithorn, in the far southwest

and suitably hairy actors to re-create the Viking world. Take in the Homestead, with its Viking smells, and the Hall of the Gods. There's an entertaining film show with shouting and sword-clanging, then the Hall of Knowledge with replica carvings, information boards and a touch-screen computer. Great for adults as well as kids.

THE WHITHORN STORY

312 F15 • 45–47 George Street, Whithorn DG8 8NS ☎ 01988 500508 Apr–end Oct daily 10.30–5 Adult £2.70, child £1.50 (under 5 free), family £7.50
www.whithorn.com

It took an Act of Parliament in 1581 to stop the pilgrims from flocking to Whithorn. Royals and commoners were drawn to the shrine of St. Ninian, Scotland's first Christian missionary, who built a stone church here in AD397. He followed it with a priory, but the existing ruins are from a later, 12th-century construction. Excavations have turned up stone carvings and smaller, more personal treasures left by the pilgrims; ongoing archaeological work is uncovering the remains of a 5th-century village. The centre includes audio-visual presentations and access to the main sites.

WIGTOWN

312 F15 Machars Information Office, 26 South Main Street DG8 9EH, tel 01988 402036
www.wigtown-booktown.co.uk

Wigtown brands itself as Scotland's Book Town. The neat buildings in black and white that line the broad main street have an upbeat air, and more than 20 specialist and antiquarian booksellers and many other related outlets offer a wide choice for literary browsers.

A corner of the library in this most ancient Scottish house

TRAQUAIR

An unassuming treasure, and the oldest inhabited house in Scotland.

314 J12 • Innerleithen EH44 6PW ☎ 01896 830323 Jun–end Aug daily 10.30–5.00; mid-Apr to end May and Sep 12–5; Oct 11–4 House and grounds: adult £5.80, child £3.25, family £16.80. Grounds only: adult £2.50, child £1.25 £3.50 Home baking at the 1745 Cottage Restaurant in the Old Walled Garden Gift shop sells souvenirs and ale; antique shop; craft workshops including jewellery
www.traquair.co.uk

An air of romance and ancient secrecy surrounds Traquair, a beautiful old castle buried in the trees 6 miles (9.7km) southeast of Peebles. It started out as a royal hunting lodge at

RATINGS			
Good for kids	●	●	● ●
Historic interest	●	●	● ●
Photo stops	●	●	●
Specialist shopping	●	●	● ●

the time of James III—its 'modern' extensions were made way back in 1680, and today it presents a serene, grey-harled face to visitors. Once the Tweed ran so close that the laird could fish from his windows. That changed when the river was re-routed by Sir William Stuart, who also built most of what we see now, in 1566.

Part of Traquair's sense of mystery comes from its connections with the doomed Stewart cause: Mary, Queen of Scots, stayed here in 1566 (her bed is now in the King's Room), and the famous Bear Gates have not been opened since 1745, when Bonnie Prince Charlie last rode through. There are secret stairs to the hidden Priest's Room, and touching relics of a time when Catholics were persecuted in Scotland. An impressive modern venture has been the revival of a brewery at Traquair: Re-established in 1965, it has proved highly successful, and now

produces three rich, dark ales for export worldwide—sample them in the brewery shop.

At the heart of Traquair is a former royal hunting lodge

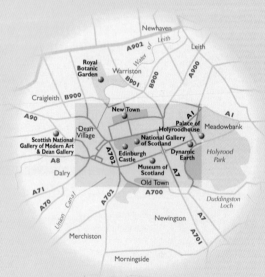

EDINBURGH

Scotland's capital city has a genteel, cultured outlook reflected in the magnificent 18th-century architecture of its so-called New Town. Some of the country's major visitor attractions are found here, including national museums, galleries and the city's famous castle on top of a rocky crag overlooking the city.

KEY SIGHTS

Edinburgh

i VisitScotland Edinburgh Information Centre, 3 Princes Street EH2 2QP, tel 0131 473 3800
www.visitscotland.com
The tourist board's main website for the whole of Scotland

HOW TO GET THERE

✈ Airport
Edinburgh's airport is located at Ingliston, 6 miles (9.6km) west of the city, off the A8.

🚆 Train stations
Waverley is the main station for the city centre, at the west end of Princes Street. Haymarket lies to the west of the centre.

You'll get great views of the city from Calton Hill (above). Deacon Brodie's (right) is one of the Old Town's many enticing pubs

TIPS

● Four operators run bus tours from Waverley Bridge, following different routes. Pick the route that suits you and you can hop on and off all day.
● With its steep cobbled streets and sometimes irregular pavements Edinburgh is hard on the feet, so wear comfortable shoes for a day's exploring.
● Allow extra time to get about during the Festival, when the streets are particularly busy and cafés fill up quickly.
● A free bus links the four main art galleries, including the out-of-centre modern art venues. It operates between 10.45am and 5pm.

SEEING EDINBURGH

Central Edinburgh is relatively compact, and divides into two halves: the narrow, steep, curving streets of the Old Town to the south of Princes Street Gardens, and the neat grid, broad boulevards and crescents of the New Town to the north of Princes Street. The Old Town is built along a ridge of rock that stretches from the castle for around a mile eastwards to Holyrood Palace, which lies in the shadow of the tilted volcanic hill of Arthur's Seat. All the main streets run parallel to this line—Queen Street, George Street (for boutique shopping) and Princes Street (high street shopping) to the north; Castle Hill, Lawnmarket, High Street and Canongate (which together form the famous 'Royal Mile') on the top of the ridge; and Grassmarket, Cowgate and Chambers Street (with the Royal Museum and Museum of Scotland) to the south. The best places to get your bearings are from the top of Calton Hill, at the east end of Princes Street, or from the castle esplanade. Views extend north to the Firth of Forth, the Forth bridges and the hills of central Scotland, south to the Pentland Hills and east to the conical mound of Berwick Law.

The tour buses that congregate on Waverley Bridge, by the main train station, offer the best introduction to the city, with four different routes taking in the main attractions and linking you to sites outside the city centre such as the Botanic Gardens and the old port of Leith (good for shopping, trendy bars and the Royal Yacht *Britannia*). A day's ticket allows you to hop on and off as you fancy, and the commentaries from the guides are thoroughly informative and entertaining. The national museums and the main local museums are free. If you plan to visit several of the more expensive attractions in a short time, the Edinburgh Pass, available from tourist offices or via www.edinburghpass.org, may save you money (from 1 day, £26, to 3 days, £40).

DEACON BRODIES

BACKGROUND

Edinburgh grew up in medieval times as a warren of narrow streets around the castle (▷ 71–73). Wealth led to expansion in the 18th century and the development of the gracious New Town (▷ 84–85). Today it is the home of the new Scottish Parliament (join a guided tour and wonder at how the money was spent, tel 0131 348 5200), and is the financial, legal and tourism hub of Scotland. Its annual arts festivals are world renowned, and in 2005 it was declared the first ever literary capital of Europe for its numerous connections with esteemed writers over the centuries, from Sir Walter Scott and R. L. Stevenson to J. K. Rowling and Alexander McCall Smith.

DON'T MISS

CALTON HILL
The views from the top say it all (▷ 70)
EDINBURGH CASTLE
Still dominating the city, and its best-known landmark (▷ 71–73)
MUSEUM OF SCOTLAND
The national treasure store, in a fabulous modern building (▷ 78–81)
NEW TOWN
Edinburgh's elegant 18th-century development (▷ 84–85)

The tilted ridge of Salisbury Crags, by Arthur's Seat, loom above Holyroodhouse at the eastern end of Edinburgh's Old Town

Edinburgh's own museum is on the Royal Mile

THE SIGHTS

ARTHUR'S SEAT

🔢 309 off F2 🚌 24, 25
🚉 Edinburgh Waverley

The bare green hill of Arthur's Seat is a great landmark in the city, 251m (823ft) high and visible for miles around. It's the remains of a volcano 325 million years old, with seven smaller hills around it and the high cliffs of Salisbury Crags, tilted in a later ice age. It forms the bottom of the Old Town ridge which leads up to the castle Mound. There is open access to the hills and four small lochs, which are part of the Royal Park of Holyrood, with good walks and great views down over Holyrood Palace itself. You'll find car parks at the palace, in Duddingston village, and by the man-made pools of St. Margaret's Loch and Dunsappie Loch. Duddingston Loch is a bird reserve.

CALTON HILL

🔢 309 E1 ℹ️ Edinburgh Lothian Tourist Information Centre, 3 Princes Street EH2 2QP, tel 0131 473 3800 🚌 40 🚉 Edinburgh Waverley

In the 18th century Edinburgh was known as the Athens of the North; this reached absurd proportions when a reproduction of the Parthenon was planned, as a grand memorial to those killed in the Napoleonic Wars. The story goes that the money ran out in 1829, but the remaining folly is part of the distinctive skyline of Calton Hill, at the east end of Princes Street.

It shares the spot with the City Observatory, founded in 1776, the 1807 tower of the Nelson Monument (Apr–end Sep Mon 1–6, Tue–Sat 10–6; rest of year Mon–Sat 10–3) and various other monuments. It's well worth the climb to the windy park at the top (350ft/107m), for a superb view over the city.

CAMERA OBSCURA AND WORLD OF ILLUSIONS

🔢 308 C2 • Castlehill, The Royal Mile EH1 2ND ☎ 0131 226 3709
🕐 Apr–end Jun, Sep, Oct daily 9.30–6; Jul, Aug daily 9.30–7.30; rest of year daily 10–5 💷 Adult £6.50, child £4.20 (5–15) 🚌 23, 27, 41, 42, 45
🚉 Edinburgh Waverley 🖥️
www.camera-obscura.co.uk

The Camera Obscura is lodged at the top of the Royal Mile in a castellated building known as the Outlook Tower. It started life in 1853 as Short's Popular Observatory, and grew into the Victorian equivalent of today's hands-on science centres.

The Camera Obscura is like a giant pin-hole camera, with no film involved: It projects on to a viewing table a fascinating panorama of the city outside, which of course changes minute by minute. It can zoom in impressively, to catch details of what's happening, including all the action in Princes Street Gardens (▷ 77).

There are also great views through the Superscope, the most powerful telescope in Britain, and displays of old photographs and cameras.

CANONGATE KIRK

🔢 309 E2 • Canongate EH8 8BR
☎ 0131 556 3515 🕐 Jun–end Sep Mon–Sat 10.30–4, Sun 10–12.30; rest of year Sun 10–12.30 💷 Free 🚌 35
🚉 Edinburgh Waverley

When James VI/II converted the abbey church at Holyrood (▷ 83) to a chapel for the Knights of the Thistle in 1687, the Canongate district needed a new church. It was built up the hill, next to the Tolbooth (see right), in the following year, its distinctive Dutch gable and plain interior reflecting the Canongate's trading links with the Low Countries. At the

gable top, note the gilded stag's head, traditionally a gift of the monarch.

Some of Edinburgh's finest are buried in the graveyard, including economist and philosopher Adam Smith (1723–90), and David Rizzio, favourite of Mary, Queen of Scots, murdered in 1566. Robert Burns paid for a headstone for fellow poet Robert Fergusson (1750–74) to show his admiration—Fergusson died tragically young of insanity, but his vernacular poetry about the city gave it one of its nicknames, Auld Reekie.

CANONGATE TOLBOOTH/ THE PEOPLE'S STORY MUSEUM

🔢 309 E2 • 163 Canongate EH8 8BN
☎ 0131 529 4057 🕐 Mon–Sat 10–5; Aug also Sun 12–5 💷 Free 🚌 35
🚉 Edinburgh Waverley 🖥️
www.cac.org.uk

Just up the hill from the Canongate Kirk, the French-style old Tolbooth dates from 1591 and served as the council chamber for the independent burgh of Canongate until its incorporation into the city in 1856. It also served time as a prison. The huge boxed clock that projects above the street was added in 1884.

The building is now the home of The People's Story, a museum dedicated to everyday life and times in Edinburgh since the 18th century and up to the present day. Tableaux and objects, sounds and smells evoke life in a prison cell, a draper's shop, of a servant at work and a tramcar conductor (a 'clippie', who clipped the tickets). With a host of other everyday details, it portrays the struggle for better conditions, better health, and better ways to enjoy what little leisure the citizens had.

Edinburgh Castle

One million visitors a year come to view Scotland's oldest castle.
See the powerful symbols of Scottish nationalism:
the crown jewels and the Stone of Destiny.
There are several military museums within the castle, including
the National War Museum.

The Military Tattoo show takes over the Esplanade in summer

St. Margaret's Chapel is perched near the top of the rock

The One o'Clock Gun booms out every day except Sunday

SEEING EDINBURGH CASTLE

To enter the castle you must first cross the Esplanade, which in summer is bedecked with seating for the Military Tattoo (▷ 175). Pass through the gate and up the steep, cobbled ramp for great views over the city and various attractions. Once you step inside the thick walls, the castle feels like a complete community, remote, powerful, and cut off from the rest of Edinburgh.

HIGHLIGHTS

ARGYLE BATTERY

This great terrace offers the first chance to catch your breath and enjoy the view north over the city as you wind your way up the Castle Rock. Behind you is the Lang Stairs—a steep, curved flight of steps which was the main entrance in medieval times, before the shifting of heavy guns necessitated the building of a wider, gentler approach. The cannons along the battery were a picturesque improvement suggested by Queen Victoria—in fact, they are front-loading naval guns, and totally impractical in this setting. The One o'Clock Gun, a 25-pounder field gun from World War II, fires from nearby Mills Mount Battery at precisely 1pm in a tradition dating from 1861.

ST. MARGARET'S CHAPEL

The oldest structure in the castle is also the simplest and most moving. It's the 12th-century chapel, dedicated to St. Margaret by her son, King David I. Margaret was the wife of Malcolm III and died here in 1093. The chapel, with its single, whitewashed chamber and tiny Norman arched windows, survived intact through several razings of the castle, and is still used for occasional weddings and baptisms. The chapel is almost overshadowed by the huge cannon on the rampart outside—Mons Meg, a gift in 1457 to James II from the Duke of Burgundy. Despite a firing distance of 2.5 miles (4km), it proved too heavy to be really useful, and blew up its own barrel in 1681.

RATINGS				
Good for kids	●	●	●	●
Historic interest	●	●	●	●
Photo stops	●	●	●	●
Value	●	●	●	

TIPS

● A courtesy minibus is available to take less mobile people to the top of the castle site—check when you buy your ticket.
● Historic Scotland members can skip the ticket queues and go straight into the castle.
● The huge esplanade in front of the castle doubles as a pay-and-display parking area, but note that this is not available Jun–end Oct.

Mighty Mons Meg (top) fired stone cannonballs weighing 150kg (330lb)

✚ 308 C2 • Castle Hill EH1 2NG
☎ 0131 225 9846
◉ Apr–end Sep daily 9.30–6; rest of year daily 9.30–5
💰 (HS) adult £9.80, child £3.50
🚌 23, 27, 28, 45, 35
🚉 Edinburgh Waverley
🎫 Free guided tours every half-hour, from just inside the main gate. Hand-held audio guide in six languages
☕ Cafés in the castle
🎁 Gift shops stock books, Scottish souvenirs and exclusive jewellery 📖

SCOTTISH NATIONAL WAR MEMORIAL

One of the newest buildings on Castle Rock, the National War Memorial was designed by Sir Robert Lorimer in 1923–28 to honour the 150,000 Scottish personnel who died in World War I, and was later amended with the names of the 50,000 who died in World War II. Its impressive entrance, flanked by a stone lion and unicorn, is to your right as you enter Crown Square. Inside, the dark stone gives the building a sombre air. Each of the 12 Scottish regiments is commemorated in its own bay in the Hall of Honour, with the bays at either end dedicated to sailors and airmen respectively. In an open chamber at the heart of the building, the highest peak of the 70-million-year-old rock on which the castle stands has been polished into a shrine, on which stands a casket containing the names of the dead. The figure above is of St. Michael.

The castle stands high on a volcanic plug of basalt rock

The Colours (flag) of the Glengarry Fencibles

The Honours of Scotland are the oldest regalia in the UK

www.historic-scotland.gov.uk
Practical and efficient site tells everything you need to know about Historic Scotland, its activities and 300 properties. Good for latest events.

CROWN ROOM

The Crown Room is on the first floor of the Royal Palace, and comes at the end of a winding route past endless static tableaux of historical scenes. Skip these (unless you are into the audio commentary) to reach the real treasures: the ancient Honours of Scotland, consisting of crown, sceptre and sword. The crown dates from 1540, and is made of Scottish gold, studded with semi-precious stones from the Cairngorms. It was made by James Mosman, who lived in the John Knox House (▷ 76). Both the sword and sceptre were papal gifts. The regalia were locked away after the union with England in 1707, and largely forgotten about until unearthed by Sir Walter Scott in 1818.

The Stone of Destiny shares the same display case. Originally at Scone Palace (▷ 99), it was the stone on which Scottish kings were crowned until it was pinched by Edward I and taken to London. Recovered from Westminster Abbey in 1996, it is a poignant symbol for the revival in Scottish nationalism.

TIP

● Personal audio tours slow visitors down on the route to see the crown jewels, giving the impression of a queue—move straight through if your time is limited and you don't want to see the static tableaux.

'PRISONERS OF WAR'

This exhibition reveals the vaults where American, French, Spanish, Dutch and Irish prisoners of war were held during the 18th-century American War of Independence. French prisoners carved their names on the doors, and the graffiti can be seen in parts restored to their appearance as it was in 1781.

SCOTTISH NATIONAL WAR MUSEUM

The history of the Scottish soldier is told in this fascinating museum, in the former Ordnance Storehouse. There's a bit of everything in here, from an oath of allegiance to Charles Edward Stewart signed by Jacobite soldiers for the Duke of Perth's Regiment in 1745 (▷ 28), to a tunic worn by Earl Haig when he commanded the British army in France in 1916. On the way, there are uniforms and badges, an explanation of the phrase 'iron rations', and weapons galore. The most bizarre exhibit is three elephant's toes, which belonged to a regimental mascot who died around 1840. The creature had been a living symbol of the elephant badge worn by the 78th Highland Regiment of Foot, and lived at the castle. It shared with its keeper a deep thirst for beer, which hastened its early demise.

Army recruiting poster of 1910

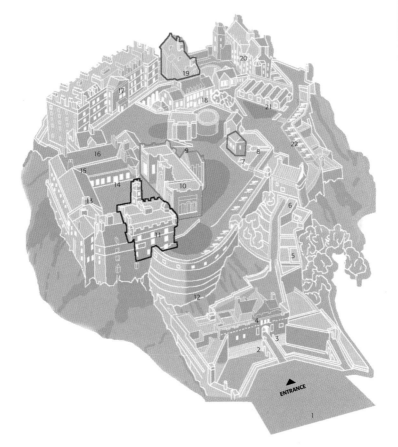

THE SIGHTS

BACKGROUND

Edinburgh Castle towers over the city from its perch high on a wedge of volcanic rock, a solid symbol of the Scottish nation which has withstood centuries of battering. It owes its defensive position to a volcano, which became extinct 70 million years ago. The plug of volcanic rock withstood the Ice-Age glaciers, which scoured the landscape around it, creating near-vertical faces to the north and south and leaving a descending 'tail' of rock to the east—the ridge which is occupied today by the Royal Mile.

Bronze-Age people settled on the top around 850BC, and in AD600 it was occupied by an army who called it Din Eidyn. By the Middle Ages it was a heavily fortified site and royal residence.

A key event in the castle's history was the Lang (long) Siege of 1567–73, by the regent of James VI. James had been born in the castle in 1566, and it was occupied by supporters of his mother, Mary, Queen of Scots. They held out for two years against the forces of regent James Douglas, Earl of Morton (c1516–81) and his English back-up. Much of the castle was destroyed, and it was the victorious Morton who instigated the rebuilding, including the Half Moon Battery.

Later royalty preferred the comforts of Holyroodhouse (▷ 83), and Oliver Cromwell's army converted the 16th-century Great Hall into a barracks for his soldiers when he took the castle in 1650 (since restored, its hammerbeam roof is notable). The castle's primary function has been as a garrison fortress ever since.

1 Esplanade
2 Statue of Robert the Bruce
3 Statue of William Wallace
4 Gatehouse
5 Old Guardhouse (now the gift shop)
6 Portcullis Gate (with Argyle Tower above)
7 St. Margaret's Chapel
8 Mons Meg
9 Foog's Gate
10 Scottish National War Memorial
11 Royal Palace
12 Half Moon Battery
13 Great Hall
14 Queen Anne Building
15 Vaults
16 Military prison
17 New Barracks
18 Governor's House (now the Officers' Mess)
19 Ordnance Storehouse (now the Scottish National War Museum)
20 Hospital
21 Cartshed (now the restaurant)
22 One o'Clock Gun

Boating on the River Almond at Cramond

Simulated lava flow in Restless Earth fills the senses

CRAIGMILLAR CASTLE

➕ 309 off E3 • Craigmillar Castle Road EH16 4SY ☎ 0131 661 4445 ⏰ Apr–end Sep daily 9.30–6.30; Oct–end Mar Sat–Wed 9.30–4.30 💷 (HS) adult £3, child £1.20 🚌 33 ☕ 🏛
www.historic-scotland.gov.uk

Lying 2.5 miles (4km) southeast of the city centre off the A7, this splendid medieval castle is often forgotten, in the shadow of its more famous Edinburgh neighbour. Craigmillar fell into ruin after its abandonment in the mid-18th century. At its core is a stout 15th-century L-plan tower house with walls up to 2.7m (9ft) thick, constructed on the site of an older fortification by the Preston family. Defensive features include massive doors, a spiral turnpike stair, narrow passageways and two outer walls to fend off English attackers. Mary, Queen of Scots, fled here on several occasions when the pressures of life at Holyroodhouse became too great, notably after the murder of David Rizzio in 1566, and the tiny chamber where she slept bears her name.

CRAMOND

➕ 308 off A1 ℹ VisitScotland Edinburgh Information Centre, 3 Princes Street EH2 2QP, tel 0131 473 3800 🚌 41, 42

Edinburgh is made up of many villages, some of which retain their own identity and appeal. One such is Cramond, to the west of the centre, near Queensferry: It was a hive of water-powered industry in the 18th century thanks to its location at the mouth of the River Almond. All sorts of useful items were manufactured here at one time, with four separate iron works, and later a papermill, but all is peaceful today on the

DYNAMIC EARTH

Fun science and the perfect antidote to Edinburgh's more staid attractions.

➕ 309 F2 • 112 Holyrood Road EH8 8AS ☎ 0131 550 7800 ⏰ Apr–end Jun, Sep, Oct daily 10–5; Jul, Aug daily 10–6; rest of year daily Wed–Sun 10–5 💷 Adult £8.95, child £5.45 (under 5 free), family from £24.50; may be additional charges for special exhibitions 🚌 35, 64; also stop on Edinburgh Tour and City Sightseeing tour routes 🚉 Edinburgh Waverley 🚇 £4 🍴 The Food Chain restaurant, licensed to sell alcohol 🎁 Well-stocked themed gift shop 🚻 ❓ Allow at least 90 minutes to explore
www.dynamicearth.co.uk

The tented roof of this science park rises like a spiked white armadillo on the edge of Holyrood Park: It's like nothing else in the city, and has proved a popular and successful millennium project. It tells the story of the Earth and its changing nature, from the so-called Big Bang (as viewed from the bridge of a space ship) to the present day (exactly who lives where in the rainforest), in slick, bite-sized chunks of virtual reality science—ideal entertainment for kids with a short attention span, but it may prove a bit too whizzy for some.

The underlying message—that the world is a fascinating and ever-changing place—is unarguable. The planet is explored inside out through 11 galleries, from the effect of erupting volcanoes to the icy chill of the polar regions, and including a 'submarine' exploration of strange creatures and coral reefs along the way. In the Restless Earth section you'll feel the tremors of a simulated earthquake while lava apparently boils below, and you may get caught (and a bit damp for real) in a rain storm in the Tropical Rainforest. You can even experience a sense of infinity in the Time Machine, where numberless stars are created using lights and mirrors. A multi-screen flight over mountains and glaciers is a dizzying highlight.
Don't miss Virtual flight in Shaping the Surface.

RATINGS				
Good for kids	●	●	●	● ○
Photo stops	●	●	●	
Specialist shopping	●	●	●	● ○
Value for money	●	●	●	●

MAKE A DAY OF IT
Arthur's Seat; Holyroodhouse

The Fruitmarket was redesigned in 1994 by Richard Murphy

Plush 18th-century furnishings at the Georgian House

A gilded hawk above the entrance to Gladstone's Land

secluded tree-lined walk by the stream, which leads up to a venerable 17th-century bridge. The Romans built a port here in the second century to supply troops stationed along the Antonine Wall. A ferry still transports passengers across to Dalmeny, and pleasure boats occupy the space today. **Don't miss** On a summer's evening, join local people on the riverside stroll, followed by a drink at the Cramond Inn.

DYNAMIC EARTH

See page 74

EDINBURGH CASTLE

See pages 71–73

EDINBURGH ZOO

🟥 308 off A3 • 134 Corstorphine Road EH12 6TS ☎ 0131 334 9171 🕓 Apr–end Sep daily 9–6; Oct, Mar daily 9–5; Nov–end Feb daily 9–4.30 💷 Adult £9, child £6 (under 3 free), family £28; special events extra 🚌 12, 26, 31; Airport Bus 🚻 🚽 www.edinburghzoo.org.uk

In an era when zoos have to work hard to justify themselves, Edinburgh remains an excellent example of its type, allowing close access to a wide variety of animals while at the same time promoting conservation and education. The site is at Corstorphine, 3 miles (4.8km) west of the city centre, and on the side of a steep hill. Highlights include the swinging-gibbon enclosure, the hilltop safari to the African Plains exhibit (admire zebras and antelopes against the distinctly Scottish backdrop of Edinburgh Castle!), and the ever-popular penguins. Look out for special events such as night tours. **Don't miss** The daily stroll outside their enclosure by the penguins at 2.15, Apr–end Sep, weather permitting.

FRUITMARKET GALLERY

🟥 309 D2 • 45 Market Street EH1 1DF ☎ 0131 225 2383 🕓 Mon–Sat 11–6, Sun 12–5 💷 Free 🚉 Edinburgh Waverley 🚻 🚽 www.fruitmarket.co.uk

As the name tells you, this contemporary art gallery, found behind Waverley Station, is built in the original fruit market. With the separate and more populist City Art Centre just opposite (Mon–Sat 10–5, Sun 12–5), it forms part of a chic artistic enclave at the heart of the city. The wide expanse of glass frontage on this handsome old building reveals a minimum of its exhibits to the street—but entices with its excellent and buzzing café. Inside, changing exhibitions showcase the work of new Scottish artists and also international work in a Scottish context. The bookshop has a good selection of art books.

GEORGIAN HOUSE

🟥 308 B1 • 7 Charlotte Square EH2 4DR ☎ 0131 226 3318 🕓 Mar, Nov daily 11–3; Apr–end Jun, Sep, Oct daily 10–5 💷 (NTS) adult £5, child £4 (under 5 free), family £14 🚌 36 🚉 Edinburgh Waverley 🚽 www.nts.org.uk

The north side of Charlotte Square is the epitome of 18th-century New Town elegance (▷ 84–85), designed by architect Robert Adam (1728–92) as a single, palace-fronted block. With its symmetrical stonework, rusticated base and ornamented upper levels, it is an outstanding example of the style. For a feel of gracious Edinburgh living in 1800, visit the Georgian House, a preserved residence right in the middle. It is a typically meticulous re-creation by the National Trust for Scotland, reflecting all the fashionable

details of the day. The NTS also owns No. 28, with exhibition space, a café and shop. **Don't miss** For contrast, the kitchen—in the basement.

GLADSTONE'S LAND

🟥 309 D2 • 477b Lawnmarket EH1 2NT ☎ 0131 226 5856 🕓 Easter–end Jun, Sep, Oct daily 10–5; Jul, Aug daily 10–7 💷 (NTS) adult £5, child £4 (under 5 free), family £10 🚌 23, 27, 41, 42, 45 🚉 Edinburgh Waverley 🚽 www.nts.org.uk

This fascinating example of 17th-century tenement housing is a highlight of the Old Town. Its narrowness was typical of the cramped Old Town conditions—the only space for expansion was upwards, and its eventual height of six floors reflects the status of its merchant owner, Thomas Gledstanes, who extended the existing tenement in 1617.

The building is unique for its stone arcading, once common along the High Street but now vanished elsewhere. Inside, the National Trust for Scotland has reconstructed 17th-century shop-booths on the ground floor, and there are original painted ceilings to admire, adorned with flowers and birds. The first floor is furnished as a typical home of the period.

GRASSMARKET

🟥 308 C2 ℹ VisitScotland Edinburgh Information Centre, 3 Princes Street EH2 2QP, tel 0131 473 3800 🚌 2 🚉 Edinburgh Waverley

The old road into the city from the west used to run (via the West Port, or gate, which survives in a street name) into this long open space below Castle Rock. The Grassmarket was used for various activities—from 1477, corn and cattle markets were held here, and it was the site of public executions until 1784.

Alfresco dining in the broad street of the Grassmarket

The John Knox House projects into the Royal Mile

Edwardian elegance in the dining room of Lauriston Castle

THE SIGHTS

A stone disc marks the location of the old gibbet, and commemorates the Covenanting martyrs who died here. The Grassmarket was also a haunt of the notorious 19th-century 'body-snatchers' Burke and Hare, who murdered their victims to sell on to the anatomists of the city's hospitals. Today it has good shops and eating places, and several excellent pubs, including the ancient White Hart Inn.

GREYFRIARS BOBBY

309 D3 • At the junction with George IV Bridge 2, 23, 27, 35, 41, 42, 45 Edinburgh Waverley

At the top of Candlemaker Row, opposite the Museum of Scotland (▷ 78–81), stands a favourite Edinburgh landmark: a bronze statue of a little Skye terrier, which has stood here since 1873. The dog's story was memorably told by American Eleanor Atkinson in her sentimental novel of 1912, *Greyfriars Bobby*. He was the devoted companion of a local farmer who dined regularly in Greyfriars Place. After 'Auld Jock' died, faithful Bobby slept on his grave in the nearby churchyard for 14 years, while returning to the same pie-shop for his dinner. A later version suggests he was owned by a local policeman, and taken in by local residents when his owner died. A nearby pub is named after the celebrated hound.

GREYFRIARS KIRKYARD

309 D3 • Greyfriars Tolbooth and Highland Kirk, Greyfriars Place EH1 2QQ 0131 226 5429 Apr–end Oct Mon–Fri 10.30–4.30, Sat 10.30–2.30; rest of year Thu 1.30–3.30 Free 23, 27, 35, 41, 45 Edinburgh Waverley

Greyfriars Bobby, right, was buried in Greyfriars Kirkyard

The Kirk of the Grey Friars was built on the site of the garden of a former Franciscan monastery in 1620. Just 18 years later it was the scene of a pivotal event in Scottish history, when Calvinist petitioners gathered to sign the National Covenant, an act of defiance against the King (▷ 26–27). The church itself was trashed by Cromwell's troops in 1650, and later accidentally blown up. The kirkyard made a makeshift prison for hundreds of Covenanters captured after the battle of Bothwell Bridge in 1679; they were kept here for five dreadful months. Today it is full of elaborate memorials, including the grave of architect William Adam (1689–1748).

JOHN KNOX HOUSE

309 E2 • 43–45 High Street EH1 1SR 0131 556 9579 Mon–Sat 10–6, Sun 12–6 Adult £3, child £1 (under 7 free) 8, 35 Edinburgh Waverley

It is said that John Knox (c1505–72), the great Protestant reformer and founder of the Church of Scotland, used to preach from the front window of this handsome old corner house on the Royal Mile. Whether he actually lived here is less certain. The house dates back to 1490, and with its gables projecting out above the street, it gives a clear impression of how crowded the city's medieval High Street must have been. Inside and upstairs, you can admire the painted ceiling of the Oak Room, dating from 1600. There are exhibitions about Knox, a focused and surprisingly witty man, and also about goldsmith James Mossman, who lived in the house in the mid-16th century.

LAURISTON CASTLE

308 off A1 • 2A Cramond Road South EH4 5QD 0131 336 2060 Apr–Oct Sat–Thu tours every hour 11.20–4.20; rest of year Sat–Sun at 2.20, 3.20 Castle: adult £4.50, child £3 (under 5 free). Grounds: free Edinburgh Waverley www.cac.org.uk

This gabled and turreted mansion, in a leafy setting overlooking the Firth of Forth near Cramond (▷ 74–75), offers up a slice of neatly preserved Edwardian comfort and style. Once a simple tower house, Lauriston was remodelled and extended several times, most notably in 1827 by architect William Burn (1789–1870), before it came into the hands of William Robert Reid. He was the wealthy head of a firm of cabinetmakers, and an avid collector of fine furniture and precious objects—his collection of pieces made from the fluorspar mineral called Blue John is particularly unusual. He left the castle to the City of Edinburgh in 1926, on condition that it remained just as it was, for the edification and education of the public.

Strolling in the park: Princes Street Gardens run parallel to the famous shopping street and were planned as part of the New Town

Ghost stories abound in the spooky Mary King's Close

LEITH

➕ 309 off E1 ℹ️ VisitScotland Edinburgh Information Centre, 3 Princes Street EH2 2QP, tel 0131 473 3800 🚌 1, 7, 10, 12, 14, 16, 22, 25, 32, 32A, 34, 35, 36, 49, N22

Leith is Edinburgh's seaport, connected to the city centre by Leith Walk, and was for many years a prosperous town in its own right. As the shipbuilding industry began to wane in the 20th century the town went into decline, but in recent years it has come up in the world, and now it buzzes with fashionable eating places. Edinburgh's river, the Water of Leith, flows through the middle.

The town has witnessed its share of history—Mary, Queen of Scots, landed here from France in 1561 and stayed at Lamb House, in Water Street, and Charles I played golf on the links in the park. Where Tower Street meets The Shore, look for the Signal Tower, built in 1686 as a windmill. The Royal Yacht *Britannia* is a major draw (▷ 86).

MUSEUM OF CHILDHOOD

➕ 309 E2 • 42 High Street EH1 1TG ☎ 0131 529 4142 🕐 Mon–Sat 10–5; Sun 12–5 🎟️ Free 🚌 35 🚉 Edinburgh Waverley 🏛️ www.cac.org.uk

Edinburgh claims the first museum in the world dedicated to the history of childhood, and what a delight it is, too, for visitors of all ages. It was the brainchild of bachelor Joseph Patrick Murray (*d*1981), a town councillor, who argued that the museum presented a specialized branch of social science, and was about children rather than for them. It opened in 1955, and has grown into the collection seen today, a nostalgic treasure-trove of dolls and doll's houses,

train sets, tricycles, board games and, of course, tribes of teddy bears.
Don't miss The re-created 1930s schoolroom—it wasn't all fun.

MUSEUM OF EDINBURGH

➕ 309 E2 • Huntly House, 142 Canongate, Royal Mile EH8 8DD ☎ 0131 529 4143 🕐 Mon–Sat 10–5; Aug also Sun 12–5 🎟️ Free 🚌 35 🚉 Edinburgh Waverley 🏛️ www.cac.org.uk

Just across the road from the Canongate Tolbooth (▷ 70), Edinburgh's own museum occupies Huntly House, a 16th-century dwelling much altered through the years, and at one time occupied by a trade guild, the Incorporation of Hammermen. Its three pointed gables mark it out. Inside, the museum is a treasure-house of local details which bring the history of the city to life. Items on display include maps and prints, silver, glass and old shop signs, and Greyfriars Bobby's collar (▷ 76).
Don't miss The original National Covenant (▷ 27), signed in 1638.

MUSEUM OF SCOTLAND

See pages 78–81

NATIONAL GALLERY

See page 82

NEW TOWN

See pages 84–85

PALACE OF HOLYROODHOUSE

See page 83

PRINCES STREET GARDENS

➕ 308 C2 • Princes Street ☎ 0131 3322 368 🕐 Summer 7am–10pm; winter 7–5 🎟️ Free 🚉 Edinburgh Waverley 🚌

This long thin park lies at the heart of the city, in a sound-muffling dip between Castle Rock and noisy Princes Street. It's a great place to take a break, sit down and admire the backs of the Old Town tenements across the steep-sided valley. In summer there are band concerts to enjoy, and an Edinburgh institution since 1902, the floral clock—a flowerbed planted up as a clock, complete with moving hands, at the Waverley Station end.

In 1460 this valley was dammed and flooded to form the Nor' Loch, an extra defence for the castle which quickly filled up with the city's detritus. It was drained in the mid-18th century, and the public gardens first laid out in 1820. Now it is an oasis of relative peace, giving a touch of grace to one of the city's busiest shopping streets.

THE REAL MARY KING'S CLOSE

➕ 309 D2 • 2 Warriston's Close, High Street EH1 1PG ☎ 08702 430160 🕐 Apr–end Oct daily 10–9; rest of year Sun–Fri 10–4, Sat 10–9 🎟️ Adult £8, child £6 (under 5 not admitted) 🚌 23, 27, 41, 42, 45 🚉 Edinburgh Waverley 🏛️ www.realmarykingsclose.com

Mary King's Close is a narrow alleyway that once led between the tall houses of 17th-century Edinburgh, part of the rabbit warren of the Old Town. It is now preserved under the City Chambers, which were built over the top in 1753. Archaeological research has produced insights into the lives of the people who lived here. Guided tours help to create the atmosphere of what the Old Town was like—you can walk through the houses, see the cramped living conditions, and learn about the outbreak of plague in 1644. Tours run every 20 minutes; reserve ahead.

THE SIGHTS

Museum of Scotland

**An entertaining introduction to Scottish history and culture.
A national collection of more than 10,000 objects, from Bonnie Prince Charlie's
silver travelling canteen to chairs designed by Charles Rennie Mackintosh.**

*The museum is at the western
end of Chambers Street*

*The tiny Monymusk Reliquary
dates from the eighth century*

*18th-century ebony and ivory
quaich (drinking bowl)*

SEEING THE MUSEUM OF SCOTLAND

Treasures abound in this superb collection, but the multiple levels
of the fortress-like building mean it can be confusing to find your
way around. However, armed with the knowledge that the floors
work chronologically, you can work your way up from the
basement through history from the earliest beginnings, or start at
the top and work down. Alternatively, use the plan on page 80 to
go straight to the things that interest you most, and explore from
there. Objects are grouped according to colour-coded themes.

HIGHLIGHTS

PICTISH SCULPTURED STONE

The chief legacy of the Pictish period is vivid relief carvings in stone,
generally depicting figures and strangely intertwined beasts. The
displays on level 0 contrast these nicely with more regular Roman
stonework. Among the noble groups of horsemen engaged in
hunting or fighting there is one less gallant figure worthy of special
note. He rides alone, bearded and bare-headed. His drooping nag is
ambling along at a walking pace, and no wonder—for this warrior is
quaffing deeply from a drinking horn, and drunk. The stone, from
Bullion in Angus, reads as a skilled stonemason's joke.

HUNTERSTON BROOCH

The Hunterston Brooch dates to around AD700, and is a potent
symbol of wealth and power. No contemporary clasp in the museum's
collection can touch it in terms of size (about 12cm/5in high) or
craftsmanship, which suggests that it was made as a gift to impress a
king. A runic inscription on the back claims the brooch for Melbrigda,
a Viking, but the brooch predates the Viking period and the identity of
its original owner is lost in time. Although the lighting is dim, you can
walk around both sides of the display case, to admire close up the
detail of the gold, amber and gilded silver worked into exquisite curling,
intertwined Celtic motifs. The brooch was found at Hunterston, on
the Ayrshire coast, but is believed to have been made at Dunadd, in
Argyll, the heart of the ancient Scots kingdom of Dalriada.

RATINGS				
Good for kids	●	●	●	○
Historic interest	●	●	●	●
Specialist shopping	●	●	●	●

TIPS

● Don't expect to see
everything in the museum in
one hit. Focus first on the
things that interest you most,
and come back another day to
enjoy the rest—entry is free.
● Only one lift stops at all
levels in the museum: Find it
at the far side of the building
from the entrance.
● To explore in comfort, leave
coats and shopping bags at the
cloakroom just next door in
the Royal Museum. It is
located on the first floor (street
level), near the gift shop, with
direct access from the
Hawthornden Court.

*Top, 11 of the 82 Lewis Chess
Pieces are held here, including
2 kings and 3 queens. The rest
are in the British Museum,
London*

Left, the Hunterston Brooch

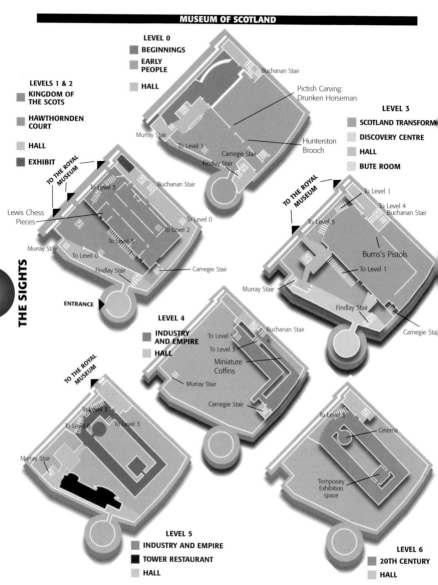

THE SIGHTS

LEVEL 0
- BEGINNINGS
- EARLY PEOPLE
- HALL

LEVELS 1 & 2
- KINGDOM OF THE SCOTS
- HAWTHORNDEN COURT
- HALL
- EXHIBIT

TO THE ROYAL MUSEUM

Lewis Chess Pieces

Murray Stair
To Level 0
Findlay Stair
Carnegie Stair
To Level 3
Buchanan Stair
To Level 0
To Level 2
To Level 3

ENTRANCE

Murray Stair
To Level 1
Carnegie Stair
Findlay Stair

Pictish Carving: Drunken Horseman

Hunterston Brooch

LEVEL 3
- SCOTLAND TRANSFORM
- DISCOVERY CENTRE
- HALL
- BUTE ROOM

TO THE ROYAL MUSEUM

To Level 1
To Level 4
Buchanan Stair
To Level 5

Burns's Pistols
To Level 1

Murray Stair
Findlay Stair
Carnegie Sta

LEVEL 4
- INDUSTRY AND EMPIRE
- HALL

Buchanan Stair
To Level 5
To Level 3
Miniature Coffins
Murray Stair
Carnegie Stair

TO THE ROYAL MUSEUM

To Level 6
To Level 3
To Level 3
Murray Stair

To Level 3
Cinema

Temporary Exhibition space

LEVEL 5
- INDUSTRY AND EMPIRE
- TOWER RESTAURANT
- HALL

LEVEL 6
- 20TH CENTURY
- HALL

GALLERY GUIDE

LEVEL 0 (BASEMENT)
Beginnings (formation of the land and natural history); Early People 8000BC–AD1100

LEVEL 1 (STREET LEVEL)
The Kingdom of the Scots 900–1707
Also main entrance and information point; access to the Royal Museum; Hawthornden Court central exhibition hall; exhibIT (computer access to detailed information about exhibits on-screen, and to SCRAN, an archive of Scottish history and culture)

LEVEL 2 (ACCESS FROM LEVEL 1 ONLY)
Burghs (an insight into the formation of Scotland's trading towns)

LEVEL 3
Scotland Transformed 1707–19th century
Also access to the Royal Museum; Discovery Centre (hands-on fun for children)

LEVEL 4 AND LEVEL 5
Industry and Empire 19th century–1914
Also access from level 5 to the Royal Museum; Tower Restaurant

LEVEL 6
20th Century (changing exhibitions to reflect the last century)

LEVEL 7
Roof Terrace (open-air views over the city)

The mysterious coffins are sophisticated in their construction, and inset with metal fragments—clearly miniatures, not toys

BASICS

309 D3 • Chambers Street, EH1 1JF

0131 247 4422

All year Mon and Wed–Sat 10–5, Tue 10–8, Sun 12–5

Free; may be charge for some temporary exhibitions

35

Check at the information desk on arrival for times of free daily tours. Free audio guides available in English, Gaelic, French, Italian, Spanish and German

£4.99

The Tower Restaurant is the place to be seen, booking essential at weekends. Various cafés available in the next door Royal Museum (▷ 86)

Gift shop, shared with the Royal Museum, stocks unusual presents

www.nms.ac.uk
Site for Scotland's six national museums, including excellent virtual tour of National Museum plus online shop.

LEWIS CHESS PIECES

In 1831 a collection of 82 carved chess pieces was discovered in the sands of Uig, on Lewis (▷ 135). They had been hidden there 700 years before, possibly by a merchant, during a time of upheaval and violence when the islands were subject to an influx of Viking settlers from Denmark and Norway. Clearly treasured by their original owner, they form one of the most popular exhibits in the museum today. Find them on the street level (level 1) near the Monymusk Reliquary.

The small, greyish pieces are carved from walrus ivory, and were probably made by a Scandinavian craftsman in the 12th century. They include kings and queens, pop-eyed bishops, 'berserker' warders chewing on their shields, and knights on horseback. The carving of the solemn facial expressions reflects minute attention to detail, and is carried through even to the patterns on the fabric worn by the kings.

BURNS'S PISTOLS

For an unusual view of Scotland's national bard, look out for a pair of pistols on level 3, part of an opulent display about the emergence of a monied society in the 18th century. The reputation of Robert Burns (1759–96) is as a poet and writer of songs, many with an anti-establishment bias. Poetry was a poor basis for making a living, however: Burns needed paid employment and took a job as a collector of taxes. The pair of wooden-handled and wooden-barrelled pistols which he carried with him for self-protection—tax collectors were no more popular then than now—give further insight into this well-loved character. More regular Burns items are shown on level 5.

MINIATURE COFFINS

One of the most mysterious displays here was brought to public attention by Ian Rankin in his 2001 novel, *The Falls*. It is the group of tiny wooden coffins, each holding a body not much longer than an adult finger, that was discovered on Arthur's Seat in Edinburgh in 1836. Each body fits its own coffin precisely. The figures have been carved with some care, including facial features, feet that stick out, and moving joints, and some are clothed.

Eight have survived of the original 17 coffins, but nobody knows who made this gruesome little collection, or why. They may represent a mock burial for the 17 victims of murderers Burke and Hare, who provided bodies for the local medical school from 1827 to 1828.

BACKGROUND

The museum showcases the Scottish collections from the Royal Museum (▷ 86). The structure of the building, designed by Gordon Benson and Alan Forsyth, is impressively modern. A lofty central courtyard, narrow slit windows and a round tower at the entrance contribute to the feeling of being in a fortified castle, built to protect a precious heritage.

The wit of this Pictish carving, depicting a drunken man on his lazy horse, reaches across more than 1,000 years (▷ 79)

John Singer Sargent's portrait of Gertrude, Lady Agnew of Lochnaw

The gallery building was designed to complement the New Town

NATIONAL GALLERY OF SCOTLAND

A breathtaking collection of artistic masterpieces displayed on a friendly, human scale.

Scotland's National Gallery stands prominently on the Mound, the raised road that bisects Princes Street Gardens. Designed by New Town architect William Playfair (1789–1857), and completed in the year of his death, it is easily spotted from the huge golden stone pillars of its neoclassical flanks (and should not be confused with its linked neighbour, the Royal Scottish Academy building). Its collection of paintings, sculptures and drawings runs to more than 20,000 items and in the UK is second only to London's National Gallery in importance, but it is smaller and feels much more accessible. At its heart are paintings by the great masters of Europe, including Vermeer, Hals, Tiepolo, Van Dyck, Raphael and Titian. Look out for Monet's *Haystacks* (1891), Vélasquez's *Old Woman Cooking Eggs* (1618) and Botticelli's masterpiece, *Virgin Adoring the Sleeping Christ Child* (c1485). The display is boosted by loans from the Queen's collection, and from that of the Duke of Sutherland. A fabulous collection of watercolours by English landscape artist J. M. W. Turner (1775–1851), bequeathed in 1900, is displayed each January.

THE SCOTTISH COLLECTION

Not surprisingly, the gallery has an outstanding collection of works by Scottish artists, which are displayed in their own section downstairs. Favourites here include Sir Henry Raeburn's unusual 1795 portrait of *The Reverend Robert Walker Skating*; Allan Ramsay's delicate portraits of his first wife, *Anne Bayne* (c1740), and his second wife, *Margaret Lindsay* (1757); and the sweeping land- and seascapes of William McTaggart (1835–1910). Look out for the vivid scenes of everyday life among the common people, as captured on canvas by Sir David Wilkie (1785–1841), such as *Pitlessie Fair* (1804) and *Distraining for Rent* (1815).

Don't miss Raeburn's over-the-top tartan clad chieftain, *Colonel Alasdair Macdonnell of Glengarry* (1812).

RATINGS

Good for kids	●●
Historic interest	●●●●●
Specialist shopping	●●●●

BASICS

✚ 308 C2 • The Mound EH2 2EL
☎ 0131 624 6200 🕐 Fri–Wed 10–5, Thu 10–7 💷 Free 🚌 Free bus runs between all four national galleries. Also 23, 27, 41, 42, 45 🚆 Edinburgh Waverley 🎧 £12.95 🛍 Shop stocks cards, books and gifts 🍴 🛍 ♿

www.nationalgalleries.org
Site covers Scotland's five national galleries. Limited information, but good for latest exhibitions.

Looking down the Royal Mile, with the John Knox House ahead

ROYAL BOTANIC GARDEN

See page 86

ROYAL MILE

309 D2

This is the name given to the long, almost straight route linking Holyroodhouse with the castle, up the spine of rock on which the Old Town was built. About 60 narrow closes lead off between the buildings on either side (there were once 300), many with names indicating the trades once carried out there. The Writers' Museum (▷ 88) is in Lady Stair's Close.

The route consists of four streets, each with its own identity. At the bottom, Canongate feels practical and workaday, the dressed stone of its façades giving way to rough and ready stonework on the sides of the buildings. Drop into the Museum of Edinburgh (▷ 77) for a view of the interiors of these old houses. Look for a board outside the Canongate Church, indicating celebrities buried there—including Handel's preferred bassoon player, John Frederick Lampe.

Where St. Mary's Street and Jeffrey Street cross over, you enter High Street, and sweet shops and tea rooms give way to boutiques and the postmodern pastiche of the Radisson SAS Hotel. Above the Tron Kirk the road retains its setts (cobbles) and broadens out. Buildings are more regular in appearance, with fewer baronial towers and turrets. After St. Giles's (▷ 87), with the Heart of Midlothian in the cobbles marking the site of a prison, the street becomes the Lawnmarket, where linen (lawn) was manufactured. The final stretch, Castle Hill, lies above Café Hub (a converted church), as the road narrows on the steep approach to the castle.

The name derives from the Holy Rood, a piece of Christ's cross

PALACE OF HOLYROODHOUSE

A royal palace rich with historical associations.

309 F1 • EH8 8DX ☎ 0131 556 5100 ⏰ Apr–end Oct daily 9.30–6; rest of year daily 9.30–4.30. May close at short notice 💷 Adult £8.50, child £4.50 (under 5 free), family £21.50 🚌 35 🚉 Edinburgh Waverley ▭ Free audio tour available 🎧 £4.50 🛍 Gift shop stocks cards, books and commemorative china 👫
www.royal.gov.uk

This pepperpot-towered castle at the foot of the Royal Mile is the Queen's official residence in Scotland, which means it may be closed for odd days at short notice to make way for investitures, royal garden parties and other state occasions. It offers all the advantages of exploring a living palace steeped with history and filled with works of art from the Royal Collection. More precious artworks are on view in the stunning Queen's Gallery, by the entrance and opposite the Scottish Parliament, which is also where you'll find the well-stocked gift shop.

RATINGS			
Good for kids	●	●	●
Historic interest	●	●	●	●
Photo stops	●	●	●	●
Specialist shopping	●	●	●

The palace was probably founded in 1128 as an Augustinian monastery. In the 15th century it became a guesthouse for the neighbouring Holyrood Abbey (now a scenic ruin), and its name is said to derive from the Holy Rood, a fragment of Christ's cross belonging to David I (c1080–1153). Mary, Queen of Scots, stayed here, and a brass plate marks where her favourite, David Rizzio, was murdered in her private apartments in the west tower in 1566. After serious fire damage in 1650 during the Civil War, major rebuilding was required. Bonnie Prince Charlie held court here in 1745, followed by George IV on his triumphant visit to the city in 1822, and later Queen Victoria on her way to Balmoral (▷ 120). The state rooms, designed for Charles II by architect William Bruce (1630–1710) and hung with Brussels tapestries, are particularly elaborate and splendid.

Don't miss The fun of 110 preposterous royal portraits painted in a hurry by Jacob de Wet in 1684–86.

New Town

Explore the streets and squares of the capital city
to understand why elegant 18th-century Edinburgh was
a planner's dream.

The second building phase can be recognized in window details

The dining room of the Georgian House

Adam's Charlotte Square was the epitome of style

RATINGS	
Historic interest	●●●●○
Photo stops	●●●○
Shopping	●●○
Walkability	●●●●○

BASICS
✚ 308 C1 🛈 Edinburgh Lothian Tourist Information Centre, 3 Princes Street EH2 2QP, tel 0131 473 3800
🚉 Edinburgh Waverley

SEEING THE NEW TOWN

Edinburgh's so-called New Town covers an area of about
1 square mile (2.6sq km) to the north of Princes Street, and is
characterized by broad streets of spacious terraced (row) houses
with large windows and ornamental door arches. The original
area comprised three residential boulevards to run parallel with
the Old Town ridge: Princes Street, George Street and Queen
Street. With a square at each end (St. Andrew and Charlotte),
they were also linked by smaller roads which would take shops
and other commercial services: Rose Street and Thistle Street.

Fenced, private gardens make green havens in the city

HIGHLIGHTS

CHARLOTTE SQUARE
While Princes Street has lost its shine in the glare of modern commerce, the wide Charlotte Square, with its preserved Georgian House (▷ 75), is the epitome of the planners' intentions.

THE MOUND
The North Bridge was needed to enable pedestrians to reach the new city without foundering in the muddy valley (the Nor' Loch was still being drained at the time). A second link, the Mound, came about by accident, when a clothier in the Old Town started to dump earth rubble in the marsh. Soon the builders from the New Town joined in, as they dug out foundations for the new buildings. It took 2 million cartloads of rubble to complete the job, and the causeway became the Mound, later home to the National Gallery of Scotland (▷ 82) and the Royal Scottish Academy.

STOCKBRIDGE
Stockbridge, a former mining village, was developed as part of the second New Town, on land owned by painter Sir Henry Raeburn. It became a Bohemian artisans' corner, and Ann Street, named after Raeburn's wife and with the unusual bonus of front gardens, is now one of the city's most exclusive addresses.

BACKGROUND
Until the mid-18th century, Edinburgh had been contained on the narrow ridge of rock between Arthur's Seat and the castle. Conditions were overcrowded and insanitary, and as a new age of scientific advance and intellectual enlightenment dawned, so the need for expansion became clear. A competition was held in 1766 to design a new city on the windy fields to the north. The winner was unknown architect James Craig (1744–95), and within three years the first house was ready.

The first New Town was so successful that a second one was laid out in 1802, extending north. Highlights of this period are William Playfair's Royal Circus, and Moray Place.

Hallways in Moray Place were built to take a sedan chair

TIP
● Comfortable shoes are essential for a walking tour of the cobblestones and pavements.

MAKE A DAY OF IT
Georgian House museum; also walk ▷ 208–209

Fine Georgian door

Royal quarters for lavish entertaining on Britannia

ROYAL MUSEUM

309 D2 • Chambers Street EH1 1JF
0131 247 4422 Mon and Wed–Sat 10–5, Tue 10–8, Sun 12–5
Free; may be a charge for special temporary exhibitions 35
Edinburgh Waverley
Free tours available daily
www.nms.ac.uk

This huge museum houses a world-class collection of international treasures, and is undergoing major redevelopment. The main entrance hall, dating from 1861, is a vast, airy space. It has a high (23m/78ft) glazed roof, and is ringed with galleries supported on slender iron pillars. One of two cafés is also here. Passages lead off to the galleries, and the scale is bewildering—ask about free tours at the information desk, or pick up an audio tour guide. A highlight of the decorative arts displays is the Ivy Wu Gallery of East Asian Art, with carved jade from China, swords from Japan and lacquer-ware from Korea. Look out for world-class temporary exhibitions.
Don't miss The chiming of the weird and wonderful animated Millennium Clock.

ROYAL YACHT *BRITANNIA*

309 off E1 • Ocean Terminal, Leith EH6 6JJ 0131 555 5566 Apr–end Oct daily 9.30–4.30; rest of year daily 10–3.30 Adult £9, child £5 (under 5 free), family £25 11, 22; also on Majestic Tour route Edinburgh Waverley
www.royalyachtbritannia.co.uk

It is said that many a royal tear was shed when *Britannia* was decommissioned in 1997 after a cut in government funds. Since its launch at Clydebank in 1953, it had carried the Queen and her family on 968 official voyages to all parts of the world. Now it's a

Giant lily pads in the Tropical Aquatic House

ROYAL BOTANIC GARDEN

A green oasis in a busy capital, with year-round interest and ten big glasshouses for wet days.

308 off B1 • 20A Inverlieth Row EH3 5LR 0131 552 7171 Mar, Oct daily 10–6; Apr–end Sep daily 10–7; rest of year daily 10–4 Free; glasshouses adult £3.50, child £1 (under 5 free), family £8 8, 17, 22, 27, also on Majestic Tour route Edinburgh Waverley Tours lasting around 90 minutes leave the West Gate at 11 and 2, Apr–end Sep, £4 £3; audiopass 50p Terrace Café Extensive Botanics gift shop with stationery, plants and related souvenirs
www.rbge.org.uk

RATINGS	
Good for kids	● ● ● ●
Photo stops	● ● ●
Specialist shopping	● ● ●
Walkability	● ● ● ● ●

TIP

• To find your way about, pick up a map at the West or East gates (small charge or free from website).

The Botanics, as it is known locally, boasts 15,500 plant species on display, lending weight to its claim to be one of the largest collections of living plants in the world. This total includes some 5,000 species in the rock garden alone (seen to best advantage in May). Occupying this site since 1823, it covers over 28ha (70 acres) of beautifully landscaped and wooded grounds to the north of the city centre, forming a minutely maintained green oasis.

There are ten glasshouses alone to explore, collectively called the Glasshouse Experience Windows on the World and offering the perfect escape on chilly days. They include an amazingly tall palm house dating back to 1858, and the Tropical Aquatic House, where you can enjoy an above-the-waterline view of giant waterlilies, and then go downstairs for an underwater view of fish swimming through the roots.

Outdoors, the plants of the Chinese Hillside and the Heath Garden are particularly interesting, and in summer the herbaceous border, backed by a tall beech hedge, is breathtaking. A great place for a break, and for children to let off steam and feed the inquisitive squirrels.

Exhibitions of contemporary art and photography are held in the different buildings around the site.
Don't miss The West Gate, also known as the Carriage Gate, is the main entrance, but don't miss the stunning inner east side gates, designed by local architect Ben Tindall in 1996. A silvery riot of electroplated steel, they depict rhododendron foliage.

View of the Balmoral Hotel through the Scott Monument

A mosaic frieze adorns the entrance to the Portrait Gallery

St. Giles Cathedral stands near the top of the Royal Mile

floating museum at Edinburgh's port of Leith (▷ 77), accessed via the Ocean Terminal shopping and leisure complex. While bigger than most 'yachts', *Britannia* is surprisingly compact, just 125.6m (412ft) long. She carried a crew of 240, including a Royal Marine band and topped up with around 45 household staff when the royal family were aboard.

SCOTCH WHISKY HERITAGE CENTRE

⊞ 308 C2 • 354 Castlehill, Royal Mile EH1 2NE ☎ 0131 220 0441 ⊙ Sep–end May daily 10–5; Jun–end Aug daily 9.30–7 ⊘ Adult £8.50, child £4.50 (under 5 free), family £19.95 ⊟ 23, 27, 41, 42, 45 ⊟ Edinburgh Waverley ⊟ ⊞ ⊟ ⊞ www.whisky-heritage.co.uk

Learn all about Scotland's national liquor at this popular attraction, at the top of the Royal Mile immediately below the castle. Tours set off every 15 minutes and last around an hour. They include a short film, a slow-moving barrel-ride through history, and a talk through the manufacturing process. With models and a 'ghost', it's a better all-round family experience than most distillery tours. Adults get a free taste (juice for children), and can then explore more than 300 whiskies and liqueurs at the Amber Bar.

SCOTT MONUMENT

⊞ 309 D2 • East Princes Street Gardens EH2 2EJ ☎ 0131 529 4068 ⊙ Apr–end Sep Mon–Sat 9–6, Sun 10–6; Oct–end Mar Mon–Sat 9–3, Sun 10–3 ⊘ £3 (one price) ⊟ Edinburgh Waverley www.cac.org.uk

This Gothic sandstone pinnacle 61m (200ft) high dominates the eastern end of Princes Street, and is well worth the drafty climb up 287 steps to the top for the magnificent views over the city. It was built between 1840 and 1846, to the design of George Meikle Kemp, as a memorial to the novelist and poet Sir Walter Scott (1771–1832), and was later encrusted with stone figures based on characters from his novels. A marble statue of Scott, with his deerhound Maida, sits at the bottom. It is by sculptor John Steell (1804–91).

SCOTTISH NATIONAL PORTRAIT GALLERY

⊞ 309 D1 • 1 Queen Street EH2 1JD ☎ 0131 624 6200 ⊙ Fri–Wed 10–5, Thu 10–7 ⊘ Free, may be charges for temporary exhibitions ⊟ Edinburgh Waverley ⊟ Free galleries bus; also 4, 8, 15, 15A, 16, 17, 26, 44 ⊟ ⊞ ⊞ www.nationalgalleries.org

The faces of the men and women who shaped Scotland hang here, forming a fascinating group of the great and the good, the vain and the bad, the beautiful and the long-forgotten. Scottish artists are well represented, including locals Allan Ramsay (1713–84) and Henry Raeburn (1756–1823). This is also where you'll find the original and much copied portrait of poet Robert Burns by Alexander Nasmyth (1758–1840), as well as a host of other familiar faces.

The national photography collection is also held here, including the body of work by Edinburgh pioneers Hill and Adamson (▷ 31).

SCOTTISH PARLIAMENT

See page 173

ST. GILES CATHEDRAL

⊞ 309 D2 • Royal Mile EH1 1RE ☎ 0131 225 9442 ⊙ May–end Sep Mon–Fri 9–7, Sat 9–5, Sun 1–5; rest of year Mon–Sat 9–5, Sun 1–5 ⊘ Free ⊟ 23, 27, 41, 42, 45 ⊟ Edinburgh Waverley ⊞ www.stgiles.net

The dark stonework of the High Kirk of Edinburgh, near the top of the Royal Mile, is forbidding on first sight. The columns inside, which support the 49m (160ft) tower with its distinctive crown

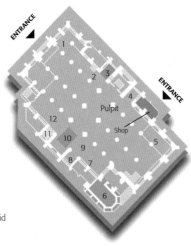

ST. GILES CATHEDRAL

1 Albany Aisle
2 John Knox statue
3 St Eloi's Chapel
4 Chambers Aisle
5 Holy Cross Aisle
6 Thistle Chapel
7 Royal Pew
8 Chapman Aisle
9 Preston Aisle
10 Rieger Orgelbaum organ
11 Regent Moray
12 Moray Aisle (with memorial plaques to R. L. Stevenson and David Livingstone)

Burns memorabilia at the Writers' Museum

top, are a relic of the 12th-century church which occupied the site. The tower itself dates from 1495, and the rest of the church from the 15th and 16th centuries. Presbyterian reformer John Knox (c1505–72) became minister here in 1559, arguing openly against Mary, Queen of Scots' attempts to revive the Roman Catholic cause. Inside, the exquisitely carved Thistle Chapel is by architect Robert Lorimer (1864–1929). The body of the great soldier James Graham, Marquis of Montrose (1612–50) is interred here, and there is a bronze memorial to writer Robert Louis Stevenson (1850–94), who died in Samoa.

WRITERS' MUSEUM

🕂 309 D2 • Lady Stair's Close, Lawnmarket, Royal Mile EH1 2PA ☎ 0131 529 4901 🕔 Mon–Sat 10–5, Aug also Sun 2–5 💷 Free 🚌 23, 27, 41, 42, 45 🚉 Edinburgh Waverley 🏛 www.cac.org.uk

Robert Burns (1759–96), Sir Walter Scott (1771–1832) and Robert Louis Stevenson (1850–94) are three of Scotland's most famous authors, and this little museum, in the narrow 17th-century Lady Stair's House, is dedicated to them. Burns wrote 'Ae Fond Kiss' while staying at the White Hart in the city's Grassmarket (▷ 75–76).

Scott and Stevenson were both born in Edinburgh, and both studied law at the university. Displays to the former include a reconstruction of his New Town drawing room. Unlike the others, Stevenson has no museum elsewhere dedicated to him, and he died abroad, so this collection of memorabilia, including his hand-printing press, is particularly significant.

Don't miss Quotations by more famous Scottish writers set into the paving slabs of Maker's Court, outside the museum.

Duane Hanson's lifelike Tourists *(1970) are a rotating exhibit*

SCOTTISH NATIONAL GALLERY OF MODERN ART AND DEAN GALLERY

Scottish painting and sculpture flourished in the 20th century—and this is the place to view it.

🕂 308 off A1 • 75 Belford Road EH4 3DR ☎ 0131 624 6200 🕔 Daily 10–5 💷 Free, but may be charges for temporary exhibitions 🚌 Free bus links all four national galleries 🚉 Edinburgh Haymarket 🚻 🏛 Shop stocks books, cards, gifts 🚻 www.nationalgalleries.org

A sweeping, living sculpture of grassy terraces and semi-circular ponds is the first thing you see as you arrive at the main gallery, an installation called *Landform UEDA* by Charles Jencks. After that, the gallery itself feels quite small, but it has an enviable and varied collection of modern art treasures from around the world.

RATINGS	
Good for kids	●●●
Specialist shopping	●●●●●

TIP

● If you're on the free galleries bus, visit the main gallery first and return to the town centre from the Dean Gallery.

Temporary exhibitions occupy the ground floor, with a changing display from the permanent collection on the first floor. Among these pieces, look out for works by Picasso, Braque and Matisse, Hepworth and Gabo. The work of the early 20th-century group of painters known as the Scottish Colourists is particularly striking, with canvases by Samuel John Peploe (1871–1935), George Lesley Hunter (1877–1931), Francis Cadell (1883–1937) and John Duncan Fergusson (1874–1961). Look out for Fergusson's dramatic *Portrait of a Lady in Black* (c1921), the vibrant colours of Cadell's *Blue Fan* (c1922) and Peploe's later, more fragmentary work such as *Iona Landscape, Rocks* (c1927).

Cross the road to the Dean Gallery, an outstation of the Gallery of Modern Art. Housed in a former orphanage and surrounded by picturesque allotment gardens, the collection majors on Dada and the Surrealists, and the Scottish sculptor Eduardo Paolozzi (1924–2005). Paolozzi's striding *Vulcan* statue of welded stainless steel, half man and half machine, takes up an entire two-floor gallery on its own. A chamber on the ground floor gives an insight into how a sculptor works, with a re-creation of Paolozzi's London studio, including 3,000 plaster casts and moulds.

CENTRAL SCOTLAND

Central Scotland takes in the wooded heart of the country, extending eastward across the fertile Perthshire farmland into Fife. The area has a rich history of rebellion and skirmish and there is plenty to explore—mansions, fishing villages and a remarkable show of modern engineering at the Falkirk Wheel.

KEY SIGHTS

William Adam's five-arched bridge at Aberfeldy

ABERFELDY

⊞ 317 H9 🛈 The Square PH15 2DD, tel 01887 820276; seasonal
www.perthshire.co.uk

Aberfeldy is a pleasant stone-built town on the River Tay in the heart of Perthshire. It has two claims to fame: a handsome hump-backed bridge with decorative obelisks, designed by architect William Adam for road-builder General Wade in 1733, which still carries the traffic, and a literary allusion by poet Robert Burns. He wrote of the 'Birks of Aberfeldie', referring to the birchwoods above the town, and signs point the way to walking trails there. Dewar's World of Whisky offers a distillery tour and visitor centre (Easter–end Oct Mon–Sat 10–6, Sun 12–4; rest of year Mon–Fri 10–4).

ARBROATH MUSEUM

⊞ 318 K9 • Ladyloan DD11 1PU ☎ 01241 875598 ⏰ Mon–Sat 10–5; also Jul, Aug Sun 2–5 💷 Free
🚉 Arbroath 🏛
www.angus.gov.uk/history

The signal tower is a significant building to the south of the town, and was the shore station for the Bell Rock Lighthouse (1811). It is a small Regency-style complex topped by a tower that was used as a signalling station. Inside, the museum tells the epic story of the lighthouse's construction on a submerged sandstone reef 12 miles (19.3km) offshore, and other aspects of Arbroath's history, including fishing and engineering, are shown in talking tableaux. On a clear day, don't forget to look out to the Bell Rock Lighthouse—a pencil-thin line on the horizon.
Don't miss The local delicacy, Arbroath 'smokies'—smoked haddock, lightly grilled and served hot.

The Atholl Highland regiment has its own exhibition at the castle

BLAIR CASTLE

A postcard-perfect castle in a beautiful setting.

⊞ 317 H8 • Blair Atholl, Pitlochry PH18 5TL ☎ 01796 481207 ⏰ Easter–end Oct daily 9.30–4.30 💷 House and grounds: adult £7.20, child £4.50 (5–16), family £18.50. Grounds only: adult £2.30, child £1.20, family £5.40 🚉 Blair Atholl Village 📷 £3.50 ☕ Café and restaurant 🎁 Gift shop includes many Blair Castle themed items, plus other Scottish-made souvenirs ♿
www.blair-castle.co.uk

This white-harled and turreted mansion, set against a background of dark green forestry 8 miles (12.9km) north of Pitlochry, seems the archetypal romantic Scottish castle, admired on shortbread tins the world over. It's been the ancestral home of the Murray and Stewart Dukes and Earls of Atholl for over 700 years, and boasts its own private army, the Atholl Highlanders, thanks to a favour granted by Queen Victoria in 1845.

RATINGS				
Good for kids	●	●	●	
Historic interest	●	●	●	●	●
Photo stops	●	●	●	●	
Walkability	●	●	●	●	●

MAKE A DAY OF IT
Killiecrankie; Pitlochry

The medieval castle occupied a strategic position on the main route to Inverness, so it's no surprise that in 1652 Cromwell's army seized it. The castle also played a role in the Jacobite uprisings of 1715 and 1745, when the Murray family's loyalties were tragically divided. In more peaceful times, the castle was recast as a Georgian mansion by the 2nd Duke, and with the coming of the railway in 1863, a Victorian-style remodelling took place, leaving the picturesque building seen today.

There's lots to see in the castle, from portraits and rich furnishings to an original copy of the National Covenant (▷ 27) and the small tartan-clad tower room where Bonnie Prince Charlie slept in 1745. Look for Raeburn's portrait of the legendary fiddler Neil Gow (1727–1807), and Gow's own fiddle, in the ballroom. Leave time to explore the mature gardens and grounds, including Diana's Grove, with conifers up to 59m (188ft) high.
Don't miss The Treasure Room at the end, stuffed with Jacobite relics, jewellery and intriguing personal items.

Restored 17th-century gardens at Drummond Castle

Picking out a seahorse souvenir at Deep Sea World

Doune Castle starred in the film Monty Python and the Holy Grail

CALLANDER

➕ 317 G10 🛈 Ancaster Square FK17 8ED, tel 01877 330342
www.incallander.co.uk

Callander is a bustling little town, the eastern gateway to the Trossachs (▷ 98). The architecture of its long main street reflects the town's heyday in the late 19th century as a holiday resort, and today it is lined with interesting shops. In the square, the former church is occupied by the tourist information office with, upstairs, the audio-visual Rob Roy Story (Mar–end May, Oct daily 10–5; Jun–end Sep daily 10–6). Rob Roy MacGregor (1671–1734) was a folk hero and outlaw, who took refuge with his clanspeople in the Trossach hills.

Ben Ledi looms at one end of the street, and there are good walks signed to Callander Crags and Bracklinn Falls.

CRIEFF

➕ 317 H10 🛈 Muthill Road PH7 4HQ, tel 01764 654014; seasonal
www.perthshire.co.uk

The old town of Crieff lies west of Perth on the very edge of the Highlands, and its shops buzz with visitors in high summer. It's a hub for activities including fishing, bicycling, watersports on nearby Loch Earn, and walking in the surrounding hills—Knock Hill, signposted from the town centre, offers the best views. Crieff Visitor Centre tells the story of ancient drovers' roads (daily 10–4.30). To the west of the town, the Glenturret Distillery dates from 1775 and claims to be Scotland's oldest (daily 9.30–6). Two miles (3.2km) south, Drummond Castle has an extensive formal garden, laid out in the 17th century, and restored in the 1950s (garden only: Easter, May–end Oct daily 2–6).

CULROSS

See page 92

DEEP SEA WORLD

➕ 317 J11 • North Queensferry KY11 1JR ☎ 01383 411880 ◷ Apr–end Oct daily 10–6; rest of year Mon–Fri 11–5, Sat–Sun 10–6 💷 Adult £8.55, child £6.30 (3–16), family £29.50 🚆 North Queensferry ◻ ▦
www.deepseaworld.com

This mega-aquarium and seal sanctuary lies just off the north side of the Forth road bridge, and is an underwater wonder-world. It has the world's longest underwater walkway (112m/360ft), where a perspex tunnel allows you to share the elements of the sharks without getting wet. Beware—it's easy to lose small children on the conveyor belt as you step off to ogle the fish. You can explore tanks full of piranhas, sharks, stingrays and deadly poisonous frogs, and get your hands wet in the rock pools with safer creatures such as starfish. If you're over 16, try joining an incredible shark dive by night.
Don't miss The free Behind the Scenes tour—book on arrival.

DOUNE CASTLE

➕ 317 G10 • Castle Road, Doune FK16 6EA ☎ 01786 841742 ◷ Apr–end Sep daily 9.30–6.30; Oct–end Mar Sat–Wed 9.30–4.30 💷 (HS) Adult £3, child £1.20 ▦
www.historic-scotland.gov.uk

The village of Doune lies 8 miles (12.9km) northwest of Stirling, and it would be easy to pass through and miss the castle—look out for signs which lead down a narrow road to this substantial grey ruin, hidden in the trees on a curve of the River Teith. Built by the powerful regent of Scotland, Robert Stewart, Duke of Albany, in the late 14th century, it is comparatively simple in construction, with a main block of buildings set with a courtyard, and contained by a great curtain wall. It is an admirable example of medieval concerns for security, with gates to secure the courtyard, further gates to defend the buildings should the courtyard be lost, and separate stairs to the lord's hall and the retainers' hall to ensure that each could be defended in its own right. Even the Duke's bedroom has an emergency exit.
Don't miss The climb up to the curtain wall-walk for the views.

DUNDEE

See page 93

DUNKELD AND HERMITAGE

See page 94

EAST NEUK

See pages 96–97

THE FALKIRK WHEEL

➕ 317 H11 • Lime Road, Tamfourhill, Falkirk FK1 4RS ☎ 08700 500208 ◷ Apr–end Oct daily 9–6; rest of year daily 10–5 💷 Free. Boat ride: adult £8, child £4.25 (under 3 free), family £21.50 🚆 Falkirk Grahamston ◻ ▦
www.thefalkirkwheel.co.uk

Is it engineering or is it art? That's one of the questions you'll ask on first sight of this unique structure, 35m (115ft) high. It opened in 2002 to link the canals that run across the centre of Scotland, replacing 11 locks. The wheel is a state-of-the-art means of raising and lowering boats between two very different levels of the Forth and Clyde ship canal and the Union Canal. Watch from the glass-sided visitor centre as the great beaked structure rotates, and take a 1-hour boat ride up on to the higher canal, through a tunnel and back down again on the eerily silent Wheel.

The twin towers of Falkland Palace's gatehouse

FALKLAND PALACE

🔲 317 J10 • Falkland, Cupar KY15 7BU
☎ 01337 857397 🕐 Mar–end Oct
Mon–Sat 10–6, Sun 1–5.30 🎫 (NTS)
adult £10, child £7, family £25 🏛
www.nts.org.uk

Stuart monarchs used this handsome Renaissance-fronted fortress in the heart of Fife as a hunting lodge and cosy retreat. The palace dates to the 15th century, with major additions between 1501 and 1541. Mary, Queen of Scots, spent part of her childhood here, but when Charles II fled to exile on the Continent in 1651, it fell into ruin. In 1887 its fortunes changed when John Patrick Crichton Stuart started rebuilding and restoring, work that continued in the 20th century. A series of rooms reflects the different periods of occupation, including the Chapel Royal and the King's Room. The gardens are outstanding.

GLAMIS CASTLE

🔲 318 J9 • by Forfar DD8 1RJ
☎ 01307 840393 🕐 Mid-Mar to end Oct daily 10–6; Nov, Dec selective opening 🎫 Adult £7.30, child £4.10 (5–16), family £21 🏛 🏛
www.glamis-castle.co.uk

A grand, turreted pile 5 miles (8km) west of Forfar, Glamis (pronounced 'Glahms') has been the seat of the Earls of Strathmore and Kinghorne since 1372. It's essentially a medieval tower house extended and remodelled to palatial proportions. Visitors explore the castle on a guided tour, which lasts around 1 hour, and are then free to roam the beautiful park, landscaped in the 18th century, which includes a 0.8ha (2 acre) Italian garden. Glamis was the childhood home of Queen Elizabeth, the Queen Mother (1900–2002).

CULROSS

A preserved Scottish burgh on the north shore of the River Forth, west of Dunfermline.

🔲 317 H11 ℹ 1 High Street, Dunfermline KY12 7DL, tel 01383 720999
www.culross.org

Your first impression of this quaint little town may be one of familiarity: Culross (pronounced 'Cure-oss') looks like the paintings of very old Scottish burghs, all winding, cobbled streets and crow-stepped gables. It had an early involvement in coal-mining and salt panning, mostly through George Bruce, the town's 16th-century entrepreneur. As the local coal was gradually worked out, the emphasis on industrial activity swung to other parts of the Forth Valley and Culross became a backwater, overlooked on the muddy estuary shores. Significantly, many of the substantial merchants' and workers' houses dating from the 17th and 18th centuries were never replaced by later buildings. Paradoxically, it was Culross' poverty which created the picturesque groupings so admired today.

In the 1930s the National Trust for Scotland started buying up properties which were by that time approaching dereliction. Decades later, many of the houses, fully restored, are lived in by ordinary folk. Really exceptional buildings, such as the ochre Culross Palace (Bruce's mansion of 1597), and the Town House (1626, where suspected witches were locked in the attic), are open to the public (NTS, Easter–end Sep daily 12–5).
Don't miss A self-guided tour of all the historic buildings in the NTS's guidebook (£3).

RATINGS	
Historic interest	●●●●
Photo stops	●●●●
Shopping	●●●
Walkability	●●●●●

MAKE A DAY OF IT
South Queensferry; Deep Sea World

At one time the ground floor of the 17th-century Town House served as a prison

Scott's ship Discovery *returned here from its London berth in 1986*

DUNDEE

An historic ship and a fascinating industrial museum spearhead the renaissance of Scotland's fourth city.

Dundee was founded on a 19th-century industrial base that was famously reduced to the three 'J's: jam, jute and journalism. Today it sprawls untidily along the northern shore of the Firth of Tay. Speed past on the ring road, however, and you'll miss a treat, for Dundee's waterfront has undergone a transformation. The focus is Discovery Point, centring on a famous heroine of polar exploration, the three-masted Royal Research Ship *Discovery*, which was built here in 1900–01. The story of her planning and construction is told in the museum alongside, with models, audio clips and objects that bring the city's shipbuilding to life (Easter–end Oct Mon–Sat 10–6, Sun 11–6; rest of year Mon–Sat 10–5, Sun 11–5). *Discovery*'s maiden voyage, under the command of a young Robert Falcon Scott (1868–1912), was to Antarctica, where in 1902 she became frozen in the pack ice. She was to remain there for two long winters, while scientific research was undertaken and Scott made an unsuccessful attempt to reach the South Pole. It's a fascinating story, and makes the tour of the ship all the more interesting, as you see the cramped quarters and realize the supplies needed for such an expedition.

FURTHER MAIN ATTRACTIONS

On the other side of the train station, Sensation: Dundee is a tribute to modern research (Apr–end Oct daily 10–6; rest of year daily 10–5). It's a hands-on science centre dedicated to understanding the five senses. There's something for everybody, from an explanation of 3D technology and Roboreatic, to a climb-through nose to explain snot. In the heart of the city is a former jute factory, the Verdant Works (Easter–end Oct Mon–Sat 10–6, Sun 11–6; rest of year Wed–Sat 10.30–4.30, Sun 11–4.30). This is more fun than it sounds, so allow a couple of hours for the full tour, taking in the origin of the fibre (grown in India), the manufacture and uses of jute, and its considerable impact on the people of Dundee.

RATINGS				
Chainstore shopping	●	●	●	●
Historic interest	●	●	●	●
Good for kids	●	●	●	●
Photo stops	●	●		

BASICS

⊞ 318 J9

🛈 21 Castle Street DD1 3AA, tel 01382 527527

🚇 Dundee

www.angusanddundee.co.uk
Regional tourist board site, with events.

TIPS

● At the Verdant Works, see the short Juteopolis film before starting the tour, and it will all make more sense.
● Save money by buying a joint ticket for both *Discovery* and the Verdant Works, or *Discovery* and Glamis Castle.

Dundee, above, is a university city on the River Tay

Hill House, the only Mackintosh house built during his lifetime

Dunkeld was preserved under the Trust's 'Little Houses' scheme

GLEN LYON

✚ 317 G9 🛈 The Square, Aberfeldy PH15 2DD, tel 01887 820276; seasonal **www.perthshire.co.uk**

This long and beautiful hidden valley lies sandwiched in the mountains between Loch Tay and Loch Rannoch, and stretches for 34 miles (55km) to the hydroelectric dam at the eastern end of Loch Lyon. Entry is via the mountain pass at Ben Lawers (1,214m/3,982ft) or through the dramatic, steep-sided pass at Fortingall. The road is single track and follows the route of the River Lyon, through scenery of woodland and little farms, backed by sweeping hills. In winter the valley is quickly cut off by snow; in summer it can be a sun trap, with red cattle standing in the river shallows to cool down.

HILL HOUSE

✚ 316 F11 • Upper Colquhoun Street, Helensburgh G84 9AJ ☎ 01436 673900 🕐 Easter–end Oct daily 1.30–5.30 💷 (NTS) Adult £8, child £5 (under 5 free), family £20 🚉 Helensburgh Central ▯ ▯ **www.nts.org.uk**

Set among the 19th-century villas of Helensburgh, this 'Dwelling House' is one of architect Charles Rennie Mackintosh's (▷ 114–115) finest achievements. The house was designed with a free hand for publishing magnate Walter Blackie, and completed in 1904. Mackintosh and his wife also saw to much of the interior design, including the exquisite, calm white space of the drawing room, with its stencilled motif of roses and trellis in restrained shades of pink, green and grey. Look for domestic details such as light fittings.
Don't miss A walk around the exterior to admire the changing pattern of shadows and rooflines.

DUNKELD AND HERMITAGE

A pretty 18th-century town with a tiny Gothic cathedral and superb woodland setting.

✚ 317 H9 🛈 The Cross, Dunkeld PH8 0AN, tel 01350 727688 🚉 Dunkeld and Birnham

With the exception of the diminutive 13th-century cathedral, the original settlement of Dunkeld was destroyed by the Jacobites after their victory at Killiecrankie in 1689 (▷ 95). It was rebuilt, with terraced houses packed into a compact centre of just two main streets: Cathedral Street and High Street, with a neat little square, the Cross. Many of the houses are whitewashed, and its pleasing uniformity owes much to restoration by the National Trust for Scotland.

RATINGS				
Good for kids	●	●	●	
Historic interest	●	●	●	
Photo stops	●	●	●	●
Walkability	●	●	●	●	●

MAKE A DAY OF IT
Killiecrankie; Blair Castle

At the far end of the partly restored cathedral stands the 'Parent Larch', a tree imported from Austria in 1738 and the source of many of the trees in the surrounding forests, planted between 1738 and 1830 by the Dukes of Atholl. A walk beside the River Braan leads past the tallest Douglas fir in Britain (64.3m/211ft) to the Hermitage, an 18th-century folly. The celebrated 18th-century fiddler Neil Gow was born across the river, and his grave is at Little Dunkeld.

To the east, the Loch of the Lowes is in the care of the Scottish Wildlife Trust and noted for breeding ospreys (Apr–end Sep daily 10–5).
Don't miss The black 'ell' marked on the wall of a house in Dunkeld's square, dated 1706; the ell was a unit of measurement equivalent to 37 inches (92.5cm).

Beechwoods by the River Braan

Port of Menteith, the access point for Inchmahome Priory

Admiring the Falls of Dochart, in the middle of Killin

A statue of the fictional Peter Pan, Kirriemuir

HILL OF TARVIT MANSIONHOUSE

➕ 318 J10 • Cupar KY15 5PB ☎ 01334 653127 🕐 House: Easter–end Sep daily 1–5; Oct Sat–Sun 1–5. Garden and grounds: all year daily 🅿️ (NTS) House and garden: adult £8, child £5 (under 5 free), family £20. Gardens only: £2–£4 🔲 🚻
www.nts.org.uk

The influence of Edinburgh-born architect Robert Lorimer (1864–1929) is seen in many of Scotland's great houses, but none more effectively than this, the Edwardian house that he remodelled in 1906 for Frederick Bower Sharp. Sharp had made his money in the Dundee jute trade, and commissioned a house that would show off his collection of fine art, including magnificent paintings, tapestries and furniture. The result is grandeur without pomposity, a comfortable harmony of taste and style that reflects a golden age of Scottish craftsmanship.
Don't miss The Raeburn and Ramsay portraits in the library, the plasterwork ceiling in the dining room and the Remirol toilet in the bathroom—Lorimer spelled backwards.

INCHMAHOME PRIORY

➕ 317 G10 • Port of Mentieth, by Kippin FK8 3RA ☎ 01877 385294 🕐 Apr–end Sep daily 9.30–4.30 🅿️ (HS) Adult £3.30, child £1.30 (under 5 free) 🚢 Ferry from Port of Menteith, 4 miles (6.4km) east of Aberfoyle 🚻
www.historic-scotland.gov.uk

Augustinian monks made their home on a beautiful tree-covered island on the Lake of Menteith in 1238. Today you can catch a little ferry to reach the romantic grey stone ruins of their priory, where a church and the shells of various other domestic buildings are ranged around a cloister. The priory is associated with the infant Mary, Queen of Scots, who took refuge here for three weeks in 1547 before her flight to France. The flamboyant Scottish Nationalist politician Robert Bontine Cunninghame Graham (1852–1936) is buried in the church with his Chilean wife.

KILLIECRANKIE

➕ 317 H8 • near Pitlochry PH16 5LG ☎ 01796 473233 🕐 Visitor centre: Easter–end Oct daily 10–5.30 🅿️ Free; parking £2 🔲 🚻
www.nts.org.uk

This spectacular wooded gorge is worth a visit for its scenery alone. Deciduous woodland of oak and beech lines the steep sides of the valley, with the waters of the River Garry flowing through the rocks below. Wild flowers are abundant, and you may be lucky enough to see the rare native red squirrels.

Yet Killiecrankie's fame is twofold: As well as natural beauty, it is celebrated for its significance as the site of a momentous battle in 1689, when John Graham of Claverhouse, or 'Bonnie Dundee' (c1649–89), swept down here at the head of a rebel Jacobite army. The superior government force was defeated, but Dundee was mortally wounded in the conflict.
Don't miss The Soldier's Leap, below the visitor centre, where a fleeing soldier, Donald McBean, jumped 18ft (5.5m) across the gorge to safety.

KILLIN

➕ 317 G9 ℹ️ Breadalbane Folklore Centre, Falls of Dochart, Main Street FK21 8XE, tel 01567 820254
www.incallander.co.uk

The flower-bedecked village of Killin lies at the western end of Loch Tay, in the ancient district of Breadalbane, and is a popular touring, walking and fishing centre for the area. It has its own attractions, notably the Falls of Dochart, which run through the middle; parties of visitors viewing these from the old stone bridge regularly bring the holiday traffic to a standstill. The surrounding hills abound with legends, which are brought to life at the Breadalbane Folklore Centre in St. Fillan's Mill (Mar–end May, Oct daily 10–5; Jun, Sep daily 10–6; Jul, Aug daily 9.30–6.30)—if you can't tell your fairies from your kelpies and urisks, this is the place to find out.
Don't miss The preserved, simple 19th-century farmhouse north of the village, Moirlanich Longhouse (NTS, May–end Sep Wed, Sun 2–5).

KIRRIEMUIR AND THE GLENS OF ANGUS

➕ 318 J9 ℹ️ Cumberland Close, Kirriemuir DD8 4EF, tel 01575 574097; seasonal
www.angusanddundee.co.uk

Kirriemuir is a proud little town built of red sandstone. It is associated with writer J. M. Barrie (1860–1937), whose most famous creation was Peter Pan, the boy who never grew up. Barrie was born here, the son of a handloom weaver, and his birthplace on Brechin Road is now an evocative museum (NTS, Easter–end Jun, Sep Fri–Wed 12–5; Jul, Aug Mon–Sat 11–5, Sun 1–5).

The town's position makes it the natural gateway to the great Glens of Angus, the long valleys which stretch north into the open moorland of the Grampian Mountains. They include Glen Esk, Glen Clova and Glen Prosen, and all three offer good hill-walking, with Glen Clova giving access to the remote Glen Doll.

East Neuk

A string of antique fishing villages with pretty corners and southerly views.

Crowded cottages face the sea, Pittenweem

Mooring in the harbour at Anstruther

Anstruther has the Scottish Fisheries Museum

RATINGS

Good for kids	● ● ●
Historic interest	● ● ●
Outdoors	● ● ●
Photo stops	● ● ● ● ●

BASICS

✛ 318 K10

🛈 Museum and Heritage Centre, 62–64 Marketgate, Crail KY10 3TL, tel 01333 450869; seasonal

🛈 Tourist Information Office, Harbourhead, Anstruther KY10 3AB, tel 01333 312996; seasonal

❓ The Fife Coastal Path (▷ 236) links the villages

SEEING THE EAST NEUK

'Neuk' is the Scots word for a corner, and the East Neuk is the name given to eastern Fife. Today it has a prosperous, well-farmed look, with rich grainfields beyond the hedgerows, but in the 15th century James II of Scotland referred to its poverty as a 'beggar's mantle, fringed with gold'. The East Neuk is noted for its charming old fishing villages, which are linked by the A917 road.

HIGHLIGHTS

CRAIL

The most easterly of the string, Crail has a charter dating back to 1178 and a much-photographed 16th-century harbour. Former trading links

Houses with crow-step gables tumble down to the harbour at Crail

Fishy details in glass, above, and plaster, top

with the Low Countries show up in the architecture, characterized by pantile roofs and high, stepped gables. The square-towered tolbooth even has a Dutch bell, cast in 1520. In nearby Marketgate there are some fine 17th- and 18th-century townhouses, with a mercat (market) cross to complete the picture. To the southeast is a good view of the Isle of May, 6 miles (9.7km) offshore, with its lighthouse.

ANSTRUTHER

Next west is Anstruther, a larger resort town and former herring port, where seafront shops sell fish and chips and colourful beach toys. The Scottish Fisheries Museum is housed in historic waterfront buildings around a central courtyard, and illustrates the past and present life of Scottish fishermen and their families (Apr–end Sep Mon–Sat 10–5.30, Sun 11–5; rest of year Mon–Sat 10–4.30, Sun 12–4.30). The town also has a history of smuggling, which centred on the Dreel burn (stream) and the 16th-century Smuggler's Inn.

PITTENWEEM

Continue west to Pittenweem, the main fisheries port for the East Neuk. The town dates back to the seventh century, when St. Fillan based himself in a cave here (in Cove Wynd) while converting the local Picts to Christianity. A priory grew up here in the 13th century, and the harbour dates from the 16th century. Artists are particularly attracted to the town, and there are plenty of small galleries to explore.

ST. MONANS AND ELIE

The tiny houses of the next village, St. Monans, crowd around its harbour, where shipbuilding as well as fish brought prosperity in the 19th century. The squat Auld Kirk (old church) standing alone at the western end dates from 1362. Elie is the most westerly of the East Neuk villages, and its golden sands made it a popular holiday resort in the late 19th century. A causeway leads to a rocky islet, with panoramic views and a busy watersports centre.

The Auld Kirk at St. Monans stands apart from the village

TIPS

● These old towns have narrow streets that quickly become congested in summer, so be prepared to park your car and explore on foot.
● Although you can see all these places in one day, allow extra time to see the Fisheries Museum.

MAKE A DAY OF IT

Scotland's Secret Bunker; Arbroath Museum

Boat painting, Pittenweem

THE SIGHTS

Beautiful Loch Katrine is the main reservoir for the city of Glasgow

RATINGS	
Good for kids	●●●●
Outdoors	●●●●●
Photo stops	●●●●●

BASICS

✚ 316 F10

🛈 National Park Gateway Centre, Loch Lomond Shores, Ben Lomond Way, Balloch G83 3QL, tel 01389 722199

🚂 Balloch, Tarbet and Ardlui on west side Loch Lomond

www.incallander.co.uk
The best site for tourist information including walks, tours.

TIP

● Some of the best scenery is on the short but winding A821 between Aberfoyle and Loch Katrine, known as the Duke's Pass. Travel from south to north for the best views.

Pleasure boats on the pebble shore of Loch Lomond

LOCH LOMOND AND THE TROSSACHS NATIONAL PARK

Magnificent scenery of woods, water and hills in the 720 square miles (1,865sq km) of Scotland's first designated national park (2002).

The romantic beauty of the Highland landscape, epitomized by this accessible and scenic area, was first 'discovered' in the late 18th century. Novelist and poet Sir Walter Scott did much to bring it to the popular eye, with his thrilling poem *The Lady of the Lake* (1810) set in identifiable locations across the Trossachs, ending at Loch Katrine. Today the national park stretches from the Argyll Forest Park in the west across to Callander (▷ 91), and from Killin (▷ 95) in the north to Balloch in the south, just 18 miles (29km) from Glasgow.

EXPLORING THE PARK

This is popular hiking country, with plenty of waymarked trails and a lovely stretch of the West Highland Way long-distance path, which runs down the eastern shore of Loch Lomond. Some 24 miles (38.6km) long, the loch is a watersports playground littered with 38 islands. It narrows to the north, where the mountains become bigger and bleaker. Ben Lomond, on the eastern shore, is a popular 'Munro' hill climb at 973m (3,192ft; ▷ 15). Luss, off the A82, is the prettiest village to explore. The Loch Lomond Shores Visitor Centre at Balloch explains the geology and history of the region (daily 10–5).

The Trossachs is the area to the east of Loch Lomond, including the wooded hills of the Queen Elizabeth Forest Park, and the peak of Ben Venue (729m/2,391ft). Some of the best scenery is around Loch Katrine, with easy walking and a steamboat ride among tree-clad islands.
Don't miss The dramatic pass to the high point of Rest and Be Thankful, on the A83 west of Arrochar.

Arched doorway at the island fortress of Lochleven Castle

The 18th-century mansion House of Dun, by Montrose

Rich furnishings displayed at Scone Palace, near Perth

LOCH LOMOND AND THE TROSSACHS NATIONAL PARK

See page 98

LOCHLEVEN CASTLE

➕ 317 J10 • by Kinross KY13 7AR
☎ 07778 040483 🕐 Apr–end Sep daily 9.30–6.30 💷 (HS) Adult £3.50, child £1.30 ⛴ Ferry from Fisherman's Pier, Kinross ♿
www.historic-scotland.gov.uk

Near the western shore of Loch Leven, the stark grey, roofless tower of Lochleven Castle stands on a small island, accessible by boat from Kinross. This 15th-century fortress gained notoriety as the prison of Mary, Queen of Scots, after her defeat in 1567. After her forced abdication she escaped and sought refuge with Elizabeth I of England, who promptly imprisoned her again. The castle was abandoned in the mid-18th century.

Loch Leven is a nature reserve noted for its huge over-wintering flocks of pink-footed geese, with the Royal Society for the Protection of Birds' Vane Farm Visitor Centre on its southern shore (daily 10–5).

MEIGLE SCULPTURED STONE MUSEUM

➕ 318 J9 • Dundee Road, Meigle, Blairgowrie PH12 8SB ☎ 01828 640612 🕐 Apr–end Sep daily 9.30–12.30, 1.30–6 💷 (HS) Adult £2.20, child 80p (under 5 free) ♿
www.historic-scotland.gov.uk

Our knowledge of the Picts, who lived in Scotland in the Middle Ages, is limited by the distance of time, and the fact that their artefacts have not survived. Much of what we do know has been gleaned from their remarkable legacy of stone carvings, and this museum in a former schoolhouse at Meigle, northeast of Coupar Angus, is a

good place to see and begin to understand. Around 25 carved stones and cross slabs are displayed, dating from the late eighth to the late tenth centuries. While salmon, dogs and horsemen can be picked out with relative ease, what can be made of the strange elephant-like creatures, camels, or birds with bulbous eyes?

MONTROSE

➕ 318 K8 ℹ Bridge Street DD10 8AB, tel 01674 672000; seasonal
🚊 Montrose
www.angusanddundee.co.uk

The harbour town of Montrose lies at the mouth of the South Esk River on Scotland's eastern seaboard, with fabulous golden sands exposed at low tide. Its comfortable prosperity was built up in the 18th century, largely on the back of trade with continental Europe, and some of its architecture echoes the style and elegance of Edinburgh's New Town (▷ 84–85).

A vast, shallow inland sea trapped behind the harbour, the Montrose Basin is important for migrant birds. The House of Dun, on its northern shore, is a mansion of 1730 designed by architect William Adam, and greatly restored by the National Trust for Scotland (NTS, Easter–end Jun, Sep Wed–Sun 12.30–5.30; Jul, Aug daily 11.30–5.30).

PERTH

➕ 317 J10 ℹ Lower City Mills, West Mill Street PH1 5QP, tel 01738 450600
🚊 Perth
www.perthshire.co.uk

The Roman settlement of Perth was founded along the banks of the sylvan River Tay in the first century; in the Middle Ages it was the capital of Scotland. Today it is a lively city at the

centre of a prosperous farming community, its compact core offering great shopping and bohemian cafés that spill on to the pavements. The Perth Mart visitor centre is housed within the old cattle market—come in February or October if you want to enjoy the sights, sounds and smells of the pedigree bull sales, the biggest of their kind in all Europe.

Balhousie Castle, along the edge of the North Inch park, houses the Black Watch Regimental Museum (May–end Sep Mon–Sat 10–4.30; rest of year Mon–Sat 10–3.30).

Open-top bus tours from the train station are a good way to see the town, linking attractions such as the Art Gallery and Museum, and the 12th-century St. John's Kirk, and travelling as far as Scone Palace, 2 miles (3.2km) to the north (Apr–end Oct daily 9.30–5.30). This sumptuously furnished stately home dates mainly from the 19th century. In the grounds is a tartan maze, and the Moot Hill, the earliest crowning place of Scottish kings. The Stone of Scone, or Stone of Destiny, on which kings were crowned, was originally here, but is now held for security in Edinburgh Castle (▷ 71–73)—the one on view is a replica.

Two notable gardens on the southern outskirts are worth exploring. Branklyn Garden, covering just 0.8ha (2 acres), has plants predominantly from China, Tibet and Bhutan, with an outstanding collection of Himalayan poppies (NTS, Easter–end Oct daily 10–5). Bell's Cherrybank Gardens, sponsored by the famous whisky manufacturer, hosts the national collection of over 900 heather species (Mar–end Oct Mon–Sat 10–5, Sun 12–4; reduced hours in winter).

The gaunt ruins of the cathedral, which was destroyed in the 16th century

RATINGS

Historic interest	●●●○
Photo stops	●●●○
Shopping	●●●●●
Walkability	●●●○

BASICS

✚ 318 K10

ℹ 70 Market Street KY16 9NU, tel 01334 472021

www.saint-andrews.co.uk
Fun site with virtual town tour.

MAKE A DAY OF IT

Scotland's Secret Bunker; East Neuk; Hill of Tarvit; walk and drive ▷ 214–217

Golf on the famous Old Course

ST. ANDREWS

A compact historic town and the heart of the golfing world

This attractive, breezy town is set on the east coast, with a sandy bay to the north (the opening scene of the 1981 movie *Chariots of Fire* was filmed here), and a narrow harbour to the south. Before the Reformation it was the ecclesiastical and scholarly centre of Scotland, and it has the country's oldest university, founded in 1413. It is also the home of the Royal and Ancient Golf Club, founded in 1754 and still the ruling authority on the game worldwide. Check out the history of the game at the British Golf Museum on Bruce Embankment (Apr–end Oct Mon–Sat 9.30–5.30, Sun 10–5; rest of year daily 10–4).

EXPLORING THE TOWN

The town received its royal charter in 1140, and the cathedral was started 20 years later. After Protestant reformer John Knox preached here in 1559, it was smashed up, and just a century later left derelict (free access; visitor centre: Apr–end Sep daily 9.30–6.30; rest of year daily 9.30–4.30). Near the gaunt ruins of the cathedral stand the remains of the 12th-century St. Rule's Church (admission fee). It is dedicated to a Greek monk, who was shipwrecked here while carrying holy relics of St. Andrew in AD347. Climb the spiral stairs of the tower (33m/108ft) for great views over the town, revealing the medieval grid of its streets. The two main roads are North Street, which leads to the famous St. Andrews Links (golf course), and South Street, with the restored city gateway of 1589, the West Port, at its far end.

Northward along the shore lie the ruins of the castle, rebuilt around 1390, which was the site of a battle and siege in 1546–47 (open as cathedral visitor centre). Look for the mine and counter-mine tunnels under the walls, which date from this time.

Don't miss The chilling bottle-shaped dungeon in the northwest corner of the castle, 7.3m (24ft) deep, cut from solid rock and impossible to escape.

Looking for salmon bypassing the dam at Pitlochry

The cascading River Devon at Rumbling Bridge

An ordinary farmhouse hid the entrance to the Secret Bunker

PITLOCHRY

🗺 317 H8 🏠 22 Atholl Road
PH16 5DB, tel 01796 472215/472751;
seasonal 🚉 Pitlochry
www.perthshire.co.uk

This bustling town in the
wooded valley of the River
Tummel is based around one
long main street, lined with
shops and eating places. The
geographical heart of Scotland,
it's been a popular holiday resort
since the 19th century, and
boasts two distilleries: Bell's Blair
Atholl Distillery (Jan–Easter, Nov,
Dec Mon–Fri 11, 1, 3; Easter–
end Sep Mon–Sat 9.30–5;
Jun also Sun 12–5; Oct Mon–Fri
10–4) and the tiny Edradour
Distillery (Mar–end Oct Mon–Sat
9.30–6, Sun 11.30–5; Jan, Feb
Sun 12–4; Nov, Dec Mon–Sat
9.30–5, Sun 12–5).

A footbridge leads across the
river to the Festival Theatre with
its Explorers' Garden, opened
in 2003 to celebrate 300 years
of botanical exploration and
collection around the world
by Scots (mid-Mar to end Oct
daily 10–5). There's a view from
the footbridge to the salmon
ladder, installed as part of the
hydroelectric dam system along
the river. Learn more about this
at the Scottish Hydro

Electric Visitor Centre (Apr–end
Oct Mon–Fri 10–5.30; Jul, Aug
also Sat–Sun), which gives free
access to a fish observation
window, as well as a paying
exhibition.

RUMBLING BRIDGE

🗺 317 H10 • At junction of A823 and
A977, access via nursing home gardens

It's not the bridge that rumbles at
this beauty spot along the River
Devon, rather the waters which
thunder through the rocky gorge
beneath when the river is in
spate. And there's not one bridge,
but two, with one built above the
other. The lower bridge dates
from 1713, the upper one,
36.5m (120ft) above the water,
from 1816. Visitors used to flock
here in such numbers that it
once had its own train station.
Now it's a peaceful backwater,
with pleasant walks to the
waterfalls of the Devil's Mill and
the Cauldron Linn.

ST. ANDREWS

See page 100

SCOTLAND'S SECRET BUNKER

🗺 318 K10 • Crown Buildings,
Troywood, near St. Andrews KY16 8QH
☎ 01333 310301 🕐 Apr–end Oct daily
10–5 💷 Adult £7.50, child £4.60 (under
5 free), family £22 🚻 📷
www.secretbunker.co.uk

Scotland's Nuclear Command
Centre, buried in a 40m (131ft)
hole between St. Andrews and
Anstruther, is a secret no longer.
The hole was originally dug out
after World War II to house a
radar installation. Instead, in the
1950s it was secretly lined with
3m (10ft) of reinforced concrete,
and a bomb-proof warren was
built inside, with an innocuous-
looking farmhouse on the top to
deter the curious.

The purpose of the secret
bunker was to house a self-
supporting military community
and seat of government in the
event of the Cold War getting out
of hand. Now you can explore
the eerie chambers, complete
with original communications
equipment, and the cramped
dormitories where as many as
300 personnel would have slept
in rotation.

SCOTTISH CRANNOG CENTRE

🗺 317 G9 • Kenmore, South Loch Tay,
near Aberfeldy PH15 2HY ☎ 01887
830583 🕐 Mid-Mar to end Oct daily
10–5.30; Nov Sat–Sun 10–4 💷 Adult
£4.75, child £3 (under 5 free), family
£14; additional charges for special
events such as storytelling 📷
www.crannog.co.uk

Crannogs were round,
communal dwellings built on
stilts above the surface of a loch,
and 2,000 years ago central
Scotland was apparently littered
with hundreds of them. One has
been reconstructed near
Kenmore at the eastern end of
Loch Tay, its design based on
ongoing underwater excavations
on the opposite side of the loch
at Fearnan. The insights it offers
are fascinating. Informative tours
show some of the remarkable
discoveries from the site, and

*Visit the reconstructed crannog
on Loch Tay*

The 19th-century Forth Bridge still carries trains daily

take you across the uneven pier into the hut itself, where you can learn how the archaeologists have gleaned clues to the way of life of the original crannog dwellers.

Back on land, there are demonstrations of ancient skills such as bodging and fire-making. It's essential to reserve ahead in midsummer.

SOUTH QUEENSFERRY

✚ 317 J11 🚹 Forth Bridges Tourist Information Centre, by North Queensferry KY11 1HP, tel 01383 417759
www.standrews.co.uk

A ferry operated across the Firth of Forth from this little royal burgh, from 1129 until 1964, when the opening of the suspended road bridge made it obsolete. Lying 10 miles (16km) northeast of Edinburgh, it is a great place to come and admire the two Forth bridges on a summer's evening.

The older, cantilevered rail bridge dates from 1890, and its striking design by William Arrol (1839–1913) and partners has made it an icon of Scotland. Fifty seven workmen died during the eight-year construction of the bridge. Its regular maintenance includes an end-to-end coating of 31,000 litres (6,817 gal) of red oxide paint (though new developments promise longer-lasting results in the future, of up to 30 years).

Hopetoun House, to the west, is a splendid early 18th-century mansion built by William Bruce and William Adam, with 40ha (100 acres) of parkland giving more great views to the bridges (Apr–end Sep daily 10–5.30). Stuffed with fine paintings, original furniture, tapestries and rococo details, the house is still the home of the Marquis of Linlithgow.

STIRLING

An interesting old town with a fighting reputation at the historic heart of Scotland.

✚ 317 H11 🚹 Royal Burgh of Stirling Visitor Centre, Castle Esplanade FK8 1EH, tel 01786 479901 🚉 Stirling
www.visitscottishheartlands.com

Stirling Castle's strategic position high on a rocky outcrop, commanding the narrow waist of land between the Forth estuary and the marshlands of the west (now drained), has given it a prominent role in Scottish history. The castle served as a royal palace and was remodelled many times (HS, Apr–end Sep daily 9.30–6; rest of year daily 9.30–5). Mary, Queen of Scots, spent her childhood here and was crowned in the Chapel Royal in 1543.

RATINGS				
Historic interest	●	●	●	●	●
Photo stops	●	●	●		
Shopping	●	●	●		
Walkability	●	●	●		

MAKE A DAY OF IT
Callander; Crieff; Doune Castle

STIRLING'S PLACE IN HISTORY

The town behind and below the castle has other interesting buildings, and was of particular importance in the Wars of Independence, fought against England in the 13th and 14th centuries. Notable Scottish victories include Stirling Bridge (1297), fought at the Old Bridge just north of the town centre, when William Wallace cleverly split the opposing army in two, and Bannockburn (1314), when Robert the Bruce took charge. Both men are commemorated as local heroes, Wallace with the 67m (220ft) tower, the National Wallace Monument on the nearby hill of Abbey Craig (Nov–end Feb daily 10.30–4; Mar–end May, Oct daily 10–5; Jun daily 10–6; Jul, Aug daily 9.30–6.30; Sep daily 9.30–5), and Bruce with a heritage centre on the field of Bannockburn, below the castle (NTS, Apr–Oct daily 10–5.30; Feb, Mar, Nov, Dec daily 10.30–4).

High on its crag, Stirling Castle is like Edinburgh in miniature

102 CENTRAL SCOTLAND S

GLASGOW

It may not have the Scottish Parliament, or the Festival, but there is no doubting that Scotland's largest city is a cultural dynamo. Its galleries and museums are a match for any in Britain and in the legacy of one of Europe's finest architects—Charles Rennie Mackintosh—it has buildings to rival Barcelona or Paris. The restaurants and vibrant nightlife make this a thoroughly modern city, but it never forgets its roots.

KEY SIGHTS

Glasgow

🛈 11 George Square G2 1DY, tel 0141 204 4400; daily 10–6
www.seeglasgow.com
A thorough guide to contemporary city life, with excellent links to other useful sites.

THE SIGHTS

HOW TO GET THERE

✈ Airport

Glasgow International airport is just 8 miles (13km) west of the city. Glasgow Prestwick International is a good (30 miles) 48km away but is served by more low-cost carriers.

🚆 Train stations

Glasgow Central is the mainline station, but there are also services to Queen Street from Greater Glasgow and Edinburgh.

Elegant design at House for an Art Lover (above) and in Cathedral Square (below)

TIPS

● Many of Glasgow's best galleries and museums are out of the centre, so be prepared to catch a bus or use the inexpensive train and subway.
● The Barras is best seen at the weekend, when it comes to life.
● Take the time to appreciate the architectural gems of Charles Rennie Mackintosh and Alexander 'Greek' Thomson. There are leaflets and guidebooks to help you.
● Visit the Clydebuilt museum to see how the Clyde made Glasgow what it is today.

SEEING GLASGOW

While Glasgow lacks the obvious tourist charm of its rival on the east coast, it makes up for this in the quality of its galleries, the warmth of its people and the vitality of its nightlife. It's worth taking at least a long weekend to visit the exceptional Burrell Collection, Kelvingrove, the Hunterian and the People's Palace. These are world-class collections and should be taken at a leisurely pace. It can feel like a long way between some of the best sights, but if you have the time, this is an exceptional city to walk across. Look above the modern shop fronts and you will see the fantastic breadth of the Victorian architects' vision. Here are Venetian palaces, Egyptian temples, Gothic wonderlands and modernist gems, all cheek by jowl with the residential streets that run almost to the centre of the city. There are some excellent walking tours with guides who will explain the architectural highlights as you go. But Glasgow is also justly famous for its night-times. Sauchiehall Street may no longer be the bawdy centre of it all, famed in music-hall song, but in the Merchant City you'll find a bar and restaurant scene to suit most tastes.

BACKGROUND

Glasgow traces its origins back to St. Mungo in the sixth century AD. The British saint established a religious community here, which later grew into a trading centre. A bishop was appointed in 1114 and the university came along in 1451. The Union of the Crowns in 1603 allowed seaborne trade with England to flourish, and later this expanded to Ireland, the Caribbean and the Americas. After the Act of Union in 1707 this trade took in the whole of the new British empire, but it was the Industrial Revolution which brought about the most dramatic changes. James Watt, it is said, conceived the steam engine while walking across Glasgow Green one Sunday morning in 1765. Textiles, dyeing, iron founding then shipbuilding all demanded labour, and this arrived in the thousands of displaced Highlanders from the glens and Irish fleeing poverty and famine in their homeland. Glasgow's heady Celtic mix began to develop its own distinctive culture and the wealth of its shipping and engineering men brought expensive art and flamboyant architecture. By the middle of the 20th century the boom years had passed, and post-industrial Glasgow looked sorry and forlorn. But with a new spirit at the end of the century, like other British cities it re-invented itself with great shopping, a metropolitan outlook and a new confidence. The 21st century has brought refurbishment to many of the city's great buildings, giving well-deserved recognition to this jewel among British cities.

DON'T MISS

THE BURRELL COLLECTION
Marvel at the fantastic detail in the 15th-century tapestry *Burgundian Peasants Hunting Rabbits with Ferrets* (▷ 106–108)

THE MACKINTOSH TRAIL
Proof that architecture can be beautiful, modern and fun (▷ 114–115)

THE TENEMENT HOUSE
See how countless Glaswegians lived in the city's iconic housing style (▷ 117)

THE PEOPLE'S PALACE
Follow the history of Glasgow's distinctive culture through original and often funny displays and exhibits (▷ 113)

Inside the Kibble Palace, a Victorian glasshouse

The City Chambers form one side of George Square

Glasgow Cathedral lies east of the city centre

THE BARRAS

311 E2 • Gallowgate and London Road, between Ross Street and Bain Street ☎ 0141 552 4601 ☻ Sat–Sun 10–5 ⦿ Free 🚆 Glasgow Central, Glasgow Queen Street
www.glasgow-barrowland.com

The famous flea market and market on the poorer east side of the city is a relic of a bygone age, a gritty, witty contrast to Glasgow's modern veneer of sleek shopping centres and debonair café society. It dates back to the 1920s, when enterprising street trader Margaret McIver raised a roof for stand-holders, who had previously sold their wares from open barrows. Today it's a sprawling hotchpotch of sheds, stands and warehouses that looks forlorn and tattered during the week, but comes raucously to life at weekends. You'll find everything from antique furniture to fortune-tellers and counterfeit designer clothing, plus a monthly farmers' market. **Don't miss** The oldest pub in town, the Saracen's Head, on Gallowgate.

BOTANIC GARDENS

310 C1 • 730 Great Western Road G12 0UE ☎ 0141 334 2422 ☻ Daily 7–dusk; glasshouses: summer daily 10–4.45; winter daily 10–4.15 ⦿ Free 🚆 Hillhead 🚌 8, 11, 18, 20, 41, 66, 89, 90 🅿 ❓ Kibble Palace closed until 2006 for restoration

Glasgow's botanic gardens grew out of a collection of plants for medical use held by the university. It moved to this site in the West End suburbs in 1842, and now covers 11ha (27 acres), with a main entrance on the corner of Great Western Road and Queen Margaret Drive, and an arboretum separated by another road. Its highlight is the Kibble Palace, a 2,137sq m (23,000sq ft) glasshouse named

after its donor, who had it moved here from his own garden in 1872. Today it houses tree ferns from Australia and New Zealand, and plants from Africa, the Americas and the Far East.

BURRELL COLLECTION

See pages 106–108

CITY CHAMBERS

311 D2 • George Square G2 1DU ☎ 0141 287 4018 ☻ Mon–Fri 9–5 ⦿ Free 🚆 Buchanan Street; St. Enoch's 🚆 Glasgow Queen Street ❓ Tours at 10.30 and 2.30
www.glasgow.gov.uk

This opulent, grandiose 'palace', the administrative heart of the city, fills one side of George Square. The building was opened by Queen Victoria in 1888. From the outside, beneath the Venetian-style central tower, pediments and corner cupolas you can glimpse the richness of the gilded ceilings and grand entrance hall. It's well worth joining one of the free tours to see the interior properly. Enjoy the murals of the vast banqueting hall, the marble staircases, and the mosaic ceiling of the loggia, rumoured to contain 1.5 million fragments. The design successfully captures the confidence of what was Britain's second city at the time, and is by architect William Young (1843–1900).

CLYDEBUILT

310 off A1 • Braehead Shopping Centre, Kings Inch Road G51 4BN ☎ 0141 886 1013 ☻ Mon–Sat 10–5.30, Sun 11–5.30 ⦿ Adult £4.25, child £2.50 (under 5 free), family £10 🚌 22, 25, 55 🚢 Water bus: Braehead from centre of Glasgow 🏛
www.scottishmaritimemuseum.org

Clydeside is synonymous with the golden age of shipbuilding in the late 19th and early 20th

centuries, when the river was dredged to allow passage for huge vessels such as the *QE2*. So it's appropriate that you can catch the water bus down to Braehead, for this, one of three outlets of the Scottish Maritime Museum (the others are at Irvine and Dumbarton). Different galleries lead you through the history of shipbuilding here, from the 18th-century wooden sailing ships which were the mainstay of Glasgow's tobacco trade, to the liners of the 1940s. On the way you can see how a liner was built, and try your hand at loading or berthing a vessel.

GALLERY OF MODERN ART (GoMA)

See page 109

GLASGOW CATHEDRAL

311 E1 • Castle Street G4 0QZ ☎ 0141 552 6891 ☻ Apr–end Sep Mon–Sat 9.30–6, Sun 2–5; rest of year Mon–Sat 9.30–4, Sun 2–4 ⦿ Free 🚌 213 🚆 High Street 🏛
www.glasgowcathedral.org.uk

With the blackness of its stonework, the high profile of its modern stained glass, and its setting below the Victorian necropolis (▷ 110), you could be forgiven for assuming that Glasgow Cathedral was also 19th century. In fact it dates from the 13th to the 15th centuries, and is a remarkable medieval survivor. The central tower and spire are replacements dating from about 1406, after the originals were struck by lightning.

The cathedral is dedicated to St. Mungo, or Kentigern, who died in AD603. His shrine, once a major pilgrimage site, is in the crypt, and the symbols of a robin, fish, bell and tree on the lamp-posts outside are references to miracles performed by the saint. **Don't miss** Carved stone ceiling bosses in the Blackadder Aisle.

Burrell Collection

Exquisite ceramics, paintings, embroidery and other treasures from around the world.
Set in a dramatic purpose-built gallery, a world away from Glasgow's centre.
Around 3,000 exhibits are on show at any one time.

The Bactrian camel dates from the third century

Collector William Burrell made his fortune in shipping

Rodin's The Thinker, *originally part of a larger composition*

TIPS

- Allow time for your eyes to adjust to the low levels of light in the inner galleries, to really appreciate the tapestries.
- On a hot summer's day the temperature in the outer galleries can become high, so visit them early in the morning, then retreat to the cooler, windowless interior.
- The Country Park also has wildlife gardens, a ranger centre, signed woodland and riverside walks and picnic places. Pollok House (▷ 113) is worth a visit on its own.

SEEING THE BURRELL COLLECTION

The Burrell Collection is housed in a modern, purpose-built museum set in leafy Pollok Park, south of the centre of Glasgow. Outside it appears modest and unassuming. Inside is a treasure-trove of decorative arts, crafts and paintings, from all corners of the world. A changing selection of objects is shown, and the overall impression in the museum is of a few outstanding items very well displayed, so they are never overwhelming. There is always something of interest around the next corner. The museum is mainly on one level, with a small mezzanine floor, and a cafeteria downstairs. Look out for the latest temporary exhibitions, which may be more interactive.

HIGHLIGHTS

MEDIEVAL TAPESTRIES

Burrell loved European art of the medieval period, and while the reconstruction of rooms from his 15th-century castle form the dullest part of the museum, the objects he collected—including furnishings and stained glass—are all together more exciting. The tapestries form the rich core of this collection, outstanding in their quality of design and workmanship, and in the preservation of their vibrant colours. The *Burgundian Peasants Hunting Rabbits with Ferrets* is a masterpiece dating from 1450–75, full of life and wit. Look for the cheeky rabbits, hiding amid the foliage while nets are prepared and ferrets released. The slightly earlier *Hercules on Mount Olympus* (c1425) shows the hero initiating the Olympic Games. While it is more formal in subject matter, there is a great vitality about the faces of both people and horses in the crowded scene, which makes this a remarkable work of art.

RODIN'S *THE THINKER*

The light and airy Central Courtyard is dominated by the massive *Warwick Vase*, an 18th-century marble reconstruction incorporating fragments of a second-century original. Around the edge of the space are set smaller statues, including an icon of modern sculpture:

Top, Chinese celadon porcelain bowl dating from AD960–1126

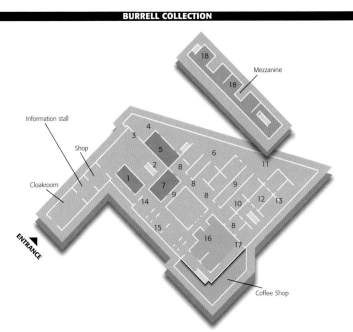

Mezzanine

Information stall

Shop

Cloakroom

ENTRANCE

Coffee Shop

Auguste Rodin's famous bronze, *The Thinker*. This was originally sculpted in 1880, one figure among hundreds in a huge commission for the entrance to a Paris museum, inspired by Dante's *Divine Comedy* and entitled *The Gates of Hell*. This brooding, muscled figure was to represent the poet himself, and reflects the inspiration of artists such as Michaelangelo and William Blake. The project was never completed, but what later became known as *The Thinker* took on its own life. Originally cast as a small bronze, the statue was scaled up between 1902 and 1904, and now exists in many different forms and sizes.

ORIENTAL ART

Although Burrell never travelled to the Far East himself, his Oriental collection is one of the best-known features of the museum, including beautiful jade carvings and magnificent porcelain figures. Rare bulbous Neolithic urns of painted earthenware date back to the Yangshao culture, which flourished more than 4,000 years ago—their survival is remarkable. Look for a comical pair of Han-dynasty earthenware bottles in the shape of startled owls. The huge Bactrian camel, glazed in brilliant orange and green, dates from slightly later; it would have been buried in the third century with its dead owner as a symbol of wealth. The soft green celadon-glazed pottery is another highlight, with delicate bowls and dishes in timeless shapes.

Manet's Women Drinking Beer, *a pastel dating from around 1878*

REMBRANDT SELF-PORTRAIT

The 16th and 17th Century Room is dominated by furniture of the period, and very British in feel. But look a little more closely, and you'll see a familiar face looking out at you from under a big, black Dutch hat. It's the face of the young Rembrandt van Rijn (1606–69), in a self-portrait of 1632, done at a time when the artist was becoming established as a portrait painter in Amsterdam, and a full ten years

1 Dining room from Hutton Castle
2 Central Courtyard (the Warwick Vase, Rodin's *The Thinker*)
3 Doorway from Hornby Castle
4 Ancient Egypt, Greece and Rome (stone sculptures, reliefs, vessels, bronze, glass etc)
5 Drawing room from Hutton Castle
6 Chinese Art and Ceramics (earthenware, porcelain, jades, furniture)
7 Hall from Hutton Castle
8 Tapestry Galleries (tapestries are displayed in four consecutive galleries, with appropriate period furniture)
9 Arms and Armour (European, 13th–17th century)
10 Needlework Room (embroidered textiles, lace)
11 Gothic Art (medieval religious art)
12 16th and 17th Century Room (paintings and furnishings)
13 Islamic Art (carpets, rugs, early ceramics and metalwork)
14 Burrell the Man, Burrell the Building (background to the collection)
15 Stained Glass
16 Temporary exhibitions
17 Montron Arch
18 Mezzanine floor: Paintings (generally including works by 19th-century French artists Degas, Cézanne and Boudin)

before he would produce his most famous work, *The Night Watch*. Rembrandt painted around 60 self-portraits during the course of his life, starting in 1629, and was the first artist to produce such a detailed autobiographical study. In the early days, he may have been saving money on models, but by the end of his life he was intrigued by the decay that he saw in his own face. A Rembrandt self-portrait of 1634 was discovered fairly recently: It had been overpainted by his students, to make it anonymous and easier to sell. In its restored form, it was valued at a cool £5 million.

DEGAS PICTURES

Burrell's collection includes many paintings and pastels by the great French artists of the 19th century. He was clearly fascinated by the work of Edgar Degas (1834–1917), who is best known for his images of ballet dancers, in paint and in bronze. The bright pastel *Les Jupes Rouges* is a notable example of this, portraying dancers in rehearsal. Degas was particularly good at capturing dancers in their private moments, in the wings at the theatre, waiting to dance, or perhaps tying on a shoe or casually stretching out a limb. Typically the women

Rembrandt's self-portrait of 1632

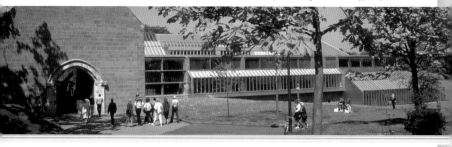

The building was designed by Gasson, Meunier and Anderson, and intriguing historic stone doorways lead into different sections

BASICS

✚ 310 B3 • Pollok Country Park, 2060 Pollokshaws Road, G43 1AT

☎ 0141 287 2550

🕐 Mon–Thu, Sat 10–5, Fri, Sun 11–5

💰 Free, but may be a charge for some special exhibitions; parking charge

🚌 34, 45, 47, 48, 57

🚉 Pollokshaws West

🍴 Self-service café and restaurant on the lower floor with views over the parkland

🎁 Extensive gift shop at the entrance, with everything from postcards to pricey ceramics

👫

❓ Free guided tours several times a day–check on arrival, and listen for the announcement

www.glasgowmuseums.com
Clunky, but a useful site for up-to-date information about temporary exhibitions.

are caught in a half-light that sums up the translucence of their costume, as well as body expression, in the act of movement. Precise paintwork gave way to more impressionistic images, and pastel became his preferred medium after 1880. The artist had learned and practised his skill by drawing race horses, and his pastel *Jockeys in the Rain* (*c*1881) is also in the collection. It shows restless horses lining up for the start of a race, and the impatience of the animals before they set off is brilliantly captured in the flowing pastel lines.

MANET SKETCHES

Degas was influenced by fellow Parisian artist Édouard Manet (1832–83), who scandalized polite society with his bohemian image of young men picnicking with a naked woman in *Déjeuner sur l'Herbe* in 1862. In later life, Manet's painting became much looser and more impressionistic, culminating in the well-known *Un Bar aux Folies-Bergères* (1881–82). A glimpse of the work that led up to that masterpiece can be seen in Manet's sketches in the Burrell Collection, which include the delightful *Women Drinking Beer*, a free-flowing pastel of women relaxing in a Paris bar.

BACKGROUND

This priceless collection of about 9,000 varied pieces of art from around the world was gifted to Glasgow in 1944 by Sir William Burrell (1861–1958) and his wife, Constance. Burrell was an eclectic magpie with a discriminating eye and excellent judgement, who had collected rare and precious works of art since his teens. It was 1983 before a suitable home for the collection could be made, away from city pollution in Pollok Country Park. Its huge feature walls of glass seem to pull the woodland greenery inside. Hundreds of panels from the stained-glass collection are incorporated into the windows of the South Gallery, where the natural daylight reveals their jewel-like colours.

Admiring *John Bellany's* Untitled, *left, and June Redfern's* From Two Paths, *right*

GALLERY OF MODERN ART (GoMA)

This is one of the most controversial and provocative contemporary art galleries in Britain.

This exceptional contemporary art gallery at the very heart of the city never fails to provoke and inspire.

GoMA occupies what was once a 1780s tobacco baron's palatial mansion. The gallery is renowned for going its own populist way, and the image it sells of itself is of the mounted statue of the Duke of Wellington outside, crowned by a traffic cone. (This icon of modern Glasgow is less frequently seen now, as the statue is better protected from the so-called vandals.)

Inside the grandiose pillored entrance, you'll find a great exhibition space, which is usually given over to some of the best contemporary works from Glasgow Museum's collection. This changes every six months or so but it may include dramatic pieces by L. S. Lowry, the Boyle family, Sir Eduardo Paolozzi, Grayson Perry or Sir Stanley Spencer. A particular favourite which appears on heavy rotation is Peter Howson's *Patriots*, a controversial painting from 1991 which depicts three baseball-hat clad thugs, wielding chains and baseball bats and accompanied by snarling bulldogs. Downstairs is a café and public library, while upstairs are two galleries that tend to showcase specific artists.

WHAT TO LOOK FOR

Because this is an ever-changing exhibition, it's difficult to pin down even a handful of works that are likely to still be there in six months' time. However, that is what makes GoMA so special, and it certainly seems to work with the public—this is the second most visited art gallery in Britain outside London. The city's museum service has a positive acquisitions policy for contemporary Scottish art, so look out for works by artists such as Roderick Buchanan, Graham Fagen and Toby Paterson in the future. For detailed accounts of what is currently on display check the gallery's website or look for the *Preview* magazine.

RATINGS	
Good for kids	● ● ● ●
Historic interest	● ● ●
Specialist shopping	● ● ● ●

BASICS

311 D2 • Royal Exchange Square, Queen Street G1 3AZ ☎ 0141 229 1996 ⏰ Mon–Wed and Sat 10–5, Thu 10–8, Fri and Sun 11–5 💷 Free 🚌 6, 12, 18, 20, 40, 41, 61, 62, 66, 75 🚇 Buchanan Street, St. Enoch's 🚆 Queen Street, Glasgow Central 🍴 Small café in basement 🛍 Shop on ground floor sells good arty souvenirs 👥 ❓ Volunteer guides provide tours most weekends (donations) www.glasgowmuseums.com Clunky, but useful for latest exhibitions.

Papier mâché figures by the Mexican Linares brothers

Over-the-top Victorian monuments at the Necropolis

The library, on the southwest corner of the School of Art

Classical cupola in the ceiling of Holmwood house

THE SIGHTS

GLASGOW GREEN

311 E2 · 11 George Square G2 1DY, tel 0141 204 4400 · Glasgow Central

This green space in the East End, recently restored to its former glory, is the oldest public park in Scotland, gifted to the people in 1450 and resonant with the city's history. For centuries it was the place where washing was dried, livestock grazed and criminals were hanged. From 1650, merchants watched the River Clyde eagerly from the top of the Steeple, to see if their ships had come in. Bonnie Prince Charlie's army received a lukewarm reception when it camped here in 1746. The obelisk of blackened brick was the first memorial anywhere to be raised to Lord Nelson (1806). The city's earliest golf club played here in the 1780s, and both Rangers and Celtic football clubs were founded on the Green.

It's the home of the People's Palace (▷ 113), and famous landmarks around the perimeter include the unlikely red and gold façade of Templeton Business Centre, a former carpet factory of 1889 by William Leiper, modelled on the Doge's Palace in Venice, and the McLennan Arch, the rescued façade of the old Assembly Rooms.

GLASGOW NECROPOLIS

311 E2 · 11 George Square G2 1DY, tel 0141 204 4400 · Daily 10–6 · Free · 213 · High Street www.glasgownecropolis.org

This is Glasgow's fascinating city of the dead, stuffed to bursting point with ostentatious and florid monuments to Victorian worthies—the wealthy industrialists and tobacco merchants who developed the city in the 19th century. Their competitive spirit showed even

after death, with extraordinary monuments commissioned from the finest architects of the day, including Alexander 'Greek' Thomson. The burial ground was set out in 1833 on a hilltop near the cathedral, where it was felt that it could be contained, thus avoiding the spread of infectious diseases such as cholera and typhus. It is said to have been based on the Père Lachaise Cemetery in Paris. There's a great view of the crowded skyline of the Necropolis from the third floor of the St. Mungo Museum (▷ 116).

GLASGOW SCHOOL OF ART

311 D1 · 167 Renfrew Street G3 6RQ · 0141 353 4526 · Tours Apr–end Sep daily 10.30, 11, 11.30, 1.30, 2, 2.30; Oct–end Mar Mon–Sat 11 and 2 · Adult £6, child £4.80 (under 10 free) · Cowcaddens · Queens Street · www.gsa.ac.uk

Glasgow's art school was founded in 1845. By 1896 it was clear that a new building was required, and a competition for a design to suit this awkward site on the side of a steep hill was announced. The winner was Charles Rennie Mackintosh (1868–1928), an innovative architect who had trained at the college and was beginning to gain a reputation in the city (▷ 114–115). The Glasgow School of Art became known as his masterpiece.

The exterior is severe, yet the stonework is adorned with a light, confident touch of wrought iron at the windows, on railings and on the roof. Inside, he designed everything down to the light fittings, creating a practical working space with a distinctive Arts and Crafts style that still, over 100 years later, looks fresh and modern. The tour includes the magnificent library, and an

exhibition of artwork by Mackintosh.

GLASGOW SCIENCE CENTRE

See page 111

GREENBANK GARDEN

310 C3 · Greenbank House, Flenders Road, Clarkston G76 8RB · 0141 616 5126 · Garden: daily 9.30–dusk. House: Apr–end Oct Sun 2–4 · (NTS) adult £5, child £4 (under 5 free), family £14 · 44 · www.nts.org.uk

Seven miles (11.3km) south of the city centre, this garden was gifted to the National Trust for Scotland in 1976 as a demonstration piece, to inspire suburban gardeners and show just what can be grown in a heavy clay soil. Set in a frost pocket, with 1ha (2.5 acres) of walled garden and extensive policies (grounds) beyond, Greenbank prides itself on being very much a garden that normal people can aspire to. That may be a little optimistic, given that it contains over 3,500 different plants. As well as ideas you should be able to take away some unusual plants, available from the shop.

HOLMWOOD

311 D3 · 61–63 Netherlee Road, Cathcart G44 3YE · 0141 637 2129 · Apr–end Oct daily 12–5 · (NTS) adult £5, child £4 (under 5 free), family £14 · 44, 66, 374 · Cathcart · www.nts.org.uk

Manufacturing and ostentation went hand-in-hand in 19th-century Glasgow. So it was that in 1857, papermill owner James Coupar commissioned fashionable architect Alexander 'Greek' Thomson (1817–75) to design a villa, 3 miles (4.8km) south of the centre. Thomson was an exponent of Classical and

Distinctive Mackintosh roses at the House for an Art Lover

Titanium cladding gives the Science Centre a space-age look

GLASGOW SCIENCE CENTRE

Hands-on edutainment for kids and adults at Scotland's flagship millennium project.

➕ 310 C2 • 50 Pacific Quay G51 1EA ☎ 0141 420 5000 🕐 Daily 10–6; late opening at IMAX cinema Thu–Sat 🎟 Science Mall: adult £6.95, child £4.95 (under 3 free); IMAX: adult £6.95, child £4.95; combination tickets available 🚌 24, 89, 90 🚇 Cessnock 🏛 Exhibition Centre 🍴 Foyer restaurant seats up to 250 ☕ Two cafés and brasserie 🎁 Extensive gift shop with pocket money toys, serious scientific bits and everything in between 👫 On ground floor and second floor ❓ Birdbot, an animated crane on the second floor, can answer your questions about the day's events www.glasgowsciencecentre.org

The Science Centre lies on the south side of the River Clyde, and has three distinct elements. The first is a 24m (80ft) screen IMAX theatre housed in the silver titanium-skinned 'egg', which shows a changing schedule of films, including some in 3D. Second is a dizzying 122m (400ft) high aerofoil-shaped viewing tower designed to turn 360 degrees in the wind.

The main attraction is the Science Mall, with four floors containing 500 interactive exhibits. This futuristic building, with its glass wall overlooking the 'Armadillo' exhibition centre to the city beyond, was designed with a curved roof to avoid problems of wind turbulence. How do we know? It's just one of the fascinating exhibits on the second floor, in Structures, which also lets you into the engineering secrets of the Forth Rail Bridge.

The biggest laughs are at the distorting mirrors (floor 1). Other highlights include using computer screens to design your own dance sequence (floor 2); seeing how an artificial arm picks up signals from your body to move (floor 3); the Kinex construction sector (floor 2) where you can race vehicles you've made on a 60m (197ft) test track; and a walk-on piano for under 7s (floor 1).
Don't miss The ScottishPower Space Theatre (planetarium).

RATINGS	
Good for kids	●●●●●
Photo stops	●●●●●
Specialist shopping	●●●●●
Value for money	●●●●

TIPS
● Can be overwhelming at peak holiday times, so check the timed shows you want to see and plan your visit around them.
● It is easy for children to get overexcited and simply run through the exhibits, hitting buttons and seeing nothing. To get the best out of the experience, slow down, find something that interests you, be prepared to wait your turn, and explore it in depth.
● To avoid some of the crowds, start at the top and work down.

Egyptian motifs, and his designs are seen throughout the city, including the United Presbyterian Church on Caledonian Road. Nowhere is his style seen to better effect than this extraordinary neoclassical mansion, where a window takes on the appearance of a bay with the use of Greek temple columns and pediment above. Crowning all is the cupola or lantern, giving light to the stairwell. The building is absurd, but beautifully executed, and rich details of the original interior decoration are gradually being revealed. (▷ 218.)

HOUSE FOR AN ART LOVER

➕ 310 B2 • Bellahouston Park, 10 Dumbreck Road G41 5BW ☎ 0141 353 4770 🕐 Apr–end Sep Mon–Wed 10–4, Thu–Sun 10–1; Oct–end Mar Sat–Sun 10–1 🎟 Adult £3.50, child £2.50 (under 10 free), family £7 🚌 9, 36, 38, 54, 56 🚇 Ibrox 🚉 Dumbreck ☕ 🎁 www.houseforanartlover.co.uk

The House for an Art Lover is a fantasy, set out on paper in 1901 without limitations of budget or client's whims, by Charles Rennie Mackintosh (1868–1928) and his wife, Margaret Macdonald (1865–1933). It was for a competition set by a German magazine for 'a grand house in a thoroughly modern style', but their entry was disqualified. The physical reality was achieved only in 1996, when artists and craftspeople were brought together by the City Council and the School of Art to build the dream in leafy Bellahouston Park. And what a dream it is, with perfect proportions, light, open spaces, a harmonious balance of straight and curved lines, and every attention to detail in the furnishings and fittings.
Don't miss Sunday afternoon recitals in the Music Room.

The Modern Art gallery at the Hunterian Museum

Kelvingrove has everything from fossils to Pre-Raphaelite art

The spiral stairway in the tower of the Lighthouse

HUNTERIAN MUSEUM AND ART GALLERY

✚ 310 C1 • University of Glasgow, 82 Hillhead Street G2 8QQ ☎ 0141 330 4221/5431 🕐 Mon–Sat 9.30–5; Mackintosh House closed daily 12.30–1.30 💷 Free. Mackintosh House £2.50 🚇 Hillhead 🚌 44, 59 🅿 🏛 www.hunterian.gla.ac.uk

William Hunter (1718–83) was a Glasgow-trained physician, who bequeathed his scientific collections to his old university. They were put on show in 1807, making this the oldest public museum in Scotland.

Hunter's coin collection formed the basis for one of the museum's specialties today. Other strengths are geology and archaeology (including Roman finds in Scotland). The magnificent art collection, in a separate building across University Avenue, began with Hunter's purchases of 17th-century Flemish, Dutch and Italian masters. Today it includes a range of more modern art, with works by the Scottish Colourists, the Glasgow Boys, and American James McNeill Whistler (1834–1903).

Don't miss The Mackintosh House, an intriguing reconstruction made long after the architect's death (▷ 114–115).

KELVINGROVE ART GALLERY AND MUSEUM

✚ 310 C1 • Argyle Street, Glasgow G3 8AG ☎ 0141 287 2699 🕐 Reopens July 2006 after refurbishment. Check website for details www.glasgowmuseums.com

This sprawling red-brick pile of Edwardiana dates from 1902 and houses outstanding art and objects. Its interiors have recently been lovingly restored. Among the fantastic paintings on display are works by Rembrandt,

Constable and Monet, as well as items by the Glasgow Boys and Scottish Colourists. The Armoury exhibits include field armour from the 15th century and the natural history displays feature Sir Roger the Elephant as well as up-to-date interactive exhibits.

THE LIGHTHOUSE

✚ 311 D2 • 11 Mitchell Lane G1 3NU ☎ 0141 221 6362 🕐 Mon and Wed–Sat 10.30–5, Tue 11–5, Sun 12–5 💷 Adult £3, child £1 (under 5 free) 🚌 9, 11, 12, 16, 18, 20, 23, 40, 41, 42, 44, 45, 47, 48, 54, 56, 57, 59, 61, 62, 64, 66, 75A 🚇 Buchanan Street 🚉 Glasgow Queen Street, Glasgow Central 🅿 🚻 🏛 www.thelighthouse.co.uk

This is Glasgow's museum of architecture and design. Completed in 1895, the building was the first public commission by Charles Rennie Mackintosh (▷ 114–115), and gets its name from the tower that dominates the structure. As well as a permanent Mackintosh display, there are extensive temporary exhibitions relating to other aspects of architecture and design in the city.

Don't miss A ride in the elevator to the viewing platform for a breathtaking Glasgow panorama.

MACKINTOSH TRAIL

See pages 114–115

McLELLAN GALLERIES

✚ 311 D1 • 270 Sauchiehall Street G2 3EH ☎ 0141 565 4137 🕐 Mon–Thu, Sat 10–5, Fri and Sun 11–5 💷 Free 🚇 Cowcaddens 🚉 Charing Cross, Queen Street, Central 🅿 🏛 www.glasgowmuseums.com

Behind an inauspicious shop front on Sauchiehall Street, the McLellan Galleries are one of Glasgow's hidden treasures. Partially destroyed by fire in the 1980s they were rebuilt in the

1990s as a top, air-conditioned exhibition space, and housed exhibits from Kelvingrove, while that gallery was being refurbished. They are now home to high-profile touring art—check *Preview* magazine for details.

MUSEUM OF PIPING

✚ 311 D1 • 30–34 McPhater Street, Cowcaddens G4 0HW ☎ 0141 353 0220 🕐 Jun–end Aug daily 10–4.30; Sep–end May closed Sun 💷 Adult £3, child £2 (under 5 free), family £10 🚌 23, 54, 66, 75 🚉 Queen Street 🚇 Cowcaddens 🅿 🏛 www.thepipingcentre.co.uk

An Italianate former church of 1872 at the top of Hope Street is the home of the National Piping Centre, Scotland's centre of excellence for the learning and performance of bagpipe music. Students from all over the world come here to study.

The building incorporates an auditorium for concerts and a sound archive as well as the small museum. This is an intriguing outpost of the Museum of Scotland (▷ 78–81), dedicated to the history of the Highland bagpipe, which dates back to the 14th century.

Don't miss A unique visual interpretation of the pipe music known as *piobaireachd* in the three windows above the main entrance (1996), by John K. Clark.

MUSEUM OF TRANSPORT

✚ 310 C1 • Kelvin Hall, 1 Bunhouse Road G3 8DP ☎ 0141 287 2720 🕐 Mon–Thu and Sat 10–5, Fri and Sun 11–5 💷 Free 🚌 6, 8,16, 18, 19, 42, 62, 64, 89, 90 🚇 Kelvinhall 🚉 Partick 🅿 🏛 www.glasgowmuseums.com

The spacious arena, opposite the Kelvingrove Museum (see left) in the West End, is packed with

A Glasgow tram preserved at the Museum of Transport

historic vehicles of all shapes, sizes and ages, from steam locomotives and horse-drawn trams to early Arrol Johnson cars. The Hillman Imp car was a less enduring rival to the Mini—look out for the first Imp ever to come off the production line in 1963 (blue, and driven by the Duke of Edinburgh). Along the way there are fire engines, motorbikes, buses, model ships, the earliest pedal bicycle, caravans (trailers) and other transport paraphernalia. There's even a whole reconstructed 1930s Glasgow street scene, complete with shops, cinema and underground station.
Don't miss The little loco, *Royal Train Pilot 123,* which used to run at the front of the Royal Train.

POLLOK HOUSE

🔢 310 B3 • Pollok Country Park, 2060 Pollokshaws Road G43 1AT ☎ 0141 616 6410 🕐 Daily 10–5 💷 (NTS) adult £6, child £4 (under 5 free), family £15, Apr–Oct; free Nov–Mar 🚌 34, 45, 47, 48, 57 🚇 Pollokshaws West 🍴 🎁 www.nts.org.uk

Pollok House is a compact grey stone mansion lying just 3 miles (4.8km) south of the city centre. It feels like another world, thanks to the 146ha (361 acres) of country park which surround it. The house was started for Sir John Stirling Maxwell, 2nd Baronet in 1747, and stayed in the family until 1966. The 10th Baronet was a co-founder of the National Trust for Scotland, which now maintains the house. Inside it is light and airy, with comfortably small-scale rooms including an elegant library with some 7,000 volumes, in which chamber concerts are given. El Greco's portrait of c1577, *Lady in a Fur Wrap,* is here, a highlight of the otherwise rather gloomy collection of Spanish paintings.

PEOPLE'S PALACE
The museum of the people of Glasgow.

🔢 311 E2 • Glasgow Green G40 1AT ☎ 0141 271 2951 🕐 Mon–Thu and Sat 10–5, Fri and Sun 11–5 💷 Free 🚌 18, 43, 61, 62, 64, 93, 96, M2 🚇 High Street, Argyle Street, Bellgrove 📖 Various guidebooks available 🍴 Winter Gardens café 🎁 Gift shop stocks items of particular local interest 🚻 www.glasgowmuseums.com

Set on Glasgow Green (▷ 110), this red sandstone building of 1898 is less a museum, more a local institution which captures the wit, eccentricity and gritty character of the city. The main exhibitions are on the second and third floors, with temporary displays and the shop at ground level. It tells the history of Glasgow through familiar objects and quotes from real people. So, a doll's house model of a prefabricated house, made by Duncan MacKenzie for his daughters, highlights the story of the post-war housing shortages, and a mock-up of a 'steamy', or communal wash-house, brings the city's social history to life.

One section asks 'what happened to Glasgow's industry?' Making It In Glasgow is a corner on the top floor devoted to famous Glaswegians, with John Byrne's portrait of comedian Billy Connolly, singer Lulu's emerald trouser suit, books by Jimmy Boyle and Iain Banks, and television scripts for Ian Pattison's *Rab C. Nesbitt* comedies. A collection of tobacco tins recalls the city's heyday, and displays of the details of everyday life bring things up to date. It's great to listen to the people around you as they recognize and reminisce.
Don't miss Smelly cheese in the reconstructed Buttercup Dairy.

RATINGS					
Good for kids	●	●	●	●	●
Historic interest	●	●	●	●	
Specialist shopping	●	●			

Billy Connolly's trademark dress sense, captured in 1973

The Winter Gardens are a great place for a break

The Mackintosh Trail

Track down the finest buildings and interiors by Scotland's
best-loved modern architect.
Understand why the Mackintosh Revival has
swept Glasgow.

*Street lamps are a modern
addition to the School of Art*

*Taking tea in the Room de
Luxe, Willow Tearooms*

*Oak beds in a reconstructed
Mackintosh bedroom, Hunterian*

RATINGS	
Good for kids	● ●
Historic interest	● ● ● ●
Walkability	● ● ●

TIP

● The Mackintosh Society
arranges guided tours of the
best sites. Contact them at
St. Matthew's Free Church,
tel 0141 353 4526.

*Top, Mackintosh in 1893
Below, the library, School of Art,
showing the narrow, high gallery*

SEEING CHARLES RENNIE MACKINTOSH'S WORK

You can hardly miss the designs of Charles Rennie Mackintosh in
Glasgow today—his stylized roses and trademark lettering (tall,
strong capitals softened by dots and lines) stare out on endless
souvenirs from mugs and tea towels to mirrors and silver jewellery. The style has become so familiar it is known affectionately
as 'Mockintosh', and Glasgow, it seems, can't get enough of it.
Yet Mackintosh's designs flourished for a relatively brief spell in
the early 20th century, and it is only in the last 30 years or so
that serious attempts have been made to preserve the major
works of this remarkable and original architect. Start your tour at
the Lighthouse on Mitchell Lane (map 311 D2; ▷ 112).

HIGHLIGHTS

GLASGOW SCHOOL OF ART (▷ 110)

If you only have limited time to visit Glasgow, then a glimpse of
the School of Art on Renfrew Street is a must. This is authentic
Mackintosh, with strong, confident lines and bold touches of unusual,
stylized decoration. Guided tours show how the architect's
confidence carried through into every detail of the interior design.

WILLOW TEAROOMS

The Willow Tearooms are a short walk away, above a jeweller's shop
at 217 Sauchiehall Street (Mon–Sat 9–5). They offer a magnificent
restored Mackintosh interior upstairs in the Room de Luxe, complete
with mirrored walls inset with purple glass, and tall-backed silver
chairs. First opened in 1904, this became the most famous of local
entrepreneur Kate Cranston's revolutionary tea rooms, where
respectable men and women could meet up, in private or in public,
without the shadow of the 'demon' drink. Mackintosh also designed
interiors for Cranston at Ingram Street, Buchanan Street and Argyle
Street (see surviving elements in the Museum of Scotland ▷ 78–81).

MACKINTOSH HOUSE

Located at the university's Hunterian Museum (▷ 112), this is
the exquisite re-creation of the interior of the home which the

Mackintoshs made together, with original furniture, as it appeared in 1906. The fittings here show clearly the influence of Japanese style on Charles's work, and its combination with his wife's flowing, organic art nouveau patterns. More Mackintosh furniture and designs from buildings now lost are on show in the gallery itself, along with paintings of Mediterranean scenes from his later travels.

HOUSE FOR AN ART LOVER (▷ 111)
Located away from the centre in Bellahouston Park, this is a modern build (1996) of a complete dream house designed by the couple in 1901.

SCOTLAND STREET SCHOOL
For another prime example of Mackintosh's architecture completed in his lifetime, travel south of the river to admire the stunning Scotland

BASICS

ℹ 11 George Square G2 1DY, tel 0141 204 4400

www.crmsociety.com
The Mackintosh Society's excellent website lists details of further buildings plus full biography and events.

TIP

• If you're a Mackintosh fan, take a trip out to Helensburgh to see the Hill House, now owned by the National Trust for Scotland (▷ 94).

A reconstructed Mackintosh interior at the Hunterian

Scotland Street School's façade is dominated by the twin staircase towers; inside, the central hall has a theatrical air

Street School (Mon–Thu, Sat 10–5, Fri, Sun 11–5, tel 0141 287 0500). Built in 1903–06, it ceased to be a school in the 1970s and is now preserved as a museum of education. The front is dominated by two tall, glazed, semicircular towers which contain the main staircases—not winding round, as you might expect from their reference to Scottish baronial style, but uncompromisingly straight and set back from the glass to create a very different light and space. The back of the building reflects a more restrained and Classical style.

ST. MATTHEW'S FREE CHURCH
Located at Queen's Cross, 870 Garscube Road, northwest of the city centre, this is Mackintosh's only complete church, designed in 1897 (Mon–Fri 10–5, also Mar–end Oct Sun 2–5). It follows a simple Gothic revival style, creating a calm interior space. Attention to detail extended to the carvings of stylized birds and foliage on the oak pulpit.

BACKGROUND
Charles Rennie Mackintosh was born in Glasgow in 1868, and at the age of 16 was apprenticed to a firm of architects. While attending evening classes at the School of Art he met Herbert McNair, who became a life-long friend, and Margaret Macdonald (1865–1933), whom he married in 1900. McNair married Margaret's sister Frances, and the two couples, known as 'the Four', came to dominate the emerging Glasgow Style.

Mackintosh's partnership with his wife extended into design, and her input became an acknowledged part of his work. Mackintosh's first project was in 1893, a workaday building for the *Glasgow Herald* newspaper, which is now the Lighthouse. His design for his most famous structure, the School of Art, was commissioned in 1896, and his best work was completed in the first years of the 20th century.

By 1914, his distinctive fusion of the abstracted, flowing lines of art nouveau with the simplicity of the Arts and Crafts movement had passed from fashion in Britain. Disillusioned, he moved to England and later toured Europe—delicate watercolour paintings which survive from this period can be seen at the Hunterian Gallery. He died in 1928.

High-backed Mackintosh chair designed for the Argyle Street Tearooms and now in the School of Art Collection

THE SIGHTS

Provand's Lordship: a house of many identities

PROVAND'S LORDSHIP

🔢 311 E1 • 3 Castle Street, G4 0RB
☎ 0141 552 8819 🕐 Mon–Thu and Sat 10–5, Fri and Sun 11–5 💷 Free
🚌 11, 12, 16, 37, 38, 42, 51, 89, 90
🚇 High Street
www.glasgowmuseums.com

The oldest house in Glasgow, Provand's Lordship lies close to the medieval cathedral (▷ 105) and opposite the St. Mungo Museum, east of the city centre. It was built around 1471 as an almshouse for the care of 12 old men, and until the end of World War I was still in use as a sweet shop. Outside, it is a simple sandstone building facing a busy road junction. Inside, the thick walls and tiny windows muffle the noise of the outside world. A lack of historic atmosphere is compensated for by the collection of beautiful 15th- and 16th-century wooden furniture. A re-created knot garden has been planted at the back.
Don't miss The story of Rab Ha', the weighty 'Glesca Glutton', amid the amusing 19th-century illustrations of Glasgow characters on the top floor. Rab would bet his appetite on horse races and even fox hunts, and was defeated only once, by a dish of oysters with cream and sugar.

SCOTTISH FOOTBALL MUSEUM

🔢 311 D3 • The National Stadium, Hampden Park G42 9BA ☎ 0141 616 6139 🕐 Mon–Sat 10–5, Sun 11–5
💷 Museum: adult £5, child £2.50 (under 5 free); museum and stadium: adult £8, child £4 🚌 5, 7, 12, 31, 34, 37, 66, 74, 75, 89, 90, M2 🚇 Mount Florida via Glasgow Central 🚇 Bridge Street 💻 🏧
www.scottishfootballmuseum.org.uk

Hampden Park is the home of Scotland's oldest football (soccer) team, Queen's Park, who claim to have invented the

Unusual perspective in Dalí's Christ of St. John of the Cross

ST. MUNGO MUSEUM OF RELIGIOUS LIFE AND ART

A thought-provoking and beautifully presented collection of religious art and objects from the major world faiths.

🔢 311 E2 • 2 Castle Street G4 0RH ☎ 0141 553 2557 🕐 Mon–Thu and Sat 10–5, Fri and Sun 11–5 💷 Free 🚌 11, 12, 16, 37, 38, 42, 51, 89, 90 🚇 High Street 🍴 £4.99 🍴 Modern restaurant on ground floor 🛍 Ground-floor gift shop stocks unusual cards, jewellery and books
www.glasgowmuseums.com

RATINGS			
Good for kids	●	●	●
Historic interest	●	●	● ●
Specialist shopping	●	●	●

Enter this modern building near the cathedral (▷ 105) through the calm space of a Zen gravel garden. The museum is on three floors, with an international art collection, objects relating to religious life, and a section about religion in Glasgow. In the Gallery of Religious Art on the first floor, a native American chilkat blanket woven with animal designs of whales, wolves and beavers rubs shoulders with an Australian Aboriginal Dreamtime painting and the popping figures of a Nigerian ancestral screen. European art is represented by exquisite stained-glass panels, backlit and hanging at eye level, including a Burne-Jones angel with crimson halo, and Salvador Dalí's 1951 painting, *Christ of St. John of the Cross*. The Gallery of Religious Life juxtaposes items associated with particular ceremonies from different cultures.

On the third floor, dedicated to religion in Glasgow, look out for the moral tale, *Buy your own Cherries*, a lantern slide show used by temperance preachers to show the evils of drink. A display tells the story of the Protestant/Catholic divide in the city, and there is a thought-provoking exhibit about religion, society and poverty. In a hands-on section, children can learn the basics of Buddhism, Christianity, Hinduism, Islam, Judaism and Sikhism.
Don't miss Third-floor views to the Necropolis (▷ 110)—binoculars are available on request.

THE SIGHTS

Admiring a trophy at the Scottish Football Museum

passing style of the game as it is played today. So it's appropriate that this is also the site of the world's first national football museum. An air of vanished glory haunts the 2,500 items on display. They include part of the original Hampden dressing room as it was known to great players of the past. You can even experience the 'Hampden roar' of the 1930s, when 140,000 men would pack in here for the big games. Tours of the modern pitch take place every hour and last 45 minutes.

TALL SHIP AT GLASGOW HARBOUR

➕ 310 C2 • 100 Stobcross Road G3 8QQ ☎ 0141 222 2513 🕐 Mar–end Oct daily 10–5; rest of year daily 10–4 💷 Adult £4.95, child £2.50 (1 free per full paying adult, under 5 free) 🚌 64 🚇 Finnieston/ Exhibition Centre 🚇 Partick, Kelvinhall 🍴 📷
www.thetallship.com

The best view of this fine old steel-hulled sailing ship, moored on the River Clyde near the 'Armadillo' exhibition centre, is from the windows of the Science Centre, opposite (▷ 111). The SV *Glenlee* was built on the Clyde in 1896, and carried mixed cargoes four times around the world before serving as a training ship for the Spanish Navy. She was eventually rescued in 1993 and brought here for refurbishment. Today she's one of only five Clyde-built sailing ships left afloat. On board, you can see the huge cargo hold, the restored crew's quarters and the galley, complete with original sounds and smells. Access is through the Pumphouse Visitor Centre, with changing exhibitions, nautical gift shop and café-bar. **Don't miss** Tales of the ship's voyages, told on board on the 'Tween Deck.

The everyday clutter of pots and dishes in the homey kitchen

THE TENEMENT HOUSE

A rewarding insight into one woman's very ordinary life in a Glasgow tenement.

➕ 311 D1 •145 Buccleuch Street, Garnethill G3 6QN ☎ 0141 333 0183 🕐 Mar–end Oct daily 1–5 💷 (NTS) adult £5, child £4 (under 5 free), family £14 🚌 11, 20, 66, 66A, 66B 🚇 Charing Cross 🚇 Cowcaddens 📖 £3.50, also in French, German and Italian 🎫 Small range of items at ticket desk ♿ ❓ Display about tenements in lower apartment, also owned by NTS
www.nts.org.uk

In the 19th and early 20th centuries, most Glaswegians lived in tenement houses, or flats, with each apartment occupying rooms on one floor level, and sharing communal facilities such as a wash-house. In poorer districts these could be horribly overcrowded, with whole families sharing one room.

This compact little house gives a clear picture of tenement life for the slightly better off. From 1911 it was the home of spinster Agnes Toward, a shorthand typist, and her mother, a seamstress. Agnes never threw anything away, and when she died in 1975, her house was found to provide a unique time capsule of social history. Remarkably, it was preserved, and is now in the care of the National Trust for Scotland.

Climb the stairs, knock at the door and you are admitted to admire the hall, with its grandfather clock and wooden Scotch chest, suggesting past family wealth; the kitchen with its curtained box bed and state-of-the-art coal-fired range, still used by Agnes in the 1960s; the parlour with its lace drapes, rosewood piano and concealed, recessed bed; the bedroom, with its pretty floral-tiled fireplace and holiday suitcases; and the bathroom, a feature of comparative luxury.
Don't miss The unusual brass and shell watch-holder on the bedroom dressing table, and the hissing gas lights that illuminate the rooms.

RATINGS			
Good for kids	●	●	●
Historic interest	●	●	●	●

TIP
● Signage at the front of the house is low key and easily missed, so check on a map before you go.

MAKE A DAY OF IT
People's Palace

HIGHLANDS AND ISLANDS

The Highlands and Islands cover the wild high country of the northern mainland and the islands along the western coast. For many this area, with its remote fortifications, lonely glens and some of Britain's last true wilderness areas, epitomizes the outstanding natural beauty of Scotland.

KEY SIGHTS

Aberdeen is known as the granite city

The high mountain pass northwards into Applecross

Pretty Findochty is particularly popular with painters

ABERDEEN

✚ 323 L7 🅸 23 Union Street AB11 5BP, tel 01224 288828 🅿 Aberdeen ✖ Aberdeen
www.agtb.org

Scotland's third city was once its biggest seaside resort, thanks to the miles of golden sands that stretch north from the mouth of the River Don. Today Aberdeen has a businesslike air and is better known as the oil capital of Europe (▷ 36). Its foundations as a royal burgh date back to the early 12th century, and it grew into a major port for access to the Continent, trading in wool, fish, and scholars from its two universities. The harbour is still the heart of the city.

North of the centre, in the Old Town, St. Machar's Cathedral, with its distinctive twin towers, dates from 1520. In the late 18th century the town expanded, and many of Aberdeen's finest granite buildings in the New Town date from the 19th century. Architect Archibald Simpson (1790–1847) is associated with many, including the Union Buildings and Assembly Rooms Music Hall on Union Street. Marischal College, on Broad Street, with its stunning Perpendicular frontage, was completed in 1895.

Provost Ross's House on Shiprow (1593) has the lively Aberdeen Maritime Museum (Mon–Sat 10–5, Sun 12–3), with exhibits that include an intriguing 8.5m (30ft) scale model of an oil rig.

The Aberdeen Art Gallery on Schoolhill has an outstanding collection of 18th- to 20th-century paintings (Mon–Sat 10–5, Sun 2–5). And if a cold wind is blowing off the North Sea, you can retreat to the warmth of the winter gardens in Duthie Park, one of Europe's largest covered gardens.

APPLECROSS

✚ 320 D6 🅸 Main Street, Lochcarron IV54 8YB, tel 01520 722357; seasonal

The strung-out settlements on this remote west-coast peninsula only became fully accessible by road in the 1970s. Today this winding single-track road is the slow, scenic route between Kishorn and Shieldaig. It takes in the dramatic mountain pass of Bealach-Na-Ba, or Pass of the Cattle, to the south, and the southern shore of Loch Torridon to the north. (Note: Bealach-Na-Ba is not suitable for vehicles towing caravans (trailers).) In between, acid moors and hummocks stretch to mountains inland, with the scattered remains of deserted villages along the coast, overlooking Raasay and Skye (▷ 138–141). Applecross Bay is a welcoming curve of pinkish sand, with an excellent little inn noted for its seafood (▷ 261).

ARDNAMURCHAN

✚ 320 C8 🅸 Kilchoan Community Centre, Pier Road, Kilchoan PH36 4LJ, tel 01972 510222 🚢 Ferry from Tobermory on Mull to Kilchoan, summer only

Ardnamurchan is a narrow finger of land that points west between the Small Isles and Mull. It remains one of Scotland's prettiest hidden corners, thanks to its remote location and narrow, winding roads, which lead through woodland of oak and birch, dripping with lichen, to more exposed country and a lighthouse on the farthest tip of rock, the most westerly point in mainland Britain (visitor centre: Apr–end Oct daily 10–5). It's a good place for spotting seals and even otters, if you're lucky.

An intriguing Natural History Centre at Glenmore explains the geological interest of this area, as well as wildlife (Easter–end Oct Mon–Sat 10.30–5.30, Sun 12–5.30).

Don't miss The silver sand dunes of Sanna Bay.

BANFFSHIRE COAST

✚ 323 K5 🅸 Collie Lodge, Low Street, Banff AB45 1AU, tel 01261 812419; seasonal

The coastline to the west and east of Banff is riddled with little fishing harbours and appealing rocky bays, as the fertile fields give way to an unexpectedly wild and rugged shore. To the west, Buckie is a sprawling fishing town, with the more charming neighbours of Findochty (pronounced 'Finechty') and Portknockie. Cullen, on a magnificent sandy bay, is picturesque, its tightly packed terraces set end-on to the sea are dominated by the arching railway viaduct.

Portsoy is a holiday town with a little stone harbour, its prosperity built on export of the local serpentine marble (it was used for fireplaces in the French palace of Versailles).

The town of Banff itself is much older than its genteel 18th-century heart, with Duff House (▷ 124) on the outskirts. To the east, the coast road continues through unlovely Macduff (but see the Marine Aquarium, ▷ 134) to the more remote villages of Gardenstown and Crovie, huddled under the red cliffs of Buchan on Gamrie Bay. The latter tiny, isolated settlement, pronounced 'Croovie', is accessible only on foot from a parking area. The road into Pennan is also steep, but well worth the difficulty. Its single row of cottages backed up against the cliff, with a small hotel in the middle, will be instantly familiar to fans of the 1983 movie *Local Hero*, which was filmed here.

THE SIGHTS

The River Dee rises in the Cairngorms before tumbling through the rocks at Braemar

RATINGS	
Historic interest	● ● ●
Outdoors	● ● ● ● ●
Photo stops	● ● ● ●
Specialist shopping	● ● ●

BASICS

✚ 322 J7

🛈 The Mews, Mar Road, Braemar
AB35 5YL, tel 01339 741600; seasonal

www.braemarscotland.co.uk
Practical and elegant guide to the town,
with fascinating insights into the
workings of the local big estates.

MAKE A DAY OF IT

Aberdeen; Crathes Castle

*The grandeur of the Old
Royal Station recalls its
Victorian heyday*

BRAEMAR AND DEESIDE

**The long valley of the Dee from Braemar to Banchory offers
scenic splendour fit for a queen.**

When, in 1852, Queen Victoria and Prince Albert picked an estate
between Ballater and Braemar on which to build their holiday home,
the entire Dee Valley acquired a cachet that it has never quite lost.
Members of the royal family, including the Queen, still spend their
summer holidays at Balmoral Castle (exhibition Apr–end Jul daily
10–5), enjoying country sports in the surrounding hills and forests.
    West of the busy town of Braemar, a narrow road leads upstream
to the Linn of Dee, where the river plunges down between polished
rocks into foaming pools. This is part of the 29,380ha (72,598 acre)
Mar Lodge Estate, managed by the National Trust for Scotland, and
including a number of signposted walks. The road ends near the Earl
of Mar's Punchbowl, another beauty spot where, it is said, the Earl
brewed punch in a natural bowl in the rocks before the Jacobite
uprising of 1715.

EAST FROM BRAEMAR

From Braemar the A93 follows the route of the river as it flows for
60 miles (96km) to the coast at Aberdeen. Ballater is a small
granite-built town, once the terminus of a branch train line. This is
celebrated at the Old Royal Station, now an information centre and
tea room (Jun–end Sep 9–6; Oct–end May 10–5) which recalls the
days when famous guests would
alight here on their way to Balmoral.
Royal provisions still come from the
town, as can be seen by the coats of
arms everywhere from the bakery to
outdoor clothing shops. To the east
lies Glen Tanar, with birch woods at
the Muir of Dinnet, and good
walking over the Grampian hills to
the Glens of Angus. Banchory marks
the shift into lower Deeside.
Don't miss The footbridge at Bridge
of Feugh, south of Banchory, from
which you can watch salmon leaping
the Falls of Feugh.

Kisimul was home to the lawless and piratical MacNeil clan

Rocks at Cape Wrath mark the northern tip of mainland Britain

Shakespeare's Macbeth was Thane (lord) of Cawdor

BARRA

➕ 319 A7 ℹ️ Main Street, Castlebay, Isle of Barra HS9 5XD, tel 01871 810336; seasonal ✈️ Flights from Glasgow and Benbecula ⛴️ Ferry from Lochboisdale on South Uist, Enskay and Oban to Castlebay

This island at the foot of the Outer Hebridean chain has an interest out of all proportion to its size, just 5 miles (8km) across and 8 miles (12.8km) long. Arriving is part of the fun—especially if you choose to come by air and land on the tidal shell beach of Traigh Mhor.

A road runs around the island but is only 12 miles (19.3km) long, making this a haven for bicycling and walking. In spring and summer the island is rich in wild flowers, with the machair (sea meadow) on the western side at its best. Barra survives on crofting and tourism, and the Gaelic culture flourishes.

Bagh a Chaisteil (Castlebay) is the main settlement, with Kisimul Castle, seat of the MacNeils since 1427 on a tiny island in the bay. (HS, Apr–end Sep daily 9.30–6.30). The heritage centre, Dualchas, explores the history of the island (Mar–end May, Sep Mon, Wed, Fri 11–4; Jun–end Aug Mon–Fri 11–4).

BLACK ISLE

➕ 322 G5 ℹ️ North Kessock Picnic Site, North Kessock, IV1 1XB, tel 01463 731505; seasonal

Neither black nor an island, the Black Isle is the broad and fertile peninsula immediately north of Inverness, bordered by three firths or river estuaries: Cromarty, Beauly and Moray. Wild sea cliffs tip down to low-lying ground in the west, with a central wooded ridge of Ardmeanach, a name which originally covered the whole area. The harbour town of

Cromarty, largely rebuilt in the late 18th century, occupies the northeast point. Its history is told in the Courthouse Museum on Church Street (Apr–end Oct daily 10–5; Nov, Dec 12–4). Cromarty's most famous son was Hugh Miller (1802–56), a geologist and fossil collector who did much to popularize natural history. His statue stands above the town, and his thatched cottage is a museum (NTS, Apr–end Sep daily 12–5; Oct Sun–Wed).

BRAEMAR AND DEESIDE

See page 120

THE CAIRNGORMS

See page 122

CAPE WRATH

➕ 326 F2 ℹ️ Durine, Durness IV27 4PN, tel 01971 511259; seasonal

The far northwestern corner of Scotland feels like another country, with silvery light reflected from the grey quartzite mountains, and everywhere emptiness and space. If you want to get to Cape Wrath, prepare for a short ferry ride over the Kyle of Durness (May–end Sep), then a minibus ride across the bleak moor called The Parph. The road passes between the peaks of Sgribhisbheinn (371m/1,217ft) and Fashven (457m/1,499ft) to reach the sheer 280m (920ft) Clo Mor cliffs and the remote lighthouse, built in 1828, which blinks out over the Atlantic. Durness is a scattered settlement, with Smoo Cave to the east. Just west of Durness, Balnakeil has a beautiful sandy beach and an unusual craft village, which occupies a former military installation.

CASTLE FRASER

➕ 323 K7 • Sauchen, Inverurie AB51 7LD ☎️ 01330 833463 🕐 Apr–end

Jun, Sep Sat–Sun, Tue–Thu 12–5; Jul, Aug daily 11–5; Nov, Dec Sat–Sun 12–4 💷 (NTS) adult £8, child £5, family £20 📷 🏛️ www.nts.org.uk

This magnificent turreted tower house, 16 miles (25.8km) west of Aberdeen, was built between 1575 and 1636. The original structure, known as Muchalls-in-Mar, was remodelled at that time to give it the distinctive Z-plan by the addition of a square tower at one corner and a round one at the opposite corner. The changes were made by the 6th Laird, Michael Fraser, and the castle remained in that family until the 20th century. Family portraits are displayed inside, along with a rich collection of carpets and drapes. The surrounding estate is extensive, with waymarked walks and a walled garden.

CAWDOR CASTLE

➕ 322 H6 • Nairn IV12 5RD ☎️ 01667 404401 🕐 Jun to mid-Oct daily 10–5.30 💷 Adult £6.80, child £4 (under 5 free), family £19.50. Gardens only, £3.50 📷 🍴 🏛️ www.cawdorcastle.com

The name of Cawdor evokes Shakespeare's *Macbeth*. It stands inland, between Inverness and Nairn, with a central tower dating back to 1454, a drawbridge, and proud turrets and wings that proclaim later additions. It is the home of Angelika, the Dowager Countess of Cawdor, and the presentation of family portraits and treasures within is refreshingly relaxed and even light-hearted. The influence of the owner and her late husband is most clearly seen in the gardens, which are symbolically themed. They include a holly maze surrounded by a tunnel of golden laburnum, and the mysterious Paradise Garden with a seven-pointed star at its core.

THE SIGHTS

Winter frosting: The Cairngorms are Britain's premier ski destination

RATINGS	
Good for kids	●●●○
Outdoors	●●●●●
Photo stops	●●●○
Specialist shopping	●○

BASICS

✚ 322 H7 🚉 Grampian Road, Aviemore PH22 1PP, tel 01479 810363
🚂 Aviemore

www.cairngorms.co.uk
Excellent National Park website, covering every aspect of life in the National Park.

MAKE A DAY OF IT

Highland Folk Museum; Strathspey

Summer brings the sailboards and boats on to Loch Morlich

THE CAIRNGORMS

The highest massif in Britain, with alpine flora and rare wildlife, attracts walkers, rock climbers and skiers.

The Cairngorm mountains lie between Speyside and Braemar (▷ 137, 120), dominated by the four peaks of Ben Macdhui (1,309m/4,295ft), Braeriach (1,295m/4,249ft), Cairn Toul (1,293m/4,242ft) and Cairn Gorm (1,245m/4,085ft). Between them runs the ancient north–south pass of the Lairig Ghru, and around the northwest edge the settlements of Speyside and the resort of Aviemore. The remoteness of the Cairngorms has left them the haunt of golden eagles, ptarmigan, capercaillie and other species that thrive in the deserted corries amid unusual alpine flora. The area was designated Scotland's second national park in 2003.

AROUND AVIEMORE

The once-sleepy train station of Aviemore was developed in the 1960s as a ski destination, and while some of the most brutal specimens of architecture from this period have been razed, it has little to recommend it unless you are part of the ski scene.

The Rothiemurchus Estate, 1.5 miles (2.4km) to the south (daily 9–5.30), offers a variety of outdoor pursuits with beautiful mountains, lochs and Caledonian pine forest. This is the remains of the Old Wood of Caledon which once covered much of the country, harbouring wolves and bears. A good walk leads around Loch an Eilean.

Aviemore is linked by the preserved Strathspey Steam Railway (tel 01479 810725 for times) to Boat of Garten. The Royal Society for the Protection of Birds (RSPB) has a visitor centre here (Apr–end Aug daily 10–6), with a camera watching the ospreys which nest on nearby Loch Garten. A funicular railway in the Cairngorm ski area east of Aviemore takes visitors up the flank of Cairn Gorm itself, terminating in the highest shop and restaurant complex in Britain (May to mid-Jun, Sep–end Nov daily 10–5.15; Jun–Sep Fri, Sat sunset dining).
Don't miss The ancient landscapes of Rothiemurchus; watching the ospreys on Loch Garten.

Gulf Stream warmth encourages growth at Benmore Gardens

Craigievar, a perfectly preserved Scottish tower house

The Crinan basin is at the seaward end of the canal

THE SIGHTS

COWAL AND BUTE

⊞ 316 E11 🛈 7 Alexandra Parade, Dunoon PA23 8AB, tel 01369 703785 🛈 Isle of Bute Discovery Centre, 55 Victoria Street, Rothesay PA20 0AH, tel 01700 502151

The Cowal peninsula points its fingers down from Arrochar, caught between Loch Long and Loch Fyne. Its top reaches are covered in forestry, and are part of the Loch Lomond national park (▷ 98). Dunoon is the only town of size, a holiday resort with a statue to Robert Burns's love, 'Highland Mary', born nearby. Benmore, 7 miles (11.3km) to the north, is an outpost of Edinburgh's Royal Botanic Garden, with particularly good autumn foliage (Apr–end Sep daily 10–6; Mar, Oct daily 10–5).

Elsewhere the landscape is of mountains and wild moorland intersected by sea lochs, including Holy Loch, formerly a submarine base. To the south, captured in the long fingers of Cowal, is the low-lying island of Bute, with the small town of Rothesay once a pleasure ground for steamers from Glasgow. Mount Stuart, in the southern sector, is a sumptuous Victorian mansion (Easter–end Sep Sun–Fri 11–5 Sat 10–2.30).

CRAIGIEVAR CASTLE

⊞ 323 K7 • Alford AB33 8JF ☎ 013398 83635 🛈 Grounds: daily 9.30–dusk 🛈 Grounds only: free (restricted access) www.nts.org.uk

The quintessential Scottish baronial tower house, Craigievar has a fairy-tale quality that makes it stand out from its fellows. It was built by merchant trader William Forbes between 1600 and 1626, and—unusually— remained unaltered in the following centuries of occupation by the Forbes and Forbes-

Sempill families. The result is a six-storey pinkish-harled fantasy of turrets on a central Great Tower, a delight to the eye in the leafy setting of the Don Valley. While the surrounding policies (gardens) remain open to the public, the castle itself is likely to be closed until spring 2007, when the scaffolding that restricts light inside (there is no electric lighting) is removed.

CRARAE GARDENS

⊞ 316 E10 • Inveraray PA32 8YA ☎ 01546 886614 🛈 Garden: daily 9.30–dusk. Visitor centre: Apr–end Sep daily 10–5 🛈 (NTS) Adult £5, child £4 (under 5 free), family £14 🛈 🛈 www.crarae-gardens.org.uk

This hillside garden lies on the shores of Loch Fyne, between Inveraray and Lochgilphead. It was the creation of Captain George Campbell, who began the transformation of a narrow Highland glen into a Himalayan gorge in 1925. Today it is cared for by the National Trust for Scotland, and boasts over 400 species of rhododendrons and azaleas, which thrive in the mild, damp climate and acid soils. This is primarily a woodland garden, with paths winding through the eucalypts and other trees. A 20ha (50 acre) forest garden is a newish development, with fresh planting of native, broadleaved species. Look out for the Neolithic chambered cairn (c2500BC) by the picnic site.

CRATHES CASTLE

See page 124

CRINAN CANAL

⊞ 315 D11 🛈 27 Lochnell Street, Lochgilphead PA31 8JN, tel 01546 602344; seasonal

Winding for 9 miles (14.5km) between Ardrishaig on Loch Fyne and Crinan harbour on the

Sound of Jura, the Crinan Canal is a narrow waterway through an attractive region of woodland and open marsh. It was built in 1793–1809 by the engineer John Rennie (1761–1821), when fishing craft and 'puffers'— the small steam-driven boats which transported vital supplies to all parts of the Scottish coast— used it to avoid the 130-mile (209km) trip around the Kintyre peninsula. Today it is still well used by yachts and small fishing boats, which must negotiate 15 locks along its course. The tow path provides good walks from Lochgilphead, Cairnbaan and Crinan itself.

Don't miss The bustle of the canal basin at Crinan, with views to Duntrune Castle and the island of Jura.

CULLODEN

See page 125

DORNOCH

⊞ 322 H4 🛈 The Square IV25 3SD, tel 845 225 5121

A stone marks the spot near the golf course in Dornoch where, in 1727, Janet Horne was tarred, feathered and burned. Accused of changing her daughter into a pony, she was the last witch in Scotland to be executed. Today, there's little sign of such outrageous practices in the quiet streets of this east-coast town, which is better known for its world-class golf course, sandy beaches and dolphin-watching expeditions. The cathedral, once the seat of the bishops of Caithness, dates from the 13th century. Skibo Castle, 4 miles (6.4km) west, was the retreat of American philanthropist Andrew Carnegie (▷ 33). Now an exclusive golf resort, it was the centre of a maelstrom in December 2000 when pop icon Madonna held her wedding there.

Duff House once served as a sanitorium, and is now restored

THE SIGHTS

DUFF HOUSE

323 K5 • Banff AB45 3SX ☎ 01261 818181 ⏰ Apr–Oct daily 11–5; rest of year Thu–Sun 11–4 💷 Adult £5.50, child £4.50, family £14 ▯ ▦
www.duffhouse.com

Tucked away in an apparently quiet corner of Banff, Duff House is the principal outstation of the National Galleries of Scotland, providing the perfect, glittering backdrop to a wealth of paintings including portraits by the Scottish painters Raeburn and Ramsay, and paintings of the Italian, Dutch and German schools of art. The house itself is a grand mansion designed by architect William Adam for the 1st Earl of Fife. It was started in 1735, but unfortunately the Earl's pride in his new house was seriously dented when a crack appeared in the structure, and he never lived there.
Don't miss El Greco's *St. Jerome in Penitence.*

DUNROBIN CASTLE

326 H4 • Golspie KW10 6SF
☎ 01408 633177 ⏰ Apr, May, 1 Oct to mid-Oct Mon–Sat 10.30–4.30, Sun 12–4.30; Jun–end Sep Mon–Sat 10.30–5.30, Sun 12–5.30; also Jul, Aug Sun 10.30–5.30 💷 Adult £6.80, child £4.70, family £18 🚉 Dunrobin ▯ ▦
www.highlandescape.com

Looming above its gardens like a French château and lying just 0.5 miles (800m) north of the east-coast village of Golspie, Dunrobin Castle boasts 189 rooms, making it the largest mansion in northern Scotland. It dates back to c1275, but its outward appearance is overwhelmingly Victorian, thanks to extensions between 1845 and 1850 by Sir Charles Barry (better known as the architect of London's Houses of Parliament).

Continued on page 126

High hedges create a micro-climate in which the gardens thrive

CRATHES CASTLE
A fairy-tale turreted castle set in stunning gardens.

323 L7 • Banchory AB31 5QJ ☎ 01330 844525 ⏰ Gardens: all year daily 9–dusk. Castle and visitor centre: Apr–end Sep daily 10.30–5; Oct daily 10–4.30 💷 (NTS) Adult £10, child £7 (under 5 free), family £25. Castle or gardens only: adult £8, child £5 🍴 ▦ 🚻
www.nts.org.uk

In 1323 Robert the Bruce gifted a parcel of land, east of Banchory, to Alexander Burnard (Burnett) of Leys, presenting him with a carved and bejewelled ivory horn as a symbol of tenure. In 1553 a castle was started on the site, which took almost 50 years to complete. It is now a delightful example of a baronial-style tower house, and famous for its Jacobean ceilings, boldly painted with figures, designs and mottoes.

RATINGS	
Historic interest	● ● ●
Photo stops	● ● ● ●

TIP
● Be prepared to wait; to contain numbers, entry to the castle itself is by timed tickets.

MAKE A DAY OF IT
Braemar; Castle Fraser; Craigievar

While the interior of the castle presents the comfortable setting of mellow furnishings, oak-carved panels and family portraits you might expect, it is the 1.5ha (3.75-acre) walled garden glimpsed from the windows which steals the show.

Massive hedges of Irish yew, planted up to 300 years ago, and carved into undulating 'egg and cup' topiary sculptures, dominate the upper garden. They frame and shelter themed 'rooms', helping to create a micro-climate in which a rich variety of plants thrive. The deep herbaceous borders of the lower garden are breathtaking in the colour and variety of their planting, with the June border linking the vistas of the castle and a venerable doocote (dovecote). In their present form, these remarkable gardens reflect a labour of love by Sir James and Lady Sybil Burnett in the early 20th century, and their work is continued by the National Trust for Scotland.
Don't miss In the High Hall of the castle, the treasured Horn of Leys.

There are few landmarks on this bleak spot, but memorial stones mark where clans fell in battle

CULLODEN

A boggy moor on a windy ridge 5 miles (8km) east of Inverness, the emotive scene of the final battle fought on Scottish soil, when Bonnie Prince Charlie made his last stand.

The Jacobite defeat at the Battle of Culloden, fought on 16 April 1746, was the dismal outcome of a civil war that had split families and hastened the end of the already disintegrating clan system in Scotland.

Prince Charles Edward Stuart (1720–88), later known as Bonnie Prince Charlie, was raised in European exile, the heir to the Scottish throne that the Catholic Stuarts still claimed through James, the Old Pretender (Jacobus in Latin, hence Jacobite as the name for the political movement). The French were keen on stirring up political matters with the Protestant Hanoverian government in Britain, and encouraged the Prince's madcap expedition to claim the throne in 1745.

Charles landed at Glenfinnan (▷ 128) and raised a mixed bag of Highland fighters, some of them coerced by their chiefs. Initially the Prince's army was successful, and reached Derby in central England before running out of steam. The Highlanders retreated northwards, but by the spring of 1746 the Hanoverian forces were closing in.

AN ARMY IN RETREAT

When the two armies met at Culloden, the Prince's outnumbered and exhausted forces faced an army of regular soldiers. A tactical blunder placed his Highlanders within range of the government artillery, and the Jacobites were blown away in under an hour. More than 1,200 Jacobites and 400 Hanoverians died in the battle. Stones and flags mark the battlefield today, to show where individual clans fell.

In the aftermath, the government leader the Duke of Cumberland earned the title of 'Butcher' when he sanctioned one of the worst atrocities ever carried out by the British Army. Military looting was legalized throughout the Highlands, irrespective of loyalties, and the Highland way of life changed for ever. Jacobite propaganda retreated into sentimentality, and the romantic figure of the Prince in hiding, never betrayed as he fled to exile, became legendary.

Don't miss Living history presentations in summer at restored Leanach Cottage, which survived at the heart of the battle.

RATINGS				
Good for kids	●	●	●	
Historic interest	●	●	●	●	●
Photostops	●	●		
Walkability	●	●	●	

BASICS

✚ 322 G6 • Culloden Moor, Inverness IV2 5EU ☎ 01463 790607

🕐 Site: all year daily. Visitor centre: Nov, Dec, Feb, Mar daily 11–4; Apr, May, Sep, Oct daily 9–5.30; Jun–end Aug daily 9–6 💷 (NTS) Adult £5, child £4 (under 5 free), family £14

📖 Guidebook £3.50; also in French and German 🍽 Restaurant in visitor centre 📽 ❓ Audio-visual programme in French, Gaelic, German, Italian, Japanese

www.nts.org.uk
Informative and efficient website for all 100 or so National Trust for Scotland properties, organized by region. Also useful for special events listings.

TIP

● See the audio-visual exhibition in the visitor centre before you explore the battlefield, to understand what you are seeing.

MAKE A DAY OF IT

Black Isle; Forres; Great Glen; Inverness

Eilean Donan, the epitome of a Highland castle

Towering Sueno's Stone is encased in protective glass

There are great views from the cable car on Aonach Mòr

Continued from page 124

Dunrobin was the seat of the Earls and Dukes of Sutherland, censured by history for their actions during the Highland Clearances (▷ 142, Strathnaver).
Don't miss Daily falconry displays in the French-style gardens.

EILEAN DONAN CASTLE

✚ 320 E6 • Dornie, by Kyle of Lochalsh IV40 8DX ☎ 01599 555202 ◷ Mar, Nov daily 10–3.30; Apr–end Oct daily 10–5.30 ▥ Adult £4.75, child £3.75 (under 6 free), family £9.75 ▢ ▦ www.eileandonancastle.com

Probably the most photographed castle in Scotland, Eilean Donan is perched on a rock near the northern shore of Loch Duich, and joined to the mainland by a bridge. There has been a fortification on the site since the 13th century, and a MacRae stronghold was destroyed here by government troops in 1719. The perfect castle as seen today, complete with stone walls up to 4.3m (14ft) thick, is the result of rebuilding between 1912 and 1932. It is said that its creator, Lt Col John MacRae-Gilstrap, saw an image of how it might look in a dream, and there is certainly an idealized quality to it, which has seen it star in many a calendar and in several films. Not to be missed.

FORRES

✚ 322 H5 ⓘ 116 High Street IV36 1NP, tel 01309 672938; seasonal ⓡ Forres

The ancient market town of Forres on the River Findhorn, 10 miles (16km) east of Nairn, was once plagued by witches. William Shakespeare made full use of this in *Macbeth* (c1606), when he set scenes with the three 'weird sisters' in the area. Three more witches are commemorated with an iron-bound stone in the town.

A huge glass box protects Sueno's Stone, on the eastern outskirts. This is a Pictish cross-slab which stands 6m (20ft) tall and is believed to date from the 9th or 10th century (free access). The sandstone is intricately carved in five sections with vivid scenes from an unidentified and bloody battle.

To the south of Forres, the Dallas Dhu Historic Distillery is preserved by Historic Scotland (Apr–end Sep daily 9.30–6.30; rest of year Sat–Wed 9.30–4.30).
Don't miss Califer viewpoint, east of town, off the A96, for superb views of the Moray coastline.

FORT WILLIAM

✚ 321 E8 ⓘ Cameron Centre, Cameron Square PH33 6AJ, tel 01397 703781 ⓡ Fort William

Fort William's location on road and train junctions at the head of Loch Linnhe and the foot of the Great Glen (▷ 128) makes it a convenient touring base for the northwest. The town's heyday as a military outpost for subduing the Highlands is long gone—the fort, which had withstood Jacobite attacks in 1715 and 1745, was knocked down in 1864 to make space for a train station. The town grew after this period, and is unappealing in itself, despite pedestrianization of the centre and other attempts to give it a clearer identity. Its strategic position makes it a popular hub for walkers and mountaineers, and shops are well stocked with outdoor gear.

Fort William's biggest attraction lies to the east: the rounded bulk of Ben Nevis. At 1,343m (4,406ft) this is Britain's highest mountain. Conditions at the top can be arctic on the best of days, and walkers should take all necessary precautions before attempting to climb it. On the first Saturday in September you may be overtaken by runners—entrants in the annual Ben Nevis Race, established in 1937. The record currently stands at 1 hour 25 minutes. There are easier walks through the more gentle landscape of Glen Nevis, west and south of the mountain, which lead to Steall Falls.
Don't miss The 15-minute gondola ride up Aonach Mòr (1,219m/3,998ft), the mountain beside Ben Nevis (Jul, Aug daily 9.30–6; Jan–end Jun, Sep to mid-Nov daily 10–5 weather permitting).

FYVIE CASTLE

✚ 323 L6 • near Turriff AB53 8JS ☎ 01651 891266 ◷ Castle: Apr–end Jun, Sep Sat–Wed 12–5; Jul, Aug daily 11–5. Grounds: all year daily 9.30–dusk ▥ (NTS) Adult £8, child £5 (under 5 free), family £20 ▢ ▦ www.nts.org.uk

This magnificent mansion, set in a landscaped park in the valley of the River Ythan, has a cream-harled frontage 46m (150ft) long, dominated by the massive gatehouse. It is said that five of Scotland's great families—the Prestons, Meldrums, Setons, Gordons and Leiths—each contributed a tower as they owned the castle in turn. The oldest part dates from the 13th century and incorporates the architectural highlight: a spiral staircase of broad, shallow stone steps known as a wheel-stair, a 16th-century addition. Opulent interiors were created in the early 20th century, making a rich backdrop to the armoury collections and portraits by Raeburn, Romney, Gainsborough and Hoppner.

THE SIGHTS

Springtime in Glencoe: heading west down the valley, past the Three Sisters, left

GLENCOE

A dramatic valley through high mountains in the west, resonant with one of the most infamous events in Scotland's history.

RATINGS				
Historic interest	●	●	●	
Outdoors	●	●	●	●
Photo stops	●	●	●	●

Whether your first approach to Glencoe is down from the wide, watery wasteland of Rannoch Moor, or up from the finger of sea that is Loch Leven, you cannot fail to be impressed by the majesty of this long, steep-sided valley. On a clear day you can see the tops of the Aonach Eagach ridge to the north (966m/3,169ft), with its sweeping sides of loose scree, and the peaks of the great spurs of rock known as the Three Sisters to the south, leading down from Bidean nam Bian (1,148m/3,766ft). At the eastern end the glen is guarded by the massive bulk of Buachaille Etive Mor, the 'Great Shepherd of Etive' (1,019m/3,343ft). On other days the tops are hidden in a smirr (mist) of rain clouds, the waterfalls become torrents and wind funnels up the glen at a terrific rate.

This is prime mountaineering country, and not for the unfit or unwary. In winter it becomes its own snow-filled world, offering an extra challenge to climbers and regularly claiming lives. There is a ski area on the flanks of Meall a'Bhùiridh (1,108m/3,635ft). Learn more at the eco-friendly visitor centre, Inverrigan (NTS, Mar daily 10–4; Apr–end Aug daily 9.30–5.30; Sep, Oct daily 10–5; Nov–end Feb Fri–Mon 10–4).

BASICS

✚ 316 E8 ℹ Ballachulish PA39 4JR, tel 01855 811296; seasonal

www.glencoe-nts.org.uk
National Trust for Scotland website includes information on Glencoe village, visitor centre and Dalness area in nearby Glen Etive.

A dreadful massacre took place here on a winter's night, 1692

MAKE A DAY OF IT
Fort William; Great Glen; Oban

CAMPBELLS AND MACDONALDS

Memories are long in the Highlands, and there is still a frisson between Macdonalds and Campbells that dates back to a February night in 1692. At a time when clan leaders were required to swear loyalty to the monarchs William and Mary, Alastair Macdonald of Glencoe left the unsavoury task as late as possible. When he missed the deadline by a few days, Campbell of Glenlyon was sent to make an example of him. Campbell's men were billeted here for two weeks before turning on their hosts in an act of cold-blooded slaughter that left 38 dead. It was a betrayal that has never been forgotten.

A low autumn mist hangs over the River Affric

The view from the viaduct at Glenfinnan is a highlight of the West Highland railway route

THE SIGHTS

GLEN AFFRIC

⊕ 321 F6 🛈 Castle Wynd, Inverness IV2 3BJ, tel 01463 234353

This peaceful valley, 30 miles (48km) southwest of Inverness and running parallel with the Great Glen, is one of the best-loved beauty spots in the Highlands. Its scenery combines forest and moorland, river and loch with mighty mountains such as Carn Eige (1,182m/3,878ft).

A narrow road leads up from Cannich to the River Affric parking area, passing the Dog Falls and a beautiful picnic area at Loch Beinn a Mheadhoin on the way up. Footpaths are marked, and for serious hikers a trail leads through to Kintail. A 1,265ha (3,100-acre) area of native woodland, incorporating fragments of ancient Caledonian pine forest, has been established. Crested tits and crossbills may be seen year-round in the woods, while golden eagles and capercaillie are rarer sightings.

GLENELG

⊕ 320 D7 ⛴ Ferry to Kylerhea on Skye, mid-May–end Oct daily; Apr to mid-May Mon–Sat

This isolated spot is reached via the steep pass of Mam Ratagan from the southern shore of Loch Duich. The village is strung out along a shallow bay, with the deserted 18th-century barracks of Bernera to the north, and overlooking the narrow Sound of Sleat to Skye. A small ferry operates in summer to Kylerhea: Look out for seals in the swirling waters. The road continues south, passing above Sandaig, where Gavin Maxwell (1914–69), author of *Ring of*

A monument at Spean Bridge recalls commandos who trained in the Great Glen

Bright Water, lived and is buried, and giving spectacular views to isolated Knoydart.

Don't miss Dun Telve and Dun Toddan, the well-preserved remains of two Iron-Age brochs—circular stone buildings with double walls—in Glen Beag.

GLENFINNAN

⊕ 320 E8 🛈 Cameron Centre, Cameron Square, Fort William PH33 6AJ, tel 01397 703781 🚇 Glenfinnan

On 19 August 1745 Prince Charles Edward Stewart raised his standard here at the top of Loch Shiel, a rallying cry to supporters of his father's claim to the throne of Scotland. It was the start of the Stuarts' final campaign, which would end in disaster at Culloden (▷ 125). The occasion is recalled by a pillar monument, topped by the statue of a kilted soldier, built here in 1815, which provides a focus for the magnificent view down the loch. The National Trust for Scotland has an informative visitor centre nearby (Apr–end Jun, Sep, Oct daily 10–5; Jul, Aug daily 9.30–5.30; Nov Sat–Sun 10–4).

GREAT GLEN

⊕ 321 F7 🛈 Castle Wynd, Inverness IV2 3BJ, tel 01463 234353 🛈 Cameron Centre, Cameron Square, Fort William PH33 6AJ, tel 01397 703781

Slashing for 60 miles (97km) across the country from Inverness in the northeast to Fort William in the southwest, the Great Glen follows the line of a

massive geological fault. A straight, sweeping trough between bare-topped mountains, it is strung with roads (chiefly the A82), a long-distance walking trail and bicycle route (▷ 236). Look out for the so-called Parallel Roads on the hillside at Glen Roy: in fact they are an entirely natural feature of terracing left behind by lakes in the ice ages. The bottom of the glen is lined by a series of lochs, of which the longest and best known is Loch Ness.

Narrow and as much as 230m (754ft) deep, Loch Ness is believed by some to hide a fishy monster, with the first recorded sighting back in the sixth century AD. Find out about more recent searches and their results at Drumnadrochit's Loch Ness 2000 visitor centre (Nov–Easter daily 10–3.30; Easter–end May daily 9.30–5; Jun, Sep daily 9–6; Jul, Aug daily 9–8; Oct daily 9.30–5.30). The long, straight nature of the loch attracts speedboat enthusiasts, and a memorial cairn at the roadside between Drumnadrochit and Invermoriston recalls racing driver John Cobb, who died here in 1952 while attempting to beat the world water speed record.

The lochs of the Great Glen are linked by the Caledonian Canal, an engineering feat planned by Thomas Telford in 1801 and completed in 1847. Loch Oich is the highest point in the chain, with a famous group of eight locks, Neptune's Staircase, at Banavie near Fort William (see also walk, ▷ 226–227).

Commando troops trained around Spean Bridge during World War II. They are commemorated in a striking memorial from 1952 by sculptor Scot Sutherland (off A82, open access).

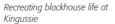
Recreating blackhouse life at Kingussie

A footbridge spans the River Ness, Inverness

The peaks of Suilven and Cul Mòr, Inverpolly reserve

HELMSDALE

⊞ 327 H3 ▨ Helmsdale

Gold fever struck this little harbour on the northeast coast in 1868, when gold was discovered in the Strath of Kildonan and up to 3,000 prospectors set up a shanty town. The excitement was brought to a halt by the local landowner, the 3rd Duke of Sutherland, who feared for the disturbances to his deer and sheep, but you can still buy gold panning equipment in the town today and try your luck.

Helmsdale grew up in the early 19th century as a resettlement site for crofters who had been moved from farther inland to make way for large-scale sheep farming in an episode which became known as the Highland Clearances—learn more at the Timespan Heritage Centre on Dunrobin Street (Apr–end Oct Mon–Sat 10–5, Sun 12–5).

Don't miss A glimpse of La Mirage Restaurant, which pays homage to romantic novelist Barbara Cartland (1901–2000), who had a home close by.

HIGHLAND FOLK MUSEUM (KINGUSSIE AND NEWTONMORE)

⊞ 322 G7 • Duke Street, Kingussie PH21 1JG ☎ 01540 661307
🅘 Kingussie: mid-Apr to end Aug Mon–Sat 9.30–5; Sep, Oct Mon–Fri 9.30–4 (guided tours hourly, Sep, Oct 4 per day). Newtonmore: mid-Apr to end Aug daily 10.30–5.30; Sep daily 11–4.30; Oct Mon–Fri 11–4.30
🖳 Kingussie: adult £2.50, child £1.50. Newtonmore: adult £5, child £3. Family season ticket gives admittance to both sites for the whole season: £15
▨ Kingussie ▣ Newtonmore only ⊞ www.highlandfolk.com

This museum occupies two sites 2.5 miles (4km) apart, clearly signed from the A9. Together they offer an unsanitized picture of rural life in the Highlands over the centuries, through reconstructed buildings, a working croft (small farm) and collections of everyday objects, from food packaging to home-made chairs.

Kingussie is the smaller site, with more of a museum feel to it. It has an extensive collection of farming implements and machinery, and a reconstructed blackhouse from Lewis. (A blackhouse is a long, low dwelling made with walls of peat, and thatched with heather. The family would live at one end, while the livestock occupied the other.) Newtonmore has a reconstructed 18th-century village, including a tailor's workshop, a church and a school. Living history actors at both sites bring things to life, including traditional farming skills and crafts such as weaving and wood-carving.

INNER HEBRIDES

See pages 130–131

INVERARAY

See page 132

INVEREWE GARDENS

See page 133

INVERNESS

⊞ 322 G6 🅘 Castle Wynd IV2 3BJ, tel 01463 234353 ▨ Inverness ❎ Inverness

The administrative capital of the Highland region, Inverness is a service town for the surrounding area, and in summer fills with visitors planning their trips to more remote places and enjoying the shops and restaurants.

Three important roads meet here: the A96 from the northeast, the A9 from the south, and the A82 which runs up the side of the Great Glen (▷ opposite). It is also the northern end of the Caledonian Canal, where the River Ness flows into the Moray Firth.

Inverness's lack of antiquities is due, the locals will tell you, to the Highlanders' habit of burning the town down at regular intervals after English Parliamentarian leader Oliver Cromwell built a fort here in 1652. The architecture of the town is predominantly 19th century, including the red sandstone castle with its monument to heroine Flora Macdonald, who helped Bonnie Prince Charlie to escape in 1746 after his defeat at nearby Culloden (▷ 125). The drum tower hosts the Castle Garrison Encounter, with costumed actors playing out scenes of Hanoverian army life at that time (Mar–end Nov daily 10.30–6).

INVERPOLLY

⊞ 326 F4 🅘 Argyle Street, Ullapool IV26 2UB, tel 01854 612135
🚢 Summer cruises twice daily from Badentarbat pier at Achiltibuie to the Summer Isles, May–end Sep Mon–Sat

The road north from Ullapool leads into a sparsely populated country of peatbog and loch, heather moorland and bare, rocky mountains that look as if they have been thrown down into the landscape at random. This is the national nature reserve of Inverpolly, which covers around 11,000ha (27,000 acres), and the prominent lumps of rock are mountains of weathered, red Torridonian sandstone: Stac Pollaidh (612m/2,008ft), Cul Beag (769m/2,523ft) and Cul Mòr (849m/2,786ft).

The area is rich in wildlife, with otters and deer, golden eagles, and salmon in the rivers. There are also sandy beaches of note at Achnahaird, Garvie, Reiff and Badentarbat.

Inner Hebrides

A chain of small islands nestles down Scotland's rugged western shoreline, each with its own character and community life. The main islands—Mull and Iona, Coll, Tiree, Colonsay, Islay, Jura and Gigha— are accessible by ferry, for a short trip or longer exploration.

Brightly painted houses are a feature of Tobermory Bay, Mull

Carved tombstones, Iona

The unusual round church at Kilarrow, Islay

RATINGS	
Historic interest	● ● ● ○
Outdoors	● ● ● ○
Photo stops	● ● ● ● ○
Specialist shopping	● ●

Top, abandoned fishing boats at Salen, Mull

Below, Duart Castle, Mull, where Cromwell's ship, the Swan, *foundered in 1653*

SEEING THE INNER HEBRIDES

The islands of the Inner Hebrides hug the western shores of Scotland (for Skye, ▷ 138–41). Also marketed as Argyll's Atlantic Islands, they are accessed via scheduled ferry services, and are within reach of day excursions from the mainland.

MULL AND IONA

Mull is the largest, covering some 350 square miles (906sq km), with high mountains in the south, and the rugged inlets of Loch Scridain and Loch na Keal in the west. The main settlement is the 19th-century fishing port of Tobermory, in the northeast. The remoteness of the western seaboard makes it an ideal habitat for the reintroduced white-tailed eagle, as well as for golden eagles, buzzards, peregrines and seabirds. To see birds of prey up close, visit Wings Over Mull, a conservation centre at Craignure (Easter–end Oct daily 10.30–5.30).

Just a short ride away on the narrow-gauge railway (Apr–end Oct daily 10–5.30), Torosay Castle is a stately home of 1858, with 4.8ha (12 acres) of Italianate gardens (house: Apr–end Oct daily 10.30–5; gardens: summer daily 9–7). On the point of Duart Bay stands a much older edifice, Duart Castle, 13th-century home of the Macleans (May to mid-Oct daily 10.30–5.30; Apr Sun–Thu 11–4). West of Ben More, Mull's highest mountain, is the Ardmeanach peninsula, the tip of which is reached via an arduous 5.5-mile (8.8km) path. Its main sight is a fossilized tree, 12m (40ft) high and up to 50 million years old.

Fionnphort is the access point for Iona, a magical island known since the sixth century AD as the cradle of Christianity in Scotland. Most visitors make straight for the abbey (Apr–end Sep daily 9.30–6.30; rest of year daily 9.30–4.30), but spare time for the remains of the 13th-century priory, built for Augustinian nuns. St. Columba founded his monastery here in AD563, and from it Christianity radiated throughout Europe. Now home to the Iona Community, the abbey welcomes pilgrims from around the world. Beside it is the ancient burial ground of Scottish kings, including Duncan and Macbeth. Excursions take in the island of Staffa, with its spectacular hexagonal basalt columns, and Fingal's Cave.

COLL, TIREE, COLONSAY AND ORONSAY
To the west of Mull, the low-lying islands of Coll and Tiree are noted for their sandy beaches, machair (sea meadow) and rare birds, including corncrakes and little terns. Colonsay and nearby Oronsay, to the south, also have fine sands and interesting birdlife.

ISLAY
By comparison, Islay is positively cosmopolitan, a working island with seven distilleries, the excellent Museum of Islay Life at Port Charlotte (Easter–end Oct Mon–Sat 10–5, Sun 2–5), and an annual festival of music and whisky. Loch Finlaggan, west of Port Askaig, was the base for the Lordship of the Isles in the 14th and 15th centuries, and is now an extensive archaeological site (May–end Sep Mon–Fri 10–4.30, Sat 1–4.30; Oct–end Apr Sun, Tue, Thu 1–4). Around 110 species of bird breed on Islay, including the chough, a black crow-like bird with startling red legs and beak. And an estimated 50,000 geese overwinter here from Greenland and Iceland.

JURA AND GIGHA
With its three high conical mountains or 'Paps', Jura is easily recognized. Standing stones and cairns date habitation here back to 7000BC. Gigha is famous for the gardens of Achamore House, noted for their camellias, azaleas and rhododendrons (all year daily).

Iona's abbey cathedral was restored in 1910

TIPS
• Ferry services to the islands are infrequent, and may change according to local weather conditions, so plan your visit carefully and allow several days.
• Visitor accommodation on the smaller islands is limited, so reserve in advance.

BASICS
✚ 315, 319, 320
ℹ The Pier, Craignure, Isle of Mull PA65 6AY, tel 01680 812377
ℹ Morrisons Court, Bowmore, Islay PA43 7JP, tel 01496 810254
ℹ Harbour Street, Tarbert PA29 6UD, tel 01880 820429
🚢 Mull: ferry from Oban, Kilchoan and Lochaline. Coll, Tiree, Colonsay: ferry from Oban. Islay and Jura: ferry from Kennacraig, near Tarbert. Gigha: ferry from Tayinloan on the Kintyre peninsula. All Caledonian MacBrayne, tel 01475 650100.
❓ Islay has its own whisky trail leaflet, detailing opening times for the distilleries, which include the famous Laphroaig, Lagavulin and Bowmore brands.

Nineteen life-size figures line the Statue Walk at Torosay Castle

THE SIGHTS

The so-called Last House at John o'Groats

JOHN O'GROATS

✚ 327 J2 ℹ️ County Road, John o'Groats KW1 4YR, tel 01955 611373; seasonal

In popular imagination, John o'Groats is the most northerly point on the British mainland, 874 miles (1,405km) from Land's End in Cornwall. It is named after a Dutchman, Jan de Groot, who lived here in 1509, and his octagonal house overlooks the wild waters of the Pentland Firth. There are craft studios, souvenir shops and a café or two to mark the location, and never mind that the inhabitants of tiny Scarfskerry, a few miles to the northwest, have been known to take exception to the claim. There are good walks to the wind-blown cliffs of Duncansby Head.

Queen Elizabeth the Queen Mother (1900–2002) restored the nearby Castle of Mey as a holiday home (May–end Jul, mid-Aug to end Sep Sat–Thu 10.30–4). It contains an appealing blend of kitsch, comfort and grandeur.

Don't miss The real most northerly point of mainland Scotland: the exposed headland of Dunnet Head, between John o'Groats and Thurso, with views to Orkney.

KILMARTIN

✚ 315 D10 ℹ️ 27 Lochnell Street, Lochgilphead PA31 8JN, tel 01546 602344; seasonal

The peaceful green glen which leads to the hamlet of Kilmartin, between Oban and Lochgilphead, is littered with piles of silvery boulders, the remains of burial cairns dating from around 3000BC. At the centre of each was a small tomb of stone slabs, and together with the standing stones at

Continued on page 134

Listen to a historic trial in the courtroom at Inveraray Jail

INVERARAY

A handsome lochside town of whitewashed buildings with a proud history and lots to see.

✚ 316 E10 ℹ️ Front Street PA32 8UY, tel 01499 302063

RATINGS	
Good for kids	●●●○
Historic interest	●●●○
Photo stops	●●●○
Walkability	●●●○

MAKE A DAY OF IT

Crarae Gardens; Loch Awe

Spread out along a bay near the head of Loch Fyne, Inveraray was for centuries the capital of Argyll. The ruling family, the Campbell dukes of Argyll, had a castle nearby, and when the untidy village threatened the view from his planned new mansion in 1743, the 3rd Duke moved the lot to its present purpose-built site. This creates a harmony in the buildings, many of which were designed by Robert Mylne (1734–1811).

They include the parish church, which causes the main street to flow around it. The tall brown stone tower is that of All Saints' Episcopalian Church, famous for its peal of 10 bells and with panoramic views from the top (mid-May to Sep daily 10–1 and 2–5). The town's courthouse and jail of 1820 are now host to an entertaining and interactive exhibition about prison life (Apr–Oct daily 9.30–6; rest of year daily 10–5).

The three-masted schooner *Arctic Penguin* is moored in the small harbour (summer daily 10–6; winter daily 10–5), and includes an exhibition about local-born novelist Neil Munro (1864–1930), author of the humorous *Para Handy* tales. (Para Handy was the roguish skipper of a 'puffer', or small steamboat, which plied the Crinan Canal.)

To the north of the town, Inveraray Castle is a splendid 18th-century mansion with pepperpot towers and a delightfully decorative interior (Apr, May, Oct Mon–Thu, Sat 10–1, 2–5.45, Sun 1–5.45; Jun–end Sep Mon–Sat 10–5.45, Sun 1–5.45). Its leafy grounds are overlooked by the watchtower on Duniquoich Hill (255m/837ft).

Don't miss The Loch Fyne Oyster Bar for fresh and smoked seafood, at the head of Loch Fyne.

THE SIGHTS

Although the garden is on a latitude more northerly than Moscow, it is rarely hit by extreme frosts

INVEREWE GARDENS

An exotic 20ha (50-acre) garden on the wild northwest coast, the most famous in Scotland.

In 1862 Osgood Mackenzie (1842–1922) acquired the sporting estate of Inverewe, and on this barren, rocky, salt-wind-blown promontory started to plant shelter belts of trees. Soil and fertilizing seaweed had to be imported by the back-breaking creel-load. It was the unpromising start to what would become Scotland's best-known woodland garden.

Mackenzie had to wait patiently for another two decades before the trees were sufficiently established for him to begin serious planting, as, with typical enthusiasm, he set to work to collect 'every rare exotic tree and shrub which I hear succeeds in Devon, Cornwall, and the west of Ireland'. Like these places, Inverewe benefits from the warmth of the Gulf Stream, and rarely suffers from serious frosts. Mackenzie's daughter Mairi Sawyer took over the garden on her father's death, and in 1953 it was passed on to the National Trust for Scotland.

EXPLORING THE GARDENS

Entry to the gardens is through the visitor centre and shop, leading past the south-facing walled garden and through the rock garden. A network of paths draws you on through the Woodland Walk, the Pond Garden and Wet Valley, to the high viewpoint of Am Ploc Ard, the jetty on Camas Glas bay and back around the Rhododendron and Jubilee Walks and the bamboo garden, Bambooselem. The planting is varied and exotic, with something flowering at almost any time of the year. Alongside great paddle-leaved rhododendrons from the Himalayas, you'll find magnolias from the Far East, Tasmanian eucalypts, olearias from New Zealand and even the Chilean flame flower—flouncing its arresting red blossoms apparently effortlessly here.

Whichever direction your approach, Inverewe is surrounded by some of the most beautiful scenery in the Highlands, including Loch Maree and Gruinard Bay, making a visit to this remote spot well worth while.

Don't miss The candelabra primulas, an Inverewe specialty.

RATINGS

Good for kids	●●
Photo stops	●●●●●
Specialist shopping	●●●●

BASICS

🔲 325 E5 • Poolewe, Achnasheen IV22 2LG ☎ 01445 781200

🕐 Garden: Apr–end Oct daily 9.30–9; rest of year daily 9.30–4. Visitor centre: Apr–end Sep daily 9.30–5; Oct daily 9.30–4 🖤 (NTS) Adult £8, child £5.25, family £16

⛴ Private jetty in the garden allows access by private or cruise boat

📖 £3.50 🍴 🎁 ❓ Free guided tours Apr–end Sep Mon–Fri at 1.30

www.nts.org.uk
Informative and efficient website for all 100 or so National Trust for Scotland properties.

TIPS

● Remember this is the west coast, and receives around 152cm (60in) of rain per year—take an umbrella!

● If the number of coaches in the parking area puts you off, take a break first in the excellent restaurant, or come back towards the end of the afternoon, when the day trippers have moved on.

● Dogs are not allowed in the gardens, and there is limited shaded parking.

Deep-cut tombstones in Kilmartin churchyard

Catch a boat to ruined Kilchurn Castle, Loch Awe

Sealife observed at nose level in Macduff's aquarium

Continued from page 132

Ballymeanoch, the stone circle at Temple Wood, and cup-and-ring carved rocks in the surrounding hills, they form one of the most remarkable collections of early monuments in Britain. Learn more at Kilmartin House, the archaeological museum by the church (daily 10–5.30).

To the south, the great rocky outcrop of Dunadd was the capital of the sixth-century Scottish kingdom of Dalriada: Look for the footprint-shaped impression in the exposed stone on the top of the rock.

Don't miss Deeply carved grave slabs in the churchyard, depicting warriors and dating from the ninth century AD.

KINTYRE

➕ 315 D12 ⓘ Harbour Street, Tarbert PA29 6UD, tel 01880 820429; seasonal ⓘ Mackinnon House, The Pier, Campbeltown PA28 6EF, tel 01586 552056 ✈ Campbeltown ⛴ Ferry: Lochranza on Arran to Claonaig (summer only) and Tarbert (winter only)

In 1098 Norse king Magnus Barelegs hauled his ship over the narrow neck of land at Tarbert to claim the beautiful Kintyre Peninsula for an island. Despite swift, modern access down its western side provided by the A83, it still has the feeling of a world apart. The eastern road, via the holiday village of Carradale, is much slower, allowing time to enjoy the views to the island of Arran (▷ 57).

The Mull of Kintyre is the lumpy southern tip, looking across to Northern Ireland, barely 12 miles (19.3km) away. Tarbert, at the top, is an appealing little port, busy with yachts and small fishing boats. Campbeltown, at the southern end, remains an important service centre for the

farming community of the peninsula, and the home of the Springbank distillery (advance reservations only, Apr–end Sep Mon–Fri 2pm).

Don't miss The golden sands in Machrihanish Bay.

LANDMARK FOREST HERITAGE PARK

➕ 322 H6 • Carrbridge PH23 3AJ, tel 01479 841613 ⓘ Apr to mid-Jul daily 10–6; mid-Jul to end Aug daily 10–7; rest of year daily 10–5 ⓘ Adult £8.95, child £6.90 (under 4 free); lower cost in winter months ⓘ Carrbridge ⓘ ⓘ www.landmark-centre.co.uk

The Landmark Forest Heritage Park is a woodland-themed park, combining serious information about the natural world with activities such as a giant water slide. It lies 6 miles (9.7km) north of Aviemore.

Follow the Timber Trail to learn about the history of the logging industry, and climb the 105 steps of the creaking wooden lookout tower for magnificent views to the Cairngorms. The Ancient Forest leads you through a venerable wood of Scots pines, with a treetop walkway and wildlife feeding area favoured by red squirrels. MicroWorld is about hands-on fun with lenses, while Ant City, a playground for all ages, includes a climbing wall and a giant slide.

LOCH AWE

➕ 316 E10 ⓘ Front Street, Inveraray PA32 8UY, tel 01499 302063 ⓘ Lochawe

A narrow loch 23 miles (37km) long, Loch Awe lies amid the dark green forested hills of Argyll surrounded by scattered small villages, castles and hotels. There are little islands and the remains of crannogs (▷ 101), and the clear waters teem with trout and pike. The Duncan Ban McIntyre Monument, signposted from

Dalmally, is a good viewpoint.

At the northern end, tantalizingly surrounded by marsh, sits the picturesque ruin of Kilchurn Castle (HS, access by ferry, summer only, tel 01838 200440/200449). It dates from 1440 and was built by Colin Campbell of Breadalbane, with additions into the 17th century.

Where the northwest corner of the loch narrows into the awesome Pass of Brander, a hydroelectric power station lies on the shore below the bulk of Ben Cruachan (1,124m/ 3,688ft). A minibus takes you 0.5 miles (800m) into the mountain to see the mighty turbines (reserve in advance 01866 822618 Easter–end Jul and Sep to mid-Nov daily 9.30–5; Aug daily 9.30–6).

MACDUFF MARINE AQUARIUM

➕ 323 K5 • 11 High Shore, Macduff AB44 1SL ☎ 01261 833369 ⓘ Daily 10–5 ⓘ Adult £4.75, child £2.25 (under 3 free), family £12.75 ⓘ www.marine-aquarium.com

This little gem on the northeast coast is a refreshing way to learn about the sealife of the Moray Firth. In a modern circular building by the shore, its centrepiece is a deep sea-water tank, open to the heavens and complete with wave machine, offering realistic conditions for its inhabitants. Clear sides enable you to see plants and creatures inhabiting the different levels in this naturalistic setting, from delicately fringed sea anemones and lurking conger eels, to commercial species of fish such as cod and whiting. Three times a week you can watch dive shows through the giant window in the theatre, when divers feed the fish. There are around 100 species of fish and invertebrate to see here.

THE SIGHTS

The stone structures at Calanais are similar in age to England's Stonehenge

LEWIS AND HARRIS

A single island in two parts, with stunning sandy bays, abundant birdlife, excellent fishing for trout and salmon, and a slower pace of life.

Lewis and Harris are joined by a narrow neck of land but retain strong individual identities. They share a strong Gaelic culture and a traditional observance of the Sabbath—so plan ahead if you're here on a Sunday, as restaurants, shops and petrol stations may be closed.

Lewis, the northern part, has great undulating blanket peat moors scattered with lochs, and a surprising density of population for such an isolated place. Steornabhagh (Stornoway) is the administrative centre, a busy fishing port and the only real town on the island. Good roads lead through the crofting communities which hug the shore, and to the mountainous southwest corner, where the white sands of Uig and Reef compete with green islands to steal the view. On a clear day, you can see the pointed peaks of St. Kilda, 50 miles (80km) away on the horizon. Harris, the southern sector, is the most beautiful of the Outer Hebrides, with high mountains and deep-cut bays. The subtle browns, greens and smoky greys of the landscape are reflected in the island's most famous export, Harris Tweed, a hand-woven wool cloth of high quality made here since the 1840s.

WHAT TO SEE

The island has many prehistoric monuments and monoliths, of which the avenue and circle of 13 stones at Calanais (Callanish), dating to around 3000BC, is outstanding (visitor centre: Apr–end Sep Mon–Sat 10–6; rest of year Wed–Sat 10–4). The stones are of the underlying rock of the island, Lewisian gneiss, some 2,900 million years old. Just up the coast, Dun Carloway Broch (HS, free access) is an excellent example of a stone-built circular Iron-Age dwelling. Set back from the beach at Bosta is a reconstructed Iron-Age house (Jun–end Aug Tue–Sat 12–6), which can be compared with the evocative 19th-century Blackhouse at Arnol (HS, Apr–end Sep Mon–Sat 9.30–6.30; Oct–end Mar 9.30–4.30). At Roghadal (Rodel), St. Clements Church dates from *c.*1500, and has curious sculptures on the stone tower. **Don't miss** The luminous sands and turquoise waters of Tràigh Luskentyre, with views to Taransay island.

RATINGS				
Historic interest	●	●	●	●
Outdoors		●	●	●
Photo stops		●	●	●

BASICS

🗺 324 C3/B4

🛈 26 Cromwell Street, Stornoway, Isle of Lewis HS1 2DD, tel 01851 703088

🛈 Pier Road, Tarbert, Isle of Harris HS3 3DG, tel 01859 502011

⛴ Ferry from Uig on Skye to Tarbert, from Otternish on North Uist to An T-ob (Leverburgh) and from Ullapool to Stornoway

✈ Flights from Glasgow and Edinburgh to Stornoway

TIPS

● If driving here, be aware that petrol (gas) stations are few and far between and may be closed on Sunday.

● Roads are good but not fast, so allow plenty of time for your journey.

● Many road signs use Gaelic spellings which can be confusing, so equip yourself with a good map, such as that published by the Western Isles Tourist Board.

● There is no scheduled public transport on Sundays.

Traditional croft house,
North Uist

Looking through the arches of
McCaig's Tower, Oban

The abbey church at Pluscarden
is the heart of the community

THE SIGHTS

MUSEUM OF SCOTTISH LIGHTHOUSES

323 L5 • Kinnaird Head,
Fraserburgh AB43 9DU ☎ 01346
511022 🕔 Apr–end Jun, Sep, Oct
Mon–Sat 10–6, Sun 12–5; Jul, Aug
Mon–Sat 10–6, Sun 11–6; rest of year
Mon–Sat 11–4, Sun 12–4 💷 Adult £5,
child £2 (under 6 free), family from
£12.40 📷 📚 Good bookshop with
postcards and souvenirs
www.lighthousemuseum.co.uk

This is the only dedicated
lighthouse museum in Britain,
and makes for a fascinating day
out. As well as the imaginative
presentation of lenses, ghostly
glass prisms and working models,
and an interactive map to show
how the lighthouse system grew
along the Scottish coastline, you
can go inside a real lighthouse to
see how it worked and how
the keepers lived.

The Kinnaird Head lighthouse
was built by the great engineer
Robert Stevenson in 1824, and
is rather oddly placed in one
corner of a square castle keep.
The views from the top are
windy but magnificent,
overlooking the busy fishing port
of Fraserburgh. Reserve your
timed place on the lighthouse
tour when you arrive at the
museum (it's included in the
entry price)—and if you're lucky,
you may be shown around by a
former lighthouse keeper.

NORTH UIST, BENBECULA, SOUTH UIST AND ERISKAY

319 🛈 Pier Road, Lochmaddy, Isle
of North Uist HS6 5AA, tel 01876
500321; seasonal 🛈 Pier Road,
Lochboisdale, Isle of South Uist HS8
5TH, tel 01878 700286; seasonal
🚢 North Uist: ferry from Uig on Skye
to Lochmaddy, and from An T-ob
(Leverburgh) on Harris to Otternish.
South Uist: ferry to Lochboisdale from
Oban and Castlebay on Barra. Ferry to
Barra from Eriskay

Part of the chain of the Outer
Hebrides, these four islands are
linked by a series of causeways.
They are characterized by low,
peaty ground glittering with a
thousand trout-stocked lochans
(small lakes), with big bare hills
and beaches of sparkling white
shell sand to the west. North Uist
is particularly rich in standing
stones and other prehistoric
remains, signs that these islands
have been inhabited for over
4,000 years. Communities are
widely scattered and surprisingly
numerous, for crofting on the
fertile machair (sea meadow) is
still viable in the 21st century.

The Kildonan Museum on
South Uist reveals the history of
the people here (Apr to mid-Oct
Mon–Sat 10–5, Sun 12–5), and
also has a welcoming café.

The islands provide vital
wetland habitat for birds
including corncrakes, red-necked
phalaropes, geese and mute
swans, with major reserves at
Balranald and Loch Druidibeg.

The Sound of Eriskay, now
crossed by a stone causeway, is
where the whisky-laden SS
Politician foundered in 1941,
giving novelist Compton
Mackenzie the idea for his comic
tale Whisky Galore (1947); the
classic film (released in the US
as A Tight Little Island) was shot
on neighbouring Barra (▷ 121)
in the following year.
Don't miss The ruined croft
house on South Uist that was
the birthplace of Jacobite
heroine Flora Macdonald
(1722–90), signed from the
main road near the turning to
Gearraidh Bhailteas.

OBAN

315 E9 🛈 Argyll Square PA34 4AR,
tel 01631 563122 🚂 Oban

A busy rail-head and ferry port
for the Western Isles, Oban
developed as a holiday resort in

the 19th century. The bustling
harbour is the start point for local
tours to the islands. It is on a
curving bay sheltered by the low
island of Kerrera, and dominated
by the circular folly of stone
arches on the hillside behind.

This is McCaig's Tower, erected
by John Stuart McCaig, a banker
and philanthropist, in 1897 as a
family memorial and to relieve
local unemployment. It was to
have held a museum, with
statues in each of the windows,
but unfortunately McCaig died
before it could be completed.
Today it provides a superb
viewpoint.

Oban is also a popular touring
centre, with good shops on the
main roads of Corran Esplanade
and George Street. The distillery
in the middle is a pleasant
diversion on a wet day (Feb
Mon–Fri 12–4; Mar–Easter, Nov
10–5; Easter–end Jun Mon–Sat
9.30–5; Jul–end Sep Mon–Fri
9.30–7.30, Sat 9.30–5, Sun
12–5; Oct Mon–Sat 9.30–5;
Nov Mon–Fri 10–5; Jan, Dec
closed).

Four miles (6.4km) to the
north lies Dunstaffnage Castle,
built in the 13th century to fight
off Norsemen, and burned down
in 1810 (HS, Apr–end Sep daily
9.30–6.30; Oct–end Mar
Sat–Wed 9.30–4.30). Beyond
that, the Scottish Sea Life
Sanctuary at Barcaldine cares for
sick and injured seals (Apr to
mid-Oct daily 10–5; winter times
vary).

PLUSCARDEN ABBEY

322 J5 • Pluscarden, Elgin IV30 3UA
☎ 01343 890257 🕔 Daily 9–5
💷 Free 📚
www.pluscardenabbey.org

This remarkable monastery is the
only medieval foundation in
Britain still used for its original
purpose. Lying in a green valley
6 miles (9.7km) southwest of

Looking across the sands at Morar to the profile of Rum

Whisky barrels spell out a welcome at Glenfiddich

A deserted croft sets the scene near Bettyhill, Strathnaver

Elgin, it is the permanent home of 27 Benedictine monks, and a haven of spiritual retreat for both men and women. The monastery was founded in 1230 for the French Valliscaudian order by Alexander II, and during the Reformation in the 16th century was gradually abandoned.

In 1943 Benedictine monks from Prinknash Abbey in Gloucestershire started to restore it, and in 1974 it received the status of abbey. Today the white-habited monks work in the grounds and workshops and care for the abbey buildings. These focus on the massive abbey church, where ancient stonework and frescoes contrast with modern stained glass.

Don't miss Gregorian chant at Sunday Mass.

SKYE

See pages 138–41

SMALL ISLES

320 C7/C8 Main Street, Mallaig PH41 4QS, tel 01687 462170; seasonal Reached via CalMac ferry from Mallaig (www.calmac.co.uk); cruises from Arisaig, tel 01687 450224

Canna, Rum, Eigg and Muck make up this island group due west of Mallaig. Each has its own distinct identity, but they share a reputation for interesting birdlife, including the rare white-tailed eagle.

Rum (or Rhum) is much the biggest, with the high mountains of Askival (810m/2,658ft) and Sgùrr nan Gillean (763m/2,503ft) to the southeast, and a reputation for particularly vicious midges. Once cleared as a private sporting island, it is now a nature reserve owned by Scottish Natural Heritage, home to red deer, feral goats and some 100,000 Manx shearwaters who nest in the hillsides. About 30 people live in the small east-coast settlement based around the deserted Edwardian castle at Kinloch, which offers hostel facilities but is otherwise not open to view.

Muck is the smallest and flattest island, occupied by just one farm, along with a craft shop, tea room and limited visitor accommodation. Canna, an early Christian settlement site, is owned by the National Trust for Scotland. Its most famous feature is Compass Hill: Iron in the basalt rock can upset compasses within a radius of 3 miles (5km). Eigg, with its high spine of pitchstone porphyry called the Sgurr, has a small pierside complex including a restaurant and craft shop. In 1997 the island was famously bought by its occupants, in a landmark venture.

SPEYSIDE

322 J6 17 High Street, Elgin IV30 1EG, tel 01343 542666 54 High

Street, Grantown-on-Spey PH26 3EH, tel 01479 872773; seasonal www.maltwhiskytrail.com

The River Spey flows from the Cairngorms near Aviemore and winds northeast through a green landscape of gentle hills and woodland, to pour into the sea between Lossiemouth and Buckie. On the way, it flows under a magnificent iron bridge at Craigellachie by engineer Thomas Telford (1757–1834), lends its name to the historic Strathspey Railway and the town of Grantown-on-Spey, and picks up a long-distance trail, the Speyside Way, which runs north from Tomintoul to Spey Bay.

Speyside is a name associated with the area between Elgin, Keith and Grantown, and more particularly with the production of some of Scotland's most famous single malt whiskies (▷ 242–243): Signposts here can read like a well-stocked bar. Eight distilleries, mostly founded in the early 19th century, are linked by the signposted Malt Whisky Trail: Glen Grant, Cardhu, Strathisla, Glenlivet, Benromach, Dallas Dhu, Glen Moray and Glenfiddich. Each offers guided tours and whisky tastings, but opening times and admissions vary so check ahead (the tourist information office has a leaflet with all the information).

Thousands of oak barrels essential to the whisky industry are maintained at the Speyside Cooperage, Craigellachie (Mon–Fri 9.30–4).

Don't miss A little cupboard cut into the rock beside the burn (stream) in the garden of Glen Grant Distillery, where the owner kept his special whisky. It's known as the Major's Safe.

Kinnaird Head lighthouse is now part of the Museum of Scottish Lighthouses

Skye

The most romantic and picturesque of the Western Isles, with good food, big mountains and historic castles. Skye is around 50 miles (80km) long, with around 350 miles (560km) of indented, rocky coastline.

Pastel painted houses crowd along the harbour in Portree

The view from Beinn Edra and the Trotternish Ridge

A glimpse of luxury in the library of Dunvegan Castle

SEEING SKYE

The Isle of Skye is the largest and best known of the Inner Hebrides, its name woven into the warp of Bonnie Prince Charlie's flight after Culloden (▷ 125) in the 18th century; and into the weft of the loss of a way of island life and emigration to the New World in the 19th century. Broadford is the main hub for the south, with access to the steep, magnificently scenic road to Elgol. Portree is a more appealing township, and centre for the north of the island.

Skye is an unlikely crossroads among the Western Isles. In summer you can reach it by ferry from Mallaig or Gairloch, or by ferry across the strong currents by Glenelg, or at any time of the year by the convenient but controversial bridge from Kyle of Lochalsh (tolls were removed in December 2004). Ferries to the Outer Hebrides leave from Uig, and to little Raasay from Sconser.

HIGHLIGHTS

THE CUILLIN

Every view of the Isle of Skye is dominated by the Cuillin (pronounced 'Coolin'), a range of jagged mountains of dark gabbro which reaches its peak in the far south with Sgùrr Alasdair (1,009m/3,309ft). They are to be treated with respect, but Munro-baggers (▷ 15) can have a field day here, with 12 mountains reaching beyond the magic figure of 3,000 ft (914m).

The southern mountains are the Black Cuillin, distinct from the scree-covered granite of the lower Red Cuillin. All are challenges for mountaineers, and the most inaccessible peaks were conquered only at the end of the 19th century. In geological terms, the Cuillin are comparatively young, formed in volcanic activity at the same time as Iceland, a mere 20 million years ago, and scoured by the ice ages.

PORTREE

The harbour town of Portree on the eastern coast is the capital of the island, and the centre of island life, its colour-washed houses around the harbour pleasing on the eye. The town was named after a royal visit in 1540 by James V—*port rig* means king's harbour—and its formal square is a miniature delight. Its Aros Experience offers an

RATINGS	
Historic interest	●●●○
Outdoors	●●●●●
Photo stops	●●●○

BASICS
✚ 320 C6
ℹ Bayfield House, Bayfield Road, Portree, Isle of Skye IV51 9EL, tel 01478 612137
⛴ Car ferry from Mallaig to Armadale (40 minutes, summer only), from Glenelg to Kylerhea (15 minutes, summer only); passenger ferry from Gairloch to Portree (1 hour 30 minutes, summer only)

www.skye.co.uk
Lots of different ways to explore this excellent community website, with good background information and useful links.

Top, grey seal at Dunvegan Left, Loch Scavaig from Elgol, in the south of the island

The Cuillin mountains

introduction to Skye's natural history with an audio-visual show about the return of the white-tailed sea eagle (all year daily 9–6).

DUNVEGAN CASTLE

The MacLeod clan have owned and fought over Skye for generations, and their home in the northwest of the island, Dunvegan Castle, is well worth a visit (mid-Mar to Oct daily 10–5; Nov to mid-Mar daily 11–4). It is a fortress built on a high rock that was once completely surrounded by the sea, and has been occupied since the 13th century. Heavy restoration in the 19th century has left it impressive, if not beautiful, but the interior is full of rich treasures. The most poignant of these is the faded and tattered talisman of the Fairy Flag, a gift to an early clan chief from his fairy lover, with potent powers to rescue the clan at times of peril.

Skye's bridge (1996) strides across Eilean Bàn

A fishing boat moored at Dunvegan village

The jagged rocky spine of the Quiraing, Trotternish

TIPS

● The voracity of Skye's midges is the stuff of legends, so be prepared with suitable insect repellent.
● The summer weather on the island is unpredictable, so be prepared for heavy rain, lowering mist and blazing sunshine—in the space of just a few hours.
● Skye looks quite small on the map, but allow several days to explore properly—the roads are slow, and the scenery big.
● Fine dining and Scottish islands don't always go together, but Skye has several excellent restaurants that make any stay here a gourmet pleasure (▷ 264–265). And at Carbost, the Talisker Distillery produces a fragrant, peaty single malt (Nov–end Mar Mon–Fri 2–4.30; Apr–end Oct Mon–Sat 9.30–4.30).

Dunvegan's gardens have taken the place of the 'bare wine-dark moorland' observed by Dr. Johnson in 1773. Helped by the benign climate of the Gulf Stream, the rhododendrons planted in the 19th century have flourished alongside a surprising range of other exotics from China, the Americas, Japan, Korea and New Zealand.

You can join a boat trip from Dunvegan to see the common and grey seals which loll about the rocks, or a mini-cruise on the loch to explore the history and wildlife of some of the many tiny islands.

TROTTERNISH

Trotternish is the name of the peninsula which sticks up like a long finger at the northern tip of Skye. Ancient flows of lava have produced sheer cliffs, with shearings and pinnacles down the spine created where softer rocks buckled under the weight of the lava. The most famous of these is the Old Man of Storr, a black obelisk 49m (160ft) high. The weird and mysterious stone formations of the area known as the Quiraing, 30.4km (19 miles) north of Portree, can be examined up close if you walk with care (▷ walk, 232–233).

Basalt columns have formed huge cliffs on the eastern coast. Perhaps the most spectacular of these is known as the Kilt Rock, from its resemblance to the pleated garment. There's a dramatic waterfall here, too, and captivating views across to the blue hills of the mainland.

EILEAN BÀN

The Skye bridge sets one massive concrete foot firmly on the little 2.4ha (6-acre) island of Eilean Bàn, a nature reserve run by a charitable trust for the local community. Access is via the Bright Water Visitor Centre on the pier at Kyleakin (May–end Oct Mon–Sat 10–4), which has information about local wildlife and history, and interactive exhibits to teach children about conservation. But Eilean Bàn is more than just a wildlife reserve. The island is home to a lighthouse, built in 1857 and decommissioned in 1993. Gavin Maxwell, the enigmatic author best known for his tale of otter-keeping, *Ring of Bright Water* (1960), bought and spectacularly refurbished the keepers' cottages in the 1960s. One of the rooms has been restored, and is now furnished with many objects that belonged to Maxwell himself.

The shapely island of Raasay, to the east of Skye, is another haven for wildlife, and benefits from fewer visitors than Skye itself.

If you are unlucky enough not to spot wild otters in the coastal waters around Skye, try the hide at the Kylerhea Otter Haven (all year daily dawn–dusk).

BACKGROUND

Arriving in Skye, you know you've left the mainland. For a start, road signs in Gaelic as well as English quickly tell you you're in a different culture. Skye retains a strong Gaelic identity, encouraged at the college, Sabhal Mor Ostaig, in Sleat, but the economic necessity of generations of emigration have made the island outward-looking and perhaps surprisingly cosmo-politan. If your ancestors came from Skye or the western Highlands, then make sure to visit Armadale Castle, in the southwest (Apr–end Oct daily 9.30–5.30). Within it is the excellent Museum of the Isles, and a library and resource centre where you can undertake your own genealogical research.

Many people's introduction to Skye is through the romantic and well-loved melody, the 'Skye Boat Song'. It recalls the flight of Charles Edward Stewart (Bonnie Prince Charlie) after the disaster at Culloden in 1746 (▷ 125), when the prince was smuggled to Skye from South Uist by Flora Macdonald, disguised as Betty Burke. He continued his journey in safety to Raasay and then exile in France.

While the prince escaped, Flora Macdonald was arrested and imprisoned briefly in the Tower of London. She later married a Skye man and emigrated to America; they eventually returned to live at Kingsborough, and her grave is there. There is also a memorial to the Jacobite heroine near ruined Duntulm Castle, a former Macdonald stronghold.

You can take a boat trip on to the loch at Dunvegan Castle

Torridon is spectacular hillwalking country

18th-century houses along the shore of Loch Broom, Ullapool

Urquhart Castle is popular with Nessie-spotters

STRATHNAVER

✚ 326 G2 🔲 Clachan, Bettyhill KW14 7SS, tel 01641 521342; seasonal

This remote valley has a forlorn air, the landscape dotted with broken walls and the grassy mounds of small homesteads. Its name is resonant with the period of the Highland Clearances, and in particular with the clearing of his land by the Duke of Sutherland and his callous factor (land agent), Patrick Sellar, between 1812 and 1819, to make way for sheep farming. It was a time when the crofters were forced to leave their homes inland to eke a living on the inhospitable coast, or join the emigration to the New World. The story is well told at Strathnaver Museum near Bettyhill (Apr–end Oct Mon–Sat 10–1, 2–5). In the valley, there is a well-marked trail at the former village of Rosal.

TORRIDON

✚ 320 E5 🔲 Auchtercairn, Gairloch IV22 2DN, tel 01445 712130; seasonal

A spectacular wilderness of massive, bare mountains, Torridon lies on the northwest coast. The 972m (3,189ft) bulk of Beinn Eighe looms above the lonely pass between Shieldaig and Kinlochewe, shedding white quartzite scree like snow. This was Scotland's first national nature reserve, celebrated with a visitor centre north of Kinlochewe, and seen at its best from Loch Clair.

To the west, Liathach (1,054m/3,456ft) is the tallest peak in the range, with seven tops along its ridge, and closely followed in size by Beinn Alligin (985m/3,232ft). The mountains are for serious walkers only, but there's a more accessible path along the north shore of Loch Torridon to Redpoint.

The National Trust for Scotland has a small visitor centre on the approach to Torridon village, with video footage showing the wildlife of the area (Easter–end Sep daily 10–6).

ULLAPOOL

✚ 325 E4 🔲 Argyle Street IV26 2UB, tel 01854 612135 🚢 Ferry to Lewis

The white-painted houses of this small town stretch along a spit of land on the shore of Loch Broom. Despite its frontier feeling, Ullapool has a dignified air brought about by its neat grid of streets, for this was a planned village, built in 1788 by the British Fisheries Society. Tourism has replaced fishing as the mainstay, and as the last settlement of size on the route up the northwest coast, it is usually busy with visitors in summer.

The MV *Summer Queen* cruises to the green bumps of the Summer Isles, 12 miles (19.3km) northwest at the mouth of the loch (for reservations, tel 01854 612472). The biggest island, Tanera Mhor, issues its own unique and collectable postage stamps. **Don't miss** The dramatic Corrieshalloch Gorge, at the head of Loch Broom, and the view from the suspension bridge below the Falls of Measach.

URQUHART CASTLE

✚ 321 G6 • Drumnadrochit, Inverness IV63 6XJ ☎ 01456 450551 🕐 Apr–end Sep daily 9.30–6.30; rest of year daily 9.30–4.30 🎟 (HS) Adult £6, child £2.40 (under 5 free) ▢ 🏛 www.historic-scotland.gov.uk

The broken battlements of this splendid castle, 3.2km (2 miles) south of Drumnadrochit, are testimony to its place in the history of the 13th to the 17th centuries. It was built on a rocky promontory sticking out into Loch Ness, offering strategic command of the Great Glen (▷ 128) to whoever could hold it. It changed hands many times between Durwards, Macdonalds and Grants, with an early spell in English hands, and in the 14th century a brief period of ownership by Robert the Bruce. It was finally blown up in 1691 to prevent its use by Jacobite rebels.

The modern visitor centre exhibits interesting medieval fragments discovered here, including an ancient harp.

WICK HERITAGE CENTRE

✚ 327 J2 • 20 Bank Row, Wick KW1 5EY ☎ 01955 605393 🕐 Jun–end Sep Mon–Sat 10–5 🎟 Adult £2, child 50p 🚻 Wick 🏛

Like Ullapool in the west, Wick, in the northeast corner of the country, was built up as a fishery town in the 19th century to take advantage of the herring boom. The new development, to a design by the great civil engineer Thomas Telford for the British Fisheries Society, was to the south of the river, complementing the older settlement on the north bank.

The Heritage Centre is a fascinating local museum, run by volunteers. It tells of the town's heyday as one of the busiest herring ports in the world, when the harbour bristled with boats and the population was swelled by migrant workers from the west coast and Ireland. Some of the boats and whole rooms are preserved here, and you can see the old smokehouse, for curing fish, complete with its original soot.

At the core of the museum is the outstanding Johnston collection of photographs. Named after three generations of a local family, they form a vivid record of life in the town between 1863 and 1977.

ORKNEY AND SHETLAND

The northern isles of Orkney and Shetland have an identity that is shared as much with Scandinavia as with the Highlands. The contrasting island groups, with the rocky and isolated island of Fair Isle between, have an independent outlook on the world that is invigorating and refreshing.

Shetland Islands
Unst
Yell
Foula
Lerwick

Westray
Orkney Islands
Sanday
Skara Brae
Stromness
Kirkwall
Hoy
South Ronaldsay
Thurso
John o'Groats
Wick

KEY SIGHT

The remarkable painted interior of the Italian Chapel

HOY

✚ 327 J4 ⓘ 6 Broad Street, Kirkwall KW15 1NX, tel 01856 872856 🚢 From Houton, on Mainland, to Lyness, and from Stromness to Moaness

The second largest of the Orkney islands, Hoy derives its name from the Old Norse term Ha-ey, meaning 'high island'. Its best-known feature is the columnar stack of red sandstone just off the western cliffs, known as the Old Man of Hoy. Standing 137m (450ft) high, it is a challenge for climbers. The heather covered hills of Cuilags (433m/1,420ft) and Ward Hill (479m/1,570ft) offer excellent walking country.

This sheltered bay was home to the Royal Navy during two world wars, and famously the site of the scuttling of the German fleet after the end of World War I, in 1919. The remains now prove popular with divers. Learn more at the fascinating Scapa Flow Visitor Centre and Museum, in the former naval base at Lyness (Mon–Fri 9–4; also Jun–end Sep Sat 9–4, Sun 10–4).

Near Rackwick, the Dwarfie Stane is a unique Neolithic chambered cairn hollowed out of a single solid rock.

ITALIAN CHAPEL

✚ 327 K4 • Dunedin, St. Mary's, Lamb Holm KW17 2RT ☎ 01856 873191 🕐 Daily dawn–dusk 🎫 Free, donations welcome

After a German U-boat successfully broke into Scapa Flow in 1939 and sank the naval vessel HMS *Royal Oak* with the loss of 833 lives, it became clear that further defences were needed to block access to this vital natural harbour. Italian prisoners of war were drafted in

Continued on page 146

Turf and stone roofs on abandoned croft buildings, Rackwick

ORKNEY

A green and fertile group of islands off the northeast tip of mainland Scotland that played a key role in both world wars.

✚ 327 ⓘ 6 Broad Street, Kirkwall KW15 1NX, tel 01856 872856 🚢 From Aberdeen (7 hours) or Scrabster, by Thurso (1 hour 30 minutes), or Lerwick (8 hours); John O'Groats (40 minutes), summer only ✈ Kirkwall www.visitorkney.com

This low-lying cluster of more than 70 islands and skerries lies off the northern coast of Scotland, usually clearly within view of the mainland, and separated by the churning waters of the Pentland Firth. Approaching on the ferry from Scrabster or Aberdeen, the first view of Hoy, with its tall rock stacks and slabby red sandstone cliffs, is misleading.

Only when the boat swings towards the harbour at Stromness is a more typical view of Orkney revealed, low and green and richly fertile, with cattle grazing and crops growing on this well-farmed land, and brown trout lurking in the lochs. On a warm summer day, the scent of wild flowers in the clear air of these islands is invigorating.

Kirkwall, on the eastern side of Mainland, the largest island in the archipelago, is the capital. There is much to explore among the islands, which are linked by causeway, ferry or air, including the shortest scheduled air route in the world—just under two minutes for the 1.5-mile (2.4km) flight between Westray and Papa Westray.

Orkney, like Shetland, shares a close history with Scandinavia and tends to regard itself as a part of Britain which is separate from Scotland, having little in common with, say, the deeply religious and Gaelic culture of the Western Isles. Orkney became part of Scotland in the 15th century, part of a dowry when Margaret of Denmark married Scottish king James III. Today these islands ring with Norse-sounding placenames, although Picts and Celts pre-dated the Vikings by at least 3,500 years, leaving extraordinary signs of their presence at Maes Howe and Skara Brae.

Reminders of a more recent history are also all around, in the remains of gun emplacements and the giant concrete blocks of the Churchill Barriers, recalling a time when the sheltered bay of Scapa Flow was a vital naval base through two world wars.

Slab stone structures like this cupboard or dresser survived when the houses were buried under sand

SKARA BRAE

The remains of a stone-built Neolithic village, concealed for centuries under the sand, are Orkney's 'must see' sight, offering a unique window into a domestic world long gone.

It is tempting to believe that our prehistoric ancestors, who left so little record of their daily existence, were not very clever and lived wretchedly in dark hovels. A visit to Skara Brae suggests otherwise, and can be an eye-opening experience. Lying 19 miles (30.6km) northwest of Kirkwall, it is the site of a village, inhabited between 3100 and 2500BC, probably originally some distance from the sea.

At some point the sands encroached and covered the houses, which lay undiscovered until a great storm in 1850 revealed the presence of stone structures. Subsequent excavation showed nine very similar houses linked by winding passageways, their dry-stone walls buried to the eaves by the surrounding midden pits, which probably provided some degree of insulation.

EXPLORING THE SITE

As you walk around the site today, you are looking down into the houses from above, through what would have been roofs of skin and turf laid over timber spars or whalebone. Slabs of the local flagstone were used to create central hearths, cupboards in the walls, bed surrounds, clay-lined troughs in the floor, and even a dresser, suggesting a level of sophistication that is as delightful as it is unexpected.

A reconstructed house by the visitor centre shows how animal skins and bracken would have helped to make the dwellings cosy, and fragments of jewellery, tools and pottery give further insights into the lives of these mysterious people.

Don't miss A walk on the sparkling white sands of Skaill Bay.

RATINGS				
Good for kids	●	●	●	●
Historic interest	●	●	●	●
Photo stops	●	●	●	●
Walkability	●	●	●	

BASICS

✚ 327 J4 • Sandwick KW16 3LR
☎ 01856 841815 ● Apr–end Sep daily 9.30–6.30; rest of year daily Mon–Sat 9.30–4.30, Sun 2–4.30 ● (HS) adult £6, child £2.40 (under 5 free)
🍴 On-site restaurant seats 90 people
🎁 Gift shop in visitor centre stocks local Orkney-made products ♿
www.historic-scotland.gov.uk

MAKE A DAY OF IT

Maes Howe

Walkways between the houses enable you to see straight down into the dwellings

St. Magnus Cathedral is Orkney's grandest building

A low stone passageway is the entrance to Maes Howe

The old harbour at Stromness, Orkney's second town

Continued from page 144

to construct massive concrete blocks, which were piled between Mainland and the eastern islands of Lamb Holm, Glimps Holm, Burray and South Ronaldsay to form impregnable causeways known as the Churchill Barriers.

The Italian workers created their own memorial, converting two Nissen huts to make a chapel and decorating it with scrap materials. The inside is beautifully painted with frescoes and *trompe-l'oeil* on plasterboard and concrete mouldings, with even a rood screen. The result is extraordinary, and a moving tribute to the ingenuity, skill and imagination of the prisoners, so far from home, which the islanders have carefully preserved.

KIRKWALL

🖪 327 K4 🖪 6 Broad Street, Kirkwall KW15 1NX, tel 01856 872856
🛇 Kirkwall

This is the main town of Orkney. There's been a settlement here since the 11th century, but most of the compact buildings seen in the narrow, paved streets of the old harbour town today date from the 16th to the 18th centuries. The long main street is lined with interesting little shops, including high-quality crafts and jewellery businesses, which thrive on the wealthy clientele of the cruise ships that call here.

Dominating all is the red sandstone bulk of St. Magnus Cathedral on Broad Street, begun by Earl Rognvald in 1137 (great-nephew of St. Magnus, murdered 20 years before) and completed in the 15th century (Apr–end Sep Mon–Sat 9–6, Sun 2–6; rest of year Mon–Sat 9–1 and 2–5). Inside, the huge

Romanesque pillars and decorative stonework create a sense of magnificent space and peace. One of the best views is from the top of the ruins of the nearby Bishop's Palace (HS, Mar–end Sep daily 9.30–6.30). **Don't miss** A taste of the local Highland Park whisky, from Scotland's most northerly distillery (tours every half-hour, May–end Aug Mon–Sat 10–5, Sun 12–5; Apr, Sep, Oct Mon–Fri 10–5; and Nov–end Mar at 2pm only).

MAES HOWE

🖪 327 J4 • By Tormiston Mill, Mainland KW16 3HA ☎ 01856 761606
🕓 Apr–end Sep daily 9.30–6.30; Oct–end Mar daily 9.30–4.30; tours every 45 mins from 9.45, advance reservations recommended 🖪 (HS) Adult £4, child £1.60 (under 5 free) 🖪
🌐 www.historic-scotland.gov.uk

A 7m (23ft) high grassy mound in a field to the south of Loch of Harray, on the road from Stromness to Finstown, Maes Howe looks unpromising at first sight. Under the turf, however, lies a chambered grave dating from around 2800BC which is a treasure of World Heritage status.

You must take your turn and bend double to walk through the 14.5m (47ft) entrance passageway, before you emerge into the beautifully formed inner chamber, which is almost 4.5m (15ft) square. The walls are lined with neatly fitting stone slabs, the roof is corbelled, and there are three small side chambers. While the contents were looted centuries ago and can only be guessed at, the structure itself has survived more or less undamaged, barring some runic graffiti left by passing Vikings.

The Ring of Brogar stone circle 5 miles (8km) northeast of Stromness

Don't miss The nearby Ring of Brogar, a magnificent stone circle with surrounding ditch.

SKARA BRAE

See page 145

STROMNESS

🖪 327 J4 🖪 Ferry Terminal Building, Ferry Road, Stromness KW16 3BH, tel 01856 850716 🖪 From Scrabster

Orkney's second town, Stromness has a history that is closely tied to the sea. Houses and stores on the waterfront date from the 18th and 19th centuries, each with its own slipway—a good view of this is from the windows of the Pier Arts Centre (Tue–Sat 10.30–12.30, 1.30–5). The Arts Centre is a gallery specializing in exhibitions of modern art.

The town's winding main street is paved with the local huge sandstone slabs, and cobbles; follow it to its southern end, to the maritime delights displayed in the excellent Stromness Museum on Alfred Street (May–end Sep daily 10–5; rest of year daily 10.30–12.30, 1.30–5). It offers a maritime history of the town. Stromness boomed in the early 19th century, a centre for Arctic whaling, and a key stopping point for vessels of the Hudson's Bay Company who took on crew and supplies here, and fresh water from nearby Login's Well. Look out for the barnacle-encrusted treasures recovered by divers from the sunken German fleet in Scapa Flow.

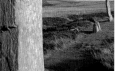

Gunnister Voe, on the north Mainland: Voes are coastal inlets

SHETLAND

A remote group of more than 100 rugged, rocky islands and exposed skerries, with a proud Viking history.

➕ 324 ℹ️ Market Cross, Lerwick ZE1 0LU, tel 01595 693434 🚢 From Aberdeen (14 hours); also summer ferries from Bergen in Norway via the Faroes and Iceland ✈️ Sumburgh, at the southern tip of Mainland www.visitshetland.com

Shetland, with a population of around 24,000, is the most northerly part of Britain, lying as close to the Faroes and Bergen in Norway as it does to Aberdeen. Its place on northern trade routes has given it an unusually cosmopolitan air, and a culture that is more Viking than Scots, with a broad dialect, the January festival of Up Helly Aa, a rich heritage of skilled knitting, and a vibrant tradition of fiddle music which has been exported around the world by musicians such as Aly Bain (1945–).

The landscape of these islands is wild and rugged, with low hills, exposed rock, and peaty, waterlogged moorland. Few trees survive the wind, but the wild flowers grow large and sublime, and nowhere is farther than 5 miles (8km) from the sea. Seals and porpoises are common sights around the indented coastline, and thousands of seabirds nest here, including puffins, black guillemots and gannets.

The capital is the harbour town of Lerwick, halfway up the east side of the main island. Scalloway, west of Lerwick, was the medieval heart of the island, and is dominated by its ruined castle, built in 1600. The Scalloway Museum features a fishing boat which took part in the secret 'Shetland Bus' sea link to resistance fighters in Norway during World War II (May–end Sep Mon 9.30–11.30, 2–4.30, Tue–Sat 10–12, 2–4.30).

Shetland's prosperity rose sharply at the end of the 20th century with the exploitation of oil and gas fields in the North Sea. The money has funded new roads, new inter-island ferries and modern community centres on many of the islands, as well as other public facilities. Sullom Voe, one of the largest oil and gas terminals in Europe, lies at the north of the main island.

Flights from the mainland come in to Sumburgh, at the southern tip. There are air and sea links to other main islands and to Fair Isle, the isolated island between Orkney and Shetland which is famous as the stopover point for more than 350 species of migrating birds (May–end Oct observatory).

Multiple layers of history are revealed at Jarlshof

JARLSHOF PREHISTORIC AND NORSE SETTLEMENT

➕ 324 A3 • Sumburgh ZE3 9JN ☎ 01950 460112 🕐 Apr–end Sep daily 9.30–12.30, 1.30–6.30 🎫 (HS) Adult £4, child £1.60 🍴 In nearby Sumburgh Hotel www.historic-scotland.gov.uk

Complex layers of history were first uncovered at this fascinating site above the sea, near the southern tip of Shetland, when a mighty storm dislodged the covering turf. The most obvious survivor is the shell of the 17th-century Laird's House, which is the only structure to stick up above ground. This overlies a prehistoric broch which, it would seem, was converted during the Iron Age into a round-house. All around the site are the remains of a Viking farm dating from the ninth century, complete with the outline of a communal longhouse that was almost 20.7m (68ft) long.

Further layers have revealed a settlement from the second century BC and a medieval farm dating from the 14th century, making an intriguing record of life here over the years. Signboards help to clarify what you're seeing. **Don't miss** Migrant whooper swans in autumn on the nearby reserve of Loch of Spiggie.

LERWICK

➕ 324 A2 ℹ️ Market Cross, Lerwick ZE1 0LU, tel 01595 693434

It was Dutch herring fishermen who made Lerwick the capital of the islands, when they started using its sheltered harbour in the 17th century. Today the compact grey town stretches out to either side, with a bustling main thoroughfare one row back, stone-flagged Commercial Street.

The old harbour is active with local ferries, fishing boats and

White sands form a tombolo at St. Ninian's Isle

The cliffs at Hermaness, on the northern tip of Unst, attract millions of nesting seabirds in the spring and early summer

pleasure craft. Bigger ferries, cruise ships and support vessels for the oil industry tend to use the less vibrant modern harbour a mile (1.6km) to the north. In the shops, knitwear produced using traditional, intricate patterns is a local specialty, and if you can't see what you want, nimble-fingered workers will soon make you a garment to your own choice of pattern or colour.

The Shetland Museum on Lower Hillhead is worth a look (due to relocate in 2006 to Hays Dock, tel 01595 695057 for times). Fort Charlotte, dating from 1665, is one of the oldest buildings in Shetland, and also worth seeing. It is still used as a barracks for the Territorial Army. There are good views to the island of Bressay.

MOUSA BROCH

✚ 324 A3 ⓘ Market Cross, Lerwick ZE1 0LU, tel 01595 693434 🚤 Boat trips on *Solan IV* Apr to mid-Sep, Mon–Thu and Sat 2pm, Fri and Sun 12.30 and 2pm. Adult £9, child (5–16) £4. Reservations essential, tel 01950 431367
www.mousaboattrips.co.uk

High and dry at Sandwick Bay

The double-skinned circular tower of Mousa Broch dates from 100BC to AD300, and is the best preserved example of its kind in Scotland. The walls stand up to 13m (43ft) high, and the small gaps between the neatly placed stones now provide nesting sites for tiny storm petrels.

The broch was built on a small island, off the eastern coast of southern Shetland, which suggests it had a defensive role at some time—but nobody quite understands how people lived in and used these structures. The island has no human inhabitants today, and is a designated Site of Special Scientific Interest (so no dogs allowed). Access in summer is via a small passenger boat from Leebitton, in Sandwick. There are good views to the broch from the main road near Sandwick.

ST. NINIAN'S ISLE

✚ 324 A3 ⓘ Market Cross, Lerwick ZE1 0LU, tel 01595 693434

St. Ninian's Isle is a green jewel, a tiny grass-covered island off the western side of southern Shetland. It is joined to the land by a curved tombolo of silvery shell sand, which permits access except during the highest tides of the year, and makes for lovely walking. St. Ninian came from the monastery at Whithorn in Dumfries (▷ 67) as the first Christian missionary to reach Shetland, and the ruins of a church dating back to the 12th century are on the island.

In 1958 a hoard of beautifully worked Pictish silver was discovered, buried under the nave. The treasure is now in the Museum of Scotland in Edinburgh (▷ 78–81), but replicas can be seen in the Shetland Museum in Lerwick.

UNST

✚ 324 B1 ⓘ Market Cross, Lerwick ZE1 0LU, tel 01595 693434 🚢 Regular ferry service to Unst from Yell

Much of Unst's fame rests on its status as the most northerly of the Shetland isles. In this way, it can claim the most northerly house in Britain at Skaw. The nature reserve at Hermaness is no gimmick, however, but home in summer to 100,000 screaming seabirds which nest on and around the 167.4m (558ft) cliffs (free access; visitor centre: mid-Apr to mid-Sep daily 9–5). Look out for puffins and guillemots, fulmars and large, creamy gannets. Beware the great brown Arctic skuas, which are inclined to dive-bomb visitors if they feel their moorland nest sites are threatened (local people know them as bonxies). **Don't miss** Views to the lighthouse (1858) on the exposed rock of Muckle Flugga.

This chapter gives information on things to do in Scotland other than sightseeing.

What to Do

SHOPPING

Scotland's main centres of population are very well served with shopping malls full of big-name brands. Outside the bigger cities shopping takes on an altogether more small-town air, with independently owned stores geared to serving the local community. Some towns still have a market once or twice a week, or a monthly farmers' market, where you can expect to find fruit and vegetables, butcher's and fishmonger's stalls and household items.

DISTINCTIVELY SCOTTISH

Scotland is particularly good for woollen goods, which are widely available in specialist and souvenir stores. Knitted goods are found everywhere, from sweaters in the intricate designs of Shetland and Fair Isle to throws and shawls of the finest cashmere.

Woven woollen cloth in the strong shades and chequered designs of tartan is, of course, one of Scotland's best-loved exports, and can be bought in the form of everything from a blanket to a kilt (and on a vast range of souvenirs). Tartan (also known as plaid) is a relatively recent invention, having first appeared at the start of the 18th century. It's particularly associated with the Highlands, and its wearing was banned after the Scots' defeat at Culloden in 1746. It was not until the end of the 18th century that tartan became established as a means of identifying Scotland's clans and districts.

There are many tartans today, both historic and modern. Scotland's oldest families may be associated with more than one, with a dress tartan for ceremonies and perhaps a hunting tartan in subdued shades.

CHAIN STORES

NAME	Women's clothing and/or shoes	Men's clothing and/or shoes	Children's clothing and items	Pharmacy and toiletries	Jewellery and accessories	Souvenirs and gifts	Books, music and magazines	Sports and outdoor kit	Food and drink	Household and electrical goods	HEAD OFFICE
BHS	✔	✔	✔		✔					✔	020 7262 3288
The Body Shop				✔							01903 731500
Boots			✔	✔					✔	✔	0131 225 4721
Burtons		✔									0845 121 4514
Clarks	✔	✔	✔								01458 443131
Debenhams	✔	✔	✔	✔	✔	✔				✔	020 7408 4444
Edinburgh Woollen Mills	✔	✔	✔			✔					01387 380611
HMV							✔				0131 225 7008
House of Fraser	✔	✔	✔	✔	✔			✔		✔	020 7963 2000
Jessops										✔	0116 232 6000
JJB Sports	✔	✔	✔					✔			01942 221400
John Lewis Partnership	✔	✔	✔	✔	✔			✔		✔	020 7828 1000
Marks & Spencer	✔	✔	✔	✔	✔				✔		020 7935 4422
Monsoon	✔				✔						020 7313 3000
Next	✔	✔	✔		✔					✔	0845 456 7777
Hector Russell	✔	✔	✔		✔	✔	✔		✔		01877 339999
Thorntons						✔			✔		01773 540550
Tiso								✔			0131 554 9101
Waterstones							✔				020 8742 3800
Whisky Shop									✔		0141 334 6666
WH Smith							✔				0141 848 6832
Woolworths			✔	✔	✔		✔		✔	✔	0845 608 1101

The cloth known as tweed is more often associated with the weaving mills of southern Scotland, and generally carries smaller designs in more subdued hues than tartan. Harris Tweed is still hand-woven by islanders in the Outer Hebrides, and has made a fashionable comeback on the catwalks in recent years.

Scotland also produces some distinctive glasswear, with firms such as Edinburgh Crystal known for its fine cut-glass, and Caithness Glass for its modern designs and beautiful coloured paperweights. Pottery from Highland Stoneware, hand-painted with Scottish scenes, is also widely available.

An ornamental tin of shortbread is perhaps the ultimate Scottish souvenir, but in recent years the choice of local food available to take home has widened to embrace such delicacies as venison and smoked salmon in vacuum packs, and specialty haggis in tins. Heather honey, sweet biscuits from the Borders and Dundee fruit cake are also popular options for a taste of Scotland back home.

TAX-FREE SHOPPING

If the goods you buy are going to be exported to a non-European Union (EU) country, you are exempt from Value Added Tax (VAT; currently 17.5 per cent), where it is applied. This can be a considerable saving (but you have to spend a minimum amount which varies from shop to shop) and it is usually reclaimed at the airport on departure rather than deducted in the shop. Most major department stores participate and will have details of their tax-free shopping policies to help with your claim.

OPENING TIMES

Core opening hours are from 9am to 5pm (with no break for lunch). In larger towns and cities most shops stay open to 5.30pm, and late opening, until 9pm or 10pm, is common in busy areas, while supermarkets are likely to remain open into the night. Many shops will open for at least a few hours on Sundays.

In addition to countless individual boutiques and specialist shops, Scotland also has several chain stores. The chart below gives details of some of them, stating the number of branches each chain has in Scotland. You will find branches of these stores in shopping areas and malls in Scotland.

NUMBER OF SHOPS	DESCRIPTION	SHOP WEBSITE
17	Mid-range clothing store with some household goods and lighting	www.bhs.co.uk
23	Pioneering retailer of cosmetic products using natural, sustainable resources	www.thebodyshopinternational.com
126	Chemists and opticians plus cosmetics, children's clothing and food	www.boots.com
52	Mid-range clothing for men	www.burtonsmenswear.co.uk
43	Retailer of shoes for men, women and children	www.clarks.co.uk
10	Dependable department store retailing fashion brands and homeware	www.debenhams.com
74	Fine woollen pullovers, accessories and other clothing	www.ewm.co.uk
15	Sells CDs in all genres of music and DVDs, videos and books	www.hmv.co.uk
6	Classy department store retailing fashion brands and homeware	www.houseoffraser.co.uk
18	Sells all kinds of photographic equipment and accessories, including digital	www.jessops.com
55	Sportswear and shoes for men and women	www.jjb.co.uk
3	Reliable department store retailing fashion brands and homeware	www.johnlewis.com
21	The mainstay of the middle classes, selling food, clothing and homeware	www.marksandspencer.com
26	Women and children's clothing, specializing in party wear	www.monsoon.co.uk
22	Smart, practical clothing for men, women and children	www.next.co.uk
6	Quality Scottish clothing and souvenirs	www.hectorrussell.com
38	Sells own-brand chocolates and toffees	www.thorntons.co.uk
11	Everything for camping, tramping and outdoor sports	www.tiso.com
12	Britain's biggest chain of bookstores with superb coverage in larger branches	www.waterstones.co.uk
10	A great selection of whiskies and related gift items	www.whiskyshop.com
56	Large shops sell countless magazines, stationery, even books and CDs	www.whsmith.co.uk
80	Stores majoring on good value clothing for children, music and homeware	www.woolworths.co.uk

ENTERTAINMENT AND NIGHTLIFE ♪ ♥

The availability of evening entertainment in Scotland varies according to your location. Edinburgh and Glasgow are well served on all levels, as you would expect, with a lively night scene and top-rank entertainment. A series of great festivals, led by the Edinburgh Festival (▷ 174–175) helps to foster a vibrant arts scene. Live music can be heard in pubs and village halls all over the country at any time of year, and if it's advertised as a ceilidh, there's probably some dancing involved. Plays and musicals may be performed in anything from a world-class venue to the tiny theatre on Mull. While most towns have a small cinema, clubs and bars are generally confined to the larger urban centres, with pubs taking over the role in smaller communities.

CLASSICAL MUSIC, OPERA AND DANCE

Scotland has three big orchestras, led by the Royal Scottish National Orchestra (RSNO), whose main season runs from September to April.

Updating Shakespeare at Dundee

Look out also for the Scottish Chamber Orchestra (mainly touring) and the BBC Scottish Symphony Orchestra. Smaller groups such as the BT Scottish Ensemble are also worth seeking out. Scottish Opera has a wide international repertoire.

Scottish Ballet performs regularly in the main cities, and contemporary dance is led by the Scottish Dance Theatre, based in Dundee.
● For more information see www.visitscotland.com/ aboutscotland/culture

POPULAR MUSIC AND COMEDY

Stadiums such as Glasgow's SECC (▷ 186) are the preserve

of household names and top pop acts. Jazz, blues and world music also get a look-in: Henry's Jazz Cellar in Edinburgh is just one well-known venue.

Home-grown pop and folk music thrives in clubs, festivals and more intimate venues around the country.

Meanwhile, live comedy has become increasingly evident in cities, where chains such as Stand Comedy Club provide live acts most nights.

CINEMA

Cities and larger towns are well served by huge, comfortable multiplexes showing the latest films, interspersed with fewer independent picture houses such as the Glasgow Film Theatre (▷ 185). In the regions, cinemas may offer fewer frills and less choice.

TICKETS

The easiest ways to buy tickets are from the venue's box office, or through a ticket agency for larger events (a fee may be added).
● Agencies include Ticketmaster, tel 0870 444 4224; www.ticketmaster.co.uk

PUBS, BARS, NIGHTCLUBS

Unlike the male-dominated bastions of the past, most pubs now encourage female customers and families, and most serve food plus coffee and tea. In the countryside

they may be the only option for a night out. City pubs can become very busy on Friday and Saturday evenings.

In some towns bars are taking over from pubs and nightclubs as the focal points

A modern multiplex at Falkirk

for socializing. During the day they resemble cafés, serving food and coffee, while at night they become small nightclubs, complete with DJ and dance floor.

Most towns and cities will have at least one nightclub, but choose carefully: Smaller towns may have just one dingy venue, playing uninspiring chart music. Dress codes vary according to the location, so check before you set out. Most places accept smart-casual, but generally not T-shirts, jeans or trainers.
● *The List* magazine appears every other Thursday (£3.50). It's a useful guide to the entertainment scenes in Edinburgh and Glasgow.

SPORTS AND ACTIVITIES

The delights of the Highlands as an outdoor venue were discovered in the 19th century, when acres of land were bought up as sporting estates for hunting, shooting and fishing. Today, influenced by the growth worldwide of adventure sports, the range of activities on offer across the country is wider than ever. It takes in white-water canoeing, diving, mountaineering, downhill skiing and other high-adrenaline pursuits, as well as more traditional activities such as hill-walking, game fishing and golf. All are a great way to see more of the countryside, and are well supported with information available at local tourist offices. Whatever you undertake, be prepared for changeable and sometimes extreme weather, and heed local advice if taking to the hills, where conditions may change rapidly.

There are plenty of opportunities to enjoy world-class spectator sports such as football (soccer) and rugby, too, and Scotland's own variations of athletic events such as hammer throwing can be seen throughout the summer at Highland games events. For information on shinty fixtures, visit www.shinty.com

BICYCLING
Forest paths, disused rail tracks and quiet rural roads

Fishing on the River Tay

make bicycling a popular holiday activity here. The National Cycle Network (Sustrans) has over 1,300 miles (2,092km) of routes marked by distinctive blue signposts, including a scenic route between Glasgow and Inverness (214 miles/344km). The National Byway is a rural bicycling route in southern Scotland. The Scottish stretch of the international North Sea Cycle Route picks up in Shetland and continues down the eastern seaboard of the mainland into England.

There are many shorter bicycle trails—see local tourist offices for details and leaflets. These include KM Cycle Trail from Dumfries to Drumlanrig

Castle. It is named after local hero Kirkpatrick Macmillan (1813–78), inventor of the bicycle.

- **www.**cycling.visitscotland. com has advice on bicycle rental.

FISHING
Scotland has an abundance of rivers, lochs and 4,000 miles (6,436km) of coastline, so you can enjoy coarse, sea and game fishing. It's essential to check the rules before fishing as many waters restrict the tackle or bait you can use. For coarse and game fishing you'll need a permit, which you can buy from the local tourist office, fishery or tackle shop.

- **www.**visitscotland.com/fish is a good source of information.
- **www.**fishing-uk-scotland.com lists a variety of fishing organizations and holiday options.

Coarse fishing
Angling for roach, pike, carp, tench or perch lacks the cachet of game fishing, but is often more accessible on a short visit—there is no closed season for coarse fishing. Lochs Ken, Lomond and Awe are known for their pike.

- Scottish Federation for Coarse Angling; **www.**SFCA.co.uk

Sea angling
No permit is required. Cod and pollock are favourites, caught

A sunny day on the links (course)

from the southeastern shores through the summer, and off more northerly shores in winter. The southeast shores of Dumfries and Galloway produce some of the best shore fishing, with pollock and wrasse in summer and cod in winter. Porbeagle sharks, skate and halibut are more adventurous catches off northern and western coasts. Fishing for mackerel with a long lure line is a great holiday pastime.

Game fishing
The brown trout season is from 15 March to 6 October. Wild brown trout are found in lochs and rivers all over the country. You can find salmon

and sea trout fishing from 15 January to 30 November, although open and close season dates vary from region to region. Note that salmon fishing is prohibited on a Sunday. Expect to pay a high price for a beat on the great salmon rivers—the Tweed, the Spey, the Tay and the Dee.

● Salmon and Trout Association, tel 020 7283 5838; **www.**salmon-trout.org

FOOTBALL (SOCCER)
The football season runs from August until May. The two big Edinburgh teams—Heart of Midlothian (Hearts) and Hibernian (Hibs)—are both worth a look. Finding tickets

Fine walking country: the Trossachs

for the Edinburgh derby may be tricky, but for all other games try the websites for match details and tickets. Celtic and Rangers are the great rivals in Glasgow. Advance reservations are essential.

GOLF
Golf is the national game, played by people of all ages and incomes. With more than 500 courses to choose from, you'll need advice to select a course and reserve a round. Tourist offices have information on all the main courses (▷ 301). The golf season is from April until mid-October; reserve in advance as far as possible.

● **www.**scottishgolf.com has a directory and reservations advice.

Most regions offer a golf pass or ticket which can be used to save money: Ask at any tourist office. For example, a three-day Perthshire Highland ticket gives access to 11 top courses for around £35. Some courses may have age restrictions.

● For information on individual courses, see the regional listings that follow.

HORSEBACK RIDING
Forest trails, sandy beaches and heather-covered hills make Scotland ideal for horseback riding. Find out about local facilities from the nearest tourist office. Go through a riding centre that has been approved by the British Horse Society (BHS) or the Trekking and Riding Society of Scotland (TRSS).

● **www.**bhsscotland.org.uk
● **www.**riding-in-scotland.com

RUGBY
International games have become a great spectacle even for the non-rugby fan. The home of Scottish rugby is Murrayfield, in Edinburgh.

WALKING
There is an established network of waymarked rights of way, and local tourist offices usually stock leaflets and books about walking in the area, whether you're looking for a level stroll or something more exacting. Detailed Ordnance Survey maps are also sold here and in most bookshops. Look out for the AA's book, *100 Walks in Scotland*, which contains mapped walks for all abilities.

Access to the hills is generally open, but during the shooting season (12 August to early December) walkers should check locally for possible restrictions. On some of the most popular hills,

Hillphones run by the Mountaineering Council give up-to-date information about stalking activities. Particularly during the lambing season (March–end May), dogs must be kept under strict control.

Hill walkers take a particular interest in ticking off the list of Munros, a set of 284 peaks classified as over 914.4m (3,000ft) and named after the climber who first categorized them. Corbetts and Grahams are lower level lists.

Look out for the 'Walkers Welcome' symbol at accommodation sites from bothies to guesthouses, where drying facilities and early breakfasts are available.

Downhill skiing at Glencoe

● For information about long-distance paths ▷ 236.

WATERSPORTS
Scotland's inshore waters are popular with sailors of small- and medium-size craft. The seas around the Western Isles and larger lakes such as Loch Lomond are particularly good. Inland waterways like the Forth & Clyde and Union Canal offer more options for holidays afloat.

● **www.**sailscotland.co.uk has information on sailing courses and boat charter.

Windsurfing takes place in a number of spots around the coast, as well as on Loch Tay, Loch Lomond and other freshwater sites. Popular

beaches include Elie and Lunan Bay in the east, Machrihanish in the west, Sandhead Bay in the southwest and Thurso in the north. Tiree claims to be the windsurfing capital of Scotland. Waterskiing takes place on larger lochs, including Loch Tay and Loch Lomond.

WINTER SPORTS

There are five main ski centres in Scotland. Tuition and ski rental are available at all, and day adult lift passes cost around £25. The season depends entirely on snowfall: so, if it snows they open the runs. The best snowfall is usually in January and February.

Nevis Range

Due to the altitude, this centre near Fort William is the best for snow late in the season. It is popular with skiers and snowboarders and has an excellent off-piste area, Back Corrie.
● www.nevis-range.co.uk

Cairngorm

The ski centre near Aviemore has a funicular railway system to take you to the top in comfort, and offers a range of runs for all ability levels.
● www.cairngormmountain.com

The Lecht

The most easterly ski centre, family-focused, with a snowboard fun park, snowtubing, quad bikes and deval karting.
● www.lecht.co.uk

Glencoe

At the inland end of the pass, this is the most alpine ski centre, with dramatic, wild scenery and the steepest on-piste run in Scotland. It's also popular with snowboarders.
● www.glencoemountain.com

Glenshee

Close to Braemar, Glenshee is the most extensive ski and snowboard area, with 21 lifts and 36 runs.
● www.ski-glenshee.co.uk

HEALTH AND BEAUTY ♥

Luxurious spas are a well-established feature of upmarket tourism in Scotland, with the top hotels offering wonderfully indulgent treatments in opulent surroundings.

The spectacular rooftop hydropool at Edinburgh's One-Spa at the Sheraton Grand, for example, has become a vital modern icon for the capital. However, the idea of self-pampering is relatively new to the Scottish spirit, and beyond the major centres you'll be lucky to find much more than the facilities of, perhaps, a local hairdresser.

Fitness is another matter, and most settlements of any size have a local gym, swimming pool and fitness centre, with training times and facilities well advertised locally.

FOR CHILDREN ☻

From outdoor activities such as go-carting and quad biking aimed at older kids to the retelling of well-loved tales in the Scots vernacular at storytelling sessions, children are well catered for in Scotland, especially in summer.

Visitor centres offer opportunities to get involved with everything from learning how ice cream is made and hand-painting pottery to getting up close to wildlife and farm animals. Glasgow's fabulous hands-on Science Centre is the biggest of several excellent such facilities around the country, and history can be explored through steam trains, sailing ships and excellent industrial museums such as Wanlockhead and Dundee's Verdant Works. The harbour town of Tobermory, on Mull, has become the hottest attraction for under-sixes since the advent of the BBC's storytelling programme for youngsters, *Balamory*—a leaflet available locally will help them identify the real houses of characters such as Josie Jump, Miss Hoolie and Spencer the Painter.

In practical terms, many attractions are free to under-fives and offer a substantial discount to children under 16. Family discount tickets are widely available, but always check ahead as details of numbers and ages included can vary enormously according to the attraction. It's well worth searching through the local free newspapers and tourist leaflets, too, as they often offer discount tickets (such as free child entry with one full-paying adult) on the day.

SPORTS AND ACTIVITIES/HEALTH AND BEAUTY/FOR CHILDREN 155

FESTIVALS AND EVENTS

Scotland has many festivals and traditions. Listed below, month by month, are the major events that take place annually. While some are free public events, most involve buying tickets which will vary in price according to the event and venue. Check for the availablility of season tickets, which may offer better value.

JANUARY

BA' GAME
Kirkwall, Orkney
www.bagame.com
An energetic game of mass soccer, when two teams from the upper and lower ends of the town (the Uppies and the Doonies) scrummage in the streets in a tradition that dates back further than anyone can remember. The main throw-in occurs at 1pm, at the Mercat Cross, with the Doonies aiming for the harbour and the Uppies for a point near the Catholic church.
⊙ 1 January

CELTIC CONNECTIONS
Glasgow, various venues
www.celticconnections.co.uk
Scotland's biggest Celtic and folk festival attracts leading musicians from all over the world. Concerts, workshops and ceilidhs over three weeks.
⊙ January

UP HELLY AA
Lerwick, Shetland
Tel 01595 693434
www.visitshetland.com
Viking celebrations on the last Tuesday of the month, with torchlight processions, 'guizers', a ceremonial ship burning and partying. Local Up Helly Aa festivals are held around the islands during February and March.
⊙ Late January

APRIL/MAY

SHETLAND FOLK FESTIVAL
Shetland, Lerwick and various venues
Tel 01595 694757
www.shetlandfolkfestival.com
Four days of some of the liveliest folk music around, in

venues as far as Fair Isle. Attracts artists such as Aly Bain and Phil Cunningham, Frances Black and Elvis Costello as well as performers from around the world. Join in sessions and workshops at the Isleburgh Community Centre.
⊙ End April/early May

SPIRIT OF SPEYSIDE WHISKY FESTIVAL
Speyside, various venues
Tel 07092 840566
www.spiritofspeyside.com
Four days of whisky-imbued fun all over Speyside, from vintage tastings on trains to tours of the distilleries.
⊙ End April/early May

JUNE

CAMANACHD CUP FINAL
Venues change annually
www.shinty.com
The Camanachd Association is the ruling body of the predominantly Gaelic sport of shinty, and the cup final is the highlight of the year's fixtures as teams compete for the silver trophy.
⊙ Mid-June

T IN THE PARK
Balado, Fife
www.tinthepark.com
Scotland's biggest rock festival boasts a line-up of around 100 of the best local and international pop bands on seven stages over one weekend, from Idlewild and Super Furry Animals to Radiohead.
⊙ Mid-June

ROYAL HIGHLAND SHOW
Ingliston, by Edinburgh
Tel 0131 335 6200
www.royalhighlandshow.org

The biggest agricultural show in Scotland offers four days of top livestock judging, show jumping, heavy horses, crafts, trade stands and other country activities. The permanent show site is near Edinburgh airport.

ST. MAGNUS FESTIVAL
Orkney, various venues
www.stmagnusfestival.com
Prestigious summer festival of music (chiefly classical, but also folk and jazz), theatre, literature and visual arts. St. Magnus Cathedral is the main setting.
⊙ Late June

JUNE/JULY

COMMON RIDINGS
Selkirk, Hawick, Galashiels
Up to 400 horseback riders take part in these traditional Borders festivals, following the town's flag as it is borne around the edge of the common land.
⊙ June/July

JULY

GLASGOW INTERNATIONAL JAZZ FESTIVAL
Glasgow, various locations
Tel 0141 552 3552
www.jazzfest.co.uk
Eight days of the best in international jazz in venues across the city. Check out the Fringe, too.
⊙ Early July

SCOTTISH TRADITIONAL BOAT FESTIVAL
Portsoy
Tel 01261 842951
www.scottishtraditionalboatfestival.co.uk
Maritime fun at this pretty, old town on the Banffshire coast when, for three days, the harbour fills with wooden

sailing boats reminiscent of the glory days of the fishing fleet. Racing, displays by the local Coastguard service, folk music, beer, food and fun.
⊙ July

AUGUST

EDINBURGH FRINGE FESTIVAL
▷ 174
⊙ August

EDINBURGH INTERNATIONAL ARTS FESTIVAL
▷ 174
⊙ August

MILITARY TATTOO
▷ 175
⊙ August

WORLD PIPE BAND CHAMPIONSHIPS
Glasgow, various venues
Pipers, drummers and pipe bands from all over the world turn Glasgow Green into a sea of tartan at this prestigious annual competition.
⊙ Mid-August

COWAL HIGHLAND GATHERING
Dunoon
Tel 01369 703206
www.cowalgathering.com
The biggest Highland games in Scotland boast 3,500 competitors from as far afield as Canada and New Zealand. Highland dancing, piping and athletics over three days.
⊙ Late August

SEPTEMBER

BRAEMAR GATHERING
Braemar, Deeside
Tel 01339 755377
www.braemargathering.org
The Queen is a regular visitor to this most famous of Highland games events. Competitive pipers, athletes and dancers are augmented by teams from HM Forces.
⊙ Early September

SCOTTISH BOOK TOWN FESTIVAL
Wigtown, various venues
Tel 01988 402036
www.wigtown-booktown.co.uk/festival
This literary festival in the relaxed setting of Scotland's 'book town' is becoming an established favourite, with guest speakers, book signings and Kidzfest for children.
⊙ Late September

OCTOBER

ROYAL NATIONAL MOD
Venues change annually
www.the-mod.co.uk
A major competition-based festival celebrating and helping

The Braemar Gathering is regularly visited by the Queen

to promote all areas of Gaelic language, arts and culture.
⊙ Early October

ACCORDION AND FIDDLE FESTIVAL
Shetland, various venues
Tel 01595 694757
www.shetland-music.com/musevnt2.htm
Dance 'til you drop at this hectic four-day festival, celebrating the music of two of Scotland's most popular folk instruments, and held in community halls all across the islands.
⊙ Mid-October

DECEMBER/JANUARY

FLAMBEAUX
Comrie, Perthshire
www.hogmanay.net/scotland/perth
An ancient hogmanay festival is celebrated at midnight when 10-ft (3m) high flaming torches are lit in the old churchyard, then processed through the streets, to be doused in the River Earn. The torch-bearers are led by a pipe band, and followed by villagers in fancy dress.
⊙ 31 December/1 January

HOGMANAY
Princes Street, Edinburgh
Tel 0131 473 3800
www.edinburghshogmanay.org
Celebrate the end of the old year and the start of the new with live music, dancing and mega-fireworks at Scotland's biggest annual party. Entry is free, but you need to obtain a pass in advance—check for details on the website.
⊙ 31 December/1 January

HIGHLAND GAMES
Highland games take place throughout the summer all across Scotland, and visitors are welcome at these lively spectacles. Historically trials of strength, today they generally include a number of athletic events such as hammer throwing and tossing the caber. In this event a tree trunk must be lifted and thrown end-over-end, to land as near as possible in a 'twelve o'clock' position on the ground.

Typically, the games also include competitions in Highland dance and bag-piping, and there may be showjumping, tug-of-war, and livestock events such as sheepdog trials, as well as food stands and other entertainments.

Check with local tourist offices for more information.

SOUTHERN SCOTLAND

Visitors who know no better often hurry through the Borders and bypass the southwest altogether in their haste to see the Highlands. But there's lots to do in this southern sweep, from the delights of small-town shopping in places such as Jedburgh, Melrose and Kelso, to world-class golf at Troon and Turnberry, and active watersports on Loch Ken. The region boasts Scotland's 'book town', galleries and arty shops in Kirkcudbright and Castle Douglas, and discount designer fashion outlets at Livingston and Gretna. If you want to get out and about, you can enjoy native wildlife at Caerlaverock, Glen Trool and Laggan o'Dee, plus exotics at Newton Stewart. Dumfries offers all the facilities of a bigger town, with Burns connections as well. There are several excellent Lowland distilleries to visit, including Glenkinchie at Tranent. And the Isle of Arran is a world of its own, complete with brewery, distillery and health and beauty products.

KEY TO SYMBOLS	
⊕	Shopping
🎭	Entertainment
▼	Nightlife
⚽	Sports
✪	Activities
♥	Health and Beauty
✿	For Children

ANNAN

🎭 LONSDALE CINEMA

Moat Road
Tel 01461 206901
www.lonsdalecitycinemas.co.uk
Mainstream cinema with twin screens, reasonably priced, in the centre of Annan. Shows mostly popular movies, but also some independent films. Snacks available. Free parking.
🎭 Daily, with screenings nightly and afternoon matinees at weekends and school holidays

✪ WESTLANDS ACTIVITIES

Westlands, Near Hollee
Tel 01461 800274
www.westlands-activities.co.uk
Go-carting, quad biking and paintballing are top of the list at this activity centre, which is located 4 miles (6.4km) east of Annan. Try a cross-country ride, with guide, on a quad bike (older children only), have a go on the go-carts for adults and children, and enjoy the mayhem of paintballing. Equipment and clothing are all supplied. Trout fishing and clay pigeon shooting are also available.
✪ Daily 9–5 ✪ Paintball from £3; go-carts from £6; quad bikes from £5

ARRAN (ISLE OF)

⊕ ARRAN AROMATICS

The Home Farm, Brodick KA27 8DD
Tel 01770 302595
www.arranaromatics.com
Natural bath and beauty products are handmade on the farm, signposted from Brodick Pier. As well as the Arran Aromatics shop, with its special offers and discounts, there is a gift shop on the site, a smokehouse, and an outlet selling home-made cheese.
⊕ Mon–Sat 9–5.30, Sun 10–5
🍴 Tea room serves snacks and lunch

☆ ISLE OF ARRAN BREWERY COMPANY

Cladach, Brodick KA27 8DE
Tel 01770 302353
www.arranbrewery.com
If beer is more your tipple than
whisky, come and see it being
brewed at Cladach, near
Brodick. The entry fee includes
a taste of the beer.
🕐 Mon–Sat 10–5, Sun 12.30–5
💷 £1.50 🏢

☆ ISLE OF ARRAN DISTILLERS

Distillery and Visitor Centre, Lochranza
KA27 8HJ
Tel 01770 830264
www.arranwhisky.com
The distillery in the north of
the island produces Arran's
own single malt whisky.
Take the guided tour, enjoy
the exhibition and buy a gift or
bottle of Arran whisky in the
shop. Tours include a taste of
the whisky.
🕐 Mid-Mar to end Oct daily 10–6; Nov
to mid-Mar check ahead 💷 Adult
£3.50, child £2.50 (under 12 free)
🍴 Restaurant serves good local food,
Italian coffee and home baking 🏢

AYR

⊕ HOURSTON'S

22–30 Alloway Street KA7 1SH
Tel 01292 267811
You can't miss the window
displays for this large
independent department
store on Alloway Street, at
the top of the High Street.
Hourston's sells fashion,
accessories, household
goods, china, glass and gifts
including china by Royal
Doulton and glassware by
Edinburgh Crystal.
🕐 Mon–Fri 9.30–5.30, Sat 9–5.30
🍴 Restaurant on the top floor
serves soup, sandwiches, teas and
hot meals

♪ GAIETY THEATRE

Carrick Street KA7 1NU
Tel 01292 611222
www.gaietytheatre.co.uk
This busy venue in the heart
of Ayr hosts a wide variety
of touring productions
throughout the year,

including comedy, jazz,
drama, pop and ballet.
🕐 Box office Mon–Sat 10–5 💷 From £8
☕ Popplewell's café bar Mon–Sat
9.30–4

🎬 ODEON

10 Burns Statue Square KA7 1UP
Tel 0871 224 4007
www.odeon.co.uk
This cinema, showing
mainstream movies, is found at
the top of the town, opposite
the train station. Snacks include
popcorn, sweets and soft drinks.
🕐 Daily from 12.30 💷 From £5

🍴 TAM O'SHANTER INN

230 High Street KA7 1RQ
Tel 01292 611684

*Enjoy one of the samples at Isle
of Arran Distillers*

Small traditional pub with a
thatched roof, dating back to
1749, on the main street of
Ayr. The snug interior has a
log fire and Burns poetry
painted directly on to the
walls.
🕐 Daily 10am–12.30am. Food daily 10–8

BIGGAR

⊕ ATKINSON-PRYCE BOOKS

27 High Street ML12 6DA
Tel 01899 221225
A small shop front at the
bottom of the High Street
conceals this charming
bookshop, tightly packed with
goodies. It has a particularly
wide range of Scottish titles
including travel, poetry and

literature. There's also a good
selection of children's books,
and classical and folk CDs.
Gift wrapping service.
🕐 Mon–Sat 9.30–5

☆ PURVES WORLD OF PUPPETS

Puppet Tree House, Broughton Road
ML12 6HA
Tel 01899 220631
www.purvespuppets.com
This puppet theatre troupe
has been going for over
35 years, and tours the world.
Catch them at the puppet
theatre in Broughton (clearly
signposted from the main
road), which has weekly
shows for all the family
and backstage tours. The
whole attraction is designed
to delight children. Check
locally for show dates
and times.
🕐 Tue–Sat 10–4.30 💷 From £2.50
☕

BLADNOCH

☆ BLADNOCH DISTILLERY AND VISITOR CENTRE

DG8 9AB
Tel 01988 402605
www.bladnoch.co.uk
Scotland's most southerly
distillery, lying 2 miles (3.2km)
south of Wigtown, dates
from 1817. Enjoy a guided
tour, see a video of how the
whisky is produced and then
taste a dram yourself. There's
a picnic area, and nearby
Cotland Wood has rare
orchids and is a pleasant
place for a walk.
💷 Adult £3 (under 18 free) 🏢 Gift
shop Easter–end Oct Mon–Fri 9–5;
summer Sat 11–5, Sun 12–5

BROUGHTON

✪ BROUGHTON GALLERY
Broughton Place ML12 6HJ
Tel 01899 830234
www.broughtongallery.co.uk
High-quality paintings, etchings and crafts are displayed in the superb setting of a Border castle, reached via a steep private road. Includes work by local and British artists. Crafts include turned and carved wood, jewellery, traditional toys and handmade glass.
🕐 Apr–end Sep, mid-Nov to Christmas Thu–Tue 10.30–6

CAERLAVEROCK

✪ CAERLAVEROCK WILDFOWL AND WETLANDS TRUST CENTRE
East Park Farm DG1 4RS
Tel 01387 770200
www.wwt.org.uk
This 560ha (1,400-acre) nature reserve is off the B725, 9 miles (14km) southeast of Dumfries. In autumn, winter and spring, thousands of wild geese and other birds can be seen from observation towers. In summer, wander along the nature trails or join one of the free wildlife safaris, which take place at 11.30am and 2.30pm.
🕐 Daily 10–5 💷 Adult £4.40, child £2.70, family £11.50 ☕ Small tea room

CASTLE DOUGLAS

⊞ DESIGNS GALLERY & CAFÉ
179 King Street DG7 1DZ
Tel 01556 504552
www.designsgallery.co.uk
This crafts shop and gallery on the main street of Castle Douglas specializes in contemporary art and design led crafts, and is well worth seeking out for the top quality designer jewellery, ceramics, sculpture, glass and paintings. There's also an excellent café downstairs, with conservatory and walled garden.
🕐 Mon–Sat 9.30–5.30

🎭 LOCHSIDE THEATRE
Lochside Road DG7 1EU
Tel 01556 504506
www.lochsidetheatre.co.uk
Local volunteers staff this theatre in a converted church. It's home to the Lochside Theatre Company and a venue for touring productions.
🕐 All year; box office Mon, Wed, Fri–Sat 12–2 💷 From £4

✪ CLOG AND SHOE WORKSHOP
Balmaclellan DG7 3QE
Tel 01644 420465
www.clogandshoe.co.uk
Shoes and clogs are made at this unusual workshop, 13 miles (21km) north of

Make your own ceramics at Dalton Pottery Art Café

Castle Douglas. In the showroom, admire the small museum collection of footwear from around the world. Shoes can be made to order.
🕐 Easter–end Oct Mon–Fri 10–5

✪ SULWATH BREWERY
209 King Street DG7 1DT
Tel 01556 504525
www.sulwathbrewers.co.uk
Six beers are brewed in this small, family-run micro-brewery in the town centre. Sample the product on a fascinating guided tour.
🕐 Mon–Sat 10–4 💷 Guided tour £3.50. Cost includes a pint of beer or, if you're driving, a bottle to take away

DALTON

✪ DALTON POTTERY ART CAFÉ
Meikle Dyke, Dalton DG11 1DU
Tel 01387 840236
See the clocks, vases, napkin rings and cat-and-fish-themed ceramics being made at this working pottery and café, or make your own. Use of the workshop is free, as are all materials and baking, so all you pay for is the pot. Fun, safe activity for children as young as four. Signposted from Carrutherstown, off the A75 between Dumfries and Annan.
🕐 Easter–end Oct daily 10–5; rest of year Tue–Sun 10–5 💷 From £3 ☕ Daily 10–5; serves home baking, including children's meals ⊞ Daily 10–5

DRUMMORE

✪ MULL OF GALLOWAY VISITOR CENTRE
Near Drummore
Tel 01776 830682
www.mull-of-galloway.co.uk
This nature reserve, famous for its seabirds, is on Scotland's most southerly point, 22 miles (35.4km) south of Stranraer. Enjoy a circular walk around the reserve. There's usually a warden on hand to answer your questions.
🕐 Apr–end Oct daily 10–4 💷 Free

DUMFRIES

🎬 ODEON
Shakespeare Street DG1 2JJ
Tel 0871 224 4007
www.odeon.co.uk
A single-screen cinema showing mainstream films. Found in the town centre, near the Theatre Royal. Snacks available.
🕐 Daily 💷 From £4.60

🎬 ROBERT BURNS FILM THEATRE
Robert Burns Centre, Mill Road DG2 7BE
Tel 01387 264808
www.rbcft.co.uk
This single-screen cinema is housed in the Robert Burns Centre, on the opposite bank of the River Nith from the main

part of the town. It shows a variety of mainstream, foreign and art house films, offering films that are a bit more unusual than what's on offer at the Odeon.

🕐 Tue–Sat. Often evening screenings only, so check beforehand 💷 £4.40 🍴 Hullabaloo Restaurant upstairs, Mon–Sat 11–4, 6–10 (not Mon eve), Sun 11–3

🎭 THEATRE ROYAL
Shakespeare Street DG1 2JH
Tel 01387 254209
www.theatreroyaldumfries.co.uk
The Theatre Royal is Scotland's oldest working theatre. In the town centre, it offers plays and pantomimes performed by the theatre's resident amateur Guild of Players, and touring productions of music and drama, including Scottish Opera.

🕐 All year 💷 From £6 🛒

🍺 THE GLOBE INN
56 High Street DG1 2JA
Tel 01387 252335
www.globeinndumfries.co.uk
This 400-year-old pub is an absolute must if you are in Dumfries, even if it is just to have a look at the place that was Robert Burns's local. It's full of character, with little oak-panelled rooms and crooked door lintels. The poet's favourite room is preserved as it was in the 1730s, and you can see his chair by the fire. You'll find the pub down an alley near the foot of the High Street. It serves home cooking, real ale and lots of malt whiskies.

🕐 Mon–Wed 10am–11pm, Thu–Sun 10am–midnight

✪ GRACEFIELD ARTS CENTRE
28 Edinburgh Road DG1 1NW
Tel 01387 262084
www.web-link.co.uk/gracefield
A 10-minute walk from the centre of town, the arts centre offers a changing series of contemporary visual art and craft exhibitions and activities. There is also a permanent

collection of Scottish paintings, which are shown at different times throughout the year.

🕐 Tue–Sat 10–5 💷 Most exhibitions free 🍴 Café serves light lunches and home baking 🛍 Shop (Tue–Sat 11–3) sells locally made crafts, jewellery, cards and postcards

GATEHOUSE OF FLEET

✪ MILL ON THE FLEET VISITOR CENTRE
High Street DG7 2HS
Tel 01557 814099
At the top end of Gatehouse of Fleet, this beautifully converted 18th-century mill has two working watermills and is now a visitor centre incorporating a café, bookshop, craft shop, art

The historic Globe Inn is one of Dumfries' finest

gallery and wildlife exhibition. It is in grounds with picnic tables and wooden sculptures.

🕐 Apr–end Oct daily 10.30–5 🍴 Café set on a veranda overlooking the river 📖 Bookshop sells new and second-hand titles

✪ CREAM O'GALLOWAY VISITOR CENTRE
Dairy Co Ltd, Rainton, Gatehouse of Fleet, Castle Douglas DG7 2DR
Tel 01557 814040
www.creamogalloway.co.uk
Watch 30 flavours of fabulous ice cream being made at this organic farm dairy, in a converted 17th-century farmstead, then choose your favourite in the shop. There are

nature trails through the surrounding woodland, a dry-stone dyking exhibition and playground. From the A75, take the road to Sandgreen; after 1.5 miles (2.4km), turn left at the sign for Carrick.

🕐 Daily 10–5; Oct daily 10–4; Nov Sat–Sun daily 10–4; Dec, Jan closed 💷 Free; small charge for playground 🍴 📖

GRETNA

🏬 GRETNA GATEWAY OUTLET VILLAGE
Glasgow Road DG16 5GG
Tel 01461 339100
www.gretnagateway.com
This extensive shopping complex in Gretna itself has a pedestrianized street with designer outlet stores on either side. Permanent discounts in stores such as Polo Ralph Lauren, Reebok, Tag Heuer, Tommy Hilfiger, Van Heusen and Marks & Spencer.

🕐 Daily 10-6 🍴 Café Vienna and Café Thorntons for tea, coffee and light lunches

🏬 THE WORLD FAMOUS OLD BLACKSMITH'S SHOP CENTRE
Gretna Green DG16 5EA
Tel 01461 338224
www.gretnagreen.com
Although Gretna Green has a romantic history, there's nothing romantic about the rampant commercialism that exists in this low, whitewashed complex today. Shops sell knitwear, Scottish food, whisky, golf wear, china, jewellery and wood carvings. Quality varies from excellent (Johnston's of Elgin cashmere and Wedgwood china) to poor (plastic, kilted dolls). Tax-free shopping for visitors from outside the European Union (EU), and post-it-home service for UK and overseas.

🕐 Daily, variable times from 9am, all year 🍴 Large café sells snacks and lunches

JEDBURGH

🌐 R & M TURNER LTD
34–36 High Street TD8 6AG
Tel 01835 863445
A huge antiques shop behind
a traditional façade on the
main street of Jedburgh, this is
an Aladdin's cave of old silver,
furniture, pictures, thimbles
and china, spread over three
floors. They can send your
purchases overseas.
🕐 Mon–Fri 9.30–5.30, Sat 10–5

⭐ CHRISTOPHER RAINBOW
8 Timpendean Cottages TD8 6SS
Tel 01835 830326
Tandems, mountain and road
touring bicycles can all be
rented here, and even
delivered to or collected for
you. Ideal for the peaceful Four
Abbeys Cycleway through
Melrose, Dryburgh and Kelso.
The route, which is 62 miles
(100km), is well signposted
and takes you along the Tweed
and Teviot rivers. Tool kit and
puncture repair kit supplied.
🕐 All year 💷 Bicycle rental from £18
a day

⭐ HARESTANES
COUNTRYSIDE VISITOR
CENTRE
By Ancrum TD8 6UQ
Tel 01835 830306
Just 3 miles (4.8km) north of
Jedburgh, the visitor centre
offers beautiful woodland
walks, an outdoor play area,
exhibitions, and craft workshops
selling leather goods, tiles and
wooden objects. Storytelling,
face-painting and other
activities for children.
🕐 Late Mar–end Oct daily 10–5
💷 Free 🍴 Tea room serves home
baking, light lunches and local ice
cream in a relaxed, child-friendly
atmosphere

⭐ JEDFOREST DEER AND
FARM PARK
Camptown, Jedburgh TD8 6PL
Tel 01835 840364
www.aboutscotland.com/jedforest
Birds of prey and deer are
to be found on this working
farm, 5 miles (8km) south

of Jedburgh. Eagles, owls
and hawks display daily.
Look for ranger-led activities
and talks on farming and
the environment. For
children there are indoor
and outdoor play areas
and special activities.
Picnic and barbecue area.
🕐 May–end Aug daily 10–5.30;
Sep–end Oct daily 11–4.30 💷 Adult £4,
child £2.50, family £12 🍴 🎁

KELSO

🌐 BORDER GALLERY
6 Bowmont Street TD5 7JH
Tel 01573 226002
www.scottishbordersartsandcrafts.co.uk
This little art gallery in a
whitewashed building just

*An antiques treasure-trove at
Jedburgh's R & M Turner*

off the main square sells
affordable modern oil
paintings, watercolours,
glass, jewellery, sculptures
and textiles.
🕐 Tue–Sat 10–5

🌐 THE HORSESHOE GALLERY
22 Horsemarket TD5 7HD
Tel 01573 224542
www.scottishbordersartsandcrafts.co.uk
An unusual combination is on
sale in this elegant dark-green
façaded shop on the corner of
Horsemarket: fine art and toys.
The historic oil and
watercolour paintings on offer
are reasonably priced, along
with sporting prints and
etchings, a large selection of

teddy bears, and a variety of
other gifts.
🕐 Mon–Sat 10–5; Jan–end Mar closed
Wed

🎬 ROXY CINEMA
Horsemarket TD5 7AE
Tel 01573 224609
www.roxy-kelso.co.uk
A small cinema in the centre
of Kelso, the Roxy manages
two shows a night of
mainstream movies, and
doubles as a bingo hall.
🕐 Tue–Wed and Sat–Sun 6 until late
💷 From £1.50

KIPPFORD

⭐ KIPPFORD HOLIDAY PARK
Kippford, Dalbeattie DG5 4LF
Tel 01556 620636
www.kippfordholidaypark.co.uk
Activities at this award-winning
nature conservation park
include guided nature walks,
bicycle rental, a 9-hole golf
course and fishing. The park
has private woodland and has
won awards for conservation,
with views to the English Lake
District 40 miles (64km) away.
Play area and assault course
for children.
🕐 Open all year, but some activities
(notably watersports) are restricted to
summer 💷 Various prices, depending
on activities 🎁 Food shop open
Easter–end Sep

KIRKCUDBRIGHT

🌐 THE CORNER GALLERY
75 St. Mary Street DG6 4DU
Tel 01557 332020
A designer knitwear shop on
the corner with Gladstone
Street, with a wide choice of
hats, sweaters, scarves and top
quality hand-knitted works of
art. Almost everything is
made by small, independent
producers from Scotland and
the islands.
🕐 Mid-Mar to mid-Jan Mon–Sat 10–5;
closed Thu from 1pm, except Jun–end
Aug

WHAT TO DO

JO GALLANT

Ironstones, 70 High Street DG6 4JL
Tel 01557 331130
www.jogallant.co.uk
Sumptuous textiles are displayed in this traditional, stone-fronted building near the Tolbooth Art Centre. The price of the machine-embroidered and quilted wall-hangings, cushions and scarves may be high, but so is the quality.
⏰ Mon–Sat 10–5 (call first if travelling specially)

TOLBOOTH ART CENTRE

High Street DG6 4JL
Tel 01557 331556
www.dumfriesmuseum.demon.co.uk
The centre, in a former prison and court house, tells the story of the Kirkcudbright colony of artists through a video presentation and a permanent display of paintings. The gallery upstairs shows exhibitions of contemporary art and crafts.
⏰ Oct–end May Mon–Sat 11–4; also Jun–end Sep Sun 2–5 💷 Free
🖼 Good selection of paintings, crafts and art books in the gift shop 🍴 Café on the ground floor serves tea, coffee and locally made cakes and biscuits

GALLOWAY WILDLIFE CONSERVATION PARK

Lochfergus Plantation DG6 4XX
Tel 01557 331645
www.gallowaywildlife.co.uk
Enjoy a free guided tour of the park, which is home to nearly 200 animals in large enclosures, including pandas, lynx, Scottish wildcats, snakes, deer and llamas. Pet and snake handling sessions, children's educational activity area, children's quiz in the summer and animal crazy golf. The park is set in 27ha (67 acres) of woodland, signed from the centre of the town.
⏰ Mar–end Nov daily 10–6; Feb–end Nov Fri–Sun 10–4 💷 Adult £4.50 child £2.50

LAGGAN O'DEE

GALLOWAY RED DEER RANGE

Laggan o'Dee, New Galloway DG7 3SQ
Tel 07771 748401
www.forestry.gov.uk
If you want to get close to the shy red deer, then this deer park, where you can walk among the animals, is the place to come. The deer range lies between New Galloway and Newton Stewart in the beautiful Galloway Forest Park, which covers 300 square miles (777sq km) of forest, moors and lochs.
⏰ Mid-Jun to end Sep Tue, Thu 11, 2, Sun 2.30 💷 Adult £3.50, child £1.25, family £8

Laggan o'Dee is the place to go to meet red deer

LIVINGSTON

MCARTHURGLEN DESIGNER OUTLET

Almondvale Avenue EH54 6QX
Tel 01506 423600
www.mcarthurglen.com
Scotland's largest designer shopping outlet, with 100 stores under one roof, as well as a cinema and lots of eating places. Shops include Jane Shilton, Mexx, Regatta and Burberry.
⏰ Mon–Wed 9–6, Thur 9–8, Fri–Sat 9–6, Sun 11–6 🍴 🍽 🚻

LOCH KEN

LOCH KEN WATER SKI SCHOOL

Loch Ken Marina, by Castle Douglas
Tel 07050 092792
www.skilochken.co.uk
Learn to waterski at this watersports centre on Loch Ken. Aquatic activities to suit all ages and abilities, and all equipment and tuition is included. Advance booking required.
⏰ Daily 💷 Prices vary with the activity; 15-minute waterski lesson from £14

GALLOWAY SAILING CENTRE

Castle Douglas DG7 3NQ
Tel 01644 420626
www.lochken.co.uk
Activities at this family owned watersports centre on beautiful Loch Ken include sailing, windsurfing, kayaking, canoeing, quad biking and gorge scrambling. Check availability in advance, and note that some activities may not be suitable for younger children. You can also camp in the grounds, or take a residential course, staying in the lodge.
⏰ Mid-Mar to end Oct 💷 Lessons from £20 🍴 Lunch, snacks and drinks available

KEN-DEE MARSHES NATURE RESERVE

Tel 01671 402861
www.rspb.org.uk
This nature reserve lies half-way down the south side of Loch Ken, near the viaduct. It has a nature trail through woods and marshes beside the loch and along the River Dee. Winter wildfowl include Greenland white-fronted geese, and in summer migrating birds such as redstarts and pied flycatchers are the stars.
⏰ Daily dawn–dusk 💷 Free

WHAT TO DO

MELROSE

⊕ ABBEY MILL
Annay Road TD6 9LG
Tel 01896 822138
This large store selling knitwear, clothes, toys and Scottish food occupies a historic corn mill just outside the town, beyond Melrose Abbey. The mill building dates back to the Middle Ages, when it supplied the abbey brewery with roasted barley.
⏰ Summer daily 9–5.30; winter times vary ⬛ Abbey Mill Tea Room serves light meals and snacks

⊕ THE CRAFTERS
The High Street TD6 9PA
Tel 01896 823714
www.melrose.bordernet.co.uk/traders/crafters
A unique co-operative of local craft workers sells handmade gifts from this small shop, including cards, ceramics, knitwear, silk, jewellery and woodwork.
⏰ Mon–Sat 9.30–5

⊕ THE WHOLE LOT
St. Dunstans, High Street TD6 9RU
Tel 01896 823039
This well-stocked antiques, art and gift shop is in a red building, set back from the road, opposite the rugby club. Antiques include jewellery, ceramics, furniture and paintings. A gift section sells quality kitchenware, toys, clothes, pottery, scarves and baskets.
⏰ Mon–Fri 9.30–5, Sat 9.30–5.30, Sun 12–5

⊕ THE WYND THEATRE
The Wynd TD6 9PA
Tel 01896 820028
www.thewynd.com
A small, local theatre just off the High Street, with films, concerts including blues, big band and folk music, plays and pantomime. Bar open on performance evenings.
⏰ All year 💷 From £5

⊗ ACTIVE SPORTS
Chain Bridge Cottage, Annay Road TD6 9LP
Tel 01896 822452
www.activitiesinscotland.com
Choose from a half-day or full-day activity at this outdoor centre, the only one of its kind in the Borders. Rent a mountain bicycle, go quad biking, or enjoy watersports such as canoeing. Most activities take place just outside Selkirk, though some may not be suitable for younger children. Advance reservations recommended.
⏰ Open all year, but watersports May–end Oct only 💷 Depends on the activity

Locally made crafts for sale at The Crafters in Melrose

◯ DOWN TO EARTH HEALTH
32 The Market Square, Melrose TD6 9PP
Tel 01896 822590
www.downtoearthhealth.co.uk
Complementary health therapy centre with various treatments available. Kinesiology (muscle testing) is a particular area of expertise. There is also a wide range of products to buy in store. Opposite the Ship public house.
⏰ Mon–Sat 10–5

NEWCASTLETON

✪ BAILEY MILL TREKKING CENTRE
Bailey TD9 0TR
Tel 01697 748617
www.holidaycottagescumbria.co.uk
Horseback riding and bicycling through the Scottish Borders and into Cumbria. After the day's activities, relax in the sauna and jacuzzi at this holiday complex, which also offers accommodation. Advance reservations recommended.
⏰ All year 💷 Trekking £12 per hour; lessons £8 per 30 minutes ⬛

NEWTON STEWART

✪ TROPIC HOUSE
Carty Port DG8 6AY
Tel 01671 404050 (day) or 01671 402485 (evening)
Enjoy the colour and spectacle of tropical butterflies and insects, and the best collection of carnivorous plants in the UK, all at this tropical plant house near Newton Stewart.
⏰ Daily 10–5 💷 Adult £3.50, child £1.50, family £8 ⬛ Tea room

PENICUIK

✪ EDINBURGH CRYSTAL VISITOR CENTRE
Eastfield EH26 8HB
Tel 01968 675128
www.edinburgh-crystal.com
See the famous Edinburgh Crystal being made in the factory and choose from beautiful decanters, vases and whisky glasses in the shop, which also has a discount on seconds. You can talk with the master craftspeople as they work, and see how glass has been made through the ages. Signposted off the A701, 30 minutes south of Edinburgh city centre.
⏰ Mon–Sat 10–5, Sun 11–5 ⬛ Coffee shop sells home baking and hot and cold snacks

PENTLAND HILLS ICELANDICS

Windy Gowl Farm, Carlops, Penicuik EH26 9NL
Tel 01968 661095/07836 729988
www.phicelandics.co.uk
Enjoy a short ride or an all-day trek in the Pentland Hills on a hardy Icelandic pony from this Trekking and Riding Society of Scotland approved centre, just south of Carlops. Warm clothes, tough shoes or boots essential (no trainers). Minimum age 6. Advance reservations advised.
🕐 All year Fri–Wed. Rides normally start at 10 and 2.30 💷 1 hour 30 minutes £25, 2 hours £30, 3 hours £40

STOBO

STOBO CASTLE

EH45 8NY
Tel 01721 725300
www.stobocastle.co.uk
Treat yourself in this luxurious health spa, which is set in a 19th-century castle, an hour's drive south of Edinburgh. State-of-the-art facilities include an ozone pool, aromatic steam room and mud room. Advance reservations essential.
🕐 All year 💷 Day visit from £160; overnight packages from £155 🍽

TRANENT

GLENKINCHIE DISTILLERY

Pencaitland EH34 5ET
Tel 01875 342004
www.malts.com
The home of the Edinburgh Malt, southeast of the city. You can see the working distillery, an exhibition of malt whisky and taste the whisky itself. Children under 8 are welcome, but are not allowed in the production area.
🕐 Jun–end Sep Mon–Sat 10–5, Sun 12–5 💷 Admission (£4) includes a discount voucher for the whisky shop

TROON

ROYAL TROON

Craigend Road KA10 6EP
Tel 01292 311555
www.royaltroon.com
You'll need to reserve months ahead if you want to play a round at this world-class Open Championship golf course. The facilities are excellent, and this is reflected in the prices. Minimum age 18.
🕐 Daily 💷 From £100 for two rounds on the Portland course, including lunch; £170 for one on the Portland and one on the Old Course. Available Mon–Tue and Thu only 🚻 🍴 Restaurant in clubhouse 🏛

The Old Bank Bookshop is a delight for bibliophiles

TURNBERRY

TURNBERRY

KA26 9LT
Tel 01655 334032
www.turnberry.co.uk
This world famous Open Championship links course is 15 miles (24km) south of Ayr. Minimum age 16 and must be accompanied by an adult. If you're with a golfing partner, the Westin Turnberry Resort has an outdoor activity centre and an award-winning spa.
🕐 Daily 💷 Summer green fees for the Ailsa course begin at £130 for non-residents 🚻 🍴 Clubhouse with restaurant 🏛

WIGTOWN

THE BOOK SHOP

17 North Main Street DG8 9HL
Tel 01988 402499
www.the-bookshop.com
A book lover's dream: the largest second-hand bookstore in Scotland, with over 0.5 mile (700m) of shelves for the stock of 65,000 books. Free coffee with a seat by the fire!
🕐 Mon–Sat 9–5

MING BOOKS

Beechwood, Acre Place DG8 9DU
Tel 01988 402625
Britain's largest dealer in second-hand crime and detective books, Ming Books also stocks naval history, natural history and books about Winston Churchill. It's set in a rambling old building in its own grounds, with books covering every available surface from the floor and up the stairs. Friendly owners Marion and Robin Richmond will also find and mail books to you.
🕐 Daily 10–6

THE OLD BANK BOOKSHOP

7 South Main Street DG8 9EH
Tel 01988 402111
A vast selection of second-hand books on subjects as diverse as ornithology, poetry, natural history, military history, biography and Robert Burns, on the site of a former bank at the foot of the high street.
🕐 Daily 10–5

READING LASSES

17 South Main Street DG8 9EH
Tel 01988 403266
www.reading-lasses.com
Medium-sized second-hand bookshop with a pale green façade, specializing in women's studies, politics and psychology. Art and crafts by local women also on sale.
🕐 Mon–Sat 10–5 ☕ Small café offers real coffee, tea, home baking

EDINBURGH

In summer the capital fairly buzzes with all the activities of the festivals and their fringes, catering for every taste and budget. In fact there's lots to do here at any time of year, whether you're into the high arts (six theatres, plenty of cinemas and a wealth of concert venues big and small) or looking for exciting nightlife in the numerous small bars and clubs. Enjoy a literary pub crawl, or a guided witch tour—or stick to the excellent tour buses, if that all sounds a little alarming. You can spend a small fortune on designer cashmere and exclusive fashion in boutiques around the centre, browse the high street shops on Princes Street, or just soak up the atmosphere of a genteel Edinburgh institution, Jenners department store (and contrast it with the ultra-modern Harvey Nichols). It's a great city to explore on foot, but why not rent a bicycle and go further, or perhaps just chill out in the Commonwealth Pool?

WHAT TO DO

KEY TO SYMBOLS

- ⊕ **Shopping**
- 🎭 **Entertainment**
- ▼ **Nightlife**
- 🏃 **Sports**
- ✪ **Activities**
- ♥ **Health and Beauty**
- ✿ **For Children**

⊕ SHOPPING

BOOKS

OLD TOWN BOOKSHOP
8 Victoria Street EH1 2HG
Tel 0131 225 9237
The place to come for second-hand books on poetry, music, travel, art and, of course, Scotland and Scottish writers. Also has a good selection of prints and maps.
🕐 Mon–Sat 10.30–5.45

WATERSTONE'S
128 Princes Street EH2 4AD (west end branch)
Tel 0131 226 2666
www.waterstones.co.uk
One of the leading bookshop chains in Britain, Waterstone's has several branches in Edinburgh. The shop at the west end of Princes Street is on several floors, with large windows and a café on the top level which gives great views to the castle. The branch at the east end of Princes Street has a well-stocked Scottish travel and literature section. Further branches on George Street and at Ocean Terminal.
🕐 Mon–Sat 8.30–8, Sun 10.30–7 ☕

DEPARTMENT STORES

FRASERS (HOUSE OF FRASER)
145 Princes Street EH2 4YZ
Tel 0870 160 7239
www.houseoffraser.co.uk
In price terms, this popular department store falls midway between John Lewis in the St. James shopping centre and Jenners. Good selection of accessories, perfumes, clothes (including labels such as DKNY and Ralph Lauren), kitchenware and accessories. On the west corner of Princes Street.
🕐 Mon, Wed–Fri 9.30–6, Tue 9.30–7, Sat 9–6, Sun 11–5 ☕ Café on the fifth floor for coffee, light lunch and three-course meals

HARVEY NICHOLS

30–34 St. Andrew Square EH2 3AD
Tel 0131 524 8388
www.harveynichols.com
Perfumes, designer handbags, accessories and clothes including Gucci, Burberry, Prada, Fendi and Dior make this an exclusive but expensive shopping experience. More designer labels are to be found in next-door Multrees Walk.
🅖 Mon–Wed 10–6, Thu 10–8, Fri–Sat 10–7, Sun 11–6 🍴 Bar, brasserie and top-floor restaurant

JENNERS

48 Princes Street EH2 2YJ
Tel 0131 225 2442
www.jenners.com
Snootier than its newest rival Harvey Nichols, Jenners is an Edinburgh institution, founded in 1838. Until it was recently bought by House of Fraser, it was the world's oldest independent department store. Inside it is a confusing rabbit warren of different levels, with a central galleried arcade reminiscent of Liberty's in London—pick up a printed store guide to help you find the bits you want, or explore and discover. It sells everything from high quality clothes and shoes to toys, glassware, groceries and perfume, and also offers online shopping from its website. On the corner of St. David Street, opposite Waverley train station. There are branches at the airport and Loch Lomond shores.
🅖 Mon, Wed and Fri–Sat 9–6, Tue 9.30–6, Thu 9–8, Sun 11–5 🍴 Four cafés on different floors serve coffee, snacks and full meals

GIFTS AND SPECIALIST CLOTHING

ANTA

93 West Row EH2 2JP
Tel 0131 225 4616
www.anta.co.uk
Upmarket independent shop selling stoneware, tiles, carpets and luggage from Scotland. Also sells high quality fabrics, throws and cushions in wool and woven tweed in a variety of contemporary and classic tartans. Stylish but expensive.
🅖 Mon–Sat 10–6, Sun 11–5

CRUISE

94 George Street EH2 3DF
Tel 0131 226 3524
31 Castle Street EH3 2DN
Tel 0131 220 4441
This is where Edinburgh's fashionistas go shopping for designer clothes, shoes and accessories, with labels such as Gucci, Prada and Paul Smith. Prices are not for the faint-hearted. Both shops are in the smart New Town area,

Jenners is Edinburgh's most distinguished department store

with menswear in George Street, and the ladies' store in Castle Street. Further stores at 80 George Street and 14 St. Mary's Street.
🅖 Mon–Wed, Fri–Sat 10–6, Thu 10–7, Sun 12–5

HAWICK CASHMERE COMPANY

71-81 Grassmarket EH1 2HJ
Tel 0131 225 8634
www.hawickcashmere.com
The 'Cashmere Made In Scotland' swing ticket indicates that the clothes in this shop at the foot of Victoria Street are of the highest quality. Sweaters and scarves in every hue.

Cashmere doesn't come cheap: sweaters start at £140.
🅖 Mon–Sat 10–6

HECTOR RUSSELL

95 Princes Street EH2 2ER
Tel 0131 225 3315; freephone order number (UK only) 0800 980 4010
www.hector-russell.com
The Princes Street branch of this well-known chain of kilt shops is a good place to rent or buy a kilt or kilt outfit, whether you're looking for a sgian dubh (small knife traditionally worn inside the sock) or the full works. A complete outfit won't cost less than £500, but purchases can be mailed home. Ladies are also well catered for. Additional branch in High Street.
🅖 Mon–Sat 9–5.30, Sun 11–5

NESS

336–340 Lawnmarket, Edinburgh
Tel 0131 225 8815
www.nessbypost.co.uk
Funky modern knitwear and accessories in vibrant tones make the most of flamboyant local design and quality Scottish wool. You'll find everything from Harris tweed handbags to long scarves in zingy shades. Also farther down the Royal Mile at 367 High Street.
🅖 Daily 10–6

PALENQUE

56 High Street, Royal Mile EH1 1TB
Tel 0131 557 9553
www.palenque.co.uk
This small jewellery shop, just below the junction with South Bridge, specializes in contemporary and silver rings, necklaces and bracelets and hand crafted accessories, all reasonably priced. There is a second shop on Rose Street.
🅖 Mon–Sat 9.30–5.30, Sun 11–5

RAGAMUFFIN

276 Canongate EH8 8AA
Tel 0131 557 6007
Eye-catching displays in the large windows of this shop on the corner of St. Mary's Street show brightly hued, handmade chunky knitwear, clothes, scarves and toys from all over England and Scotland.
🔘 Mon–Sat 10–6, Sun 12–5

ROYAL MILE WHISKIES

379 High Street, Royal Mile EH1 1PW
Tel 0131 225 3383
www.royalmilewhiskies.com
This specialist whisky shop opposite St. Giles Cathedral stocks a vast range of malt whiskies, some of which are 100 years old. It's the best place to buy rare whiskies if you want them shipped home—order by phone or online for delivery within the UK or overseas.
🔘 Mon–Sat 10–6, Sun 12.30–6 (open longer in Aug)

TARTAN WEAVING MILL AND EXHIBITION

555 Castlehill, The Royal Mile EH1 2ND
Tel 0131 226 4162 (shop)/0131 226 1555 (mill)
www.tartanweavingmill.co.uk
Walk down the floors of this massive tartan and tartanalia shop at the top of the Royal Mile to discover the source of all that clacking and burring of machinery—the weaving looms in the basement. On the way you can have your photo taken in full Highland rig, and consult the Clans and Tartans Bureau for information about your own clan history. The shop and exhibition make imaginative use of a building which once housed the Old Town's water reservoir.
🔘 Apr–end Sep Mon–Sat 9–6.30, Sun 9.30–6.30; rest of year Mon–Sat 9–5.30, Sun 10–5.30 🎟 Free 🅿

TISO

123-125 Rose Street EH2 3DT
Tel 0131 225 9486
www.tiso.com
The best outdoor clothing and equipment shop in Edinburgh.

Helpful and knowledgeable staff can give you advice on everything you need for walking, climbing, camping or skiing. There's also an excellent travel and mountaineering book section. Rose Street is in the heart of the city.
🔘 Mon, Wed, Fri–Sat 9.30–5.30, Tue 10–5.30, Thu 9.30–7.30, Sun 12–5

MARKETS AND MALLS
OCEAN TERMINAL

Ocean Drive, Leith EH6 6JJ
Tel 0131 555 8888
www.oceanterminal.com
Designed by Jasper Conran and opened in 2001, Ocean Terminal is a vast shopping

Stop off for a tipple at Royal Mile Whiskies

and cinema complex which overlooks the Firth of Forth and the Royal Yacht *Britannia* (▷ 86). The shops are mainly the high street names that you can find in the centre of Edinburgh. However, the huge, free parking area makes shopping here an attractive option. The lofty central space is the venue for exhibitions of anything from artwork to tents.
🔘 Mon–Fri 10–8, Sat 10–7, Sun 11–6
🚍 11, 22, 36 🅿 🚻 🛗 Food outlets, including Costa Coffee and Starbucks for caffeine, Zinc Bar & Grill for upmarket restaurant dining (tel 0131 553 8070), Ocean Kitchen for buffet food and Ocean Bar for stylish drinks

PRINCES MALL

Princes Street EH1 1BQ
Tel 0131 557 3759
www.princesmall-edinburgh.co.uk
This surprisingly light and spacious subterranean shopping centre next to Waverley train station has many of the usual high street names in fashion and gifts. Look out for handmade chocolates at Maxwell & Kennedy and Orkney jewellery at Ortak.
🔘 Mon–Sat 9–7, Sun 10–6 🍴 Food court in the lower mall with McDonald's, Costa Coffee, Rollover Hotdogs and Spud-U-Like (baked potatoes)

ST. JAMES CENTRE

Leith Street EH1 3SS
Tel 0131 557 0050
www.thestjames.co.uk
High street favourites such as HMV, Boots and Accessorize dominate this modern shopping mall at the east end of Princes Street. The big draw is the John Lewis department store, which has everything for the home, clothes, a large beauty counter and a café with panoramic views. Large parking area.
🔘 Mon–Wed, Sat 7.30–6.30, Thu–Fri 7.30–8.30, Sun 11–5 🅿

MUSIC
CODA MUSIC ON THE MOUND

12 Bank Street, The Mound EH1 2LN
Tel 0131 622 7246
www.moundmusic.co.uk
This small shop on the Mound stocks a fabulous collection of recordings of traditional and contemporary Scottish folk music, as well as world and country music, and is a great place to find out about the Edinburgh folk scene.
🔘 Mon–Sat 9–5.30, Sun 11–5

🎭 ENTERTAINMENT
CINEMAS
CAMEO

38 Home Street EH3 9LZ
Tel 0131 228 4141 (box office); 0131 228 2800 (24-hour recorded information)
www.picturehouses.co.uk

Small, friendly independent cinema showing low-key Hollywood, international and independent films. Near the King's Theatre. Ask for a plastic glass and you can take your drink into the cinema with you.

£5.90; all tickets £4 Mon except bank holidays Extended bar hosts exhibitions by local artists

DOMINION

18 Newbattle Terrace, Morningside EH10 4RT
Tel 0131 447 4771 (box office)
www.dominioncinema.com
This small, family-run, independent cinema in the southern suburb of Morningside is the perfect antidote to the plethora of giant multiplex cinemas. It shows independent and mainstream movies, and has traditional leather Pullman seats. The Gold Class service even offers leather sofas along with the complimentary wine or beer and nibbles. Look out for the collection of photos of famous faces that have visited the cinema over the years.
From £5.10 11, 15, 16, 23

FILMHOUSE

88 Lothian Road EH3 9BZ
Tel 0131 228 2688 (box office); 0131 228 2689 (recorded information)
www.filmhousecinema.com
This three-screen art house cinema opposite the Usher Hall has the best range of independent and international cinema in Edinburgh and hosts local film festivals.
Relaxed Filmhouse Café Bar is great for a coffee or for a full pre-film meal, 10am–10pm From £5.50

ODEON

118 Lothian Road EH3 8BG
Tel 0871 224 4007
www.odeon.co.uk
The Odeon is a five-screen cinema off the west end of Princes Street, showing mostly mainstream movies.
Light bar

VUE EDINBURGH

Omni Leisure Building, Greenside Place, Leith Street EH1 3EN
Tel 08712 240240
www.myvue.com
A huge glass-fronted building opposite John Lewis, this multiplex cinema has stadium seating and the latest in digital surround sound. The Gold Class ticket gives you luxury leather seats, waiter bar service during the film and a wall-to-wall screen. Don't miss the remarkable giraffe sculpture by Helen Denerley outside.
Screenings from lunchtime Mon–Fri; also morning screenings Sat–Sun From £5.60

Morningside's Dominion cinema is worth a trip from the centre

VUE EDINBURGH OCEAN TERMINAL

Ocean Terminal, Ocean Drive, Leith EH6 7DZ
Tel 08712 240240
www.myvue.com
This 12-screen cinema shows mainstream films on the largest multiplex screen in Scotland, with the latest in digital surround sound. The ergonomically designed seats are particularly comfortable, and give extra leg room. Free parking, and possibly the best view of Edinburgh from the top of the escalator.
From £5 Trendy Ocean Bar

EDINBURGH FESTIVAL THEATRE

13–29 Nicolson Street EH8 9FT
Tel 0131 529 6000
www.eft.co.uk
Prestigious concert venue close to the city's east end hosts a variety of international and British touring productions of dance, theatre, musicals and comedy, from contemporary ballet to Scottish Opera. Distinctive all-glass façade and the largest stage in Britain.
All year From £8.50 Café Lucia in the foyer Three further bars

EDINBURGH PLAYHOUSE

18–22 Greenside Place EH1 3AA
Tel 0870 606 3424 (Ticketmaster, 24 hours)
www.cclive.co.uk
The best venue in town for touring productions of big-budget musicals and dance. Located a five-minute walk away from the east end of Princes Street, next door to the huge Vue cinema.
All year From £10

KING'S THEATRE

2 Leven Street EH3 9LQ
Tel 0131 529 6000
www.eft.co.uk
This grand old Edwardian building is one of Edinburgh's oldest theatres. The King's is great for family entertainment, majoring on shows and musicals, pantomime, comedy and plays. Also drama, including Shakespeare. Located a short bus ride from the West End.
All year From £10 Two, for interval drinks

NETHERBOW CENTRE

43-45 High Street EH1 1SR
Tel 0131 556 9579
www.scottishstorytellingcentre.co.uk
A small, intimate venue with an innovative programme of Scottish and children's theatre, and traditional stories and poetry readings.
Phone for details

WHAT TO DO

ROYAL LYCEUM THEATRE

Grindlay Street EH3 9AX
Tel 0131 248 4848
www.lyceum.org.uk
One of the leading production theatres in Scotland, the Lyceum creates all its own shows. Contemporary and classic theatre predominate, including Shakespeare productions. Off Lothian Road near the West End of the city.
All year From £7

TRAVERSE THEATRE

10 Cambridge Street EH1 2ED
Tel 0131 228 1404
www.traverse.co.uk
The Traverse is famous for its productions of experimental theatre and dance, and is a good place to catch hot new work by Scottish playwrights. Located next to the Usher Hall, near the city's West End.
All year From £9 Traverse Bar Café downstairs warm and intimate, with a wide selection of exotic and draught lagers Blue Bar Café, upstairs, is one of the best restaurants in Edinburgh, tel 0131 221 1222

MUSIC

CORN EXCHANGE

11 New Market Road, Gorgie EH14 1RH
Tel 0131 4163 2437
www.ece.uk.com
Pop and rock music venue, 2 miles (3.2km) southwest of the city centre. Opened in 1999 by Blur, and acts have included Blur, Travis, Pulp, Fun Lovin' Criminals and Coldplay.
All year From £10

HENRY'S JAZZ CELLAR

78 Morrison Street EH3 8BJ
Tel 0131 538 7385
The best place in Edinburgh for contemporary jazz, with something to suit all tastes, including Latin, free and Jamaican jazz. There's a bar, but no food is served. Morrison Street is a short walk from the West End.
All year From £4

QUEEN'S HALL

Clerk Street EH8 9JG
Tel 0131 668 2019
www.queenshalledinburgh.co.uk
A more intimate venue than the Usher Hall, the Queen's Hall is a hot spot for jazz, blues and soul, as well as classical music and comedy, attracting names such as Courtney Pine and Ruby Turner.
All year From £8 Café on two floors, good for coffee and filled rolls Stocks good selection of real ales and malt whiskies

USHER HALL

Lothian Road EH1 2EA
Tel 0131 228 1155
www.usherhall.co.uk

The Usher Hall is one of the city's top venues

Edinburgh's most prestigious concert hall attracts high quality performers such as the English Chamber Orchestra and the Moscow Philharmonic Orchestra. A distinctive circular building towards the West End, its high dome can be seen from many parts of the city.
All year From £10 Three bars

NIGHTLIFE

CLUBS/BARS

BAILIE BAR

2 St. Stephen Street, New Town EH3 5AL
Tel 0131 225 4673
This basement pub has an unusual, triangular-shaped bar, low ceilings and sumptuous dark-red décor. There's plenty of space, and a lounge area where you can enjoy the real ales. On the corner of St. Stephen Street and North West Circus Place, in Stockbridge.
Mon–Sat 11am–1am, Sun 12.30–11pm

BELUGA

30a Chambers Street, Old Town EH1 1HU
Tel 0131 624 4545
www.beluga-edinburgh.com
The place to see and be seen: The ground-floor restaurant is a laid-back place to have lunch by day, and the basement bar is the home of the beautiful people and a packed dance floor by night. The interior is opulent and stylish, with leather seats and chrome fittings. Opposite the Royal Museum of Scotland.
Daily 11am–1am Free entry

BLUE MOON

1 Barony Street, New Town EH1 3SB
Tel 0131 557 0911
Everybody is welcome at this gay bar, noted for serving the best food in the area all day. Alongside the substantial range of beers and a wine list, try Mexican food or even vegetarian haggis, neeps and tatties. Deep red-painted walls, a coal fire and relaxing fish tanks. Off Broughton Street, a few minutes' walk from the east end of Princes Street.
Mon–Fri 11am–midnight, Sat–Sun 10am–1am

BONGO CLUB

Moray House, 37 Holyrood Road EH8 8AQ
Tel 0131 558 7604
www.thebongoclub.co.uk
The Bongo nightclub's club nights are diverse and cover different styles of live music, from hip hop to reggae and breakdancing. In daytime, it's a café, with free internet access and exhibition space.
Variable; café open from noon
Up to £10

WHAT TO DO

BOW BAR

80 The West Bow , Victoria Street,
Old Town EH1 2HH
Tel 0131 226 7667
Painted blue and located half-way down Victoria Street, this is the best bar in the city for whisky, with over 140 to choose from and usually several on special offer. Good selection of real ales too. Wood panelling and old brewery mirrors inside.
🕐 Mon–Sat 12–11.30, Sun 12.30–11

CAFÉ ROYAL CIRCLE BAR

19 West Register Street EH2 2AA
Tel 0131 556 1884
This traditional pub in a grade 'A' listed building is almost 150 years old, and boasts the most impressive pub interior in Edinburgh. It's well worth having a drink here to admire the Victorian interior with Doulton tile portraits, stained glass, ornate ceiling and comfy leather sofas. Find it down an alley behind Burger King at the east end of Princes Street.
🕐 Mon–Wed and Sun 11–11, Thu 11am–midnight, Fri–Sat 11am–1am

CASK AND BARREL

115 Broughton Street, New Town
EH1 3RZ
Tel 0131 556 3132
An unpretentious, traditional pub with plenty of constantly changing real ales served by staff who know their stuff. The Cask is well known as a soccer pub, and on the day of an important match it's shoulder-to-shoulder in here, with standing room only as locals pile in to watch the game on the TVs around the bar. At the foot of Broughton Street.
🕐 Mon–Wed 11am–12.30am, Thu–Sat 11am–1am, Sun 12.30pm–12.30am

DORIC TAVERN

15–16 Market Street, Old Town
Tel 0131 225 1084
There's a warm atmosphere in this traditional pub, and the smell of good food. Now into its fourth century, it's a very old pub indeed, but the façade is unassuming and easy to miss. A wine bar and bistro are upstairs. Market Street is behind Waverley train station.
🕐 Daily 12pm–1am

ESPIONAGE

4 India Buildings, Victoria Street, Old Town EH1 1EX
Tel 0131 477 7007
www.espionage007.com
It's late, it's free and you can dance the night away at this bar/club—small wonder it's popular with young people looking to extend their evening. Four themed bars and two dance floors spread over five floors make this an easy place to lose your friends. At

The Jolly Judge is a popular pub for lawyers

the top of Victoria Street, near George IV Bridge.
🕐 Nightly 7pm–3am (to 5am during Festival) 🎟 Free entry

GRAPE

The Capital Building, 13 St. Andrew's Square EH2 2BH
Tel 0131 557 4522
A smart and stylish city centre wine bar on George Street. There's an extensive selection of wines, but Grape is equally good for a coffee break while you're shopping. Comfy sofas and a dramatic painted ceiling.
🕐 Mon–Tue, Thu 11am–midnight, Wed 11am–11pm, Fri–Sat 11am–1am, Sun 12.30–6pm

GREYFRIARS BOBBY

34 Candlemaker Row EH1 2QE
Tel 0131 225 8328
Behind its traditional wooden façade there is a friendly pub, named after the famously loyal dog. Popular with students and visitors alike. Located in front of Greyfriars Kirk.
🕐 Mon–Sat 11am–1am, Sun 12.30pm–1am 🚌 23, 27, 103

JOLLY JUDGE

7 James Court, Old Town EH1 2PB
Tel 0131 225 2669
It's not easy to find this charming little pub, but worth seeking out for its genuine 17th-century character complete with painted, low-beamed ceiling and for its wide choice of malt whiskies. At the top of the Royal Mile look out for the sign; go down East Entry into James Court, and the pub is down some steps on the left.
🕐 Mon and Thu–Sat 12–12, Tue–Wed 12pm–11pm, Sun 12.30pm–11pm

OPAL LOUNGE

51a George Street EH2 2HT
Tel 0131 226 2275
www.opallounge.co.uk
Stylish New Town basement cocktail bar and fusion restaurant where the beautiful and famous hang out. Reputedly a favourite haunt of Prince William.
🕐 Daily 12pm–3am 🎟 Mon–Fri £3 after 11pm; Sat–Sun £5

PO NA NA

43B Frederick Street EH2 1EP
Tel 0131 226 2224
www.ponana.co.uk
A popular city centre bar/nightclub, if you fancy a dance after the pubs have closed. Moroccan themed interior, with dance floors and secluded alcoves. The queues start forming at around 10pm. Just down from George Street, below Café Rouge.
🕐 Mon–Sat 10pm–3am 🎟 From £2

RICK'S

55a Frederick Street, New Town EH2 1LH
Tel 0131 622 7800
Trendy, minimalist basement bar in the heart of the city, with over 20 types of vodka as well as a list of bar snacks. Rick's serves as restaurant, cocktail bar, breakfast café and boutique hotel, all in one. Just off Princes Street.
🕐 Daily 7am–1am

STAND COMEDY CLUB

5 York Place EH1 3EB
Tel 0131 558 7272
www.thestand.co.uk
Enjoy live comedy from new and well-known Scottish comedians, seven nights a week, at this dark and intimate basement bar. Weekend shows often sell out, so advance booking is advised.
🕐 Mon–Sat 7.30pm–1am, Sun 12.30–12.30 💷 £5–£10

THE VENUE

17–21 Calton Road EH8 8DL
Tel 0131 557 3073
This intimate, gay-friendly club and gig venue, spread over three floors, specializes in both established and up-and-coming rock, funk, pop and indie bands. A two-minute walk from the east end of Princes Street.
🕐 All year 💷 From £4; tickets from Ripping Records, 91 South Bridge, tel 0131 226 7010

⚽ SPORTS AND ⚽ ACTIVITIES

BICYCLING

BIKE TRAX

7–11 Lochrin Place, Tollcross EH3 9QX
Tel 0131 228 6633
www.biketrax.co.uk
Rent a bicycle to explore the city for yourself. Bike Trax rents mountain and hybrid bicycles, kids' bicycles, trailer bicycles and child seats, and is found to the south of the city centre, near the King's Theatre.
🕐 Summer Mon–Sat 9.30–5.30, Sun 12–5; winter Mon–Sat 9.30–5.30 💷 Mountain bicycle hire from £12 a day

FOOTBALL

HEART OF MIDLOTHIAN FOOTBALL CLUB

Tynecastle Stadium, Gorgie Road EH11 2NL
Tel 0131 200 7201
www.heartsfc.co.uk
The Hearts ground lies 1 mile (1.6km) southwest of the city centre.
🕐 Adult £10–£35, child £5–£15 🚌 1, 2, 3, 3a, 25, 33

HIBERNIAN FOOTBALL CLUB

Easter Road Stadium, 12 Albion Place EH7 5QG
Tel 0131 661 1875
www.hibernianfc.co.uk
The Hibs ground is off Easter Road, towards Leith,

See Edinburgh's sinister side on the City of the Dead Walking Tour

1 mile (1.6km) from the centre.
🕐 Adult £20–£25, child £10 🚌 1

RUGBY

MURRAYFIELD STADIUM

Off Roseburn Terrace, Murrayfield EH12 5PJ
Tel 0131 346 5000
www.sru.org.uk
Rugby is arguably Edinburgh's favourite sport, and games throughout the year are well supported, so advance reservations are essential. Located in the Murrayfield district, 1 mile (1.6km) from the city centre. No age restrictions.
💷 £10–£50 🚌 12, 31, 36

SWIMMING

ROYAL COMMONWEALTH POOL

21 Dalkeith Road EH16 5BB
Tel 0131 667 7211
www.edinburgh-leisure.co.uk
This Olympic-size indoor swimming pool below Arthur's Seat has water slides, a diving pool and a children's pool as well as a gym, sauna and Clambers—a soft, safe play area for younger children.
🕐 Mon–Tue, Thu–Fri 6am–9.30pm, Wed 6am–9am, 10–9.30, Sat 6am–7pm, Sun 10–7 💷 Adult £3.30, child £1.90, family £7.80; cheaper rates Mon–Fri before 4pm 🚌 14, 21, 33 🚗

TOURS

ADRIAN'S EDINBURGH CITY CYCLE TOUR

Tel 07966 447 206
www.edinburghcycletour.com
Enjoy a 3-hour guided bicycle tour, taking in Edinburgh's history, design, Holyrood and other top attractions. All equipment, including bicycles, helmets and waterproofs are supplied. No age restrictions, but not recommended for children under 10. Meet by Holyrood Palace gates. Advance reservations required.
🕐 Daily at 10 and 2.30 (winter by arrangement) 💷 Adult £15

CITY OF THE DEAD WALKING TOUR

40 Candlemaker Row EH1 2QE
Tel 0131 225 9044 /0771 542 2750
www.blackhart.uk.com
Enjoy a night-time guided walk through the mysterious dark lanes of the Old Town, ending up in a haunted mausoleum in Greyfriars graveyard. Meet up at St. Giles Cathedral. Advance reservations recommended. Not suitable for younger children.
🕐 Tours nightly 8.30, 9.15 and 10 💷 Adult £8.50, child (under 16) £6.50

EDINBURGH BUS TOURS

Waverley Bridge EH1 1BQ
Tel 0131 220 0770
www.edinburghtour.com
A guided open-top bus tour is a great way to see the city and,

as your ticket is valid all day, you can get off to see the attractions and catch the next bus. The live tour is in English, or there is a recorded multi-lingual version. Join the tour at Waverley Bridge, Lothian Road, Grassmarket, Royal Mile, Princes Street or George Street. Buy tickets on the bus itself or at the tourist information office.

🕐 Tours leave daily every 10–15 minutes from 9.30am; last tour Easter–end Oct 6.30pm, Nov–Easter 3.30pm 💷 Adult £8.50, child 5–15 accompanied by adult £2.50 (under 5 free), family £19.50

THE EDINBURGH LITERARY PUB TOUR

Tel 0131 226 6665
www.scot-lit-tour.co.uk
A 2-hour walking (and drinking) tour of pubs with literary associations, in the company of knowledgeable actors. Advance reservations are recommended. Meet at the Beehive Inn in the Grassmarket. Minimum age 18.

🕐 Tours start at 7.30pm each night; Oct, Mar–end Apr Thu–Sun only; Nov–end Feb Fri only 💷 £8

MANSFIELD TRAQUAIR CENTRE

15 Mansfield Place EH3 6BB
One of Edinburgh's most extraordinary hidden treasures is accessed via free guided tours, and not to be missed. It's a former church of 1885, remarkable for its decoration from floor to ceiling with murals by the Arts and Crafts artist Phoebe Anna Traquair (1852–1936). The impact of the freshly restored paintings is stunning.

🕐 2nd Sun of each month, extra dates during Festival 💷 Free

MERCAT TOURS

Niddry Street South EH1 1NS
Tel 0131 557 6464
www.mercattours.com
Take an hour-long guided tour of Edinburgh's haunted underground city, through the vaults at South Bridge, or perhaps a late-night stroll on the Ghosthunter Trail. Reservations are essential. Meet at the Mercat Cross on the Royal Mile.

🕐 Daily, times vary 💷 Adult from £6.50, child £3, family £16

SCOTTISH PARLIAMENT

Edinburgh EH99 1SP
Tel 0131 348 5200
www.scottish.parliament.uk
Take a tour of Scotland's most talked-about modern building, and get an insight into Scottish democracy at work. Guided tours take in the Debating Chamber, the Garden Lobby and views to the MSP

Rooftop relaxation in the Sheraton's outdoor hydropool

Building—advance reservations are essential. And if you just want to see what all the fuss was about, access to the Main Hall and a peep inside the Chamber (on non-business days) will cost you nothing. The public entrance is tucked around a corner, opposite Holyrood Palace.

🕐 Tours: Fri–Mon when Parliament is in session, daily during recess, every 15 minutes 10.15–3.15 (Apr–end Oct 10.15–5.15 weekdays) 💷 Adult £3.50, child £1.75 (under 5 free) 📷 🔲

THE WITCHERY TOUR

84 West Bow, EH1 2HH
Tel 0131 225 6745
www.witcherytours.com

For a glimpse of the Old Town's murkier side, including tales of witchcraft, torture and plague, join a guided walking tour. Witchery tours last 1 hour 15 minutes, and meet outside the Witchery restaurant on Castlehill. Not suitable for the very nervous. Advance reservations are essential.

🕐 Ghosts and Gore tour nightly May–end Aug 7, 7.30; Murder and Mystery tour nightly all year 9, 9.30, according to demand 💷 Adult £7.50, child £5 (price includes *Witchery Tales* book)

◉ HEALTH AND BEAUTY

EDINBURGH FLOATARIUM

29 North West Circus Place, Stockbridge EH3 6TP
Tel 0131 225 3350
Massage and alternative therapies are the order here. Enjoy the float tank, reflexology, therapeutic massage, aromatherapy massage and facials. Reserve well in advance.

🕐 Mon–Fri 9–8, Sat 9–6, Sun 9.30–4 💷 1-hour float £25; 1-hour aromatherapy massage £32; 2-hour Sheer Bliss £70 📷 24, 29, 36, 42 🔲 Sells pure essential oils, candles, incense, books, CDs, crystals, crystal jewellery and homeopathic remedies

ONE SPA AT THE SHERATON GRAND

8 Conference Square EH3 9SR
Tel 0131 221 7777
www.one-spa.com
This luxurious spa is equipped with an extensive range of spa treatments including massage, facials and Ayurvedic treatments. Facilities include a 19m (62ft) ozone friendly pool, gym, thermal suite and mud room. The rooftop hydropool provides spectacular views of Edinburgh's skyline. Advance reservations are recommended.

🕐 Mon–Fri 6.30am–10pm, Sat–Sun 7am–9pm; children's hours daily 3–5, and Sat–Sun 8.30–9.30am and 3–5pm 💷 Day spa break from £65; overnight residential spa package for two from £300 📷 10, 11, 16, 17 🔲 Spa Café

EDINBURGH FESTIVAL SURVIVAL GUIDE

Millions throng to the capital every year for the world's biggest arts festival and its spin-offs. Here are information and insider tips to help you plan and get the most out of your visit.

EDINBURGH INTERNATIONAL ARTS FESTIVAL

The three-week Edinburgh International Festival offers the highest quality opera, dance, classical music and theatre, and is held every August. The programme, which is free and available from the Edinburgh Festival Office, is published at the end of March and you can reserve tickets from the middle of April. Many events sell out quickly, so it's advisable to reserve as far ahead as possible to secure tickets.

Advertising your show is an integral part of Festival fun

Festival performances are held in Edinburgh's larger and more prestigious venues such as the Usher Hall.
● Edinburgh Festival Office The Hub, Castlehill EH1 2NE, tel 0131 473 2000; **www.**eif.co.uk

EDINBURGH FRINGE FESTIVAL

The ever-expanding Fringe is host to hundreds of different productions of varying quality. Performances of theatre, comedy, music and dance are held in every venue imaginable. Availability of tickets hinges on positive or negative reviews, so get in there quickly

if you hear good things about a production. The Fringe programme, which you can get from the Fringe office on the Royal Mile, comes out in June.
● Festival Fringe Office, 180 High Street EH1 1QS, tel 0131 226 0026; **www.**edfringe.com

Military Tattoo fireworks

HOW TO ENJOY THE FESTIVAL WITHOUT SPENDING A FORTUNE

● The Festival Cavalcade along Princes Street is another opportunity for acts to advertise their shows and for you to pick up the free goodies they throw to the crowd.

● Street theatre happens every day of the Festival on the Royal Mile and outside the National Gallery of Scotland.

● The Bank of Scotland Fireworks from Edinburgh Castle takes place after the last day of the Festival. Princes Street and Calton Hill are good viewing points.

● Buy unsold tickets for Official Festival productions for half price on the day of the performance. Available 1–5 from The Hub, or from the venue an hour before curtain-up. Similarly, last-minute tickets for Fringe events are available at a discount from the Fringe box office on the High Street or outside the tourist office on Princes Street.

● The *Scotsman* newspaper offers free tickets to Fringe shows every day, to the first person bearing a copy of their paper to present him/herself at the Fringe Office.

● Bigger venues tend to have more established, well-known acts. For 'more established' read 'more expensive'. Ergo, smaller venue, smaller price.

● Not officially part of the Festival, but the charming Cameo independent cinema has every film for £3.50 on a Monday.

● Edinburgh's art galleries often start new exhibitions at this time of year. Entrance is free, but there may be a charge for exhibitions.

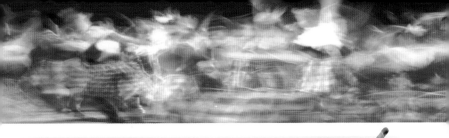

TOP FESTIVAL TIPS

- When in the queue at the Fringe office, note the acts that have sold out for that day (usually written on a blackboard). Reserve tickets for that show for the next night. With so many acts to choose from, a sell-out show is going to be good.
- If going to the Tattoo, take as many of the following as you can find: binoculars, hip flask, waterproofs, cushion and rug. It may be summer but this is still Scotland.
- The best venues for that 'I'm sure I've seen him on TV' moment are the Pleasance, and the Assembly Rooms on George Street.
- Give yourself enough time to have a good look at the Fringe programme. It may be the size of a telephone book but it's free and lists every show in the Fringe.
- Try to see a play performed in the Royal Botanic Gardens. It's rare to be allowed into the gardens at night and it's a wonderfully atmospheric location for theatre. Also, dress warmly and bring a rug to sit on.
- Take a punt. The Mongolian throat singers were the surprise hit of 2000. Yes, really.
- Book your accommodation before you arrive. It's not unheard of for every hotel, B&B and hostel in the city to be fully booked on certain days in August.

WHAT TO DO

Military bands from all over the world take part in the Tattoo on the castle esplanade

EDINBURGH INTERNATIONAL BOOK FESTIVAL

The two-week bookfest, held in the green calm of Charlotte Square Gardens, is near to, but separated from, the madness of the Fringe. You can hear talks and readings, join in question and answer sessions with famous writers and of course, meet your favourite authors and buy books at signing sessions. The Book Festival has many events specifically for children.

- Tel 0131 718 5666; www.edbookfest.co.uk

EDINBURGH INTERNATIONAL FILM FESTIVAL

The Film Festival has been going for more than 50 years, showing international and independent films in Edinburgh's art house cinemas. Highlights include screenings followed by question and answer sessions with the director. Just don't expect anything from Hollywood.

- Filmhouse Cinema, 88 Lothian Road EH3 9BZ, tel 0131 228 4051; www.edfilmfest.org.uk

EDINBURGH INTERNATIONAL JAZZ AND BLUES FESTIVAL

Lasting ten days, the Jazz Festival hosts musicians from all over the world who play in pubs and clubs throughout the city.

- Tel 0131 225 2202; www.jazzmusic.co.uk

EDINBURGH MILITARY TATTOO

The Tattoo—the annual outdoor military spectacle on the castle esplanade—runs for three weeks in August. Pipe bands, soldiers in kilts—they're all here. The show sells out most nights so buying your ticket well in advance is recommended.

- Tattoo Office, 32–34 Market Street EH1 1QB, tel 0131 225 1188; www.edintattoo.co.uk

EDINBURGH ART FESTIVAL

Held for the first time in 2004, this is the newest of the city's festivals, with art, crafts and photography highlighted in galleries and other venues throughout August.

- www.edinburghartfestival.com

CENTRAL SCOTLAND

Family and outdoor activities abound in the beautiful and accessible landscapes of the central region, from archery, falconry, watersports, guided hikes, bicycle routes, quad biking and fishing, to clay pigeon shooting and adrenaline sports. You can witness Formula 3 racing at Knockhill, or play a round of golf in the game's spiritual home, St. Andrews. Its great country for horseback riding, and many centres offer guided treks lasting a day or half a day. If you want a slower pace, join a scenic cruise of Loch Lomond or Loch Katrine, or perhaps catch the boat to the Isle of May to watch puffins and other seabirds. Dundee and Perth are the major cities, with the facilities and nightlife you might expect, while St. Andrews, Stirling and Pitlochry offer a quieter lifestyle. Among the localized shopping, look out for good value knitwear and woollen goods, and pottery and crafts outlets.

ABERFELDY

✪ ABERFELDY GALLERY
39 Kenmore Street PH15 2BL
Tel 01887 829129
www.aberfeldygallery.co.uk
High quality paintings, photography, woodwork, sculpture and pottery by over 100 Scottish-based artists.
🕐 Mon–Sat 10–5, Sun 1–4

✪ DEWAR'S WORLD OF WHISKY
PH15 2EB
Tel 01887 822010
www.dewarswow.com
Just outside Aberfeldy, this distillery has an impressive visitor centre. Enjoy a video and tour of the production area. Hand-held audio guides are available in seven languages.

🕐 Easter–end Oct Mon–Sat 10–6, Sun 12–4; rest of year Mon–Fri 10–4
💷 Adult £5, child £2.50 (5–17), family £12 ☕ Small café serves coffee and cakes 🎫 Whisky and memorabilia

✪ HIGHLAND ADVENTURE SAFARIS
Drumdewan PH15 2JQ
Tel 01887 820071
www.highlandadventuresafaris.co.uk
Explore the high mountain country on a Land Rover tour, reaching a height of nearly 1,000m (3,300ft). Local wildlife includes grouse, mountain hares, red deer and golden eagles. Advance reservations are essential. Binoculars and telescopes provided.

🕐 All year 💷 2 hour 30 minute tour: adult £35, child £14; 1 hour 30 minute tour: adult £17.50, child £8

ANSTRUTHER

✪ EAST NEUK OUTDOORS
Cellardyke Park KY10 3AX
Tel 01333 311929
www.eastneukoutdoors.co.uk
This popular seaside centre offers activities for the whole family such as archery, abseiling, canoeing and orienteering. You can also rent mountain bicycles and play on a putting green. Minimum age 8 for activities. Advance reservations recommended.

🕐 Apr–end Sep daily 10–5 💷 From £18 for a half-day of different activities 🎫

ISLE OF MAY

From Anstruther harbour
Tel 01333 310103 (24-hour recorded information line)
www.isleofmayferry.com

The round trip to the national nature reserve on the tiny Isle of May takes 5 hours. The rugged island is home to seabirds including razorbills, eider ducks and puffins. Paths lead around the remains of a 12th-century monastery. Buy tickets at Anstruther harbour up to 1 hour before sailing.
🕐 May–end Oct once a day
✋ Adult £15, child £7
☕ Snack bar on board

BLAIRGOWRIE

⚽ MILLHORN FARM RIDING CENTRE

Rosemount, Blairgowrie PH13 9HT
Tel 01828 626172/07884 060648

Day hacks, riding lessons and tailor-made holiday programmes can be arranged at this rural riding centre. Suitable for adults and teenagers. Advance reservations recommended.
🕐 All year ✋ Lesson from £20; 2-hour hack from £30

BO'NESS

⚽ BO'NESS & KINNEIL RAILWAY

Bo'ness Station, Union Street EH51 9AQ
Tel 01506 822298
www.srps.org.uk

Enjoy a 3.5-mile (5.6km) ride on a historic steam train from Bo'ness, west of Edinburgh, to the caverns of Birkhill Mine. At Bo'ness station, locomotives are displayed at the Scottish Railway Exhibition. At the mines you can take a guided tour to see 300-million-year-old fossils. Look for special events for children.

🕐 Easter, end Mar–end Jun, Sep, Oct Sat–Sun; Jul, Aug Tue–Sun ✋ Adult £4.50, child £2; with fireclay mine: adult £7.50, child £3.70 🍴 Carriages Restaurant

BRACO

⚽ PHOENIX FALCONRY SERVICES

Gardeners Cottage, Braco Castle Estate
FK15 9LA
Tel 01786 880539
www.scottishfalconry.co.uk

Learn about the ancient sport of falconry, and how to handle the birds yourself on half-day, full-day or evening trips. Longer trips include lunch. The Eagle Odyssey package, which involves handling birds of prey, is for those age 16 and over.

Striking art at the excellent Aberfeldy Gallery

Advanced reservations essential. Braco lies just off the A9.
🕐 Daily, dawn–dusk ✋ 3-hour Meet the Birds experience £55; 2-hour evening field trip £49.50

CLUNY

⚽ CLUNY CLAYS

Cluny Mains Farm, Cluny, by Kirkcaldy
KY2 6QU
Tel 01592 720374
www.clunyclays.co.uk

Try your hand at clay pigeon shooting, archery and air rifle shooting, or golf at the driving range or on the 9-hole course. Instruction and lessons are available for all activities but must be reserved in advance.

Some activities are not suitable for children.
🕐 Summer daily 11–5.30, winter daily 11–4 ✋ Clay pigeon shooting from £19; golf from £11; archery from £17 🍴 Licensed restaurant open for lunch Mon–Thu and lunch and dinner Fri–Sun ☕ Café serves cakes and coffee all day

COMRIE

⚽ AUCHINGARRICH WILDLIFE CENTRE

PH6 2JS
Tel 01764 679469

An extensive wildlife park set in 40.5ha (100 acres) of the Perthshire hills, with animals such as Highland cattle, llamas, chipmunks, beavers, rabbits, porcupines and meerkats. It also has Scotland's largest collection of waterfowl, including both ornamental and game birds. There's a huge playbarn with real tractors, a sandpit and swings, a 'flying fox' aerial runway, a playground, and opportunities for bird and animal handling. Picnic areas and barbecue sites. You can also fish for trout on three lochs, with rod rental and tuition available, tel 07796 232885.
🕐 Mid-Mar to mid-Nov ✋ ☕

⚽ DRUMMOND TROUT FARM AND FISHERY

PH6 2LD
Tel 01764 670500
www.drummondtroutfarm.co.uk

There's a choice of six pools for trout fishing at this fishery, 1 mile (1.6km) west of Comrie. An underwater camera allows fish-eye views, and food to feed the fish is free. Tuition is also free Monday to Friday and children on the beginners ponds get a badge and certificate for their first ever fish. You keep everything you catch, and pay for the fish at the end by weight. Picnic areas.
🕐 Winter daily 10–5; summer daily 10–10 ✋ 2 hours: adult £3.50, child £3 🏪 Farm shop sells snacks as well as fresh trout, pâté and fishcakes

WHAT TO DO

CUPAR

✪ GRISELDA HILL POTTERY
Kirkbrae, Ceres KY15 5ND
Tel 01334 828273
www.wemyss-ware.co.uk
This family pottery has revived the famous Wemyss Ware style of curious cats and floral pigs, popular in the 19th century. Hand-painting ensures that every piece is unique. To find it, follow signs with a grinning, pop-eyed yellow cat.
🕒 Mon–Fri 9–5, Sat–Sun noon–5

✪ SCOTTISH DEER CENTRE
Bow-of-Fife KY15 4NQ
Tel 01337 810391
www.tsdc.co.uk
Wolves, birds of prey and, of course, nine species of deer are the big attraction at this wildlife park, 12 miles (19.3km) west of St. Andrews. You can get close to all the animals. Falconry displays are given three times daily in summer, once a day in winter. There is also a playground, and picnic spots.
🕒 Easter–end Sep daily 10–5.30; rest of year daily 10–4.30 💷 Adult £5.10, child £3.55, family £15.60 ☕ Café has light lunches and home baking
🏬 Several high quality shops, including outdoor clothing and golf equipment

DUNDEE

🏬 OVERGATE
DD1 1UQ
Tel 01382 314201
www.overgate.co.uk
Bright, modern shopping mall on two levels, with household name stores and more unusual ones, such as Ortak, the Orkney jewellers. Tax-free shopping widely available.
🕒 Mon–Wed, Fri–Sat 9–6, Thu 9–7.30, Sun 12–5 ☕ Options include Costa Coffee and a baked potato outlet

🎭 DUNDEE CONTEMPORARY ARTS (DCA)
152 Nethergate DD1 4DY
Tel 01382 909900
www.dca.org.uk
The DCA and the Dundee Rep theatre together form the core of the arts revival in the city's cultural quarter. As well as housing exhibitions of contemporary art, the DCA is Dundee's only city-centre cinema, showing mainstream and international films.
🕒 DCA and exhibitions free; cinema from £3.50 ☕ Trendy Jute Café Bar

🎭 DUNDEE REP
Tay Square DD1 1PB
Tel 01382 223530
www.dundeereptheatre.co.uk
Scotland's leading repertory theatre is set in Dundee's up-and-coming cultural quarter. As well as the summer repertory season, the theatre hosts touring productions. The building is also home to

Feline ceramics at Griselda Hill Pottery in Cupar

the contemporary Scottish Dance Theatre.
🕒 From £5 ☕ Intimate café-bar with varied menu 🍷 Two bars

🎭 SOCIAL
10 South Tay Street DD1 1PA
Tel 01382 202070
The glass-walled side of this trendy bar overlooks Tay Square and the Dundee Rep theatre. Cool, contemporary decoration inside, with different events each night, including quiz nights and live music from R&B to reggae.
🕒 Daily 12–12

✪ OLYMPIA LEISURE CENTRE
Earl Grey Place, Dundee DD1 4DF
Tel 01382 432300
www.dundeecity.gov.uk/olympia
If you're crossing the road bridge to Dundee, you can't miss this glass-fronted sports centre with its three giant water slides, right on the waterfront. There's a 25m (75ft) training pool, a dive pool and a wave pool, as well as a gym and health suite. Opening times for different facilities vary according to age group, so check ahead.
🕒 Leisure pool term time Mon–Fri 12–7.30pm; other times 10–5.30; Sat–Sun 10–5.30 💷 Adult from £3.60
🍴

✪ CAMPERDOWN WILDLIFE CENTRE
Camperdown Country Park, Coupar Angus Road DD2 4TF
Tel 01382 432661
www.dundeecity.gov.uk/camperdown
This wildlife park just outside the city has 85 species of native Scottish and other European wildlife including lynx, bears, wolves, bats, Arctic foxes and pine martens. In the summer you can see the animals being fed. Seasonal pitch and putt and kiddie bicycles. Special events year-round include animal handling and feeding days.
🕒 Mar–end Sep daily 10–4.30; rest of year daily 10–3.30 💷 Adult £2.20, child £1.70, family £6.50

✪ DUNDEE ICE ARENA
Camperdown Leisure Complex, Kingsway West DD2 3SQ
Tel 01382 889369
www.dundeeicearena.co.uk
A popular ice rink just outside the city, with ice skating shows, ice discos, lessons, public skating sessions and professional ice hockey games. The ice discos for children have special lighting effects.
🕒 All year daily, but check that there is a public skating session on the day of your choice 💷 Skating from £3.10; disco session £3.80; skate hire £1.10 ☕

DUNKELD

⊕ BROUGHTON-STUART JEWELLERY LTD

25 Atholl Street, Dunkeld PH8 0AR
Tel 01350 727888
www.broughton-stuartjewellery.co.uk
Craig Stuart uses an ancient technique called Mokume Gane to achieve a delicate wood-grain effect on his jewellery, combining gold, platinum and diamonds into unique miniature works of art.
🕐 Mon–Wed, Fri 9.30–4, Sat 10–4.30

✪✪ NAE LIMITS

14 The Cross, Dunkeld PH8 0AJ
Tel 01350 727242
www.naelimits.co.uk
This adventure sports centre offers water-, land- and snow-based activities. Try everything from whitewater rafting to cliff-jumping, according to the season. Full instruction and safety kit are included. Age restrictions apply, so check ahead.
🕐 All year 🚇 From £35 for half-day activity, £75 full day

✪ GOING POTTIE

Cathedral Street, Dunkeld PH8 0AW
Tel 01350 728044
www.goingpottie.com
From daubing a plaster frog to decorating your own dinner service, there's something to appeal to all ages at this friendly ceramic painting centre, with expert tuition to help you make the most of your project. The perfect activity for a wet day.
🕐 Mon–Sat 10–5, Sun 11–4
🚇 From £5

ELIE

✪ ELIE WATERSPORTS

Elie Harbour
Tel 01333 330962
www.eliewatersports.com
Sheltered Elie Bay is a great place to learn watersports, and this centre near the Ship Inn offers windsurfing, sailing and canoeing courses. There are also mountain bicycles to rent. Advance reservations advised.

🕐 May–end Sep 🚇 Windsurfer rental and instruction £18 per hour; canoe rental and instruction £14 per hour; mountain bicycle rental from £7 for half-day.

FALKIRK

🎬 CINEWORLD CINEMA

Central Retail Park, Old Bison Works FK2 7AN
Tel 08712 208000 (reservations and information)
www.cineworld.co.uk
Falkirk's 12-screen multiplex cinema has a policy of showing British films.
🕐 All year 🚇 Adult from £5.40; reduced tickets Tue

There's a wide range of motorsports at Knockhill

KENMORE

✪ CROFT-NA-CABER

Loch Tay PH15 2HW
Tel 01887 830588
www.croftnacaber.com
This lively outdoor activities centre beside the Scottish Crannog Centre offers river rafting, fishing, quad biking, sailing, power boating, loch cruises on the *Maid of the Tay* and waterskiing. Minimum age 8 for canoeing and kayaking, 16 for quad biking. Advance reservations recommended.
🕐 Open all year, but restricted activities in winter 🚇 Canoe rental from £15; archery from £12; loch cruise adult £6.50, child £2.50 🍴 🚻

KNOCKHILL

✪ KNOCKHILL RACING CIRCUIT

By Dunfermline, Fife KY12 9TF
Tel 01383 723337
www.knockhill.co.uk
Come and watch weekend superbike and Formula 3 racing at Scotland's National Motor-sport Centre (Apr–end Oct). You can also take part in quad biking, driving racing or rally cars, 4x4s and motorcycling. Children can drive at the carting centre. Advance booking advised.
🕐 Summer 9–7; winter 9–6 🚇 Entry £7–£20 🚻

LAKE OF MENTEITH

✪ LAKE OF MENTEITH FISHERIES

'Ryeyards', Port of Menteith FK8 3RA
Tel 01877 385664
www.menteith-fisheries.co.uk
Lake Mentieth has excellent fly fishing for rainbow trout. Rent a boat through the booking office (advance reservations recommended); a qualified instructor can also be arranged.
🕐 End Mar–end Oct Mon–Sat 9.30–5.30 🚇 Day session from £37 per boat

LARBERT

⊕ BARBARA DAVIDSON DESIGNER POTTERY

Muirhall Farm FK5 4EW
Tel 01324 554430
The hand-thrown pottery for sale at this working pottery includes mugs, dinner sets, vases and candle-holders. You can paint your own pots, and in July and August you can make your own pot for a small charge (book ahead). Larbert is 9 miles (14.4km) south of Stirling.
🕐 Mon–Sat 10–5

LOCH KATRINE

⭐ SS *SIR WALTER SCOTT*
Trossachs Pier Complex FK17 8H2
Tel 01877 376316
www.lochkatrine.co.uk
Take a steamship cruise around beautiful Loch Katrine, at the heart of the Trossachs, aboard the 100-year-old *Sir Walter Scott*. Sailing times vary, so check ahead. Can be combined with a lochside bicycle ride, contact Katrinewheelz on the same number.
⏰ Sailings Mar–end Oct daily 11, 1.45 and 3.15 💷 Adult £7.25, child £5.25 (5–16) 🍽 Captains Rest Café ♿

LOCH LOMOND

🏛 LOCH LOMOND OUTLET SHOPPING CENTRE
Main Street, Alexandria G83 0UG
Tel 01389 710077
www.lochlomondoutletcentre.co.uk
This impressive Edwardian building is now a shopping mall with clothes, sportswear, books, gifts and things for the home. Famous brands such as Adidas, Nike and Ecco, with items discounted up to 50 per cent. Look out for weekend events such as antiques and chocolate fairs, and the monthly farmers' market. There's also a vintage motor museum. Located off the A82.
⏰ Mon–Sat 9.30–5.30, Sun 10–5 🍽 Gallery Café serves home baking

🏛 LOCH LOMOND SHORES
Ben Lomond Way, Balloch G83 8QL
Tel 01389 721500
www.lochlomondshores.com
This pedestrianized crescent of shops has beautiful views over Loch Lomond. The main draw is Jenners, a branch of the famous Edinburgh department store, which has clothing, a food hall and a good selection of whiskies. Balloch is at the southern end of the loch.
⏰ Daily 10–6 🍽 Conservatory restaurant in Jenners 📖 In bookstore

⭐ DRUMKINNON TOWER
By Loch Lomond Shores, Ben Lomond Way, Balloch G83 8QL
Tel 01389 721500
www.lochlomondshores.com
A modern interpretation of an ancient castle, the tower has beautiful views over Loch Lomond. Currently being refitted to house an aquarium and sealife centre.
⏰ To reopen mid-2006

⭐ GLENGOYNE DISTILLERY
Dumgoyne, near Killearn, Glasgow G63 9LB
Tel 01360 550254
www.glengoyne.com
Taste the whisky at this notably picturesque distillery in the

Cruise on Loch Katrine aboard the SS Sir Walter Scott

reception room overlooking the loch and waterfall, enjoy a guided tour, and visit the heritage room and shop. Located 14 miles (22.4km) north of Glasgow on the A81.
⏰ Mon–Sat 10–4, Sun 12–4. All tours start on the hour 💷 Adult £4.50, under 18 free; specialized tours from £5.95

⭐ *MAID OF THE LOCH*
The Pier, Pier Road, Balloch G83 8QX
Tel 01389 711865
www.maidoftheloch.co.uk
Loch Lomond's paddle steamer, *Maid of the Loch*, is docked at Balloch. Volunteers are on hand to answer questions about the craft, built in 1953, as you look around.

⏰ Easter–end Oct daily 10–4; winter weekends only 💷 Free 🍽 ♿ 🚻

PERTH

🏛 ONCE A TREE
255 Old High Street PH1 5QN
Tel 01738 636213
www.onceatree.co.uk
This charming gift shop specializes in items made from wood, including carvings, ornaments, chess sets and secret boxes.
⏰ Mon–Sat 9.30–5.30

🏛 P. D. MALLOCH
259 Old High Street PH1 5QN
Tel 01738 632316
www.pdmalloch.com
If you enjoy fishing, then this is the shop for you. Everything from permits for trout fishing on the rivers Tay and Almond to specialist clothing and equipment, including maggots, worms and dead bait! Can also advise on where to buy permits for salmon fishing.
⏰ Mon–Sat 9–5.30

🏛 PERTHSHIRE VISITOR CENTRE
Bankfoot PH1 4EB
Tel 01738 787696
www.macbeth.co.uk
Lying 7 miles (11.3km) north of Perth on the A9, this covered centre has a collection of shops selling clothes, Scottish food and gifts including whisky and wines. The Macbeth Experience is a multimedia production.
⏰ Daily 9–8 💷 Macbeth Experience: adult £2, child £1 🍽 Specializes in local produce

🎭 PERTH THEATRE
185 High Street PH1 5UW
Tel 01738 621031
www.horsecross.com
Behind an art deco frontage on the High Street lies Perth's only theatre, home to a resident company of actors, and visiting shows. Film star Ewan McGregor learned his craft here. Music and comedy as well as drama.
⏰ All year 💷 From £10 🍽 🍴 🚻

ⓨ THE FAMOUS BEIN INN
Glenfarg PH2 9PY
Tel 01577 830216
www.beininnmusic.com
This pub, 5 miles (8km)
south of Perth and just
off the M90, is famous for its
intimate concert room, which
attracts international and UK
artists performing folk, country,
rock, Americana and
alternative country music.
There are about ten
performances a month.
🕐 Daily to 11pm 🎫 Tickets from £6
🍴 Basement bar serves food

ⓨ GIG@BYTES
5 St. Paul's Square PH1 5QW
Tel 01738 451580
www.gig-at-bytes.com
Enjoy a tea, coffee or hot
chocolate while you surf the
net, email, print, fax, scan and
write documents. Located off
the Old High Street, behind
the former St. Paul's Church.
🕐 Mon–Sat 10–6.30 💻 Internet from
£1.50 for 15 minutes

ⓨ TWA TAMS
79–81 Scott Street PH2 8JR
Tel 01738 634500
The best pub in the city for
live music from, rock to
reggae. No cover bands, just
home-grown talent, usually
at weekends. The pub also
serves food, with a beer
garden for summer and a
log fire for winter.
🕐 Mon–Thu 11am–11pm, Fri–Sat
11am–11.45pm, Sun 12.30–11 💷 From
£3 on band nights

✪ CAITHNESS GLASS
VISITOR CENTRE
Inveralmond PH1 3TZ
Tel 01738 492320
www.caithnessglass.co.uk
Watch the famous glassware
being made, then stock up on
vases, whisky tumblers,
decanters and paperweights
at discount prices in the
factory shop. Glassmaking can
be seen on weekdays
throughout the year. The shop
offers overseas posting and
engraving.

🕐 Jun to mid-Sep Mon–Fri 9–6, Sat
9–5; rest of year Mon–Sat 9–5; also
Mar–end Nov Sun 10–5; Dec–end Feb
12–5 💷 Free 🍴 Open all day 🏛

PITLOCHRY
⊞ HERITAGE JEWELLERS
104 Atholl Road PH16 5BL
Tel 01796 474333
www.heritage-jewellers.co.uk
This small, exclusive shop
sells gold and silver jewellery,
cultured pearls, Celtic
jewellery made in Orkney,
and Scottish gold.
🕐 Mon–Sat 9–5, Sun 12–4; Nov–end
Mar may close Thu, Sun

*Edradour Distillery resembles a
miniature village*

⊞ THE SHEEP SHOP
69 Atholl Road PH16 5BL
Tel 01796 473559
www.thesheepshop.uk.com
If you love sheep, then this is
definitely the shop for you.
Slippers, mugs, T-shirts and
anything you can think of with
a sheep on it.
🕐 Mon–Sat 10–5.30, Sun 11.30–4

♪ PITLOCHRY FESTIVAL
THEATRE
PH16 5DR
Tel 01796 484626/484600
www.pitlochry.org.uk
A modern venue with lovely
views across the River Tummel
to the town, the Festival
Theatre is open in summer

and autumn, with different
concerts and touring theatre
productions every night.
🕐 May–end Oct 💷 From £15.50 🎫
🍴 Reserve in advance 🏛

✪ EDRADOUR DISTILLERY
Moulin PH16 5JP
Tel 01796 472095
www.edradour.co.uk
Scotland's smallest distillery
produces a mere 12 casks of
malt whisky a week, and is set
in a picturesque location east
of Pitlochry.
🕐 Mar–end Oct Mon–Sat 9.30–6, Sun
11.30–5; Nov, Dec Mon–Sat 9.30–5, Sun
12–5; Jan, Feb Mon–Sat 10–4, Sun 12–4
💷 Free 🏛

✪ ESCAPE ROUTE
3 Atholl Road PH16 5BX
Tel 01796 473859
www.escape-route.biz
Staff at this bicycle rental shop
are real enthusiasts and can
give you maps and advice
about local routes. Mountain
and hybrid bicycles, tandems,
trailers and child seats are
available. A full range of
walking gear is also available.
🕐 Mon–Sat 9–5.30, Sun 10–5

ST. ANDREWS
⊞ DAVID BROWN GALLERY
9 Albany Place KY16 9HH
Tel 01334 477840
The gallery is worth a visit if
you love antiques—but if you
love antiques and golf, then
it's a must. Unassuming on the
outside, it's an Aladdin's cave
within, crammed full of
silverware, prints and vintage
golfing books. Don't leave
without hearing one of owner
David Brown's anecdotes.
Located on the corner with
North Street.
🕐 Easter–end Sep Mon–Sat 9–6; rest
of year Mon–Sat 10–5

DI GILPIN DESIGN STUDIO
Hansa House, Burghers Close,
141 South Street KY16 9UN
Tel 01334 476193
www.handknitwear.com
Unique, handmade designer jewellery, knitwear and accessories. The high quality is reflected in the prices. The shop also stocks a wide range of knitting yarns and patterns.
🅖 Mon–Wed, Fri–Sat 10–5, Thu 10–8, Sun 12–5

BYRE THEATRE
Abbey Street KY16 9LA
Tel 01334 475000
www.byretheatre.com
The Byre Theatre hosts various theatre productions and touring shows, including dance, music, comedy and poetry.
🅦 From £12.50 🄱 Byre café-bar open until midnight

NEW PICTURE HOUSE
117 North Street KY16 9AD
Tel 01334 474902/01334 473509 (recorded information line)
www.nphcinema.co.uk
This cinema shows mainstream, independent and some foreign films. Drinks and snacks available.
🅖 Daily 🅦 From £4

YOUNGER HALL
University of St. Andrews, North Street KY16 6YD
Tel 01334 462226
www.st-and.ac.uk/services/music
Venue for professional and student-led classical, jazz, musicals and choir concerts. Concerts are also held in the more intimate college chapels, so check when you reserve your ticket.
🅖 Lunchtime concerts Wed 1.15pm during term time 🅦 From £1

CENTRAL BAR
79 Market Street KY16 9NU
Tel 01334 478296
A St. Andrews institution in the town centre, popular with students and local people. Food including sandwiches and sausage and mash is served until 9pm. Located on

the corner of College Street and Market Street.
🅖 Mon–Thu 12–12, Fri–Sat 12pm–1am, Sun 12.30–12

ST. ANDREWS LINKS
Pilmour House KY16 9SF
Tel 01334 466666
www.standrews.org.uk
The largest golf complex in Europe consists of six public golf courses. The three championship courses include the legendary Old Course. There are also two clubhouses, a golf practice centre and two shops. Advance reservations are essential—the waiting list is anything from weeks to years. Check the website for rules

Track down some excellent music at Stirling's Tolbooth

and requirements, which vary widely according to the course. For example, to play the Old Course you need a handicap of 24 (men) or 36 (women), and must reserve at least a year ahead or enter the daily lottery early on the day on which you want to play.
🅖 All year; Old Course closed Sun 🅦 Strathtyrum Course £20; Old Course £105 🍴 🄿

ORIGINAL ST. ANDREWS WITCHES TOUR
3A Drybriggs, Balgarvie Road, Cupar KY15 4AJ
Tel 01334 655057
Enjoy a thrilling night-time guided walk through the

centre of St. Andrews, with spooky tales of local witches. Advance reservations recommended.
🅖 Apr–end Oct Fri 8; Jun Fri, Sun 8; Jul, Aug Thu–Fri, Sun 8; rest of year Fri 7.30 🅦 Adult £6, child £4

STIRLING
CRAWFORD ARCADE
King Street FK8 1AX
Tel 07710 086076
Twenty-four independent shops lie within this covered Victorian shopping arcade in the town centre, including a well-stocked bookshop and The Changing Room, Stirling's contemporary art gallery.
🅖 Mon–Sat 8–5.30 🍴 🄲

TOLBOOTH
Jail Wynd FK8 1DE
Tel 01786 274000
www.stirling.gov.uk/tolbooth
The Tolbooth dates from 1705 and used to be a jail and court house. It's now a lively music venue which hosts world music, ceilidhs, jazz, comedy and storytelling events. Look out for the hidden stairway outside the toilets. Opposite the old jail.
🅖 Tue–Sat 10–6 🅦 Free 🄲 🍴 Tolbooth Restaurant open Tue–Sun for lunch and dinner

BLAIR DRUMMOND SAFARI AND ADVENTURE PARK
Blair Drummond, near Stirling FK9 4UR
Tel 01786 841456
www.safari-park.co.uk
Safari park to the west of Stirling, where you can drive among animals which roam free, including elephants, giraffes, lions and camels. The pets' farm has llamas, donkeys and ponies, and there are sea lion shows, a boat safari and a playground. Adventure and climbing area for children of all ages, plus pedal boats and 'astraglide' funfair ride. Picnic and barbecue areas.
🅖 End Mar–end Sep daily 10–5.30 🅦 Adult £8.50, child £4.50 (under 3 free) 🄲 Ranch Kitchen

WHAT TO DO

GLASGOW

WHAT TO DO

Scotland's second city used to be best known for its flea market, the Barras. While that is still going strong, today the city centre is completely dominated by designer shops and huge, classy shopping malls selling everything from top quality modern furniture to luxury chocolate and pricey must-have jewellery. Take your ease in the new breed of pavement cafés, or perhaps retreat to a classic tea room—a Glasgow speciality. There are guided horror tours to chill the blood, and pub tours with a ceilidh at the end to warm it up again. Glasgow has a happening nightlife of clubs and bars, including the famous King Tut's Wah Wah House, plus six theatres, lots of cinemas and concert venues, and changing exhibitions and events at the massive Scottish Exhibition and Conference Centre. And if the city gets a bit too much, you can hop on a vintage paddle steamer for a tour of the River Clyde.

🏛 SHOPPING

BOOKS

BORDERS
98 Buchanan Street G1 3BA
Tel 0141 222 7700
www.borders.com
Overlooking Royal Exchange Square, this massive branch of the well-known chain sells all the latest books, CDs and DVDs.
🕒 Mon–Sat 8.30am–10pm, Sun 10–8
☕ Starbucks on the first floor

DEPARTMENT STORES

FRASERS (HOUSE OF FRASER)
45 Buchanan Street G1 3HR
Tel 0141 221 3880
www.houseoffraser.co.uk
This huge department store on the corner of Buchanan Street and Argyle Street sells fashion, cosmetics, perfume, china, glassware and the best selection of menswear in the city.
🕒 Mon–Wed, Fri 9.30–6, Thu 9.30–8, Sat 9–6, Sun 12–5.30 ☕ Cappuccino bar on first floor, café on the top floor

GIFTS AND SPECIALIST CLOTHING

ARGYLE ARCADE
Buchanan Street G2 8BD
This elegant glass-covered shopping centre opposite Fraser's specializes in jewellery, with 25 different shops selling modern and antique jewellery and other items in gold and silver.
🕒 Mon–Sat 9–6, Sun 12–5

CRUISE
180–187 Ingram Street G1 1DN
Tel 0141 572 3232
If you're into designer clothes, prepare for designer heaven and bring your credit card. Three floors of labels like Gucci, Prada and Fendi clothes, shoes, bags and accessories for men and women. East of the city centre.
🕒 Mon–Wed, Fri 10–6, Thu 10–7 Sat 9.30–6, Sun 12–5

KEY TO SYMBOLS

🏛	Shopping
🎭	Entertainment
🍸	Nightlife
⚽	Sports
✪	Activities
♡	Health and Beauty
✿	For Children

GEOFFREY (TAILOR) KILTMAKERS & WEAVERS

309 Sauchiehall Street G2 3HW
Tel 0141 331 2388
www.geoffreykilts.co.uk

One of Scotland's top kilt-makers and Highland dress specialists. This big store has every kind of kilt, tartan and accessory, for sale or to rent, including the exclusive fashion range, 21st Century Kilts. Made-to-measure outfits can be sent to you abroad. On the corner of Sauchiehall and Pitt streets.
☺ Mon–Wed, Fri–Sat 9–5.30, Thu 9–7, Sun 11–5

GLASGOW PRINT STUDIO

22 and 25 King Street G1 5QP
Tel 0141 552 0704
www.gpsart.co.uk

The artists' studio at number 22 is a fully equipped print-making workshop, with a shop at number 25. There are exhibitions of art by contemporary local and international artists throughout the year, much of which is for sale. Near the Tron theatre, southeast of the centre.
☺ Tue–Sat 10–5.30

ITALIAN CENTRE

Ingram Street G1 1DN
Tel 0141 552 6368

This is the place to come for famous name designer clothes and accessories. Shops are based around a stylish piazza and include Italian designer stores such as Armani and Versace. Popular with style-conscious Glaswegians.
☺ Mon–Wed, Fri–Sat 10–6, Thu 10–8, Sun 12–5

MERCHANT SQUARE

71–73 Albion Street G1 1NY
Merchant City, east of George Square, is a small mall with the exclusive Gift Merchant shop, restaurants and bars. Look for Kshocolat's handmade and organic chocolates.
☺ Mon–Wed, Fri–Sat 9.30–6, Thu 9.30–7, Sun 12–5

SOLETRADER

164a Buchanan Street G1 2LW
0141 353 3022
www.soletrader.co.uk

Every type of shoe you can think of on two floors, from the latest trainers to smart, designer shoes. Labels include Hugo Boss, Paul Smith, Diesel and Adidas.
☺ Mon–Wed, Fri–Sat 9–6, Thu 9–7.30, Sun 11.30–5.30

TIM WRIGHT ANTIQUES

Richmond Chambers, 147 Bath Street G2 4SQ
Tel 0141 221 0364
www.timwright-antiques.com

The biggest and best selection of antiques in Glasgow is to be

Princes Square is an excellent shopping choice

found in this emporium, a family business for over 30 years. Showrooms either side of the entrance hall are packed full of furniture, ceramics, china, jewellery and other decorative items. On the corner of Bath and West Campbell streets.
☺ Mon–Fri 10–5, Sat 10–2

TISO GLASGOW OUTDOOR EXPERIENCE

50 Couper Street, off Kyle Street G4 0DL
Tel 0141 559 5450
www.tiso.com

A great selection of outdoor equipment, clothing, books and bicycles make this one of the top outdoor stores in

Britain. The 15m (49ft) rock pinnacle, waterfall and 7m (23ft) real ice wall enable you to try out the equipment in the environment where you are likely to use it. Couper Street is north of the centre.
☺ Mon–Tue, Fri–Sat 9–6, Wed 9.30–6, Thu 9–7, Sun 11–5

URBAN OUTFITTERS

157 Buchanan Street G1 2JX
Tel 0141 248 9203
www.urbanoutfitters.com

This vast store on three levels specializes in fashionable, quirky clothes and accessories for the home, all with a funky, retro feel. Allow plenty of time, it's full of unusual things. There's also a music section, Carbon Records, where a live DJ plays the latest music.
☺ Mon–Thu 10–8, Fri 10–7, Sat 10–7, Sun 12–6

VICTORIAN VILLAGE

93 West Regent Street G2 2BA
Tel 0141 332 9808

A collection of little antiques shops, selling porcelain, silver, clothes, costume jewellery and trinkets at affordable prices. Located in an old tenement house in the middle of West Regent Street.
☺ Mon–Sat 10–5

MARKETS AND MALLS

BARRAS

Gallowgate and London Road, between Ross Street and Bain Street
Tel 0141 552 4601
www.glasgow-barrowland.com

Glasgow's famous indoor and outdoor flea market on Gallowgate has around 150 shops inside and 1,000 traders' stands outside. Many items are second-hand, so the quality varies. The Barras is safe, but with such large crowds, beware of pickpockets. (▷ 105)
☺ Sat–Sun 10–5

BUCHANAN GALLERIES

220 Buchanan Street G1 2FF
Tel 0141 333 9898
www.buchanangalleries.co.uk
One of Glasgow's biggest shopping malls, with over 80 high-street stores on four levels. The quality of the stores, which include John Lewis, Next and Gap, is generally higher than in the St. Enoch Centre. It's at the top of Buchanan Street.
🕐 Mon–Wed, Fri–Sat 9–6, Thu 9–8, Sun 11–5 🍴 Food gallery on the second floor

PRINCES SQUARE

48 Buchanan Street G1 3JX
Tel 0141 204 1685
www.princessquare.co.uk
An art deco style doorway on Buchanan Street announces this smart indoor shopping centre. High quality shops sell clothes, shoes and gifts. Shops include Jo Malone perfumes and the Scottish Craft Centre.
🕐 Mon–Wed, Fri 9.30–6, Thu 9.30–8, Sat 9–6, Sun 12–5 🍴 Cafés and restaurants on the top floor, with bars and restaurants open until midnight

ST. ENOCH SHOPPING CENTRE

55 St. Enoch Square G1 4BW
Tel 0141 204 3900
www.stenoch.co.uk
A huge mall on two floors with over 80 high street stores housed in the largest glass building in Europe.
🕐 Mon–Wed and Fri–Sat 9–6, Thu 9–8, Sun 11–5.30 🚇 St. Enoch

AVALANCHE RECORDS

34 Dundas Street G1 2AQ
Tel 0141 332 2099
This large, independent music store near Queen Street station stocks a wide range of new and rare, second-hand CDs and some vinyl, with the emphasis on indie, rock and punk.
🕐 Mon–Wed, Fri–Sat 9.30–6, Thu 9–7, Sun 12–6

TEA ROOMS
MISS CRANSTON'S

33 Gordon Street G1 3PF
Tel 0141 204 1122
www.misscranstons.com
Tea rooms are a genteel Glasgow institution, and not to be missed. Miss Cranston's is an outlet of Glasgow's famous local Bradford bakery, and named after Kate Cranston, who commissioned Charles Rennie Mackintosh to design the interior (▷ 114–115). The tea room, with its tall windows, glass tabletops and a good view over the street, is above a ground-floor patisserie and bakery. Tea

Cutting-edge exhibitions at the Centre for Contemporary Arts

and a scone with jam and cream costs £2.75.
🕐 Mon–Sat 8–5.30

WILLOW TEAROOMS

217 Sauchiehall Street G2 3EX
Tel 0141 332 0521
www.willowtearooms.co.uk
The famous tea room, designed in white, purple and silver by Charles Rennie Mackintosh, is in a gallery above Hendersons jewellery shop. What you really want to see is the front room, the Room de Luxe, its confident design restrained and strong. The menu is extensive, and afternoon tea costs £9.50 (sandwiches, scone and cake).
🕐 Mon–Sat 9–5, Sun 11–4.15

🎭 ENTERTAINMENT

CINEMAS
CENTRE FOR CONTEMPORARY ARTS (CCA)

350 Sauchiehall Street G2 3JD
Tel 0141 352 4900 (cinema tickets)
www.cca-glasgow.com
Various contemporary art forms, including music, visual art and alternative cinema are catered for at this cutting-edge centre. Everything from classics to foreign films. Worth a visit for the architecture alone.
🕐 All year; free tours Sat 2pm
🎬 Cinema from £4; many exhibitions free 🚇 Cowcaddens 🍴 Café serves interesting food, 9–11 🍷 Dark and stylish bar on the first floor, 12–11pm
📋

GLASGOW FILM THEATRE

12 Rose Street G3 6RB
0141 332 8128
www.gft.org.uk
The best art house cinema in Glasgow, the Film Theatre has a retro feel to the interior. Contemporary and classic, independent and foreign films are shown on its two screens. On the corner of Rose Street and Sauchiehall Street.
🕐 Daily 🎬 From £3.50 🍴 Café Cosmo serves food daily until 5pm

THEATRES
ARCHES

253 Argyle Street G2 8DL
Tel 0870 240 7528
www.thearches.co.uk
An unusual venue built under the arches of a railway bridge in the city centre, the Arches has a schedule of theatre, music and cultural festivals, and also serves as a nightclub.
🕐 All year Mon–Sat 11am–12am, Sun 12–12 🎬 From £4 🍷

CITIZENS THEATRE
119 Gorbals Street G5 9DS
Tel 0141 429 0022
www.citz.co.uk
The resident company at this Victorian theatre, south of the river in the Gorbals area, produces a wide range of British and European classics.
All year 🕐 Adult from £12, reduced rate Tue 🚌 5, 7, 12, 20, 31, 37, 66, 74, 75, 267 🍺 Two bars

KING'S THEATRE
297 Bath Street G2 4JN
Tel 0141 240 1111; Ticketmaster (24 hours, fee) 0870 400 0680
www.kings-glasgow.co.uk
Big budget touring musicals dominate at this theatre, along with some comedy and lighter plays. At the junction of Bath and Elmbank streets.
All year From £8 🚌 18, 42, 57 Café-bar

PAVILION THEATRE
121 Renfield Street G2 3AX
Tel 0141 332 1846
www.paviliontheatre.co.uk
Expect to find comedy, musicals and pantomime at this, the last bastion of Glasgow music hall tradition.
All year From £10 Open on performance nights

SCOTTISH MASK AND PUPPET THEATRE
8-10 Balcarres Avenue, Kelvindale G12 0QF
Tel 0141 339 6185
www.scottishmaskandpuppetcentre.co.uk
Puppet show for children every Saturday and accompanying mask and puppet exhibition. Northwest of the city centre, off Great Western Road.
Shows usually Sat 2pm, and sometimes 12pm Adult £4.50, child £3.50

THEATRE ROYAL
282 Hope Street G2 3QA
Tel 0141 240 1133
www.theatreroyalglasgow.com
www.scottishopera.org.uk
www.scottishballet.co.uk
The best in opera, ballet, dance and theatre at the home of Scottish Opera and Scottish Ballet. Located at the top of Hope Street, on the corner of Cowcaddens Road.
All year From £4 Café Royal open for pre- and post-performance dining Circle Café is good for a pre-show snack

TRAMWAY
25 Albert Drive G41 2PE
Tel 0845 330 3501
www.tramway.org
Cutting-edge art, dance and theatre and contemporary art exhibitions at this theatre, south of the River Clyde.
All year, closed Mon From £5;

The Theatre Royal offers a wide range of productions

exhibitions free 🚌 28, M29, 38, 45, 47, 48, 57, 59 🚉 From Central station, take the train to Pollokshields East, 3 minutes Tramway Café on ground floor

TRON THEATRE
63 Trongate G1 5HB
Tel 0141 552 4267
www.tron.co.uk
Contemporary Scottish and international drama, comedy, music and dance are the fare at this theatre at the eastern end of Argyle Street, easy to spot from its church steeple.
From 10am From £4 Two bars serve lunch and dinner

CONCERT HALLS

BARFLY
260 Clyde Street G1 4JH
Tel 0141 204 5700/08709 070999 (ticketline)
www.barflyclub.com
Rock and indie venue for up-and-coming rock, punk and indie bands, on the north bank of the River Clyde.
Open on gig nights, which are most nights of the week. Bar open until 11pm weekdays, 3am weekends From £4

BARROWLAND
244 Gallowgate G4 0TS
0141 552 4601/0870 903 3444 (credit card bookings)
www.glasgow-barrowland.com
Big name pop and rock acts play at this atmospheric venue to the southeast of the city centre. Get tickets from Ticket Scotland, tel 0141 204 5151.
From £9 5-minute walk from St. Enoch Bar open on concert nights

GLASGOW ROYAL CONCERT HALL
2 Sauchiehall Street G2 3NY
Tel 0141 353 8000
www.grch.com
The most prestigious venue in the city, with a varied programme of classical, pop and rock music. In January and February it hosts the international Celtic Connections music festival.
All year £5–£30 The Green Room for a pre-show meal, tel 0141 353 8000 Café Bar on the ground floor (Mon–Sat from 10am), plus four more bars

KING TUT'S WAH WAH HUT
272a St. Vincent Street G2 5RL
Tel 0141 221 5279/0870 169 0100 (Ticketmaster)
www.kingtuts.co.uk
The heart of the Glasgow music scene. It's an unpretentious, relaxed venue playing cutting edge indie, pop and rock. Tickets from Ticket Scotland, tel 0141 204 5151.
All year From £4.50 Modern bar or functional bar with pool table

WHAT TO DO

QUEEN MARGARET UNION
22 University Gardens G12 8QN
Tel 0141 339 9784
www.qmu.org.uk
Less well-known pop, rock and indie bands and some bigger names play occasional gigs at this university venue, to the west of the city centre. Get tickets from Ticket Scotland, tel 0141 204 5151.
⏰ Open for 1 or 2 concerts a week
🚇 Hillhead 🔣 Student Union bar, so the drinks are always cheap

SCOTTISH EXHIBITION & CONFERENCE CENTRE (SECC)
G3 8YW
Tel 0870 040 4000
www.secctickets.com
This huge venue on the north bank of the River Clyde, opposite the Science Centre, is nicknamed the Armadillo, for its great segmented silver shell. It has big-league rock and pop concerts.
💷 From £6–£50 🚇 Exhibition Centre
🚌 Various 🔣 Various

🔽 NIGHTLIFE
BARS
BABBITY BOWSTER
16–18 Blackfriars Street, Merchant City G1 1PE
Tel 0141 552 5055
This traditional pub is known for its simple Scottish food. There's live folk music early evening on Saturdays, a good range of real ales, and it's the only pub in the city centre with a licenced beer garden. The building is by Robert Adam (c1790). Over 18s only.
⏰ Mon–Sat 11am–12am, Sun 12.30–12

BACCHUS
80 Glassford Street G1 1UR
Tel 0141 572 0080
A stylish, friendly bar with a good lunch menu, a big screen TV for soccer matches, and relaxed funk/soul DJs at the weekend. Tasteful cool, blue interior. Glassford Street is east of the centre. Over 18s only after 7pm.
⏰ Daily 11am–12am

BLACKFRIARS
36 Bell Street, Merchant City G1 1LG
Tel 0141 552 5924
A relaxed pub with an excellent selection of hand-pulled real ales, bottled beers, a malt of the month and live jazz at weekends. You'll feel like you're at home with the candles, patterned upholstery and posters. Over 18s only.
⏰ Mon–Sat noon–midnight, Sun 12.30–12

DELMONICAS
68 Virginia Street G1 1TX
Tel 0141 552 4803
Cheesy tunes are the order of the day in this mainstream gay bar at the heart of

Babbity Bowster is a popular city-centre pub

Glasgow's gay village. Look for karaoke and quizzes too. Over 18s only.
⏰ Daily 12–12

HORSE SHOE BAR
17 Drury Street G2 5AE
Tel 0141 229 5711
This city centre pub boasts the longest continuous bar in the UK, real ale, karaoke and reasonably priced food. Over 18s only.
⏰ Mon–Sat 11am–12am, Sun 12.30–12

OCTOBER
Rooftop, Princes Square Shopping Mall, 48 Buchanan Street G1 3JX
Tel 0141 221 0303
www.princessquare.co.uk

During the day the top of Princes Square is full of shoppers having coffee or lunch. But at night it transforms into a smart cocktail bar where the rules are: take advantage of the discounted cocktails, and dress up. A glass elevator takes you to the mahogany bar under a glass roof. Over 18s only.
⏰ Mon–Wed 11am–12am, Thu–Sun 11am–12am

SCOTIA BAR
112 Stockwell Street G1 4LW
Tel 0141 552 8681
This traditional old pub serves real ale and hearty food until 3pm, seven days a week. It's Glasgow's oldest pub (1792), with snug corners for a quiet drink. Live music on most evenings. Patrons must be over 18.
⏰ Mon–Sat 11am–12am, Sun 12–12

STAND COMEDY CLUB
333 Woodlands Road G3 6NG
Tel 0870 600 6055
www.thestand.co.uk
This bar is the venue for live Scottish and international comedy, most nights. Northwest of the city centre, on the other side of the M8 motorway. Over 18s only.
⏰ Check listings. Doors open at 7.30, shows start at 8.30–9 💷 From £1
🚇 Kelvin Bridge

UISGE BEATHE
232–246 Woodlands Road, West End G3 6ND
Tel 0141 564 1596
With a name that is Gaelic for whisky, you wouldn't expect anything less than the 100 or more malt whiskies that are on offer in this specialist pub. Wooden pews, low ceilings, a bizarre selection of bric-à-brac and old portraits on the walls. Well worth seeking out, northwest of the city centre. Over 18s only.
⏰ Mon–Sat 12–12, Sun 12.30–12
🚇 St. George's Cross 🚌 411, 44
🚇 Charing Cross

CLUBS

ARCHES

253 Argyle Street G2 8DL
Tel 0870 240 7528
www.thearches.co.uk
The nightclub in the Arches centre, with its industrial-style interior, is one of Glasgow's most popular. The music might include hip-hop, house, soul or big name DJs. Over 18s only.

◉ Club nights Fri–Sun, open until late
🎟 From £5

BUDDHA

142a St. Vincent Street G2 5LA
Tel 0141 248 7881
There's always up-to-the-minute music in this popular pre-club venue in the centre of town, with a DJ on Saturday nights. Decorated in Turkish-cave style, the bar is dark and comfortable. Over 18s only.

◉ Sun–Thu 12–late, Fri 12–3am

JONGLEURS

11 Renfrew Street G2 3AB
Tel 0141 332 2815
www.jongleurs.com
This city-centre venue is part of a UK-wide chain of comedy clubs, offering live comedy three nights a week. In the basement of the UGC building, which is one of the tallest in Europe. Over 18s only.

◉ Thu–Sat; doors open 7pm, show starts at 8.30 🎟 From £7

⊗ SPORTS AND ✪ ACTIVITIES

BICYCLING

CLYDE TO LOCH LOMOND CYCLEWAY

Tel 0141 287 9171 (Glasgow City Council), 0845 113 0065 (Sustrans)
www.nationalcyclenetwork.org.uk
Several bicycle paths start in the centre of Glasgow. The Clyde to Loch Lomond Cycleway is a dedicated bicycle route 20 miles (32km) long, taking in Clydebank, Dumbarton, the Vale of Leven and Balloch. The path, which is also suitable for walkers, follows forest trails, minor roads, old train tracks and canal tow paths. Pick up a Cycling in Scotland brochure from any tourist office.

SOCCER

CELTIC FOOTBALL CLUB

Celtic Park, Glasgow G40 3RE
Tel 0870 060 1888 (tickets)/0141 551 4308 (tour)
www.celticfc.net
Celtic enjoys passionate support both at home and worldwide. Take a tour of the stadium to the east of the city, one of Europe's largest, or go to see the team in action.

◉ Tours daily except match days
🎟 Tour: adult £8.50, child £5.50,

Take a trip along the Clyde on the Waverley

family £20. Match: adult from £15
🎫 Superstore sells Celtic memorabilia

RANGERS FOOTBALL CLUB

Ibrox Stadium, 150 Edmiston Drive, Glasgow G51 2XD
Tel 0870 600 1993 (tickets)/0870 600 1972 (tour)
www.rangers.co.uk
Take a tour of the stadium or go and see a game. South of the River Clyde. Tickets for an 'Old Firm' game (the Glasgow derby between Rangers and Celtic) are notoriously difficult to get hold of.

◉ Thu–Fri 11, 12.30, 2.30, Sun 10.30, 11.15, 12, 12.45, 1.30, 2.15, 3, 3.45, 4.30
🎟 Tour: adult £7, child £5. Match: adult from £22 🍴

TOURS

GUIDE FRIDAY

Tel 0141 248 7644
www.guidefriday.com
Guided tours of the city on an open-top bus are a great way to get your bearings. Tours leave from George Square, near the tourist information office, and take in all the main sights around the city. Tickets are valid all day, so you can get on and off the bus as often as you like. Buy your ticket on the bus.

◉ Daily 9.20–4.45 every 20 minutes
🎟 Adult £8.50, child £3 (under 5 free), family £20

JOURNEYMAN TOURS

Tel 0800 093 9984 (free)
www.journeymantours.co.uk
Take a guided walk to an old Glasgow pub, with stories of the city's past and its people. At weekends the tour goes on to a ceilidh for traditional Scottish dancing. Advance reservations essential. Meet at the war memorial on George Street.

◉ Sun–Thu 7.30–9pm, Fri–Sat 7–12am
🎟 Midweek tour £5; pub tour and ceilidh £15 ❑ Glasgow Cross pub and Scotia Bar

WAVERLEY EXCURSIONS LTD

33 Landsfield Quay G3 8HA
Tel 0845 130 4647
www.waverleyexcursions.co.uk
Built in Glasgow in 1947, the Waverley is the only sea-going paddle steamer in the world. Join it for a day, afternoon or evening cruise along the River Clyde to the lochs and islands of the west coast.

◉ Apr–end Sep 🎟 From £20
❑ Snacks, lunch and full meals available on board 🎫 🚉 Anderston, Central

HIGHLANDS AND ISLANDS

The scattered population of northern Scotland means that facilities may be few and far between—but none the less welcome for that. Aberdeen and Inverness are the main centres for the bigger shops and entertainment, with Oban also ranking well for its shopping, its diving and its town centre distillery. Otherwise, nightlife tends to centre on local activities and may be thin on the ground—look out for notices of music nights in pubs and local dances. Mull is a rare exception, with its own tiny theatre. Crafts flourish, and there is a wealth of small-scale jewellers, weavers, potters and artists to discover, especially on the islands. Outdoor activities are of the active sort, with Fort William the main base for walkers and climbers, and Aviemore the centre of the winter sports scene. Estates such as Rothiemurchus offer more family oriented activities, and there's lots of wildlife to enjoy, from dolphins, seals and otters to deer, and rare breeding ospreys at Loch Garten. If the Loch Ness Monster is more your sort of thing, then head for Drumnadrochit. Explore the scenic delights of the Cairngorm Mountain Railway, the Strathspey Steam Railway and the West Highland line. Many of the great distilleries offer visitor trips, including Glenfiddich and Glenmorangie. And for variety, there's even a winery and a brewery to discover.

ABERDEEN

🌐 ESSLEMONT & MACINTOSH

26–38 Union Street AB10 1GD
Tel 01224 647331
Founded in 1873, this large independent department store on the 'Granite Mile' is an Aberdeen institution. On a site split between two buildings, linked by a covered walkway, discover emporia of clothes, cosmetics, perfume, china, gifts and things for the home.
🕐 Mon, Wed, Fri–Sat 9–5.30, Tue 9.30–5.30, Thu 9–7.30, Sun 12–4
🍴 Cafés on ground and top floors

🎬 THE BELMONT

49 Belmont Street AB10 1JS
Tel 01224 343536 (bookings); 01224 343534 (24-hour recorded information)
www.picturehouses.co.uk
Opened in 2000, this popular art house cinema shows independent, foreign and classic films. It also has French and Italian film festivals.
🕐 Daily 💷 From £3.70 🍴 The Belmont café bar also hosts art exhibitions, live bands and has a pub quiz every Tue

🎬 HIS MAJESTY'S THEATRE ABERDEEN

Rosemount Viaduct AB25 1GL
Tel 0845 270 8200/01224 641122 (box office)
www.hmtheatre.com
The main theatre in Aberdeen, this is the venue for shows, plays, musicals, dance, opera and pantomimes.
🕐 All year 💷 From £6.50 🍸 Two bars for pre-performance and interval drinks

🎭 LEMON TREE

5 West North Street AB24 5AT
01224 642230
www.lemontree.org
The best music venue in Aberdeen, with classical, traditional Irish, drum 'n' bass, funk, blues and rock concerts. Also contemporary theatre, dance and comedy.
🎭 from £5 (though many gigs are free) 🍴 Relaxed café-bar serves food Thu–Sun 12–3; live jazz Fri and Sun

🎭 MUSIC HALL

Union Street AB10 1QS
Tel 01224 641122 (box office)
www.musichallaberdeen.com
Big classical concerts are held here, including performances by the Royal Scottish National Orchestra. Also jazz, big band music, pop music and Christmas pantomime.
🎭 All year 🎫 From £6 🎭

🍷 OLD BLACKFRIAR'S

52 Castle Street AB11 5BB
Tel 01224 581922
This pub in the city centre dates back to the time of Mary, Queen of Scots. It has a good selection of cask beers, is family-friendly and serves food. In its own words 'Centuries of history for the price of a pint.'
🍷 Mon–Sat 11am–12am, Sun 12.30–11.30

🍷 SLAINS CASTLE

14–18 Belmont Street AB10 1JE
Tel 01224 631877
One of the more unusual bars in the Belmont Street drag, Slains Castle occupies a former church and takes its name from the famous ruins up the coast near Cruden Bay.
🍷 Daily, until 1am Fri–Sat

ACHNASHEEN

🏬 THE STUDIO

Achnasheen, by Strathconon Forest IV22 2EE
Tel 01445 720227
www.studiojewellery.com
This contemporary, gallery-style shop has been in business for 25 years and stocks the largest selection of gold and silver jewellery anywhere in the Highlands. All the pieces are made in the studio. There is another branch on High Street, Fortrose.
🏬 Daily 9.30–5
🍴 Great views from the Studio café

Make a new friend at the Cairngorm Reindeer Centre

ARDFERN

☺ ARDFERN RIDING CENTRE

By Lochgilphead PA31 8QR
Tel 01852 500632
www.aboutscotland.com/argyll/appaloosa
Day rides, hacks, lessons and cross-country jumps are all available from this centre, overlooking Craobh Haven yacht harbour and with views to the Inner Hebrides. The horses are Appaloosas. Advance reservations advised.
☺ All year 🕐 1 hour £20, 2 hours £30; tuition £25 per hour

AVIEMORE

🏬 ELLIS BRIGHAM

9–10 Grampian Road PH22 1RH
Tel 01479 810175
www.ellis-brigham.com
This large shop on the main street stocks ski and snowboarding clothes and equipment, as well as mountain and outdoor sports gear.
🏬 Daily 9–6

☺ CAIRNGORM MOUNTAIN RAILWAY

CairnGorm Mountain Ltd PH22 1RB
Tel 01479 861261
www.cairngormmountain.com
The highest in the UK, the 1.25-mile (2km) funicular Mountain Railway is a great way for people of all ages and physical abilities to reach the top of Cairn Gorm to enjoy the spectacular views. Advance reservations advised during peak holiday periods.
☺ May–end Oct daily 10–5.15; trains depart every 15 minutes; last train up 4.30 🎫 Adult £8.50, child £5 (under 5 free), family £23 🍴 The Ptarmigan Restaurant, with a viewing terrace, is the UK's highest restaurant, open for lunch; dinner served Fri–Sun, summer only 🎁 Gift shop at the top

☺ CAIRNGORM REINDEER CENTRE

Glenmore PH22 1QU
Tel 01479 861228
www.reindeer-company.demon.co.uk
Wear sensible footwear and suitable outdoor clothes to visit the only herd of reindeer in Britain (you can hire wellington boots if needed). You can get close up and even stroke the reindeer by taking a tour out into the hillside, where they roam freely. Located 6 miles (10km) southeast of Aviemore.
☺ Daily 10–5; visits to the herd at 11am, all year; and at 2.30, May–end Sep 🎫 Adult £8, child £4 (under 5 free), family £20 🎁

WHAT TO DO

✪ LOCH MORLICH WATERSPORTS

Glenmore Forest Park, by Aviemore
PH22 1QU
Tel 01479 861221
www.lochmorlich.com
This watersports centre on
Loch Morlich, in the
Cairngorms National Park,
offers canoeing, kayaking,
windsurfing, mountain
bicycling, sailing and walking.
Advance reservations essential.
🕐 Apr–end Sep 💷 Kayak £8 per
hour; rowing boat £14 per hour;
windsurfer £15 per hour 🍴 Café by
the loch

✪ ROTHIEMURCHUS ESTATE

By Aviemore PH22 1QH
Tel 01479 812345
www.rothiemurchus.net
The 10,125ha (25,000 acre)
Rothiemurchus Estate to the
south of Aviemore has forests,
rivers, lochs and mountains,
and is home to rare native
animals such as capercaillies
and red squirrels. The multi-
activity outdoor centre offers
activities such as guided walks,
hill-walking, fishing, clay
pigeon shooting, bicycling and
off-road driving. Hill-walking
and use of the bicycle trails are
free; phone for prices of all
other activities. Advance
reservations advised.
🕐 Daily 9–5.30 🅿

✪ STRATHSPEY STEAM RAILWAY

Aviemore Station, Dalfaber Road
PH22 1PY
Tel 01479 810725
www.strathspeyrailway.co.uk
This classic steam railway was
reopened by enthusiasts in
1978 and is still run almost
entirely by volunteers. Travel in
first, second or third class from
the centre of Aviemore
through Boat of Garten and on
to Broomhill Station. Look for
the Santa Train in December.
🕐 Apr–early Jan 💷 Adult from £9,
child £4.50 (under 5 free), family
£22.50 🍴 Buffet car on most services

BARCALDINE

✪ ARGYLL POTTERY

Barcaldine, by Oban PA37 1SQ
Tel 01631 720503
www.scottishpotters.org
Simple, high quality stoneware
pottery is hand-thrown on the
wheel at this pottery workshop
and shop on the southern
shore of Loch Creran, 8 miles
(12.8km) north of Oban.
🕐 All year Mon–Fri 10–6, Sat 2–5

✪ SCOTTISH SEA LIFE SANCTUARY

Barcaldine, by Oban PA37 1SE
Tel 01631 720386
www.sealsanctuary.co.uk
This is Scotland's leading
marine animal rescue centre,

*Travel in style on the Strathspey
Steam Railway*

caring for seals, fish and
otters. There are feeding
displays, talks, an outdoor
children's play area and an
underwater observatory.
🕐 Daily from 10am in summer; often
only Sat–Sun in winter, check ahead
💷 Adult £9.50, child £6.95, family
£27.95 🍴 🅿

BEAULY

✪ MADE IN SCOTLAND

Station Road IV4 7EH
Tel 01463 782578
www.madeinscotlanddirect.com
This large specialist Scottish
food and gift shop sells
high-quality goods on two
floors, including crafts,
knitwear, jewellery, ceramics,

furniture, food and drink.
Tax-free shopping for visitors
from outside the EU.
🕐 Mon–Sat 9.30–5.30, Sun 10–5 🅿

BLACK ISLE

✪ BLACK ISLE BREWERY

Old Allangrange, Munlochy IV8 8NZ
Tel 01463 811871
www.blackislebrewery.com
Located just 10 minutes from
the A9 north of the Kessock
Bridge, this small, independent
brewery in an 18th-century
house produces bottled light,
dark and organic beers. Free
tours every half-hour.
🕐 Mon–Sat 10–5; also Sun 12–5

CARRBRIDGE

✪ THE ARTIST STUDIO

Main Street PH23 3AS
Tel 01479 8413328
www.carrbridgestudios.com
This gallery sells paintings and
prints of local Cairngorm
scenery, decorative pottery and
ceramic jewellery. The pots are
produced at nearby Carrbridge
Studios, and by appointment
you can visit the workshop.
Carrbridge is 7 miles (11km)
north of Aviemore.
🕐 Apr–end Oct Mon–Fri 9–5, Sat
10–2, Sun 12–4; rest of year Mon–Fri
10–4.30, Sat 10–2

✪ LANDMARK FOREST HERITAGE PARK

▷ 134

CORPACH

✪ SNOWGOOSE MOUNTAIN CENTRE

The Old Smiddy, Station Road,
Corpach, by Fort William PH33 7JH
Tel 01397 772467
www.highland-mountain-guides.co.uk
This outdoor activities centre,
on the A830 to Glenfinnan,
offers abseiling (rappelling),
hill-walking, kayaking and rock
climbing in summer, with
winter mountain sports and
hill-walking in winter (Oct–end
Apr). Suitable for age 8 and
above. Advance reservations
essential.
🕐 Daily, all year 💷 Prices depend on
activities

CRAIGELLACHIE

✪ THE MACALLAN DISTILLERY

Easter Elchies, Craigellachie, Aberlour
AB38 9RX
Tel 01340 872280
www.themacallan.com
Enjoy a guided tour and tasting at the distillery, 13 miles (21km) from Elgin, and home of one of Scotland's favourite single malts.
🕐 Easter–Oct 9.30–5 Mon–Sat; Nov–Easter Mon–Fri 11–3 💷 Free

DRUMNADROCHIT

✪ LOCH NESS CRUISES

The Original Loch Ness Visitor Centre
IV3 6UR
Tel 01456 450395
www.lochness-cruises.com
Join a hunt for the Loch Ness Monster on a cruise of the loch, with skippers who have studied these waters for years. The boat is equipped with Nessie-finding gear such as sonar and radar and there is an excellent photo opportunity as the cruise passes Urquhart Castle.
🕐 Tours run all year, hourly in summer 💷 Adult £10, child £6. Reservations advised

DUFFTOWN

✪ GLENFIDDICH DISTILLERY

Dufftown, Keith AB55 4DH
Tel 01340 820373
www.glenfiddich.com
Take a tour of the famous whisky distillery and then try a dram yourself. Manufactured since 1887, it is the only Highland malt to be distilled, matured and bottled at the distillery, north of Dufftown.
🕐 All year Mon–Fri 9.30–4.30; also Easter to mid-Oct Sat 9.30–4.30, Sun 12–4.30 💷 Free

EASDALE

✪ SEA.FARI

Easdale Harbour, Seil Island, near Oban
PA34 4RF
Tel 01852 300003
www.seafari.co.uk
Enjoy an exhilarating adventure trip on a rigid inflatable boat to see wildlife such as deer, wild goats, seals, seabirds, porpoises, dolphins and the occasional minke whale. Waterproof clothing provided. Minimum age 4. Advanced booking essential. Easdale (Ellanbeich) village is on the bridge-linked island of Seil.
🕐 Trips run all year, mainly Easter–end Oct, and are weather dependent 💷 2-hour Corryvreckan Special: adult £26, child £19.50, family £82.50

ELGIN

✪ JOHNSTON'S OF ELGIN CASHMERE VISITOR CENTRE

Newmill IV30 4AF
Tel 01343 554099
www.johnstonscashmere.com

Sea.Fari in Easdale offers exciting wildlife trips

Take a tour of the only Scottish mill still to transform cashmere from fibre to clothes. There is an exhibition area, and a huge shop sells high quality cashmere and lambs wool clothes. Tax-free shopping for visitors from outside the EU.
🕐 Mon–Sat 9–5.30; Jun–end Dec also Sun 11–4.30 💷

FOCHABERS

✪ BAXTERS HIGHLAND VILLAGE

IV32 7LD
Tel 01343 820666
www.baxters.com
In whitewashed buildings beside the A96, this is the home of the Baxter family's food business, best known for its range of canned soups. You can see how food is prepared in the factory, enjoy cookery demonstrations and even taste new products. Several shops on the site sell food, kitchen items and Scottish gifts.
🕐 Jan–end Mar daily 10–5; Apr–end Dec 9–5.30 🍴

✪ MORAY FIRTH WILDLIFE CENTRE

Tugnet, Spey Bay IV32 7PJ
Tel 01343 820339
www.mfwc.co.uk
Spey Bay and the nearby nature reserve are home to many birds, animals and plants including otters, ospreys, seals and bottlenose dolphins. Explore the dolphin exhibition with videos of the Moray Firth and farther afield. Follow the B9014 for 5 miles (8km) and head left at the Spey Bay Hotel.
🕐 Apr–end Oct daily 10.30–5; mid-Feb to end Mar, Oct to mid-Dec Sat–Sun 10.30–5 💷 Free 🔲 🔲

FORRES

⊕ BRODIE COUNTRYFARE

Brodie IV36 2TD
Tel 01309 641555
www.brodiecountryfare.com
This group of shops in low, whitewashed buildings, sells high-quality Scottish gifts, outdoor clothes, kitchen and tableware, toys, games and Scottish foods. Located between Forres and Nairn.
🕐 Mon–Sat 9.30–5.30 (5 in winter), Sun 10–5.30 (5 in winter) 🔲 Family restaurant serves coffee, snacks and meals

⊕ LOGIE STEADING VISITOR CENTRE

IV36 2QN
Tel 01309 611278
www.logie.co.uk
Shops in these converted former farm buildings, in the Findhorn Valley 6 miles (9.7km) south of Forres, sell second-hand books, antique furniture, crystal, plants and contemporary Scottish art. The

visitor centre has information about the River Findhorn.

🔆 Mid-Mar to end Dec daily 10.30–5 ▫

FORT WILLIAM

🍴 HEBRIDEAN JEWELLERY
95 High Street PH33 6DG
Tel 01397 702033
www.hebridean-jewellery.co.uk
The distinctive jewellery in this small shop is adorned with Celtic designs and handmade in the Hebrides. The shop also stocks CDs of Scottish folk music. Other branches are found in South Uist, and Stornoway on the Isle of Lewis. Tax-free shopping for customers from outside the EU.

🔆 Mon–Sat 9–5.30

🍴 NEVISPORT
High Street PH33 6EJ
Tel 01397 704921
www.nevisport.com
A distinctive triangular glass atrium opposite the Alexandra Hotel holds the best outdoor clothing and equipment shop in the area. There's a huge selection to choose from, including waterproof jackets, boots, tents, books and maps, and there is also a craft shop. Staff can advise on outdoor activities in the area, and can also organize ski or mountain rental for you.

🔆 Mon–Sat 9–5.30 (7pm in summer), Sun 9.30–5 ▫ 🎫 Open from 11am

🍴 SCOTTISH CRAFTS & WHISKY CENTRE
135–139 High Street PH33 6EA
Tel 01397 704406
This is the best craft shop in Fort William, with a range of very high-quality knitwear, rugs, pottery, glassware and books on offer, and a separate whisky shop.

🔆 Summer daily 9–8; winter Mon–Fri 9.30–4

🍷 BEN NEVIS
103 High Street PH33 6DG
Tel 01397 702295
A large, friendly pub on the main street in Fort William, with comfortable leather chairs, a pool table, a real fire and real ales. Bar meals are available until 5pm and there is a restaurant upstairs.

🔆 Mon–Wed 11am–11.30pm, Thu–Sat 11am–1am, Sun 12.30pm–11.30pm

⭐ NEVIS RANGE
Torlundy PH33 6SW
Tel 01397 705825
www.nevisrange.co.uk
Ski and snowboarding centre north of Fort William, with the highest skiing in Scotland. Ski runs from easy to very difficult, snowboard fun areas, off-piste skiing, a ski and snowboard school and equipment rental.

Visit Hebridean Jewellery for a range of Celtic designs

The mountain gondola (pictured on page 189) takes you up Aonach Mor.

🔆 Daily; closed early Dec 🎿 Gondola: adult £8, child £4.90; ski rental: £15.50 per day; snowboard rental £17.50 per day; day tickets from £9.50 ▫ 🍴 Snowgoose restaurant and bar at the top gondola station

⭐ JACOBITE STEAM TRAIN
Fort William Railway Station
Tel 01463 239026
www.steamtrain.info
The steam train (similar to the one featured as the 'Hogwarts Express' in the 2002 movie *Harry Potter and the Chamber of Secrets*) follows the scenic Road to the Isles. The train goes to Mallaig via Glenfinnan (where film scenes were shot at the great viaduct) and returns the same way.

🔆 Mid-Jun to early Oct Mon–Fri 10.20am; also Sun in Aug 🎫 Day return: adult £26, child £15 ▫ 🛍 On-board souvenir shop

INVERNESS

🎭 EDEN COURT
Eden Court, Bishop's Road IV3 5SA
Tel 01463 234234
www.eden-court.co.uk
The premier arts venue in the Highlands and Islands district. Currently undergoing extensive refurbishment (until 2007), it continues to promote film, theatre and dance in a variety of alternative venues.

🔆 All year 🎿 Closed for refurbishment ▫ Closed for refurbishment

🍷 CLACHNAHARRY INN
17–19 High Street, Clachnaharry IV3 8RB
Tel 01463 239806
There's a great view of the Moray Firth from the garden of this 17th-century coaching inn, which offers a good selection of whiskies and cask conditioned beers, and bar meals throughout the day. Over-18s only in the evening. Located 2 miles (3km) out of town on the A862, towards Beauly.

🔆 Mon–Wed 11–11, Thu–Fri 11am–1am, Sat 11am–11.45pm, Sun 12.30–11pm

🍷 HOOTANANNY
67 Church Street IV1 1ES
Tel 01463 233651
A friendly town centre bar with traditional music and good food. After dinner enjoy the live music on most evenings. Wooden floors, red walls and exotic, carved door frames inspired by the owner's travels. Over 18s only after 8pm.

🔆 Mon–Fri 10am–1am, Sat 10am–12.30am, Sun 7pm–12am. Food: Mon–Sat 12–3, 6–9.30

🍸 JOHNNY FOXES
26 Bank Street IV1 1QU
Tel 01463 236577
www.johnnyfoxes.co.uk
The music is the main
attraction at this welcoming
riverside pub, with karaoke on
a Wednesday night and live
music every other night.
Especially busy at weekends.
The pub also offers a wide
variety of food, from steak to
veggie burgers. Over 18s only
after 8pm.
🕐 Mon–Thu 11am–1am, Fri–Sat
11am–1.30am, Sun 12.30–12am

✪ CASTLE GALLERY
43 Castle Street IV2 3DU
Tel 01463 729512
www.castlegallery.co.uk
This outstanding contemporary
art gallery has paintings,
sculpture, prints, ceramics,
glass, wood, textiles and
jewellery by British artists. It's
in an 18th-century building
with exposed walls of wattle
and daub.
🕐 Mon–Sat 9–5

ISLAY

✪ ARDBEG DISTILLERY
Port Ellen PA42 7EA
Tel 01496 302244
www.ardbeg.com
Learn about this famous Islay
malt in the visitor centre, then
sample the whisky. The
distillery was founded in 1815
and completely restored in
1997. Today it is one of seven
remaining distilleries on Islay
(there used to be 21!).
🕐 Jun–end Aug daily 10–5; rest of year
Mon–Fri 10–4; tours 11.30 and 2.30
💷 Tours: adult £2.50, child free 🔲
🈺

KINGUSSIE

✪ HIGHLAND WILDLIFE
PARK
Kincraig PH21 1NL
Tel 01540 651270
www.highlandwildlifepark.org
The reserve has a viewpoint
shelter where you can view
red deer, Highland cattle and
even some animals that are
now extinct in the wild such as

huge bison and ancient breeds
of sheep and horses. A raised
walkway takes you over the
wolf enclosure. There is a
children's trail and play area.
Check ahead in winter, as the
park may not open in bad
weather. Located 7 miles
(11km) south of Aviemore.
🕐 Apr, May, Sep, Oct daily 10–6;
Jun–end Aug 10–7; rest of year10–4
💷 Adult £8.50, child £6.50 🔲 🈺

LEWIS (ISLE OF)
🌐 MOSAIC CRAFTS AND
GIFTS
21 North Beach, Stornoway HS1 2XQ
Tel 01851 700155
High-quality Scottish and
international ethnic crafts and

*Try a wee dram at Islay's
Ardbeg Distillery*

jewellery, sold by friendly,
Gaelic-speaking staff in this
little shop by the harbour.
🕐 Mon–Tue, Thu–Fri 9.30–5.30, Wed
10–5.30, Sat 10–5

✪ HIGHLAND AIRWAYS
Stornoway Airport HS2 0BN
Tel 0845 450 2245
www.highlandairways.co.uk
For stunning views of the
Hebrides from the air, join a
flight from Stornoway airport
on Lewis. Scenic flights take
in Harris, Uist and Taransay.
Flights are dependent on the
weather. Advance reservations
essential.
💷 From £46

✪ OISEVAL GALLERY
Brue HS2 0QW
Tel 01851 840240
www.oiseval.co.uk
Enjoy beautiful photographs of
Hebridean landscapes by
James Smith, displayed in a
gallery in the photographer's
house. All of the framed work
on display is for sale. Brue is
on the west coast.
🕐 Mon–Sat 10.30–5.30

LOCH GARTEN

✪ LOCH GARTEN OSPREY
CENTRE
Tulloch, Nethy Bridge PH25 3EF
Tel 01479 821409
www.rspb.org.uk
Part of the RSPB's Abernethy
Forest reserve, Loch Garten is
famous for its ospreys, which
feed on the fish here, and nest
nearby. Watch the nest on a
closed-circuit camera link at
the RSPB centre.
🕐 Apr–end Aug daily 10–6 💷 Reserve
free; Osprey Centre: adult £3, child 50p,
family £6 🈺

LOCH INSH

🅐 LOCH INSH
WATERSPORTS
By Loch Insh, Kincraig PH21 1NU
Tel 01540 651272
www.lochinsh.com
Join a half-day or full day of
activities at this busy centre.
Watersports include canoeing,
windsurfing and sailing; try
your hand at fishing, archery
and skiing on the dry ski slope,
or go for a mountain bicycle
ride. An adventure area for
children includes a climbing
wall. Advance reservations
essential. Loch Insh is 7 miles
(11km) south of Aviemore.
🕐 All year daily 8.30–5.30; watersports
mid-Apr to mid-Oct 💷 Ski rental 1 day
£16; sailing, 2 hours: adult £26.75
🍴 Boathouse bar and restaurant, open
Feb–end Oct daily 10–10, rest of year
daily 10–6 🈺

MONIACK CASTLE

MONIACK CASTLE WINERIES

Moniack Castle, Inverness IV5 7PQ
Tel 01463 831283
www.moniackcastle.co.uk
Country-style wines, liquors and preserves are made from a variety of plants at this historic 16th-century castle, which lies 7 miles (11km) west of Inverness. See the wines being made and then make your choice in the shop.
Mar–end Oct Mon–Sat 10–5; rest of year 10–4 Tours: adult £2, child free

MULL (ISLE OF)

TOBERMORY CHOCOLATE COMPANY

56–57 Main Street, Tobermory PA75 6NT
Tel 01688 302526
www.tobchoc.co.uk
This specialist sweet shop is above the handmade chocolate factory on the main street of Tobermory. Children under 12 can join a 45-minute workshop and make their own chocolates to take away.
Mon–Sat 9.30–5; also Sun 11–5, summer

MULL THEATRE

Royal Buildings, Tobermory PA75 6NU
Tel 01688 302828
www.mulltheatre.com
Established in 1966, the theatre on Mull has a reputation much bigger than its size—the main theatre building outside the village of Dervaig seats just 43. The resident theatre group performs original and established plays in summer, and may also tour productions around the Highlands. Advance reservations essential.
May–end Sep, and some winter dates Vary from £8

ISLAND ENCOUNTER

Arla Beag, Aros PA72 6JS
Tel 01680 300441
www.mullwildlife.co.uk
Join a full-day wildlife tour of the island, with a chance to see golden eagles, peregrine falcons, owls, otters, seals and porpoises. Lunch, snack and binoculars are provided. Advance reservations essential. Not suitable for very young children.
All year, according to demand
£29.50

NORTH UIST

UIST OUTDOOR CENTRE

Cearn Dusgaidh, Lochmaddy HS6 5AE
Tel 01876 500480
www.uistoutdoorcentre.co.uk
This outdoor activities centre offers diving, canoeing, rowing, sea kayaking, rock climbing and abseiling (rappelling), which you can do as a day visitor. Lochmaddy is noted for the richness of its birdlife. Advance reservations essential. Accommodation is also available.
All year Full day: adult £50, child (under 12) £35; half-day: adult £25, child £17.50

Sailing is just one of the options at Loch Insh Watersports

OBAN

OBAN INN

1 Stafford Street PA34 5NJ
Tel 01631 562484
A large, white building on the seafront, this venerable pub dates from 1790, offers around 50 malt whiskies and a changing selection of real ales. Food is also served, with moules marinière the specialty of the house. Children welcome in the upstairs bar until 8pm.
Mon–Sat 11am–12.45am, Sun 12.30pm–12.45am

O'DONNELL'S IRISH BAR

Breadalbane Street PA34 5NZ
Tel 01631 566159
This Irish-themed pub in the town centre is popular with all ages, with live music most nights during the summer. Bar meals are available, and the restaurant is in a banqueting hall which dates from 1882. Over 18s only in the pub.
Sun–Wed 5pm–1am, Thu–Sat 2pm–2am

OBAN DISTILLERY

Stafford Street PA34 5NH
Tel 01631 572004
www.malts.com
There's been a distillery in the centre of Oban since 1794. Take a tour and see how the coastal location affects the taste of the whisky—it's rich and sweet, with a subtle hint of sea salt. Children are welcome, but under 8s are not admitted to production areas.
Feb Mon–Fri 12–4; Mar–Easter, Nov 10–5; Easter–end Jun Mon–Sat 9.30–5; Jul–end Sep Mon–Fri 9.30–7.30, Sat 9.30–5, Sun 12–5; Oct Mon–Sat 9.30–5; Nov Mon–Fri 10–5; Jan, Dec closed
Adult £4, child free

PUFFIN DIVE CENTRE

Port Gallanach PA34 4QH
Tel 01631 566088
Booking office: George Street PA34 5NY
Tel 01631 571190
www.puffin.org.uk
For an underwater view of Scotland's marine wildlife including fish, crabs and plants, try a shallow dive with an experienced instructor at this dive centre, 1.5 miles (2.4km) south of Oban at Port Gallanach. All equipment, including dry suits, is included. Advance reservations essential. Not suitable for children under 8.
Daily 8am–late 1.5-hour Try-a-Dive: £57.50

WHAT TO DO

OBAN RARE BREEDS FARM PARK

Glencruitten PA34 4QB
Tel 01631 770608
www.obanrarebreeds.com

Children can meet, feed, stroke and touch the geese, llamas, alpacas, rabbits, donkeys, deer, cattle, ducks and pigs at this farm park designed especially for children. There is also a woodland walk, and picnic areas. Located 2 miles (3.2km) east of Oban via the golf course on the Glencruitten road.

🕐 Mid-Mar to end Oct daily 10–6
💷 Adult £6, child £4 🅿 🚻

RAASAY

RAASAY OUTDOOR CENTRE

Raasay House IV40 8PB
Tel 01478 660266
www.raasayoutdoorcentre.co.uk

On the little island of Raasay, off Skye (home to otters, deer, eagles and seals), the centre offers a range of activities such as fishing, walking, abseiling (rappelling), archery, canoeing and sailing. Advance reservations advised. Accommodation and camping also available.

🕐 Apr–end Oct 💷 Half-day courses from £12 🍴 Dolphin Café and Bar open 9am–11pm 🚢 Ferries from Sconser on Skye run Mon–Sat, every hour 8am–7pm, and take 15 minutes

ROY BRIDGE

FISHING SCOTLAND

Roy Bridge PH31 4AG
Tel 01397 712812
www.fishing-scotland.co.uk

Tuition and equipment are provided on the day and evening fly fishing excursions for wild brown trout and rainbow trout around Lochaber. Advance reservations essential. Minimum age 8.

🕐 Fishing trips run all year, according to fish seasons 💷 Private fishing excursion for two people: £160

SKYE (ISLE OF)

SKYE BATIKS

The Green, Portree IV51 9BT
Tel 01478 613331
www.skyebatiks.com

This shop sells a range of batik garments with ancient Celtic designs. It also stocks tweed clothes, leather bags and jewellery.

🕐 Summer Mon–Fri 9–9, Sat–Sun 9–6; winter Mon–Fri 9–5

SKYE SILVER

The Old School, Colbost, Dunvegan IV55 8ZT
Tel 01470 511263
www.skyesilver.com

This shop sells silver and gold jewellery, ceramic tiles and

Pick up some unique gifts at Skye Silver

other gifts, most with unique Celtic-style designs. Tax-free shopping for customers from outside the EU. Located 7 miles (11km) from Dunvegan, on the B884 to Glendale.

🕐 Mar–end Oct daily 10–6

SPEAN BRIDGE

SPEAN BRIDGE MILL

PH34 4EP
Tel 01397 712260
www.foreverscotland.com/mini_sites/spean_bridge

An extensive old mill has been converted to a bright Scottish goods shopping centre selling whisky, specialist foods, knitwear, cashmere, souvenirs, Harris Tweed and outdoor clothing. Regular weaving demonstrations are held during the week, and you can trace your clan history at the tartan centre. Located 10 miles (16km) north of Fort William.

🕐 Mon–Sat 9.30–5, Sun 10–5 🚻

STRATHDON

LECHT 2090

Lecht 2090 Ski and Multi Activity Centre AB36 8YP
Tel 01975 651440
www.lecht.co.uk

This ski and snowboarding centre is ideal for families, and also offers tubing, quad biking and carting. A points card system means you decide how much you want to spend and this is converted into points and loaded on to your card. Swipe the card to pay for your chosen activity. Fun carts are for age 10 and over, quad bikes for age 6 and over, kiddie karts are for age 4–10. The centre is on the A939 between Cockbridge and Tomintoul.

🕐 Daily 10–5; skiing daily from 8.30am, dependent on snowfall
💷 Day ski rental: adult £14, child £8.50; 2-day package including lift pass, skis and instruction: adult £75, child £65. Other activities from £4 🅿

ULLAPOOL

HIGHLAND STONEWARE

North Road IV26 2UN
Tel 01854 612980
www.highlandstoneware.com

See this distinctive pottery being made and hand-painted by skilled craftspeople at the Ullapool factory and also on the shoreline at Lochinver. The full range of tableware is available in the shops and you can even commission your own tiles.

🕐 Mon–Fri 9–6; shop only also open Easter–end Oct Sat 9–5

ORKNEY AND SHETLAND

Most visitors come here for peace and quiet, and to enjoy the seabirds and other wildlife. Scapa Flow is also a mecca for divers, eager to explore the wrecks which lurk there. These northern islands celebrate their rich traditions and distinctive heritage in a series of lively music festivals throughout the year. Otherwise, nightlife tends to be on a local scale— check for folk music evenings and ceilidhs advertised in village halls. Shopping is also limited, but look out for signs advertising traditional handmade Shetland knitwear.

KEY TO SYMBOLS

- 🌐 Shopping
- 🎭 Entertainment
- ♦ Nightlife
- ⚐ Sports
- ✪ Activities
- ◯ Health and Beauty
- ✪ For Children

ORKNEY

🌐 JUDITH GLUE
25 Broad Street, Kirkwall KW15 1DH
Tel 01856 874225
www.judithglue.com
Rich hues and strong design mark out the high quality knitwear, designed by Judith Glue and made in the islands. The extensive shop also sells local crafts and jewellery, and hampers filled with food made in Orkney. Opposite St. Magnus Cathedral. Mail order service, online shopping and tax-free for visitors from outside the EU.
🕐 Mon–Sat 9–5.30; also Jun–end Sep Sun 10–5.30

🌐 ORTAK
Hatston, Kirkwall KW15 1RH
Tel 01856 872224
www.ortak.co.uk
Orkney has a tradition of jewellery making which dates back 5,000 years. This jewellery shop and visitor centre is in the Hatston area to the west of Kirkwall. You can watch the silver jewellery being made, see a permanent exhibition and then explore the shop.
🕐 Mon–Sat 9–5 ⚑ Free

🎭 NEW PHOENIX CINEMA
Muddisdale Road, Kirkwall KW15 1LR
Tel 01856 879900
www.pickaquoy.com
Britain's most northerly cinema is in the Pickaquoy leisure centre, to the west of the town centre. The centre also has a gym, sports arena and athletics track.
🕐 Daily ⚑ Adult from £4.40 🖼 📷

🎭 ORKNEY ARTS THEATRE
Mill Street, Kirkwall
Tel 01856 872047
This small theatre in the town centre hosts a variety of amateur theatre, opera and touring productions through the year. Check locally for show information. Drinks are available on performance nights.

✪ HIGHLAND PARK
Holm Road, Kirkwall KW15 1SU
Tel 01856 874619
www.highlandpark.co.uk
Explore the most northerly malt whisky distillery in the world, founded in 1798. Watch the audio-visual presentation 'The Spirit of Orkney' and then take a guided tour.
🕐 Apr–end Jun, Oct Mon–Fri 10–5; Jul, Aug Mon–Fri 10–5, Sat–Sun 12–5; tour only Mon–Fri at 2pm and shop open Nov–end Mar 1–5 ⚑ Adult £5, child (over 12) £2.50 ☕ Small café for tea, coffee and snacks 🌐

⭐ PIER ARTS CENTRE

28–30 Victoria Street, Stromness KW16 3AA
Tel 01856 850209
www.pierartscentre.com
Contemporary visual art from local, Scottish and international artists, in two converted buildings on the harbour side. Temporary exhibitions are shown alongside the permanent collection of modern art, which include works by Barbara Hepworth and Ben Nicholson.
🕐 Tue–Sat 10.30–12.30, 1.30–5
📅 👤 Free

⭐ ROVING EYE ENTERPRISES

Westrow Lodge, Orphir KW17 2RD
Tel 01856 811309
www.orknet.co.uk/rov
Take a 3-hour boat tour (pictured on page 197) to see the wrecked German war ships that sank in Scapa Flow. A remotely operated vehicle is sent down to explore the wrecks and video pictures are transmitted back to the boat. The return journey concentrates on spotting wildlife such as seals and seabirds. Advance reservations essential.
🕐 May–end Sep daily at 1.20 👤 Adult £25, child (under 12) £12.50

SHETLAND

⊕ ANDERSON & CO

62 Commercial Street, Lerwick ZE1 0BD
Tel 01595 693714
www.shetlandknitwear.com
Overlooking Lerwick harbour, this large shop is full of vibrant sweaters, scarves and hats, knitted by outworkers to traditional Shetland patterns and in many different styles. Mail order service and tax-free shopping for customers from outside the European Union (EU).
🕐 Mon–Sat 9–5

⊕ HIGH LEVEL MUSIC

1 Gardie Court, Lerwick ZE1 0GG
Tel 01595 692618
A great place to buy toe-tapping Shetland and traditional

music on CD and cassette, and also musical instruments and accessories. Some music books also available.
🕐 Mon–Sat 9–5

⊕ SHETLAND TIMES BOOKSHOP

71–79 Commercial Street, Lerwick ZE1 0AJ
Tel 01595 695531
www.shetlandtoday.co.uk
This wonderful store near the market cross stocks thousands of books on Shetland, Orkney and the rest of Scotland, covering subjects as diverse as archaeology, knitting and history. There is some sheet music for traditional tunes, and

The Garrison Theatre in Lerwick is an important arts centre

CDs of Scottish music. Mail order also available.
🕐 Mon–Fri 9–6, Sat 9–5

🎭 GARRISON THEATRE

Isleburgh Community Centre, King Harald Street, Lerwick ZE1 0EQ
Tel 01595 692114
www.islesburgh.org.uk
The main performing arts venue in Shetland, with everything from touring theatre productions to dance, music and a wide variety of lively community events. Films are also shown here. Refreshments are available on performance evenings.
🕐 All year 👤 Cinema £5, theatre from £4

⭐ CLICKIMIN LEISURE COMPLEX

Lochside, Lerwick ZE1 0PJ
Tel 01595 741000
www.srt.org.uk
One of eight well-equipped leisure complexes scattered throughout Shetland, Clickimin provides great facilities, including a 25m (82ft) pool, river ride and flumes and a toddlers' pool, as well as health and fitness suites.
🕐 Complex: Mon–Fri 7.30am–11pm
Main pool: adult £1.60–£2.60, child £1.60 👤

⭐ ISLAND TRAILS

Tel 01950 422408
www.island-trails.co.uk
Several guided walking tours are offered, including an exploration of historic Lerwick. The tour to St. Ninian's Isle, famous for its sand bar, history and tales of smuggling, takes 3 hours, including a 3-mile (5km) walk—strong shoes or boots and waterproofs are required. Advance reservations essential, via the tourist office in Lerwick.
🕐 St. Ninian's Isle: all year by arrangement. Historic Lanes walking tour of Lerwick May–end Sep Tue 11am
👤 Historic Lanes: adult £6, child £3.50

⭐ SEABIRDS-AND-SEALS

Tel 01595 693434/07831 217042 (after hours)
www.seabirds-and-seals.com
Cruise to the Noss and Bressay national nature reserves in the company of an expert wildlife guide. The twin-engined boat has a heated cabin and underwater TV cameras to help you to spot seals and seabirds. All tours leave from the small boat harbour in Lerwick. Advance reservations essential.
🕐 Mid-Apr to mid-Sep daily 9.30 and 2; Jun, Jul also daily 7pm 👤 3-hour tour: adult £35, child £25

WHAT TO DO

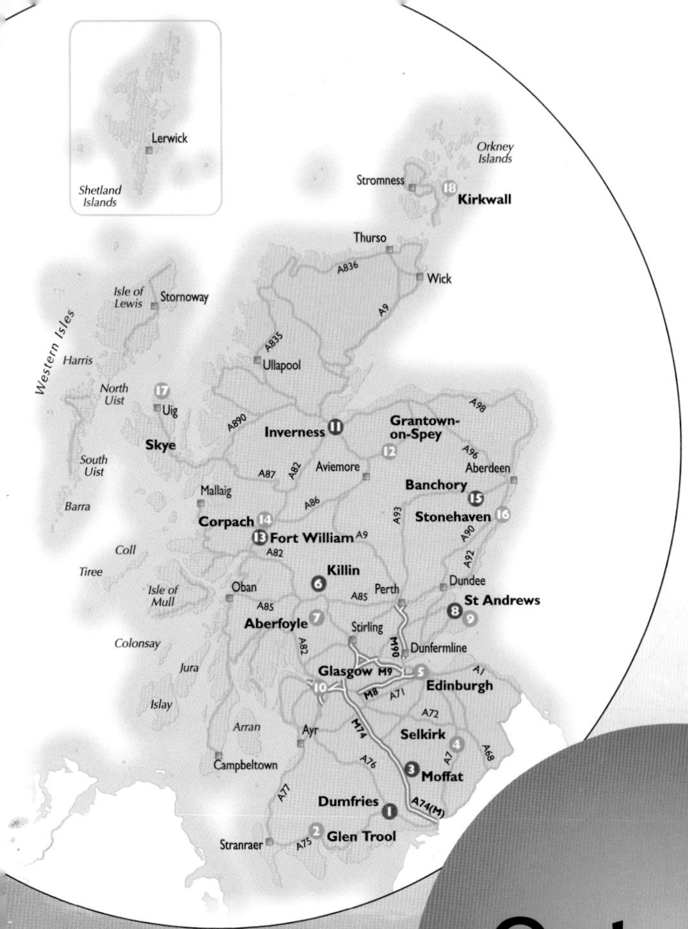

Shetland Islands

Lerwick

Orkney Islands

Stromness

Kirkwall 18

Thurso

A836

Wick

A9

Isle of Lewis

Stornoway

Western Isles

Harris

A835

Ullapool

North Uist

17 Uig

A890

Skye

Inverness 11

Grantown-on-Spey

12

A98

A96

Aberdeen

South Uist

A87 A82

Aviemore

Banchory 15

Barra

A96

A93

Stonehaven 16

Mallaig

Corpach 14

13 **Fort William** A9

A82

Killin

6

A90

A92

Coll

Tiree

Oban

Perth

Dundee

Isle of Mull

A85

A85

St Andrews

Aberfoyle

7

Stirling

8 9

A82

A90 M90

Colonsay

Jura

Glasgow M9 5

Dunfermline

10

M8 A71

A1

Edinburgh

Islay

A72

Arran

Ayr

M74

Selkirk 4

A68

A76

3 **Moffat**

Campbeltown

A7

Dumfries 1

A74(M)

Stranraer

A75

2 **Glen Trool**

Out and About

Walks and drives are numbered sequentially. The start point of each is shown above, with red dots for drives and green for walks. For accommodation along driving routes, ▷ 269–288.

SOUTHWEST COAST

This scenic drive from the ancient city of Dumfries takes in some of the prettiest townships along the southwest coast, returning inland via the Galloway Forest Park.

THE DRIVE

Distance: 118 miles (193km)

Allow: 1–2 days

Start/end: Dumfries, map 313 H14

Tourist information office:
64 Whitesands, Dumfries DG1 4TH,
tel 01387 253862

Dumfries itself ❶ is worth exploring for its connections with the poet Robert Burns (1759–96), who lies buried in St. Michael's kirkyard. Learn more about the connections at the Robert Burns Centre, beside the River Nith (Apr–end Sep Mon–Sat 10–8, Sun 2–5; rest of year Tue–Sat 10–1 and 2–5).

Leave Dumfries by the A710 (the Solway Coast road) and follow it south for 7 miles (11km) to New Abbey (▷ 64). Continue along the A710 beside the northern shore of the Solway Firth. After 19 miles (31km) reach Dalbeattie.

The mudflats and salt marshes of the shallow Solway Firth are famous for their birdlife. Sandyhills Bay has a particularly good sandy beach. Dalbeattie is a quarrying town noted for its sparkling grey granite. Stone from here was exported as far as the island of Malta, to build the Grand Harbour at Valetta.

Leave the town via the A711, then turn right on to the A745. After 6 miles (10km) reach Castle Douglas ❷.

Castle Douglas is a pleasant old market town, with a high street broad enough to take horse and cattle fairs in the past, and some interesting little shops to explore. The town's prosperity was built on a limey clay called marl, which was extracted from Carlingwark Loch for use as fertilizer. The National Trust for Scotland's Threave Garden (▷ 66) is on the outskirts.

Leave the town on the B736, and turn left when the A75 is met. Turn left at the A711 and follow this towards Kirkcudbright.

Pass Tongland Hydroelectric Power Station on the River Dee, one of several power stations in the Galloway Hydroelectric Scheme. Tongland Bridge, built by the great engineer Thomas Telford (1757–1834) lies downstream.

Reach the pretty artists' town of Kirkcudbright ❸ (▷ 62). Leave by the A755 and turn left at the A75. Turn right at the B796 to reach Gatehouse of Fleet.

This was a planned industrial spinning and weaving village, and it is said that Burns composed the rallying song 'Scots Wha Hae' in the Murray Arms hotel.

Return along the B796 and turn right at the A75, passing Cardoness Castle on the right at the junction.

Cardoness overlooks Fleet Bay and was a prominent 15th-century stronghold of the McCullochs.

Follow this road towards Creetown. After 8 miles (13km)

turn right on to a narrow road, signposted to Cairn Holy.

There are two ancient burial sites at Cairn Holy ❹ (free access) more than 3,000 years old, which may also have had some ceremonial role. The main site, Cairn Holy I, is 52m (170ft) long. It has a pillared façade and two tombs which would have originally been covered by a huge mound of stones, something like the cairns at Kilmartin (▷ 132).

Return to the A75 and turn right. Leave the A75 on the right at the signposted road to Creetown.

The ruined tower house of Carsluith Castle is on the left before entering the town. Creetown's best attraction is the Gem Rock Museum (Easter–end Sep daily 9.30–5.30; Oct, Nov, Mar–Easter 10–4; Dec, Feb Sat–Sun 10–4), with a fascinating collection of minerals, fossils and other exhibits from all over the world. To the north of the town lies the lonely hill of Cairnsmore of Fleet (710m/2,331ft), a prominent landmark associated with Richard Hannay's flight in John Buchan's novel *The Thirty-nine Steps* (1915).

Rejoin the A75 and turn right. Turn right at the A712, and continue to the artificial Clatteringshaws Loch and the Forest and Wildlife Centre ❺.

The loch is part of the Galloway Forest Park, and surrounded by moorland and conifer plantations, home to herds of wild deer and wild goats. A memorial stone to Robert the Bruce (1274–1329) recalls a battle here in 1307, when the Scots soldiers out-witted their English foe by burying them in a landslide.

National bard Robert Burns died at Dumfries in 1796

OUT AND ABOUT

The Neolithic chambered tomb, Cairn Holy I

Moniaive's square has a 17th-century mercat (market) cross

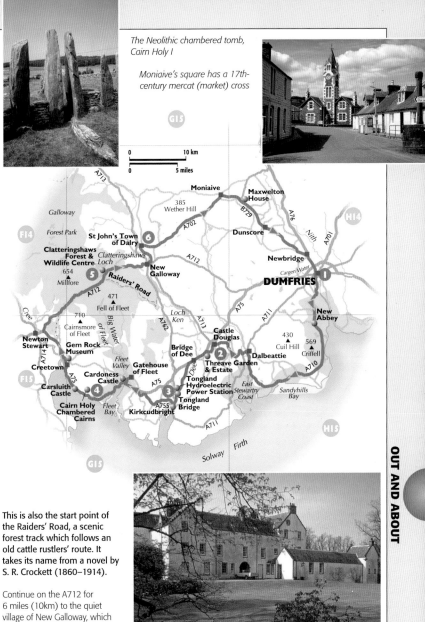

0 ——— 10 km

0 ——— 5 miles

Map labels:
A713
Galloway
Forest Park
Clatteringshaws Forest & Wildlife Centre
Clatteringshaws Loch
St John's Town of Dalry
385 Wether Hill
Moniaive
Maxwelton House
B729
A76
A701
H14
Dunscore
A702
Newbridge
A712
Nith
Cargen Water
DUMFRIES
New Galloway
654 ▲ Millfore
Raiders' Road
A712
471 ▲ Fell of Fleet
Loch Ken
A762
A713
A75
A711
New Abbey
710 ▲ Cairnsmore of Fleet
Big Water of Fleet
Castle Douglas
430 Cuil Hill ▲
569 ▲ Criffel
Newton Stewart
Gem Rock Museum
Bridge of Dee
Threave Garden & Estate
Dalbeattie
A710
Creetown
Cardoness Castle
Fleet Valley
Gatehouse of Fleet
A75
Dee
Tongland Hydroelectric Power Station
East Stewartry Coast
Sandyhills Bay
Carsluith Castle
F15
Cree
A714
Cairn Holy Chambered Cairns
Fleet Bay
A755
Kirkcudbright
Tongland Bridge
A711
Solway Firth
H13
G15
F14

This is also the start point of the Raiders' Road, a scenic forest track which follows an old cattle rustlers' route. It takes its name from a novel by S. R. Crockett (1860–1914).

Continue on the A712 for 6 miles (10km) to the quiet village of New Galloway, which stands above the 9-mile (15km) long Loch Ken. Leave by the A712, then turn left at the A713 to reach St. John's Town of Dalry ⑥.

Dalry has a main street of whitewashed houses. At the top stands an unusual stone seat, known as St. John the Baptist's Chair, and placed here by an acquaintance of Sir Walter Scott. The Southern Upland Way long-distance footpath passes through here on its long route from

Maxwelton House is still owned by the Laurie family

Portpatrick, on the west coast, to Cockburnspath on the east (▷ 236).

Leave the village via the A702, and follow this for 11 miles (18km) to Moniaive.

Moniaive is notable as the birthplace of the last Covenanter to be hanged,

James Renwick, executed in 1688 at the age of 26. A monument to him stands at the edge of the village. White-harled Maxwelton House, to the east, dates from 1370 (private). It was the home of Annie Laurie, born in 1682, about whom a famous ballad was composed.

Continue on the A702, then turn right at the B729. Turn right at the A76 to return to Dumfries.

GLEN TROOL—WHERE A BATTLE MARKED THE ROAD TO INDEPENDENCE

Forest trails lead to the site of Robert the Bruce's turning point during the bitter Wars of Independence.

THE WALK

Distance: 5 miles (8km)

Allow: 2 hours

Start/end: Parking area at entrance to Caldons Campsite, Loch Trool OS Explorer 318 Galloway Forest Park Grid reference NX 396791

How to get there: 13 miles (21km) north of Newton Stewart, off the A714; map 312 F14

Robert the Bruce's famous victory over the English forces at Bannockburn (▷ 24) in 1314 is regarded as the culmination of the Wars of Independence. But Bannockburn was not the end of the conflict—an earlier skirmish, when the two nations clashed at Glen Trool, was a far more important step on the road to independence.

Scotland was an independent country before these wars, but had been left without a monarch following the death of Alexander II in 1286. The Guardians of Scotland asked Edward I of England to adjudicate on the various claimants to the succession. He agreed but also used it as an excuse to re-assert his claim as overlord of Scotland, and the country was run by English officials.

Armed resistance to English occupation was led by Sir William Wallace, a shadowy figure about whom little is really known prior to his uprising. He was in turn appointed Guardian of Scotland by the nobility and

then betrayed by them in 1305, taken to London and executed there.

Meanwhile Robert the Bruce was advancing his claim to the Scottish throne. He murdered his rival claimant, John, the Red Comyn, in Greyfriars church at Dumfries and launched a series of attacks on the English in the southwest. He was crowned King of Scots at Scone on 25 March 1306 (▷ 99). Following a series of defeats, Bruce fled to Rathlin Island, off the Antrim coast, where he regrouped his followers before returning to Scotland early in 1307.

After the attack on English forces in Galloway, an army was dispatched to capture him. But this wild part of Scotland was Bruce's home territory and he set up an ambush in Glen Trool that was successful. It marked the turning point in Bruce's fortunes and he went from here to further victories, culminating in the Battle of Bannockburn.

Edward I counterattacked between 1317 and 1319, seizing the town of Berwick on the Scottish–English border. In 1322 the Scottish nobility appealed to the Pope to support independence in the Declaration of Arbroath (▷ 24). Support was granted in 1324, and in 1328 England finally recognized Scotland as an independent nation in the Treaty of Edinburgh.

Leave the parking area ❶ and follow the obvious waymarkers for the Loch Trool Trail. Cross the bridge over the Water of Trool to enter the Caldons Campsite, then take a left turn on to a footpath that runs along the banks of the river. Cross over a bridge and go past some toilet blocks ❷.

Follow this well waymarked trail through the Caldons Campsite picnic area, across a green bridge, then head right across a grassy area to pick up the trail as it heads uphill and into the forest.

Keep on the path ❸ uphill and through a clearing, then go through a kissing gate and re-enter the woodland. Continue along the southern side of Loch Trool until you reach an interpretation board near the loch end ❹.

This marks the spot where Robert the Bruce and his army lured the superior English forces to a well-planned ambush and routed them. Using part of his force to lure the English on to the southern shores of Loch Trool, Bruce concealed the bulk of his men on the slopes above the loch. The English were forced to follow in single file, the Scots blocked the path and hurled heavy boulders down on them.

Follow the path from here, leaving the woodland and heading downhill and to the left, briefly joining the Southern Upland Way. Turn left, go through two gates and over a wooden bridge. Cross the bridge over Gairland Burn and continue. Eventually reaching the bridge over the Buchan Burn, cross over and take the path to the left, branching off uphill ❺.

Spectacular autumn colour in the bracken, Glen Trool

OUT AND ABOUT

The Galloway Forest park at Glen Trool is owned and managed by the Forestry Commission

Tumbling waterfalls, Glen Trool

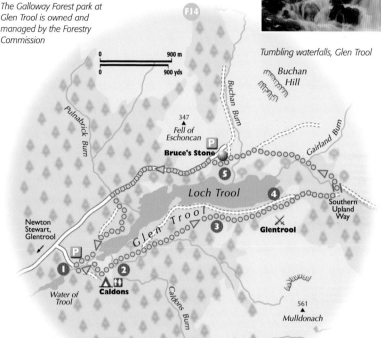

F14

0 — 900 m
0 — 900 yds

Pulnabrick Burn

Buchan Burn

Buchan Hill

347 ▲
Fell of Eschoncan

P

Bruce's Stone

Gairland Burn

5

Loch Trool

4

Southern
Upland
Way

Newton
Stewart,
Glentrool

Glen Trool

3

✕ **Glentrool**

P

🔺🏠 **Caldons**

Water of Trool

Caldons Burn

561 ▲
Mulldonach

F14

Follow this to the top of the hill.

At the top, Bruce's Stone was raised to commemorate the victory at the Battle of Glentrool, the first victory in the Independence Wars. From here, across the clear waters of the loch to the tree-clad hills opposite, is one of the finest views in Scotland.

Follow the track past the stone, then turn left on to the narrow road and head through the parking area. Keep going until you reach a waymarker on the left which leads to a forest trail, and take this to return to the start of the walk.

WHERE TO EAT

Eating places are few and far between but you'll find lots of suitable picnic spots on the walk, so come prepared.

The nearest tea room is a few miles back on the road to Glen Trool at the Stroan Bridge visitor centre. With friendly staff serving a variety of snacks, light meals and delicious hot soup, it's a popular place to stop.

The monolith of Bruce's Stone marks a famous viewpoint across the loch

LITERARY MEANDERINGS IN THE BORDERS

This circular tour from Moffat takes in some of the loveliest landscapes of the Scottish Borders, chasing literary connections with novelists John Buchan (1875–1940) and Sir Walter Scott (1771–1832), and poets William Wordsworth (1770–1850) and James Hogg (1770–1835).

THE DRIVE

Distance: 120 miles (193km)
Allow: 1–2 days
Start/end: Moffat, map 313 H13
Tourist information office:
Churchgate, Moffat DG10 9EG,
tel 01683 220620

Leave the attractive 17th-century spa village of Moffat ❶ by the A701, which follows the course of the Tweed Valley. Turn right at the B712 to Dawyck Botanic Garden.

This is an outpost of the Royal Botanic Garden, Edinburgh. Established over 300 years ago, it is noted for its trees, with spectacular autumnal displays from the magnificent beeches and maples (Apr–end Sep daily 10–6; Mar, Oct daily 10–5; rest of year daily 10–4).

Return along the B712, turn right at the A701, and follow this to Broughton ❷.

In a converted church in Broughton, the John Buchan Centre (May to mid-Oct daily 2–5) details the history of the master storyteller whose best-known novel is _The Thirty-nine Steps_. Buchan was also a historian, and wrote notable biographies of Sir Walter Scott and the Marquis of Montrose. He took the title Lord Tweedsmuir when he became Governor-General of Canada in 1935. Don't miss Broughton Gallery, set in a fairy-tale castle up the hill.

Continue on the A701 and turn right at the A72. Turn left at the A721 and right at the A702. Follow this into the narrow streets of West Linton ❸.

In the 17th century West Linton became famous for its stonemasons, who were the chief gravestone carvers in the area. Gifford's Stone, a well-worn _bas relief_ on a wall in the main street, is by James Gifford. Opposite it is another of his works, the Lady Gifford Well, which was carved in 1666. The Cauld Stane Slap, an ancient drove road across the Pentland Hills, passes nearby.

Leave the village by the B7059. Turn right at the A701 and left at the B7059. Turn left at the A72 for Peebles.

Pass the solid tower of Neidpath Castle on the right ❹, above the River Tweed, as you enter the town of Peebles (▷ 64). Leave the town on the A72, passing the Kailzie Gardens. After 6 miles (10km) reach Innerleithen.

This is the oldest spa in Scotland. It boomed in the 19th century when Sir Walter Scott named one of his novels, _St. Ronan's Well_ (1823), after the mineral wells in the town. In the High Street, Robert Smail's Printing Works is a tiny print shop that started in 1840, when the press was powered by water (NTS, Easter, Jun–end Sep Thu–Mon 12–5, Sun 1–5). Historic Traquair House (▷ 67) lies just over 1 mile (2km) to the south.

Stay on the A72 for 12 miles (19km) to reach the busy textile town of Galashiels ❺.

Galashiels is famous for its weaving. The story of the mills is told in the Lochcarron Cashmere Wool of Scotland Visitor Centre;

entertaining factory tours show the entire process of tartan manufacture (Mon–Sat 9–5; also Jun–end Sep Sun 12–5). Look for Old Gala House, founded around 1583. The nearby mercat (market) cross, which marks the centre of the old town, dates from 1695. It features in the Braw Lads Gathering, an annual festival dating from 1599, during which the boundaries of the town are confirmed by being ridden on horseback.

Leave by the A7, signposted to Selkirk. Turn right at the B7060, then left at the A707 at Yair Bridge. Continue on this road, which becomes the A708 near Selkirk. Follow Ettrick Water and then Yarrow Water on the A708 to Yarrowford ❻, a distance of 13 miles (21km).

This scattered village lies on the lovely Yarrow Water river, which inspired English Romantic William Wordsworth to compose no fewer than three poems in its praise. The former royal hunting lodge of Newark Tower lies downstream, and dates from 1423. Hunting took place in the surrounding hills of Ettrick Forest until the 16th century, when sheep farming was introduced and developed into the cornerstone of local industry.

The ruins of Foulshiels House also lie this way. It was the birthplace of explorer Mungo Park (1771–1806), who died in his search for the source of the River Niger in Africa (▷ 206–207). Bowhill House is a 19th-century mansion with fine French furniture and a good collection of paintings, surrounded by a scenic country park (house: Jul daily 1–5; park: mid-Apr to end Aug Sat–Thu 11–5).

A bronze ram tops the fountain at Moffat, prime sheep country

OUT AND ABOUT

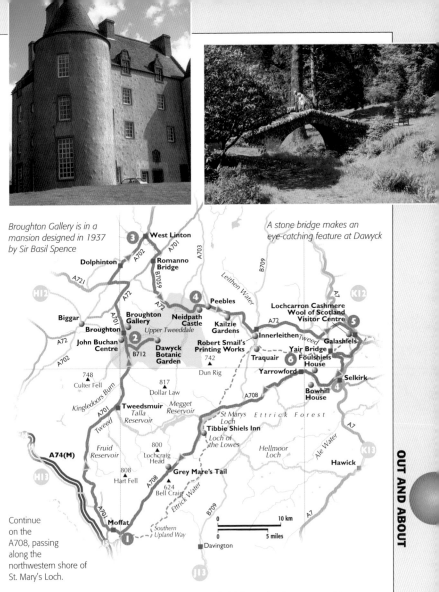

Broughton Gallery is in a mansion designed in 1937 by Sir Basil Spence

A stone bridge makes an eye-catching feature at Dawyck

Continue on the A708, passing along the northwestern shore of St. Mary's Loch.

At around 3 miles (5km) long, this is one of the best places in southern Scotland for sailing. At the southern end of the loch, on a spit of land which separates it from the smaller Loch of the Lowes, a red sandstone monument recalls local poet James Hogg, known as the Ettrick Shepherd. Hogg spent many an evening in the nearby Tibbie Shiels Inn with his friend Sir Walter Scott.

Continue on the A708 for 9 miles (15km) and follow signs to the parking at the Grey Mare's Tail waterfall (▷ 61). Continue on the A708 for 10 miles (16km) to return to Moffat.

Writer John Buchan tramped these rolling Border hills in his youth

FROM SELKIRK TO THE WILDS OF AFRICA

A gentle walk by Ettrick Water, laced with memories of the great explorer Mungo Park (1771–1806).

THE WALK

Distance: 3 miles (5km)
Allow: 1 hour 40 minutes
Start/end: West Port Car Park, Selkirk.
OS Explorer 338 Galashiels
Grid reference NT 469286
How to get there: On the A707 on the western outskirts of Selkirk; map 314 K13

The statue on Selkirk's High Street commemorates Mungo Park, the noted surgeon and explorer, who was born nearby at Foulshiels. Park was educated at Selkirk Grammar, trained as a doctor and took a post as surgeon's mate on a ship bound for the East Indies. He returned from the voyage and promptly set off again, this time heading for Africa to map the River Niger.

Park's journey lasted more than 2.5 years. He became desperately ill from fever and hunger, and was robbed many times. He was even captured and held prisoner by a tribal leader. He escaped and continued his travels, following the River Niger to Sillis and only abandoning his journey when he became too ill to carry on.

When Park returned to Scotland he published an account of his explorations, *Travels in the Interior Districts of Africa* (1799), which became a bestseller. Shortly afterwards he married and took a post as a doctor in Peebles (▷ 64).

In 1805, Park set sail again for Africa, accompanied by his friend George Scott and brother-in-law Alexander Anderson, intending to complete the journey along the Niger.

The intrepid explorers never came home. Scott, Anderson and others died from fever.

The Selkirk bannock is a local delicacy—a sweet bread made with dried fruit

Park refused to give up, writing 'I shall…discover the termination of the Niger or perish in the attempt.' He continued his journey with a few soldiers and bearers, but fate was against him. While trying to escape from hostile tribesmen, he threw himself into the waters of the Niger and drowned.

Sadly, when his son followed in his footsteps some 20 years later, he too disappeared without trace.

From Park's statue in the High Street ❶ walk to the Market Place, go left down Ettrick Terrace, left at the church, then sharp right down Forest Road. Follow this downhill, cutting off the corners using the steps, to Mill Street. Go right, then left on to Buccleuch Road. Turn right following the signs for the riverside walk and walk across Victoria Park to join a tarmac track.

Turn left ❷, walk by the river, then join the road and continue to cross the bridge. Turn left along Ettrickhaugh Road, passing a row of cottages on your left. Just past them turn left, cross a tiny footbridge, then take the indistinct track on the left. Walk to the riverbank and turn right ❸.

Follow the path along the river margin; it's eroded in places so watch your feet. In spring and summer your way is sprinkled with wild flowers. Eventually join a wider track and bear left. Follow this to reach a weir and a salmon ladder. Turn right to cross the tiny bridge ❹.

Immediately after this go left and continue walking alongside the river until you reach a point at which the Yarrow Water joins the Ettrick Water. Retrace your steps for about 91m (100 yards), then turn left at a crossing of tracks ❺.

Your route now takes you through the woods, until you cross over the little bridge by the weir again. Take the footpath to the left and follow the grassy track around the meadow until you come to the mill buildings ❻.

Bear right (but don't cross the bridge) and continue, walking with the mill lade (small canal) on your left. Where the path splits, take the track on the left to follow a straight, concrete path beside the water to reach the fish farm ❼ (you'll smell it).

Walk around the buildings, then bear left to continue following the mill lade. Go left over the footbridge, then right, passing the cottages again. At the main road go right to reach the bridge. Don't cross the bridge but join the footpath on the left ❽.

OUT AND ABOUT

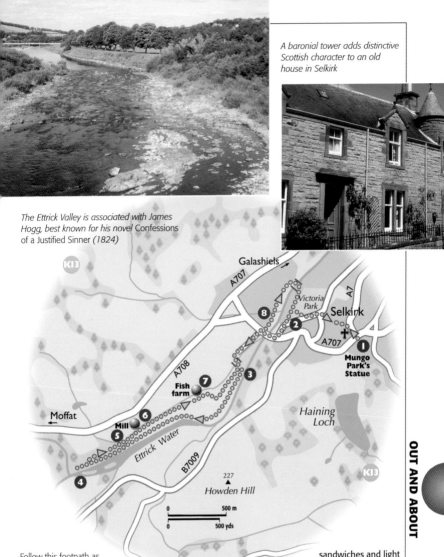

A baronial tower adds distinctive Scottish character to an old house in Selkirk

The Ettrick Valley is associated with James Hogg, best known for his novel Confessions of a Justified Sinner *(1824)*

Galashiels

A707

Victoria Park

Selkirk

A7

8

2

A707

Mungo Park's Statue

A708

3

Fish farm

7

Haining Loch

Moffat

6

Mill

5

Ettrick Water

B7009

227
Howden Hill

4

K13

0   500 m
0   500 yds

Follow this footpath as it goes past a sports ground, then skirts a housing estate. Continue walking until you reach the pedestrian footbridge on your right-hand side, where you cross over the river, bear right, then retrace your footsteps back over Victoria Park and uphill to the Market Place at the start of the walk.

WHERE TO EAT

There are several places to try in the centre of Selkirk. Among the hotels offering bar meals is the Cross Keys by the Market Place, which serves toasted sandwiches and light snacks. There's also a small tea room. Look out for the famous Selkirk bannock on sale in the town bakeries.

Sir Walter Scott was a sheriff of Selkirk; his statue stands in the town square

OUT AND ABOUT

EDINBURGH'S ELEGANT NEW TOWN

A walk in the footsteps of a fistful of literary giants.

THE WALK

Distance:	3 miles (5km)
Allow:	1 hour 30 minutes
Start/end:	Tourist Information Centre, Princes Street, Edinburgh Grid reference NT 257739
How to get there:	By Waverley train station; map 317 J11

Edinburgh's New Town is an elegant, 18th-century planned development of wide airy streets, sweeping crescents and soft grey Georgian buildings. The New Town soon became the haunt of the Scottish literati, many of whom are celebrated in the paving stones around the Writers' Museum (▷ 88).

The city has long held a fascination for writers and many meetings have taken place here, including that between literary giants Sir Walter Scott and Robert Burns. The war poet Wilfred Owen (1893–1918) often came into Edinburgh while he was recuperating from shell shock at nearby Craiglockhart War Hospital, and it was here that he met fellow poet Siegfried Sassoon, who encouraged him in his writing.

From the tourist information office ❶, turn left and walk along Princes Street.

Princes Street marks the dividing line between the medieval Old Town, on your left, and the Georgian New Town (▷ 84–85), which spreads out to your right.

Just after you pass the Scott Monument (▷ 87) on your left, cross the road to reach Jenners, the famous Edinburgh department store. Continue along Princes Street, then take a right turn up Hanover Street.

Milne's Bar on Hanover Street was a popular haunt of several of Scotland's most influential modern poets. Hugh MacDiarmid, Norman MacCaig and Sorley MacLean are just some of the figures who used to meet here in the last century. The pub walls are still covered with their memorabilia.

Take the second turning on your left ❷ and walk along George Street.

English Romantic poet Percy Bysshe Shelley (1792–1822) stayed at 60 George Street with his young bride, Harriet Westbrook, in 1811.

Reach Charlotte Square, the epitome of Georgian elegance in the city, and turn right and right again to go along Young Street. At the end, turn left and walk down North Castle Street to reach Queen Street ❸.

Kenneth Grahame (1859–1932), author of the classic book for children, *The Wind in the Willows*, was born at 30 Castle Street. Novelist and poet Sir Walter Scott (1771–1832) was also born in the city, and kept a town residence at 39 Castle Street.

Cross the road, turn left, then right down Wemyss Place and

The Scott Monument, on Princes Street

right into Heriot Row.

Robert Louis Stevenson (1850–94), best known as the author of the adventure stories *Treasure Island* and *Kidnapped,* and for the macabre tale of *Dr Jeykyll and Mr Hyde*, spent his childhood at 17 Heriot Row.

At Howe Street turn left and, before you reach the church in the middle of the street, turn left and walk along South East Circus Place. Walk past the sweep of Royal Circus and down into Stockbridge.

Cross the bridge ❹, then turn left along Dean Terrace. At the end, turn right into Ann Street. At Dean Park Crescent turn right and follow the road round into Leslie Place and into Stockbridge again. Cross the road to walk down St. Bernard's Row (almost opposite). Follow this, then bear left into Arboretum Avenue ❺.

Continue past the Water of Leith and down to Inverleith Terrace. Cross over and walk up Arboretum Place to reach the entrance to the Botanic Garden on the right (▷ 86). Turn left after exploring the gardens and retrace your steps to Stockbridge.

The sparkling east gates of the Royal Botanic Garden

Turn left at Hectors Bar ⑥ and walk uphill, then turn left along St. Stephen Street. At the church follow the road, then turn left along Great King Street. At the end, turn right, then immediately left to walk along Drummond Place, past Dublin Street and continue ahead into London Street.

At the roundabout ⑦ turn right and walk up Broughton Street to Picardy Place. Turn left and go past the statue of Sherlock Holmes.

The statue of the great fictional detective is a tribute to his Edinburgh-born creator Sir Arthur Conan Doyle, who lived nearby at 11 Picardy Place (now demolished). Conan Doyle studied medicine at Edinburgh University and modelled Holmes on one of his former lecturers—Dr Joseph Bell, who helped the police in solving several murders in the city. Many believe that Conan

The view from Calton Hill is one of the best in the city

Doyle assisted Bell with his work in this capacity, acting as Dr. Watson to his Holmes.

Bear left towards the Playhouse Theatre. Cross over, continue left, then turn right into Leopold Place and right again into Blenheim Place. After the church turn right and keep right up the hill. Turn left at the meeting of paths.

Go up the steps on the right ⑧, walk over Calton Hill, then turn right to pass the cannon. Go downhill, take the steps on your left and walk down into Regent Road. Turn right and walk back into Princes Street.

WHERE TO EAT

Apart from Milne's Bar on Hanover Street there are plenty more pubs and bars to choose from in the New Town. George Street has several bistros and restaurants.

Down in Stockbridge you can relax in a coffee bar such as Patisserie Florentin, which serves great cakes, or have a light snack and a cappuccino in Maxi's or Hectors.

OUT AND ABOUT

THE TROSSACHS TRAIL

This drive explores the varied and magnificent scenery of Scotland's first designated national park of Loch Lomond and the Trossachs (▷ 98).

THE DRIVE

Distance: 159 miles (256km)

Allow: 2 days

Start/end: Killin, map 317 G9

Tourist information offices:
Breadalbane Folklore Centre, Falls of Dochart, Main Street, Killin FK21 8XE, tel 01567 820254; seasonal Trossachs Discovery Centre, Main Street, Aberfoyle FK8 3UQ, tel 01877 382352

Leave the hill-walking centre of Killin ❶ (▷ 95) on the A827, and follow this northeast for 17 miles (27km) to Kenmore.

As you pass Loch Tay on the right, the big, bare-looking mountain of Ben Lawers (1,214m/3,984ft) is up to your left. A National Nature Reserve, it is celebrated for its Arctic and alpine flora, which thrives on the lime-rich soils. Look for mountain hares on the high ground. The National Trust for Scotland has a visitor centre, signposted from the road (May–end Sep daily 10.30–5). Glen Lyon (▷ 94) runs parallel, on the other side of the mountain ridge. Kenmore is a small resort and watersports centre, dominated by the 19th-century pile of Taymouth Castle (private). Sticking into the loch is a reconstruction of an Iron-Age roundhouse, the focus of the intriguing Scottish Crannog Centre (▷ 101).

Continue on the A827 for 6 miles (10km) to Aberfeldy ❷ (▷ 90).

Pass a memorial of 1887 to the men of the Black Watch on the southern side of the bridge. The Black Watch regiment was enrolled into the British Army in 1739, and took its name from the soldiers' dark tartan, which was carefully selected to differentiate them from the Guardsmen, or 'Red Soldiers'.

Leave by the A826, and follow this wild road up over the high moors. Turn right at the A822, then right at the A85 and follow this into Crieff (▷ 91). Continue on the A85 for 19 miles (31km) through Comrie to Lochearnhead ❸.

This small town at the western tip of Lochearn grew when the railway was built through Glen Ogle, which lies to the north and links up with Killin, passing to a height of 289m (948ft). Edinample Castle, a castellated mansion of 1630, lies where the Burn of Ample runs into the loch.

Leave by the A84 and follow it for 14 miles (23km) southward to Callander (▷ 91), passing a turning right to Balquhidder, where outlaw Rob Roy MacGregor (1671–1734) is buried in the churchyard. Return along the A84 and then turn left at the A821. After passing the Trossachs Hotel, follow the signs (right) to Loch Katrine.

Leave your car in the parking area at the end ❹ and take a walk or bicycle ride beside this lovely loch, 9 miles (15km) long, whose island-studded beauty became legendary after Sir Walter Scott's description in *The Lady of the Lake*. While recreation is to the fore as visitors come in droves to enjoy the scene and take a ride on the steamer, the loch also has a serious practical function, supplying central Glasgow with fresh water via an underground pipeway some 35 miles (56km) long.

Return to the A821 and turn right. Follow the A821 for 7 miles (11km) over the hills on the Duke's Pass, and through the Achray Forest to Aberfoyle.

Aberfoyle is surrounded by the pine trees of the Queen Elizabeth Forest Park, and the extensive visitor centre 1 mile (1.6km) to the north has information about the many walking routes in the area. This little stone-built town bustles at the heart of the Trossachs, its Scottish Wool Centre (May–end Sep daily 9.30–6; rest of year daily 10–5), signposted from the main road, attracting a steady flow of visitors throughout the year, to enjoy the lively Sheep Show and the shopping. A good place for woollens, but also other clothing, books and gifts.

Continue on the A821 and the A81. At the intersection with the A811, turn right to pass Drymen, and then go through the small village of Gartocharn.

Gartocharn is best known, not for itself, but rather for the superb view up Loch Lomond from the hill behind the village, Duncryne (142m/462ft).

Continue on the A811 through Balloch and turn right at the A82.

Rob Roy's grave, Balquhidder

The Black Watch memorial at Aberfeldy was raised in 1887

A view of snow-capped Ben Lawers, from Glen Lyon

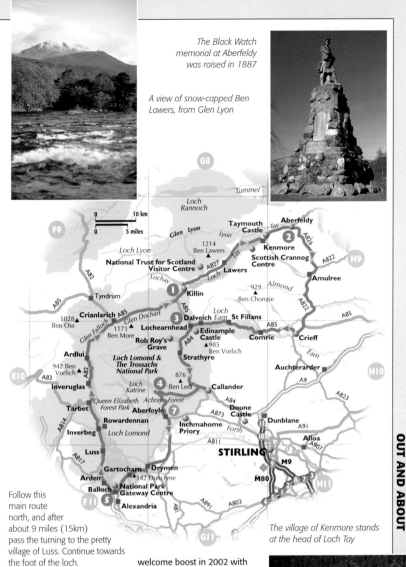

Tummel

Loch Rannoch

G8

0   10 km
0   5 miles

F9

Glen Lyon

Loch Lyon

Lyon

1214 Ben Lawers

National Trust for Scotland Visitor Centre

Lochay

A827

Loch Lawers

Tay

Aberfeldy

2

A826

Taymouth Castle

Kenmore

Scottish Crannog Centre

A822

H9

Amulree

929 Ben Chonzie

Almond

A822

Tyndrum

A82

1

Killin

A85

A85

1028 Ben Oss

Crianlarich

A85

Glen Dochart

3

Dalveich

Loch Earn

St Fillans

Lochearnhead

1171 Ben More

Glen Falloch

Rob Roy's Grave

Edinample Castle

985 Ben Vorlich

Comrie

A85

Crieff

Earn

Ardlui

942 Ben Vorlich

A82

A84

Strathyre

Loch Lomond & The Trossachs National Park

876 Ben Ledi

Auchterarder

H10

E10

A83

Inveruglas

Loch Katrine

4

Callander

A9

A823

Tarbet

A814

Queen Elizabeth Forest Park

Achray Forest

7

Aberfoyle

A84

Doune Castle

A873

A85

Rowardennan

Inverbeg

Loch Lomond

Inchmahome Priory

Forth

Dunblane

A91

10

Alloa

A907

Luss

A817

STIRLING

M9

Arden

Gartocharn

142 Duncryne

Drymen

M80

Balloch

National Park Gateway Centre

5

F11

Alexandria

A81

A891

A803

G11

H11

OUT AND ABOUT

The village of Kenmore stands at the head of Loch Tay

Follow this main route north, and after about 9 miles (15km) pass the turning to the pretty village of Luss. Continue towards the foot of the loch.

Lying near the foot of Loch Lomond, the village of Balloch **5** received a

welcome boost in 2002 with the opening of the visitor centre, Loch Lomond Shores, and its companion ultra-modern shopping centre, which together form the National Park Gateway Centre (daily 10–5, extended hours in summer). The Thistle Bagpipe Works are nearby. Pass Inverbeg, from where it is possible to catch a ferry across the loch to the isolated settlement of Rowardennan.

Rejoin the A82 and continue up the west shore of the loch. After Ardlui, the mountains become

The steamer is the only powered boat on Loch Katrine

more rugged as you continue up Glen Falloch to Crianlarich. At Crianlarich, turn right on to the A85, driving through Glen Dochart. Pass Loch Lubhair on the left, with Ben More looming on the right (1,171m/3,842ft). Turn left at the A827 to return to Killin.

QUEEN ELIZABETH FOREST PARK

A woodland walk with spectacular views across a geological fault.

THE WALK

Distance: 4 miles (6km)

Allow: 3 hours

Start/end: Visitor Centre, Aberfoyle
OS Explorer 365 The Trossachs
Grid reference NN 519014

How to get there: Aberfoyle is on the
A821 22 miles (35.4km) west of Stirling;
map 316 G10

This walk crosses the Highland Boundary Fault, a geological line stretching from Arran to Stonehaven, just south of Aberdeen. It is one of Britain's most important geological features and it separates the Highlands from the Lowlands.

This weak line in the crust of the earth formed around 390 million years ago when the old rocks of the Highlands were forced up and the Lowland rocks pushed down. North of the fault lie Highland rocks, created over 500 million years ago. Whinstone, used extensively as a building stone, formed from extreme pressure on mud and sand. Slate was also formed in this fashion but was compressed into layers and was valued as a roofing material. Near the walk is the Duke's Pass, one of the largest slate quarries in Scotland.

From the front of the visitor centre ❶ turn left, go down

Waymarked trails in the park take in the geological feature, the Highland Boundary Fault

some steps on to a well-surfaced footpath and follow the blue waymarkers of the Highland Boundary Fault Trail. Continue on this trail to reach the Waterfall of the Little Fawn with its 16.7m (55-ft) drop. Shortly after this turn left to cross a bridge, then turn right following the white arrow left again on to a forest road ❷.

This forest road is part of the National Cycle Network (NCN), so look out for bicyclists.

Head uphill on this waymarked road following the blue Highland Boundary Fault markers and the NCN Route 7 signs. When the road forks at a junction, keep left continuing uphill until you reach a crossroads ❸.

Turn right, at the blue waymarker, on to a smaller and rougher road. The Boundary Fault Trail parts company with the NCN Route 7 at this point. The going is easy along this fairly level section. Keep on until you eventually reach a viewpoint on the right with a strategically placed seat ❹.

Most of the higher mountains in this area are formed from a rock known as Leny Gritt, which started life as sand and gravel before being moulded into shape by intense heat and pressure. Another group of rocks includes Achray Sandstone, formed when this high mountain area was under the sea.

From here the road heads uphill until it reaches a waymarker near a path heading uphill towards a mast. Turn right, then go through a barrier and start descending. Although this is a well-made path, it is a very steep descent through the woods and great care should be taken.

Given the quality and variety of the rocks found in this part of the forest park it is not surprising that a great deal of quarrying once took place

here. This steep downhill path follows the line of the Limecraigs Railway, an inclined railway that dates from the beginning of the 19th century and was used for transporting stone from Lime Craig Quarry. The limestone was carried on wooden wagons to the lime kilns at the bottom of the hill. Heavy wooden sleepers supported the three rails of the wagon way. Full wagons went down using the centre and one outside rail, while the empties returned on the centre and other outside rail. The wagons were attached to a wire rope, and the weight of the full wagons and gravity provided the power to return the empty ones to the top. By 1850 the quarry was worked out.

Stay on the path down the hill ❺, and go through another barrier where the path is intersected by a forest road. Cross this road, go through another barrier and once again head downhill.

At the bottom of the hill is a set of steps ❻ leading to a forest

OUT AND ABOUT

The park, owned by the Forestry Commission, was designated in 1953 in honour of the coronation of Elizabeth II

The visitor centre includes a restaurant and gift shop

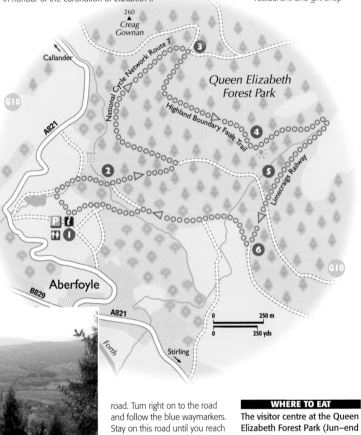

road. Turn right on to the road and follow the blue waymarkers. Stay on this road until you reach a green signpost on the left pointing to the visitor centre. Turn left on to a downhill track and head through the woods.

Eventually you will reach a board announcing the end of the trail. From here the route is signed back to the visitor centre. When the trail forks take the right-hand turning and head uphill beside a handrail and return to the start.

A bench seat makes the most of a scenic viewpoint on the trail

WHERE TO EAT

The visitor centre at the Queen Elizabeth Forest Park (Jun–end Aug daily 10–6; Easter–end Jun, Sep–end Dec daily 10–5; rest of year Sat–Sun daily 10–5) contains an excellent restaurant where you can enjoy a bowl of hot soup, a selection of drinks and a host of other delights ranging from sandwiches to hot meals. As an accompaniment to the food there are extensive views over the forest park.

OUT AND ABOUT

A CIRCUIT OF FIFE

This circular tour takes in the highlights of an east-coast peninsula with a strong tradition of farming, fishing and mining, known as the Kingdom of Fife.

THE DRIVE

Distance: 97 miles (156km)
Allow: 1 day
Start/end: St. Andrews, map 318 K10
Tourist information office:
70 Market Street, St. Andrews KY16 9NU, tel 01334 472021

From the ancient university town of St. Andrews ❶ (▷ 100), home of golf, take the A917 southeast along the coast towards Crail, passing a turning to Scotland's Secret Bunker (▷ 101).

Crail's picturesque harbour is at the bottom of a steep lane. The town is the start of the fishing villages of the East Neuk (▷ 96–97), a chain of charming old fishing harbours strung out along the southeast coast of Fife. They share views out to the Isle of May, and across the Firth of Forth to the flat lands of North Berwick.

Follow the A917 for 4 miles (6km) to Anstruther, where the Scottish Fisheries Museum on the seafront is an added attraction (Apr–end Sep Mon–Sat 10–5.30, Sun 11–5; rest of year Mon–Sat 10–4.30, Sun 12–4.30). Continue on the A917 for 1 mile (1.6km) to Pittenweem ❷, the busiest of the harbours.

To the north, Kellie Castle is worth a short diversion (NTS, gardens open all year daily 9.30–5.30; house May–end Sep daily 1–5). A venerable tower house, it dates back to 1360, but most of what is seen today is from 1606. The interior was restored by the family of architect Robert Lorimer at the end of the 19th century, and has a comfortable, eccentric air, with painted panels and some beautiful plaster ceilings upstairs. From the house there are views south towards the sea, and down the back to the beautiful walled gardens, planted with old-fashioned roses, fruit and vegetables, and herbaceous flowers.

Continue on the A917 to explore first St. Monans and then Elie, with its golden sands. Stay on the A917 to Upper Largo, then join the A915 towards Windygates, passing Largo Bay and the holiday and golfing resort of Lundin Links. Leven and Methil are also holiday towns on the edge of the industrial and mining district which stretches towards Kirkcaldy.

At Windygates ❸, join the A911 and head towards Glenrothes, a planned 'new town' established in 1949. Turn right at a roundabout at the intersection with the A92 and head northwards. Turn left when the A912 is met and follow this to the ancient village of Falkland (▷ 92), which has several good eating places. Continue on the A912 and turn left at the A91 and left again at the B919. Turn left at the A911 and follow it to Scotlandwell ❹.

Scotlandwell lies on the flat land to the east of Loch Leven, and records dating back to AD84 show that Roman soldiers drank from the holy well here. In medieval times, it was a place of pilgrimage; the current stone cistern marking the well is 19th century. Today the village is better known for the nearby gliding centre.

Leave by the B920 and turn right at the B9097, following the southern shore of Loch Leven, a nature reserve noted for its birdlife. Pass the Royal Society for the Protection of Birds' Vane Farm visitor centre on the left (daily 10–5). At the intersection with the B996, turn right and follow this road to Kinross ❺.

Standing on the northwest shore of Loch Leven, Kinross is a former county town and a popular centre for anglers. It is also the access point for Lochleven Castle (▷ 99). The gardens of 17th-century Kinross House are open in summer (Apr–end Sep daily 10–7), and were designed by William Bruce (1630–1710), better known for his work on Holyrood Palace in Edinburgh.

Continue on the B996 and join the A922. After Milnathort, follow the B996 then the A91. Turn left at the A912 and right at the A913 to Abernethy.

Pictish carved stones discovered in the area suggest that this quiet little village was once a centre of some significance, and it is said that Malcolm II of Scotland knelt to

Enjoying the sands and the views by the village of Elie

OUT AND ABOUT

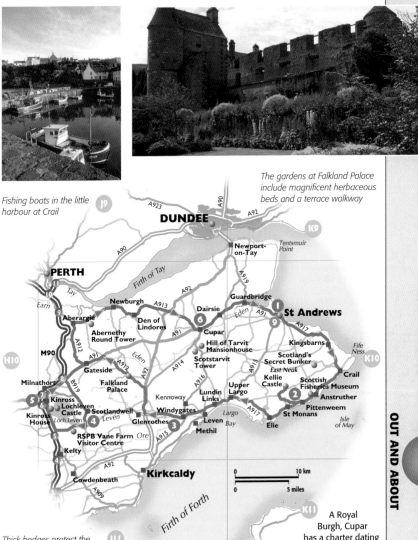

The gardens at Falkland Palace include magnificent herbaceous beds and a terrace walkway

Fishing boats in the little harbour at Crail

DUNDEE

PERTH

Newport-on-Tay

Tentsmuir Point

Firth of Tay

Guardbridge

St Andrews

Newburgh

Dairsie

Cupar

Aberargie

Den of Lindores

Abernethy Round Tower

Hill of Tarvit Mansionhouse

Scotstarvit Tower

Kingsbarns

Fife Ness

M90

Gateside

Scotland's Secret Bunker

East Neuk

Kellie Castle

Scottish Fisheries Museum

Crail

Milnathort

Falkland Palace

Kennoway

Lundin Links

Upper Largo

Anstruther

Kinross Lochleven Castle

Scotlandwell

Windygates

Pittenweem

St Monans

Kinross House

Loch Leven

Glenrothes

Largo Bay

Leven

Elie

Isle of May

RSPB Vane Farm Visitor Centre

Methil

Kelty

Cowdenbeath

Kirkcaldy

| 0 | 10 km |
| 0 | 5 miles |

Firth of Forth

OUT AND ABOUT

Thick hedges protect the gardens at Kellie Castle from salt-laden winds off the sea

William I of England here in 1072. Its biggest claim to fame is the curious round tower, 22.5m (74ft) high and dating from the 11th century. It is only the second example of such an Irish Celtic church tower in Scotland (the other is at Brechin). Abernethy village, incidentally, has nothing to do with Abernethy biscuits, which were named after an English doctor.

Continue on the A913 and follow it for 13 miles (21km) to the busy town of Cupar **6**.

A Royal Burgh, Cupar has a charter dating back to 1363, and an unusual claim to fame in the annals of Scottish theatre. It was here, in 1535, that poet David Lyndsay's morality play, *Ane Pleasant Satire of the Three Estates*, received its first performance. As a lively attack on church corruption of the day, it was welcomed by reformers, and versions of the drama are still staged today. To the south, off the A916, lies Scotstarvit Tower, a ruined tower house dating back to 1579 and part of the estate of Hill of Tarvit (▷ 95).

Leave by the A91 and follow it back into St. Andrews.

UNIVERSITY TRADITIONS AT ST. ANDREWS

An easy town trail reveals some unusual customs.

OUT AND ABOUT

THE WALK

Distance: 4.5 miles (7.2km)

Allow: 2 hours

Start/end: Martyrs Monument, The Scores, St. Andrews

OS Explorer 371 St. Andrews & East Fife Grid reference No 506170

How to get there: St. Andrews is on the A911 14 miles (22.4km) south of Dundee; map 318 K10

The historic town of St. Andrews (▷ 100) is famous as the home of golf and of an ancient university. The university was established in 1410 and is the oldest in Scotland, and third oldest in Britain—after Oxford and Cambridge. The town's relatively isolated location on the Fife coast may be one of the reasons why Prince William chose to study here.

The university is proud of its traditions and you may spot students around the town in their distinctive scarlet gowns. First-year students wear them over both shoulders, gradually casting them off each year, until in their fourth and final year the gowns hang down, almost dragging behind them.

Elizabeth Garrett, the first woman in Britain to qualify as a doctor, was allowed to matriculate at St. Andrews in 1862 but was then rejected after the Senate declared her enrolment illegal. Following this the university made efforts to encourage the education of women, who were finally allowed full membership of the university in 1892.

With the Martyrs Monument on The Scores in front of you ❶, walk left past the bandstand. At the road turn right, walk to the British Golf Museum, then turn left. Pass the clubhouse of the Royal and Ancient Golf Club on your left and the Aquarium, right, then bear right at the burn (stream) to reach the beach ❷.

Walk along the West Sands as far as you choose, then either retrace your steps along the beach or take one of the paths through the dunes to join the tarmac road. Walk back to the Golf Museum, then turn right and walk to the main road ❸.

Turn left along the road and walk to St. Salvator's College.

In medieval times students could enter the university at the age of 13, and a system of seniority arose among the student body. New students were initiated into the fraternity on Raisin Monday, when they were expected to produce a pound of raisins.

The tradition persists today, when they are taken under the wings of older students who become their 'academic parents'. On Raisin Sunday, in November, academic 'fathers' take their charges out to get drunk. The next day, Raisin Monday, the 'mothers' put them in fancy dress before they congregate in St. Salvator's quad for a flour and egg fight.

Peek through the archway at the quadrangle and look at the initials PH in the cobbles outside. They commemorate Patrick Hamilton, who was martyred here in 1528—it is said that students who tread on the site will fail their exams.

Cross over and walk to the end of College Street ❹. Turn right and walk along Market Street. At the corner turn left along Bell Street, then left again on South Street. Just after you pass Church Street, cross over into the quadrangle of St. Mary's College. Join the path on the right and walk up to reach Queen's Terrace ❺.

Turn right to reach the red-brick house, then left down steeply sloping Dempster Terrace. At the end cross the burn, turn left and walk to the main road. Cross over and walk along Glebe Road. At the park, take the path that bears left, walk past the play area and up to Woodburn Terrace ❻.

Turn left to join St. Mary Street, turn left again, then go right along Woodburn Place. Bear left beside the beach.

You'll get good views of the Long Pier, where students traditionally walked on Sunday mornings after church, until the pier was closed for repair. Another tradition is a mass dawn swim in the icy sea on May morning (1 May).

Golfers at the 18th hole on the famous Old Course

The gaunt ruins of the castle, which was destroyed in the 16th century

Stonework from the once fine cathedral was reused in other town buildings over centuries

St Andrews Bay

The Links

West Sands

Cupar

British Golf Museum

Martyrs Monument

Royal and Ancient Golf Club

THE SCORES

& Castle
St Salvator's College

Cathedral

NORTH ST

Long Pier

MKT ST

University

St Andrews

St Mary's College

SOUTH ST

ABBEY WALK

East Sands

B939

GARDENS

HEPBURN

Kinness Burn

GLEBE ROAD

LAMOND DRIVE

Crail

Leven

Cross the footbridge and join the road ⑦. Bear right for a few paces, then ascend the steps on the left.

The steps bring you up to the remains of a church and on to the ruined cathedral (free access). A gate in the wall on the left gives access to the site.

Pass the ancient castle on the right ⑧ (Apr–end Sep daily 9.30–6.30; rest of year daily 9.30–4.30).

A former royal palace and fortress, the castle was at the forefront of the Reformation— Protestant leader John Knox preached here.

Pass the castle visitor centre, then continue walking along

The Scores to return to the start of the route.

WHERE TO EAT

There are plenty of pubs in St. Andrews catering for all those eternally thirsty students, as well as a choice of cafés. Brambles, on College Street, is a very popular restaurant which serves soups, snacks and great home-made cakes, as well as more filling main courses.

Fisher and Donaldson, on Church Street, is a bakery famous for its fudge dough-nuts (they're very sweet, so hang on to your fillings).

A glimpse through the gateway of St. Salvator's College

IN THE FOOTSTEPS OF ALEXANDER 'GREEK' THOMSON

Discover a Victorian city and the architect who shaped it.

Distance: 6.5 miles (10.4km)

Allow: 3 hours 30 minutes

Start/end: Central Station, Glasgow
OS Explorer 342 Glasgow
Grid reference NS 587653

How to get there: Central Station;
map 317 G11

Architect Alexander Thomson, with his innovative use and interpretation of Classical Greek designs, helped shape 19th-century Glasgow. Born in 1817, he was apprenticed to an architect and studied the plans, drawings and engravings of Classical architecture. Their influence on his own designs earned him the nickname 'Greek' Thomson, although he never travelled abroad.

Thomson's buildings ranged from churches to villas, warehouses, tenements and even a set of steps. Much of his work was destroyed during World War II and more disappeared in the modernization of Glasgow during the 1960s and 1970s. However, the 24 buildings that have survived provide a fine cross-section of his work.

Thomson's own home was at No. 1 Moray Place,

Strathbungo, a terrace that was built to his design in 1858. Like most of the houses he designed, it is privately owned.

One exception is Holmwood house (▷ 110–111) in Cathcart, 4.5 miles (7.2km) from the city centre, now owned by the National Trust for Scotland. It is probably Thomson's finest work and is undergoing complete restoration.

Although he gained prominence during his lifetime and was a major influence on later architects such as Charles Rennie Mackintosh and Frank Lloyd Wright, Thomson is little known today.

Exit Central Station ❶ and turn right. At the intersection with Union Street turn right.

The structure on the opposite corner is the Ca' d'Oro building, a late 19th-century Italianate warehouse by John Honeyman, based on the Golden House in Venice. A little way down Union Street from here and on the same side as the Ca' d'Oro is Thomson's Egyptian Halls

(1871–73), an enormous stone-fronted building that started life as an early form of shopping centre, and is now in need of renovation.

Cross over then head down Union Street, turning left into Argyll Street at the next intersection ❷. Cross Argyll Street, then walk along to the intersection with Dunlop Street.

Here you will find the Buck's Head building, named after an inn that previously stood on this spot.

Cross Argyll Street again, retrace your steps, turning right into Buchanan Street. Turn left into Mitchell Lane, pass the Lighthouse (▷ 112), then turn right ❸.

Walk up Mitchell Street, continue along West Nile Street then turn left into St. Vincent Street. Continue on this for just under 0.5 mile (800m), going uphill to the junction with Pitt Street.

You are now standing in front of Thomson's St. Vincent Street church (1857–59), one of his greatest achievements. It is a remarkable building, adorned with Grecian columns and an

Holmwood showed Thomson at the pinnacle of his architectural career, and is worth a visit in its own right

OUT AND ABOUT

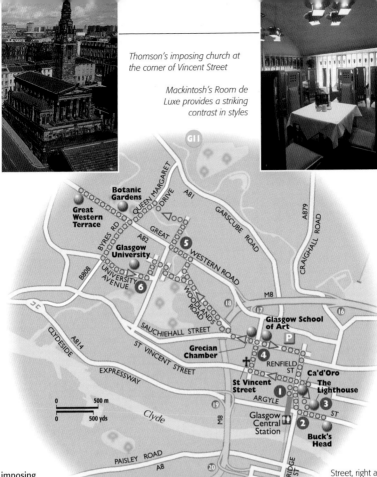

Thomson's imposing church at the corner of Vincent Street

Mackintosh's Room de Luxe provides a striking contrast in styles

imposing tower, built on the side of Blythswood Hill.

Cross St. Vincent Street here, then head up Pitt Street to Sauchiehall Street **4**.

On the opposite corner is Thomson's Grecian Chamber (1865) and to the right along Scott Street is Rennie Mackintosh's Glasgow School of Art (▷ 110).

From the front of the Grecian Chamber turn left, head down Sauchiehall Street to Charing Cross, then take the pedestrian bridge over the motorway to Woodlands Road. Go along here until it ends at Park Road, turn right, then left again into Great Western Road.

Turn right into Belmont Street **5**, left at Quad Gardens, then left again at Queen Margaret Drive. Cross the road and head

down past the Botanic Gardens (▷ 105) to turn right, back into Great Western Road. Cross the road and continue to Great Western Terrace.

This is another Thomson masterpiece (1869), and known as the grandest terrace in Glasgow. Note how he placed the tallest buildings in the middle of the row, rather than at the ends.

Trace your steps back from here to the top of Byres Road and turn right then, near the bottom, turn left into University Avenue.

Turn left into Oakfield Avenue **6**, pass Eton Terrace on the corner with Great George Street. Turn right into Great George

Street, right at Otago Street, left into Gibson Street and keep going when it becomes Eldon Street. Finally turn right into Woodlands Road and return to Sauchiehall Street.

Follow this to the intersection with Renfield Street, turn right and head downhill to Central Station.

WHERE TO EAT

On a tour of Glasgow's architecture there can be only one place to dine. The Willow Tearooms in Sauchiehall Street (▷ 114) were designed by Charles Rennie Mackintosh for Kate Cranston who had a string of tea rooms. Entry is through a jeweller's shop. There is always a queue for the 1904 Room de Luxe, where everything—including the chairs and tables—is by Mackintosh. It's worth the wait, and the food is good and reasonably priced.

CASTLES, FORTS AND BATTLEFIELDS

Legend and history come to life in this scenic Highland tour to the east of Inverness.

THE DRIVE

Distance: 106 miles (171km)

Allow: 1–2 days

Start/end: Inverness, map 322 G6

Tourist information offices:
Castle Wynd, Inverness IV2 3BJ,
tel 01463 234353
High Street, Grantown-on-Spey PH26
3EH, tel 01479 872773; seasonal

Leave Inverness ❶ (▷ 129) on the A96, travelling through the flatlands south of the Moray Firth. Turn left at the B9039 to reach the fishing village of Ardersier, then take the B9006 to Fort George, a distance of 12 miles (19km).

Fort George was built between 1748 and 1769 on a narrow spit of land which sticks out into the Moray Firth, facing Chanonry Point on the Black Isle (▷ 121). With extensive landward defences, the site originally covered 29.6ha (12 acres), and was designed to accommodate a garrison of over 2,000 men. The fort, named after George II, was set here to protect Inverness from seaward attack, and as part of the backlash to subdue the Highlands following Culloden (▷ 125). It remains unaltered, a superb example of an artillery fort (HS, Apr–end Sep daily 9.30–6.30; rest of year daily 9.30–4.30).

Return to Ardersier, then follow the B9006 and the B9090 to Cawdor Castle ❷.

This magnificent 14th-century castle is associated with Shakespeare's play *Macbeth* (▷ 121). Kilravock Castle (private) stands to the west, the 15th-century family seat of the Roses and overshadowed by its famous neighbour. It can number both Bonnie Prince Charlie and his nemesis, the Duke of Cumberland, among its visitors in the hours before Culloden (1746).

18th-century Fort George

Continue on the B9090 and follow it to Nairn.

Comic actor Charlie Chaplin (1889–1977) liked to take his holidays at this prosperous resort town, with its fine beach, good golf course and activities for all the family. Villas and hotels spread back from the old Fishertown by the shore, where the former fishermen's houses are packed tightly together. The harbour dates from 1820, and was designed by engineer Thomas Telford.

Leave by the A96, passing Auldearn, site of a major battle between Covenanters and Royalists in 1645. Continue on this road through the shady plantation of Culbin Forest. Turn left to visit Brodie Castle.

A Z-plan tower house dating back to 1567, Brodie Castle is set in attractive parkland that is famous for its spring show of daffodils (NTS, Apr, Jul, Aug daily 12–4; May, Jun, Sep Sun–Thu daily 12–4). Remodelled into a comfortable home in the 19th century, it remained in the private hands of the Brodie family until 1980, when it passed to the National Trust for Scotland. The family's collection of fine art, books and furniture is outstanding, and includes works from 17th-century Dutch masters to the Scottish Colourists.

Regain the A96, and stay on this road into the floral town of Forres (▷ 126). Continue on the A96, then turn left at the B9011 and follow this to Findhorn ❸.

Ever-vulnerable from the sea and shifting sand dunes, this is the third village on the site to be called Findhorn—the first was buried in 1694, the second washed away in 1701. It was once a major port, but the harbour is now given over to pleasure craft. In 1962 the Findhorn Community was founded here by Peter and Eileen Caddy and Dorothy Maclean to find an alternative, more spiritual and sustainable way of living. The community is still going strong, with some 400 residents, an extensive holistic educational programme and an eco-village (tours Mar–end May, Sep, Oct Mon, Wed, Fri, 2pm; also Jun–end Aug Sat, Sun).

Return along the B9011 and A96 to Forres. Head south on the A940 and join the A939 for Grantown-on-Spey, a distance of 27 miles (43km).

Grantown-on-Spey ❹ lies at the edge of the Speyside whisky country (▷ 137), and makes a useful touring centre. The village was planned in the late 18th century by Sir James Grant, and the arrival of the railway in 1863 heralded its popularity as a health resort. The railway was lost in the

OUT AND ABOUT

The central tower of Cawdor Castle dates back to the 14th century

Above, a picnic spot beside the old Spey Bridge at Grantown, which was built in 1754. It is a much more solid affair than the single span at Dulnain, below, which was constructed less than 40 years earlier

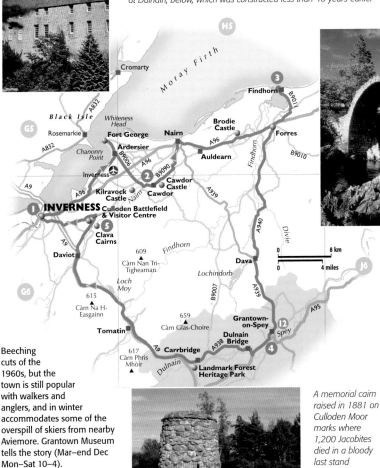

OUT AND ABOUT

A memorial cairn raised in 1881 on Culloden Moor marks where 1,200 Jacobites died in a bloody last stand

Beeching cuts of the 1960s, but the town is still popular with walkers and anglers, and in winter accommodates some of the overspill of skiers from nearby Aviemore. Grantown Museum tells the story (Mar–end Dec Mon–Sat 10–4).

Leave on the A95 towards Aviemore, and at Dulnain Bridge turn on to the A938 to Carrbridge, noted for its picturesque old bridge of 1717, and the Landmark Forest Heritage Park (▷ 134). Continue on the A938 and join the A9, heading towards Inverness. Just after Daviot, turn right on the B851. Turn left at the B9006 and follow it to the major battle site of Culloden Moor **5** (▷ 125).

Just east of Culloden, a minor road (B9091) passes Clava Cairns, three of the most important chambered cairns in the country, dating from the Bronze Age (free access). The two outer ones are passage graves, topped with a massive flat slab. The perimeters of all three are marked by a ring of standing stones, often carved with 'cup' marks.

Continue along the B9006 to the A9. Join the A9 and return to Inverness.

CASTLES, FORTS AND BATTLEFIELDS 221

SIR JAMES GRANT'S TOWN

Explore an ancient pine wood on the banks of the Spey, and an 18th-century planned town.

THE WALK

Distance: 7 miles (11km)	
Allow: 3 hours	
Start/end: Grantown-on-Spey Museum	
OS Explorer 419 Grantown-on-Spey	
Grid reference NJ 035280	
How to get there: Grantown-on-Spey is	
on the A939; map 322 H6	

Around the year 1750, young James Grant returned to Speyside (▷ 137) from his Grand Tour of Europe. He'd seen Edinburgh New Town, just then being built, and thought Speyside could do with something similar. Somehow he persuaded his father, Sir Ludovic Grant, and a new town was set out above the new military bridge over the Spey.

Merchants, tradesmen and artisans were invited to build their own houses, to a set pattern, roofed with slate and walled with pale, speckled granite. The town was to be supported by a linen factory.

In 1766 the market cross was moved in procession from old town to new. To persuade the townsfolk away from whisky, a brewery was set up. The Grants put up a handsome orphanage, and established a modern school.

However, James Grant was obliged to subsidize the building of most of the houses, and then had to pay for the linen factory. The Industrial Revolution in England was just starting to produce cheap cloth and in 1774 the linen factory failed. By 1804 the town was threatened with economic collapse, and Grant had to sell his London house to buy meal for the villagers.

Grantown continued as a market town, serving the barley lands of the Spey valley. With the arrival of the railway, middle-class visitors came in the wake of a visit by Queen Victoria. The inhabitants of Grantown moved into cottages set in their own gardens, while the middle-class families of doctors and lawyers moved in for the summer. And Sir James Grant's handsome granite town has been attracting tourists ever since.

Go down past the museum ❶ (▷ 137). Turn left into South Street, then right into Golf Course Road. A tarred path crosses the golf course to a small gate into Anagach Wood ❷.

The wide path ahead has a blue/red waymarker. At a junction, the blue trail departs to the right; turn left, following a Spey Way marker and red-top poles. Keep following the red markers, turning left at the first intersection and bearing left at the next. When the track joins a new fence and a bend in a stream is on the left, keep ahead, following a Spey Way marker.

The track emerges into open fields ❸. After crossing a small bridge, turn right through a chained gap stile. A path with pines on its left leads to a track near the River Spey. (Bridge of Cromdale is just ahead here.)

Turn sharp right on this track ❹, alongside the river. At a fishers' hut it re-enters forest. About 0.75 mile (1.2km) later it diminishes to a green path and slants up past the cottage of Craigroy to join its entrance track.

At Easter Anagach ❺, a grass track on the right has red waymarkers and runs into a birchwood. With a barrier ahead, follow marker poles to the left, on to a broad path beside a falling fence.

At the next intersection, turn right, following the red poles, over a slight rise. Descending, turn left just before a blue-top post, on to a smaller path with blue and red posts. This runs along the top of a ridge, to reach a bench above a lane ❻.

To the left down the lane is the handsome stone bridge built by Major Caulfield in the mid-18th century as part of the military road system constructed in the aftermath of the Jacobite uprising (▷ 28–29).

The path bends right, alongside the road, to meet a wide track (the former military road). Turn right, to a path on the right with green-top posts. At a small pool, the main path bends left for 137m (150 yards), with blue and green posts; take the path ahead, with green posts. At a five-way intersection bear left to find the next green post. At the edge of the golf course turn left to a parking area and information board ❼.

OUT AND ABOUT

The Spey is one of the great salmon rivers of Scotland

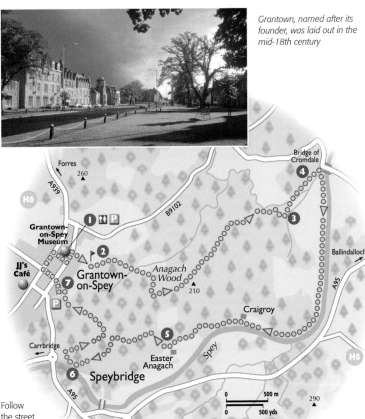

Grantown, named after its founder, was laid out in the mid-18th century

Follow the street uphill, past the end of the golf course, to the High Street. Turn right to the Square, and the Grant Arms Hotel.

In September 1860, when Queen Victoria stopped off at the Grant Arms, her ghillies got rather drunk. Meanwhile, her secretary General Grey went shopping and bought himself a watch, and the Queen enjoyed some excellent porridge.

Just past the Grant Arms, a sign points right, to return to the museum.

The Old Spey Bridge, built for military use, was a catalyst for the construction of the new town

OUT AND ABOUT

THE WESTERN HIGHLANDS

'The Road to the Isles', an old cattle drovers' road, leads into the western Highlands at the start of one of the most scenic routes in Scotland.

THE DRIVE

Distance: 205 miles (330km)
Allow: 2–3 days
Start/end: Fort William, map 321 E8
Tourist information offices:
Cameron Centre, Cameron Square, Fort William PH33 6AJ, tel 01397 703781
Main Street, Mallaig PH41 4QS, tel 01687 462170; seasonal

Leave Fort William ❶ (▷ 126) on the A82 towards Inverness, then turn left at the A830, signposted to Mallaig. Turn right at the B8004 to Banavie, to admire the flight of locks on the Caledonian Canal called Neptune's Staircase (▷ 226–227). Return to the A830. Turn right and follow the road along Loch Eil to Glenfinnan ❷.

Glenfinnan, at the head of Loch Shiel, is famous for its links with the ill-fated Jacobite rebellion of 1745 (▷ 28–29). Take the short path behind the National Trust for Scotland's visitor centre to view the 21-arch Glenfinnan viaduct, by Sir Robert 'Concrete Bob' MacAlpine (1847–1934), which carries the scenic West Highland Railway to Mallaig. The railway runs parallel with the road for much of the way—look out for steam locomotives in summer.

Follow the A830, passing the shores of Loch nan Uamh.

A cairn marks the spot from where, after defeat at Culloden

in 1746 (▷ 125) and months in hiding in the Western Isles, Bonnie Prince Charlie finally fled to exile in France. He was helped during this time by many ordinary people, and despite a well-publicized reward of £30,000, nobody betrayed him.

Continue on the A830, passing through woodland of beech, oak and birch to the village of Arisaig.

During World War II, agents of the Special Operations Executive (SOE) trained in this area, honing their fieldcraft skills before being dropped behind enemy lines in Europe. Their base was nearby Arisaig House, a manor house in a magnificent setting (private).

Continue on the A830 up the coast to Morar, with views out to the islands of Eigg and Skye.

Morar is famous for its silvery silica sands, and for its very own monster, Morag, who is believed to live in the murky depths of Loch Morar, 310m (1,017ft) down.

Continue on the A830 to Mallaig ❸.

This busy fishing harbour faces the island of Skye across the Sound of Sleat, and is the mainland terminal for ferries to the Inner Hebrides, including the group of Rum, Eigg, Muck

and Canna, known as the Small Isles (▷ 137). Mallaig grew to prominence after the arrival of the railway in 1901, which provided swift access south for fishing catches. That was during the herring boom— now prawns are a mainstay. See them in Marine World, an aquarium on the harbour front (all year daily 9–5; may close Jan, Feb; extended hours in summer). At the end of the road, Mallaigvaig looks across to the hills of Knoydart, one of the remotest areas of Scotland.

Return along the A830 to Lochailort. Turn right at the A861 and follow it to Kinlochmoidart and Acharacle ❹.

The village lies at the south-west tip of Loch Shiel. A detour on to the B8044 leads to the dramatic ruin of Castle Tioram, on Loch Moidart (free access, restricted for safety reasons). It lies on a rocky islet at the end of a sandy spit, and dates from the early 13th century, although the central keep is later. It was the seat of the Macdonalds of Clanranald, and deliberately burned down when Allan, the 14th Chief, set off in 1715 to join the Jacobite uprising, to prevent its use by Campbell enemies.

Continue on the A861 to Salen, then turn right at the B8007, to explore the Ardnamurchan Peninsula (▷ 119). Continue on the B8007, passing through the scattered community of Kilchoan, to Ardnamurchan Point ❺.

The most westerly point on the British mainland is marked with a lighthouse, and has superb views out to the islands of the Inner Hebrides.

Return to Salen along the B8007, then turn right at the A861 to Strontian ❻.

This Highland village gives its name to the element

A stone cairn marks the spot on the shore of Loch nan Uamh where Bonnie Prince Charlie last set foot in Scotland

OUT AND ABOUT

Watching the sunset over Rum and Eigg, from the cliffs by Mallaig

Mallaig's fishing has survived by changing tack, and prawns are now a staple

The Jacobite Express steam train pulls out of Glenfinnan

The shell of Castle Tioram watches over Loch Moidart

strontium, extracted from the mineral strontianite, discovered here in 1764. Strontium has a deep crimson flame when burned, and is used in the manufacture of fireworks. The area was extensively mined between 1722 and 1904 for lead, zinc and silver; it now supplies barytes for the lubrication of North Sea drilling rigs. There are pleasant walks through the nearby Ariundle woods.

Continue on the A861, then turn right on to the A884. Follow this to Lochaline **7**.

Lochaline stands on the Sound of Mull, with a ferry service to Fishnish, and views down to the ruins of Ardtornish Castle, and Duart Castle on Mull. Silica sand is extracted here, for use in the production of high-grade optical glass.

Return on the A884 to the junction (right) with the B8043. Follow this unclassified road to meet the A861. Turn right and follow this up Loch Linnhe to Ardgour. Take the Corran ferry across the loch. At the other side turn left on to the A82 and return to Fort William.

DISCOVERING THE CALEDONIAN CANAL

A walk alongside—and underneath—Thomas Telford's masterpiece of civil engineering.

THE WALK	
Distance: 4.5 miles (7.2km)	
Allow: 1 hour 45 minutes	
Start/end: Kilmallie Hall, Corpach	
OS Explorer 392 Ben Nevis, Fort William Grid reference NN 097768	
How to get there: Corpach is on the A830, 3 miles (4.8km) northwest of Fort William; map 321 E8	

The first survey for a coast-to-coast canal across Scotland, linking the lochs of the Great Glen, was made by James Watt, inventor of the steam engine, in 1767. But it was the economic and military necessities of the Napoleonic War that finally sent the men with the wheelbarrows up to Fort William in 1803.

For this great enterprise, only one name was seriously considered: Thomas Telford (1757–1834). Apprenticed to a stonemason, Telford worked on a new bridge for his home town of Langholm, while educating himself in the poetry of Burns and Milton, and chemistry out of books lent by the local gentry. As well as the old-style stonework, Telford became a master of two entirely new techniques—the cast iron arch and the first suspension bridges. While

working on the Caledonian Canal, he was also building 600 miles (nearly 1,000km) of new roads and enlarging most of Scotland's harbours.

The canal was a tremendous feat of civil engineering. Some 200 million wheelbarrow loads of earth were shifted over the next 19 years. Four aqueducts let streams and rivers pass below the waterway, and there was a dam on Loch Lochy and diversion of the rivers Oich and Lochy. Loch Oich needed to be deepened, and for this task a steam dredger had to be not just built, but invented and designed.

After falling into a state of neglect in the 20th century, the canal was on the verge of closure when, in 1996, the government promised £20 million for a complete refurbishment.

From the hall **1**, go down past Corpach Station to the canal and cross the sea lock that separates salt water from fresh water.

Each of the 29 locks on the Caledonian Canal was designed to accommodate the width and length of a 40-gun frigate of Lord Nelson's navy.

Follow the canal (on your left) up past another lock, where a path on the right has a blue footpath sign and a Great Glen Way marker. It passes under tall sycamores to the shore. Follow the shoreline path past a soccer pitch and then turn left, across damp grass to a road sign that warns motorists of a nearby playground. A path ahead leads up a wooded bank to the tow path **2**.

Turn right along the tow path, for 0.5 mile (800m). Just before the Banavie swing bridge, a path down to the right has a Great Glen Way marker.

The Great Glen Way is a Long Distance Route that runs parallel to the tow path (▷ 236). This has been resurfaced as a cycleway running from coast to coast.

Follow waymarkers on street signs to a level crossing, then turn left towards the other swing bridge, the one with the road on it.

Just before the bridge **3**, turn right at signs for the Great Glen Way and the Great Glen Cycle Route, and continue along the tow path to Neptune's Staircase **4**.

Eight locks, each big enough to take an 18th-century ship of war, make up the flight of Neptune's Staircase

OUT AND ABOUT

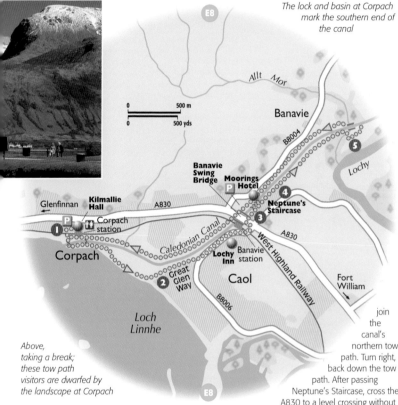

The lock and basin at Corpach mark the southern end of the canal

*Above,
taking a break;
these tow path
visitors are dwarfed by
the landscape at Corpach*

The fanciful name was given to the group of eight locks by Thomas Telford himself. It takes about 90 minutes for boats to work through the system. As each lock fills, slow roiling currents come up from underneath, and as each empties, water forced under pressure into the banks emerges from the masonry in little fountains. The 18m (60ft) of ascent alongside the locks is the serious uphill part of this walk.

A gate marks the top of the locks. About 183m (200 yards) later, a grey gate on the right leads to a dump for dead cars; ignore this one. Over the next 91m (100 yards) the canal crosses a little wooded valley, with a black fence on the right. Now comes a second grey gate. Go through, to a track turning back sharp right and descending to ford a small stream **5**.

On the right, the stream passes right under the canal in an arched tunnel, and alongside is a second tunnel which provides a walkers' way to the other side. Water from the canal drips into the tunnel, which has a fairly spooky atmosphere. At the tunnel's end, a track runs up to join the canal's northern tow path. Turn right, back down the tow path. After passing Neptune's Staircase, cross the A830 to a level crossing without warning lights. Continue along the right-hand tow path. After a mile (1.6km) the tow path track leads back to the Corpach double lock.

WHERE TO EAT

The Moorings Hotel at Banavie offers restaurant and bar meals to canal users and visitors. On the other side of both the A830 and canal, the unassuming Lochy family pub has picnic tables and promises 'massive portions'.

At the walk start, a Spar shop on the main road sells hot pies, and the Kilmallie Hall has a community garden with picnic tables to eat them at.

A CIRCUIT OF CASTLE COUNTRY

This circuit from the pleasant little town of Banchory takes in some of the best castles in northeast Scotland.

THE DRIVE

Distance: 143 miles (230km)	
Allow: 2 days	
Start/end: Banchory, map 323 K7	
Tourist information offices:	

Bridge Street, Banchory AB31 5SX,
tel 01330 822000; seasonal
St. Nicholas House, Broad Street,
Aberdeen AB9 1DE, tel 01224 632727

Before leaving Banchory, call in at the local history museum on Bridge Street (Apr, Oct Sat 11–1, 2–4.30; May, Jun, Sep Mon–Sat 11–1, 2–4.30). It includes displays about local hero James Scott Skinner (1843–1927), known as the Strathspey King for his virtuoso fiddle playing and prolific composition of tunes, many of which are still played.

Leave Banchory ❶ on the A93, and after 3 miles (5km) turn left to visit Crathes Castle (▷ 124). Continue on the A93 and turn left at an unclassified road to reach Drum Castle ❷.

The big, grey stone keep of Drum Castle is one of the oldest tower houses in Scotland, dating to the 13th century. Beside it is a fine Jacobean house of 1619, and the whole was embellished in the 19th century. The wooded grounds include an ancient oak forest (NTS, Apr–end May, Sep daily 12.30–5.30; Jun–end Aug daily 10–5.30).

Return to Crathes and turn left on the A957. Soon turn right on to a minor road and follow this along the southern bank of the River Dee to Bridge of Feugh. Turn left on to the B974 and follow this south to Fettercairn ❸, passing over the high pass of Cairn o'Mount (450m/1,475ft).

The heart of this pleasant red sandstone town is dominated by an elaborate Gothic arch, erected in honour of a visit by

The historic mansion of Fasque is surrounded by a deer park

Queen Victoria in 1861. To the north lies the castellated mansion of Fasque, adopted home of 19th-century prime minister William Gladstone (open to group visits only).

Leave Fettercairn, heading east, on the B966. Turn left on to the A90 and follow this to Stonehaven. On the outskirts, turn right and left on to a minor road that leads into the town.

Modern Stonehaven spreads back from the harbour, where the Carron and Cowie waters flow into the sea. The Tolbooth on the wharf, with its Dutch-style crow-stepped roof, dates from the 17th century. This was a difficult period of history for the town, when it endured being burned by Montrose's army, then occupied for eight long, weary months by Cromwellian troops (who were besieging Dunnottar Castle, to the south).

Rejoin the A90 and continue for 15 miles (24km) to Aberdeen ❹ (▷ 119).

Leave Aberdeen on the A944. Turn right at the B977, then left on to an unclassified road to Castle Fraser (▷ 121). On leaving the castle grounds, turn right and follow the minor road to Craigearn. Turn left, and left again on to the B993, and continue to Monymusk. Turn right at a minor road to explore the village.

Monymusk is a quiet village, neatly laid out around a grassy centre. It has a notable Norman church dating back to 1140, making it contemporary with an Augustinian priory. The priory has long since disappeared, its stonework absorbed into the wings of Monymusk House (private). The famous Monymusk Reliquary, believed to contain the bones of St. Columba, was held here for many years—it's now in the Museum of Scotland in Edinburgh (▷ 78–81).

Return to the B993 and turn right by the former toll house. At the A944, turn right and follow this to Alford ❺.

This small town (pronounced 'Afford') has two transport museums. The eclectic Grampian Transport Museum (Apr–end Sep daily 10–5; Oct daily 10–4) has vintage cars, lorries and motorcycles, as well as trams and the extraordinary Craigivar Express, a steam-powered tricycle built locally in 1895. Modern eco-friendly vehicles gather here each August for trials and competitions. Steam trains operate on the narrow-gauge Alford Valley Railway between Alford station and Haughton Country Park (Jun–end Aug daily 1.15–4.15; Apr, May, Sep Sat–Sun 1.15–4.15).

Continue on the A944, then turn left on the A97 to Kildrummy.

OUT AND ABOUT

The Falls of Feugh are a beauty spot on the River Dee

The Gothic arch at Fettercairn celebrates the visit of Queen Victoria

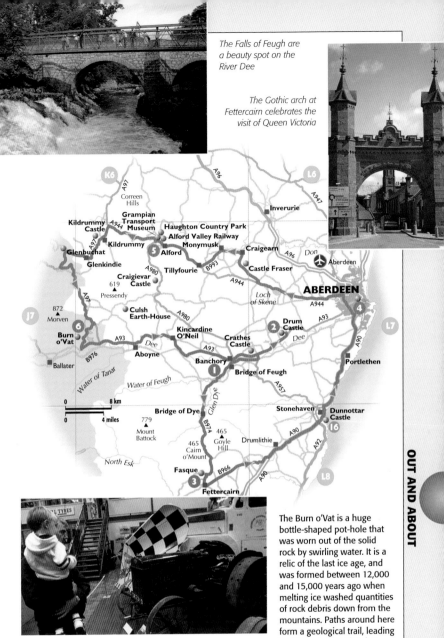

Admiring an early Austin tractor, Grampian Transport Museum

The Burn o'Vat is a huge bottle-shaped pot-hole that was worn out of the solid rock by swirling water. It is a relic of the last ice age, and was formed between 12,000 and 15,000 years ago when melting ice washed quantities of rock debris down from the mountains. Paths around here form a geological trail, leading to different examples that show how the landscape was formed.

Kildrummy was started in around 1230 for the Earl of Mar, and grew to be one of the biggest castles in Scotland. With sturdy circular towers at the gate and placed at the four corners of linking curtain walls, its structure is reminiscent of Harlech Castle in Wales. The chapel, part of the original building phase, sticks awkwardly through the walls.

Besieged by the English in 1306, Kildrummy changed hands several times before its final destruction in 1715 (HS, Apr–end Sep daily 9.30–6.30).

Continue on the A97, passing 16th-century Glenbuchat Castle on the right (private), and after 18 miles (29km) turn right at the B9119 to reach the oddly named Burn o'Vat **6**.

The nearby Culsh Earth-House is a well-preserved chamber and underground passage, roofed by stone slabs and believed to be 2,000 years old (free access).

Continue on the B9119 and turn left at the A93. Follow this via Kincardine O'Neil to return to Banchory.

THE HIDDEN TREASURE OF STONEHAVEN

A bracing walk along the cliffs to ruined Dunnottar Castle.

THE WALK

Distance: 3.5 miles (5.7km)

Allow: 1 hour 30 minutes

Start/end: Market Square, Stonehaven
OS Explorer 273 Stonehaven
Grid reference NO 874858

How to get there: Stonehaven is on the
A90 south of Aberdeen; map 318 L8

Stonehaven's most attractive quarter is around the old harbour

Dunnottar Castle is a deliciously picturesque, glowering ruin perched on the edge of the cliffs and sprayed by the chilly northern seas. It was the setting for one of the most fascinating and little known episodes in Scotland's history, for Dunnottar Castle was the hiding place of the priceless Scottish regalia, or crown jewels.

Scotland's crown jewels are among the oldest in Europe. Also known as the Honours of Scotland, they comprise a crown, a sword of state and a silver sceptre. Together they are powerful symbols of Scotland's independence, and today the Honours are on display in the safety of Edinburgh Castle (▷ 71–73), along with the famous Stone of Destiny.

English Parliamentarian Oliver Cromwell invaded Scotland in 1650 and determined to destroy them, as he had done with the English crown jewels. His plan was foiled when they were spirited away from Edinburgh and taken to George Ogilvie,

the King's Earl Marischal, at Dunnottar Castle for safe keeping.

Cromwell's men besieged the castle for nearly a year, but when it finally fell the jewels disappeared. They had been smuggled out by the wife of James Granger, the minister of nearby Kinneff, and her maid.

The jewels remained secreted in the church at Kinneff, farther down the coast, and though Cromwell's men imprisoned the Grangers and tortured Ogilvie's wife, nobody gave the secret away. (Visit Kinneff Old Church today and you can see a memorial to these brave souls.)

The crown jewels were returned to Edinburgh after the Restoration of the Monarchy in 1660. Following the Act of Union with England in 1707, they were walled up in a sealed room in a tower in Edinburgh Castle. People eventually forgot where they were, and many believed they had been stolen by the English. Sir Walter Scott rediscovered them, locked inside a dusty chest.

From the Market Square in Stonehaven ❶, walk back on to Allardyce Street, turn right and cross the road. Turn left up Market Lane and, when you come to the beach, turn right to cross over the footbridge. Turn

right at the signs to Dunnottar Castle to reach the harbour. Cross here to continue down Shorehead, on the east side of the harbour. Pass the Marine Hotel, then turn right into Wallis Wynd ❷.

Turn left into Castle Street. Emerge at the main road, then maintain your direction, walking along the road until it bends. Continue ahead, following the enclosed tarmac track, between arable fields and past a war memorial on the right-hand side. Cross the stile at the end of the track ❸.

Make your way across the middle of the field, cross a footbridge and two more stiles. Pass a track going down to Castle Haven and continue following the main path around the cliff edge. Cross another footbridge and bear uphill. Soon you reach steps on your left that run down to Dunnottar Castle ❹ (Easter–end Oct daily 9–6; Nov–Easter Fri–Mon 9–dusk).

The ruined castle stands on a flat-topped rock stack, 50m (160ft) above the sea, dominated by the remains of a 14th-century tower house. Further buildings reflect 17th-century domestic life, including stables and a ballroom. Scenes from Mel Gibson's 1990 movie of *Hamlet* were filmed here.

Bear right here, past a waterfall, through a kissing gate and up to a house. Pass the house to reach the road into Stonehaven by the Mains of Dunnottar, turn right, then take the first turning on the left, walking in the direction of the radio masts. Follow this wide, metalled track past the masts and East Newtonleys on the left-hand side, to the A957 ❺.

Turn right and walk downhill, then take the first turning on the left. Follow this track to a sign on the right, 'Carron Gate'.

OUT AND ABOUT

Dunnottar Castle made a dramatic film location in 1990

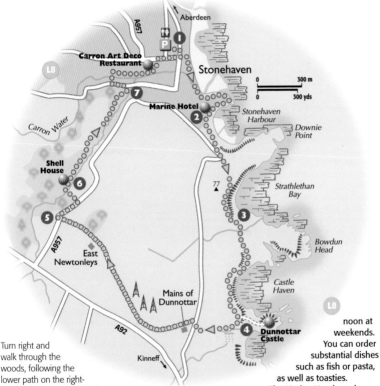

OUT AND ABOUT

Turn right and walk through the woods, following the lower path on the right-hand side that runs by the burn (stream). Soon reach the little Shell House on the left **6**.

Pass this on the left, continue along the lower track, then climb uphill to join a wider track. Bear right, to maintain direction and reach the edge of the woods. Walk through the housing estate to join Low Wood Road and the river **7**.

Turn left, then right to cross the footbridge with the green railings. Turn right and walk by the water. Pass the stylish Carron Restaurant on the left-hand side, and then come to a cream-coloured iron bridge. Bear left here, then turn first right to return to the Market Square.

WHERE TO EAT

The Ship Inn by the harbour in Stonehaven is a popular spot and serves food all day from noon at weekends. You can order substantial dishes such as fish or pasta, as well as toasties.

The Marine Hotel nearby serves lunches from 12 to 2pm, and supper from 5 to 9.15pm, as well as coffee. It's worth noting that the hotel has won awards for the quality of its ale.

You can also try the fantastically art deco Carron Restaurant, which has seats outside and serves light meals including seafood, baguettes, baked potatoes and toasted sandwiches.

THE HIDDEN TREASURE OF STONEHAVEN **231**

PRISON AND PINNACLE

Exploring the weird lava landscape of Skye's northern peninsula.

THE WALK

Distance: 5.25 miles (8.4km)

Allow: 3 hours

Start/end: Pull-off at the top of the pass on the Staffin-Uig road, Isle of Skye OS Explorer 408 Skye Grid reference NG 440679

How to get there: On minor road 2 miles (3.2km) west of Brogaig; map 324 C5

The rocks of Scotland vary from ancient—about 400 million years—to a great deal older than that, but along the western edge is something quite different. The great eye of the Atlantic Ocean opened at a time that, geologically speaking, is this morning just before breakfast.

A mere 60 million years ago, the mid-Atlantic ridge lay just off the Scottish coast. And all along that ridge, new seabed emerged in exotic and interesting volcanic rocks that now form the Arran granite, the basalt of Mull and Skye, and the Skye gabbro. Basalt lava is a slippery liquid, like milk rather than treacle; it spreads in wide, shallow layers across the country. After erosion, you get a flat-topped landscape, with long low cliffs at the edges and wide grassy plateaux.

North of Portree, the lava flowed out over older, softer rocks of Jurassic (dinosaur) age. All along the Trotternish peninsula, the sea has been steadily removing those softer rocks, and the basalt above has been breaking off in hill-sized chunks and slipping downhill and eastwards. The chunks lean over, split apart and erode: The result is some extraordinary scenery, of which the queerest is the Quiraing.

Some of its rock forms, with intriguing names such as the Prison, the Needle and the Fingalian Slab, have been a tourist must-see since Victorian times. As a result, a wide, well-made path leads below these pinnacles, then back along the top. Spread your picnic cloth on the Table, and then peep out between the rock architecture to the Sound of Raasay and the distant mainland hills of Torridon.

Take the well-built path that starts at a 'bendy road' sign opposite the lay-by (pull-off) **1**.

The jagged tower of grass and rock on the skyline is grimly named the Prison.

The path crosses the steep landslip slope towards the Prison, with an awkward crossing of a small stream gully on bare rock, then passes a small waterfall high above and heads to the right rather than up into a rocky gap. It turns uphill into the wide col to the left of the Prison **2**.

The main path does not drop, but goes forward, slightly uphill, crossing an old fence line at a crag foot. Follow as it crosses the foot of steep ground, then passes above a small peat pool. Ignore a path forking down right; the main path slants up left into a col where an old wall runs across **3**.

The path descends into a landslip valley that runs across rather than down the hillside, then slants up left to a col with a stile **4**. Cross over the stile and turn right for the excursion to Sron Vourlinn.

Follow the crest over a slightly rocky section with a short descent beyond, then join the main path along a grassy meadow with a very sudden edge on the right. After the highest point, continue slightly downhill to reach the north top **5**.

Here at Sron Vourlinn you can see that the land is still slipping, with a crevasse beside the cliff edge where another narrow section is shortly to peel away.

Return to the col with the stile (**4**) and continue uphill.

The drops are now on your left, as you look down towards the pinnacles surrounding the Table, a gently undulating lawn.

After passing broken ground on the right, you come to a fallen wall, part of which appears from below as a cairn. The path continues next to the cliff edge on the left; you can fork off right, directly uphill, to the summit trig point on Meall na Suiramach **6**.

Follow a broad, gentle path slightly downhill to a cairn at the cliff edge.

You now look straight down on to the grassy feature known

While the Cuillin mountains are best left to expert walkers and climbers, Trotternish offers more opportunity for gentler exploration

OUT AND ABOUT

The Old Man of Storr is a landmark in these mountains, and visible from the main road—it's a basalt monolith standing 19.5m (65ft) tall

In spring look out for flowers of the Scottish primrose (Primula scotia)

Sron Vourlinn **5**

492 ▲ Sgurr Mor

4 Fir Bhreugach

244 ▲ Loch Hasco

3

0   500 m
0   500 yds

Loch Fada

6 543 ▲
Meall na Suiramach

The Table

30 ▲ Quiraing

The Needle

Loch Fada

Maoladh Mor

2 The Prison

Dun Mor

Brogaig, Staffin →

Uig ↓

I

P

P

Loch Leum na Luirginn

C5

as the Table, 30m (100ft) below.

Turn right on the wide path. After a mile (1.6km), the path starts to descend alongside the cliff edge.

As the edge turns half right, you should turn fully right. The path is faint, but reappears ahead contouring around the fairly steep grass slope. Once above the parking area it turns straight downhill for a final steep descent.

WHERE TO EAT

The Pieces of Ate café at Brogaig lies at the foot of the

The vast raised plateau of the Table, amid the jagged peaks of the Quiraing

hill road. It serves homemade snacks and soup from a small shack. Magnificently sited below the Quiraing crags, the

Flodigarry Hotel offers evening meals and Sunday lunch at its restaurant, specializing in local lobster and other seafood. Bar meals are available in the public bar and conservatory.

THE GLOUP LOOP

A circular walk around the nature reserve of Mull Head.

THE WALK

Distance: 4 miles (6.4km)

Allow: 2 hours 30 minutes

Start/end: Mull Head parking area
(free), Mainland Orkney
OS Explorer 461 Orkney
Grid reference HY 590079

How to get there: North of the B9050;
map 327 K4

The parish of Deerness is a peninsula joined to Orkney's Mainland only by a very narrow spit, and the land has been affected constantly by people and the climate. Nearby archaeological excavations have turned up an Iron-Age settlement, a Pictish farm, obvious Norse remains and a hog-back gravestone in the kirkyard dating from AD1100.

This walk follows the story of the landscape to explore a remarkable feature formed entirely by the force of the North Sea. The Gloup—from the Old Norse word *gluppa* meaning chasm—is not the only collapsed cave in Orkney, but at 30m (100ft) deep, it is the most visited.

Mull Head was declared a Local Nature Reserve by Orkney Islands Council in 1993, the ninth in Scotland, and because it has been spared modern agricultural 'improvement' it is now very rich in interesting plantlife. Mull Head has never been ploughed, although Clu Ber, the first range of cliffs you will see, has been burned, cultivated and fertilized to allow grazing for stock. Even though this work was done generations ago, the heather's destruction means that grass and different herb species thrive on this land.

The plants which survive here are determined by the location—how close to the sea they are, how fertile the soil is where they grow, how marshy it is and how influenced by humans. Plants that have to withstand the salt spray at the cliff edge, such as sea pink or thrift, will hug the ground. As well as salt tolerators and salt haters, plants which prefer marshy conditions, such as grass of Parnassus, grow here.

Another influence on the plants are the activities of some of the birds. Islands of lush grass have grown up on the heath where great black-backed gulls roost each night, the grasses benefiting from the natural fertilizer.

Leave the parking area ❶ at the right-hand corner and follow the direction sign along the gravel path to the Gloup, where you will find two viewing platforms and an information plaque ❷.

The rocks which you see as you walk the headland are 350 million years old. There are two types: Eday flags, which are coarse red sandstone, and Rousay flags at the south end of the reserve, both formed from conditions when Lake Orcadie covered this land.

Past the Gloup you will see a red-painted kissing gate and a directional sign pointing left; this leads you along a grassy footpath to the Brough of Deerness (pronounced 'broch'), but a more interesting route, perhaps, is straight ahead and then left along the cliff edge, also following a grassy path.

At the Brough ❸ is another information plaque. In the cliff edge, a precipitous stone staircase takes you down the cliff and, by turning right at the beach, into a sheltered stony bay, Little Burra Geo. You will see, in the edge of the Brough wall, a steep dirt path which you can climb with the help of a chain set into the rock. This leads to the top of the Brough, where you can explore the ancient site.

The first people to have an impact on Mull Head were Neolithic. The ancient scrubland was grazed by animals, then Norsemen played their part, followed in their turn by folk 'paring'— stripping off the top soil for use elsewhere—during the 18th century. The result of this and continuous grazing is a mature heather heath and very impoverished soil.

Continue along the coast, and at ❹, another red-painted kissing gate on your right shows the footpath that leads to the cairn at Mull Head.

From the cairn the path turns left and becomes much narrower,

An aerial view of Deerness shows its tenuous connection to the northeastern tip of mainland Orkney

OUT AND ABOUT

The Gloup is a deep crevice in the rocks, the result of a collapsed cave

Nature
Reserve

48 ▲
Mull Head

K4

300 m

300 yds

Little
Burra
Geo

Brough of
Deerness

DEERNESS

East
Denwick

Clu Ber

43 ▲

P

The
Gloup

56 ▲

Gritley,
Kirkwall

K4

although still clear, taking you along the northern cliff edge. The path turns sharp left just before a wire fence **5**, and climbs uphill through moorland to another red-painted kissing gate **6**.

Turn right here and go down to yet another gate, visible in the fencing above the derelict farmhouse of East Denwick. Here turn left along a wide track and climb the hill. Where the track becomes very overgrown, take the left turn downhill to a small red-painted gate on your left **7**.

Follow the narrow grass path through the gate and between wire fences, to turn sharp right and continue back into the parking area.

Look out for great skuas (Stercorarius skua); 2,000 pairs of them nest in Orkney, around a quarter of the UK population

WHERE TO EAT

There is nowhere in Deerness to eat and drink and you will need to take your own provisions. The nearest pub, the Quoyburray (at Tankerness), is open all year, although lunches are available only on Saturday and Sunday in the winter. It's best to book, tel 01856 861255.

LONG-DISTANCE FOOTPATHS

Scotland has four officially designated national walking trails, known as Long Distance Routes: the West Highland Way, the Great Glen Way, the Speyside Way and the Southern Upland Way. Walking the full distance of any of these trails takes careful planning and a high level of fitness, but they can also be enjoyed in shorter stretches. There are many other opportunities for longer walks, which may or may not be waymarked on the ground, and for which leaflets and guidebooks are widely available at tourist offices. Part of the European Footpath Network, the E2, also passes through southern Scotland.

THE COWAL WAY

Portavadie to Ardgarten
Distance: 47 miles (75km)
Time: allow 6 days
www.colglen.co.uk

Traverses the beautiful Cowal peninsula from Portavadie on Loch Fyne to Ardgarten near Arrochar on Loch Long. On the way it passes through moorland and forestry in remote Glendaruel.

FIFE COASTAL PATH

Forth Bridge to Tay Bridge
Distance: 81 miles (130km)
Time: allow 4–5 days
www.fifecoastalpath.com

Relatively easy walking along the scenic coast, with extensions to St. Andrews and beyond.

GREAT GLEN WAY

Fort William to Inverness
Distance: 73 miles (117km)
Time: allow 4–6 days
www.greatglenway.com

This spectacular route is along Scotland's massive natural fault line, the Great Glen. The walking is relatively easy, on low-level woodland tracks and the tow path which runs alongside the Caledonian Canal. The start point is the Old Fort in Fort William, and highlights include Neptune's Staircase, Fort Augustus and Urquhart Castle, before it reaches Inverness Castle. A bicycle trail follows a similar route.

THE KINTYRE WAY

Tarbert to Southend
Distance: 89 miles (142km)
Time: allow 10–12 days
www.kintyre.org

From Tarbert in the Highlands, walk the entire length of Scotland's 'mainland island' to Southend near the famous Mull of Kintyre, where the more rounded lowland scenery gives way to dramatic views across the North Channel to Ireland.

PILGRIMS WAY

Glenluce Abbey to the Isle of Whithorn
Distance: 25 miles 40km
Time: allow 2–3 days

A waymarked medieval pilgrimage route in southwest Scotland.

ROB ROY WAY

Drymen to Pitlochry
Distance: 79 or 92 miles (127 or 148km)
Time: allow 6–7 days
www.robroyway.com

A dramatic route through the heart of Scotland, following the outlaw, Rob Roy MacGregor (1671–1743). The longer route takes a diversion into Glen Almond.

ST. CUTHBERT'S WALK

Melrose to Lindisfarne
Distance: 62 miles (100km)
Time: allow 7 days
www.st-cuthberts-way.co.uk

Follow the waymarked trail of the seventh-century monk, St. Cuthbert, via Jedburgh to his burial place on Lindisfarne (Holy Island), Northumberland.

SOUTHERN UPLAND WAY

Portpatrick to Cockburnspath
Distance: 212 miles (341km)
Time: allow 10–20 days
www.dumgal.gov.uk/southernupland way; www.sirwalterscottway.fsnet.co.uk

Britain's first official coast-to-coast footpath runs through the rolling hills and gentler farmland of southern Scotland. Highlights include industrial history at Wanlockhead, the ancient mansion of Traquair, and Melrose. The 92-mile (148km) section from Moffat to Cockburnspath overlaps with the Sir Walter Scott Way, which links places associated with the novelist.

SPEYSIDE WAY

Buckie to Aviemore
Distance: 84 miles (135km)
Time: allow 5–7 days
www.speysideway.org

This route follows the River Spey from the Moray coast south to the edge of the Cairngorms. The route from Buckpool harbour winds via Craigellachie Forest, Cromdale, Grantown-on-Spey and Boat of Garten to the police station at Aviemore. Additional spurs divert to Dufftown and Tomintoul.

WEST HIGHLAND WAY

Milngavie to Fort William
Distance: 95 miles (153km)
Time: allow 7–10 days
www.west-highland-way.co.uk

This is Scotland's most popular long-distance trail, taking in some of the finest west Highland scenery, including Loch Lomond and Rannoch Moor. Usually walked from south to north, it is most taxing in its later stretches. The start is at Milngavie, on the northern outskirts of Glasgow, and it uses ancient cattle drovers' roads, military roads instituted by General Wade to help tame the country after Culloden, old coaching routes, and redundant railway as it winds its way to Fort William.

THE WEST ISLAND WAY

Kilchatton Bay to Port Bannatyne, Isle of Bute
Distance: 30 miles (48km)
Time: allow 2–4 days
www.visitbute.com

This waymarked trail across the Isle of Bute in the Firth of Clyde offers easy walking with fantastic views of Kintyre, Arran and the Cowal Peninsula.

This section gives general information on places to eat and places to stay in Scotland, followed by a regional breakdown of local information.

Eating and Staying

EATING OUT IN SCOTLAND

Scotland has a clear identity apart from the rest of the UK which also shows in its food. In recent years, as the public has become more discerning and chefs higher profile, the country has developed clear culinary trends, traditions and undercurrents of its own based around distinctive local and seasonal ingredients.

Edinburgh's famous confection; checking the nets; barley, vital to the distillers

Britain's colonial past has made it a culinary melting pot, and curry has been described as Scotland's alternative national dish. The rise of Thai cuisine, the continued popularity of Chinese food and the arrival of a host of other ethnic cuisines in the cities mean that the culinary explorer can be spoiled for choice.

Continental style cafés have sprung up in most well-to-do towns, selling freshly prepared food, drink and coffee. In rural areas, you're more likely to find yourself eating at a country pub or hotel. Most pubs serve food, and a new breed of so-called gastro pubs has set about catering for guests who rate good food as highly as a good pint of beer.

It has to be said that amid all this innovation, standards are still variable and it's not uncommon to find menus that read well but simply don't deliver. Use our list of recommended eating places to avoid disappointment and you'll find that culinary excellence exists as far afield as Ullapool, Skye and Harris. And wherever you are, you'll find the tea rooms associated with many visitor attractions a useful stand-by.

WHAT TO EAT

When it comes to cooking, Scotland's historical links with France can be seen in names such as Tartan Purry (tarte en purée) and sooty bannock (sauté bannock). While it's easy to find traditional dishes such as Cullen skink or haggis with tatties and neeps, many modern chefs are once again looking to the classical techniques of French cookery—and to the spices of the Pacific Rim—for inspiration. 'Modern Scottish' menus combine all these influences.

Fresh, high-quality ingredients are a major feature. From the coastal waters come boatloads of fish and shellfish including herring, halibut, cod, lobsters, mussels, scallops and crabs. Treats include some of the largest langoustines you'll ever see, Loch Fyne oysters and the delicately flavoured Arbroath smokies—haddock smoked hot over oak chips for a gentle, smoky taste and a soft, cooked flesh. The Scots excel at curing fish: Other specialities include Finnan haddock (salted then smoked), and smoked herring (kippers), both of which may be served at breakfast.

Scottish salmon is renowned, but beware of the difference between wild (caught) salmon and farmed varieties. Salmon farming is awash with controversy thanks to revelations about fish kept in overcrowded sea cages, the use of dye to colour the flesh, and the presence of various chemicals and pollutants. Many salmon farmers have cleaned up their acts, but wild salmon is still seen as superior. Trout, both wild and farmed, is another popular option.

Other distinctive game includes grouse and venison. Aberdeen Angus beef is prized throughout Britain, and lamb is also widely available.

Oats have been grown in Scotland for centuries, and continue to thrive in the cool, damp climate. Ground into oatmeal, they are at the heart of foods such as porridge, oatcakes and haggis.

Comfort is perhaps a key word for describing Scottish food: A leisurely breakfast or an elegant high tea (served in the late afternoon or evening) can include a mouth-watering array of cakes, biscuits and scones (American biscuits). Spread them with local honey or the famous Dundee orange marmalade. And if that awakens your sweet tooth, you're in the right place: Summer brings a supply of excellent soft fruit from the Lowlands, and all year round the country could stock a sweet shop with its crunchy toffees, buttery mints and pretty pastel sticks of rock.

EATING

Arbroath smokies: small hot-smoked haddock, with a more delicate flavour than kippers (see below)

Atholl brose: drink prepared from oatmeal and water, with whisky and honey

bannock: see oatcake, below; see also Selkirk bannock

black bun: tea-time treat made from dried fruits and spices cooked within a pastry case, served in slices

black pudding: blood sausage made from pig's blood, suet and oatmeal

butterscotch: hard golden candy made from sugar, water and butter

clapshot: a blend of cooked turnip and potato (neeps and tatties), mashed up with a little butter and milk, often served as an accompaniment to haggis

clootie dumpling: steamed sweet and spicy pudding, traditionally cooked in a cloth ('cloot'), and associated with New Year

cock-a-leekie soup: stock-based soup of chicken, leeks and other vegetables

cranachan: dessert of raspberries, cream and toasted oatmeal

crowdie: light curd cheese

Cullen skink: creamy fish broth based on 'Finnan haddie' or smoked haddock

drop scone: see Scotch pancake, below

Dundee cake: rich fruit cake, traditionally decorated with almonds on the top

Forfar bridie: meat pasty made with beef, onion and potato

Edinburgh rock: crumbly sweet made into round, pastel-hued sticks with flavours such as vanilla, ginger and lemon

haggis: Scotland's national dish, a sort of large mutton sausage based on the ground-up liver, lungs and heart of a sheep, mixed with oatmeal, onion and spices, and cooked up in the sheep's stomach

hot toddy: warming drink made with boiling water, a little sugar and whisky, flavoured with lemon, nutmeg and cinammon

kedgeree: mildly curried dish of 'Finnan haddie' or smoked haddock, with hard-boiled eggs, onion and rice

kipper: smoked, cured herring

neeps and tatties: see clapshot, above

oatcake: thin, crumbly savoury biscuit made of oatmeal

partan bree: crab soup ('partan' means crab, 'bree' means broth)

porridge: a hot and filling breakfast dish of stewed oatmeal or rolled oats, served with milk and sugar, or salt to taste

potato scone: hot, flat, savoury cake made from potato and flour

reestit mutton: mutton preserved in salt, used as the basis of soups and stews in Shetland

Scotch broth: a hearty soup, with lamb, pearl barley and winter vegetables

Scotch egg: boiled egg wrapped in pork sausage meat and breadcrumbs, then deep-fried; popular cold for picnics

Scotch pancake: small, thick pancake, eaten hot or cold with butter and syrup or jam

Scotch pie: small meat pie (traditionally mutton) with hot-water crust pastry, and served hot or cold

Selkirk bannock: round fruit bread with sultanas

shortbread: thick, pale golden biscuit with a firm texture, made from butter, sugar and flour

tablet: hard fudge

Cheesemaking, another Scottish tradition, is still going strong thanks to a handful of post-war revivalists. Look out for Crowdie (a Highland soft curd cheese probably of Viking or Pictish origin) and Caboc (a soft, buttery cheese rolled in toasted oatmeal). Other classics include sharp, creamy Dunsyre Blue, and Lanark Blue—a blue-veined ewes' milk cheese.

INTERNATIONAL DINING

Recent surveys investigating the taste of the British public have found that, while native dishes are still highly rated, they are at least matched in popularity by more ethnic menus. Most towns have an Indian or Chinese restaurant or 'carry oot' ('carry out', or take-away). Newer international trends include Moroccan, Turkish and most notably Thai cuisine, but visit a big city and you may also find Indonesian, Caribbean, Vietnamese, Hungarian, Russian, Mongolian and Mexican. In many places you can now find exciting modern Indian restaurants that offer traditional Indian dishes, fusions of Indian and European cooking or the very latest innovations from Mumbai (Bombay).

Another long-standing favourite is Italian food, be it the genuine article or pizza chains. Large numbers of Italians immigrated to Scotland in the early 20th century, and Italian ice cream makers have become local heroes—look out for Nardini's in Irvine. Italian-run cafés, restaurants and coffee bars are usually a good bet if you're looking for a decent cup of coffee.

VEGETARIAN FOOD

Dedicated wholefood vegetarian restaurants are scarce since most non-vegetarian restaurants caught on to the demand and started to offer meat-free options. These choices may be limited, so telephone in advance and check what's available, especially as some restaurants do not include a vegetarian option on the menu but are happy to prepare one if the customer requests it. The international restaurants—especially Thai, Vietnamese and Indian—generally offer a wide selection of non-meat dishes.

EATING

WHERE TO EAT

Restaurant dining reflects the diversity of British culture, and there are options to suit most tastes and pockets. The one thing many have in common is their opening hours—between 12 and 2, and from 6 until 9—but in most larger towns and cities you can find food at any time of day. Later at night, only a few restaurants carry on serving.

Many top restaurants are based in hotels, particularly in the major cities. Farther afield, hotel restaurants are mixed in quality. Some of the establishments that particularly pride themselves

Café culture is now widespread; reserve ahead for the best

on their food describe themselves as 'restaurants with rooms' to indicate that the emphasis is on the dining experience.

Scotland's dining pubs are quintessentially British: Bare stone walls, open fires and low beams typify the environment, so much so that modern chain pubs are often decorated in the same quaint fashion. Most (but not all) pubs welcome families and many stay open throughout the day, though food is often only available from 12 to 2 and from 6 until 9.

Pub menus traditionally include 'bar snacks'—lighter, cheaper meals including sandwiches, toasties (toasted sandwiches), filled baked potatoes and ploughmens' lunches (a cold platter of bread, meat, cheese and salad)—but these days most pubs also serve dishes such as curry, steak and ale pie, bangers and mash, and steak and chips (french fries).

Local high-street cafés are homely establishments selling teas and (usually fried) snacks. More recently, the word café has started to be used for the more stylish continental-style establishments (once called brasserie or bistro) found in increasing numbers in cities and towns including Glasgow, Perth and Inverness. These bridge the gap between pubs, restaurants and coffee bars by selling coffees, snacks, wines and meals.

A traditional stalwart, tea shops may be found just about anywhere and are usually open from mid-morning until 4 or 5pm. They specialize in teas, home-made cakes and light meals. Find them in larger department stores, on the high street, at garden centres and at many tourist attractions. National Trust for Scotland tea rooms have a particularly good reputation for the high quality of their fresh home-baking.

RESTAURANT TIPS

● In some restaurants it is possible to walk in off the street and get a table, but if you have your heart set on dining in a particular place, it's always advisable to reserve a table in advance by telephone or email.

● Less formal establishments, especially pubs, may work on a 'first come, first served' basis.

● Smoking is totally banned in some restaurants, but many have an area where smoking is allowed, and some establishments will tolerate cigarettes but not pipes or cigars. Make sure you specify a smoking or non-smoking table when you book.

● It's fairly common for a table booking to last only a couple of hours, after which time guests will be expected to move on to make way for the next sitting.

● It's also worth noting that many restaurants stop serving food earlier than on the Continent. Don't expect to turn up at 10.30pm and be fed unless you've checked in advance. The most notable exceptions to this rule are Thai, Chinese and Indian restaurants, which are often still serving food at midnight.

● In the past the British loved to dress for dinner and the more formal restaurants tended to have strict dress codes, especially where jackets and ties were concerned. These days things are more flexible, though it's unwise to turn up at a pricey restaurant wearing jeans and a T-shirt. If you're in doubt, it's quite acceptable to telephone and ask.

● You can expect excellent service in Scotland's top restaurants, but lower down the price scale things are less consistent. If you are happy with the service, it is usual to leave a tip of about 10–15 per cent at the end of the meal.

● If you pay by credit card you may find that when you sign the receipt, it includes a section in which to add an extra amount as a tip. It is acceptable to cross this section through and leave a cash tip instead.

ALCOHOL

Scotland's licensing laws are different to those in England. Pubs can serve alcohol 11am–11pm, Monday–Saturday, and 12.30–2.30, 6.30–11 on Sundays (the afternoon gap may be bridged by a license extension). Extensions to these hours may allow premises to open late. From spring 2007, new laws allowing premises to apply for 24-hour licenses are likely to be in place.

● Children age 16–18 can drink alcohol only if it accompanies a meal.

● A bottle of wine in a restaurant usually costs significantly more than in a shop.

● Some restaurants—especially those not licensed to sell alcohol—operate a 'bring your own' system (BYO), in which case diners may pay a small corkage fee.

FAST FOOD

'Fast food' usually means take-away food, and in many cases it's possible to buy a meal for under £6. American fast food chain outlets have reached most corners of the country, so in the bigger towns and cities you won't have to look far for a hamburger or a pizza. In remoter areas the population year-round is not large enough to support this, and you are unlikely to find anything.

Other fast food outlets are likely to be independently owned, or local chains. They include local pizza delivery shops, fish-and-chip shops (which may also sell pies, burgers and pizzas) and a wide variety of multicultural take-aways. Haggis and chips (french fries) is also found on some fast food menus, and the Scots are infamous for inventing the deep-fried Mars bar. In rural areas, 'fast food' may be mobile—that is, served from the back of a van.

Service stations on motorways and major trunk roads also supply fast food, from sandwiches and pre-packed snacks to take with you, to light restaurant meals. The quality is variable, but on a long drive it's a good excuse to stop for a break. Motorway chains include Little Chef, Granada and Welcome Break.

THE LISTINGS

In the listings that follow, we have included a variety of inspected, recommended restaurants/pubs serving good food. Establishments are listed under the name of their nearest town.

QUICK GUIDE TO RESTAURANT AND FAST FOOD CHAINS

Beefeater: British steakhouse restaurants
Burger King: high-street hamburger chain
Di Maggio's: chain of restaurants and tapas bars in Glasgow and west central region
Deep Pan Pizza: winning combination of pizza, pasta and salad
Domino's Pizza: pizza to go or to your door
Harry Ramsden's: British franchise selling fried fish and chips (french fries)
Howies: Scottish chain of affordable restaurants

KFC: fried chicken, fish and fries to take away
McDonald's: ubiquitous fast food burger chain
Pizza Express: pizza restaurant chain
Pizza Hut: wide range of pizzas to eat in
Subway: the popular American chain selling filled rolls and sandwiches
T.G.I. Friday's: lively American-style restaurant chain
Wimpy: British burger restaurant chain, established in 1954

ROSETTE AWARDS

EATING

The Automobile Association's (AA's) restaurant inspectors award rosettes annually on a scale of one to five. The following gives an indication of the levels of quality you can expect:

❀ Excellent local restaurants serving food prepared with care, understanding and skill, using good-quality ingredients.
❀❀ The best local restaurants, which aim for and achieve higher standards, better consistency and greater precision in the cooking.
❀❀❀ Outstanding restaurants that demand recognition well beyond their local area. The cooking will be underpinned by the selection and sympathetic treatment of the highest-quality ingredients. Timing, seasoning and the judgement of flavour combinations will be consistently excellent. Intelligent service and a well-chosen wine list.
❀❀❀❀ Among the very best restaurants in Britain. These restaurants exhibit ambition,

excellence, superb technical skills and remarkable consistency. They combine an appreciation of culinary traditions with a desire for further exploration and improvement.
❀❀❀❀❀ Some of the finest restaurants in Britain, where the cooking stands comparison with the best in the world. These restaurants are highly individual, show exceptional culinary skills and set the standards to which other restaurants aspire.

The restaurants, cafés and pubs in the listings that do not have a rosette rating have not been inspected by the AA and are not part of its classification scheme.

WHISKY

Scotland's landscape and history are inextricably linked with whisky, the golden distilled liquor made from malted grain, especially barley or rye, and drunk as a single malt or a blend. (In contrast, American whiskey, or bourbon, is made with rye or maize.)

See the process on a distillery tour; oatcakes accompany a 'dram'; famous names among the blends

The first clear written record of the production of whisky was in 1494 during the reign of James IV, when the exchequer roll granted 'to friar John Cor, by order of the King, to make aqua vitae, eight bolls of malt.' Aqua vitae was the original term for spirits (alcoholic liquor made by distillation) and translates into Gaelic as *uisce beatha*, from which we get the word whisky.

By the 16th century whisky was being produced by everyone in Scotland from landowners to crofters. The key ingredients were close at hand: barley (which grows well in the northern climate), pure water and peat. And the tax paid on wine from continental Europe was high, making this a cheap alternative for ordinary people.

After the Battle of Culloden in 1745 the fortunes of Highland whisky changed dramatically. Legislation was introduced that made small-scale whisky production illegal. In 1774 it was legalized again, but its export beyond the Highlands was forbidden. Smuggling became rife, but by the time the final restrictions on Highland distilling were lifted in 1816, malt whisky production had been all but destroyed as a cottage industry.

In 1827 the invention of the continuous still heralded a major upturn in business. In the Lowlands large-scale whisky production had continued to flourish, although the quality of the drink, distilled from wheat, corn or unmalted barley, was considered inferior. It was now possible for the Lowland distillers to produce a better quality—and quantity—of grain whisky. When this was blended with the flavoursome Highland malts, an easy-drinking Scotch was created that would sell well both in Scotland and abroad.

The master blenders who emerged at the forefront of the new industry were men whose names are still known today, including William Teacher, Johnnie Walker and Arthur Bell.

In the later 20th century whisky's popularity took a downturn, as it went out of fashion. Then, in 1971, William Grant & Sons decided to market its single malt, Glenfiddich. A huge success, it heralded the beginning of a resurgence of interest in the single malts that had been blotted out by blends over a century earlier.

Today single malts tend to be favoured by connoisseurs. No two malt whiskies are the same—it can seem that each bottle contains the distilled essence of the place in which it was created.

WHAT'S IN A MALT?

In order to malt barley, the grain is soaked until it starts to germinate, releasing starches. It is then heated and dried out to stop germination, traditionally by burning peat, whose smoke imparts a distinctive flavour into the malt. Hot water is added to the grain and the resulting wort (into which the barley's sugars have dissolved) is drained off, cooled and pumped into fermenting vessels. Yeast is added to the wort and a bubbly fermentation begins.

SCOTCH COCKTAILS

Whisky Mac: one or two measures of Scotch and one of green ginger wine

Rusty Nail: one measure of Drambuie to one or two of Scotch

Rob Roy: three parts whisky to one part sweet vermouth and a dash of Angostura bitters

Flying Scotsman: three measures of whisky, two and a half of Italian Vermouth, one tablespoon of bitters and a tablespoon of sugar syrup

Robbie Burns: one measure of Scotch with Martini and three dashes of Benedictine

Around two days later, the resulting low strength liquor is distilled in large, copper pot stills. It is distilled for a second time and 'the cut' is made to separate the 'heart' of the spirit from the volatile 'heads' (the first alcohol that condenses) and 'tails' (the heavier alcoholic compounds). The heart is transferred to a vat where it is mixed with water before being sealed into oak casks and left to mature for three years or longer.

Every detail of the manufacture affects the taste of the finished whisky, including the amount of peat used in the malting, the composition of the local water, the design of the still, the length of maturation and the type of cask in which this takes place—often used sherry casks, which lend a distinctive flavour and colour to the whisky.

Different flavours of the single malts do not fall neatly into regions, and while there are certainly patterns—the peaty flavours in the whisky of the Western Isles, for example—there are also many exceptions. The better-known brand names are a good starting point, but investigate further and you'll quickly discover different ages and distillations of the familiar name which carry their own mystique.

REGIONAL VARIATIONS: LOWLANDS
Historically linked with large distilleries and blended whiskies, the Lowlands also produce easy drinking malts with light peat levels. Look out for the names Auchentoshan, Springbank and Rosebank.

ISLAY
Some say this is the birthplace of Scotch whisky. Numerous distilleries include excellent peaty malts such as Ardbeg, Lagavulin and Laphroaig. The latter has a salty tang, as do Bruichladdich and Bunnahabhain.

SPEYSIDE
Big names and plenty of them. This is the golden triangle of malt, and there's (literally) a dizzying amount to sample—Cragganmore, Knockando, Glenfiddich, Tamdhu, Glenfarclas and Macallan to name just a few. The area is often linked with a mellow sweetness, though in truth there are numerous variations.

HIGHLANDS
The reputation of Highland whisky lives on. Malts from the southern Highlands and Perthshire have a honeyed lightness and a lack of peat—Glengoyne, for example. Towards the east coast, a malty flavour comes to the fore, as in the Royal Lochnagar. West coast sea air permeates the whisky produced in Oban, while north Highland malts have a dry, fruity sweetness (as in Glenmorangie) and a hint of salt near the coast in whiskies such as Pulteney and Clynelish.

WESTERN ISLES AND NORTHERN ISLES
The distilleries may be fewer, but there are still at least five good reasons to make a pilgrimage. One of the best is Orkney's Highland Park, which takes its smoky, heathery tones from the island's peat. Another is Skye's characterful Talisker.

BLENDED WHISKY
It was blended Scotch that took over the world and it still accounts for the vast majority of worldwide whisky sales, but these days it's often overlooked by aficionados. In fact, there's a real art to the blending—probably as much as there is to making a single malt. A blender mixes grain whisky with any number of different malts (popular brands such as Famous Grouse and Bell's may have between 20 and 50 different varieties in their make-up) and has to keep the flavour consistent, even though the constituent malts may change in character or stop being produced altogether.

Major whisky distilleries

Highland Park — Kirkwall
Orkney Islands
Thurso
Pulteney
Western Isles
Clynelish
Ullapool
Glenmorangie   Glen Grant   Baxters
Dallas Dhu   Glenfarclas   Strathisla
Inverness   Cragganmore   Macallan
Talisker   Tomatin   Glenlivet   Glenfiddich
Skye   Kyle of Lochalsh   Knockando   Tamdhu   Aberdeen
Royal Lochnagar
Edradour
Fort William
Coll
Tiree   *Mull*   *Jura*   Oban   Dundee
Perth
Glengoyne   Stirling
Islay   Auchentoshan   Rosebank   EDINBURGH
Bruichladdich   Bunnahabhain   GLASGOW   Glenkinchie
Lagavulin   Bowmore   Isle of Arran   Galashiels
Laphroaig   Ardbeg   *Arran*   Kilmarnock
Springbank   Ayr
Dumfries
Stranraer
Bladnoch

EATING

SOUTHERN SCOTLAND

ARRAN, ISLE OF

AUCHRANNIE COUNTRY HOUSE ✿✿

Brodick, KA27 8BZ
Tel 01770 302234
www.auchrannie.co.uk

Superior local ingredients star on the short dinner menu. Try freshly caught langoustines served in a butter and coriander (cilantro) sauce or guinea fowl with pearl barley risotto. Hearty desserts are popular, and the wine list is good.

🕐 D, 6.30–9.30
🍷 D from £25.95, Wine from £13
🚗 From ferry terminal turn right and follow coast road through Brodick, then take 2nd left past golf club

KILMICHAEL ✿✿

Glen Cloy KA27 8BY
Tel 01770 302219
www.kilmichael.com

Chef Antony Butterworth delivers contemporary dishes with an often ingenious use of ingredients. You might start with roast garlic and chestnut soup, and then try lamb with rosemary, redcurrants and a red pepper marmalade. A concise

four-course menu changes daily. No children under 12.

🕐 D only, 7–8.30; closed Tue, Nov–end Feb
🍷 D £38, Wine from £11.15 🚭
🚗 Turn right on leaving ferry terminal through Brodick, left at golf club. Go past church and follow signs

AUCHENCAIRN

BALCARY BAY ✿✿

DG7 1QZ
Tel 01556 640217
www.balcary-bay-hotel.com

Local produce features strongly on this French and

European menu. Imaginative starters include sautéed collops and spiced monkfish, with mains of bacon-wrapped pork fillet, perhaps, and a dessert of pannacotta in mulled red wine.

🕐 12–2, 7–8.30; L by prior booking only Mon–Sat; closed mid-Dec to mid-Feb
🍷 L from £16, D from £29, Wine from £13.85 🚭
🚗 On A711 between Dalbeattie and Kirkcudbright. From Auchencairn follow signs to Balcary, along Shore Road

AULDGIRTH

AULDGIRTH INN

DG2 0XG
Tel 01387 740250

This 500-year-old inn's typical menu includes medallions of pork fillet, beef braised in ale, pot roast supreme of guinea fowl and noisettes of Dumfriesshire lamb.

🕐 Daily 11.30–11. Bar meals: daily 12–9pm. Restaurant: daily 12–9pm
🍷 L from £10, D from £13.50, Wine £8.95
🚗 8 miles (12.9km) northeast of Dumfries on A76 Kilmarnock road

EATING

AYR

FAIRFIELD HOUSE ❀❀
12 Fairfield Road KA7 2AR
Tel 01292 267461
www.fairfieldhotel.co.uk
The ambitious kitchen at this friendly hotel delivers modern French dishes with plenty of flavour. Baby poussin is marinated in Madeira and served with basil ravioli; while halibut is accompanied by vanilla pea purée, lobster nage and salmon tartare.
🕐 L 12–2, D 7–9
🍴 L from £14, D from £30, Wine from £12.95 💳
🚗 From A77 to Ayr South. Follow signs for town centre, turn left into Miller Road. At lights turn left, then right into Fairfield Road

FOUTERS ❀❀
2A Academy Street KA7 1HS
Tel 01292 261391
www.fouters.co.uk
A degree of panache lifts the international, modern cooking out of the ordinary at this long-established restaurant. Expect delights such as chicken supreme with mushroom and nut mousseline. No children under 5 at lunch, or under 10 at dinner.
🕐 12–2.30, 5–10; closed Sun–Mon, 4–11 Jan
🍴 L from £12.50, D from £18, Wine from £14.75 💳
🚪 Opposite Town Hall, down Cobblestone Lane

BALLOCH

DE VERE CAMERON HOUSE HOTEL ❀❀❀
Loch Lomond G83 8QZ
Tel 01389 755565
www.devereonline.co.uk
This hotel's restaurant has access to some of the finest local ingredients. Diners have a choice of two menus: a daily market menu or six courses of surprises from the tasting menu. Expect mains such as thyme scented breast of chicken with a ballotine of the leg and a Madeira-based jus. Desserts may include

steamed lemon sponge with a fresh lemon curd and black cherry compote.
🕐 L 12–2.30 (Sun only), D 7–9.30; closed Mon
🍴 L from £23.50, D from £49.50, Wine from £23 💳
🚗 M8/A82 to Dumbarton; take road to Luss, hotel signed 1 mile (1.6km) past Balloch on right

BANKNOCK

GLENSKIRLIE HOUSE RESTAURANT ❀❀
Kilsyth Road FK4 1UF
Tel 01324 840201
www.glenskirliehouse.com
Modern innovative Scottish cuisine is served in this elegant restaurant. Dishes may include

Elegant dining at Glenskirlie House Restaurant

organic chicken breast with braised chicory and a herb glaze, and Swedish-style salmon with hot buttered noodles.
🕐 12–2, 6–9.30; closed D Mon, 26–27 Dec, 1–3 Jan
🍴 L from £15.75, D from £32, Wine from £13.95 💳
🚗 From Glasgow take A80 towards Stirling. At exit 4 take A803 signed Kilsyth/Bonnybridge. At T-junction (intersection) turn right. Hotel 1 mile (1.6km) on right

BIGGAR

SHIELDHILL CASTLE ❀❀
Shieldhill Road, Quothquan
ML12 6NA
Tel 01899 220035
www.shieldhill.co.uk

Modern European dishes display clear, rich flavours which might include scallops with cauliflower purée, and venison with duck foie gras and wild mushroom jus.
🕐 12–1.45, 7–8.45
🍴 L from £12.95, D from £17.95, Wine from £15 💳
🚗 From Biggar take B7016 to Carnwath. After 2.5 miles (4km) turn left on to Shieldhill Road. Castle is 1.5 miles (3km) on right

CASTLE DOUGLAS

PLUMED HORSE RESTAURANT ❀❀
Main Street, Crossmichael DG7 3AU
Tel 01556 670333
www.plumedhorse.co.uk
This tiny restaurant has just six tables; pricing levels seem rather high. Starters may include tian of marinated salmon, sour cream, two caviars and dill oil; meat dishes might include chicken and fresh herb sausage. Vegetarian menu on request.
🕐 12.30–1, 7–9; closed D Sun–Mon, 25–26 Dec, 2 weeks Jan, 2 weeks Sep
🍴 L from £19, D from £35, Wine from £16 💳
🚗 3.5 miles (5.7km) northwest of Castle Douglas on A713

CLYDEBANK

BEARDMORE HOTEL ❀❀
Beardmore Street G81 4SA
Tel 0141 951 6000
www.bw-beardmorehotel.co.uk
In the circular Citrus Restaurant classical French cooking takes on some twists: Garden pea soup with crispy wontons and pistachio brûlée with lemon shortbread are some of the tempting options. No children under 12.
🕐 Restaurant 7–10; closed Sun
🍴 D from £25, Wine from £15 💳
🚗 M8 exit 19, follow signs for Dumbarton then follow tourist signs. Turn left on to Beardmore Street then follow signs

DALRY

BRAIDWOODS ❀❀

Drumastle Mill Cottage KA24 4LN
Tel 01294 833544
www.braidwoods.co.uk
Keith Braidwood's unfussy
restaurant delivers simply
balanced food. Dine on seared
hand-dived scallops with
cucumber spaghetti and
tomato vierge, and baked fillet
of west coast turbot in an
Arbroath smokie and saffron
stew. Follow up with an iced
Agen prune and Armagnac
parfait with caramelized
orange sauce. No children
under 12 at dinner.
🕐 12–2.15, D 7–9.30; closed Mon,
L Tue, D Sun, 1st 3 weeks Jan, 2 weeks
Sep
🍴 L from £16, D from £32, Wine from
£14.95 🅂
🚗 1 mile (1.6km) from Dalry on the
Saltcoats road

DALRYMPLE

KIRKTON INN

1 Main Street KA6 6DF
Tel 01292 560241
Menus include roast sirloin of
beef and Yorkshire pudding,
steak pie, pork with pineapple
in a Malibu and cream sauce,
lobster thermidor, battered
haddock and roast pheasant.
🕐 Daily 11am–midnight. Bar meals:
daily 11–9. Restaurant: daily 11–9
🍴 L from £6, D from £14, Wine from
£9.75
🚗 Between A77 and A713, 5 miles
(8km) from Ayr

DIRLETON

THE OPEN ARMS HOTEL ❀

EH39 5EG
Tel 01620 850241
www.openarmshotel.com
Choose from the Library
dining room or Deveau's
brasserie. Dishes might
include fillet of Aberdeen
Angus beef stuffed with
home-made parfait, served
with oatmeal oyster
mushrooms on Orkney
Hramsa (cheese) mash, or
pan-fried Barbary duck breast
baked on lemon grass and
served with couscous and
peppercorn and black cherry
coulis.
🕐 12–2, 7–9; closed D Sun
🍴 L from £12, D from £20, Wine from
£12.95 🅂
🚗 From A1 (south) take A198 to North
Berwick then follow signs for Dirleton
2 miles (3.2km) west. From Edinburgh
take A6137 leading to A198

ESKDALEMUIR

HART MANOR ❀

DG13 0QQ
Tel 01387 373217
www.hartmanor.co.uk
The blackboard menu lists
three dishes at each course,
including lightly puréed
mushroom soup with a swirl
of cream, ham and chicken pie

*The Cally Palace Hotel dates
from the 17th century*

with vegetables, and bread
and butter pudding. No
children under 10.
🕐 D only, 6.30–8.15 (reservations
required); closed Christmas
🍴 D from £28, Wine from £13.95 🅂
🚗 From M74 J17 follow signs for
Eskdalemuir for 14 miles (22.5km).
Through Eskdalemuir village Hart
Manor is 1 mile (1.6km) left on road to
Langholm

ETTRICK

TUSHIELAW INN

TD7 5HT
Tel 01750 62205
This 18th-century inn serves
wholesome meals, including
steak and stout pie, deep-fried
breaded haddock, Aberdeen
Angus sirloin steaks, grilled
lamb cutlets and local trout.
Gluten-free and vegetarian
options are always available.
🕐 Daily 12–2.30, 6.30–11. Bar meals:
12–2, 7–9.30
🍴 L from £10, D from £14, Wine from
£8.50
🚗 At junction (intersection) of B709
and B711, west of Hawick

GATEHEAD

COCHRANE INN

45 Main Road KA2 0AP
Tel 01563 570122
This pub specializes in
contemporary British cuisine,
say a starter of soused herring
and grilled goat's cheese,
followed by a pan-fried trio of
seafood with tiger prawns.
🕐 12–2, 5.30–11. Bar meals: 12–2, 6–9.
Restaurant: 12–2, 6–9; closed 1 Jan
🍴 L from £15, D from £15, Wine from
£12.95

GATEHOUSE OF FLEET

CALLY PALACE HOTEL ❀

DG7 2DL
Tel 01557 814341
www.callypalace.co.uk
Dinner here is a formal affair
(jacket and tie required). On
offer is a balance between
simple, traditional and
adventurous, modern. Pan-
fried Gressingham duck,
griddled pork fillet and
steamed fillet of salmon are
typical main courses; the
chocolate and orange tart is
deliciously decadent.
🕐 12–1.30, 6.45–9.30; closed 3
Jan–early Feb
🍴 L from £10, D from £28, Wine from
£14.50 🅂
🚗 From A74(M) take A75, at
Gatehouse take B727. Hotel on left

GIFFORD

GOBLIN HA'

EH41 4QH
Tel 01620 810244
A patio for summer eating,
a play area and dolls' house
for children, plus a varied
range of home-cooked dishes
including breast of duck, fillet
of salmon, chef's curry, shank
of lamb and beer-battered
haddock.

EATING

🕐 11–2.30, 5–11 (11–11 Jun–end Sep). Bar meals: 12.30–2, 6.30–9. Restaurant: 12.30–2, 6.30–9.

🍽️ L from £10, D from £15, Wine from £10

🚗 On A846, near village square on shore side of the road

GRANGEMOUTH

THE GRANGE MANOR ❀ ❀
Glensburgh Road, Glensburgh FK3 8XJ
Tel 01324 474836
www.grangemanor.co.uk
Starters could include home-cured herrings with pickled vegetables and Bloody Mary sauce; venison, rabbit and pigeon terrine studded with lychees; or poached pear with stilton and walnut in a red cherry soup. Slow-cooked veal in a rich tomato and herb sauce, roast monkfish fillet, and loin of lamb dressed with sweet herbs are possible main courses.

🕐 12–2.30, 7–9.30; closed L Sat, Sun, 26 Dec, 1–2 Jan

🍽️ L from £13.95, D from £26.85, Wine from £14

🚭 No pipes

🚗 M9 (eastward) exit 6, 200m (220 yards) on right; M9 (west) exit 5, then A905 for 2 miles (3.2km)

GULLANE

LA POTINIÈRE ❀ ❀
Main Street EH31 2AA
Tel 01620 843214
The four-course dinner menu is modern British that includes an amuse-bouche and a palate-cleanser. A sample menu might include warm parmesan tart, followed by seared guinea fowl on Puy lentils, and finished off with Calvados pannacotta.

🕐 12.30–2, 7–9; closed Mon–Tue, Christmas, bank holidays

🍽️ L from £16.50, D from £36.50, Wine from £15.50 🚭

🚗 On A198

INNERLEITHEN

TRAQUAIR ARMS HOTEL
Traquair Road EH44 6PD
Tel 01896 830229
The food has a distinctive Scottish flavour with dishes of

Finnan savoury, salmon with ginger and coriander (cilantro), and fillet of beef Traquair. Omelettes, salads and baked potatoes are also available.

🕐 Mon–Sat 11–12am, Sun 12–11. Bar meals: daily 12–9. Restaurant: daily 12–9; closed 25–26 Dec, 1–3 Jan

🍽️ L from £10, D from £18, Wine from £9.50

🚗 6 miles (9.7km) east of Peebles on A72. Pub 91m (100 yards) from junction (intersection) with B709

ISLE OF WHITHORN

THE STEAM PACKET INN
Harbour Row DG8 8LL
Tel 01988 500334
The inn makes good use of seafood straight off the boats

Livingston's Restaurant is in a cottage with exposed stone walls

on its menu. Expect whole, locally caught lemon and Dover sole or roast breast of pheasant among the main courses.

🕐 Summer daily 11–11; winter Mon–Thu 11–3, 6–11; closed 25 Dec. Bar meals: 12–2, 6.30–9. Restaurant: 12–2, 6.30–9

🍽️ L from £10, D from £15, Wine from £10.50 🚭

🚗 From Newton Stewart take A714, then A746 to Isle of Whithorn

LINLITHGOW

CHAMPANY INN ❀ ❀
EH49 7LU
Tel 01506 834532
www.champany.com
Described as a temple to beef, this inn serves Pope's eye,

BURT'S ❀ ❀
Market Square, TD6 9PL
Tel 01896 822285
www.burtshotel.co.uk
The bar is popular for informal lunches and suppers. In the restaurant try parfait of Border game to begin, while typical mains range from halibut, pheasant and chicken through lamb chops and steaks to a vegetarian platter. Selkirk Bannock Pudding is served with shortbread ice cream. No children under 10.

🕐 12–2, 7–9; closed 26 Dec

🍽️ L from £15.50, D from £31.50, Wine from £12.75

🚭 No smoking in dining room

porterhouse, Châteaubriand or rib-eye steaks among others. The cellar contains around 25,000 wine bottles. The house starter is hot-smoked salmon with hollandaise sauce, and there's chicken, duck and lobster, too. No children under 8.

🕐 12.30–2, 7–10; closed Sun, L Sat, 25–26 Dec

🍽️ L from £16.75, D from £33, Wine from £14.50

🚗 2 miles (3.2km) northeast of Linlithgow at junction (intersection) of A904 and A803

LIVINGSTON'S RESTAURANT ❀ ❀
52 High Street EH49 7AE
Tel 01506 846565
At this intimate restaurant typical mains include saddle of Highland venison with bramble and honey sauce, along with seared loin of tuna with tomato and olive champ. No children under 8.

🕐 12–2.30, 6–9.30; closed Sun–Mon, 2 weeks Jan, 1 week Jun, 1 week Oct

🍽️ L from £14.95, D from £33.95, Wine from £7 🚭

🚗 Opposite post office

EATING

NEWTON STEWART

CREEBRIDGE HOUSE
Minnigaff DG8 6NP
Tel 01671 402121
Bridge's Bar and Brasserie
offers a menu that might
include home-made ravioli
filled with local lobster in
seafood broth, and steaks
cut from Buccleuch beef.
The Garden Restaurant
offers a short, fixed-price
menu of modern Scottish
cooking.
🕐 Mon–Sat 12–2.30, 6–11; Sun 12–11.
Bar meals: 12–2, 6–9.30. Restaurant:
dinner only, 7–9
🍷 L from £12, D from £25, Wine from
£10
🚗 Take A75 into Newton Stewart, turn
right over the bridge, hotel is 200m
(200 yards) on left

PEEBLES

CASTLE VENLAW HOTEL ❀❀
Edinburgh Road EH45 8QG
Tel 01721 720384
www.venlaw.co.uk
The food at this romantic,
family-owned castle in the
Borders is traditional British
cooking boosted by the
occasional Mediterranean
influence. Black pudding
brioche might be followed
by Scottish salmon with
roast sweet potato and a
lobster bisque. No children
under 5.
🕐 12–2.45, 7–9
🍷 L from £10, D from £28.50, Wine
from £14.95
🚗 From east end of Peebles High
Street turn left at roundabout,
signed A703 to Edinburgh. After
0.75 mile (1.2km) hotel is signed
on right

PORTPATRICK

CROWN
9 North Crescent DG9 8SX
Tel 01776 810261
The extensive menus are
based on fresh local produce,
with an emphasis on seafood
including whitebait,
langoustine, herring, lobster,
crab and mussels. Selected as
the AA's Seafood Pub of the
Year for 2005.

🕐 11am–12am. Bar meals: 12–9.30.
Restaurant: 12–2.30, 6–9.30
🍷 L from £11, D from £14, Wine from
£10.95

SORN

SORN INN ❀❀
35 Main Street KA5 6HU
Tel 01290 551305
www.thesorninn.com
At this late 18th-century inn,
chef Craig Grant provides
brilliant value fixed prices. Try
the warm pheasant salad or
pavé of beef with wild
mushroom polenta, or go for
the chef's tasting menu.
🕐 12–2.30, 6.30–9; closed L Sat, Mon
🍷 L from £11.95, D from £23.50, Wine
from £11.50 🅂

*Malin Court enjoys views across
the Clyde estuary*

🚗 From A77 take the A76 to
Mauchline, join B743, Sorn is 4 miles
(6.4km) farther on

SWINTON

WHEATSHEAF RESTAURANT
❀❀
Main Street TD11 3JJ
Tel 01890 860257
The lunch menu at this country
inn changes daily and offers
good value; the dinner menu
is equally appealing: breast of
wild wood pigeon on a
medallion of Scotch beef fillet
with black pudding in Madeira
sauce, or fillet of salmon on a
crayfish, tomato and coriander
(cilantro) sauce.
🕐 12–2.30, 6–9.30; closed D Sun,
Dec–end Jan; 24, 26, 31 Dec, 1 Jan

🍷 L from £16, D from £20, Wine from
£12.95 🅂
🚗 In village centre

TIBBIE SHIELS INN

TIBBIE SHIELS INN
St. Mary's Loch TD7 5LH
Tel 01750 42231
Menus reflect the seasons with
winter game and fresh fish, as
well as more exotic dishes
such as cashew nut loaf with
tomato and herb salad.
Children welcome.
🕐 Mon–Sat 11–11, Sun 12.30–11. Bar
meals: daily 12.30–8.15. Restaurant:
daily 12–8.15
🍷 L from £10, D from £11.25, Wine
from £8
🚗 From Moffat take A708. Inn is 14
miles (22.5km) on right

TURNBERRY

MALIN COURT ❀
KA26 9PB
Tel 01655 331457
www.malincourt.co.uk
Lunch leans towards no-
nonsense comfort food—
home-made burgers or lamb's
liver with onion gravy and
mash—but in the evening the
menu might include baked
halibut in a herb crust with
roasted celery and grain
mustard sauce, or fillet of beef
accompanied by herb mash
and truffle jus.
🕐 12.30–2, 7–9
🍷 L from £12, D from £15, Wine from
£10.25
🚗 On A719 1 mile (1.6km) from A77,
on north side of village

TWEEDSMUIR

THE CROOK INN
ML12 6QN
Tel 01899 880272
First licensed in 1604, the
unusual 1930s art deco
interior is the setting to enjoy
shepherd's pie, haggis,
Arbroath haddock fillet or
pan-fried sirloin steak.
🕐 Daily 9–12am; closed 25 Dec, 3rd
week Jan. Bar meals: daily 12–2.30,
5.30–8.30. Restaurant: daily 12–2.30,
7–9
🍷 L from £11, D from £16, Wine
from £9.95 🅂

EATING

EDINBURGH

ATRIUM ❀❀
10 Cambridge Street EH1 2ED
Tel 0131 228 8882
www.atriumrestaurant.co.uk
White bean soup with confit duck garnish characterizes the starters, while roast chicken with chive mash and roasted root vegetables is a typically robust main course; desserts include chocolate orange tart with crème fraîche.
🕐 12–2, 6–10; closed Sun, L Sat except Aug; 25–26 Dec, 1–2 Jan
🍴 L from £13.50, D from £25, Wine from £14 🚭
🚇 From Princes Street turn into Lothian Road, 2nd left and 1st right, by the Traverse Theatre

BALMORAL HOTEL, NUMBER ONE ❀❀
1 Princes Street EH2 2EQ
Tel 0131 557 6727
The stylish modern restaurant specializes in simple dishes created from high-quality local ingredients, both à la carte and a regularly changing menu. Expect a range of meats and seafood with a list of accompaniments such as

PRICES AND SYMBOLS
The restaurants are listed alphabetically. The prices are for a two-course lunch (L) and a three-course à la carte dinner (D). Prices in pubs are for a two-course lunchtime bar meal and a two-course dinner in the restaurant, unless specified otherwise.

For a key to the symbols, ▷ 2.

sautéed spinach or creamed cabbage. For dessert try prune d'Agen parfait with caramel whisky sauce.
🕐 12–2, 7–10; closed L Sat–Sun; 1–7 Jan
🍴 L from £16.95, D from £43, Wine from £20
🚭 No pipes, no cigars
🚇 At the east end of Princes Street, by Waverley Station

BENNETS BAR
8 Leven Street EH3 9LG
Tel 0131 229 5143
Established in 1839, Bennets serves straightforward home-made food at a reasonable

price. Typical menu features steak pie and breaded haddock fillet.
🕐 Mon–Wed 11am–12.30am, Thu–Sat 11am–1am, Sun 12.30–11.30. Bar meals: Mon–Sat 12–2, 5–8.30, Sun 11.30–4
🍴 L from £8, Wine from £9.90

BLUE ❀
Cambridge Street EH1 2ED
Tel 0131 221 1222
www.bluebarcafe.com
This modern brasserie has a menu that is flexible, good value and imaginative. Lunch could be as simple as a bowl of white bean and chorizo soup. A more substantial meal would be carpaccio of beef with Parmesan followed by corn-fed chicken with wild mushroom ragout. Desserts include chocolate tart with caramelized oranges.
🕐 12–3, 6–11; closed Sun, 25–26 Dec
🍴 L from £9.95, D from £13.95, Wine from £13.95
🚇 From Princes Street turn into Lothian Road, 2nd left, 1st right, above the Traverse Theatre

EATING

THE BOW BAR
80 The West Bow EH1 2HH
Tel 0131 226 7667
The huge selection of whiskies in the bar features 140 malts on tap, and eight cask ales. Bar snacks only, and there are no gaming machines or music to distract from good conversation.
🕐 Mon–Sat 12–11.30, Sun 12.30–11; closed 25–26 Dec, 1–2 Jan
🍴 L from £2.80, Wine from £2.60

THE BRIDGE INN
27 Baird Road, Ratho EH28 8RA
Tel 0131 333 1320
Dating back to about 1750 the Bridge Inn is famous for its fleet of restaurant boats and sightseeing launches. Local produce is freshly prepared and served, and top-quality Scottish meat has been a specialty for over 30 years. Typical dishes are shank of Lothian lamb, roast Barbary duck breast, Thai green curry, and salmon and asparagus pie. Principal beers include Bellhaven 80/-.
🕐 Mon–Fri 12–11, Sat 11am–12am, Sun 12.30–11pm; closed 26 Dec, 1–2 Jan. Bar meals: daily 12–9. Restaurant: daily 12–2, 6.30–9
🍴 L from £10, D from £22, Wine from £12.50
🚗 From Newbridge B7030 junction (intersection) follow signs for Ratho

LE CAFÉ ST. HONORÉ ❀
34 NW Thistle Street Lane EH2 1EA
Tel 0131 226 2211
Intimate, chilled-out dining at this bistro. Plenty of fine Scottish produce, majoring on fish, in tempting combinations like warm salad of scallops, monkfish, chorizo and cashew nuts, mixed with some sublime French classics, such as boeuf bourguignon with mash. The wine list is extensive.
🕐 12–10; closed 24–26 Dec, 3 days New Year
🍴 L from £12, D from £20, Wine from £12.45

DORIC TAVERN
15–16 Market Street EH1 1DE
Tel 0131 225 1084
A bustling bistro, pub and wine bar, built in 1710. Classics and innovative modern dishes include fillet of venison, steaks and pastas, and sweet potato pie, with traditional pub snacks like sausage and mash, hamburger and bruschetta.
🕐 12–1am; closed 25–26 Dec, 1 Jan. Bar meals: daily 12–7. Restaurant: daily 12–4, 5–11
🍴 L from £10, D from £15, Wine from £11.50

Iggs restaurant is situated in the heart of the Old Town

DUCK'S AT LE MARCHÉ NOIR ❀
2–4 Eyre Place EH3 5EP
Tel 0131 558 1608
www.ducks.co.uk
Well-established Edinburgh staple offering pleasingly direct cooking in a relaxed setting. Game sausage on a blue cheese mash might come with sweet onions and a red wine reduction, smoked haddock fishcakes with a chilli sauce on a dressed rocket salad. White chocolate mousse and raspberry tart or coffee ricotta and pine nut crêpes are among the desserts.
🕐 12–2.30, 7–10.30; closed L Sat–Mon, 25–26 Dec

HALDANES ❀❀
39A Albany Street EH1 3QY
Tel 0131 556 8407
Refined Scottish country house cooking hardly comes better than this. Scottish fare is prominent in the guise of west coast king scallops, along with Highland venison and Scottish beef. Starters might include a glazed tartlet of Shetland crab and oak-smoked salmon with a main course of saddle of lamb. Coffee is served with homemade truffles and creamy fudge.
🕐 12–2.15, 6–10; closed L Sat–Sun, 25–26 Dec
🍴 D from £30, Wine from £15 🚭

🍴 L from £12, D from £22, Wine from £14.50
🚗 Follow the Mound across Princes Street, George Street, Queen Street to bottom of Dundas Street

LA GARRIGUE ❀❀
31 Jeffrey Street EH1 1DH
Tel 0131 557 3032
www.lagarrigue.co.uk
La Garrigue is named after an area of the Languedoc, and is an authentic showcase for the region's food. Chef Jean Michel Gauffre combines hearty no frills Gallic cooking with presentation that's full of finesse but never fussy. Mains might include boneless leg of rabbit filled with juniper berries and thyme flavoured stuffing or the famous cassoulet, and both wines and cheeses are sourced from the region.
🕐 12–3, 6–10.30; closed 25–26 Dec, 1–2 Jan
🍴 L from £6, D from £27.50, Wine from £12
🚗 Half-way down Royal Mile towards Holyrood Palace, turn left at lights into Jeffrey Street

IGGS ❀
15 Jeffrey Street EH1 1DR
Tel 0131 557 8184
A convivial restaurant where the food is Mediterranean/

EATING

Spanish, with a choice of four dishes at each course. Best Scottish produce stars in starters of Loch Fyne oysters with white wine sabayon, and a main course of poached lobster on truffled leeks with lobster caviar sauce. Other options include roast ballotine of goose or, for vegetarians, Spanish Gypsy vegetable stew. Excellent selection of Spanish wines.

🕐 12–2.30, 6–10.30; closed Sun
🍴 L from £12.50, D from £18.50, Wine from £13.75 🚭
🚇 Just off the Royal Mile

MALMAISON HOTEL & BRASSERIE ✿

One Tower Place, Leith EH6 7DB
Tel 0131 468 5001
www.malmaison.com

A chic hotel priding itself on simple brasserie food and memorable wine selections. Cod brandade with paprika aïoli and cucumber salsa, and braised guinea fowl with Savoy cabbage and girolles with a side order of broccoli and hollandaise.

🕐 12–2, 6–11; closed D 25 Dec
🍴 L from £16, D from £22, Wine from £14.95
🚭 No pipes
🚇 From the city centre follow Leith Docklands signs through 3 sets of traffic lights and left into Tower Street

MELVILLE CASTLE HOTEL ✿

Melville Gate, Gilmerton Road EH18 1AP
Tel 0131 654 0088
www.melvillecastle.com

At this candle-lit brasserie restaurant local produce dominates the menu, with favourites such as seasonal game casserole, or perhaps roast halibut with bacon and cabbage, followed by sticky toffee pudding.

🕐 12–2.30, 7–9.30
🍴 L from £13, D from £24, Wine from £16.95
🚇 2 minutes from city bypass (A720) via Sheriffhall roundabout

NORTON HOUSE ✿✿✿

Ingliston EH28 8LX
Tel 0131 333 1275
www.handpicked.co.uk/nortonhouse

Choose from lighter meals at the brasserie or a real treat in the stylish Usher's Restaurant, where top-quality food is simply and brilliantly prepared. You might start with lobster ravioli, followed by fillet of Buccleuch beef, and round off with rosewater crème brûlée and poached pear in ginger wine.

🕐 Dinner only, 7–9.30; closed Sun–Mon, 1 Jan
🍴 D from £32, Wine from £17 🚭

Haldanes displays its heritage with a dash of tartan furnishings

OFF THE WALL RESTAURANT ✿✿✿

105 High Street, Royal Mile EH1 1SG
Tel 0131 558 1497
www.off-the-wall.co.uk

An uncomplicated approach to cuisine, with no fussiness and unnecessary flourishes. Expect modern cooking: beef fillet, perhaps, with red cabbage, port sauce and buttery truffle mash; or venison with celeriac and a chocolate sauce.

🕐 Jun–end Sep 12–2.30, 6–10; Oct–end May 7–10; closed Sun, 25–26 Dec, 1–2 Jan
🍴 L from £16.50, D from £35, Wine from £13.95
🚇 On Royal Mile near John Knox House. Entrance via stairway next to Baillie Fyfes Close

RESTAURANT MARTIN WISHART ✿✿✿✿

54 The Shore, Leith EH6 6RA
Tel 0131 553 3557
www.martin-wishart.co.uk

At this tiny, minimalist restaurant the short menus change daily with lunch a more low-key affair than dinner. Your evening meal might begin with duck consommé or ravioli of lobster, followed by braised shin of beef with celeriac purée and glazed vegetables or succulent roast squab pigeon. In season, warm apricot tart with crème anglaise is hard to beat. The wine list includes a selection by the glass.

🕐 12–2, 7–10; closed Sun, Mon, L Sat, 25 Dec, bank holidays
🍴 L from £18.50, D from £45, Wine from £20 🚭

THE RESTAURANT AT THE BONHAM ✿✿

35 Drumsheugh Gardens EH3 7RN
Tel 0131 623 9319
www.thebonham.com

Stylish dining is on offer at this fashionable boutique hotel. Main courses are simple contemporary dishes with well-matched flavours (Scottish beef with seared foie gras and porcini sauce, or seared polenta cake with curried mushroom and tomato). Desserts like orange blossom pannacotta with lavender tuile are (almost) too pretty to eat.

🕐 12–3, 6.30–10
🍴 L from £13.50, D from £26, Wine from £12
🚇 West end of Princes Street

EATING

SPECIAL

RHUBARB, THE RESTAURANT AT PRESTONFIELD ❀❀❀

Prestonfield, Priestfield Road EH16 5UT

Tel 0131 225 7800

www.prestonfield.com

Rhubarb makes a frequent appearance at this theatrical restaurant. A meal here might start with shank of sea bass on citrus-braised endive, followed by roast saddle of rabbit, and perhaps a rhubarb and gingerbread crème brûlée.

12–3, 6–11

L from £14.95, D from £28, Wine from £19

Leave the city centre on Nicholson Street, join Dalkeith Road. At traffic lights turn left into Priestfield Road, hotel is on the left.

SANTINI ❀❀

8 Conference Square EH3 8AN

Tel 0131 221 7788

Santini's first restaurant in the UK outside London is situated at Edinburgh's city spa and the concept includes the Bistro, a relaxed all-day option serving pizza, pasta and lighter dishes. Dishes are authentic Italian in the main restaurant such as creamy porcini mushroom risotto.

12–2.30, 6.30–10.30; closed Sun, L Sat, New Year

L from £23, D from £25, Wine from £16

No pipes or cigars

THE SHERATON GRAND HOTEL AND SPA ❀❀❀

1 Festival Square EH3 9SR

Tel 0131 221 6422

www.sheraton.com/grandedinburgh

Here there's a clear focus on traditional French cuisine with some Scottish overtones. Choose from a fairly extensive menu, which includes appetizers of roasted scallops with leek fondue, potato parmentière and caviar beurre blanc; and mains of tuna loin, cassoulet and fennel. Wines are available by the glass.

12–2, 7–10; closed Sun–Mon, L Sat

L from £21, D from £30.50, Wine from £17

Off Lothian Road. Entrance to hotel behind Standard Life building

STAC POLLY ❀

8–10 Grindlay Street EH3 9AS

Tel 0131 229 5405

www.stacpolly.co.uk

Modern Scottish cuisine dominates the menu—for example, baked supreme of Scottish salmon served with braised leeks, bacon dumplings and a lemon butter sauce, or sliced crown of Scottish lamb with Parma ham, tomato farci and balsamic and red wine reduction. Appealing desserts

The Witchery by the Castle is popular with locals and tourists

and an interesting wine list. A second restaurant is at 29–33 Dublin Street.

12–2, 6–11; closed L Sat–Sun

L from £10, D from £25.85, Wine from £17.95

No pipes, no cigars

Beneath the castle near Lyceum Theatre

THE STARBANK INN

64 Laverockbank Road EH5 3BZ

Tel 0131 552 4141

The bar menu typically offers roast lamb with mint sauce, poached salmon, a vegetarian dish of the day, and chicken with tarragon cream sauce. Principal beers include Bellhaven 80/- and Timothy Taylor Landlord.

SPECIAL

TOWER RESTAURANT & TERRACE ❀

Museum of Scotland, Chambers Street EH1 1JF

Tel 0131 225 3003

www.tower-restaurant.com

Chic and elegant, the Tower aims for a classic and contemporary take on quality Scottish ingredients. The menu is an interesting mix: from oysters to prawn cocktail to sushi, and from seared yellowfin tuna to fish and chips (french fries), a top recommendation is the fillet of Angus beef.

12–11; closed 25–26 Dec

L from £9.95, D from £22, Wine from £15

Museum of Scotland at corner of George IV Bridge and Chambers Street

Mon–Wed 11–11, Thu–Sat 11–12am, Sun 12.30–11 (food served weekends 12–9.30). Bar meals: daily 12–2.30, 6–9.30. Restaurant: daily 12–2.30, 6–9.30

L from £8, D from £10, Wine from £8

THE WITCHERY BY THE CASTLE ❀

Castlehill, Royal Mile EH1 2NF

Tel 0131 225 5613

www.thewitchery.com

Heavy with theatrical, Gothic charm, the entire restaurant is candlelit. The menu provides a contemporary spin on modern classics: Typically, game, fish and shellfish feature highly, and there is an extensive global wine list.

12–4, 5–11.30; closed 25–26 Dec

L from £9.95, D from £25, Wine from £15.95

At the gates of Edinburgh Castle at the top of the Royal Mile

CENTRAL SCOTLAND

ABERFELDY

FARLEYER RESTAURANT WITH ROOMS ❀

Farleyer House PH15 2JE
Tel 01887 820332
www.farleyer.com

Sample bold modern French cuisine. Rosemary smoked pork cutlet with turnip and sage sponge and apple mash, followed by passionfruit parfait, are typical of the skilful menu.

🕐 12–3, 6–9.30; closed Mon in winter, and 2 weeks Feb

🍴 L from £13, D from £18, Wine from £14 🚭

AUCHTERARDER

ANDREW FAIRLIE AT GLENEAGLES ❀❀❀❀

PH3 1NF
Tel 01764 694267
www.gleneagles.com

Located in Gleneagles (▷ 277), the Andrew Fairlie restaurant is a dinner-only affair, with an element of theatre throughout the classical French menu. Creamy veal sweetbreads come with perfect pink slices of kidney and a fondant potato, or try assiette of apples (millefeuille,

charlotte and parfait). The wine list offers a lengthy list by the glass. Advance booking recommended. No children under 12.

🕐 Dinner only, 7–10; closed Sun, 3 weeks Jan

🍴 D from £55 🚭

🚗 Just off A9, well signposted

STRATHEARN AT GLENEAGLES ❀❀

PH3 1NF
Tel 01764 694270

The dining's on a grand scale at this legendary resort hotel (▷ 277). The Strathearn is the traditional option, offering an extensive classic menu. The wine list features the odd £2,000 gem. Expect simple, classic dishes: a terrine of goose liver infused with Sauternes wine perhaps, or braised oxtails with sauce bourguignon.

🕐 12.30–2.30, 7–10; closed L Mon–Sat

🍴 L from £35, D from £47

🚭 No pipes

🚗 Just off A9, well signposted

CELLAR RESTAURANT ❀❀❀

24 East Green KY10 3AA
Tel 01333 310378

At this renowned seafood restaurant there is an à la carte menu, and a well-priced set lunch. Fresh local seafood includes crayfish bisque gratin, and fillet of roast cod with a pesto crust, pine nuts and bacon. No children under 8.

🕐 12.30–1, 7–9.30; closed Mon in winter, L Mon, Tue, Christmas

🍴 L from £16.50, D from £32.50, Wine from £14.50 🚭

EATING

BALQUHIDDER

MONACHYLE MHOR ❀ ❀
FK19 8PQ
Tel 01877 384622
www.monachylemhor.com
Tom Lewis provides refreshingly honest cooking. Expect modern Scottish cooking with a French influence and some Asian touches. Begin with crostini of capered polenta with wilted red chard, curried egg and parsley perhaps, then move on to west coast scallops with smoked haddock and wild rice kedgeree. No children under 12.
🕐 12–1.45, 7–8.45; closed 4 Jan–14 Feb
🍴 L from £20, D from £38, Wine from £17.50 ⓢ
🚗 On A84, 11 miles (17.7km) north of Callander turn right at Kingshouse Hotel. Continue for 6 miles (9.7km)

BRIDGEND OF LINTRATHEN

LOCHSIDE LODGE AND ROUNDHOUSE RESTAURANT ❀ ❀
DD8 5JJ
Tel 01575 560340
www.lochsidelodge.com
On offer here is accomplished modern British and European cuisine—tuck into a dish of cod layered with potato scale, and then indulge in chocolate fondant pudding for dessert, served with Jaffa cake ice cream, or perhaps a passion fruit iced parfait. Hard to find, so phone ahead for directions.
🕐 12–2, 6.30–9; closed D Sun, Mon, 1–25 Jan
🍴 L from £12, D from £29.50, Wine from £13.95 ⓢ

CALLANDER

ROMAN CAMP COUNTRY HOUSE ❀ ❀ ❀
FK17 8BG
Tel 01877 330003
www.roman-camp-hotel.co.uk
Highly accomplished cooking draws on excellent Scottish produce. The four-course dinner menu changes daily, and the shorter lunch menu offers good value.

🕐 12.30–2, 7–8.30
🍴 L from £16, D from £39, Wine from £17.50
🚗 Turn left at east end of Callander High Street, go down a 274m (300 yards) driveway into the hotel grounds

CRIEFF

THE BANK RESTAURANT ❀
32 High Street PH7 3BS
Tel 01764 656575
Food is simple and fresh at this former bank, and demonstrates good technical skills—roasted courgette (zucchini), garlic and shallot risotto; noisette of lamb with dauphinoise potato and braised red cabbage; and a

Roman Camp Country House is in beautiful grounds

decent crème brûlée.
🕐 12–1.30, 7–9.30; closed Sun–Mon, 24–26 Dec, 2 weeks mid-Jan
🍴 L from £13, D from £20, Wine from £13.50

CUPAR

OSTLERS CLOSE RESTAURANT ❀ ❀
Bonnygate KY15 4BU
Tel 01334 655574
www.ostlersclose.co.uk
The modern Scottish menu changes almost daily and reflects a classical background with Mediterranean influences. Choose from a starter of pot roast breast of wood pigeon with a cassoulet of haricot beans and pancetta, or a main course of a selection of local

seafood served with steamed farm seakale on a langoustine butter sauce. No children under 6 in the evening.
🕐 12.15–1.30, 7–9.30; closed Sun, Mon, L Tue–Fri, 25–26 Dec, 1–2 Jan, 2 weeks Oct
🍴 L from £15, D from £20, Wine from £14.50
ⓢ
🚗 In small lane off main street, A91

DRYMEN

CLACHAN INN
2 Main Street G63 0BG
Tel 01360 660824
This is believed to be the oldest licensed pub in Scotland. Try staples such as filled baked potatoes, salads, fresh haddock in breadcrumbs and vegetable lasagne. Beers include Caledonian Deuchars IPA and Belhaven Best.
🕐 Mon–Sat 11–12am, Sun 12.30–12. Bar meals: 12–4, 6–10. Restaurant: 12–4, 6–10; closed 25 Dec, 1 Jan
🍴 L from £9, D from £20, Wine from £11.50

DUNFERMLINE

HIDEAWAY LODGE AND RESTAURANT
Kingseat Road, Halbeath KY12 0UB
Tel 01383 725474
The expansive menu makes good use of local produce—a typical meal might start with grilled goats' cheese salad or Oban mussels, then move on to chargrilled tuna steak or fillet of venison, and finish with steamed ginger pudding.
🕐 Mon–Sat 12–3, 5–11, Sun 12–9. Bar meals: 12–2, 5–9.30. Restaurant: 12–2, 5–9.30
🍴 L from £7.95, D from £15, Wine from £11.25

KEAVIL HOUSE ❀
Crossford KY12 8QW
Tel 01383 736258
www.keavilhouse.co.uk
Artistic presentation is an important part of the menu, with international cooking offering temptations such as smoked haddock cheesecake wrapped in nori, and venison

EATING

with turnip dauphinoise and thyme mash.

🕐 12–2, 7–9.30
🍴 L from £9, D from £25, Wine from £14.95 🚭
🚗 2 miles (3km) west of Dunfermline on A994

TOWN HOUSE RESTAURANT ❀

48 Eastport KY12 7JB
Tel 01383 432382
www.townhouserestaurant.co.uk
The cuisine is Scottish with a hint of European—try the hot smoked duck breast with kumquat gravy, followed by mango pannacotta.

🕐 12–6, 6–10; closed 25 Dec, 1 Jan
🍴 L from £9.95, D from £19.95, Wine from £13.95
🚭 Non-smoking area
🚗 200m (220 yards) from Carnegie Hall

ELIE

SANGSTERS ❀❀

51 High Street KY9 1BZ
A husband-and-wife team run this rising star of a restaurant. High-quality local produce makes the menu, from halibut with minted pea purée and chorizo to pan-seared venison with a red wine and thyme sauce. No children under 12.

🕐 12.30–1.30, 7–9.30; closed L Tue and Sat, D Sun, Mon; 25–26 Dec, 1–2 Jan, 2 weeks mid-Feb and Oct
🍴 L from £15.75, D from £30, Wine from £19 🚭

GLAMIS

CASTLETON HOUSE ❀❀❀

Castleton of Eassie DD8 1SJ
Tel 01307 840340
www.castletonglamis.co.uk
The menu draws on influences from all over the world, cooked with impressive flair—try saltimbocca of corn-fed chicken with roasted salsify, and perhaps the banana tart tatin.

🕐 12–2, 7–9
🍴 L from £30, D from £35, Wine from £14
🚗 On A94 midway between Forfar and Cupar Angus, 3 miles (4.8km) west of Glamis

GLENDEVON

TORMAUKIN HOTEL

FK14 7JY
Tel 01259 781252
At this 18th-century inn, bar lunches and suppers cover a range of snacks, children's choices and daily blackboard specials. Dishes could include fillet steak with sauté mushrooms and onions, or pork and apple sausages with lamb loin. On the main menu expect the likes of pan-seared fillet of Scottish salmon on mash, topped with spring onion crackling. Round off with desserts such as iced Drambuie soufflé with marmalade sauce. Principal

The Castleton in Glamis occupies a fine Victorian house

beers include Harviestoun Brooker's Bitter & Twisted.

🕐 Mon–Sat 11–11, Sun 12–11; closed 25 Dec. Bar meals: daily 12–2.15, 5.30–9.30. Restaurant: D only, daily 6.30–9.30
🍴 L from £14.50, D from £18, Wine from £12.95
🚗 On A823 between M90 and A9

GLENISLA

GLENISLA HOTEL

PH11 8PH
Tel 01575 582223
The Glenisla specializes in hunting and fishing parties in season. Inveralmond Ales and robust meals are served—expect excellent fish and game, and local hill-farmed lamb. Aberdeen Angus steaks are

SPECIAL IN ELIE

THE SHIP INN

The Toft KY9 1DT
Tel 01333 330246
At this lively free house, fresh fish takes pride of place on the specials board to supplement offerings of filled rolls (smoked salmon, prawns and cream cheese perhaps), bangers and mash in 80/- beer gravy or prime Scottish beef steaks, served plain or sauced with haggis and whisky. Alternatively, in summer, try a seafood salad that makes best use of the day's catch. There are children's choices and summer barbecues in the garden.

🕐 Mon–Sat 11–11, Sun 12.30–11; closed 25 Dec. Bar meals: daily 12–2, 6–9. Restaurant: daily 12–2, 6–9
🍴 L from £14.50, D from £36.50, Wine from £11.80
🚗 Follow A915 and A917 to Elie. Follow signs from High Street to Watersport Centre to the Toft

a permanent feature, and puddings are generous.

🕐 Mon–Fri 11–11, Sat 11–1am, Sun 11–12am. Bar meals: 12–2.30, 6–9. Restaurant: 12–2.30, 6–9.30; closed 25–26 Dec
🍴 L from £16, D from £18, Wine from £9.95
🚗 On B954

INVERKEILOR

GORDON'S RESTAURANT ❀❀

Main Street DD11 5RN
Tel 01241 830364
The menu is relatively traditional, although there are plenty of imaginative touches: A cappuccino of smoked tomato and roast red pepper soup is served with Parmesan ice cream, while Angus beef is accompanied by mushroom and smoked bacon ravioli and the intriguing 'kiln dried cherry polenta'.

🕐 12–1.45, 7–9; closed Mon, L Sat and Tue, D Sun, first 2 weeks Jan
🍴 L from £25, D from £37, Wine from £11.95 🚭
🚗 Just off A92, follow Inverkeilor signs

EATING

KINNESSWOOD

LOMOND COUNTRY INN
Main Street KY13 9HN
Tel 01592 840253
The restaurant offers
sophisticated fare, such as
supreme of guinea fowl on
creamed mash with Calvados
sauce, or chicken with a leek
and Stilton sauce.
🕐 Mon–Thu 11–11, Fri–Sat 11–12.45,
Sun 12.30–11. Bar meals: 12.30–2, 6–9.
Restaurant: 12–2.30, 6–9.30; closed 25
Dec
🍽 L from £12, D from £20, Wine from
£10.90
🚗 From M90, exit 5, follow signs for
Glenrothes then Scotlandwell,
Kinnesswood is next village

KIRKCALDY

THE OLD RECTORY INN
West Quality Street, Dysart KY1 2TE
Tel 01592 651211
In the restaurant at this old inn
a seemingly endless choice is
offered. From the carte come
starters like Manhattan clam
chowder and roast duck with
three fruits. The chef might
recommend curried egg
Madras, and tiger prawns au
Pernod, while from the lunch
menu you can try haggis
Drambuie, venison and
mushroom casserole.
🕐 Mon–Sat 12–3, 7–12am, Sun
12.30–3.30; closed 1 week Jan, 2 weeks
mid-Oct, 1 week early Jul. Bar meals
and Restaurant: Tue–Sat 12–2, 7–9.30,
Sun 12.30–2.30.
🍽 L from £12, D from £24, Wine from
£11.55
🚗 From Edinburgh take A92 to
Kirkcaldy, then A907/A955 to Dysart.
Turn right at National Trust sign

PERTH

HUNTINGTOWER HOTEL ❀
Crieff Road PH1 3JT
Tel 01738 583771
www.huntingtowerhotel.co.uk
The restaurant of this stately
hotel is a great place for
formal dining. Two menus
provide choice and value, with
simpler specials and a more
hearty contemporary menu
including Scottish seafood and
game. Thai-spiced mussel and

sweet potato broth, and roast
beef with foie gras and herb
rösti are just two selections.
🕐 Dinner only, 6–9.30
🍽 D from £21.95, Wine from £13.95
🚭
🚗 10 minutes from Perth on A85,
towards Crieff

LET'S EAT ❀❀
77–79 Kinnoull Street PH1 5EZ
Tel 01738 643377
www.letseatperth.co.uk
This restaurant has built up a
good reputation for its light,
modern bistro food. Dishes
include fillet of halibut with
Skye langoustines, Glamis sea
kale, asparagus and a prawn
essence, and Valrhona

*The menu at The Peat Inn
reflects the best of local produce*

chocolate tart with a white
chocolate sorbet. Advance
reservations recommended.
🕐 12–2, 6.30–9.45; closed Sun–Mon,
2 weeks Jan, 2 weeks Jul
🍽 L from £13, D from £21
🚗 On corner of Kinnoull Street and
Atholl Street, close to North Inch

63 TAY STREET ❀❀
63 Tay Street PH2 8NN
Tel 01738 441451
Good food using quality
ingredients is well cooked,
and the simpler lunchtime
menu is affordably inspiring.
The three-course menu with
prices fixed per course might
include herb risotto with rocket
(arugula) salad and chive oil, or
pan-fried halibut fillet with stir-

SPECIAL IN PEAT INN

THE PEAT INN ❀❀❀
Peat Inn KY15 5LH
Tel 01334 840206
www.thepeatinn.co.uk
The Francophile owners have
developed a robust Gallic
menu. From a tasting menu,
a fixed-price menu and a
short carte select the likes of
pan-fried venison liver served
with kidneys, poached quails'
eggs and a bitter orange
sauce, and a traditional
cassoulet filled with duck,
pork, sausage and beans.
🕐 12.30–1, 7–9.30; closed Sun–Mon,
25 Dec, 1 Jan
🍽 L from £22, D from £32, Wine
from £18 🚭
🚗 At junction (intersection) of
B940/B941, 6 miles (9.7km) southwest of St. Andrews

fried greens and potato rösti.
The wine list is notable.
🕐 12–2, 6.30–9; closed Sun–Mon, 1st
2 weeks Jan, last week Jun, 1st week Jul
🍽 L from £14.45, D from £26.95, Wine
from £14 🚭
🚗 On the Tay River in Perth centre

PITLOCHRY

MOULIN HOTEL
11–13 Kirkmichael Road, Moulin PH16
5EW
Tel 01796 472196
This hotel produces its own
Braveheart beer, which
appears on the food menu
too, giving local venison dishes
that extra flavour.
🕐 Sun–Thu 12–11, Fri–Sat 12–11.45.
Bar meals: 12–9.30. Restaurant: D only,
6–9
🍽 L from £10, D from £19.95, Wine
from £9.50
🚗 From A924 at Pitlochry take A923

ST. ANDREWS

THE INN AT LATHONES ❀❀
Largoward KY9 1JE
Tel 01334 840494
www.theinn.co.uk
Select from several menus—
including an eight-course
gastronome's option—all
offering modern Scottish and
European cuisine: a tartare of

EATING

ROAD HOLE GRILL ❀ ❀ ❀

Old Course Hotel KY16 9SP
Tel 01334 474371
www.oldcoursehotel.co.uk

Enjoy classic fine dining in sumptuous surroundings. The menu is marked out by clear flavours and quality Scottish produce—such as Highland venison with wild mushroom fricasée—and the wine list has 235 choices. There's a smart dress code.

🕐 Dinner only, 7–10; closed 24–28 Dec
🍽 D from £40, Wine from £33 🅂

---

salmon starter; rib-eye of mature Glenfarg Angus beef with a Lagavulin, smoked bacon and wild mushroom sauce; with a simple red berry soup to finish.

🕐 12–2.30, 6–9.30; closed Christmas, 2 weeks Jan
🍽 L from £12.50, D from £25, Wine from £12.50 🅂
🚗 5 miles (8km) south of St. Andrews on A915. In 0.5 mile (800m) before Largoward on left just after hidden dip

MACDONALD RUSACKS HOTEL ❀ ❀

Pilmour Links KY16 9JQ
Tel 0870 400 8128
www.macdonaldhotels.co.uk

The menu changes daily, with a mixture of styles from traditional British, through French, Mediterranean, and a hint of Thai. Grills and main courses include pork loin steak with braised cabbage, cocotte potatoes and tarragon and Puy lentil jus.

🕐 12–2.30, 7–9.30; closed L Mon–Sat
🍽 L from £12.95, D from £24.95, Wine from £12.95 🅂
🚗 From M90 exit 8 take A91 to St. Andrews. Hotel on left on entering the town

SANDS BAR AND RESTAURANT ❀

The Old Course Hotel KY16 9SP
Tel 01334 474371/468228
www.oldcoursehotel.co.uk

This stylish brasserie offers a crisp, upbeat menu. Start your

---

meal with home-cured bresaola and roasted figs, perhaps followed by a classic salad and cinnamon pannacotta. Dishes are thoughtfully marked out for healthy eating.

🕐 12–6, 6–10
🍽 L from £21, D from £35, Wine from £20 🅂

ST. FILLANS

THE FOUR SEASONS ❀ ❀

Loch Earn PH6 2NF
Tel 01764 685333
www.thefourseasonshotel.co.uk

Many dishes have a modern edge. Try a trio of hill lamb cutlets with pink grapefruit salsa and mint sabayon, or

St Andrews' The Inn at Lathones boasts an intimate restaurant

pan-seared guinea fowl with an unusual mango and coriander (cilantro) salsa.

🕐 12–2.30, 6–9.30; closed Jan, Feb
🍽 L from £15, D from £30, Wine from £13.95 🅂
🚗 From Perth take A85 west through Crieff and Comrie. Hotel at west end of village

STIRLING

STIRLING HIGHLAND ❀

Spittal Street FK8 1DU
Tel 01786 272727
www.paramount-hotels.co.uk

At the Scholars Restaurant and adjoining Headmaster's Study Bar dishes include roasted spring chicken supreme with baby pak choi in a sweet and sour sauce, and haunch of

---

SEAFOOD RESTAURANT ❀ ❀ ❀

The Scores KY16 9AS
Tel 01334 479475
www.theseafoodrestaurant.com

Chosen as the AA's Restaurant of the Year for Scotland 2005, this glass-walled restaurant offers a creative blend of British and European cuisine, and while there's an emphasis on seafood, other dishes such as duck with roast parsnip and fondant potato are also available.

🕐 12–2.30, 6.30–10; closed 25–26 Dec, 1 Jan
🍽 L from £20, D from £40, Wine from £19

---

venison set on cheese gnocchi, with black pepper glaze and red onion marmalade.

🕐 12.30–2, 7–9.30; closed L Sat
🍽 L from £10.95, D from £24.50, Wine from £16 🅂
🚗 On road leading to Stirling Castle, follow Castle signs

THE SEAFOOD RESTAURANT ❀ ❀

16 West End KY10 2BX
Tel 01333 730327
www.theseafoodrestaurant.com

The bar is in a 400-year-old fisherman's dwelling (principal beers include Bellhaven Best), and seafood specialties include seared scallops with mango and sweet chilli salsa, grilled turbot with red onion marmalade and mustard sauce, and carpaccio of albacore tuna with hoi sin dressing.

🕐 12–2.30, 6–9.30; closed Mon, D Sun, 25–26 Dec, 1–2 Jan
🍽 L from £29, D from £35, Wine from £19 🅂
🚗 Take A595 from St. Andrews to Anstruther, then west on A917 through Pittenweem. At St. Monans harbour turn right

EATING

GLASGOW

ARISAIG RESTAURANT AND BAR ✹

Merchant City, 24 Candleriggs G1 1LD
Tel 0141 552 4251
www.arisaigrestaurant.com
The cooking is authentic Scottish and specializes in resurrecting traditional ingredients such as kale, nettles and red seaweed. No children under 14.

🕐 12–3, 5–12am; closed L Mon–Thu, 26 Dec, 1 Jan
🍽 L from £13, D from £25, Wine from £15 ⊗

ÉTAIN ✹✹

Princes Square G1 3JX
Tel 0141 225 5630
The AA's Restaurant of the Year for 2006, the British and French contemporary menu includes grilled rib of beef with bacon and wild mushrooms. Try the six-course epicurean tasting menu.

🕐 12–2.30, 7–11; closed L Sat, D Sun, 25 Dec and 1 Jan
🍽 L from £21, D from £32, Wine from £18 ⊗

PRICES AND SYMBOLS

The restaurants are listed alphabetically. The prices are for a two-course lunch (L) and a three-course à la carte dinner (D). Prices in pubs are for a two-course lunchtime bar meal and a two-course dinner in the restaurant, unless specified otherwise.

For a key to the symbols, ▷ 2.

GAMBA ✹✹

225a West George Street G2 2ND
Tel 0141 572 0899
www.gamba.co.uk
The menu has a Mediterranean feel: Try crisp fried organic salmon with sweet Thai sauce, prawns and black beans. No children under 14.

🕐 12–2.30, 5–10.30; closed Sun, 25–26 Dec, 1–2 Jan, bank holidays
🍽 L from £15.95, D from £26, Wine from £14.95.
⊗ No pipes, no cigars
🚇 Near Blythswood Square

SPECIAL

THE BUTTERY ✹✹

652 Argyle Street G3 8UF
Tel 0141 221 8188
Chef Willie Dean cooks modern, seasonal Scottish fare, including a roasted quail starter, confit shank of Perthshire lamb, and a warm marbled chocolate and sour cream tart with candied kumquat ice cream.

🕐 12–2, 7–10; closed L Sat–Mon, 25–26 Dec, 1–2 Jan
🍽 L from £16, D from £38, Wine from £20 ⊗
🚇 From St. Vincent Street in the city centre take first left on to Elderslie Street, at roundabout go left on to Argyle Street; restaurant is 600m (600 yards) on left

LANGS ✹✹

2 Port Dundas Place G2 3LD
Tel 0141 333 1500
An unpretentious mixture of Mediterranean and French cuisine. Seafood fishcake with pesto might be followed by breast of chicken stuffed with black pudding, served with a

port jus and a spring onion potato mash.
🔵 D only 5–10
🍷 D from £15.50, Wine from £12.95
🚭

LUX ❀ ❀
1051 Great Western Road G12 0XP
Tel 0141 576 7576
www.lux-stazione.co.uk
Lux serves Scottish produce cooked by adventurous chef/proprietor, Stephen Johnson, such as pan-fried fillet of Scottish beef with red Thai paste and bean sprouts with a coriander (cilantro) sour cream. No children under 12.
🔵 D only from 6; closed Sun, 25–26 Dec, 1–2 Jan
🍷 D from £35.50, Wine from £16.50
🚭 No pipes, no cigars
🚗 At the traffic lights signed Gartnavel Hospital

MALMAISON ❀
278 West George Street G2 4LL
Tel 0141 572 1001
www.malmaison.com
Expect accomplished French brasserie cuisine, such as venison with juniper juice and Puy lentils. Wines available by the glass. (For hotel, ▷ 283.)
🔵 12–2.30, 5.30–10.30
🍷 L from £10.95, D from £13.95, Wine from £15.95
🚗 From George Square take Vincent Street to Pitt Street. Hotel on corner of this and West George Street

PAPINGO RESTAURANT ❀
104 Bath Street G2 2EN
Tel 0141 332 6678
www.papingo.co.uk
A reasonably priced menu of modern Scottish food with a fusion influence provides variations on familiar dishes such as pan-fried Barbary duck breast with apricots, bacon and port sauce.
🔵 12–2.30, 5–10.30; closed L Sun, 25–26 Dec, 1–2 Jan, bank holiday Mon
🍷 L from £7.95, D from £15, Wine from £14.95
🚭 No pipes
🚗 City centre at junction (intersection) of Bath Street and Hope Street

QUIGLEY'S ❀
158 Bath Street G2 4TB
Tel 0141 331 4060
www.quigleysglasgow.com
Local chef John Quigley's cooking style is a mix of East, West, the Med and the traditional, in confit chicken and ham hock terrine, roast monkfish with saffron mussels, and Armagnac tart with mascarpone.
🔵 D only 5–10.45; closed Sun, 25 Dec, 1 Jan
🍷 D from £19.50, Wine from £16.50
🚗 5 miles (8km) from M8, Charing Cross exit, southbound

Rococo is a chic restaurant with works by local artists

SHISH MAHAL ❀
60–68 Park Road G4 9JF
Tel 0141 339 8256
www.shishmahal.co.uk
Fast and friendly restaurant cooking meals in the classic Asian tradition: lamb favourites like Kashmiri, Rogan Josh and Bhoona; baltis in cast iron bowls; and Tarka Daal. Advance reservations essential.
🔵 12–2, 5–11; closed L Sun
🍷 L from £5.50, D from £15.95, Wine from £14.95
🚗 Exit 8 at Charing Cross junction (intersection) and proceed down Woodland Road

ROCOCO ❀ ❀
202 West George Street G2 2NR
Tel 0141 221 5004
www.rococoglasgow.com
Cuisine is modern Scottish with French and rustic Italian. Dishes include honey-roasted Barbary duck with cauliflower cream, salardaise potatoes, glazed shallots and sherry juslie.
🔵 12–3, 5–10; closed Sun, 1 Jan
🍷 L from £14, D from £36.50, Wine from £23
🚭 No pipes
🚗 City centre

UBIQUITOUS CHIP ❀ ❀
12 Ashton Lane G12 8SJ
Tel 0141 334 5007
www.ubiquitouschip.co.uk
This city institution applies a modern slant to Scottish cuisine. Dishes include vegetarian haggis with neeps and tatties, and free-range Perthshire pork with truffle oil.
🔵 12–2.30, 5.30–11; closed 25 Dec, 1 Jan
🍷 L from £21.80, D from £37.80, Wine from £14.95
🚗 In the West End of Glasgow off Byres Road. By Hillhead underground station

STRAVAIGIN ❀ ❀
30 Gibson Street G12 8NX
Tel 0141 334 2665
www.stravaigin.com
On the exotic menu a demitasse of spiced consommé is a possible taster, and achiote marinated breast of Gressingham duck with orange, coriander (cilantro) and polenta stack, refried beans and Poncho Caballero gravy a main course. Puddings regularly feature chocolate.
🔵 12–2.30, 5–11; closed Mon, L Tue–Thu, 25–26 Dec, 1 Jan
🍷 L from £11.95, D from £13.95, Wine from £13.25 🚭
🚗 Next to Glasgow University. 183m (200 yards) from Kelvinbridge underground

EATING

HIGHLANDS AND ISLANDS

EATING

ABERDEEN

MARYCULTER HOUSE ❀
South Deeside Road, Maryculter
AB12 5GB
Tel 01224 732124
www.maryculterhousehotel.com
Enjoy a candle-lit dinner with
fillet of Aberdeen Angus with
potato and celeriac purée, rack
of lamb on fried potatoes with
wild mushroom ragout, and
venison with pommes
dauphinoise, red cabbage
and Madeira jus. No children
under 4.
🕐 D only, 7–9.30; closed Sun
🍽 D from £15, Wine from £15.35 🚭
🚗 From Aberdeen take B9077 (South
Deeside Road) for 8 miles (12.9km)

NORWOOD HALL ❀
Garthdee Road, Cults AB15 9FX
Tel 01224 868951
www.norwood-hall.co.uk
Dishes are classic with the odd
Scottish twist: Breast of
pheasant is stuffed with
haggis, while Grampian
chicken is accompanied by
black pudding mousse and a
whisky sauce.
🕐 12–2, 6.30–9.30

🍽 L from £13.75, D from £18.50, Wine
from £17.50 🚭
🚗 From the south, leave the A90 at 1st
roundabout, cross bridge and turn left
at roundabout into Garthdee Road;
continue for 1.5 miles (2.4km)

SILVER DARLING ❀
Pocra Quay, North Pier AB11 5DQ
Tel 01224 576229
French cuisine includes locally
landed seafood—try turbot,
clams and mussels in a veal
jus, with a starter of seared
scallops served with Parmesan
and balsamic syrup.

🕐 12–2, 6.30–9.30; closed L Sat, Sun,
Christmas, New Year
🍽 L from £28, D from £36, Wine from
£16.50 🚭

ACHILTIBUIE

THE SUMMER ISLES HOTEL
❀ ❀
by Ullapool IV26 2YG
Tel 01854 622282
www.summerisleshotel.co.uk
The style is broadly European,
the daily changing five-course
menu could include goats'
cheese crouton on black olive
tapenade, and langoustine and
spiny lobsters with hollandaise
sauce. Lighter lunches are
served in the bar. No children
under 8.
🕐 12.30–2, D at 8; closed mid-
Oct–Easter
🍽 L from £10, D from £49, Wine from
£12 🚭
🚗 10 miles (16km) north of Ullapool.
Turn left off A835 on to single-track
road. 15 miles (24km) to Achiltibuie.
Hotel 91m (100 yards) after post office
on left

APPLECROSS INN

Shore Street IV54 8LR
Tel 01520 744262

Favourites include king scallops in garlic butter with crispy bacon on rice, and fresh monkfish and squat lobster in a rich prawn sauce on home-made tagliatelle. Or try venison casserole with braised red cabbage on apple and wholegrain mustard mash, and raspberry cranachan or cardamom pannacotta.

🕐 Mon–Sat 11–11, Sun 12.30–11; closed 25 Dec, 1 Jan. Bar meals: daily 12–9. Restaurant: D only, daily 6–9
🍴 L from £11, D from £15, Wine from £11.25 🚭
🚗 From Lochcarron to Kishorn, then left on to unclassifed road to Applecross

BOAT OF GARTEN

BOAT HOTEL ❀❀

Deshar Road PH24 3BH
Tel 01479 831258
www.boathotel.co.uk

Medallions of halibut, slices of veal and chargrilled lamb cutlets might feature as mains, with desserts like warm orange and toffee pudding on an apricot brandy sabayon. No children under 12.

🕐 D only, 7–9.30; closed 3 weeks Jan
🍴 D from £32.50, Wine from £16.50 🚭
🚗 Turn off A9 north of Aviemore on to A95. Follow signs to Boat of Garten

CAWDOR

CAWDOR TAVERN

The Lane IV12 5XP
Tel 01667 404777

Arbroath smokie and citrus mousse to start, then the traditional haggis, neeps and tatties. A daily specials menu might focus on confit of pheasant leg on a bed of clapshot, collops of Scottish beef fillet, and warm banana crêpe with rum butterscotch cream.

🕐 May–end Oct daily 11–11; rest of year daily 11–3, 5–11; closed 25 Dec, 1 Jan. Bar meals: Mon–Sat 12–2, 5.30–9,

Sun 12.30–3, 5.30–9. Restaurant: Mon–Sat 12–2, 6.30–9, Sun 12.30–3, 5.30–9
🍴 L from £12, D from £20, Wine from £12.95
🚗 From A96, Inverness–Aberdeen road, take B9006 and follow signs for Cawdor Castle. Pub is in village centre

CLACHAN

BALNAKILL COUNTRY HOUSE HOTEL ❀

PA29 6XL
Tel 01880 740206
www.balnakill.com

Sample fresh (and often organic) produce with a French twist: Fillet of Kintyre sika venison in a claret reduction, and warm organic chocolate tart are two of the possibilities.

The Boat Hotel provides a stylish setting for dinner

🕐 D only, 7–9
🍴 D from £26.95, Wine from £18.50 🚭
🚗 10 miles (16km) south of Tarbert, on Loch Fyne, off A83

CLACHAN-SEIL

TIGH AN TRUISH INN

Oban PA34 4QZ
Tel 01852 300242

Seafood pie, moules marinière, salmon steaks and locally caught prawns feature, while other options might include steak and ale pie, followed by chocolate puddle pudding.

🕐 May–end Sep all day; rest of year 11–3, 5–11; closed 25 Dec, 1 Jan. Bar meals: daily 12–2, 6–8.30. Restaurant: daily 12–2, 6–8.30

CRAIGELLACHIE HOTEL ❀❀

AB38 9SR
Tel 01340 881204
www.craigellachie.com

A meal here could include a starter of smoked, whisky-marinated beef followed by baked fillet of sea bass on a sweet pimento and saffron salsa, with warm lemon dressing.

🕐 12–2, 6–10
🍴 L from £8.90, D from £34.50, Wine from £17.50 🚭
🚗 On A95 in the village centre

🍴 L from £8, D from £13, Wine from £10.80. No credit cards 🚭
🚗 14 miles (22.5km) south of Oban take A816. After 12 miles (19.3km) turn off B844 towards Atlantic Bridge

DORNOCH

2 QUAIL RESTAURANT ❀❀

Inistore House, Castle Street IV25 3SN
Tel 01862 811811
www.2quail.com

A limited number of unfussy dishes form a set-price, three-course meal. Cheese and chive soufflé might be followed by a main of poached halibut supreme with an oyster ravioli and vermouth sauce. Advance reservations essential.

🕐 D only, 7.30–9.30; closed Sun and Mon, Christmas, 2 weeks Feb–Mar
🍴 D from £35.50, Wine from £16.95 🚭
🚗 Just before cathedral

FORT WILLIAM

INVERLOCHY CASTLE ❀❀❀

Torlundy PH33 6SN
Tel 01397 702177
www.inverlochycastlehotel.com

Creative, seasonal Scottish food is on offer. Roast loin of roe deer with a fig crust, and baked rice pudding with spiced pineapple are just two examples.

🕐 12.30–1.30, 7–9.15; closed 5 Jan–12 Feb
🍴 L from £23.50, D from £52.50, Wine from £30 🚭
🚗 Hotel is 3 miles (4.8km) north of Fort William on A82

EATING

MOORINGS ❀
Banavie PH33 7LY
Tel 01397 772797
www.moorings-fortwilliam.co.uk
The menu is modern and multicultural, and West Coast seafood and Highland game are regular features. Pan-seared duck breast with orange noodles and balsamic cream are typical.

🕐 D only, 7–10
🍴 L from £13, D from £18, Wine from £12.75 🅂
🚗 3 miles (4.8km) north, off A830. Take A830 for 1 mile (1.6km), cross the Caledonian Canal, then take 1st right

GLENELG
GLENELG INN
IV40 8JR
Tel 01599 522273
Local produce is used for such dishes as fresh scallops pan-fried with organic garlic butter and roast lemon, followed by fresh West Coast collops of monkfish, prawns and smoked haddock in flaked pastry with white wine, slow roasted broccoli and dill sauce. Meat dishes include roast chicken with lime, garlic and chilli on spiced lentils with a citrus sauce. Vegetarian dishes are also available.

🕐 12–11 (bar closed lunchtimes during winter). Bar meals: daily 12.30–2, 6–9.30. Restaurant: daily 12.30–2, 7.30–9
🍴 L from £19, D from £35, Wine from £15 🅂
🚗 From Shiel Bridge (A87) take unclassified road to Glenelg

GLENFINNAN
THE PRINCE'S HOUSE ❀
PH37 4LT
Tel 01397 722246
www.glenfinnan.co.uk
The restaurant offers local food, with a short menu reflecting the best of seasonal cooking. Leave space for tasty desserts.

🕐 D only, 7–9. Closed Christmas, Jan–Feb; by reservation only in winter
🍴 D from £23 🅂
🚗 On A830, 17 miles (27km) north of Fort William

GRANTOWN-ON-SPEY
THE PINES ❀
Woodside Avenue PH26 3JR
Tel 01479 872092
www.thepinesgrantown.co.uk
The menu at this large Victorian house features traditional British and Scottish fare, with an emphasis on game. Local produce is used whenever possible. Pre-order during the afternoon the likes of warm pigeon salad with lentils and bacon, followed by sea bass and herb risotto.

🕐 D only from 7; closed Nov–end Feb
🍴 D from £30, Wine from £18
🚗 Woodside Avenue is off A939 to Tomintoul, on outskirts of town

Glenmoriston Town House is on the banks of the River Ness

HARRIS, ISLE OF
SCARISTA HOUSE ❀ ❀
Scarista HS3 3HX
Tel 01859 550238
The set menu might feature a rich and intense squat lobster bisque, followed by locally produced fillet steak, gratin dauphinoise and béarnaise sauce. No children under 7.

🕐 D only, Tue–Sun at 8; closed 25 Dec
🍴 D from £32.50, Wine from £18
🚗 On A859 15 miles (24km) south of Tarbert

INVERNESS
BUNCHREW HOUSE ❀ ❀
Bunchrew IV3 8TA
Tel 01463 234917
www.bunchrew-inverness.co.uk

THE OLD INN
IV21 2BD
Tel 01445 712006
Locally caught seafood is used for Mediterranean-style bouillabaisse, or home-made seafood ravioli. Highland game also features. Children welcome.

🕐 Daily 11–12am. Bar meals: daily 12–9.30. Restaurant: daily 12–9.30
🍴 L from £10, D from £15, Wine from £9.95 🅂
🚗 Just off A832, near harbour at southern end of village

Expect West Coast crab cake with braised scallops, roast loin of west Highland lamb, and caramelized lemon tart with an Armagnac sauce.

🕐 12.30–2.15, 7–9.15; closed 22–28 Dec
🍴 L from £21, D from £34.50, Wine from £15 🅂
🚗 2.5 miles (4.4km) from Inverness on A862 towards Beauly

RIVERHOUSE ❀
1 Greig Street IV3 5PT
Tel 01463 222033
Start with fresh oysters served with lemon, red wine and shallot dressing. Mains range from Dover sole and pan-seared scallops to Aberdeen Angus fillet steak. No children under 8.

🕐 12–2.15, 5.30–10; closed Mon
🍴 L from £10.50, D from £28.95 🅂
🚗 On the corner of Huntly Street and Greig Street

ISLAY
THE HARBOUR INN ❀ ❀
The Square, Bowmore PA43 7JR
Tel 01496 810330
www.harbour-inn.com
Local specialities might include pheasant, partridge and woodcock, or a special recipe fish chowder. Many dishes are paired with whiskies from local distilleries.

🕐 12–2.30, 6–9.30; closed L Sun
🍴 L from £20, D from £25, Wine from £11.65 🅂
🚗 8 miles (12.9km) from the ports of Port Ellen and Port Askaig

EATING

GLENMORISTON TOWN HOUSE ❀ ❀

20 Ness Bank IV2 4SF
Tel 01463 223777
www.glenmoriston.com

The sophisticated restaurant at this stylish hotel offers a range of modern French dishes, with top-quality local produce. Try a starter of scallops and asparagus in frothy fennel milk, followed by wild duck served in two sauces.

⏰ 12–2, 7–9.30
🍴 L from £14, D from £42, Wine from £14.50 🅢
🚗 On the riverside opposite the theatre, five minutes from the town centre

KILCHRENAN

THE ARDANAISEIG ❀ ❀

PA35 1HE
Tel 01866 833333
www.ardanaiseig-hotel.com

The classical French cuisine on offer might feature Inverawe smoked trout with potato salad, trout caviar and herb oil, followed by herb crusted saddle of lamb with Provençale vegetables. The wine list is impressive. No children under 7.

⏰ 12.30–2, 7–9; closed 2 Jan–10 Feb
🍴 L from £10, D from £42, Wine from £18 🅢
🚗 Take A85 to Oban. At Taynuilt turn left on to B845 towards Kilchrenan. In Kilchrenan turn left by pub. Hotel in 3 miles (4.8km)

TAYCHREGGAN ❀ ❀

PA35 1HQ
Tel 01866 833211
www.taychregganhotel.co.uk

The five-course dinner menu is based largely on traditional recipes and fresh local ingredients: Loch Awe rainbow trout served with a bouquet of asparagus tips might be followed by monkfish with smoked haddock dauphinois and a black cauliflower fricassée. No children under 14.

⏰ 12.30–2, 7.30–8.45
🍴 L from £12.50, D from £37.50, Wine from £14.95 🅢
🚗 West from Crainlarich on A85 to Taynuilt. Then on B845 to Kilchrenan and Taychreggan

KINGUSSIE

THE CROSS ❀ ❀ ❀

Tweed Mill Brae, Ardbroilach Road
PH21 1LB
Tel 01540 661166
www.thecross.co.uk

Chef David Young's cooking is simple with an emphasis on seasonality. Scallops served with pannacotta and fennel oil might be followed by fillet of beef with red onion marmalade and chips (french fries), and the

The Albannach in Lochinver offers spectacular loch views

meal rounded off by lemon tart. The wine collection is notable.

⏰ D only, at 7; closed Sun–Mon, Christmas and Jan
🍴 D from £35, Wine from £18
🚗 From traffic lights in town centre go uphill along Ardbroilach Road for 330m (330 yards), turn left into Tweed Mill Brae

LOCHGILPHEAD

CAIRNBAAN ❀

Cairnbaan PA31 8SJ
Tel 01546 603668
www.cairnbaan.com

The carte specializes in the use of fresh local produce, notably scallops, langoustines and game. Loch Etive mussels, smoked salmon and smoked trout pâté for starters, while

KILBERRY INN

PA29 6YD
Tel 01880 770223

Everything served here is home-made. Menu favourites include Kilberry sausage pie, spinach and ricotta pasta and venison game pie.

⏰ 11–3, 6.30–10.30; closed Nov–end Mar. Bar meals: Tue–Sat 12.30–2, 7–8.30, Sun 12.30–1.30. Restaurant: Tue–Sat 12.30–2, 6.30–8.30, Sun 12.30–2
🍴 L from £11, D from £20, Wine from £11.75
🚗 From Lochgilphead take A83 south. Take B8024 signposted Kilberry

mains might include breast of pheasant with haggis en croûte, lobster and fillet of halibut. For a lighter meal there's a bistro-style menu.

⏰ 12–6. Bar meals: daily 12–2.30, 6–9.30. Restaurant: D only, daily 6–9.30
🍴 L from £9, D from £14, Wine from £11.90 🅢
🚗 2 miles (3.2km) north of Lochgilphead on A816, bear left, hotel off B841

LOCHINVER

THE ALBANNACH ❀ ❀

Baddidarroch IV27 4LP
Tel 01571 844407
www.thealbannach.co.uk

The fixed five-course menu is unmistakably Scottish with French subtleties. Local fish and shellfish feature, as do game in season and local free-range lamb and beef. Lochinver-landed turbot might follow on from carpaccio of Highland beef with rocket and pine-nut salad and tapenade. The cheese course gives way to, perhaps, vanilla parfait with rhubarb and Sauternes compote, orange and ginger sauce and a berry fruit basket. No children under 12.

⏰ D only, at 8; closed Mon, mid-Nov to mid-Mar
🍴 D from £45, Wine from £13 🅢
🚗 In Lochinver follow signs for Baddidarroch. In 0.5 mile (800m) take left turn after Highland Stoneware (after cattle grid)

EATING

LUSS

COLQUHOUN'S
Lodge on Loch Lomond Hotel G83 8PA
Tel 01436 860201
www.loch-lomond.co.uk
The cooking style is simple: A sample menu includes lobster ravioli with creamed leeks and tarragon, followed by roast wild venison with red cabbage and black pudding, rounded off by hot chocolate fondant.
12–5, 6–9.45
L from £15, D from £24.95, Wine from £13.95
30 miles (46km) north of Glasgow on A82

NETHY BRIDGE

MOUNTVIEW HOTEL
Grantown Road PH25 3EB
Tel 01479 821248
Imaginative dinners include layered wild mushroom pancake with a hazelnut cream, roast monkfish with a butter bean and vanilla stew, then warm pecan nut tart with ginger sauce.
D only, 6–11; closed Mon–Tue, Christmas
D from £20, Wine from £11.95
From Aviemore follow signs for Nethy Bridge through Boat of Garten. Go through Nethy Bridge, hotel on right

OBAN

EEUSK
North Pier PA34 5QD
Tel 01631 565666
All but two of the varieties of wet fish on offer are landed in the harbour here, and the fish is simply prepared. Halibut with creamed leeks and sautéed potatoes followed by clootie dumpling are bound to warm you on a breezy day.
12–2.30, 6–9.30; closed 25–26 Dec, 1 Jan
L from £14, D from £19, Wine from £12.75

ONICH

ONICH
PH33 6RY
Tel 01855 821214
The menu features traditional and more contemporary takes on Scottish specialties. The bar

food, in particular, offers good value for money.
D only, 7–9
D from £22, Wine from £12
Beside A82, 2 miles (3.2km) N of Ballachulish Bridge

PLOCKTON

PLOCKTON INN & SEAFOOD RESTAURANT
Innes Street IV52 8TW
Tel 01599 544222
Local fish and shellfish are smoked locally. Lunch includes a seafood platter from the smokery and moules marinière. A more extensive dinner menu might include venison collops with bramble and port sauce.

The Three Chimneys Restaurant overlooks Loch Dunvegan

Mon–Sat 11am–1am, Sun 12.30–11. Bar meals: daily 12–2.30, 5.30–9.30. Restaurant: daily 12–2.30, 5.30–9.30
L from £15, D from £15, Wine from £10

SHIELDAIG

SHIELDAIG BAR
IV54 8XN
Tel 01520 755251
Traditional bar food (rib-eye steaks, steak and Guinness pie, smoked haddock omelettes) and daily specials such as Shieldaig crab bisque with home-made bread or fresh Loch Torridon langoustines with garlic mayonnaise.
Mon–Sat 11–11, Sun 12.30–10; closed 25 Dec, 1 Jan. Bar meals: daily

THREE CHIMNEYS RESTAURANT AND HOUSE OVER-BY
Colbost IV55 8ZT
Tel 01470 511258
www.threechimneys.co.uk
Starters might include crab risotto cake with langoustines, while mains might include beef with caramelized onions and pommes Anna. For dessert try brioche bread and butter pudding with Seville orange anglaise. Advance reservations recommended.
12.30–2.30, 6.30–10; closed L Sun, 1 week Dec, 3 weeks Jan
L from £18, D from £48, Wine from £17.95
From Dunvegan take B884 to Glendale

12–2.30, 6–8.30. Restaurant: daily 7–8.30
L from £13, D from £37.50, Wine from £9.50

SKYE, ISLE OF

CUILLIN HILLS HOTEL
Portree IV51 9QU
Tel 01478 612003
www.cuillinhills.demon.co.uk
Local meat, fish and game feature largely: Steamed Loch Eilort mussels might be followed by braised saddle of venison and pigeon with red wine, topped off with a dark chocolate terrine.
12–2, 6.30–9; closed L Mon–Sat
L from £10.50, D from £31.50, Wine from £13.50
0.25 mile (0.5km) north of Portree on A855

DUISDALE COUNTRY HOUSE
Isle Ornsay IV43 8QW
Tel 01471 833202
The short five-course dinner menu brings subtle spicing to the Highland ingredients. Try salmon fishcakes and grilled sea bass, roasted loin of hill lamb, and chocolate tart with chocolate cake and pistachio ice cream.
No children under 4.

EATING

THE CEILIDH PLACE

14 West Argyle Street IV26 2TY
Tel 01854 612103

Locally landed fish is always available in dishes like fillet of cod on garlic mash and rocket purée, or monkfish wrapped in bacon with sauerkraut and chorizo sausage, or try lamb casserole with Heather Ale, and a vegetable pie.

🕑 Mon–Sat 11–11, Sun 12.30–11; closed 2nd week Jan for 2 weeks. Bar meals: daily 12–6, 6.30–9.30. Restaurant: D only, daily 7–9.30

🍴 L from £8, D from £22, Wine from £11.50 🟢

🚗 Go along Shore Street, pass the pier and take 1st right. Hotel is straight ahead at top of hill

🕑 D only, at 7.30; closed Nov–end Mar
🍷 D from £18.45, Wine from £14 🟢
🚗 7 miles (11km) north of Armadale ferry and 12 miles (19.3km) south of Skye Bridge on A851

ROSEDALE ❀

Beaumont Crescent, Portree IV51 9DB
Tel 01478 613131
www.rosedalehotelskye.co.uk

Emphasis is placed on fresh, local and organic produce in the imaginative set-price menu.

🕑 D only, 7–9; closed Nov–end Mar
🍷 D from £22, Wine from £14.95 🟢
🚗 On harbour front

STONEHAVEN

TOLBOOTH ❀

Old Pier Road AB3 2JU
Tel 01569 762287
www.tolboothrestaurant.co.uk

At this award-winning seafood restaurant, the day's catch is marked up on a blackboard, and locally sourced fish and seafood is the mainstay—although non-fish eaters are also catered for.

🕑 Tue–Sat 12–2, 6–9.30; closed 3 weeks after Christmas
🍷 L from £12, D from £17, Wine from £14.50 🟢
🚗 15 miles (24km) south of Aberdeen on A90

STRACHUR

CREGGANS INN ❀

PA27 8BX
Tel 01369 860279
www.creggans-inn.co.uk

The fixed-price dinner offers three or four dishes per course, such as saddle of lamb, with bacon, mushrooms and Savoy cabbage; and roast fillet of beef with tian of black pudding.

🕑 D only, 7–9
🍷 D from £28, Wine from £12.50 🟢
🚗 Follow A82 along Loch Lomond to Arrochar, then west on A83 and A815 to Strachur

The Ceilidh Place is an Ullapool institution

TARBERT

STONEFIELD CASTLE HOTEL ❀

PA29 6YJ
Tel 01880 820836
www.stonefieldcastle.co.uk

Seafood, lamb, venison and beef all feature strongly, with grilled Loch Fyne herring perhaps followed by pan-fried medallions of beef fillet served with a wild mushroom risotto.

🕑 12–2, 7–9
🍷 L from £15, D from £25, Wine from £12.50 🟢
🚗 2 miles (3km) north of Tarbert, Loch Fyne

TAYVALLICH

TAYVALLICH INN

PA31 8PL
Tel 01546 870282

Good seafood choices include pan-fried Sound of Jura scallops and warm salad of smoked haddock with prawns. Meat choices include grilled prime Scottish sirloin steak, and honey and mustard glazed rack of lamb.

🕑 Closed 25–26 Dec, 1–2 Jan. Bar meals: daily 12–2, 6–8. Restaurant: D 7–9
🍷 L from £15, D from £26.50, Wine from £10
🚗 From Lochgilphead take A816 then B841/B8025

ORKNEY AND SHETLAND

BRAE

BUSTA HOUSE HOTEL

Busta, Shetland ZE2 9QN
Tel 01806 522506

The beamed bar and restaurant at Britain's most northerly country-house hotel serve fresh, home-cooked local and Scottish produce. Children welcome.

🕑 Mon–Sat 11.30–11, Sun 12.30–11. Bar meals: 12–2.30, 6–9.30. Restaurant: 12.30–2, 7–9.30
🍷 L from £14, D from £30, Wine from £12

ST. MARGARET'S HOPE

CREEL RESTAURANT ❀❀

Front Road, Orkney KW17 2SL
Tel 01856 831311
www.thecreel.co.uk

Simple use of fresh local produce, particularly fish and seafood: velvet crab bisque or steamed lemon sole; sea scallops and roasted monkfish tails served with leeks, fresh ginger and beans; or grilled chicken fillet with roasted red pepper marmalade.

🕑 D only, 6.45–9.30; closed Jan–end Mar, Nov
🍷 D from £30, Wine from £13.50 🟢
🚗 13 miles (21km) south of Kirkwall. On A961 on waterfront in village

STAYING IN SCOTLAND

Hotels and guesthouses offer a wide range of accommodation across Scotland, from the plushest luxury at Gleneagles to more modest retreats. While you'll have the full choice of styles and ranges in the main cities and holiday centres, the choice may be more limited and the standard more modest in the remoter areas of the country.

A wide range of accommodation is available to suite your taste and your budget

The Automobile Association (AA) is Britain's leading organization for the classification of hotels and restaurants. The facilities of AA-inspected hotels are classified using a system of stars (see opposite). Diamond ratings provide a similar classification for guest accommodation and bed-and-breakfasts (B&Bs). Rosettes are awarded as an indication of the quality of food served by restaurants and hotels (▷ 241). The selection that follows is based on some of the AA's top recommendations.

RESERVING ACCOMMODATION

It's always worth making reservations as early as possible, particularly for the peak summer holiday period (Jun–end Sep), and ski season (Dec–end Feb). Bear in mind that New Year (Hogmanay), Easter and other public holidays (▷ 295) may be busy too.

Some hotels will ask for a deposit or full payment in advance, especially for one-night reservations, and not all hotels will take reservations for B&B, overnight or short stays. Some hotels charge half-board (bed, breakfast and dinner) whether you eat the meals or not, while others may accept only full-board reservations.

Once a reservation is confirmed, let the hotel know at once if you are unable to keep your reservation. If the hotel cannot re-let your room you may be liable to pay about two-thirds of the room price. In Scotland a legally binding contract is made when you accept an offer of

THE LISTINGS

In the listings that follow, we have included a variety of inspected, recommended hotels and B&Bs. Establishments are listed under the name of their nearest town.

accommodation, either in writing or by telephone, and illness is not accepted as a release from this contract. You are advised to take out insurance against possible cancellation.

EN SUITE

B&B accommodation offers the opportunity to stay in somebody's home, and sometimes in some remarkable historical buildings. Be aware that en suite facilities are not always available, and bathroom facilities may be shared. And if a choice of bath or shower is important to you, check at the time of reserving.

BED-AND-BREAKFAST

The B&B price generally includes a full cooked breakfast, which in Scotland may consist of any combination of porridge, eggs, fried bread, potato scones, sausage, bacon, mushroom and tomato. Lighter alternatives are usually available. Some establishments offer an evening meal, but you may need to order in advance. In Scotland, high tea is sometimes served instead of dinner—this usually consists of a savoury dish followed by bread and butter, scones and cakes. While inns and some guesthouses will have a licence to serve alcohol, few B&Bs do.

PAYING

Most hotels and restaurants accept the majority of British and international credit cards, such as Access, MasterCard, Visa, American Express and Diners Club. Debit cards and cheques are also widely accepted, but you are advised to carry some cash in case of difficulty.

Many smaller accommodation establishments, such as B&Bs, are unlikely to accept any form of credit card, so always ask about payment methods when making a reservation.

STAYING

SYHA

The Scottish Youth Hostels Association (SYHA) offers self-catering accommodation in over 60 locations. The hostels are good value, are convenient for walking or bicycling holidays, and many have family rooms. Some are open all year round; advance reservations are recommended.
● SYHA, 7 Glebe Crescent, Stirling FK8 2JA, tel 0870 155 3255; www.syha.org.uk

SELF-CATERING

The main single source of listings of self-catering (with kitchen) properties is VisitScotland's *Scotland: Where to Stay Self-Catering* guide, published annually and available on www.visitScotland.com

There are also many private agencies specializing in self-catering property rental. These include Country Cottages in Scotland, which offers a range of up-scale properties in castles as well as more rural locations.
● Country Cottages in Scotland, Stoney Bank, Earby, Barnoldswick BB94 0AA, tel 08700 781100; www.scottish-country-cottages.co.uk

The National Trust for Scotland offers a small number of unusual places to stay in or around its historic properties.

● Holidays Department, National Trust for Scotland, Wemyss House, 28 Charlotte Square, Edinburgh EH2 4ET, tel 0131 243 9331; www.scotlandforyou.co.uk

Forest Holidays, part of the Forestry Commission, offers family accommodation in wooden cabins in beautiful woodland settings at Strathyre (near Callander), as well as campsites.
● Forest Holidays, Forestry Commission, 231 Corstorphine Road, Edinburgh EH12 7AT, tel 0131 314 6100; www.forestholidays.co.uk

CAMPING AND CARAVANNING

There are over 400 licensed and recognized camping and caravan (RV) parks in Scotland. All area tourist boards carry listings of parks within their own area. The AA's annual publication *Camping and Caravanning in Britain and Ireland* is also a good source of information. Note that most local authorities do not permit overnight parking of caravans in lay-bys and other parking areas.
● Camping and Caravanning Club, tel 0247 669 4995; www.campingandcaravanningclub.co.uk
Note: if you hold a Camping Card International (CCI) you are entitled to camp on club sites at members' rates.

HOTEL AND BED-AND-BREAKFAST CLASSIFICATIONS

All hotels recognized by the AA should have the highest standards of cleanliness, proper records of reservations, give prompt and professional service, assist with luggage on request, accept and deliver messages, provide a designated area for dinner (if available) and breakfast, with drinks available in a bar or lounge, provide an early morning call on request, have good-quality furniture and fittings, adequate heating and lighting and proper maintenance. A guide to some of the general expectations for each star classification is as follows:

The AA Top 200 Hotels
☆☆ Marked with open (or red) stars, these stand out as the very best hotels in Britain and include large luxury hotels, country houses, town houses, restaurants with rooms and smaller country inns.

★ A relatively informal yet competent style of service and adequate range of facilities, including a television in the lounge or bedroom. The majority of bedrooms are en suite with a bath or shower room always available. At least one designated eating area for breakfast and dinner.

★★ As above plus smartly and professionally presented management, with at least one restaurant or dining room for breakfast and dinner. Last orders for dinner no earlier than 7pm.

★★★ As above plus direct dial telephones, remote control television, en suite bath or shower and WC, a wide selection of drinks in the bar and last orders for dinner no earlier than 8pm.

★★★★ As above plus a range of high-quality toiletries and en suite bath with fixed overhead shower and

WC. Uniformed, well-trained staff with additional services, a night porter and a serious approach to cuisine. Well-appointed public areas. Last orders for dinner no earlier than 9pm.

★★★★★ These are the most luxurious hotels, offering many extra facilities and services, attentive staff, spacious, top-quality rooms and a full concierge service. A wide selection of drinks, including cocktails, is available in the bar and the menu reflects and complements the hotel's own style of cooking. Last orders for dinner no earlier than 10pm.

The quality of all B&B accommodation in the UK is rated using diamond symbols (◆) on a scale from one to five, five diamonds representing the best. The criteria for a higher rating are guest care and quality rather than choice of extra facilities.
At all grades, guests can expect: a prompt and professional check in and out; comfortable accommodation equipped to modern standards; regularly changed bedding and towels; a sufficient hot water supply at all times; adequate storage, heating, lighting and comfortable seating; a full Scottish or continental breakfast. Evening meals may or may not be available.

◇◇◇◇◇ The very best B&Bs in the AA's listings of the top three quality ratings (five, four and three diamonds) are identified with open (or red) diamonds.

The establishments in the listings that do not have a diamond or star rating have not been inspected by the AA and are not part of its classification scheme.

Company logo	Company statement	Telephone number and website
Best Western	Britain's largest group has more than 30 independently owned and managed hotels in Scotland. Buildings may be modern or traditional and many have leisure facilities and rosette awards.	08457 737373 www.bestwestern.co.uk
travel inn	The largest budget group in the UK, offering high-quality, modern accommodation in key locations throughout the country. Every Premier Travel Inn is located adjacent to a family restaurant and bar.	0870 242 8000 www.premiertravelinn.co.uk
Travelodge	Good quality, modern, budget accommodation across the UK. Almost every lodge has an adjacent family restaurant—often a Little Chef, Harry Ramsden's or Burger King.	08700 850950 www.travelodge.co.uk
SCOTLAND'S HOTELS OF DISTINCTION	Scotland's Hotels of Distinction is a consortium of independent hotels, in the three- and four-star market.	01333 360888 www.hotels-of-distinction.com
Express by Holiday Inn	Express by Holiday Inn offers superior budget accommodation with complimentary breakfast at modern hotels across the UK.	0800 434040 www.chotelsgroup.com
MACDONALD HOTELS	Macdonald Hotels are a large group of predominantly four-star hotels, traditional and modern in style, located across the UK.	0871 522 8417 www.mcdonaldhotels.co.uk
THE INDEPENDENTS	The Independents is a consortium of independently owned, mainly two- and three-star hotels across Britain.	0800 885544 www.theindependents.co.uk
Marriott HOTELS · RESORTS · SUITES	Marriott is an international brand which offers four-star hotels in primary locations. Most are modern and have leisure facilities; some have a focus on golf.	0800 221 222 0800 699 996 www.marriott.com
Holiday Inn HOTELS · RESORTS	Holiday Inn is an internationally known group which offers a wide range of hotels throughout the UK.	0800 405060 www.chotelsgroup.com
SLH SMALL LUXURY HOTELS OF THE WORLD	Small Luxury Hotels of the World is an international consortium of mainly privately owned hotels, often in the country house style.	0800 525 48000 00 49 69 664 19601 www.slh.com
PARAMOUNT GROUP OF HOTELS	Paramount is a group of predominantly four-star hotels, many with leisure facilities.	0500 342543 www.paramount-hotels.co.uk
RELAIS & CHATEAUX	Relais et Chateaux is an international consortium of rural, privately owned hotels, mainly in the country house style	00 800 2000 00 02 www.relaischateaux.com
Malmaison HOTELS	Malmaison is a growing brand of high quality three-star city centre hotels.	020 7479 9512 www.malmaison.com
GOLDEN TULIP HOTELS · INNS · RESORTS	This established European brand now has one hotel in Glasgow.	01765 658911 www.tulipinn.co.uk

STAYING

SOUTHERN SCOTLAND

AYR

ENTERKINE COUNTRY HOUSE
★★★
Annbank KA6 5AL
Tel 01292 521608
www.enterkine.com
A gracious country mansion dating back to the 1930s, Enterkine House retains many original features—notably the luxurious bathroom suites. In keeping with country-house tradition there is no bar, drinks being served in the elegant lounge and library. Food is notably good, and many of the spacious bedrooms have lovely views over the surrounding countryside.
🛏 Double from £130–£150
🛌 6
🚗 Follow A77 to Ayr, then B743 Mossblown/Mauchline for hotel on Coylton Road, on outskirts of Annbank

SAVOY PARK ★★★
16 Racecourse Road KA7 2UT
Tel 01292 266112
www.savoypark.com
This friendly, traditional hotel is handy for the town's race

course. There are impressive panelled walls in the public rooms, along with ornate ceilings and open fires, and the restaurant is reminiscent of a Highland shooting lodge. Superior bedrooms are large and classically elegant, while others are smart and modern.
🛏 Double from £95–£115
🛌 15 (non-smoking)
🚗 From A77 follow Holmston Road (A70) for 2 miles (3km), through Parkhouse Street, then turn left into Berresford Terrace, and take 1st right into Bellevue Road

SPECIAL IN BALLANTRAE
GLENAPP CASTLE ☆☆☆
KA26 0NZ
Tel 01465 831212
www.glenappcastle.com
Impressively restored over a six-year period, this magnificent castle lies in well-tended grounds and gardens with fine views towards Ailsa Craig and Arran. The all-inclusive price covers a set five-course dinner with matched wines (dinner for non-residents by arrangement), and afternoon tea, aperitifs and liqueurs. Bedrooms are adorned with antiques and period pieces and there are a number of suites. Service is both attentive and welcoming.
🛏 Double from £365–£515
🛌 17 (non-smoking)
🚫 Closed Nov–end Mar
🚗 1 mile (1.6km) from A77, south of Ballantrae

STAYING

SPECIAL IN BALLANTRAE

COSSES COUNTRY HOUSE ◊◊◊◊◊

Cosses KA26 0LR
Tel 01465 831363
www.cossescountryhouse.com
A delightful country house in 4.8ha (12 acres) of woodland and gardens. Two bedrooms have their own lounges, and all rooms are on the ground floor. Guests meet for pre-dinner drinks with hosts in the lounge, and award-winning dinners, served at an elegant communal table, include home-grown and local produce, Scottish cheese and fine wines. Breakfast offers a choice of dishes, home-made yoghurt, preserves and bread. Facilities include a games room and table tennis. No children under 6.
🛏 Double from £95
🚫 2 (non-smoking)
⊘ Closed Nov–end Feb
🚗 South of Ballantrae on the A77, take the inland road at the caravan sign. House is 2 miles (3.2km) on the right

CASTLE DOUGLAS

CRAIGADAM ◆◆◆◆◆

Craigadam DG7 3HU
Tel 01556 650233
www.craigadam.com
Set on a working sheep farm, this elegant guesthouse offers gracious living in a relaxed environment. The large bedrooms—most of which are around a courtyard to the rear—are all individual in style and very comfortable. Public areas include a lounge and a panelled dining room with a magnificent 15-seater table. Private fishing and shooting are available.
🛏 Double from £76
🚫 10 (non- smoking)
⊘ Closed Christmas and New Year
🚗 Leave Castle Douglas east on A75 to Crocketford. In Crocketford turn left on to A712 for 2 miles (3.2km). House is on hill

CRAILING

CRAILING OLD SCHOOL B&B ◊◊◊◊

TD8 6TL
Tel 01835 850382
www.crailingoldschool.co.uk
The village school until the mid-1980s, this late 19th-century property has been imaginatively converted. An open-plan lounge and dining room overlooks the garden and is the perfect setting for excellent meals (dinner by arrangement). There are three individual bedrooms in the spacious loft, while a house in the garden provides self-contained accommodation that is easily accessible for

Craigadam near Castle Douglas offers a farm setting

visitors with disabilities. No children under 9.
🛏 Double from £50–£64
🚫 4 (non-smoking)
⊘ Closed 24–27 Dec and 2 weeks Feb and Nov
🚗 Off A698 Jedburgh to Kelso road on the B6400 signposted Nisbet, Harestanes Visitor Centre

EAST CALDER

ASHCROFT FARMHOUSE ◆◆◆◆◆

EH53 0ET
Tel 01506 881810
www.ashcroftfarmhouse.com
With nearly 40 years' experience of caring for their guests, Derek and Elizabeth Scott ensure that a stay at their farmhouse will be memorable.

Their modern home is in lovely landscaped gardens, and provides attractive ground-floor bedrooms. The residents' lounge includes a video library. Breakfast, with home-made sausages, is served at individual tables. No children under 5.
🛏 Double from £64–£70
🚫 6 (non-smoking)
🚗 On the B7015, off the A71, 0.5 miles (800m) east of East Calder near to Almondell Country Park

EAST LINTON

KIPPIELAW FARMHOUSE ◆◆◆◆◆

EH41 4PY
Tel 01620 860368
www.kippielawfarmhouse.co.uk
Kippielaw is in an elevated position, sheltered by well-tended gardens, and enjoys views of the Tyne valley. The country-cottage style bedrooms are prettily decorated. The lounge has an open staircase and log fire; excellent meals are served in the dining room. No children under 13.
🛏 Double from £60–£64
🚫 3 (non-smoking)
🚗 Leave A1 at East Linton, follow Traprain sign for 0.75 mile (1.2km), then take single-track road on right after farm. B&B 0.5 mile (800m) on left

GULLANE

GREYWALLS ☆☆☆

Muirfield EH31 2EG
Tel 01620 842144
www.greywalls.co.uk
A dignified Edwardian country house designed by Sir Edwin Lutyens, Greywalls overlooks Muirfield Golf Course. Public rooms look on to beautiful gardens, and freshly prepared cuisine may be enjoyed in the restaurant. Tennis courts are also available for guests. Bedrooms, whether intimate singles or spacious master rooms, are mostly furnished in period style and many command views of the celebrated course. A gatehouse lodge is ideal for golfing parties.

JEDFOREST HOTEL ★★★

Camptown TD8 6PJ
Tel 01835 840222
www.jedforesthotel.com

A tour of the central Borders would not be complete without a visit to this country house hotel in 14ha (35 acres) of woodland and pasture. Immaculately presented throughout, it offers an attractive dining room, a bright and comfortable brasserie and a relaxing lounge with open fire. The bedrooms are very smart, with the larger ones being particularly impressive. Service is very attentive, and facilities include private fishing. No children under 12.

🍽 Double from £140–£180 including dinner
🛏 12 (non-smoking)
🚗 4 miles (6.4km) south of Jedburgh, off A68

🍽 Double from £230–£270
🛏 23
🔆 Closed Nov–end Mar
🚗 On A198, the hotel is signed at the east end of the village

JEDBURGH

THE SPINNEY ◆◆◆◆◆

Langlee TD8 6PB
Tel 01835 863525
www.thespinney-jedburgh.co.uk

Two cottages have been transformed into this attractive modern home in the foothills of the Cheviots, surrounded by landscaped gardens. Bedrooms are bright and cheerful. Breakfast is served at individual tables in the dining room, and there is a welcoming lounge. Self-catering (with kitchen) lodges are also available on site.

🍽 Double from £50–£52
🛏 3 (non-smoking)
🔆 Closed Dec–end Feb
🚗 2 miles (3.2km) south of Jedburgh on A68

KELSO

THE ROXBURGHE HOTEL & GOLF COURSE ★★★

Heiton TD5 8JZ
Tel 01573 450331
www.roxburghe.net

Surrounded by 202.5ha (500 acres) of mature wood and parkland, this impressive Jacobean mansion is owned by the Duke of Roxburghe. An impressive range of sporting pursuits is available for guests, including shooting, fishing, tennis and golf. Some of the bedrooms come complete with a real fire. The comfortably furnished lounges provide a perfect setting for the lavish afternoon teas,

Jedforest Hotel is one of the finest in the Borders

while the restaurant serves carefully prepared Scottish and other British fare.

🍽 Double from £140–£280
🛏 22 (1 non-smoking)
🚗 3 miles (4.8km) southwest of Kelso off A698

KILWINNING

MONTGREENAN MANSION HOUSE ★★★

Montgreenan Estate KA13 7QZ
Tel 01294 557733
www.montgreenanhotel.com

This peaceful mansion is in 19ha (48 acres) of parkland and woods. Gracious public areas retain original features such as ornate ceilings and marble fireplaces, and include a drawing room, a library, a

club-style bar and a restaurant. Bedrooms come in a variety of sizes. Facilities include tennis and a croquet pitch.

🍽 Double from £159–£219
🛏 21 (16 non-smoking)
🚗 4 miles (6.4km) north of Irvine on A736

KIRKBEAN

CAVENS ★★

DG2 8AA
Tel 01387 880234
www.cavens.com

Dating back to 1752, this country house has been home to many notable figures over the years, and is in 2.4ha (6 acres) of parkland. Outdoor pursuits on offer include shooting, fishing and horseback riding. A set four-course dinner menu uses quality local produce.

🍽 Double from £80–£150
🛏 6 (non-smoking)
🚗 Hotel signed from A710 in Kirkbean

KIRKCUDBRIGHT

BAYTREE HOUSE ◆◆◆◆◆

110 High Street DG6 4JQ
Tel 01557 330824
www.baytreehouse.net

You can stay close to the centre of this appealing artists' town in this beautifully restored Georgian bed-and-breakfast. The bedrooms are thoughtfully equipped, and furnished in keeping with the style of the house. The magnificent upstairs drawing room is not to be missed. No children under 12, no credit cards.

🍽 Double from £60–£64
🛏 3
🚗 Take A711 into middle of Kirkcudbright, turn right at crossroads into Cuthbert Street, left at Castle Street, and Baytree is facing at the end of Castle Street

STAYING

EAST LOCHHEAD ◇◇◇◇◇
Largs Road PA12 4DX
Tel 01505 842610
www.eastlochhead.co.uk
A relaxed country-house atmosphere prevails at this former farmhouse, which dates back over 100 years and has magnificent views over Barr Loch. The stylish bedrooms are all superbly equipped, and enjoyable home-cooking is served in the dining room/lounge. A barn has been converted into five self-contained units.

🛏 Double from £70–£80
🛌 3 (non-smoking)
🚗 From Glasgow take M8 exit 28a for A737 Irvine. At Roadhead roundabout turn right on to A760. Guesthouse 2 miles (3.2km) on the left

LOCKERBIE
THE DRYFESDALE ★★★
Dryfebridge DG11 2SF
Tel 01576 202427
www.dryfesdalehotel.co.uk
Convenient for the M74, yet suitably screened from it, this hotel offers its guests superb care. Facilities include clay pigeon shooting and private fishing. Bedrooms, some with access to patio areas, vary in size. Dinner makes good use of local produce and is served in the airy restaurant overlooking the gardens. A warm welcome is offered by the enthusiastic young staff.

🛏 Double from £95–£125
🛌 16 (8 non-smoking)
🚗 From M74 take exit 17 signed Lockerbie North. Take 3rd exit at 1st roundabout, 1st exit at next round-about. Hotel is 183m (200 yards) on left

KINGS ARMS HOTEL ★★
High Street DG11 2JL
Tel 01576 202410
www.kingsarmshotel.co.uk
Built in the 17th century as a coaching inn, this venerable family-run hotel lies at the heart of the town, providing attractive and well-equipped bedrooms, and a choice of

two homey bars serving food—one is non-smoking.

🛏 Double from £70
🛌 13 (1 non-smoking)
🚗 In town centre, opposite Town Hall

SOMERTON HOUSE ★★
35 Carlisle Road DG11 2DR
Tel 01576 202583
This friendly, family-run Victorian mansion has been sympathetically preserved and beautiful woodwork—particularly in the dining room—is a feature. Two attractive conservatories add a new dimension and are popular for bar meals and functions. Bedrooms are notably stylish, and well equipped.

New Lanark Mill Hotel has outstanding river views

🛏 Double from £60–£75
🛌 11 (7 non-smoking)
🚗 Off A74

MAYBOLE
LADYBURN ☆☆
KA19 7SG
Tel 01655 740585
www.ladyburn.co.uk
This country house is the elegant home of the Hepburn family. It nestles in open countryside and attractive gardens. Classically styled bedrooms, two with four-poster beds, offer every comfort and are complemented by the library and the drawing room. There's a three-course set dinner menu, discussed

beforehand, served in a gracious candlelit setting. The genuine hospitality and care is a hallmark. No children under 16.

🛏 Double from £130–£170
🛌 5 (non-smoking)
🚗 Turn off A77 on to B7023, at Crosshill turn right at war memorial on to B741, signed Kilkerran. After 2 miles (3.2km) turn left, hotel is 1 mile (1.6km) farther on

MOFFAT
MOFFAT HOUSE ★★★
High Street DG10 9HL
Tel 01683 220039
www.moffathouse.co.uk
At the heart of this picturesque town the hotel has a good level of trade from both visitors and locals. The spacious bar lounge serves a variety of lunches and dinners; the restaurant offers a more formal environment. Bedrooms are generally spacious and quiet.

🛏 Double from £103–£104
🛌 20 (14 non-smoking)
🚗 From M74 exit 15, take A701 for 1 mile (1.6km). Hotel at end of High Street

NEW LANARK
NEW LANARK MILL HOTEL ★★★
Mill One, New Lanark Mills ML11 9DB
Tel 01555 667200
www.newlanark.org
This converted 18th-century cotton mill offers the opportunity to stay in the restored model village of New Lanark, now designated a World Heritage Site (▷ 65). Bright, modern styling throughout contrasts with features from the original mill, and there are stunning views over the River Clyde.

🛏 Double from £99
🛌 38 (28 non-smoking)
🚗 Signed from all major roads, M74 exit 7 and M8

NEWTON STEWART

KIRROUGHTREE HOUSE
☆☆☆
Minnigaff DG8 6AN
Tel 01671 402141
www.kirroughtreehouse.co.uk
This 17th-century mansion
enjoys a peaceful location in
3.2ha (8 acres) of landscaped
gardens, next to Galloway
Forest Park. Facilities include
tennis and a 9-hole pitch and
putt. Sumptuous day rooms
are furnished with deep,
cushioned sofas and antique
and period pieces. Individually
styled spacious bedrooms
are thoughtfully equipped.
Dinners are served in the
elegant dining rooms by a
friendly, attentive team. No
children under 10.
🛏 Double from £142–£200
🚪 17
🌙 Closed 4 Jan–16 Feb
🚗 From A75 take A712, New Galloway
road. Entrance to hotel is 274m
(300 yards) on left

PEEBLES

CRINGLETIE HOUSE ★★★
Edinburgh Road EH45 8PL
Tel 01721 725750
www.cringletie.com
This impressive baronial
mansion has a superb walled
garden that provides much of
the kitchen's produce. Public
rooms include a cocktail lounge
with adjoining conservatory,
and the first floor restaurant
has a fine painted ceiling.
Bedrooms are all individual and
several are notably spacious.
🛏 Double from £115–£160
🚪 14 (non-smoking)
🌙 Closed early Jan to early Feb
🚆 2 miles (3.2km) north on A703

PORTPATRICK

FERNHILL ★★★
Heugh Road DG9 8TD
Tel 01776 810220
www.fernhillhotel.co.uk
Splendid harbour views are
the chief delight of this hotel—
and you can make the most of
them from the conservatory
restaurant and many of the
bedrooms. A modern wing

offers particularly spacious and
well-appointed rooms, some
with balconies. Leisure
facilities are available at a
sister hotel in Stranraer.
🛏 Double from £100–£204
🚪 36 (10 non-smoking)
🌙 Closed mid-Jan to mid-Feb
🚗 Just past Portpatrick village sign on
A77, turn right before war memorial,
hotel is 1st on left

ST. BOSWELLS

DRYBURGH ABBEY ★★★
TD6 0RQ
Tel 01835 822261
www.dryburgh.co.uk
An imposing red sandstone
mansion in an attractive
riverside setting next to the

*Lochgreen House is in
extensive grounds*

ruined abbey. Private fishing is
available. The inviting public
areas include a choice of
lounges, and the elegant first
floor dining room overlooks the
river. There is a good choice of
accommodation, with suites
and many spacious rooms.
🛏 Double from £130–£210
🚪 38 (non-smoking) 🏊
🚗 From A68 at St. Boswells turn on to
B6404 through village. Continue for
2 miles (3.2km), turn left on to B6356
for Scott's View. Go through Clintmains
village, hotel in 2 miles (3.2km)

LOCHGREEN HOUSE ☆☆☆
Monktonhill Road, Southwood
KA10 7EN
Tel 01292 313343
www.lochgreenhouse.co.uk
This impressive country
house hotel offers spacious
bedrooms and is peacefully
in 53ha (30 acres) of
immaculate grounds,
including a tennis court.
There is a choice of lounges
with open fires. The brasserie
menu includes interesting
options for a light lunch, with
the restaurant providing the
main dining experience.
🛏 Double from £130
🚪 40
🚗 From the A77 follow signs for
Prestwick Airport; 0.5 mile (800m)
before the airport take B749 to Troon.
Hotel is 1 mile (1.6km) on left

TURNBERRY

WESTIN TURNBERRY RESORT
☆☆☆☆☆
KA26 9LT
Tel 01655 331000
www.turnberry.co.uk
This world-famous hotel
enjoys magnificent views over
to Arran, Ailsa Craig and the
Mull of Kintyre. Facilities
include a superb
championship golf course, the
Colin Montgomerie Golf
Academy, a luxurious spa and
a host of outdoor and country
pursuits. Elegant bedrooms
and suites are located in the
main hotel, while the lodges
provide spacious, well-
equipped accommodation.
As well as the stylish main
restaurant for dining, there
is a Mediterranean Terrace
Brasserie, or the relaxed
Clubhouse.
🛏 Double from £220–£475
🚪 221 (28 non-smoking)
🌙 Closed 12–27 Dec
🏊 🏋
🚗 From Glasgow take the A77/M77
south. Beyond Kirkoswald, follow signs
for A719 Turnberry village, hotel 500m
(550 yards) on right

STAYING

EDINBURGH

ABBOTSFORD GUEST HOUSE
◊◊◊
36 Pilrig Street EH6 5AL
Tel 0131 554 2706
www.abbotsfordguesthouse.co.uk
Within walking distance of the city centre, this guesthouse offers individually decorated and thoughtfully equipped bedrooms.
🛏 Double from £60–£120
ⓘ 8 (non-smoking)

BEST WESTERN BRUNTSFIELD
★★★
69–74 Bruntsfield Place EH10 4HH
Tel 0131 229 1393
www.thebruntsfield.co.uk
Overlooking Bruntsfield Links, this smart hotel has stylish public rooms including lounge areas and a lively pub. Dinner and hearty Scottish breakfasts are served in the conservatory restaurant. Bedrooms come in a variety of sizes.
🛏 Double from £170–£225
ⓘ 73 (49 non-smoking)
🅿 25
🚗 From the south enter Edinburgh on A702. The hotel is 1 mile (1.6km) south of the west end of Princes Street

BEST WESTERN EDINBURGH CITY ★★★
79 Lauriston Place EH3 9HZ
Tel 0131 622 7979
www.bestwesternedinburghcity.co.uk
On the site of the old maternity hospital, this tasteful conversion is close to the city centre. Spacious rooms are smartly modern, and equipped with fridges. There's a bright contemporary restaurant.
🛏 Double from £85–£190
ⓘ 52 (37 non-smoking)
🚗 Follow signs for city centre, A8. Get on to the A702, take 3rd exit on left, hotel is on right

BONNINGTON GUEST HOUSE
◆◆◆◆◆
202 Ferry Road EH6 4NW
Tel 0131 554 7610
This delightful Georgian house offers individually furnished bedrooms that retain many of their original features. The comfortable lounge has a grand piano. The kilted proprietor serves a fine Scottish breakfast.
🛏 Double from £50–£76
ⓘ 6 (non-smoking)
🅿 9
🚗 On A902

BRAID HILLS ★★★
134 Braid Road EH10 6JD
Tel 0131 447 8888
www.braidhillshotel.co.uk
This long-established hotel enjoys panoramic views. Bedrooms are smart, stylish and well equipped, and there's a choice of the restaurant or brasserie and bar.
🛏 Double from £90–£145
ⓘ 67 (8 non-smoking) 🅿 38
🚗 2.5 miles (4.8km) south on A702, opposite Braidburn Park

STAYING

THE BONHAM ☆☆☆☆
35 Drumsheugh Gardens EH3 7RN
Tel 0131 226 6050
www.thebonham.com
This stylish, contemporary hotel sets high standards of luxury. Comfortable day rooms and bedrooms combine Victorian architecture with 21st-century technology. Imaginative dinners highlight good use of local fresh produce.
🛏 Double from £146–£195
🕐 48 (24 non-smoking)
🚗 Close to West End and Princes Street

CHANNINGS ☆☆☆☆
South Learmonth Gardens EH4 1EZ
Tel 0131 332 3232
www.channings.co.uk
Classical elegance and contemporary style define this hotel, with sumptuous day rooms and Channings Restaurant. The bedrooms vary in size but are well equipped and individually designed.
🛏 Double from £125–£185
🕐 41 (34 non-smoking)
🚗 Approach from A90 from Forth Road Bridge, follow signs for city centre

DALHOUSIE CASTLE & AQUEOUS SPA ★★★
Bonnyrigg EH19 3JB
Tel 01875 820153
www.dalhousiecastle.co.uk
Bedrooms in this 13th-century castle include opulently decorated themed rooms. Dinner is served in the Dungeon restaurant, while the less formal Orangery is open all day. Facilities include a sauna and solarium, fishing and falconry by arrangement.
🛏 Double from £165–£325
🕐 33 (non-smoking) 🚗 110
🚗 Take A7 south through Lasswade and Newtongrange. Turn right at Shell garage on to the B704, the hotel is 800m (0.5 mile) from intersection

DUNSTANE HOUSE ◆◆◆◆◆
4 West Coates, Haymarket EH12 5JQ
Tel 0131 337 6169
www.dunstane-hotel-edinburgh.co.uk

This splendid hotel combines architectural grandeur with an intimate country-house atmosphere. The Skerries restaurant serves fish with lighter meals and a selection of malt whisky in the bar.
🛏 Double from £98–£138
🕐 16 (non-smoking) 🚗 12
🚗 On A8 between Murrayfield Stadium and Haymarket train station

EGLINTON ◆◆◆◆
29 Eglinton Crescent EH12 5DB
Tel 0131 337 2641
www.eglinton-hotel.co.uk
The smart bedrooms in this stylish Georgian property vary in size, the larger ones being very elegant and comfortable.

Holyrood Hotel is next to the Scottish Parliament

The breakfast room highlights the period features of the house, and there is a small public bar.
🛏 Double from £60–£120
🕐 12
🕐 Closed Christmas
🚗 From A720 (city bypass) turn right at Glasgow roundabout on to A8. After 3 miles (4.8km) turn left after Donaldson college, then take 1st right. Hotel 46m (50 yards) on left

ELMVIEW ◇◇◇◇◇
15 Glengyle Terrace EH3 9LN
Tel 0131 228 1973
www.elmview.co.uk
Bedrooms and smart bathrooms are comfortable and equipped with thoughtful extras. No children under 15.

🛏 Double from £80–£110
🕐 3 (non-smoking) 🚭
🚗 2
🚗 Take A702 south up Lothian Road, turn first left past King's Theatre into Valley Field Street one-way system leading to Glengyle Terrace

GLENALLAN ◇◇◇◇
19 Mayfield Road EH9 2NG
Tel 0131 667 1667
www.glenallan.co.uk
Glenallan is ideally located for access to the city centre. It offers stylishly decorated and well-equipped bedrooms. No children under 8.
🛏 Double from £80–£120
🕐 5 (non-smoking)
🚗 4
🚗 From A720 at Straiton intersection travel north along A701. At traffic lights turn left into West Mayfield, then left into Mayfield Road—B&B is on the left

HOLYROOD HOTEL ★★★★
Holyrood Road EH8 6AE
Tel 0131 550 4500
www.macdonaldhotels.co.uk
Air-conditioned bedrooms are comfortably furnished, and the Club floor also boasts full butler service and a private lounge. There is also a spa.
🛏 Double from £99–£250
🕐 156 (140 non-smoking)
🏊
🚗 70
🚗 Parallel to the Royal Mile, near Dynamic Earth

THE HOWARD ☆☆☆☆
34 Great King Street EH3 6QH
Tel 0131 557 3500
www.thehoward.com
There are some suites and well-proportioned rooms in this quietly elegant hotel. The Atholl Dining Room contains hand-painted murals dating from the 1800s.
🛏 Double from £180–£275
🕐 18
🚗 10
🚗 Travelling east on Queen Street take the 2nd left, Dundas Street. Continue through three sets of traffic lights, turn right and the hotel is on the left

KEW HOUSE ◆◆◆◆◆
1 Kew Terrace, Murrayfield EH12 5JE
Tel 0131 313 0700
www.kewhouse.com
Meticulously maintained, the
attractive bedrooms at this
Victorian hotel suit both
business and tourist guests.
The lounge offers a supper
and snack menu.
🛏 Double from £76–£130
🚭 6 (non-smoking)
🅿 6
🚌 On A8 Glasgow road, 1 mile
(1.6km) west of city centre

KILDONAN LODGE ◆◆◆◆◆
27 Craigmillar Park EH16 5PE
Tel 0131 667 2793
www.kildonanlodgehotel.co.uk
This is a carefully restored
Victorian house. Bedrooms are
beautifully decorated and well
appointed, and some have four-
poster beds. The hospitality is
superb. Dinner is served in the
Potters Fine Dining Restaurant,
while pre-dinner drinks are
available from the honesty bar
in the lounge.
🛏 Double from £78–£145
🚭 12 (non-smoking)
🔵 Closed Christmas
🅿 16
🚌 From city bypass (A720) exit A701
to city centre. Continue for 2.75 miles
(4.4km) to large roundabout, go
straight on, hotel located six buildings
along on right-hand side

THE LODGE ◆◆◆◆◆
6 Hampton Terrace, West Coates
EH12 5JD
Tel 0131 337 3682
www.thelodgehotel.co.uk
This charming Georgian house
is within easy walking distance
of the city centre and is also
on the main bus route.
Bedrooms are beautifully
decorated and presented.
There is a comfortable lounge
and a bar; evening meals are
by prior arrangement. No
children under 8.
🛏 Double from £75–£125
🚭 10 (non-smoking)
🅿 10
🚌 On the A8, 0.75 mile (1.2km) west
of Princes Street

MARRIOTT DALMAHOY HOTEL & COUNTRY CLUB ★★★★
Kirknewton EH27 8EB
Tel 0870 400 7299
This imposing Georgian
mansion offers two
championship golf courses
and a health and beauty club.
Bedrooms are spacious and
most have wonderful views.
Public rooms offer both formal
and informal drinking and
dining options.
🛏 Double from £110–£136
🚭 215 (136 non-smoking)
♨ 🎾
🅿 350
🚌 7 miles (11.3km) west of Edinburgh
on A71

*The Marriott Dalmahoy is set in
the Pentland Hills*

PARKLANDS ◇◇◇
20 Mayfield Gardens EH9 2BZ
Tel 0131 667 7184
A friendly, long-established
guesthouse, south of the
centre, on a main bus route.
Comfortable bedrooms are
well equipped, and hearty
breakfasts are served.
🛏 Double from £40–£70
🚭 6 (2 non-smoking)
🅿 1
🚌 1.5 miles (2km) south of Princes
Street on A7/A701

PRESTONFIELD ☆☆☆☆
Priestfield Road EH16 5UT
Tel 0131 225 7800
www.prestonfield.com
A centuries-old landmark,
this hotel has been restored

and enhanced to provide
comfortable and dramatically
furnished bedrooms. There is a
tapestry lounge and a whisky
room. Meals are served in the
Rhubarb restaurant (▷ 252).
🛏 Double from £195–£275
🚭 24 (3 non-smoking)
🚌 Off A7, Priestfield Road is 200m
(200 yards) beyond the Royal
Commonwealth Pool

THE STUARTS ◆◆◆◆◆
17 Glengyle Terrace EH3 9LN
Tel 0131 229 9559
www.the-stuarts.com
This centrally located
guesthouse offers spacious,
immaculately maintained
bedrooms with luxury private
bathrooms. Bedrooms are
equipped with extras such as
CD and video players, and
fridge. The dining room looks
on to the courtyard garden.
🛏 Double from £80–£105
🚭 3 (non-smoking)
🔵 Closed Christmas
🚌 East of A702 between King's Theatre
and Bruntsfield Links

THE SCOTSMAN ☆☆☆☆☆
20 North Bridge EH1 1YT
Tel 0131 556 5565
www.thescotsmanhotel.co.uk
This architectural Victorian
icon was previously the head
office for *The Scotsman*
newspaper. The building has
since been transformed into
a state-of-the-art boutique
hotel. Bedrooms vary in size
and style. The North Bridge
Brasserie offers an informal
dining option, or try the
opulent Vermilion Restaurant.
The leisure club has a unique
stainless steel swimming
pool.
🛏 Double from £180–£700
🚭 69 (25 non-smoking)
♨ 🎾
🚌 A8 to city centre, left on to
Charlotte Street. Right on to Queen
Street, right at roundabout on to Leith
Street. Keep straight on, left on to
North Bridge, hotel on right

STAYING

CENTRAL SCOTLAND

ANSTRUTHER

THE GRANGE ♦♦♦♦♦
45 Pittenweem Road KY10 3DT
Tel 01333 310842
www.thegrangeanstruther.fsnet.co.uk
Close to the centre of the village this Victorian house is convenient for the many golf courses in the area. Bedrooms are equipped with many thoughtful extra touches. There is a spacious, comfortable lounge, a sun lounge with sea views and a charming dining room where breakfasts are served at a large communal table. No children under 10.
🛏 Double from £64
🚭 4 (non-smoking)
🚗 In Anstruther go along Shore Street, then up Rodger Street to mini-roundabout. Turn left along A917, pass Craws Nest Hotel on the left and the Grange is slightly farther on

THE SPINDRIFT ◇◇◇◇
Pittenweem Road KY10 3DT
Tel 01333 310573
www.thespindrift.co.uk
This Victorian villa is located at the western edge of the

village. Bedrooms are brightly decorated and offer many extra touches. The Captain's Room, a replica of a cabin, is a particular feature. The lounge, with its honesty bar, invites relaxation, and home-cooked fare is served at individual tables in the dining room. No children under 10.
🛏 Double from £55–£72
🚭 8 (non-smoking)
🚗 Approaching from the west, the hotel is the first building on left on entering town

SPECIAL IN AUCHTERARDER
GLENEAGLES HOTEL
☆☆☆☆☆
PH3 1NF
Tel 01764 662231
www.gleneagles.com
With its international reputation for high standards, this grand hotel provides something for everyone. Gleneagles offers a peaceful, tranquil retreat, as well as many sporting activities, including the championship golf courses, private fishing, riding stables, shooting and off-road facilities. Afternoon tea is a treat, and cocktails are prepared with flair and skill at the bar. You will find some inspired cooking at the two restaurants (▷ 253). Service is always professional and staff are friendly.
🛏 Double from £340–£795
🚭 270 (149 non-smoking)
🏊 🏋
🚗 Just off A9, well signposted

STAYING

AUCHTERARDER

CAIRN LODGE ★★
Orchil Road PH3 1LX
Tel 01764 662634
www.cairnlodge.co.uk
This charming hotel stands in wooded grounds on the edge of the town and the friendly staff provide good levels of service. There is a choice of lounges, one with a bistro menu, and the Capercaillie Restaurant. Bedrooms include four luxury rooms providing extra quality and comfort.
🍽 Double from £90
ⓘ 10
🚗 From A9 take A823, pass entrance to Gleneagles Hotel and take 2nd turning towards Auchterarder on Orchil Road

BLAIR ATHOLL

ATHOLL ARMS ★★
Old North Road PH18 5SG
Tel 01796 481205
www.athollarmshotel.co.uk
This extensive and appealing old hotel, conveniently close to both the train station and Blair Castle, has historically styled public rooms, including a choice of bars and a splendid baronial dining room. The staff are particularly friendly, and nothing is too much trouble. Outdoor pursuits available to guests include fishing and rough shooting.
🍽 Double from £50–£75
ⓘ 30
🚗 In village, close to castle entrance

CALLANDER

ARDEN HOUSE ◇◇◇◇
Bracklinn Road FK17 8EQ
Tel 01877 330235
www.ardenhouse.org.uk
This large Victorian villa lies in mature gardens in a quiet area of the town. It starred in the 1960s TV series *Dr. Finlay's Casebook* and is a friendly, welcoming house. The bedrooms are thoughtfully furnished and equipped with little extra touches. There is a stylish lounge in addition to the

breakfast room. No children under 14.
🍽 Double from £60–£70
ⓘ 6 (non-smoking)
🅲 Closed Nov–end Mar
🚗 From A84 into Callander from Stirling, turn right into Bracklinn Road signed to golf course and Bracklinn Falls. House 183m (200 yards) on left

COMRIE

ROYAL ★★★
Melville Square PH6 2DN
Tel 01764 679200
A traditional façade gives little indication of the total refurbishment that has brought much style and elegance to this long-established hotel in the village

Killiecrankie House has a historic setting

centre. Public areas include a bar and a library, a bright modern restaurant and a conservatory brasserie. Bedrooms are furnished with smart reproduction antiques. Fishing and shooting by arrangement.
🍽 Double from £120–£160
ⓘ 11
🚗 Hotel in main square of Comrie, on A85

DUNBLANE

CROMLIX HOUSE ☆☆☆
Kinbuck FK15 9JT
Tel 01786 822125
www.cromlixhouse.com
Nestling in sweeping gardens and surrounded by a 810ha (2,000-acre) estate, Cromlix

KINLOCH HOUSE ☆☆☆
PH10 6SG
Tel 01250 884237
Idyllically amid the trees, this charming small hotel offers the highest standards of care. Inviting public areas include a choice of lounges, a conservatory bar with an impressive range of malt whiskies, and a beauty and fitness centre. Many of the spacious bedrooms have notably opulent bathrooms, and the restaurant serves high quality local produce cooked with skill.
🍽 Double from £250–£360 including dinner
ⓘ 18
🅲 Closed 18–29 Dec
🚗 2 miles (3.2km) west of Blairgowrie on A923

House is an imposing Victorian mansion, with gracious and inviting public areas. Two dining rooms serve the creative and skilled output from the kitchen. Bedrooms are classically styled and many have a private sitting room. Facilities include tennis, private fishing and archery.
🍽 Double from £220–£280
ⓘ 14
🅲 Closed 2–29 Jan
🚗 Off A9 north of Dunblane. Exit B8033 to Kinbuck village, then after village cross narrow bridge, drive 183m (200 yards) on left

DUNDEE

APEX CITY QUAY HOTEL & SPA ★★★★
1 West Victoria Dock Road DD1 3JP
Tel 01382 202404
This stylish, purpose-built modern hotel lies at the heart of Dundee's regenerated city centre. Bedrooms, including some smart suites, reflect the very latest in design, and warm hospitality and professional service are an integral part of the appeal. Open-plan public areas with panoramic windows and contemporary

STAYING

food options complete the package.

🛏 Double from £80–£170

🏠 153 (122 non-smoking)

🎱 📺

🗺 Take the A85 to Discovery Quay, exit roundabout for City Quay

DUNFERMLINE
GARVOCK HOUSE ★★★
St John's Drive, Transy KY12 7TU
Tel 01383 621067
A warm welcome is assured at this impeccably presented Georgian-house hotel, standing in beautifully landscaped gardens. Modern, stylish bedrooms include DVD players, and contemporary cuisine is served in the restaurant.

🛏 Double from £120–£130

🏠 12 (non-smoking)

🗺 From M90 exit 3, take A907 to Dunfermline. Turn left after soccer stadium, then 1st right, hotel on right

DUNKELD
KINNAIRD ☆☆☆
Kinnaird Estate PH8 0LB
Tel 01796 482440
www.kinnairdestate.com
This Edwardian mansion stands on a majestic estate. Public rooms are furnished with rare antiques and paintings. Sitting rooms have deep-cushioned sofas and open fires. Bedrooms are furnished with rich, luxurious fabrics, as are the marble bathrooms. Cooking is creative and imaginative, whether a breakfast using local ingredients, or lunch and dinner with produce from farther afield. Private fishing and shooting are available. No children under 12.

🛏 Double from £295–£450

🏠 9

🗺 From Perth, take the A9 north. Keep on A9 past Dunkeld and continue for 2 miles (3.2km), then take B898 left

GLENROTHES
RESCOBIE HOUSE ★★
6 Valley Drive, Leslie KY6 3BQ
Tel 01592 749555
www.rescobie-hotel.co.uk
Hospitality and guest care are second to none at this relaxing country house, which lies in secluded gardens on the fringe of Leslie. Period architecture is enhanced by a combination of contemporary and art deco styling—a theme which carries through to the bright, airy bedrooms. An intimate restaurant serves memorable meals.

🛏 Double from £75–£99

🏠 10

🗺 Come off A92 at Glenrothes on to

Kinclaven's Ballathie House overlooks the River Tay

A911, through Leslie. At end of High Street go straight ahead, then take 1st left. Hotel entrance 2nd on left

KILLIECRANKIE
KILLIECRANKIE HOUSE ★★
PH16 5LG
Tel 01796 473220
www.killiecrankiehotel.co.uk
A long-established hotel set in mature grounds close to the historic Pass of Killiecrankie. Owners Tim and Maillie Waters and their staff provide friendly and attentive service. Inviting public areas include an attractive restaurant looking on to the gardens. The bar and sun lounge are popular, or you can relax in the quiet lounge full of books and board games.

🛏 Double from £158–£198

🏠 10 (non-smoking)

🕐 Closed 3 Jan–14 Feb

🗺 Off A9 at Killiecrankie, hotel 3 miles (4.8km) along B8079 on the right

KINCLAVEN
BALLATHIE HOUSE ☆☆☆
PH1 4QN
Tel 01250 883268
www.ballathiehousehotel.com
In extensive grounds, this splendid Scottish mansion house combines classical grandeur with modern comfort. Bedrooms range from well-proportioned master rooms to modern standard rooms and many have antique furniture and period bathrooms. For the ultimate in quality, request one of the Riverside Rooms. The elegant restaurant has views over the River Tay, and private fishing is available.

🛏 Double from £159–£179

🏠 42

🗺 From A9 2 miles (3.2km) north of Perth, take B9099 through Stanley, hotel signed; or off A93 at Beech Hedge follow signs for Ballathie 2.5 miles (4km)

KINROSS
GREEN ★★★
2 The Muirs KY13 8AS
Tel 01577 863467
www.green-hotel.com
This long-established hotel offers a wide range of activities, both indoor (including a sauna and solarium) and outdoor (golf, pétanque, tennis, fishing and curling in season). There's a choice of bars and a classical restaurant, and even a well-stocked gift shop on site. The spacious bedrooms are enhanced by smart modern furnishings.

🛏 Double from £160–£190

🏠 46 (12 non-smoking)

🎱 📺

🕐 Closed 23–24, 26–28 Dec

🗺 On A922 in middle of village

STAYING

MARKINCH

BALBIRNIE HOUSE ☆☆☆☆
Balbirnie Park KY7 6NE
Tel 01592 610066
www.balbirnie.co.uk
This hotel is a listed Georgian country house, and is the centrepiece of a 168ha (416-acre) estate that provides a peaceful setting in an area of breathtaking scenery. Day rooms include three luxurious lounges, one with a bar, and a conservatory restaurant. Bedrooms are spacious, and feature some lovely furnishings. Views from the house encompass picturesque borders and Balbirnie Park golf course.
🛏 Double from £190–£250
🚭 30 (non-smoking)
🚗 Off A92 on to B9130, entrance 800m (0.5 mile) on left

PERTH

MURRAYSHALL COUNTRY HOUSE HOTEL & GOLF COURSE ★★★
New Scone PH2 7PH
Tel 01738 551171
www.murrayshall.co.uk
This imposing country house is in grounds which include two golf courses, one of which is of championship standard. Bedrooms come in two distinct styles; modern suites in a purpose-built building contrast with more traditional rooms in the main building. The Clubhouse bar serves a range of meals all day, while more accomplished cooking can be enjoyed in the Old Masters Restaurant. Facilities include a sauna and spa.
🛏 Double from £130–£180
🚭 41 (1 non-smoking)
🛆
🚗 From Perth take A94 Coupar Angus road. After 1 mile (1.6km) turn right to Murrayshall just before New Scone

PARKLANDS HOTEL ★★★
2 St Leonards Bank PH2 8EB
Tel 01738 622451
www.theparklandshotel.com
There are great views from this hotel over the city centre park

known as the South Inch. Bedrooms are smart and furnished in contemporary style. There's a choice of restaurants, with fine dining offered in Acanthus.
🛏 Double from £99–£159
🚭 14 (4 non-smoking)
🚗 From M90 exit 10, after 1 mile (1.5km) turn left at end of park area at traffic lights, hotel is on the left

PITLOCHRY

DONAVOURD HOUSE ★★
PH16 5JS
Tel 01796 472100
Amid the peace of its own gardens and overlooking Strathtummel, this is a quiet country house in a splendid,

Pitlochry's Pine Trees retains many Victorian features

elevated position. Public rooms reflect period style, and bedrooms are spacious and well appointed. The dining room, equipped with crisp linen and fine glassware, serves notable food.
🛏 Double from £47–£75
🚭 9 (non-smoking)
🕐 Closed 25 Dec, 5 Jan–end Feb
🚗 From A9 sliproad take immediate right under railway, continue for 0.5 mile (0.75km) then left up hill; at junction (intersection) turn left, hotel 0.5 mile (0.75km) on left

GREEN PARK ★★★
Clunie Bridge Road PH16 5JY
Tel 01796 473248
www.thegreenpark.co.uk
This hotel is stunningly set in lovely landscaped gardens on the shore of Loch Faskally, within strolling distance of the town centre. Many of the bright, spacious bedrooms share the view, and the restaurant menu includes produce from the hotel's own kitchen garden.
🛏 Double from £112–£158
🚭 39 (non-smoking)
🚗 Turn off A9 at Pitlochry, follow signs 0.25 mile (0.5km) through the town, hotel on banks of Loch Faskally

KNOCKENDARROCH HOUSE ★★
Higher Oakfield PH16 5HT
Tel 01796 473473
www.knockendarroch.co.uk
This immaculate Victorian mansion overlooks the town and the Tummel Valley. There is no bar, but guests can enjoy a drink in the lounge while studying the daily menu of freshly prepared dishes. Bedrooms are tastefully furnished, comfortable and well equipped. Those on the top floor are smaller but are not without character and appeal. No children under 10.
🛏 Double from £108–£152 including dinner
🚭 12 (non-smoking)
🕐 Closed 2nd week Nov to mid-Feb
🚗 Off A9 going north at Pitlochry sign. After railway bridge, take 1st right then 2nd left

PINE TREES ★★★
Strathview Terrace PH16 5QR
Tel 01796 472121
www.pinetreeshotel.co.uk
In extensive tree-studded grounds high above the town, this Victorian mansion has many original features, including wood panelling, ornate ceilings and a marble staircase. Public rooms overlook the lawns, and the mood is refined and relaxing.

STAYING

Staff are notably friendly and helpful.

🛏 Double from £112–£156 including dinner

ℹ 20 (non-smoking)

🚗 From the high street turn into Larchwood Road and follow hotel signs

ST. ANDREWS

EDENSIDE HOUSE ◊◊◊

Edenside KY16 9SQ
Tel 01334 838108

This modernized 18th-century house is family run and offers a home from home, over-looking the Eden estuary and nature reserve. Bedrooms are bright and cheerful, and are for the most part accessed externally. There is a homey lounge, and hearty breakfasts are served.

🛏 Double from £48–£64

ℹ 8 (non-smoking)

🚗 Clearly visible from A91, 2 miles (3km) west of St. Andrews, directly on estuary shore

OLD COURSE HOTEL, GOLF RESORT AND SPA ☆☆☆☆☆

KY16 9SP
Tel 01334 474371

A haven for golfers, this internationally renowned hotel sits right beside the 17th hole of the championship course. Bedrooms range from traditional in style to contemporary fairway rooms, with course-facing balconies. Facilities include a well-equipped spa, and a range of golf shops, as well as several excellent eating options.

🛏 Double from £295–£316

ℹ 146 (non-smoking)

🏊 🍴

⊘ Closed 24–26 Dec

🚗 Close to A91 on outskirts of the city

THE PADDOCK ◆◆◆◆◆

Sunnyside, Strathkinness KY16 9XP
Tel 01334 850888
www.thepadd.co.uk

Located in a peaceful village outside St. Andrews, this friendly, family-run guesthouse overlooks rolling countryside. Superbly maintained exotic fish tanks—

one with fresh water, the other salt—line the entrance hall, making a very unusual feature. The combined lounge/dining room is in a bright, airy conservatory, making it lovely for delicious breakfasts.

🛏 Double from £48–£64

ℹ 4 (non-smoking)

🚗 Signed from the middle of Strathkinness village

RUFFLETS COUNTRY HOUSE ☆☆☆

Strathkinness Low Road KY16 9TX
Tel 01334 472594
www.rufflets.co.uk

Owned and run by the same family for over 50 years, this imposing country mansion is

Rufflets Country House boasts award-winning gardens

in extensive gardens. The committed, friendly team ensures a memorable stay. The individually decorated bedrooms are bright and airy and many have impressive bathrooms. The Garden Room is a great setting in which to enjoy meals that utilize produce from the hotel's own gardens.

🛏 Double from £199–£305

ℹ 24 (13 non-smoking)

🚗 1.5 miles (2km) west on B939

CREAGAN HOUSE ☆

FK18 8ND
Tel 01877 384638

This delightful small hotel dates back to the 17th century and has been sympathetically restored and upgraded to provide comfortable accommodation. You'll find CD players, mineral water and bathrobes in the bedrooms, and the baronial dining room is the backdrop for memorable restaurant meals.

🛏 Double from £110

ℹ 5 (non-smoking)

⊘ Closed 23 Jan–5 Mar, 6–25 Nov

🚗 North of Strathyre on A84

ST. ANDREWS GOLF ☆☆☆

40 The Scores KY16 9AS
Tel 01334 472611
www.standrews-golf.co.uk

Friendly attentive service is a particular feature of this recently refurbished hotel, which overlooks the bay and has outstanding views of the coastline and the world-famous links. The bedrooms reflect a crisp, clean, contemporary design. The public rooms remain traditional, with comfortable and relaxing lounge areas and a choice of bars. The restaurant makes excellent use of local produce.

🛏 Double from £180–£215

ℹ 21

🚗 Follow signs for Golf Course into Golf Place and after 183m (200 yards) turn right into The Scores

STAYING

GLASGOW

STAYING

GLASGOW MOAT HOUSE
★★★★
Congress Road G3 8QT
Tel 0141 306 9988
Instantly recognizable from its
mirrored glass exterior, most of
the bedrooms at this modern
hotel have panoramic views.
There are two restaurants.
🍴 Double from £75–£150
ⓘ 283 (171 non-smoking)
🏊 📺
🅿 300
🚌 From M8 exit 19 follow signs for
SECC, hotel adjacent to centre

HOLIDAY INN ★★★
161 West Nile Street G1 2RL
Tel 0141 352 8300
www.higlasgow.com
This hotel includes the Bonne
Auberge restaurant, a bar area
and conservatory. Some suites
are available.
🍴 Double from £90–£170
ⓘ 113 (79 non-smoking)
📺 Mini gym
🚌 M8 exit 16, follow signs for Royal
Concert Hall, hotel is opposite

PRICES AND SYMBOLS
Prices are the starting price
for a double room for one
night, unless otherwise
stated. Breakfast is included
unless noted otherwise. All
the hotels listed accept
credit cards unless otherwise
stated. Note that rates vary
widely throughout the year.

For a key to the symbols, ▷ 2.

KELVIN PRIVATE HOTEL ◆◆◆
15 Buckingham Terrace, Great Western
Road, Hillhead G12 8EB
Tel 0141 339 7143
www.kelvinhotel.com
Bedrooms are comfortably
proportioned, attractive and
well equipped. The dining
room serves traditional
breakfasts.
🍴 Double from £44–£62
ⓘ 21
🚌 From M8 exit 17 take A82 to
Kelvinside and Dumbarton. Hotel is
1 mile (1.6km) from motorway on right,
just before Botanic Gardens

KELVINGROVE HOTEL ◆◆◆◆
944 Sauchiehall Street G3 7TH
Tel 0141 339 5011
www.kelvingrove-hotel.co.uk
A private, well-maintained and
friendly hotel. Bedrooms,
including several family rooms,
are well equipped with private
bathrooms. There is a
breakfast room and reception
is staffed 24 hours.
🍴 Double from £55–£80
ⓘ 22 (non-smoking)
🚌 400m (0.25 mile) west of Charing
Cross. From M8 exit 18 follow signs for
Kelvingrove Museum

LANGS ★★★★
2 Port Dundas Place G2 3LD
Tel 0141 333 1500
A contemporary-style city
centre hotel, the facilities
include a sauna and two
restaurants.
🍴 Double from £90–£148
ⓘ 100 (60 non-smoking)
📺

MALMAISON ★★★

278 West George Street G2 4LL
Tel 0141 572 1000
www.malmaison.com

Bedrooms are spacious, with facilities such as CD players and minibars. There is also a range of split level suites. Dining is European brasserie style; there is a small gym.

🛏 Double from £129–£165
🛈 72 (30 non-smoking)
🈂

🚗 From south and east: M8 exit 18, Charing Cross; from west and north: M8, City Centre Glasgow

MENZIES GLASGOW ★★★★

27 Washington Street G3 8AZ
Tel 0141 222 2929

Centrally located, this modern hotel has spacious bedrooms with internet access. Facilities include a Jacuzzi, sauna and solarium.

🛏 Double from £185
🛈 141 (121 non-smoking)
🈂 🈂 🅿 50

🚗 From M8 exit 19 follow signs for SECC, then Broomielaw. Turn left at traffic lights

MERCHANT LODGE ◆◆◆

52 Virginia Street G1 1TY
Tel 0141 552 2424
www.hotelsglasgow.com

This hotel is spread over five floors, and fully modernized with pleasant, understated décor. Breakfast is self-service in a lower level room.

🛏 Double from £57
🛈 40

🚗 From George Square enter North Hanover Street, head towards Ingram Street. Turn into Virginia Place, which leads into Virginia Street

MILLENNIUM HOTEL GLASGOW ★★★★

George Square G2 1DS
Tel 0141 332 6711
www.millennium-hotels.com

The whole property has a contemporary air and public areas include a glass veranda. There is a brasserie, and a separate wine bar.

🛏 Double from £165–£245
🛈 117 (54 non-smoking)

🚗 From M8 exit 15 follow road through four sets of traffic lights, at 5th set turn left into Hanover Street. George Square is directly ahead, hotel is on the right-hand corner

NOVOTEL GLASGOW CENTRE ★★★

181 Pitt Street G2 4DT
Tel 0141 222 2775
www.accorhotels.com

Bedrooms include a number of larger family rooms. The all-day Brasserie and bar provide good value and are also available on room service. Facilities include a sauna. A limited amount of free parking.

The Uplawmoor Hotel offers a convenient, village location

🛏 Double from £99
🛈 139 (90 non-smoking)
🈂 🅿 19

🚗 Next to Strathclyde Police HQ. Close to the Scottish Conference and Exhibition Centre just off Sauchiehall Street

RADISSON SAS GLASGOW ★★★★

301 Argyle Street G2 8DL
Tel 0141 204 3333

This large city-centre hotel offers contemporary design as well as comfort and style, with two restaurants, leisure centre and bars.

🛏 Double from £135–£190
🛈 247 (200 non-smoking) 🈂 🈂

🚗 From M8, exit 19, take 1st right, continue to Argyle Street, 1st left. Hotel on left opposite Central train station

ONE DEVONSHIRE GARDENS ☆☆☆☆

1 Devonshire Gardens G12 0UX
Tel 0141 339 2001
www.onedevonshiregardens.com

This famous townhouse hotel offers bedrooms—including a number of suites and four-poster rooms—that are individually designed. There are also drawing rooms, and a smart restaurant.

🛏 Double from £135–£495
🛈 36 🈂

🚗 From M8 exit 17 follow signs for A82. After 1.5 miles (2.4km) turn left into Hyndland Road, take 1st right, go right at mini-roundabout, right again at the end and continue to end of road

UPLAWMOOR HOTEL ★★

Neilston Road, Uplawmoor G78 4AF
Tel 01505 850565
www.uplawmoor.co.uk

At this attractive and friendly village hotel there is a formal restaurant, with cocktail bar, and the separate lounge bar serves bar meals. The modern bedrooms are well equipped.

🛏 Double from £59–£79
🛈 14 (8 non-smoking)
🅿 40

🚗 From M77 exit 2 take the A736 signposted to Barrhead and Irvine. Hotel is located 4 miles (6.4km) beyond Barrhead

VICTORIAN HOUSE ◆◆◆

212 Renfrew Street G3 6TX
Tel 0141 332 0129
www.thevictorian.co.uk

This raised terraced (row) house offers a range of well-equipped bedrooms, in both modern and traditional décor. The breakfast room serves buffet style meals.

🛏 Double from £46–£56
🛈 58

🚗 Turn left into Garnet Street at 1st set of traffic lights on Sauchiehall Street, east of Charing Cross. Go right into Renfrew Street, hotel is 91m (100 yards) on left

STAYING

HIGHLANDS AND ISLANDS

STAYING

ABERDEEN

THE MARCLIFFE AT PITFODELS ★★★★
North Deeside Road AB15 9YA
Tel 01224 861000
www.marcliffe.com
Set in attractive landscaped grounds, bedrooms are well proportioned and equipped, and there is a restaurant, and a cocktail lounge.
🍴 Double from £130–£325
🛏 42 (26 non-smoking)
🚗 Turn off A90 on to A93 signposted Braemar. Hotel 1 mile (1.6km) on right after turn-off at traffic lights

ARDUAINE

LOCH MELFORT ★★★
by Oban, PA34 4XG
Tel 01852 200233
www.lochmelfort.co.uk
This popular, family-run hotel has outstanding views; and the cuisine is based around fresh seafood. The skerry bistro serves lighter meals and afternoon teas.
🍴 Double from £78–£158
🛏 27 (11 non-smoking)
🚗 On A816, midway between Oban and Lochgilphead

PRICES AND SYMBOLS
Prices are the starting price for a double room for one night, unless otherwise stated. Breakfast is included unless noted otherwise. All the hotels listed accept credit cards unless otherwise stated. Note that rates vary widely throughout the year.

For a key to the symbols, ▷ 2.

AVIEMORE

THE OLD MINISTER'S HOUSE ◇◇◇◇◇
Rothiemurchus PH22 1QH
Tel 01479 812181
www.theoldministershouse.co.uk
Beautifully furnished and immaculately maintained, bedrooms are spacious. There is a lounge, and hearty breakfasts are served. No children under 12.
🍴 Double from £60–£80
🛏 4 (non-smoking)
🚗 From Aviemore take the B970, signed Glenmore and Coylumbridge. B&B is 0.75 miles (1.2km) from Aviemore at Inverdruie

BALLATER

BALGONIE COUNTRY HOUSE ☆☆
Braemar Place AB35 5NQ
Tel 01339 755482
www.royaldeesidehotels.com
There is a bar and lounge, and a dining room. Comfortable bedrooms and public areas are immaculately maintained.
🍴 Double from £100–£140
🛏 9
🕐 Closed 6 Jan–end Feb
🚗 Off A93, on the western outskirts of Ballater. Hotel is signed

DARROCH LEARG ☆☆☆
Braemar Road AB35 5UX
Tel 01339 755443
Elegant day rooms include a drawing room and separate smoking room. The restaurant serves modern Scottish cuisine. Some bedrooms have four-poster beds.
🍴 Double from £155–£230 including dinner
🛏 17 (non-smoking)
🕐 Closed Christmas and Jan (except New Year)
🚗 Hotel on the A93, at western edge of Ballater

BALLACHULISH HOUSE
◇◇◇◇◇
PH49 4JX
Tel 01855 811266
www.ballachulishhouse.com
Bedrooms are tastefully decorated, with many thoughtful touches, and the atmosphere is friendly and welcoming. The sitting room has an open fire, and top Scottish cuisine is served in the dining room.
🛏 Double from £80
ⓘ 8 (non-smoking)
🚗 Off A82 on to A825 Oban road. Guesthouse is 400m (440 yards) on left just beyond Ballachulish Hotel

BRORA

GLENAVERON ◆◆◆◆◆
Golf Road KW9 6QS
Tel 01408 621601
www.glenaveron.co.uk
Two bedrooms are pine-furnished and one has lovely period pieces. There is a lounge, and breakfasts are served house-party style.
🛏 Double from £56–£66
ⓘ 3 (non-smoking) 🔲
🚗 From the south, cross bridge in the middle of Brora, turn right off A9 into Golf Road and take 2nd left. Second house on the right

ROYAL MARINE ★★★
Gold Road KW9 6QS
Tel 01408 621252
www.highlandescape.com
This splendid mansion has a leisure centre (with solarium and Jacuzzi), 18-hole golf course, tennis court and ice rink for curling in season. There's a restaurant and a café-bar. Part of the Classic British group of hotels.
🛏 Double from £120–£160
ⓘ 22
🏊 🔳
🚗 Off A9 in village, towards beach and golf course

CARDROSS

KIRKTON HOUSE ◆◆◆◆◆
Darleith Road G82 5EZ
Tel 01389 841951
www.kirktonhouse.co.uk

Bedrooms are individual in style with lots of extras, and home-cooked meals are served in the dining room. Riding stables are nearby.
🛏 Double from £50–£60
ⓘ 6 (non-smoking)
◉ Closed Dec–end Jan
🚗 0.5 mile (800m) north of village, turn north off A814 into Darleith Road at west end of village. Kirkton House is 0.5 mile (800m) on the right

CLACHAN-SEIL

WILLOWBURN ★★
PA34 4TJ
Tel 01852 300276
www.willowburn.co.uk
Friendly, attentive service and fine food. There is a homey

Ballachulish House is a 17th-century laird's residence

bar with a veranda, a formal dining room and a lounge. No children under 8.
🛏 Double from £152 including dinner
ⓘ 7 (non-smoking)
◉ Closed Dec–end Feb
🚗 0.5 mile (800m) from Atlantic Bridge, on left

DUNDONNELL

DUNDONNELL ★★★
Little Loch Broom IV23 2QR
Tel 01854 633204
www.dundonnellhotel.com
A beautiful but isolated location offers a range of attractive and comfortable public areas and a choice of eating options and bars. Many of the bedrooms enjoy fine views.

RAEMOIR HOUSE ★★★
Raemoir AB31 4ED
Tel 01330 824884
www.raemoir.com
Public rooms include sitting rooms, a cocktail bar and a dining room. The bedrooms are individual in style and size. Facilities include tennis, shooting, deer stalking and a 9-hole golf course.
🛏 Double from £95–£138
ⓘ 20
🚗 Take A93 to Banchory, turn right on to A980 to Torphins. The main drive is 2 miles (3.2km) ahead at the T-junction (intersection)

🛏 Double from £90–£120
ⓘ 32
🚗 Off A835 at Braemore junction (intersection) on to A832. Hotel is 14 miles (22km) farther on

ELGIN

MANSION HOUSE ★★★
The Haugh IV30 1AW
Tel 01343 548811
www.mansionhousehotel.co.uk
Facilities include a lounge, a bar, a leisure centre with spa, a bistro and a formal restaurant. Many bedrooms are spacious and feature four-poster beds.
🛏 Double from £143–£175
ⓘ 23
🏊 🔳
🚗 In Elgin turn off the A96 into Haugh Road, the hotel is at the end of the road by the river

FORT WILLIAM

ASHBURN HOUSE ◇◇◇◇◇
8 Achintore Road PH33 6RQ
Tel 01397 706000
www.highland5star.co.uk
The bedrooms are spacious, and there is a conservatory lounge and a dining room; breakfast is cooked on an Aga.
🛏 Double from £70–£100
ⓘ 7 (non-smoking)
🚗 At the junction (intersection) of the A82 and Ashburn Lane, 457m (500 yards) from the large roundabout at the southern end of High Street; or 366m (400 yards) on the right after entering 30mph zone from the south

STAYING

ISLE OF ERISKA ☆☆☆☆
Ledaig PA37 1SD
Tel 01631 720371
www.eriska-hotel.co.uk
Situated on its own private island with beaches and walking trails, spacious bedrooms are comfortable with some antique pieces. Local produce features on the restaurant menu, as do vegetables and herbs grown in the hotel's kitchen garden. An indoor swimming pool and spa treatment rooms are available, along with private fishing and nature trails.
🛏 Double from £260–£360
ℹ️ 17
🄲 Closed Jan 🏊 🐾
🚌 Leave A85 at Connel, join A828; continue for 4 miles (6.4km) through Benderloch, then follow signs

THE GRANGE ◇◇◇◇◇
Grange Road PH33 6JF
Tel 01397 705516
www.thegrange-scotland.co.uk
Two of the bedrooms have loch views. The dining room serves hearty breakfasts. No children under 13.
🛏 Double from £96–£110
ℹ️ 4 (non-smoking)
🄲 Closed Nov–end Mar
🚌 Leave Fort William on the A82 south. 274m (300 yards) from the roundabout go left on to Ashburn Lane. The Grange is at the top on the left

GRANTOWN-ON-SPEY

CULDEARN HOUSE ★★
Woodlands Terrace PH26 3JU
Tel 01479 872106
www.culdearn.com
This hotel has the atmosphere of a relaxed country house. No children under 10.
🛏 Double from £170 including dinner
ℹ️ 7 (non-smoking)
🄲 Closed Jan–end Feb
🚌 Enter Grantown on A95 from the southwest and turn left at 30mph sign

MUCKRACH LODGE ★★★
Dulnain Bridge PH26 3LY
Tel 01479 851257
There's a homey bar, bistro and a restaurant. Facilities

include beauty and aromatherapy treatments, and fishing.
🛏 Double from £120–£160
ℹ️ 10 (non-smoking)
🄲 Closed 5–20 Jan
🚌 Leave A95 at Dulnain Bridge exit, follow A938 towards Carrbridge; hotel 500m (500 yards) on right

HARRIS, ISLE OF

SCARISTA HOUSE
Scarista HS3 3HX
Tel 01859 550238
Food lovers will know of this restaurant with rooms. The house is run in a relaxed country house manner, so expect wellies (rubber boots) in the hall

Raemoir House near Banchory is in extensive parkland

and books and CDs in one of the two lounges.
🛏 Double from £150–£170
ℹ️ 5 (non-smoking)
🄲 Closed Christmas
🚌 On A859, 15 miles (24km) south of Tarbert

INVERNESS

BALLIFEARY GUESTHOUSE ◆◆◆◆◆
10 Ballifeary Road IV3 5PJ
Tel 01463 235572
www.ballifearyhousehotel.co.uk
This house in its own grounds offers comfortable bedrooms. There is a lounge and the breakfasts use local produce. No children under 15.
🛏 Double from £60–£70
ℹ️ 6 (non-smoking)

🄲 Closed Christmas
🚌 Off A82, 0.5 mile (800m) from the town centre, turn left into Bishops Road and sharp right into Ballifeary Road

CRAIGSIDE LODGE ◆◆◆◆
4 Gordon Terrace IV2 3HD
Tel 01463 231576
Bedrooms are bright and well proportioned. There is a lounge and a conservatory. Hearty Scottish breakfasts are served at individual tables.
🛏 Double from £44
ℹ️ 5 (non-smoking)
🚌 From the town centre take Castle Street, then 1st left into Old Edinburgh Road, then next three left turns

CULLODEN HOUSE ★★★★
Culloden IV2 7BZ
Tel 01463 790461
www.cullodenhouse.com
Some bedrooms are located in a separate house. No children under 10.
🛏 Double from £130–£210
ℹ️ 28 (8 non-smoking)
🄲 Closed 24–28 Dec
🚌 Take A96 from town and turn right for Culloden. After 1 mile (1.5km), turn left at White Church after 2nd traffic lights

MOYNESS HOUSE ◆◆◆◆◆
6 Bruce Gardens IV3 5EN
Tel 01463 233836
www.moyness.co.uk
This elegant villa offers beautifully decorated bedrooms and well-fitted bathrooms. There is a sitting room, a dining room where traditional Scottish breakfasts are served, and a garden.
🛏 Double from £76
ℹ️ 7 (non-smoking)
🚌 Off A82 Fort William road, almost opposite Highland Regional Council headquarters

TRAFFORD BANK ◇◇◇◇◇
96 Fairfield Road IV3 5LL
Tel 01463 241414
Bedrooms in this impressive Victorian villa are furnished with restored traditional furniture, and thoughtful extras. Dinner is available on request.
🛏 Double from £70–£88

SPECIAL IN INVERNESS

GLENMORISTON TOWN HOUSE ★★★
20 Ness Bank IV2 4SF
Tel 01463 223777
www.glenmoriston.com
Bold contemporary designs blend seamlessly with the classical architecture. Bar and restaurant. The bedrooms are well equipped.
🛏 Double from £130–£180
🚭 30 (15 non-smoking)
📍 On the riverside opposite the theatre, five minutes from the town centre

🚭 5 (non-smoking)
📍 Turn off A82 at Kenneth Street, take 2nd left, Fairfield Road, Trafford Bank is 549m (600 yards) on left

KINGUSSIE

OSPREY HOTEL ◆◆◆◆◆
Ruthven Road PH21 1EN
Tel 01540 661510
www.ospreyhotel.co.uk
Dinner uses local produce, and hearty breakfasts include home-baked breads and preserves. Bedrooms vary in size and style.
🛏 Double from £60–£74
🚭 8 (non-smoking)
🚭
📍 Turn off A9 into Kingussie, hotel is at the southern end of the main street

LOCHINVER

INVER LODGE ☆☆☆
IV27 4LU
Tel 01571 844496
www.inverlodge.com
Local ingredients are used in the restaurant. Bedrooms have ocean views. Facilities include fishing and a sauna.
🛏 Double from £150
🚭 20
🕐 Closed Nov–Easter
📍 Take A835 to Lochinver, continue through the village and turn left after the village hall. Follow the private road for 0.5 mile (800m)

MELVICH

SHEILING ◆◆◆◆◆
KW14 7YJ
Tel 01641 531256

SPECIAL IN NAIRN

BOATH HOUSE ☆☆
Auldearn IV12 5TE
Tel 01667 454896
www.boath-house.com
Five-course dinners are matched only by the excellence of the breakfasts. The house itself is delightful, with inviting lounges and a dining room overlooking a trout loch. Bedrooms include many fine antique pieces.
🛏 Double from £170–£220
🚭 6 (non-smoking)
🕐 Closed Christmas 📺
📍 2 miles (3.2km) past Nairn on A96 driving east towards Forres, signposted on main road

Moyness House is convenient for Inverness city centre

The attractive bedrooms are equipped with thoughtful extras. The two lounges offer a range of leisure pursuits. No children under 12.
🛏 Double from £64
🚭 3 (non-smoking)
🕐 Closed Nov–end Mar
📍 17 miles (27km) west of Thurso on A836 coastal road

MULL, ISLE OF

DRUIMARD COUNTRY HOUSE
Dervaig, PA75 6QW
Tel 01688 400345
www.druimard.co.uk
Attractive decoration schemes feature in the bedrooms, there is a lounge and conservatory bar, and the dining room serves five-course dinners.

🛏 Double from £100–£125
🚭 7
🕐 Closed Jan and Nov
📍 From Craignure ferry terminal turn right towards Tobermory; go through Salen village. After 1.5 miles (2.4km) turn left to Dervaig, hotel on right before village

HIGHLAND COTTAGE ☆☆
Breadalbane Street, Tobermory PA75 6PD
Tel 01688 302030
www.highlandcottage.co.uk
Bedrooms feature antique beds and a range of extras. Public areas include a lounge, an honesty bar, and a conservatory. No children under 10.
🛏 Double from £120–£150
🚭 6 (non-smoking)
📍 A848 Craignure/Fishnish ferry terminal, pass Tobermory signs, go ahead at mini-roundabout across narrow bridge, turn right. Hotel on the right opposite the fire station

OBAN

GLENBURNIE HOUSE ◇◇◇◇
The Esplanade PA34 5AQ
Tel 01631 562089
Bedrooms include a four-poster room and a mini suite. There is a lounge and traditional breakfasts are served in the dining room. No children under 12.
🛏 Double from £70–£90
🚭 14 (non-smoking)
🕐 Closed Nov–end Mar
📍 Directly on Oban waterfront, follow signs for Ganavan

MANOR HOUSE ★★★
Gallanach Road PA34 4LS
Tel 01631 562087
www.manorhouseoban.com
The Georgian Manor House has a welcoming atmosphere. A daily-changing five-course dinner is served in the dining room. Many of the bedrooms have views across the bay. No children under 12.
🛏 Double from £134–£180
🚭 11 (non-smoking)
🕐 Closed 25–26 Dec
📍 Follow signs for MacBrayne Ferries, go past ferry entrance, hotel is on right

POOL HOUSE HOTEL ☆☆☆

IV22 2LD
Tel 01445 781272
www.poolhousehotel.com
The bedrooms are spacious
and comfortable suites. Local
produce features strongly on
the menus. No children
under 8.
🛏 Double from £240
🚭 5 (non-smoking)
🚫 Closed Jan–end Feb
🚗 6 miles (9.7km) north of Gairloch
on A832. Located in the middle of
Poolewe village

PORT APPIN

AIRDS ☆☆☆

Appin PA38 4DF
Tel 01631 730236
www.airds-hotel.com
The front-facing bedrooms
enjoy the views, as do the
lounges and restaurant.
🛏 Double from £230–£280 including
dinner
🚭 12 (non-smoking)
🚫 Closed 5–26 Jan
🚗 From Ballachulish Bridge take the
A828 south for 16 miles (25.7km), turn
right and continue for 2 miles (3.2km)

SHIELDAIG

TIGH AN EILEAN ☆

IV54 8XN
Tel 01520 755251
There are three comfortable
lounges and an honesty bar.
The dinner menu features
seafood and quality local
produce, with lighter snacks
served in the bar at lunchtime.
🛏 Double from £130
🚭 11
🚫 Closed late Oct–end Mar
🚗 From A896 take the village road
signposted Shieldaig. The hotel is in the
village centre on loch front

SKYE, ISLE OF

HOTEL EILEAN IARMAIN ★★

Isle Ornsay IV43 8QR
Tel 01471 833332
www.eileaniarmain.co.uk
Bedrooms are individual and
traditional, and there are four
suites. Public rooms are
homey. Facilities include

private fishing and whisky
tasting.
🛏 Double from £120
🚭 16 (10 non-smoking)
🚗 A851, A852, right to Isle Ornsay
harbour front

STRONTIAN

KILCAMB LODGE ☆☆

PH36 4HY
Tel 01967 402257
www.kilcamblodge.co.uk
Bedrooms in this former
hunting lodge are well
decorated. The short choice of
dishes uses local produce.
🛏 Double from £110–£220
🚭 11 (non-smoking)
🚗 Off A861, via Corran Ferry

TAIN

GLENMORANGIE HIGHLAND HOME AT CADBOLL ☆☆

Cadboll, Fearn IV20 1XP
Tel 01862 871671
www.glenmorangie.com
This highly individual hotel has
bedrooms in both the main
house and in converted farm
cottages. Prices include
afternoon tea, a four-course
dinner and wines.
🛏 Double from £280–£370 including
dinner
🚭 9 (non-smoking)
🚗 From A9 turn on to B9175 towards
Nigg and follow signs

TORRIDON

LOCH TORRIDON COUNTRY HOUSE HOTEL ☆☆☆

by Achnasheen IV22 2EY
Tel 01445 791242
www.lochtorridonhotel.com
Most bedrooms enjoy
Highland views, the day rooms
are comfortable, and the
whisky bar stocks over 300
malts. Wide range of outdoor
activities include shooting,
bicycling, horseback riding and
walking.
🛏 Double from £152–£376
🚭 19 (non-smoking)
🚫 Closed 3–27 Jan
🚗 From A832 at Kinlochewe, take
A896 towards Torridon; do not turn into
village, instead carry on for 1 mile
(1.6km). Hotel on right

ULLAPOOL

DROMNAN ◆◆◆◆◆

Garve Road IV26 2SX
Tel 01854 612333
This friendly modern house
offers attractive bedrooms with
private facilities. The
lounge/breakfast room
overlooks Loch Broom.
🛏 Double from £50–£60
🚭 7 (non-smoking)
🚗 From the A835 south on entering
the town, turn left at 30mph sign

ORKNEY AND SHETLAND

BRAE

BUSTA HOUSE ★★★

Brae, Shetland ZE2 9QN
Tel 01806 522606
Day rooms at this country-
house hotel include a
comfortable lounge. Food is
served in the traditional bar,
and in the Pitcairn restaurant.
🛏 Double from £100–£150
🚭 20 (non-smoking)
🚫 Closed 23 Dec–5 Jan
🚗 Take A970 north through village,
follow signs to hotel 0.75km (0.5 mile)
farther on

LERWICK

GLEN ORCHY HOUSE ◆◆◆◆

20 Knab Road, Shetland ZE1 0AX
Tel 01595 692031
www.guesthouselerwick.com
Bedrooms are modern and
there is a choice of lounges.
Daily-changing dinner menu.
🛏 Double from £69
🚭 24 (11 non-smoking)
🚗 Next to the coastguard station

LERWICK ★★★

15 South Road, Shetland ZE1 0RB
Tel 01595 692166
www.shetlandhotels.com
Smartly presented, it offers
an attractive brasserie and a
formal restaurant. Well-
furnished rooms.
🛏 Double from £90
🚭 34
🚗 Near the town centre, on main road
southwards to/from the airport

Planning

CLIMATE AND WHEN TO GO

Scots will tell you that Scotland does not have a climate: it only has weather. This is by far the most mountainous area of Britain, and the only part to reach over 1,350m (4,000ft), so weather conditions can be extreme. Its position on the edge of the continental land mass of Europe, surrounded on three sides by sea, means that the weather is always varied.

● The eastern side of the country tends to be cool and dry, the western side milder and wetter. Conditions can change dramatically in just a short distance, and the occasional outbreak of haar (sea mist) along the coast is often a sign of bright sunshine only a little way inland.

DAYLIGHT HOURS	
January	7 hrs 45 mins
February	9 hrs 31 mins
March	11 hrs 51 mins
April	14 hrs 12 mins
May	16 hrs 15 mins
June	17 hrs 24 mins
July	16 hrs 52 mins
August	14 hrs 53 mins
September	12 hrs 43 mins
October	10 hrs 26 mins
November	8 hrs 20 mins
December	7 hrs 11 mins

● At any time of year you are likely to meet rain, but with Scotland's ever-changing weather patterns, the chances are that it will not last for long. Weather fronts move in from the west across the Atlantic, low pressure bringing wind, rain and changeable conditions, and high pressure bringing more settled weather.

● The best times of the year for sunny weather are in spring and early summer (April and June). In high summer (July and August) the weather is changeable—it may be hot and sunny, but it can also be cloudy and wet. Late summer and early autumn (September and October) are usually more settled and there's a better chance of good weather, but nothing is guaranteed, and mist can settle in the glens for days at a time. Late autumn and winter, from November to March, can be cold, dark, wet and dreich (dreary), but you can also have sparkling, clear, sunny

EDINBURGH

Average temperature per day
per night

GLASGOW

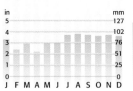

Average temperature per day
per night

LERWICK

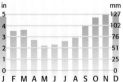

Average temperature per day
per night

Average no. of days above 70°F
below 32°F

Average no. of days above 70°F
below 32°F

Average no. of days above 70°F
below 32°F

Average rainfall

Average rainfall

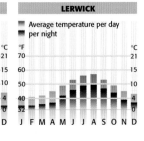

Average rainfall

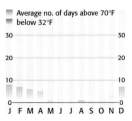

WEATHER WEBSITES		
ORGANIZATION	NOTES	WEBSITE
BBC	London, UK and world weather reports and forecasts, plus many related topics. Includes satellite imagery	www.bbc.co.uk/weather/
The Met Office (UK)	Clear, professional site with good specialist links	www.metoffice.com

PLANNING

Scotland, like the rest of Britain, is on GMT (Greenwich Mean Time—also known as Universal Time or UTC) during winter. In summer (late March to late October) clocks go forward 1 hour to British Summer Time (BST). The chart below shows time differences from GMT.

CITY	TIME DIFFERENCE	TIME AT 12 NOON GMT
Amsterdam	+1	1pm
Auckland	+10	10pm
Berlin	+1	1pm
Brussels	+1	1pm
Chicago	-6	6am
Dublin	0	12am
Johannesburg	+12	2pm
Madrid	+1	1pm
Montreal	-6	6am
New York	-5	7am
Paris	+1	1pm
Perth, Australia	+8	8pm
Rome	+1	1pm
San Francisco	-8	4am
Sydney	+10	10pm
Tokyo	+9	9pm

days of frost, when the light is brilliant. Winter can bring severe conditions of wind and snow to the Highlands and high ground, and these should not be underestimated.
● Note that many tourist sites close in winter (October to Easter), including most National Trust for Scotland properties, but major city museums stay open year round.
● Scotland's indigenous biting insect, the midgie, is active from late May to mid-September, predominantly on the west coast and the islands. Though its bite is profoundly irritating, it is not life-threatening. If the widely available midge repellents don't work for you, veils can be bought at outdoor stores.

WEATHER REPORTS
Daily forecasts are given at the end of television and radio news. They are also available by phone, fax, text or on the internet.
● Telephone 09003 444900 for regional forecasts over the phone, or fax 09060 100400 for a list of regions covered by faxed forecasts.
● For forecasts texted to a mobile phone type wthr4 followed by a UK town or city. Send this message to 8638 (Vodafone) or 2638 (O₂).

CUSTOMS
Goods you buy in the European Union (EU)
If you bring back large quantities of alcohol or tobacco, a Customs Officer is more likely to ask about the purposes for which you hold the goods. This applies particularly if you have with you more than the following amounts:

● 3,200 cigarettes
● 400 cigarillos
● 200 cigars
● 3kg of smoking tobacco

● 110 litres of beer
● 10 litres of spirits
● 90 litres of wine (of which only 60 litres can be sparkling wine)
● 20 litres of fortified wine (such as port or sherry)

The EU countries are: Austria, Belgium, Cyprus, Czech Republic, Denmark, Estonia, Finland, France, Germany, Greece, Hungary, Irish Republic, Italy, Latvia, Lithuania, Luxembourg, Malta, Netherlands, Poland, Portugal, Spain, Sweden and the United Kingdom.

Travelling to the UK from outside the EU
You are entitled to the allowances shown below only if you travel with the goods and do not plan to sell them. For further information see HM Revenue and Customs website: www.hmrc.gov.uk

● 200 cigarettes; or
● 100 cigarillos; or
● 50 cigars; or
● 250g of tobacco

● 60cc/ml of perfume
● 250cc/ml of toilet water

● 2 litres of still table wine
● 1 litre of spirits or strong liqueurs over 22 per cent volume; or
● 2 litres of fortified wine, sparkling wine or other liqueurs

● £145 worth of all other goods including gifts and souvenirs

WHAT TO TAKE
Dress in Scotland is generally casual, unless you are part of a special or formal occasion, when it can go well over the top. Use the following checklist as a starting point, but if you forget or need to replace any items there's every chance that you'll be able to buy its equivalent in Scotland.
● For a summer visit, lightweight clothing and sandals may be fine for daytime, but bring socks, long-sleeved shirts, long trousers, a lightweight sweater and water-proof jacket for cooler evenings or when the wind blows.
● On bright days the light can be dazzlingly clear, so take sunglasses and sunscreen.
● An umbrella may be useful at any time of year, and can usually be bought inexpensively if you don't want to carry it with you.
● In winter, when the wind can be particularly chilling, make sure you have layers of warm clothing for outdoors.
● If you are planning any serious walking you should be properly equipped with stout walking boots and waterproofs.

And don't forget to bring the following:
● Your driver's licence or permit. An International Driving Permit may be useful if your licence is in a language other than English.
● Photocopies of passport and travel insurance.
● Travellers' cheques and credit cards, and a small amount of cash in sterling.
● Numbers of credit/debit cards, registration numbers of mobile phones, cameras and other expensive equipment (in case of theft).

PASSPORTS
● Visitors from outside the UK must have a passport valid for at least six months from the date of entry into the country.
● The United Kingdom (England, Wales, Scotland and Northern Ireland), the Channel Islands, the Isle of Man and the Republic of Ireland form a common travel area. Once you have entered through immigration control into any part of it, you do not need further clearance to travel within it.

PLANNING

● If you are a citizen of the US, Australia, Canada or New Zealand, you do not require a visa for stays of up to six months.
● Those wishing to stay longer than six months and nationals of some other countries need a visa.
● You are usually allowed to enter and leave the UK as many times as you like while your visa is valid. On arrival in the UK you must be able to produce documentation establishing your identity and nationality.

TRAVEL INSURANCE
This is recommended for insuring your possessions and legal liability, and also for medical expenses.

HEALTH DOCUMENTS
● EHIC form, ▷ 296.

● However, you may be required to show photographic ID, such as a passport or a driver's licence with a photo, for internal flights.

VISAS
● Passport and visa regulations can change at short notice, so you should always check the current situation before you travel. For general information on visas see www.ukvisas.gov.uk
● Citizens of countries in the European Economic Area (EEA)—the EU, Switzerland, Norway and Iceland—can enter the UK for purposes of holiday or work for any length of stay, without a visa.

PRACTICALITIES

ELECTRICITY
Britain is on 240 volts AC, and plugs have three square pins. If you are bringing an electrical appliance from another country where the voltage is the same, a plug adaptor will suffice. If the voltage is different, as in the US—110 volts—you need a converter.
● Small appliances such as razors and laptops can run on a 50-watt converter, while heating appliances, irons and hair-dryers require a 1,600-watt converter.
● Telephone sockets are also different and will require an adaptor.

LAUNDRY
● When you reserve your accommodation, ask about laundry facilities.
● Telephone directories list launderettes and dry cleaners. Some launderettes offer service washes, where the washing and drying is done for you (typically £5–£6 for a small bag), either within a day or with a 24–48-hour turnaround.
● Dry cleaning is widely available: A jacket or skirt individually cleaned will cost around £4. Some dry cleaners also offer clothes-mending services such as zipper replacement.

MEASUREMENTS
Britain officially uses the metric system. Fuel is sold by the litre, and food in grams and kilograms. However, imperial

CLOTHING SIZES
The chart below shows how British, European and US clothes sizes differ.

UK	Metric	US	
36	46	36	SUITS
38	48	38	
40	50	40	
42	52	42	
44	54	44	
46	56	46	
48	58	48	
7	41	8	SHOES
7.5	42	8.5	
8.5	43	9.5	
9.5	44	10.5	
10.5	45	11.5	
11	46	12	
14.5	37	14.5	SHIRTS
15	38	15	
15.5	39/40	15.5	
16	41	16	
16.5	42	16.5	
17	43	17	
8	36	6	DRESSES
10	38	8	
12	40	10	
14	42	12	
16	44	14	
18	46	16	
20	46	18	
4.5	37.5	6	SHOES
5	38	6.5	
5.5	38.5	7	
6	39	7.5	
6.5	40	8	
7	41	8.5	

CONVERSION CHART
FROM	TO	MULTIPLY BY
Inches	Centimetres	2.54
Centimetres	Inches	0.3937
Feet	Metres	0.3048
Metres	Feet	3.2810
Yards	Metres	0.9144
Metres	Yards	1.0940
Miles	Kilometres	1.6090
Kilometres	Miles	0.6214
Acres	Hectares	0.4047
Hectares	Acres	2.4710
Gallons	Litres	4.5460
Litres	Gallons	0.2200
Ounces	Grams	28.35
Grams	Ounces	0.0353
Pounds	Grams	453.6
Grams	Pounds	0.0022
Pounds	Kilograms	0.4536
Kilograms	Pounds	2.205
Tons	Tonnes	1.0160
Tonnes	Tons	0.9842

measures are used widely in everyday speech, and road distances and speed limits are in miles and miles per hour respectively.
● Beer in pubs is still sold in pints (one pint is slightly less than 0.5 litres).
● Note that the British gallon (4.5460 litres) is larger than the US gallon (3.7854 litres).

PUBLIC TOILETS
Generally these are well located, plentiful and free in built-up areas. There may be a small charge to use toilets at certain

PLANNING

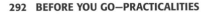

large train stations. Some unpleasant facilities survive, but most are modern and well maintained.

● All major road service stations and filling stations have free toilets. In rural areas toilets can be found at some roadside pull-offs and parking areas.

● It is not acceptable for those who are not customers to use the toilets in pubs, cafés and restaurants.

SMOKING

● Most restaurants have non-smoking areas, and an increasing number forbids smoking altogether.

● In pubs you can generally smoke, but there are sometimes dedicated non-smoking zones within dining areas.

● Smoking is banned on most local trains and buses, although long-distance trains usually have areas for smokers.

● For an online guide to smoke-free pubs, restaurants and hotels see www.ash.org.uk

TRAVEL WITH CHILDREN

Some hotels, restaurants and pubs have a strict no-children policy or serve children only over a certain age. Some places offer excellent facilities for children, including babysitting services and baby monitors.

● Many tourist attractions offer reduced admission fees or are free for children, and some sell family tickets.

● In pubs children must be accompanied by an adult (if allowed in at all). Children under 14 are not allowed in the bar area and it is illegal for anyone under 18 to purchase alcohol. Some restaurants and pubs provide high chairs.

● Major department stores, shopping centres and public venues such as theatres have changing tables for babies, but these tend to be located in the women's toilet areas. Changing facilities are provided aboard most aircraft.

VISITORS WITH DISABILITIES

Most tourist attractions and public places have facilities for visitors with disabilities, but it is always wise to check in advance. See also the information for visitors with disabilities, ▷ 53–54.

● Any special needs should be mentioned when reserving accommodation, as many places may not be suitable for wheelchairs or for visitors with visual impairments. The Holiday Care Service (tel 08451 249971, www.tourismforall.org.uk) provides information on accommodation suitable for visitors with disabilities.

● The Royal National Institute for the Blind (tel 020 7388 1266) publishes a hotel guidebook.

CAR RENTAL

Arranging a rental car through your travel agent before arriving saves money and allows you to find out about deposits, drop-off charges, cancellation penalties and insurance costs well in advance. Larger, mainstream rental companies have offices in cities and major airports, but local firms serve a wider variety of destinations, including the islands. A selection of contacts appears in the table below. More information about car rental can be supplied by the local tourist offices (▷ 301).

● The majority of rental cars have manual rather than automatic transmission, so ask if you want an automatic.

● You must have a driver's licence. An International Driving Permit may be useful if your licence is not in English.

● Most rental firms require the driver to be at least 23 years old and with at least 12 months of driving experience. If you are under 25 you may be charged an increased premium.

● Rental rates usually include unlimited mileage. A cheaper option is to opt for a limited mileage allowance, which makes an extra charge for additional mileage thereafter.

● It is important to have some form of personal insurance along with Collision Damage Waiver (CDW). Many companies also offer Damage Excess Reduction (DER) and Theft Protection for an additional premium. Expect to pay more for any additional drivers.

● Make sure you find out what equipment comes as standard (air-conditioning and automatic transmission are not always available) and check that the price quoted includes VAT, the sales tax levied on most goods and services.

● Ask about optional extras such as roof racks and child seats before collecting the car.

● Budget for about £45 per day for an economy car (such as a Ford Fiesta), £55 per day for a mid-range vehicle (such as a Ford Focus) or £70 upwards for a premium car.

● Most cars use unleaded fuel; make sure you know what's required (unleaded or diesel) before refilling the tank.

● When the car is returned, fuel should be topped up to the level shown when you first picked it up—otherwise you will be charged extra.

CAR RENTAL CONTACTS		
NAME	**LOCATIONS**	**CONTACT**
Alamo	Aberdeen, Dundee, Edinburgh, Glasgow, Prestwick, Hamilton, Inverness, Stirling	Tel 0870 400 4562 www.alamo.co.uk
Avis	Aberdeen, Edinburgh, Glasgow, Inverness, Oban, Prestwick, Stirling	Tel 0870 606 0100 www.avis.co.uk
Budget	Aberdeen, Edinburgh, Glasgow, Inverness	Tel 0870 153 9170 www.budget.co.uk
Europcar BCR	Aberdeen, Edinburgh, Glasgow, Prestwick, Inverness, Orkney, Shetland	Tel 0845 722 2525 www.europcar.co.uk
Hertz	Aberdeen, Dundee, Edinburgh, Fraserburgh, Glasgow, Inverness, Perth, Prestwick, Stranraer	Tel 0870 844 8844 www.hertz.co.uk
Arnol Motors	Isle of Lewis	Tel 01851 710548

PLANNING

MONEY

MONEY MATTERS

Expect to spend a minimum of about £45 per day if you're travelling independently. It's not hard to spend more than £100 in a day.

You are advised to carry money in a range of forms—cash, at least one credit card, bank card/charge/Maestro card and travellers' cheques.

CASH

Britain's currency is the pound sterling (see panel below).

● Scottish banks issue their own notes, and some examples are illustrated on the left, below. These are acceptable throughout the UK, but their unfamiliarity south of the Scottish border means their validity is sometimes questioned. If this becomes a problem, they may be exchanged in any bank or post office for Bank of England notes.

LOST/STOLEN CREDIT CARDS

American Express
01273 696933

Diners Club
01252 513500/0800 460800

MasterCard/Eurocard, Maestro, Visa/Connect
0113 277 8899

● Bank of England notes (shown on the right, below) are generally accepted in Scotland.
● There is no limit to the amount of cash you may import or export.
● It is worth keeping a few 10p, 20p, 50p and £1 coins handy for pay-and-display parking machines, and for parking meters.

CASHPOINTS (ATMS)

ATMs are widely available across the country. Check with your bank if you are uncertain whether you will be charged for using another bank's cash machines.

● LINK is the UK's only branded network of self-service cash machines. Use of LINK machines is free, except for credit, charge and store cards, for which you pay a cash advance fee.
● You are also charged for the use of convenience machines installed by cash machine-owners in certain private locations (such as garages); usage fees are clearly displayed, and are usually around £1.25–£2.50.

CREDIT CARDS

Credit cards are widely accepted; Visa and MasterCard are the most popular, followed by

CASH

There are 100 pence (p) to the pound (£).
Coins are in denominations of
1p, 2p, 5p, 10p, 20p, 50p, £1 and **£2.**
Banknotes are in denominations of
£1 (Scottish only), £5, £10, £20 and **£50.**

2 pounds – £2

1 pound – £1

50 pence – 50p

20 pence – 20p

10 pence – 10p

5 pence – 5p

2 pence – 2p

1 penny – 1p

PLANNING

Although banks and businesses close on the public (bank) holidays listed below, major tourist attractions and some shops may open on these dates, except on 25 and 26 Dec, and 1 and 2 Jan, when almost everything shuts. If any of these days falls on a Saturday or Sunday, the next Monday is a holiday.

New Year's Day (1 January)
New Year's Holiday (2 January)
Good Friday
Easter Monday
First Monday in May
Last Monday in May
First Monday in August
Last Monday in August
Christmas Day (25 December)
Boxing Day (26 December)

American Express, Diners Club and JCB.

● Credit cards can also be used for withdrawing currency at cashpoints (ATMs) at any bank displaying the appropriate sign, for changing banknotes and cashing travellers' cheques. If your credit cards or travellers' cheques are stolen call the issuer immediately, then report the loss to the police.

TRAVELLERS' CHEQUES
These are the safest way to carry money, as you will be refunded in the event of loss (keep the counterfoil separate from the cheques themselves), usually within 24 hours.

BANKS
Most banks open Monday–Friday, 9.30–4.30; some also open on Saturday morning.

● It pays to shop around for the best exchange and commission rates on currency. You do not pay commission on sterling travellers' cheques, provided you cash them at a bank affiliated with the issuing bank.

● You need to present ID (usually a passport) when cashing travellers' cheques.

POST OFFICES
Most post offices are open Monday–Friday, 9–5.30, with reduced hours on Saturday.

● Apart from the main post offices in urban centres which offer full postal services, there are many smaller sub-post offices around the country, often forming part of a newsagent or general store.

● Some post offices offer commission-free bureaux de change services (tel 08458 500900), with an online ordering service available through www.postoffice.co.uk. Payment can be made in cash, or by cheque, banker's draft, Visa, MasterCard, Maestro, Delta, Solo or Electron.

BUREAUX DE CHANGE
These money-changing operations can be found at main stations and airports, and at on-street locations in the bigger cities, and are mostly open 8am–10pm. Rates of exchange may vary; it pays to shop around. Commission rates should be clearly displayed.

DISCOUNTS
● Reduced fares on buses, underground services and trains are available for the under 16s.
● Over 60s can purchase Senior Citizens' Railcards for £20, giving a one-third reduction on off-peak rail services. See also ▷ 48–50.

THE EURO
It is possible to spend euros in Britain: The problem is knowing where. Generally, the bigger the city, the more places will accept euros. Ask before you shop.
● Many major chain stores, including the Body Shop, Clarks, Debenhams, Habitat, HMV, Marks & Spencer, Miss Selfridge, Topshop, Virgin and Waterstone's accept euros in some or all of their branches.

● Some pubs owned by J D Wetherspoon, Scottish & Newcastle and Shepherd Neame take euros, as do some BP and other fuel stations.
● Train tickets on Virgin trains can also be paid in euros.
● One euro is made up of 100 cents. Euro notes come in denominations of 5, 10, 20, 50, 100, 200 and 500 euros. Coins come in denominations of 1 and 2 euros, and 1, 2, 5, 10, 20 and 50 cents.

WIRING MONEY
Money wired from your home country can be expensive (agents charge fees for the service) and time consuming. Money can be wired from bank to bank, which takes up to two working days, or to agents such as Travelex (tel 01733 318922, www.travelex.co.uk) and Western Union (tel 0800 833833, www.westernunion.com).

VAT REFUNDS
See page 151.

MAJOR UK BANKS		
NAME	HEAD OFFICE ADDRESS	TELEPHONE
Barclays	1 Churchill Place, Canary Wharf, London E14 5HP	020 7699 5000
HSBC	8 Canada Square, London E14 5HQ	020 7991 8888
Lloyds TSB	25 Gresham Street, London EC2V 7HN	020 7626 1500
NatWest	135 Bishopsgate, London EC2M 3UR	0870 240 1155
Royal Bank of Scotland	36 St. Andrew Square, Edinburgh EH2 2YB	0131 556 8555

TIPPING	
Restaurants (where service is not included)	10%
Tour guides	£1–£2
Hairdressers	10%
Taxis	10%
Chambermaids	50p–£1 per day
Porters	50p–£1 per bag

10 EVERYDAY ITEMS AND HOW MUCH THEY COST	
Take-away sandwich	£2.50
Bottle of water	£1.00
Cup of tea or coffee	£1–£2
Pint of beer	£2.40
Glass of house wine	£3.50
National daily newspaper	40p–£1.30p
Roll of camera film	£5
20 cigarettes	£4.80
Ice cream	£1.20
Litre of petrol	89p

PLANNING

HEALTH

Britain's National Health Service (the NHS) provides healthcare for the country's citizens based on need rather than the ability to pay. It is funded by the taxpayer and managed by a government department.

● While NHS care for British citizens is free, private health care can also be bought from organizations such as BUPA, which owns a number of hospitals and other health care facilities.

● Visitors from the European Union (EU) are entitled to free treatment on the NHS (see below), but medical insurance is still recommended.

BEFORE YOU DEPART

● It is sensible to consult your doctor at least six to eight weeks before leaving.

● Free medical treatment is available through the NHS for visitors from EU countries with reciprocal agreements. The E111 form has been replaced by European Health Insurance Card (EHIC), available via post offices.

● Several countries have reciprocal healthcare agreements with the UK (see below). In most cases a passport is sufficient identification for hospital treatment. Most countries, however, including the US and Canada, do not have agreements with the UK, and a comprehensive travel insurance policy is advisable.

● No inoculations are required on entering Britain. However, it is advisable to have an anti-tetanus booster before travelling. Check with your doctor whether you need immunization or health advice for: meningococcal meningitis; hepatitis B; diphtheria; or measles/MMR.

COUNTRIES WITH RECIPROCAL HEALTH AGREEMENTS WITH THE UK

Anguilla, Australia, Barbados, British Virgin Islands, Bulgaria, Channel Islands, Falkland Islands, Gibraltar, Isle of Man, Montserrat, New Zealand, Romania, Russia, St. Helena, Turks and Caicos Islands, Republics of the former USSR (except Latvia, Lithuania, Estonia), Yugoslavia (i.e. Serbia and Montenegro) and successor states (Croatia, Bosnia and Herzegovina, and Macedonia).

WHAT TO TAKE WITH YOU

● Visitors from the EU should bring an EHIC card and a photocopy which should be kept in a safe place.

● Those from outside the EU should bring their travel insurance policy and a spare copy.

● Visitors with existing medical conditions and allergies, for example, to commonly used drugs, should wear a warning bracelet or tags.

IF YOU NEED TREATMENT

● If you are injured go to a hospital casualty department (emergency room).

● If you are staying at a hotel or bed-and-breakfast, members of staff should be able to help you contact a doctor urgently. In many cases emergency telephone numbers are posted on a noticeboard in a central area or in your room.

● If you are on your own call NHS 24 (tel 0845 424 2424) and explain the problem. Free medical advice from a qualified nurse is available to everyone over the phone through this government service or via the internet at www.nhs24.com. You do not have to give personal details.

● Non-urgent appointments can be made with any doctor listed in the Yellow Pages. Initial advice, such as if you need to go to hospital, will be given but those visitors without a reciprocal arrangement with the UK, such as the US and Canada, will be charged to speak to a nurse (£25) or doctor (£55) and for any prescription drugs deemed necessary. You will be issued with a receipt to present to your insurance company on your return home.

● To find the nearest doctor, dentist or pharmacy, ask at your hotel, or call NHS 24.

● Major pharmacies and large supermarkets have a wide range of medicines that you can buy over the counter, although items such as antibiotics require a prescription from a doctor.

● Pharmacists operate a roster system of out of hours opening in many areas, with times of the duty pharmacist displayed in the shop window and in the local newspaper.

● Dial 999 for an ambulance in an emergency.

WATER

Tap water is safe to drink if it is from the main water distribution supply. Avoid drinking water that comes from a tank, for example, in a train toilet.

DENTAL TREATMENT

You will have to pay for dental treatment, either as a private patient or (slightly cheaper) as an NHS patient. It is sensible to go for a dental check-up before you depart.

● In the UK dentists are listed in telephone directories. Alternatively you can use the British Dental Association's online service at www.bda-findadentist.org.uk

OPTICIANS		
NAME	TELEPHONE	WEBSITE
Boots Opticians	0845 070 8090	www.wellbeing.com/bootsopticians
Dollond & Aitchison	0121 706 6133	www.danda.co.uk
Specsavers	01481 236000	www.specsavers.co.uk
Vision Express	0115 986 5225	www.visionexpress.com

MAJOR HIGH-STREET PHARMACIES		
NAME	TELEPHONE	WEBSITE
Boots the Chemist	0115 950 6111	www.wellbeing.com
Co-op Pharmacy	0161 654 4488	www.co-oppharmacy.co.uk
Lloyds Pharmacy	024 7643 2400	www.lloydspharmacy.co.uk
Sainsbury's Pharmacy	0800 636262	www.sainsburys.co.uk
Superdrug	020 8684 7000	www.superdrug.com
Tesco Pharmacy	0800 505555	www.tesco.com

PLANNING

FINDING HELP

PERSONAL SECURITY

Levels of violent crime remain relatively low, but there are hot spots to avoid in any city. In most tourist areas, however, the main danger is petty theft.

● Be particularly wary of thieves on railway trains, in crowded public places and at busy public events.

● Avoid unlit urban areas at night, and carry bags close to you. If someone tries to grab your bag, never fight back; let go.

● If you are going out late, arrange a lift home or a taxi, and use only reputable and licensed minicab firms or black cabs.

● If you are driving alone, take a mobile phone with you if possible, but be aware that reception may be poor or limited in remoter parts of the country.

● Lock your doors when your car is stuck in stationary traffic, particularly at night. Always lock your vehicle when it is parked, and don't leave valuables in a parked car.

● Don't pick up hitchhikers.

● Sit near the driver or conductor on buses and avoid empty carriages (cars) on trains.

LOST PROPERTY

If you lose an item, contact the nearest police station and complete a lost property form. Give as much detail as possible, such as identifying marks, registration numbers and credit card numbers.

● www.lostandfound.co.uk and www.virtualbumblebee.co.uk are free 'lost and found' services, where you can log a loss or search a database of lost and found items throughout the UK.

● At airports, dedicated offices deal with lost property within terminal buildings, but contact

individual airlines if you lose belongings on board aircraft (▷ 38–40).

LOST PASSPORT

If you lose your passport, contact your embassy in the UK (see below). It helps if you have your passport number; either carry a photocopy of the opening pages or scan them and email them to yourself at an email account which you can access anywhere, such as www.hotmail.com.

SEEKING HELP

Telephone 999 or 112 in an emergency. The operator will ask you which service you require. State where you are, the number of the phone you are using, what the problem is and where it has occurred.

● If your police enquiry is not an emergency, contact the nearest police station (for directory inquiries, ▷ 298).

● If you have non-urgent health concerns, contact NHS 24 (National Health Service, tel 0845 424 2424), where trained medical staff listen to your problem, give advice and tell you where to find the nearest non-emergency doctor. This free service is available to all visitors.

● Policemen patrolling the streets on foot will readily give information and directions.

● The British Transport Police work on Britain's railways. Report any non-emergency crimes experienced on trains to them, tel 0800 405040.

● If you are the victim of a crime, Victim Support offers support and legal advice, tel 0845 303 0900.

THE LAW

● There are serious penalties for driving while under the influence of alcohol. If you drink, don't drive.

● If you are involved in a motoring incident you are obliged to give your name and address.

● On-the-spot fixed penalty notices (traffic tickets) are given out for speeding, driving in a bus lane, driving through a red light and other motoring offences (starting at about £40).

● Even if you're not driving, you can be fined if you are found to be excessively drunk or drunk and disorderly in a public place, in licensed premises or on a highway.

● Police have the power to give on-the-spot fines for a few offences involving antisocial behaviour or wasting police time.

FOREIGN CONSULATES, EDINBURGH		
COUNTRY	**ADDRESS**	**TELEPHONE**
American Embassy	3 Regent Terrace EH7 5BW	0131 556 8315
Australian Consulate	Melrose House, 69 George Street EH2 2JG	0131 624 3333
Canadian Consulate	Burness, 50 Lothian Road, Festival Square EG3 9WJ	0131 473 6320
French Consulate	11 Randolph Crescent EH3 7TT	0131 225 7954
New Zealand Consulate	5 Rutland Square EH1 2AS	0131 222 8109

PLANNING

COMMUNICATION

With technology rapidly changing the way we communicate, the humble postcard is in danger of looking old-fashioned. But however you want to keep in touch with friends and family, there is a multitude of generally swift, convenient and reliable options.

TELEPHONES
The main public phone company, British Telecom (BT), operates hundreds of payphones throughout Scotland.

Area Codes, Country Codes and Telephone Directories
● Most area codes are four- or five-digit numbers beginning with 01.
● For Edinburgh the code is 0131. Telephone directories (phone books) and *Yellow Pages* show the code in brackets for each telephone number.
● There is a full list of area codes and country codes in every phone book.
● When making a local call you can omit the area code.
● When making an international call dial the international code followed by the telephone number minus the 0 of the area code.

Public Phones
Phone boxes (booths) are generally silver or red and are found at all major bus and train stations, on the street in town centres, and in many villages and more rural locations.
● You can use credit and debit cards to make calls from many BT payphones (95p minimum charge; 20p per

minute for all inland calls).
● Payphones accept 10p, 20p, 50p and £1 coins; some also accept £2 coins. Only unused coins are returned, so avoid using high denomination coins for short calls.
● Some establishments, such as hotels and pubs, have their own payphones, for which they set their own profit margin. These can be exorbitant and are recommended only in an emergency. Similarly, phone calls made from hotel rooms often incur higher charges.

USING A MOBILE PHONE
Britain has embraced mobile phone technology wholeheartedly, although mobiles are sometimes discouraged in some pubs and elsewhere (some trains have dedicated quiet areas). There's a proliferation of mobile phone shops in almost every shopping area.
● If you are visiting from overseas and already have a mobile phone, you can purchase a sim card for between £10 and

£20, which gives you access to one of the main networks such as BT, Orange or Vodafone.
● A 'pay as you go' option allows you to top up your account at supermarkets and

COUNTRY CODES FROM THE UK	
Australia	00 61
Belgium	00 32
Canada	00 1
France	00 33
Germany	00 49
Ireland	00 353
Italy	00 39
Netherlands	00 31
New Zealand	00 64
Spain	00 34
Sweden	00 46
US	00 1

USEFUL TELEPHONE NUMBERS
Directory inquiries: competing services from several companies: try **118500** (BT) and **118111** (One.Tel)
International directory inquiries: competing services from several companies: try **118505** (BT) and **118211** (One.Tel)
International operator: 155
Operator: 100
Time: 123

DIALLING CODE PREFIXES	
00	international codes
01	area codes
02	area codes
07	calls charged at mobile rates
080	free calls
084	calls charged at local rates
087	calls charged at national rates
09	calls charged at premium rates

For details of charges, call the operator on 100.

To dial Scotland from abroad, dial 00 44 and omit the first 0 of the area code.

CALL CHARGES FROM BT PAYPHONES	
Minimum charge	30p (20p with BT Chargecard)
All UK calls	30p for first 15 mins, then 10p per 7 mins thereafter
Calls to mobile phones	60p per minute Mon–Fri 8–6, 40p per minute Mon–Fri after 6pm and before 8am
Italy, US and Canada	£1 per minute at all times
Belgium, France, Germany, Netherlands and Sweden	£1 per minute at all times
Australia and New Zealand	£1 per minute at all times
Call charges	These are lower after 6pm on weekdays and all day Saturday and Sunday. Local calls are cheaper than long-distance calls within Britain, and calls to mobile phones are generally more expensive than other calls

PLANNING

other shops when necessary. You are usually given a choice of accounts, depending on how much and when you are likely to make calls. A subscription-type account is more useful if you are staying in the country for a substantial period.

● It is also possible to use your own phone and sim card, depending on what sort of phone you have. You need to know whether your phone operates on a GSM (Global System for Mobile Communications) frequency. Single band GSM phones, which work on 900MHz frequency, can be used in more than 100 countries, but not in the US or Canada.

● Most phones sold in the US work on 1900MHz and need a new sim card for use in the UK.

● Dual (900 and 1900MHz) and tri band phones can be used in most countries around the world without alteration.

● Note that there are still 'black holes' across Scotland where you cannot get a mobile phone signal, and that these vary for each network.

● Remember to pack a plug adaptor for the charger.

INTERNET ACCESS
Multimedia web phones (e-payphones, or blue boxes) are being installed by BT in shopping areas, train stations, airports and road service stations across the country. These enable users to surf the internet and send emails and text messages. Internet and email access costs £1 for up to 15 minutes and 10p per 90 seconds thereafter. Text messages cost 10p a message.

● Web phones may threaten the future of the internet cafés (charges typically £1–£2 per hour) in major cities and towns.

● Some payphones allow you to send text messages and email—look for the sign that indicates this.

● Many public libraries have free internet access; for details see www.peoplesnetwork.gov.uk

● BT has introduced more than 400 wireless hot spots in locations such as airports, hotels and service stations across the UK. The hubs allow laptop and pocket PC users within a 100m (109-yard) radius broadband access to the internet using

wireless technology, or 'Wi-Fi'. You need a laptop or pocket PC PDA running Microsoft Windows XP, 2000 or Microsoft Pocket PC 2002, and a wireless LAN card. Any Wi-Fi approved card should work with BT Openzone.

● Note that the service remains an expensive, if convenient, way of surfing the internet.

USING A LAPTOP
If you are coming from abroad and intend to use your own laptop in the UK, remember to bring a power converter to recharge it and a plug adaptor (see Electricity, ▷ 292). A surge protector is also a good idea.

● To connect to the internet you need an adaptor for the phone socket, available (in the UK) from companies such as Teleadapt (www.teleadapt.com). If you use an international service provider, such as Compuserve or AOL, it's cheaper to dial up a local node rather than the number in your home country.

● Wireless technology, such as Bluetooth, allows you to connect to the internet using a mobile phone; check beforehand what the charges will be. Dial tone frequencies vary from country to country so set your modem to ignore dial tones.

POST
● For all post office information, call customer services, tel 0845 774 0740.

● Post boxes are painted bright red (except some in post offices) and are either set into walls, on posts or are stand-alone circular pillar boxes. Collection times are shown on each post box.

● Stamps are available from newsagents and supermarkets as well as post offices.

● Generally airmail is preferable for mail sent outside Europe; for bulky items surface mail is substantially cheaper but typically takes around eight weeks outside Europe. Airmail to Europe takes around three days, and from five days to the rest of the world.

● Large post offices have poste restante services. This service enables mail addressed to the recipient at that address and inscribed with the words poste restante to be kept at the specified post office until collected by the addressee.

● To send items within the UK for next-day delivery, use special delivery. This service also enables you to insure the items in case of loss.

POSTAGE RATES		
First class within UK	Up to 60g (2oz)	30p
	(usually arrives next day, but not guaranteed)	
Second class within UK	Up to 60g (2oz)	21p
	(usually two days)	
Proof of posting	Free	
Airmail Rates		
Americas, Middle East, Africa,	Letter (100g/3.5oz)	£2.16
India, Southeast Asia	Postcard	47p
Europe	Letter (100g/3.5oz)	£1.14
	Postcard	42p
Australasia	Letter (100g/3.5oz)	£2.44
	Postcard	47p

MEDIA

TELEVISION

- There are five main national terrestrial channels in Britain (see right). Scotland's mainstream television choice is essentially what is broadcast from south of the border, with local interest, home-based material slotted in.
- There is no advertising on the BBC channels, which are funded by a licence fee from all viewers.
- BBC1 and 2 are available on terrestrial television and BBC News 24 is broadcast on BBC1 throughout the night.
- BBC4, featuring cultural programming, BBC News 24, BBC Parliament and BBC Choice, which transmits extended coverage of shows featured on BBC1 and 2, are all available on cable networks and via digital television.
- Satellite television, dominated by Sky TV, is widely available, sometimes bringing TV to regions that had trouble with terrestrial reception in the past.

RADIO

Scotland is served by the UK's national radio stations (BBC), and has some of its own for more partisan coverage.
- BBC Radio Scotland has a loyal following; it broadcasts a broadly based mix of news, discussion, travel, magazine format and music programmes, and is useful for weather forecasts.
- Local radio stations take over the frequency at particular times—for example, on weekdays you may hear local news bulletins from the local region where you are at 7.50am, 12.54pm and 16.54pm.
- There are also several local

BBC1 Shows soaps, chat shows, lifestyle programmes, documentaries and drama, and children's shows.
International news and national weather: 6am–9am, 1pm, 6pm, 10pm weekdays and BBC News 24 4.15am–6am. Reporting Scotland at 6.30pm is the news flagship for Scotland, with further regional broadcasts after main news programmes.

BBC2 Specializes in comedy, natural history, history and cultural programmes.
News: Newsnight 10.30pm weekdays

ITV1 Shows a variety of programmes including soaps, quiz shows, children's programmes, drama and films. Commercial networks include Border Television (covering the border region), Scottish Television (central and western Scotland) and Grampian Television (covering the north and northeast).
International news and national weather: 12.30pm, 6.30pm, 10pm weekdays. Regional news updates are shown after main news broadcasts. Scotland Today is the main news programme at 6pm. Saturday afternoon's Scotsport is ever popular.

Channel 4 Broadcasts include films, documentaries, comedy and quiz shows along with science and natural history programmes.
News and weather: 7pm weekdays

Channel 5 Shows children's programmes, game shows, popular films and reruns of soaps and well-known series. Not every area of the country can receive Channel 5.
News and weather: 6am, 11.30am, 5pm, 7pm weekdays

commercial radio stations, including Radio Forth (serving Edinburgh) and Beat 106 FM (serving Glasgow and eastwards).
- Digital radio is not yet widely available in Scotland outside Glasgow, Edinburgh and the central Borders.

NEWSPAPERS, MAGAZINES

- At the quality end of the market, *The Scotsman*, based in Edinburgh, aspires to the crown as Scotland's national newspaper, though challenged by its Glasgow-based competitor, *The Herald*.
- Both are exceeded in circulation by the unashamedly regional, if not downright parochial, Aberdeen-based *Press*

and Journal, while the central region is dominated by the weekly *Dundee Courier*.
- Scotland's popular tabloid daily newspaper is the *Daily Record*.
- The *Sunday Post* is a top selling institution peddling its own unique brand of homespun, Conservative, family-oriented journalism, and featuring two evergreen cartoon strips, 'Oor Wullie' and 'The Broons'.
- *Scotland on Sunday* is a heavyweight which vies with the *Sunday Herald* for the more serious readership.
- Scotland also has many local weekly newspapers, from the radical *West Highland Free Press* to the *Shetland Times*—worth dipping into to see what entertainment is on offer in your chosen holiday locality.
- *The List* is a lively fortnightly listings magazine, giving excellent coverage for both Edinburgh and Glasgow.
- Newspapers from around the world, including foreign language papers, can be purchased at airports, larger train stations and some newsagents such as WH Smith.
- The *Scots Magazine* is a national institution, unashamedly 'for people who love Scotland'. Its small size and thick spine set it apart on the rack. A monthly stalwart, it first appeared in 1739.

BBC Radio 1 (98–99.5 FM): the latest pop music
BBC Radio 2 (88–90.2 FM): wide variety of popular music, including folk and jazz, plus lunchtime news magazine, comedy etc on the UK's favourite station
BBC Radio 3 (90.3–92.3 FM): classical music
BBC Radio 4 (92.4–95.8 FM; 198kHz LW): topical news, current affairs, drama, travel, shipping news etc
BBC Radio Five Live (693–909 kHz/693 MW): current sport
BBC World Service (648 AM and digital; 198 kHz LW): 24-hr worldwide news and current affairs
BBC Radio Scotland (92.4–94.7 FM/585 or 810 MW): mixture of news, chat, music, weather
BBC Radio nan Gaidheal (103.5–105 FM/990 MW): Gaelic radio station
Classic FM (100–102 FM): classical music with a popular twist on Britain's most successful commercial station

TOURIST INFORMATION

VISITSCOTLAND

The official source of information for tourists, VisitScotland (formerly the Scottish Tourist Board) supports the publication of free promotional brochures on everything from where to play golf to how to get around the Western Isles. It publishes various inspected accommodation and camping guides, and much of its information is available on the very useful website, www.visitScotland.com

TOURIST INFORMATION CENTRES (TICS)

There is a network of around 120 tourist information offices across the country, which are a friendly source of knowledgeable advice and free brochures, as well as official publications and maps to help you get the best out of a local area. All can advise on places to stay, and many will reserve accommodation ahead for you. Around half of the tourist offices are open only between Easter and October; standard opening hours of 9–5 may be shortened in winter. Several are located at service stations on main routes within the country, including exit 13 off the M74, exit 6 off the M90 and exit 9 off the M9. Contact details for some of the main offices, open all year, are listed here.

SOUTHERN SCOTLAND

Ayr
22 Sandgate KA7 1BW
Tel 0845 225 5121

Dumfries
64 Whitesands DG1 2RS
Tel 01387 253862

Melrose
Abbey House, Abbey Street
TD6 9LG
Tel 0870 608 0404

North Berwick
Quality Street EH39 4HJ
Tel 0845 225 5121

EDINBURGH

Edinburgh & Scotland
Information Centre,
3 Princes Street EH2 2QP
Tel 0845 225 5121

CENTRAL SCOTLAND

Aberfoyle
Trossachs Discovery Centre,
Main Street FK8 3UQ
Tel 0870 720 0604

Dundee
21 Castle Street DD1 3AA
Tel 01382 527527

Perth
Lower City Mills, West Mill Street
PH1 5QP
Tel 01738 450600

Pitlochry
22 Atholl Road PH16 5BX
Tel 01796 472215/472751

St. Andrews
70 Market Street KY16 9NU
Tel 01334 472021

GLASGOW

11 George Square G2 1DY
Tel 0141 204 4400

HIGHLANDS AND ISLANDS

Aberdeen
23 Union Street AB11 5BP
Tel 01224 288828

Aviemore
Grampian Road PH22 1PP
Tel 0845 225 5121

Fort William
Cameron Centre, Cameron
Square PH33 6AJ
Tel 0845 225 5121

Grantown on Spey
54 High Street PH26 3AS
Tel 0845 225 5121

Inverness
Castle Wynd IV2 3BJ
Tel 0845 225 5121

Lewis
26 Cromwell Street, Stornoway
HS1 2DD
Tel 01851 703088

Loch Lomond
Gateway Centre, Loch Lomond
Shores, Balloch G83 8QL
Tel 0870 720 0631

Oban
Argyll Square PA34 4AR
Tel 0870 720 0630

Skye
Bayfield House, Portree IV51 9EL
Tel 0845 225 5121

Ullapool
Argyle Street IV26 2UB
Tel 0845 225 5121

ORKNEY AND SHETLAND

Kirkwall
6 Broad Street, Orkney
KW15 1DH
Tel 01856 872856

Lerwick
The Market Cross, Shetland
ZE1 0LU
Tel 0870 199 9440

GUIDE TO OPENING TIMES	
Banks	Mon–Fri 9.30–4.30; larger branches may open Sat am
Doctors/dentists	Mon–Fri 8.30–6.30; some may open Sat am
Pharmacies	Mon–Sat 9–5 or 5.30
Post offices	Mon–Fri 9–5.30, Sat 9–12
Pubs	These vary, but are generally daily, 12–2.30pm and 6–11pm; some may stay open all afternoon
Restaurants	These vary, but are typically daily, 12–2.30pm and 6pm–11pm; many will close on one or two days in the week
Shops	Mon–Sat 9–5 or 5.30. Newsagents and some shops may open on a Sunday
Supermarkets/ convenience stores	Mon–Sat 8am–8pm or later and for six hours (such as 10–4) on Sunday
Visitor attractions	These vary widely, so always check ahead. Note that last admission is usually at least 30 min before closing time

PLANNING

Australia
Level 16, 1 Macquarie Place, Sydney,
NSW 2000
Tel 02 9377 4400
Fax 02 9377 4499

Canada
Suite 120, 5915 Airport Road,
Mississauga, Ontario L4V 1T1
Tel 0905 405 1840/1 888 VISIT UK
Fax 0905 405 1835

New Zealand
151 Queen Street, Auckland 1
Tel 09 303 1446
Fax 09 377 6965

South Africa
Lancaster Gate, Hyde Park Lane, Hyde
Park, Johannesburg 2196 (visitors);
PO Box 41896, Craighall 2024 (mail)
Tel 011 325 0343
Fax 011 325 0344

US
7th Floor, 551 Fifth Avenue at 45th
Street, New York, NY 10176-0799
Tel (1) 212 986 2200/1 800 GO 2
BRITAIN

Website for Americans visiting Britain:
www.travelbritain.org

USEFUL WEBSITES

Touring information
www.visitScotland.com
www.undiscoveredscotland.
co.uk

**Maps and guides to buy
on line**
www.theAA.com
www.estate-publications.co.uk
www.ordnancesurvey.co.uk
www.ukho.gov.uk
www.amazon.com

**General information about
Scotland**
www.electricscotland.com
www.geo.ed.ac.uk/scotgaz

**Scottish Executive/
Parliament**
www.scotland.gov.uk

Gaelic interest
www.cnag.org.uk
www.ambeile.org.uk
www.smo.uhi.ac.uk
www.the-mod.co.uk

Heritage groups
www.nts.org.uk
www.historic-scotland.net

Weather
www.onlineweather.com
www.metoffice.com
www.bbc.co.uk/weather
www.onlineweather.com
www.sais.gov.uk/about_forecasts

Travel links
www.traveline.org.uk
www.citylink.co.uk
www.nationalexpress.com
www.postbus.royalmail.com
www.scotrail.co.uk
www.nationalrail.co.uk
www.britrail.com
www.eurostar.com
www.baa.com
www.gpia.co.uk
www.hial.co.uk

www.calmac.co.uk
www.seacat.co.uk
www.stenaline.co.uk
www.poirishsea.com
www.superfast.com
www.smyril-line.com
www.jogferry.co.uk

Accommodation
www.visitScotland.com
www.theAA.com
www.syha.org.uk
www.countrycottagesinscotland.
com
www.forestholidays.co.uk
www.campingandcaravanningclub.
co.uk

Events
www.edinburgh-festivals.co.uk
www.eif.co.uk
www.edfringe.com
www.edintattoo.co.uk
www.edinburghshogmanay.org
www.the-mod.co.uk
www.celticconnections.co.uk
www.sffs.shetland.co.uk
www.shetland-
music.com/musevent2.htm
www.spiritofspeyside.com
www.tinthepark.com
www.rhass.org.uk
www.stmagnusfestival.com
www.scottishtraditionalboat
festival.co.uk
www.jazzfest.co.uk
www.wigtown-
booktown.co.uk/festival
www.braemargathering.com
www.cowalgathering.com

Sports
www.shinty.com
www.cycling.visitscotland.com
www.fish.visitscotland.com
www.scottishgolf.com
www.ridingscotland.com
www.nevis-range.co.uk
www.cairngormmountain.com
www.lecht.co.uk
www.ski-glencoe.co.uk

www.ski-glenshee.co.uk
www.heartsfc.co.uk
www.hibs.co.uk
www.celticfc.co.uk
www.rangers.co.uk
www.sru.org.uk

Banking and postal services
www.postoffice.co.uk
www.travelex.co.uk
www.westernunion.com

Embassies (London)
www.australia.org.uk
www.canada.org.uk
www.nzembassy.com/uk
www.southafricahouse.com
www.usembassy.org.uk

Miscellaneous
www.bbc.co.uk
www.uk.visas.gov.uk
www.ramblers.org.uk
www.royal.gov.uk
www.fiddlersbid.com

HERITAGE ORGANIZATIONS

National Trust for Scotland (NTS)
membership is excellent value if you
wish to visit more than one or two NTS
properties. Join at any NTS site.
● National Trust for Scotland, 28
Charlotte Square, Edinburgh EH2 4ET,
tel 0131 2265922; www.nts.org.uk

Historic Scotland (HS) also manages
hundreds of historic properties, statues
and monuments. Join at any HS-staffed
property for free entry.
● Historic Scotland, Longmore House,
Salisbury Place, Edinburgh EH9 1SH,
tel 0131 668 8800;
www.historic-scotland.net

PLANNING

BOOKS, FILMS AND MAPS

BACKGROUND READING

For a solid historical read, try the *New Penguin History of Scotland* (2001), which includes photos from the national museum collections. Christopher Harvie offers a refreshingly concise and sharply observed portrait in the pocket-size *Scotland—A Short History* (2002). Scoular Anderson's *1745 And All That: The Story of the Highlands* (2001) is an excellent cartoon introduction to Scottish history, and not just for children.

For browsing, the hefty *Collins Encyclopaedia of Scotland* by John Keay and Julia Keay (2000) is a mine of fascinating information about individuals, events and places.

PERSONAL ACCOUNTS

It seems that people can't stop writing about their experiences in Scotland, and every year brings a new crop of memoirs that provide insights into special places. Samuel Johnson and James Boswell started it all, with their *Journey to the Western Isles of Scotland* (1775), which is still in print and a surprisingly good read.

More recently, Adam Nicolson's *Sea Room* (2002) paints a memorable portrait of the Western Isles; Alison Johnson's *A House by the Shore* (1986) is an entertaining account of setting up a hotel on Harris, and Alasdair Maclean's lyrical *Night Falls on Ardnamurchan* (1984) is a powerful, melancholy account of the crofters' demise.

Muriel Gray's *The First Fifty* (1991) is an irreverent account of Munro-bagging, and an antidote to more pompous mountaineering guides. Mairi

Hedderwick has written entertaining stories of several tours, illustrated with her own watercolours; the most recent, *Sea Change* (1999), describes a six-week sailing voyage down the Caledonian Canal and around the western coast. Archie Cameron's *Bare Feet and Tackety Boots* (1988) is a humorous account of an Edwardian boyhood on Rum. And the late poet George Mackay Brown's autobiography, *For the Islands I Sing* (1997), is a vivid memory of Orkney.

SCOTTISH FICTION

Scotland has a long history of great storytelling, and a rich literary heritage that has produced writers as varied as Sir Walter Scott (the *Waverley* novels), R. L. Stevenson (*Dr. Jekyll and Mr Hyde*), Neil Gunn (*The Silver Darlings*), Muriel Spark (*The Prime of Miss Jean Brodie*), Iain Crichton Smith (*Consider the Lilies*) and Irvine Welsh (*Trainspotting*). (Not forgetting doggerel rhymer William McGonagall, 1830–1902, known to some as the worst poet in the world.)

Right is a selection of lighter Scottish classics and modern favourites, intended as a starting point for holiday reading.

MAP BASICS

For exploring by car, arm yourself with an up-to-date atlas such as the AA's *Great Britain Road Atlas,* widely available from bookshops, or purchase online.
● www.theAA.com

Around 20 more detailed touring maps of individual regions of Scotland, called Official Tourist Maps, are available from tourist information centres, or via the publisher, Estate Publications. At a scale of around 1:125,000, they provide good tourist information. Particularly recommended for exploring the islands.
● Estate Publications, Bridewell House, Tenterden, Kent TN30 6EP, tel 01580 764225; www.estate-publications.co.uk

For exploring on foot, the Ordnance Survey publishes detailed maps in the Explorer series at a scale of 1:25,000. These are available from local

tourist offices and bookshops, or buy online.
● www.ordnancesurvey.co.uk

The free literature available from tourist offices includes themed maps, such as the Speyside Whisky Trail.

Standard navigational charts of the coastline are supplied by the Hydrographic Office (UKHO).
● UK Hydrographic Office, Admiralty Way, Taunton, Somerset TA1 2DN, tel 01823 723366; www.ukho.gov.uk

10 BEST SCOTTISH READS

Kidnapped, by R. L. Stevenson (1886): Gripping 18th-century adventure, with a memorable chase across the Highlands.

Para Handy, by Neil Munro (1931): Anthology of comic tales of the skipper of a Clyde puffer (steamboat), the *Vital Spark,* and his motley crew.

A Scots Quair, by Lewis Grassic Gibbon (1934): A trilogy of novels set in the rural northeast, following the story of Chris Guthrie.

Ring of Bright Water, by Gavin Maxwell (1960): Enchanting real life story of raising otters in the idyllic but unforgiving setting of the western coast.

The Prime of Miss Jean Brodie, by Muriel Spark (1961): The fortunes of a 1930s Edinburgh schoolmistress and her talented pupils.

The Bruce Trilogy, by Nigel Tranter (1971): One of the most enduring popular histories by this evergreen historical storyteller.

The Crow Road, by Iain Banks (1992): Prentice McHoan returns to the bosom of his dysfunctional family.

Black and Blue, by Ian Rankin (1997): Crime in the oil industry for Edinburgh's Inspector Rebus—a good introduction to the Rebus series.

One Fine Day in the Middle of the Night, by Christopher Brookmyre (1999): Black humour, violent and funny, as a school reunion on an oil rig is rudely interrupted.

In Another Light, by Andrew Greig (2004): a man is haunted by his father's story, from Orkney to Penang.

10 TOP SCOTTISH FILMS

The 39 Steps (1935)
Whisky Galore (1949)
The Master of Ballantrae (1953)
Local Hero (1983)
Shallow Grave (1994)
Trainspotting (1995)
Braveheart (1995)
Rob Roy (1995)
Mrs. Brown (1997)
Morvern Callar (2002)

PLANNING

SPEAKING SCOTTISH

Standard English is the official language of Scotland, and spoken everywhere. However, like other corners of Britain, the Scottish people have their own variations on the language and the way it is spoken.

SCOTS

The Scots language, which stems from an older form of Lowland Scots, varies across the country from a barely detectable accent on certain words and phrases, to the broad (and very individual) patois of inner-urban Glasgow and northeast Aberdeenshire.

The Scots language has its own traditions of literature, poetry (including Robert Burns) and songs (including the Border ballads), and Aberdeen University Press publishes Scots dictionaries that celebrate the richness of the language. But it was only in 1983 that the first complete translation of the *New Testament* into Scots was published, the work of scholar William Laughton Lorimer (1885–1967).

NORN

In Orkney and Shetland, you'll hear a completely different accent again with long 'a's and many unusual words, influenced by the Nordic languages. At its thickest, among the local people, it can sound more akin to Danish than English.

GAELIC

In the Western Isles you'll hear another accent, sometimes described as soft and lilting, which is a legacy of an entirely separate language—Gaelic (pronounced Gaallic in Scotland), still spoken by around 65,000 people.

Visitors without prior knowledge of Gaelic are most likely to see it first in placenames on the map—especially of mountains—and on bilingual road signs in the west. You may hear it spoken naturally as a first language between local people in the Western Isles, see a Gaelic church service advertised, or hear it sung. And if you see 'ceud mile failte', you might recognize a warm welcome.

Gaelic language and culture arrived here with the Irish around the fifth century. It was the main tongue of northern and western Scotland until the dramatic changes of the 18th century brought about by the opening up of the Highlands after the Jacobite Rebellions, and the later land clearances which uprooted whole communities.

In the 20th century, while Gaelic might be the language spoken at home, English was the imposed language of education in schools and colleges. The whole culture might have died out, but a revival of interest in the early 1970s (spurred on by the example of more militant Welsh language revival) helped to sustain it.

With the more recent development of interest in a separate Scottish identity, led by the emergence of the Scottish Parliament in the 1990s, Gaelic is firmly back in vogue. While native speakers are steadily declining in numbers, understanding is increasing as the language is taught in schools and universities, the culture celebrated in an annual festival, the Mod (▷ 157), Gaelic books and newspapers are published, and Gaelic speakers get their own air-time on radio and television (▷ 300). And as part of the wider interest in Celtic roots, Gaelic is also learned and passionately celebrated worldwide.

For more information about learning Gaelic, contact the Gaelic college Sabhal Mór Ostaig (Teangue, Isle of Skye IV44 8RQ, tel 01471 888000; www.smo.uhi.ac.uk). Comunn na Gàighlig is a government-sponsored development agency, with useful links and information (5 Mitchell's Lane, Inverness IV2 3HQ; www.cnag.org.uk). The Am Baile (Gaelic Village) project is a developing website sponsored by the Highland Council offering a wide variety of resources relating to Gaelic language and culture (www.ambaile.org.uk).

PRONOUNCING SCOTTISH PLACE NAMES

Apparently complicated place names—such as Craigellachie, Wanlockhead, Clackmannan and Ecclefechan—can usually be broken down into their syllables to find the correct pronunciation. Below are some examples of Scottish place names that often cause confusion.

Ayr: Air
Breadalbane: Bred-al-bane
Cuillins: Cool-ins
Culross: Cure-oss
Culzean: Cull-ane
Edinburgh: Ed-in-burra
Eilean Donan: Ellen Donnan
Findochty: Fin-echty
Forres: Forr-es
Glamis: Glahms
Hebrides: Heb-rid-ees
Islay: Eye-la
Kirkcudbright: Kir-coo-bree
Kyleakin: Ky-lack-in
Kylerhea: Kyle-ree
Moray: Murr-ay
Roxburgh: Rox-burra
Scone: Scoon
Stac Pollaidh: Stack Polly
Sumburgh: Sum-burra
Tiree: Tye-ree
Wemyss: Weems

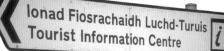

SCOTTISH WORDS IN COMMON USAGE

aye: always
bairn: baby, child
ben: hill, mountain
birle: spin, turn
bonny: pretty
brae: hill
braw: fine, beautiful
burn: stream, creek
cairn: stones forming a
landmark
canny: cunning, clever
ceilidh: gathering, party, dance
croft: smallholding, small farm

doocote: dovecot
dram: measure of whisky
een: eyes
factor: estate or farm manager
fash: bother
gae: go
gillie: hunting guide
glaur: mud
glen: valley
greet: weep
kirk: church
laird: land owner
loch: lake

machair: coastal grassland
manse: minister's house
messages: shopping
nicht: night
och: oh
partan: crab
piece: sandwich
pinkie: little finger
pirrie/peerie/peedy: small
puffer: antique steamboat
Sassenach: English-speaker
stay: live
tattie-bogle: scarecrow

GLOSSARY FOR US VISITORS

anticlockwise — counterclockwise
aubergine — eggplant
bank holiday — a public holiday that falls on a Monday; there are two in May and one in August
bill — check (at restaurant)
biscuit — cookie
bonnet — hood (car)
boot — trunk (car)
busker — street musician
car park — parking lot
caravan — house trailer or RV
carriage — car (on a train)
casualty — emergency room (hospital department)
chemist — pharmacy
chips — french fries
coach — long-distance bus
concessions — discount tickets
courgette — zucchini
crèche — day care
crisps — potato chips
dual carriageway — two-lane highway
en suite — a bedroom with its own private bathroom; may also just refer to the bathroom
football — soccer
full board — a hotel tariff that includes all meals
garden — yard (residential)
GP — doctor
half board — hotel tariff that includes breakfast and either lunch or dinner
high street — main street
hire — rent
inland — within the UK
jumper/jersey — sweater
jelly — Jello™
junction — intersection
lay-by — pull-off, rest stop
level crossing — grade crossing
licensed — a café or restaurant that has a licence to serve alcohol (beer and wine only unless it's 'fully' licensed)
lift — elevator

lorry — truck
main line station — a train station as opposed to an underground or subway station (although it may be served by the underground/subway)
nappy — diaper
note — paper money
off-licence — liquor store
pants — underpants (men's)
pavement — sidewalk
petrol — gas
petrol station/garage — gas station
plaster — Band-Aid or bandage
post — mail
public school — private school
pudding — dessert
purse — change purse
pushchair — stroller
return ticket — roundtrip ticket
rocket — arugula
roundabout — traffic circle or rotary
self-catering — accommodation including a kitchen
single ticket — one-way ticket
stalls — (in theatre) orchestra seats
subway — underpass
surgery — doctor's office
tailback — traffic jam
takeaway — takeout
taxi rank — taxi stand
tights — panty-hose
T-junction — an intersection where one road meets another at right angles (making a T shape)
toilets — restrooms
torch — flashlight
trolley — cart
trousers — pants
way out — exit

PLANNING

BRITISH FLOOR NUMBERING

In Britain the first floor of a building is called the ground floor, and the floor above it is the first floor. So a British second floor is a US third floor, and so on. This is something to watch for in museums and galleries in particular.

TRACING YOUR ANCESTORS

Family and clan identities persist in the 21st century, and there is great pride among the estimated 28 million Scottish descendants who are spread around the world in being able to say they are a Macleod or a MacKenzie, a Ferguson or a Forbes, a Cameron or a Lindsay.

● For a fascinating listing of clan histories and societies see **www.electricscotland.com**

SCOTTISH CLANS

Scotland owes its tradition of clanship (or family) to Margaret (c1046–93), the Saxon queen commemorated by the little chapel in Edinburgh Castle (▷ 71–73). The wife of Malcolm III, she persuaded her husband to adopt a feudal system of landholding by which, for the first time in Scotland, land was granted to individuals and held in tenure by their descendants.

Clan chiefs in the Highlands ruled their own people like mini-kingdoms, forming allegiances with each other and raising their own armies of men to fight in local feuds when the need arose. And the feuds were bloody: For example, in 1577 almost 400 Macdonalds were burned alive in a cave on the island of Eigg by a party of Macleods. One of the best-known feuds was that of the Campbells and Macdonalds, which came to a head in Glen Coe in 1692 (▷ 127)

The Highland clans became more separate from the Lowlanders, increasingly divided by language (Gaelic was barely spoken in the south and east) and culture. Individual chiefs became known for their dominance in certain regions, such as Macdonald of the Isles, and Campbell of Argyll.

In this patriarchal scheme, a clansman's first loyalty was to his chief, and second to the king. It was a system that allowed the rebel cause of Jacobitism to flourish in the early 18th century, but which ultimately brought about its own downfall at Culloden in 1746, where clansmen fought on both sides.

After this victory for the King, chiefs were required to swear loyalty to their monarch or suffer the bloody consequences. Other measures imposed at this time included the compulsory education of chieftains' eldest sons at the English court, and the proscription of the wearing of

tartan, which had become identified with the Jacobite cause.

The clan system of the Highlands was dealt its final blows by the Clearances which took place in the 19th century, moving tenants off the land to make way for sheep farming. Clan chiefs were not always on the side of their people in this—the tale is told on Skye, for example, of one chieftain who did his best to sell his clanspeople into slavery in the Colonies. Throughout this period, communities were broken up and thousands emigrated to Nova Scotia and the promise of the New World.

TARTAN

The use of the woven patterns of tartan to signify individual clans or families is a relatively modern phenomenon, dating to the 19th century and the romanticizing of the Highlands. Before the mid-18th century, a particular pattern (or sett) was more likely to identify the area you came from or your social rank rather than your surname.

Novelist Sir Walter Scott was partly responsible for the recovery of tartan, when he ensured that German-born monarch George IV was dressed in it from head to toe on his state visit in 1822.

WHAT'S UP, MAC?

Mac or Mc as a prefix for a surname comes from the old Gaelic, meaning 'son of'. So Macdonald is the equivalent of Donaldson. 'Nic' was a feminine equivalent prefix, meaning 'daughter of', but does not now appear in the written form.

Family names beginning with the prefix Mac or Mc usually imply an origin in the Highlands, where Gaelic was widely spoken. Other common but distinctive Scottish surnames such as Lindsay and Kennedy are more likely to originate in the Lowlands.

Surnames may be linked to several colourways of the same weave pattern, representing a subdued hunting design or perhaps a more showy dress tartan for grand occasions.

Today there are hundreds of different tartans, with new ones created every year to cater for special events and changing fashions.

TRACING YOUR RELATIVES IN SCOTLAND

If you want to trace records of your family in order to visit the places associated with them, there are several excellent sources of information.

One of the best places to begin is the national register of births, marriages and deaths, which is held by the General Register Office for Scotland (GROS) in Edinburgh. A visit in person will give you tips on how to follow up your search while you are in Scotland, but you must search for yourself. If you plan to use this facility, then reading Cecil Sinclair's *Tracing Your Scottish Ancestors* (TSO,1997) is invaluable preparation.

You can also access much of the official data via the web for a nominal fee (currently £6), on **www.scotlandspeople.gov.uk**. Information held here includes an index of births in Scotland between 1553 and 1902, marriages from 1553 to 1854 and deaths from 1855 to 1952, culled from parish records and civil registrations. Information is also available on the website from census data taken between 1881 and 1901.

Another useful website is **www.genuki.org.uk**. This includes cross-references to many different archives of material which can help you to track down information, from military service records to collections of historic newspapers. It also contains many references to books which can help you to narrow down or perhaps fill out your search.

Family history societies may also be able to help with your research. For a list of these, see the Scottish Association of Family History Societies website, **www.safhs.org.uk**

PLANNING

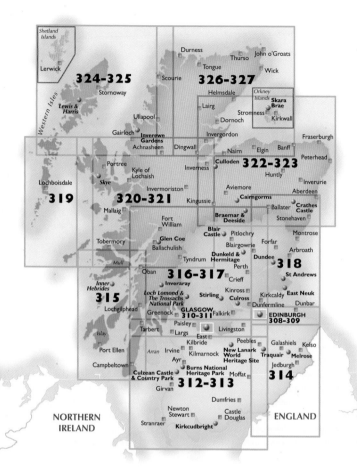

Shetland
Islands

Lerwick

324-325

Stornoway

Western Isles

Lewis &
Harris

Ullapool

Gairloch
Inverewe
Gardens
Achnasheen

Dingwall

Scourie

326-327

Helmsdale

Lairg

Dornoch

Durness

Tongue

Thurso

John o'Groats

Wick

Orkney
Islands   Skara
Brae

Stromness

Kirkwall

Invergordon

Fraserburgh

Nairn   Elgin   Banff

Peterhead

Culloden **322-323**

Inverness

Huntly

Inverurie

Portree

Kyle of
Lochalsh

Skye

Invermoriston

Aviemore

Aberdeen

Lochboisdale

319

320-321

Kingussie

Cairngorms

Ballater

Crathes
Castle

Mallaig

Braemar &
Deeside

Stonehaven

Fort
William

Blair
Castle   Pitlochry

Montrose

Tobermory

Glen Coe

Ballachulish

Blairgowrie

Forfar

Arbroath

Tyndrum

Dunkeld &
Hermitage

Dundee

318

Mull

Perth

Oban

316-317

Crieff

St Andrews

Inner
Hebrides

Inveraray

Kinross

East Neuk

315

Loch Lomond &
The Trossachs
National Park

Stirling

Culross

Kirkcaldy

Lochgilphead

Greenock

GLASGOW
310-311 Falkirk

Dunfermline

Dunbar

EDINBURGH
308-309

Tarbert

Paisley

Largs

Livingston

Islay

East
Kilbride

Peebles

Galashiels

Kelso

Port Ellen

Arran Irvine
Kilmarnock

New Lanark
World
Heritage Site

Traquair Melrose

Ayr

Jedburgh

314

Campbeltown

Culzean Castle
& Country Park

Burns National
Heritage Park

Moffat

312-313

Girvan

Dumfries

**NORTHERN
IRELAND**

Newton
Stewart

Castle
Douglas

ENGLAND

Stranraer

Kirkcudbright

	Motorway
② ●	Motorway junction with and without number
◆	Motorway service area
	Main road
	Other road
	Railway
----	Long distance footpath
	Country boundary
	County boundary
	Built-up area
■	Town / Attraction
	National park / National scenic area
●	Featured place of interest
✈	Airport
⚓	Port / Ferry route
621 ▲	Height in metres

312-327
0   15 km
0   10 miles

324 & 327
0   20 km
0   15 miles

SCOTTISH BORDERS COUNCIL

LIBRARY &

INFORMATION SERVICES

Maps

EDINBURGH

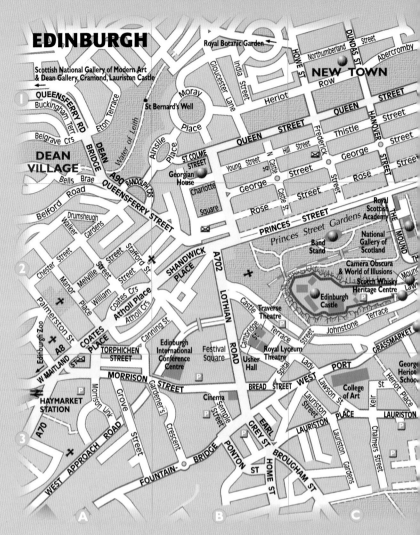

Scottish National Gallery of Modern Art & Dean Gallery, Cramond, Lauriston Castle

Royal Botanic Garden

NEW TOWN

QUEENSFERRY RD
Buckingham Terr
Belgrave Crs

DEAN VILLAGE

DEAN BRIDGE

Eton Terrace

St Bernard's Well

Moray Place

Ainslie Place

Gloucester Lane

India Street

Heriot

QUEEN STREET

Northumberland Street
Abercromby
DUNDAS ST
HOWE ST
ROW
Street

Thistle Street
Frederick Street
Hanover Street
QUEEN STREET
HANOVER STREET
THE MOUND

Belford Road
Water of Leith
Bells Brae
QUEENSFERRY STREET
RANDOLPH CRS
A90

ST COLME STREET
Georgian House
Charlotte Square
Young Street
Hill Street
Castle St
George Street
Rose Street
PRINCES STREET

Royal Scottish Academy

National Gallery of Scotland

Princes Street Gardens
Band Stand

Drumsheugh Gardens
Walker Street
Chester Street
Manor Place
Melville Street
William Street
Stafford St
Coates Crs
Atholl Place
Atholl Crts
SHANDWICK PLACE
A702

Palmerston Place
Edinburgh Zoo
A8
W MAITLAND ST
COATES PLACE
TORPHICHEN STREET
Canning St
Edinburgh International Conference Centre
Festival Square
LOTHIAN ROAD
Cambridge Street
Castle St
Terrace
Traverse Theatre
Royal Lyceum Theatre
Usher Hall
Spittal St
Lady Lawson St
Johnstone Terrace
Edinburgh Castle
Camera Obscura & World of Illusions
Scotch Whisky Heritage Centre
Mound Place
Mound
Law
GRASSMARKET
PORT
College of Art
George Heriot School
Heriot Place

HAYMARKET STATION
A70
Morrison Link
MORRISON STREET
Grove Street
Gardener's Crescent
Semple Street
Cinema
BREAD STREET
WEST
Lauriston St
Lauriston Street
PLACE
LAURISTON
Kier St
Chalmers Street

WEST APPROACH ROAD
FOUNTAIN-BRIDGE
PONTON ST
GREY ST
EARL
HOME ST
BROUGHAM ST
LAURISTON
Lauriston Gardens

A B C

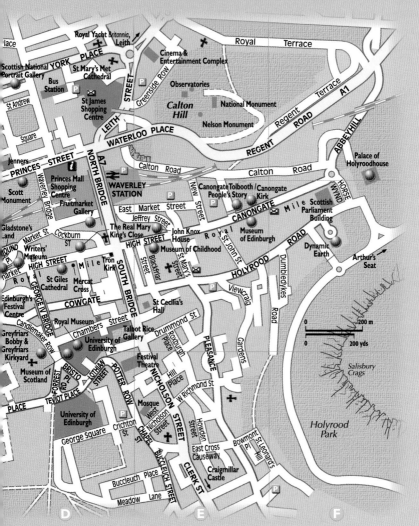

GLASGOW

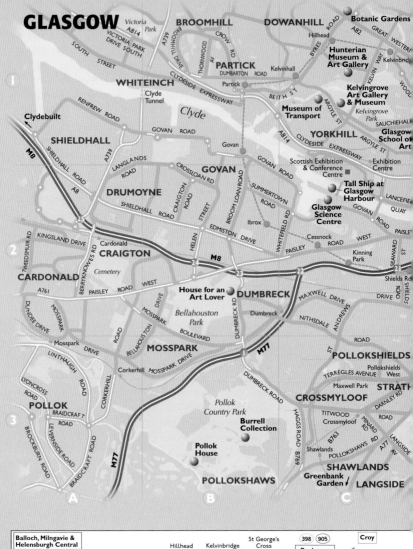

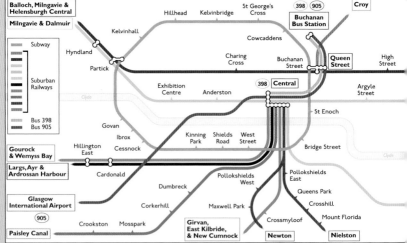

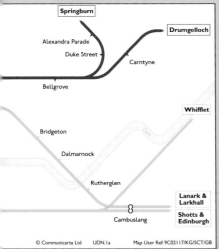

GLASGOW

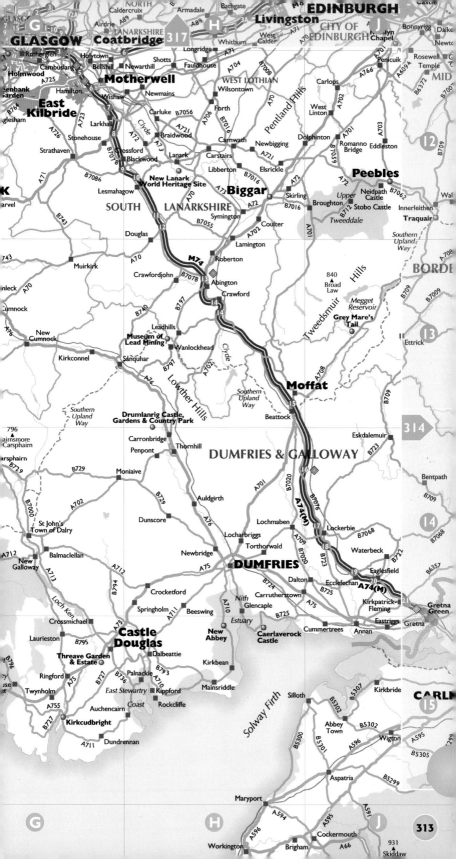

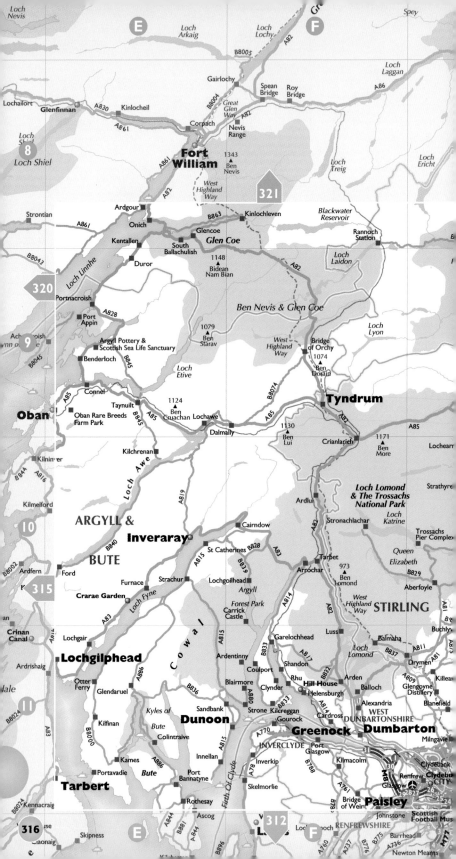

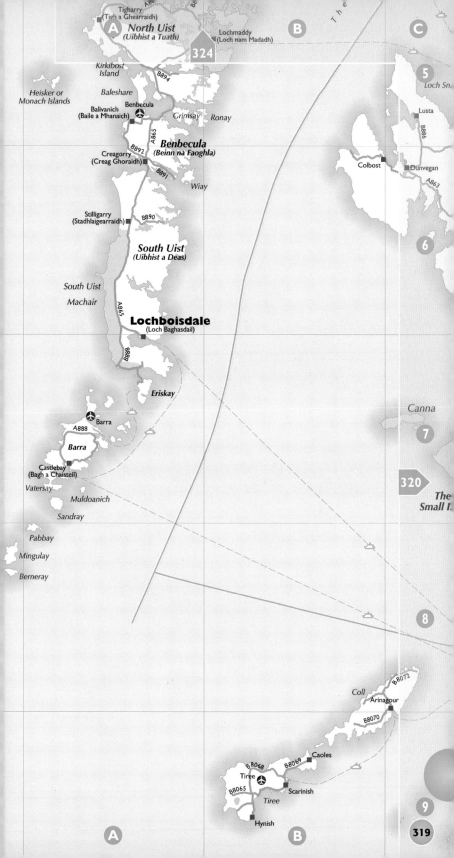

Tigharry
(Tigh a Ghearraidh)

North Uist
(Uibhist a Tuath)

Lochmaddy
(Loch nam Madadh)

The

Loch Sn.

Kirkibost
Island

B894

Heisker or
Monach Islands

Baleshare

Lusta

Balivanich
(Baile a Mhanaich)

Benbecula

Grimsay

Ronay

B886

A865

B892

Benbecula
(Beinn na Faoghla)

Colbost

Dunvegan

Creagorry
(Creag Ghoraidh)

B891

A863

Wiay

Stilligarry
(Stadhlaigearraidh)

B890

South Uist
(Uibhist a Deas)

South Uist
Machair

A865

Lochboisdale
(Loch Baghasdail)

B888

Canna

Eriskay

Barra

A888

Barra

The
Small I.

Castlebay
(Bagh a Chaisteil)

Vatersay

Muldoanich

Sandray

Pabbay

Mingulay

Berneray

B8072

Coll

Arinagour

B8070

Caoles

B8069

B8068

Tiree

B8065

Tiree

Scarinish

Hynish

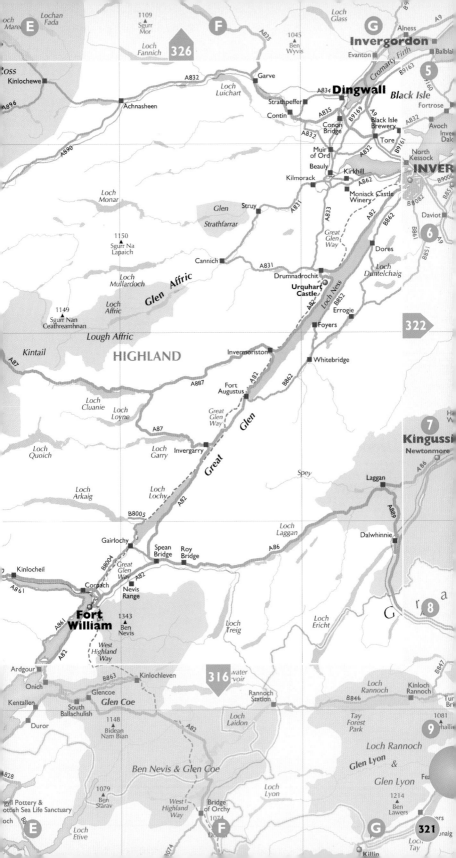

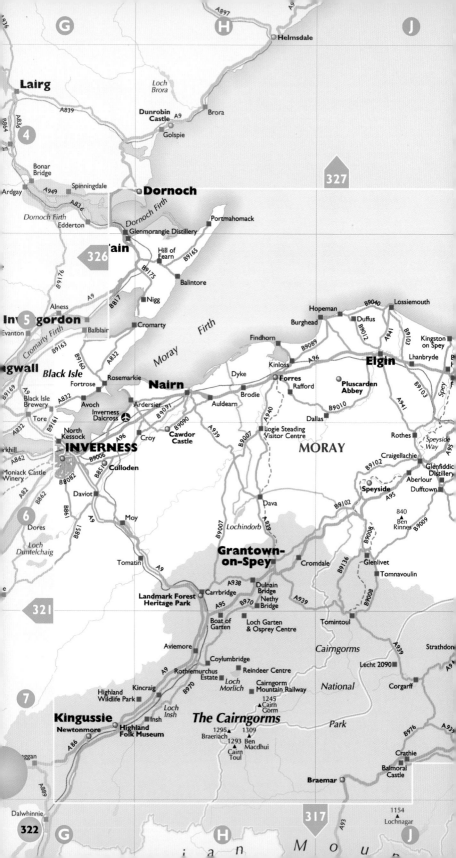

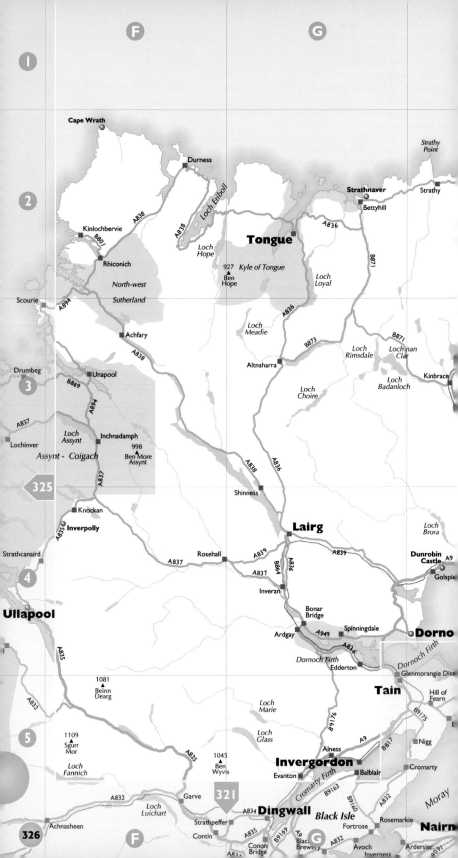

ACKNOWLEDGMENTS

Abbreviations for the picture credits are as follows:
AA = AA World Travel Library, t (top), b (bottom), c (centre), l (left), r (right)

AA/Michael Taylor; **97cr** AA/Steve Day; 97cb AA/Ken Paterson; **98t**
AA/Ronnie Weir; **98bl** AA/Peter Sharpe; **99tl** AA/Steve Day; **99tc**
AA/Jonathan Smith; **99tr** AA; **100t** Kingdom of Fife Tourist Board;
100bl AA/Jonathan Smith; **101tl**, **101tc** AA/Steve Day; **101tr**
AA/Jonathan Smith; **101bl** Barrie Andrian; **102tl** AA/Jonathan Smith;
102br AA/Stephen Whitehorne; **104clt** AA/Stephen Whithorne;
104ctr AA/Marius Alexander; **105tl** AA/Marius Alexander; **105tc**
AA/Stephen Whitehorne; **105tr** AA/Marius Alexander; **106tc** Glasgow
Museums; **106cl** Britain On View; **106cc** Glasgow Museums; **106cr**
Greater Glasgow & Clyde Valley Tourist Board; **107** Glasgow
Museums, **108tl** Glasgow Museums; **108c** AA/Douglas Corrance;
109t Greater Glasgow & Clyde Valley Tourist Board; **109br** Glasgow
Museums; **110tl**, **110tc** AA/Stephen Gibson; **110tr**, **111tl**, **111tr**
AA/Stephen Whitehorne; **112tl** Britain On View; **112tc** AA/Stephen
Whitehorne; **112tr** Greater Glasgow & Clyde Valley Tourist Board; **113t**
Glasgow Museums; **113cr** John Byrne/Glasgow Museums; **113br**
Glasgow Museums; **114tc** AA/Stephen Gibson; **114cl** Greater
Glasgow & Clyde Valley Tourist Board; **114cr** AA/Stephen Gibson;
114cr Greater Glasgow & Clyde Valley Tourist Board; **114bl** Glasgow
School of Art Collection; **115cl** Hunterian Art Gallery/University of
Glasgow; **115cr** Glasgow Museums; **115br** Glasgow School of Art
Collection; **116tl** AA/Stephen Gibson; **116tr**, **117tl** Greater Glasgow &
Clyde Valley Tourist Board; **117tr**, **119tl** AA/Stephen Whitehorne;
119tc AA/Eric Ellington; **119tr** Aberdeen and Grampian Tourist Board;
120t, **120bl** AA/Jonathan Smith; **121tl** AA/Ronnie Weir; **121tc**
AA/Stephen Whitehorne; **121tr** AA/Ronnie Weir; **122t** AA/Sue
Anderson; **122bl** AA/Ken Paterson; **123tl** AA/Jim Carnie; **123tc**
AA/Jamie Blandford; **123tr** AA/Dennis Hardley; **124tl** AA/Eric
Ellington; **124tr** AA/Ronnie Weir; **125t** Britain On View; **126tl**
AA/Stephen Whitehorne; **126tc** AA/Sue Anderson; **126tr** AA/Steve
Day; **127t** AA/Jim Henderson; **127b**, **128tl** AA/Sue Anderson; **128tr**,
128cb AA/Steve Day; **129tl** The Highland Folk Museum; **129tc** Britain
On View; **129tr** AA/Jim Henderson; **130tc** AA/Stephen Whitehorne;
130cl AA/Richard Elliot; **130cc**, **130cr** Britain On View; **130b**
AA/Stephen Whitehorne; **131cr** AA/Richard Elliot; **131b** Britain On
View; **132tl** AA/Ronny Weir; **132tr** AA/Jim Carnie; **133t** AA; **134tl**
AA/Derek Forss; **134tc** AA/Stephen Whitehorne; **134tr** AA/Eric
Ellington; **135t** Britain On View; **136tl** AA/Robert Eames; **136tc**
AA/Derek Forss; **136tr** AA/Sue Anderson; **137tl** AA/Dennis Hardley;
137tc AA/Sue Anderson; **137tr** AA/Jim Henderson; **137b** Lighthouse
Museum, Fraserburgh; **138** AA/Stephen Whitehorne; **139tc** Britain On
View; **139cl** AA/Ken Paterson; **139cc** AA/Anthony Hopkins; **139cr**
Dunvegan Castle; **140tl** The Highlands of Scotland Tourist Board;
140cl Susan Arnold; **140cc** AA/Stephen Whitehorne; **140cr**
AA/Stephen Whitehorne; **141** AA/Ronnie Weir; **142tl** AA/Eric
Ellington; **142tc** AA/Stephen Whitehorne; **142tr** AA/Michael Taylor;
144tl, **144tr** AA/Stephen Whitehorne; **145t** Britain On View; **145b**,
146tl AA/Eric Ellington; **146tc** AA/Stephen Whitehorne; **146tr** AA/Eric
Ellington; **146br** AA/Stephen Whitehorne; **147tl**, **147tr** AA/Eric
Ellington; **148tl**, **148tr** Britain On View; **148b** AA/Eric Ellington.

WHAT TO DO

149 Photodisc; **150/1** Photodisc; **152t** Brand X Pictures; **152cl**
Anthony Brannan; **152cr** Cine-UK Ltd; **153t** Photodisc; **153cl** AA/Steve
Day; **153cr** Greater Glasgow & Clyde Valley Tourist Board; **154/5t**
Photodisc; **154cl** AA/Steve Day; **154cr** AA/Ronnie Weir; **156/7t** Digital
Vision; **157c** AA/Jim Carnie; **158/9t** AA/Steve Day; **158** AA/Ted
Bowness; **159c** Arran Distillers; **160/1t** AA/Steve Day; **160c** Dalton
Pottery; **161c** AA/Marius Alexander; **162/3t** AA/Steve Day; **162c** R & M
Turner Ltd; **163c** Isobel Cameron/Forestry Commission; **164/5t**
AA/Steve Day; **164c** The Crafters; **165c** G C Books; **166/7t** AA/Steve
Day; **166** AA/Jonathan Smith; **167c** Jenners; **168/9t** AA/Steve Day;
168c Royal Mile Whiskies; **169c** Dominion; **170/1t** AA/Steve Day;

170c Usher Hall; **171c** AA; **172/3** AA/Steve Day; **172c** Black Hart
Entertainment; **173c** Greater Glasgow & Clyde Valley Tourist Board;
174/5t AA/Jonathan Smith; **174cl** AA/Jonathan Smith; **174cr**
AA/Jonathan Smith; **175cl** AA/Jonathan Smith; **175tr** AA/Jonathan
Smith; **176/7t** AA/Steve Day; **176** AA/Adrian Baker; **177c** Painting by
Georgie Young; **178/9t** AA/Steve Day; **178c** Griselda Hill Pottery; **179c**
Kingdom of Fife Tourist Board; **180/1t** AA/Steve Day; **180c** AA; **181c**
Eradour Distillery; **182t** AA/Steve Day; **182c** Tolbooth; **183t** AA/Steve
Day; **183** AA/Stephen Whitehorne; **184/5t** AA/Steve Day; **184c**
AA/Richard Elliott; **185c** Centre for Contemporary Arts; **186/7t**
AA/Steve Day; **186c** Theatre Royal; **187c** AA/Richard Elliott; **188t**
AA/Steve Day; **188c** Gerard O'Neill; **189t** AA/Steve Day; **189** M Yule;
190/1t AA/Steve Day; **190c** AA/Jim Henderson; **191c** Bill Roberton;
192/3t AA/Steve Day; **192c** Sea Fari; **193c** Hebridean Jewellery;
194/5t AA/Steve Day; **194c** Glenmorangie plc; **195c** Loch Insh
Watersports; **196/7t** AA/Steve Day; **196c** Skye Silver; **197** Roving Eye
Enterprises; **198t** AA/Steve Day; **198c** Garrison Theatre.

OUT AND ABOUT

199 AA/Sue Anderson; **200** AA/Marius Alexander; **201tl** AA/Jeff
Beazley; **201tr** AA/Cameron Lees; **201br** AA/Jeff Beazley; **202** AA/Sue
Anderson; **203tl** Forest Life Picture Library; **203tr** AA/Sue Anderson;
203br AA/Sue Anderson; **204** AA/Cameron Lees; **205tl** AA/Cameron
Lees; **205tr** AA/Cameron Lees; **205bl** Britain On View; **206b** Scottish
Borders Tourist Board; **207tl** Scottish Borders Tourist Board; **207tr**
AA/Cameron Lees; **207b** AA/Cameron Lees; **208bc** AA/Jonathon
Smith; **208br** AA/Stephen Whitehorne; **209cl** Isla Love; **210** AA/Steve
Day; **211tl** AA/Harry Williams; **211tr** AA/Jim Henderson; **211bl** AA;
211br AA/Steve Day; **212bl** AA/Ken Paterson; **212br** AA/Ken
Paterson; **213tl** Isobel Cameron/Forest Life Picture Library; **213tr**
AA/Steve Day; **214** AA/Ken Paterson; **215tl** Britain On View; **215tr**
Britain On View; **215bl** Britain On View; **216** AA/Stephen Whitehorne;
217tl Kingdom of Fife Tourist Board; **217tr** AA; **217br** AA/Jonathan
Smith; **218** Greater Glasgow & Clyde Valley Tourist Board; **219tl** Doug
Corrance/Still Digital; **219tr** AA/Rich Newton; **220** Crown Copyright
reproduced courtesy of Historic Scotland; **221tl** AA/Jim Carnie; **221tr**
AA/Ken Paterson; **221cr** AA/Jim Carnie; **221b** AA/Jim Henderson;
222 AA/Ronnie Weir; **223t** Brian Shuel/Collections; **223b** Ken
Paterson/Scottish Viewpoint; **224** AA/Jim Carnie; **225tl** AA/Jim
Carnie; **225tr** AA/Jim Carnie; **225bl** AA/Steve Day; **225cb** AA/Steve
Day; **226** AA/Steve Day; **227t** AA/Jim Henderson; **227cl** Christine
Spreiter; **228** AA/Ken Paterson; **229tl** AA/Ronnie Weir; **229tr** AA/Ken
Paterson; **229b** AA/Eric Ellington; **230** AA/Eric Ellington; **231** AA/Jim
Henderson; **232** AA/Anthony Hopkins; **233tl** Highlands of Scotland
Tourist Board www.highlandfreedom.com; **233tr** Steve
Austin/Stockscotland.com; **233br** AA/Stephen Whitehorne; **234**
Charles Tait; **235t** Colin Keldie; **235b** Charles Tait; **236** AA/Ken
Paterson.

EATING AND STAYING

239 Britain On View; **240cl** Britain On View; **242cl** AA/Ronnie Weir;
242cc Britain On View; **242cr** AA/Jonathan Smith; **244/5t** AA/Clive
Sawyer; **244** AA/S & O Mathews; **249** AA/Ken Paterson; **253**
AA/Steve Day; **260** AA/Jim Carnie; **270/1t** AA/Clive Sawyer; **274**
AA/Jonathan Smith; **277** AA/Steve Day; **282** AA/Stephen Whitehorne;
284 AA/Ronnie Weir.

PLANNING

289 AA/Clive Sawyer; **294** Scottish Banknotes: Reproduced by kind
permission of The Royal Bank of Scotland Group; **297** AA/Ken
Paterson; **298** AA/Alex Kouprianoff; **299t** AA/Jonathan Smith; **299b**
AA/James Tims; **304** AA/Richard Elliot.

Project editor
Ann F. Stonehouse

Design team
David Austin, Glyn Barlow, Alan Gooch, Kate Harling, Bob Johnson,
Nick Otway, Carole Philp, Keith Russell

Picture research
Liz Allen, Alice Earle, Serena Mellish, Chloe Butler

Internal repro work
Ian Little, Michael Moody, Susan Crowhurst

Production
Lyn Kirby, Caroline Nyman

Mapping
Maps produced by the Cartography Department of AA Publishing

Contributors
Christopher Harvie (living and history); Johanna Campbell, Gilbert Summers, Fiona Wood (sights);
Isla Love (what to do); Kate Barrett, Rebecca Ford, Moira McCrossan, Hugh Taylor, Ronald Turnbull,
David Williams (walks and tours); Jenny White (food); Pam Stagg (copy editor);
David Halford, Nicholas Lanng, Jennifer Skelley (verification)

Updaters
Chris Bagshaw, Ann F. Stonehouse

Revision Management
Cambridge Publishing Management Ltd

Published by AA Publishing, a trading name of Automobile Association Developments Limited, whose
registered office is Fanum House, Basing View, Basingstoke, RG21 4EA. Registered number 1878835.

A CIP catalogue record for this book is available from the British Library.

ISBN-10: 0-7495-4010-9
ISBN-13: 978-0-7495-4010-4

© Automobile Association Developments Limited 2004
Reprinted Sep 2006. Information verified and updated.
Reprinted Sep 2007

Key Guide is a registered trademark in Australia and is used under license.
Binding style with plastic section dividers by permission of AA Publishing.

Colour separation by Keenes
Printed and bound by Leo, China

Find out more about AA Publishing and the wide range of travel publications and services the AA
provides by visiting our website at www.theAA.com/travel

A03585

This product includes mapping data licensed from Ordnance Survey® with
the permission of the Controller of Her Majesty's Stationery Office. ©
Crown copyright 2007. All rights reserved. Licence number 100021153. Traffic signs © Crown
copyright. Reproduced with the permission of the Controller of Her Majesty's Stationery Office.
Weathercharts © Copyright 2004 Canty and Associates, LLC.

We believe the contents of this book are correct at the time of printing. However, some details,
particularly prices, opening times and telephone numbers do change. We do not accept
responsibility for any consequences arising from the use of this book. This does not affect your
statutory rights. We would be grateful if readers would advise us of any inaccuracies they may
encounter, or any suggestions they might like to make to improve the book. There is a form
provided at the back of the book for this purpose, or you can email us at Keyguides@theaa.com

COVER PICTURES

Front cover, top to bottom: Corbis/Niall Benvie; AA/S Whitehorne; AA/E Ellington; AA/J Smith
Back cover: t & b AA/Jim Carnie; ct Eilean Donan Castle AA/Stephen Whitehorn;
cb Tower Restaurant, Museum of Scotland, Edinburgh. Spine: Corbis/Niall Benvie

Dear Key Guide Reader

●

Thank you for buying this Key Guide. Your comments and opinions are very important to us, so please help us to improve our travel guides by taking a few minutes to complete this questionnaire.

You do not need a stamp (unless posted outside the UK). If you do not want to cut this page from your guide, then photocopy it or write your answers on a plain sheet of paper.

Send to: **Key Guide Editor, AA World Travel Guides FREEPOST SCE 4598, Basingstoke RG21 4GY**

Find out more about AA Publishing and the wide range of travel publications the AA provides by visiting our website at www.theAA.com/bookshop

ABOUT THIS GUIDE

Which Key Guide did you buy? _____

Where did you buy it?_____

When? _ _ month/ _ _ year

Why did you choose this AA Key Guide?
❏ Price ❏ AA Publication
❏ Used this series before; title _____
❏ Cover ❏ Other (please state) _____

Please let us know how helpful the following features of the guide were to you by circling the appropriate category: very helpful (**VH**), helpful (**H**) or little help (**LH**)

Size	**VH**	**H**	**LH**
Layout	**VH**	**H**	**LH**
Photos	**VH**	**H**	**LH**
Excursions	**VH**	**H**	**LH**
Entertainment	**VH**	**H**	**LH**
Hotels	**VH**	**H**	**LH**
Maps	**VH**	**H**	**LH**
Practical info	**VH**	**H**	**LH**
Restaurants	**VH**	**H**	**LH**
Shopping	**VH**	**H**	**LH**
Walks	**VH**	**H**	**LH**
Sights	**VH**	**H**	**LH**
Transport info	**VH**	**H**	**LH**

What was your favourite sight, attraction or feature listed in the guide?

Page _____ Please give your reason _____

_____

Which features in the guide could be changed or improved? Or are there any other comments you would like to make?

_____

_____

ABOUT YOU

Name (*Mr/Mrs/Ms*) _____

Address_____

_____

Postcode _____ Daytime tel nos _____

Email _____

Please *only* give us your mobile phone number/email if you wish to hear from us about other products and services from the AA and partners by text or mms.

Which age group are you in?

Under 25 ❏   25–34 ❏   35–44 ❏   45–54 ❏   55+ ❏

How many trips do you make a year?

Less than1 ❏   1 ❏   2 ❏   3 or more ❏

ABOUT YOUR TRIP

Are you an AA member?   Yes ❏ No ❏

When did you book?   _ _ month/_ _ year

When did you travel?   _ _ month/_ _ year

Reason for your trip?   Business ❏ Leisure ❏

How many nights did you stay?_____

How did you travel?   Individual ❏ Couple ❏ Family ❏ Group ❏

Did you buy any other travel guides for your trip?_____

If yes, which ones? _____

_____

Thank you for taking the time to complete this questionnaire. Please send it to us as soon as possible, and remember, you do not need a stamp (*unless posted outside the UK*).

AA Travel Insurance call 0800 072 4168 or visit www.theaa.com

---

Titles in the Key Guide series:

Australia, Barcelona, Britain, Brittany, Canada, Costa Rica, Florence and Tuscany, France, Germany, Ireland, Italy, London, Mallorca, Mexico, New York, New Zealand, Normandy, Paris, Portugal, Prague, Provence and the Côte d'Azur, Rome, Scotland, South Africa, Spain, Thailand, Venice, Vietnam.
Published in May 2007: Croatia   **Published in October 2007:** China

---